BLACK FREEDOM, WHITE RESISTANCE, AND RED MENACE

MAKING THE MODERN SOUTH

David Goldfield, Series Editor

BLACK FREEDOM, WHITE RESISTANCE, AND RED MENACE

CIVIL RIGHTS AND ANTICOMMUNISM

IN THE JIM CROW SOUTH

YASUHIRO KATAGIRI

Louisiana State University Press

Baton Rouge

Published by Louisiana State University Press
Copyright © 2014 by Louisiana State University Press
All rights reserved
Manufactured in the United States of America
First printing

Designer: Barbara Neely Bourgoyne
Typefaces: Gotham, display; Ingeborg, text
Printer and binder: Maple Press

Library of Congress Cataloging-in-Publication Data

Katagiri, Yasuhiro, 1960–
  Black freedom, white resistance, and red menace : civil rights and anticommunism in
the Jim Crow South / Yasuhiro Katagiri.
    pages cm. — (Making the modern South)
  Includes bibliographical references and index.
  ISBN 978-0-8071-5313-0 (cloth : alk. paper) — ISBN 978-0-8071-5314-7 (pdf) —
ISBN 978-0-8071-5315-4 (epub) — ISBN 978-0-8071-5316-1 (mobi) 1. African Americans—
Civil rights—Southern States—History—20th century. 2. Civil rights movements—Southern
States—History—20th century. 3. Communism—Southern States—History. 4. Southern
States—Race relations. 5. Southern States—Politics and government—1865–1950.
6. Southern States—Politics and government—1951– 7. White supremacy movements—
Southern States—History—20th century. I. Title.
  E185.61.K349 2013
  323.1196'073075—dc23

                                                                            2013016131

To the memory of my mentor and friend, Makoto Saito;

and dearly and gratefully dedicated to

Yasohachi, Mikiko, Charles, Shirley, Brenda,
Akira Reuben, Aya Rebekah, and Ann Rachel,

who have nurtured me and shared their lives with me
as their son, husband, and father

Demagogues start out with a great plan,
something that looks like it will be very helpful to the general people,
but if they are too demagogic,
they will run the thing into the ground. . . .
—HARRY S. TRUMAN

For what is a man profited,
if he shall gain the whole world,
and lose his own soul?
—MATTHEW 16:26

CONTENTS

Illustrations follow page 144

PREFACE

The American civil rights movement has often deservedly been regarded as one of the twentieth century's most profound dramas, identified with proud and triumphant moments, as well as courageous and inspiring characters. The drama, to be sure, also provided us with sordid and horrifying images, and a cast of "villains" who played out their unsavory roles to the bitter end. And those villains—both nationally recognized southern white segregationists and locally influential ones—were complicated men and women who, as the journalist John Blake has noted, were bound by their upbringings, personal beliefs, and the political reality and expediencies of their days.[1]

In the summer of 1959, two Tennessee writers—Wilma Dykeman and James Stokely—who had together reported on a number of civil rights events, described what the South was up against almost two years after the 1957 Little Rock, Arkansas, school desegregation crisis. They observed that as the region's racial tensions involving integration coincided with America's national survival fears in a Cold War environment, a monstrous "no-man's land of uncertainty and suspicion" had been created in the South by the cast of villains.[2] Just five years before this observation was made, in May 1954, the U.S. Supreme Court had rendered its landmark *Brown v. Board of Education* decision, outlawing legally imposed racial segregation in public schools and forcing white southerners, as the southern historian Paul M. Gaston has noted, to "face up to the consequences of the myths they had spun and by which they had lived"—the myths that racial segregation was "deeply rooted in the customs of the people" in the South and "could not be dislodged by mere law."[3]

Resenting this ruling by the nation's highest tribunal, white southerners—both politicians and ordinary citizens alike—quickly responded by organizing the region's massive resistance to the effective and meaning-ful implementation of the Supreme Court's desegregation decree. The massive resisters were determined to defy the intent of the Court, delay *Brown*'s implementation, and possibly derail the germinating civil rights movement. Summing up the resentment felt among white southerners, the John W. Hamilton–led National Citizens Protective Association in St. Louis, Missouri, whose notoriously white-supremacist and anti-Semitic publication titled the *White Sentinel* attracted considerable support in the white South, circulated what one writer sarcastically called a "poetic diamond."[4] The amateurish anti-integration "poem" read in part:

> Nine traitors to the white man's race
> Sat in our Court Supreme,
> And all agreed that whites and blacks
> Must join their mongrel scheme. . . .
>
> . . . .
>
> A hundred million white men cry
> That they will not obey
> This "traitor-law" which would destroy
> The white man's U.S.A.[5]

Racism clearly lay at the heart of this resistance movement. Some white southerners argued that, compared to whites, the black race was inherently inferior in intelligence. Many jumped to the illogical conclu-sion that the ultimate objectives of the civil rights movement were race-mixing and the spread of "miscegenation," "mongrelization," and "amal-gamation"—words that had been seldom heard before the *Brown* ruling. Furthermore, some advocated that racial segregation, perceived as crucial to perpetuating their cherished "southern way of life," was God-ordained and predestined.[6] Still others shamelessly resorted to physical intimida-tion and extreme violence to defend the South's racial status quo. Many self-described "thinking," "respectable," and "paternalistic" white leaders in the South realized, however, that racism and racial prejudice alone could not garner enough support among the general white citizenry to defend segregation or to convince the federal government to leave them alone. In addition, despite their repeated provocative and inflammatory pronouncements, these southern leaders in politics and the press under-stood that unless they could effectively make the case to the rest of the nation for the white South's resistance movement, their battle for "racial integrity" would be doomed to failure.

Even though southern segregationists utilized a broad range of weapons in waging their massive resistance, they depended upon two principal mainstays to sustain and reinforce their shared commitment to white supremacy. One of them was the resurrected theory of states' rights constitutionalism. At the center of this theory lay the constitutional doctrine of interposition, intended to protect the rights and powers of the states in relation to those of the federal government. When I published my first book in English—an acquired language of mine—in late 2001, *The Mississippi State Sovereignty Commission: Civil Rights and States' Rights,* my analysis focused primarily on how Mississippi's—and, to a larger degree, the South's—white politicians and officials carried out their massive resistance to defend racial segregation and discrimination in the name of states' rights constitutionalism.[7] To my regret, however, I paid insufficient attention in that work to the relationship between the segregationist cause and the anti-Communist discourse in the civil rights South in the Cold War environment. As Robert Cook, a British scholar of American history, has astutely observed, the Cold War, while it "could be turned to good use" by the black civil rights campaigners, should be understood as a "double-edged sword" for them. That is to say that the Cold War's stifling and punishment of political and ideological dissent within the suspicion-filled American society lent impetus to southern segregationists' tendency to label as subversive anyone who dared to attempt to undermine the existing racial and social orders in the region.[8] To be sure, a segregationist anti-Communist discourse, as the second vital mainstay of massive resistance, also decried the evils of centralized government.

Following the publication of *The Mississippi State Sovereignty Commission,* I began to explore how and to what extent southern segregationists shrewdly resorted to the assertion that black southerners' quests for social justice, political empowerment, and simple human dignity were nothing more than a foreign enterprise—the "world Communist conspiracy"—directed and dominated by despicable outside agitators, race-mixers, and, worse, outright Communists and subversives. In this way, southern segregationists ironically ended up leading their societies toward what they outwardly decried—a form of quasi-totalitarianism where freedom of conscience, freedom of speech, and freedom of assembly were all curtailed in the name of racial conformity. And my exploration of this modern southern tragedy, which encompasses what the southern historian C. Vann Woodward once termed the "burden of southern history," eventually led to the publication of this book as a sequel to my previous work.[9]

In recent years and particularly since the end of the 1990s, southern historians and civil rights scholars both in and outside of the United States have increasingly turned their attention to and investigated the complex and diverse nature of the white South's responses and resistance to the civil rights movement. And these scholars' searching historical analyses of the South's massive resistance have greatly contributed to broadening the civil rights historiography, both confirming interpretations and offering new ones to the scholarship accomplished more than four decades earlier by Numan V. Bartley's *The Rise of Massive Resistance: Race and Politics in the South during the 1950's* (1969) and Neil R. McMillen's *The Citizens' Council: Organized Resistance to the Second Reconstruction, 1954–64* (1971).[10]

In fact, since the dawn of the new millennium, this scholarly trend has also produced a few academic works specifically dealing with southern segregationists' use and abuse of anticommunism in their efforts to preserve the region's segregated societies. When Ellen W. Schrecker published her informative article entitled "Archival Sources for the Study of McCarthyism" in the June 1988 issue of the *Journal of American History,* the Cold War historian noted that an "important and largely unstudied aspect of McCarthyism is its impact on the black community" in the South. "I know of no recent work specifically in this area, yet . . . there should be a major story here," she wrote.[11] In 2004, as if to fill this void, two pathbreaking books were published by British and American civil rights historians, both of which dealt with the relationship between racial segregation and anticommunism in the South during the civil rights years—George Lewis's *The White South and the Red Menace: Segregationists, Anticommunism, and Massive Resistance, 1945–1965* and Jeff Woods's *Black Struggle, Red Scare: Segregation and Anti-Communism in the South, 1948–1968.*[12]

The bulk of my book's analysis, while partially indebted to and building upon Lewis's and Woods's works, deals with the situations in the three Deep South states of Georgia, Louisiana, and Mississippi, and in the three Peripheral South states of Arkansas, Florida, and Tennessee. Beginning with Louisiana, all of these southern states created their own versions of the House Un-American Activities Committee (HUAC) to vigorously and cruelly investigate alleged Communist influences in the civil rights movement. While I have described these states' mutual cooperation within the southern region to desperately link communism to the entire civil rights struggle, my primary objective in writing this book has been to illuminate and analyze the fact that there were sustained and mutually beneficial relations forged between professional anti-Communists in the North and segregationist politicians and officials in the South in the latter's efforts to perpetuate their crumbling caste system, a subject to which Lewis and Woods devoted either little or insufficient attention.

It is true that for a long period of time, the American South had been the nation's "exposed nerve," "feeling first and most sharply all the troubles and pains" in the sphere of black-and-white race relations.[13] And during the civil rights years, as well as in the subsequent historical narratives of the movement, the grand moral battle between almost comfortably self-righteous northerners as virtuous reformers and deplorably sinful southerners as ignorant racists was, and still is, somewhat taken for granted. However, this simplified generalization notwithstanding, there were both northerners and southerners who did not cozily fit into this regional and moral dichotomy that was "so wrapped up in artificial binaries" composed of the immaculate North and the disgraceful South.[14] And indeed, after the Supreme Court's *Brown* decision, which coincided with the demise of McCarthyism (or, more accurately, the demise of the political influence of U.S. senator Joseph R. McCarthy from Wisconsin), some northern anti-Communists suddenly found the South to be an unexplored, fertile, and promising ground, where their knowledge and expertise could be fully appreciated. In response, southern segregationists embraced the services offered by these "Yankee" collaborators and, in the years to come, they depended upon, utilized, and even canonized those whom I term "northern messiahs" in carrying out their massive resistance.

Among these messiahs, I have given special attention to two specific and notable individuals who willingly assisted the segregationist politicians and officials in those southern states equipped with their respective "little HUACs" during the latter half of the 1950s and the first half of the 1960s. One of the northern messiahs who worked for the South's segregationist cause was Myers G. Lowman. Little-known but undoubtedly the most vigorous northern collaborator for the South's racist crusade, Lowman served as the executive secretary of a Methodist laymen's anti-Communist group called the Circuit Riders, Inc., which was based in Cincinnati, Ohio. Reviving the name formerly attached to pioneer Methodist itinerant preachers who had once spread their faith in the sparsely settled areas of the nation, Lowman proliferated his paranoid version of the three Rs—Religion, the Reds, and Race—among white southerners. And what made Lowman stand out among other religious anti-Communist crusaders was his perpetual and collaborative association with the other messiah—Joseph Brown "J. B." Matthews of New York City. A former Methodist missionary, Matthews was imbued with pacifism, socialism, and racial liberalism in his younger days. Having become disillusioned with radical politics by the mid-1930s, however, Matthews then worked for the forerunner of the HUAC—the Dies Committee, which was named after its chair, U.S. representative Martin Dies Jr. from Texas—as its research director. As the Cold War commenced, he soon established himself as one of the most prominent professional anti-Communist researchers, lecturers, and witnesses, both assisting and testifying before various federal and state committees—including those of Mississippi, Arkansas, and Florida—established to investigate domestic communism.

The description and analysis of Lowman's and Matthews's activities in and for the South have occupied an important portion of this book. I have also paid substantial attention to the relationship forged between these two individuals in their association with southern states. That is to say that while Lowman counted on Matthews's voluminous information and encyclopedic knowledge in his unabashed and unabated zeal to crack down on his and the white South's enemies, Matthews also benefited from Lowman's public relations skills, which further promoted Matthews as the most reliable expert on anticommunism among southern segregationists. In her seminal work, *Turn Away Thy Son: Little Rock, the Crisis That Shocked the Nation,* published in the fiftieth anniversary year of that desegregation incident, Elizabeth Jacoway simply describes Matthews traveling the South, appearing before Communist-hunting legislative hearings, and presenting "much of the same testimony in each venue."[15]

While Jacoway's observation is not entirely false, Matthews exerted much more influence among the architects and practitioners of the white South's massive resistance than her work acknowledges. With the indispensable assistance rendered by Lowman, who functioned as Matthews's quasi-sales representative for southern states, Matthews succeeded in selling his often inflated guilty-by-association fallacies and fantasies to those who desperately needed them to perpetuate the region's racial norms. And in the early 1960s, when the progress of Parkinson's disease began to restrict Matthews's day-to-day activities and eventually prevented him from taking trips to the South, Lowman filled Matthews's shoes and funneled much sought-after information into southern audiences. From the fall of 1953 until Matthews's death in July 1966, Lowman and Matthews remained close associates, working as a team for more than a decade. In this respect, for many southern segregationists who dealt with and relied upon them, they were "Tweedledum and Tweedledee," to borrow the coinage of the eighteenth-century English poet John Byrom. Lowman and Matthews leaned on each other to enhance their reputations as credible anti-Communists, and the white South's massive resisters relied on them to maintain their region's sanctified racial orthodoxy.

After all, while the watchword of "states' rights" offered southern segregationists a seemingly respectable constitutional mantle, a cry of "Communist conspiracy" presented them with a plausible and all-purpose tool to perpetuate white supremacy in a Cold War environment. In anticommunism, white southerners found an effective and elastic weapon that they could not only mold to suit to their needs, but also use to express their rages, fears, and uncertainties. Equally important, unlike the resurrected theory of states' rights constitutionalism, anticommunism could easily garner attentive audiences beyond the confines of the South. To be sure, assessing the proper role played by anticommunism in the white South's massive resistance is far from being a simple and monolithic task because, as Lewis has accurately pointed out in his own work, examining anticommunism's role during the resistance movement era is "fraught with difficulties."[16]

Some leaders and advocates of the civil rights movement, even though they were quite small in number, might indeed have been devoted Communists or at least inclined to adopting Communist ideologies to accomplish their causes. In fact, until at least the very early 1950s, Communists could be found—in numbers that were quite "out of proportion" to the size of the Communist Party of the United States of America (CPUSA) itself—in civil rights politics and the labor movement.[17] But the civil rights historiography—scholarly books and articles, as well as memoirs penned by the movement's participants—has attested that the vast majority of civil rights leaders (including the iconic Martin Luther King Jr.), activists, and sympathizers led and supported the movement within the confinement of the American democratic system. Meanwhile, due largely to anticommunism's elasticity, divining the true intensions of southern segregationists in deploying the weapon of anticommunism for their resistance movement is not an easy endeavor. The notion of a "world Communist conspiracy" that was promoted by the white South's massive resisters was certainly a product of both their long-held racial paranoia and aversion to the civil rights movement, as well as their political pragmatism. An absolute and clear-cut line between responsible anticommunism and irresponsible racial and racist red-baiting in the South is therefore almost impossible to draw. In addition, the involvement of northern anti-Communist crusaders such as Lowman and Matthews—both of whom, to be sure, were neither outright segregationists nor peremptory racists—in the South's resistance movement makes that line of demarcation even more elusive.

In the final analysis, however, regardless of whether anticommunism was embraced sincerely or expediently by the keepers of the South's segregated societies (and despite the fact that professional anticommunism and its diabolical anti-Communist schemes eventually became much less persuasive to many excepting the most extreme southern segregationists), its effects were the same on those who were targeted as enemies, creating formidable webs of suspicion and suppression in the civil rights South. "Communism is not love!" the Chinese Communist leader Mao Tse-tung once cried out. "Communism," he dared to say, "is a hammer we use to destroy our enemies!"[18] And in the same manner, anticommunism did not embody love, either. In the civil rights South, it was used as a vicious and versatile tool to suppress enemies, sustaining "unreasoned and unreasonable resistance to free expression and experimentation" in race relations, to borrow the words of the celebrated historian John Hope Franklin.[19] In the minds of segregationist ideologues, as one Louisiana segregationist politician proclaimed in his pealing voice in 1958, "Communism and integration" were "inseparable," and "the red-tagging of Negro protest" thus became an important ingredient in guarding the white South's racist logic.[20] In summary, my objective in writing this book is to demonstrate how the white South's massive resisters relied upon those professional northern anti-Communists such as Lowman and Matthews to legitimize and vindicate their unsavory crusade against the black civil rights movement and how the massive resisters, as the keepers of the region's segregated societies, attempted during the 1950s and 1960s to nationalize their resistance not only to irresistible tides of social change but also to federal authority.

While I was in the research phase of this work in September 2005, I had an opportunity to spend a productive and memorable week at Louisiana State University in Shreveport, despite the fact that I was forced to be situated in the midst of chaos and confusion caused by Hurricane Katrina, which had just devastated New Orleans. There, at the beautiful Noel Memorial Library on the charming university campus, while I was examining the personal papers of the late Louisiana state senator William M. "Willie" Rainach—one of the most ardent segregationists that not only Louisiana, but also the entire South, had ever produced—I happened to share some of the archival boxes of the Rainach Papers with a white undergraduate who was writing her research paper on Louisiana's civil rights movement. After looking through some of those yellowed archival documents left by the state senator for some time, the student lifted her head from what she had been examining, looked at me, and asked me a short and abrupt question across our working table, as if she had been bound by a magic spell: "Was he real?" Unable to comprehend that only a half century earlier, her own native state, led by the state senator and his like-minded politicians, had fought so fiercely against the civil rights movement in the name of racial integrity, states' rights, and anticommunism, she just needed my assurance that Rainach really did exist.

This apparently casual but profound question attests that the South, four decades after the virtual demise of massive resistance, is no longer the "no-man's land of uncertainty and suspicion," having undergone tremendous changes in those years. At the same time, it also confirms and reinforces the important lesson that only by thumbing through the pages of seemingly closed chapters can we ensure that the painful past contained in those chapters will not be repeated. Thus, it is my particular and utmost wish that, along with historians and scholars, even young readers—high school and college students alike—in the South will consult this book and learn from their past, for "the past is never dead," as the Mississippi novelist William Faulkner's fictitious Gavin Stevens has reminded us, "[and] it's not even past."[21] Grappling with and confronting the dark corners of our past, whether they relate to the American South or elsewhere, is part and parcel of envisioning, encouraging, and ensuring a better future for the present generation and those who are to come. As the Pulitzer Prize–winning journalist and historian David Halberstam once said, "the less secret the past becomes, the freer we all will be."[22]

Reexamining America's civil rights years through the eyes of the villains who positioned themselves as the architects and practitioners of massive resistance in the South, as well as through the acts of northerners who lent their helping hands to southern segregationists, leads us to further understanding and appreciation of what the civil rights movement and those who fought and even made the ultimate sacrifice in the struggle really needed to overcome. Historical knowledge cannot rewrite the past, but it enables us to chart the future. And in our endeavor to move ourselves into a better future, history, even though it is saturated with many mortal blots, never fails to teach us to hope.

ACKNOWLEDGMENTS

Almost without exception, crafting a book-length manuscript is a mighty task, regardless of whether it is done in the author's mother tongue or in his/her acquired foreign languages. Though I do not presume to class myself with Oscar Wilde, I readily understand and share the troubles and trials experienced by the nineteenth-century Irish writer, who once vented his frustration with the following words: "I was working on the proof of one of my poems all the morning, and took out a comma. In the afternoon I put it back again." Preparing a book manuscript is well and truly a constant and sometimes seemingly endless string of tasks of writing, altering, deleting, and pondering the appropriateness of what has just been composed.

To be sure, any book-writing project is accomplished not only by the author's hard work, but also by what Michael Larsen, a noted literary agent in San Francisco, has called "heart work"—the calling which awakens, inspires, and sustains the author. Despite the fact that the manuscript's final form—a book—eventually bears only the author's name, in every writing project, there is an assortment of unsung heroes and heroines—both individuals and institutions—who duly deserve their recognition in having set and kept the author's "heart work" afire. Though writing a proper and inclusive acknowledgment itself is also a mighty task, in the following few pages, I wish to express my sincere and profound appreciation to those, on both sides of the Pacific, who have provided me with their unqualified support and encouragement during this book's making, as well as to those who have helped me get to the point where I stand today.

First and foremost, I would like to thank the late Makoto Saito, my mentor and friend from my graduate school days at International Christian University in Tokyo. A celebrated pioneer of American studies in Japan, he laid the solid foundations of the discipline as an academic field when

Japan still lay in ruins following the termination of World War II. As a diligent and prolific scholar and an admirable and impassioned teacher, Saito had reminded me time and time again that the ultimate raison d'être for my being a scholar was to publish—making my thoughts and interpretations public—no matter how swamped I was with teaching loads and administrative responsibilities. Saito departed this life on a cold day in January 2008, while the manuscript of this book was still in its making. For almost nineteen years, I had been truly blessed to have him not only as my mentor and friend, but also as my shining example and guiding beacon. I miss him so dearly, and the memory of him is deeply treasured.

In the course of writing this book, the American Philosophical Society in Philadelphia, Pennsylvania—the oldest learned society in the United States—most generously awarded me its 2007 Benjamin Franklin Research Grant. I am deeply grateful to Richard S. Dunn, chair of the society's Committee on Research, and other committee members, as well as its gracious research administrator, Linda Musumeci, for enabling me to complete the final phase of my research for this book.

Two other research institutions both in the United States and in Japan granted me the equally indispensable financial support. Twice in 2003 and 2006, the John Hope Franklin Collection of African and African American Documentation (presently the John Hope Franklin Research Center for African and African American History and Culture), a splendid research organ belonging to the Rare Book, Manuscript, and Special Collections Library (presently the David M. Rubenstein Rare Book and Manuscript Library) at Duke University in Durham, North Carolina, granted me generous travel grants, making it possible for me to conduct research on Duke's picturesque campus. I sincerely thank Karen Jean Hunt, director of the Franklin Collection, and the institution's selection committee, for believing in the worthiness of my project. In addition, in the spring of 2007, Duke's Special Collections Library kindly offered me the pleasant and valuable opportunity to give a public lecture there on the subject of anticommunism in the civil rights South. The generosity offered by the American Studies Foundation in Tokyo must also be mentioned. Without its graciousness, enthusiasm, and trust, my summer-long four-state research trip within the United States in 2005 could not have materialized. My heartfelt appreciation goes to Nobuyuki Nakahara, chair of the foundation's board of trustees, and two other board members, Tadashi Aruga and Hiroko Sato.

Along with these research institutions, I would like to thank the advisory committee members of an international conference entitled "The

Little Rock Desegregation Crisis: Fifty Years Later." The conference, which was held in Little Rock, Arkansas, in September 2007, generously invited me to participate in its plenary session called "The Varieties of Segregationism." Part of the chapter dealing with the situation in Arkansas in this book is based on the paper that I prepared for this international gathering. I am most grateful to the University of Arkansas at Little Rock for providing me with financial support, making my trip to the charming southern city possible. Most of all, the friendship and hospitality extended to me by the conference's cochairs—David L. Chappell at the University of Arkansas in Fayetteville (presently at the University of Oklahoma in Norman) and C. Fred Williams at the University of Arkansas in Little Rock—are deeply appreciated.

During the process of researching for this book, I was able to make a dozen trips to the United States from Japan, visiting some thirty local, state, university, and presidential libraries and archives in person. The archival material that I have examined during these research trips include the voluminous J. B. Matthews Papers, the heretofore underused Myers G. Lowman Papers and Circuit Riders, Inc., Records, and a host of personal papers and official records generated by segregationist politicians and state agencies that thrived in the Jim Crow South. I often had to convince myself that the many research trips across the Pacific were a necessary burden that I should embrace and endure. Nonetheless, this physical burden also brought me many blessings—the blessings of getting acquainted and making friends with those gifted and diligent archivists and librarians whose invaluable assistance and suggestions often broadened my historical understanding and intellectual horizons. Besides being superb professionals who made my research process much easier and pleasant, some of them were kind enough to offer me hot meals (I have learned long ago that for any traveling researcher, hot meals are true blessings) and even willing to give me rides between my accommodations and their institutions. Furthermore, a few of them, going well beyond their call of duty, kindheartedly took me on driving tours to sites of local interest and accompanied me to nearby farmers markets on weekends.

Though the acknowledgments may never be completely inclusive or fully reveal the extent of the contribution made by those archivists and librarians, I must take special note of the generosity offered by the following individuals and institutions: Patrick R. Robbins at Bob Jones University in Greenville, South Carolina; Sharon K. Perry at California State University in Fullerton; Terry S. Latour at Delta State University in

Cleveland, Mississippi (presently at Clarion University of Pennsylvania in Clarion); L. Dale Patterson at Drew University in Madison, New Jersey; Janie C. Morris, Elizabeth B. Dunn, and Eleanor A. Mills at Duke University; Miriam Gan-Spalding at the Florida State Archives (presently the State Archives of Florida) in Tallahassee; Chris Paton and Andy Phrydas at the Georgia Archives in Morrow; Liz Safly at the Harry S. Truman Presidential Library in Independence, Missouri; Judy Bolton and Jason B. Ford at Louisiana State University in Baton Rouge; Laura L. McLemore and Domenica Carriere at Louisiana State University in Shreveport; Elbert R. Hilliard, Hank T. Holmes, Anne S. Webster, Clarence Hunter, and Preston Everett at the Mississippi Department of Archives and History in Jackson; Mattie Abraham at Mississippi State University in Mississippi State; Elizabeth Odle at the Nashville Public Library in Tennessee; Wayne M. Everard at the New Orleans Public Library in Louisiana; Carol H. Holliger at Ohio Wesleyan University in Delaware, Ohio; Carol A. Leadenham, Ronald M. Bulatoff, and Nicholas C. Siekierski at Stanford University in Stanford, California; Susan L. Gordon at the Tennessee State Library and Archives in Nashville; Anne W. Prichard at the University of Arkansas in Fayetteville; Sheryl B. Vogt and Jill R. Severn at the University of Georgia in Athens; Jennifer W. Ford and Sally Leigh McWhite at the University of Mississippi in University; William K. Cawley at the University of Notre Dame in Notre Dame, Indiana; Bruce Tabb at the University of Oregon in Eugene; Andrew C. Rhodes and Elizabeth K. La Beaud at the University of Southern Mississippi in Hattiesburg; Muriel McDowell-Jackson at the Washington Memorial Library in Macon, Georgia; and Lisa R. Marine at the Wisconsin Historical Society in Madison.

Besides these adept archivists and librarians in the United States, I am also indebted to Dorothy Sheridan, head of the Special Collections, and John W. Mason, my researcher, at the University of Sussex in Brighton, United Kingdom. I first got acquainted with John when I was afforded an opportunity to offer a special lecture on the South's massive resistance at the University of Sussex in the spring of 2002. An able and considerate researcher, John endured my repeated requests for photocopying pertinent documents from the Harvey Matusow Archive housed at the university.

A great friend of mine from my graduate school days in the United States, Reid S. Derr at East Georgia College in Swainsboro, also looked into some microfilm of Georgia newspapers on my behalf. Reid was my fellow doctoral student at the University of Southern Mississippi when I was a Fulbright graduate scholar there, and the research trips that Reid and I took together to Jackson, Starkville, and some other places in Mississippi during the early 1990s were all full of fun and wonderful memories. I thank him for his graciousness and, much more than that, his unabated friendship.

I further wish to acknowledge my profound debts to some of the individuals who, in one way or the other, had helped me to keep my "heart work" afire. They include Natsuki Aruga of Tokyo; Tony Badger at the University of Cambridge in Cambridge, United Kingdom; Stephen L. Bennett at the Westwood United Methodist Church in Cincinnati, Ohio; Charles C. "Chuck" Bolton at the University of North Carolina in Greensboro; Douglas Brinkley at Rice University in Houston, Texas; Sarah Hart "Sallie" Brown at Florida Atlantic University in Jupiter; Orville Vernon Burton at the University of Illinois in Urbana; Dan T. Carter at the University of South Carolina in Columbia; Shin Chiba at International Christian University; Constance "Connie" Curry at Emory University in Atlanta, Georgia; Joe P. Dunn at Converse College in Spartanburg, South Carolina; Adam Fairclough at Leiden University in Leiden, Netherlands; Gaines M. Foster at Louisiana State University in Baton Rouge; the late John Hope Franklin at Duke University; Samuel C. Hyde Jr., at Southeastern Louisiana University in Hammond; Georg G. Iggers at the State University of New York in Buffalo; Michael J. Klarman at the University of Virginia in Charlottesville; Kevin M. Kruse at Princeton University in Princeton, New Jersey; George Lewis at the University of Leicester in Leicester, United Kingdom; Robert M. Lichtman of San Francisco, California; Martin S. Matthews of Langley, Washington; Marian McElroy of Waco, Texas; Neil R. McMillen of Hattiesburg, Mississippi; Elizabeth Gillespie McRae at Western Carolina University in Cullowhee, North Carolina; James H. Meredith of Jackson, Mississippi; Richard "Dick" Molpus of Philadelphia, Mississippi; Bo Moore at the Citadel in Charleston, South Carolina; Nisaburo Murakushi of Chiba, Japan; Naoki Onishi at International Christian University; Tom Pace at St. Luke's United Methodist Church in Houston, Texas; Jeremy Richards at Gordon College in Barnesville, Georgia; David B. Sageser of Fort Myers, Florida; Randy Sanders at Southeastern Louisiana University; William E. Saracino at the Americanism Educational League in Buena Park, California; James A. Schnur at the University of South Florida in St. Petersburg; Christopher R. "Chris" Waldrep at San Francisco State University; Peter Wallenstein at Virginia Polytechnic Institute and State

University in Blacksburg; Clive Webb at the University of Sussex; Ken Williams at the Kentucky Historical Society in Frankfort; and William F. Winter of Jackson, Mississippi.

The completion of this project would not have been possible without the guidance, enthusiasm, patience, and friendship of Paul R. "Rand" Dotson, executive editor at the Louisiana State University Press. Equally, I would like to thank the members of the University Press Committee for approving the publication of my manuscript by unanimous vote. In addition, I have immensely benefited from the generous counsel of this book's series editor, David R. Goldfield at the University of North Carolina at Charlotte, whose superb writings have made so much contribution to and broadened our understanding of the American South; and the insightful and encouraging comments of an anonymous reviewer of my book manuscript. I also take utmost pleasure in thanking my able and gracious developmental and copy editor, Susan A. Murray of York, Maine, who treated and nurtured my manuscript as if it were her own. Last but not least, the generosity of three staff members at the Louisiana State University Press—MaryKatherine Callaway, director; Lee C. Sioles, managing editor; and Lauren C. Tussing-White, marketing coordinator—needs to be mentioned here as well.

In the final stages of preparing my book manuscript, the Text and Academic Authors Association in St. Petersburg, Florida, generously awarded me its publication grant. My deepest gratitude goes to the association's executive director, Richard T. Hull, who kindly placed his trust in me and my project.

As always, my family members, who have been near and dear to me, should occupy a special place in the pages of the acknowledgments. There must be a million words to thank them, and I am afraid that I am not well versed in dexterously selecting those rare and magical few. I am immensely indebted and eternally grateful to my parents, Yasohachi and Mikiko Katagiri of Tokyo; my parents-in-law, Charles and Shirley Modesitt of Fort Worth, Texas; Hidetoshi and Harumi Katagiri of Hokkaido, Japan; the Coleman family (Jerry, Carla, Cayla, and Alexis) of Lucas, Texas; my beloved wife and a proud Texan, Brenda; and our three little (though they are no longer physically "little") ARKs—Akira Reuben, a Tokyoite by birth as I am and an adopted Texan; and Aya Rebekah and Ann Rachel, who are Mississippians by virtue of their births. I am blessed and honored to have been their son, husband, father, and friend. Each and every one of them makes me so proud, and when I count my blessings, I shall count them twice.

Last, if this book possesses any merit of being recognized as a meaning-ful addition to the civil rights historiography, all of those who are men-tioned here deserve to share the honor with me. The entire responsibility for any errors in narrative or interpretations in this book rests squarely upon me.

BLACK FREEDOM,
WHITE RESISTANCE,
AND RED MENACE

MERGING SOUTHERN PAROCHIALISM
WITH AMERICANISM

Black Monday and White Fears in the Troubled South

In the immediate aftermath of World War II, when America's struggle against the Soviet Union and its Communist bloc for the allegiance of nonwhite countries in Africa, Asia, and the Middle East commenced in earnest, a glaring inconsistency surfaced in the sphere of the nation's domestic affairs. While advocating and supporting freedom and democracy in the international realm, the United States, which President Franklin D. Roosevelt had once proudly called the "great arsenal of democracy," failed to live up to its professed ideals at home, most notably, in the southern states. In the postwar era, as black southerners increasingly demanded their rights as citizens and as the Soviets began to exploit brutal racial incidents in the South, the survival of white supremacy in the United States began to capture the attention of the world. With the values, as well as the nature and honor, of American democracy suddenly facing international scrutiny, the white South found itself on a collision course with the "great arsenal of democracy."

Along with the commencement of the Cold War came anticommunism and the accompanying fanatic conformity to American values and creeds in the United States. While anticommunism, as an ideology, certainly represented a response to the nagging stalemate overseas, it was also a reaction to new insecurities of life in the domestic sphere, where conventional values and ways of life seemed to be undergoing rapid change. Its noble pronouncements about democracy notwithstanding, the United States, through the rigidity of its foreign policy toward Soviet expansion

1

abroad, ushered in the "Communist menace" hysteria in American society, obscuring the line between a government's responsibility to defend national security and irresponsible assaults on the liberties of individuals whose views, visions, and voices were deemed unconventional. Under these circumstances, the "red-scared" American society, experiencing an unstable present and facing an uncertain future, also produced a parade of groups and individuals that attempted to link their own various agendas with the anti-Communist cause. Among those who sought to cloak their cause in the mantle of America's anti-Communist commitment, southern segregationists were conspicuous.

To be sure, the threat of international and domestic communism was used to maintain the racial status quo in the South before the 1940s. The persistent, almost obsessive belief that unwelcome changes to race relations in the region were the results of outside influences and agitation had mesmerized white southerners since the early 1930s. Not only Socialist and Communist ideas, but southern radicalism in general—which included interracialism—had often been the focus of thundering hostility expressed by the region's white leaders and elites, whose social, political, and economic status and privileges were inextricably connected with the established system of race and caste. In the wake of the Great Depression, the South witnessed the emergence of interracial agricultural union groups and labor projects espousing southern radicalism, such as the Southern Tenant Farmers' Union (STFU) and the Providence Cooperative Farm, most of which were viewed as Communist-inspired by the southern white establishment.

Incensed at their inhuman treatment by planters, a group of sharecroppers formed the biracial STFU during the summer of 1934 in Poinsett County, Arkansas, with the involvement of some Christian Socialists. As the union gradually expanded its influence throughout the fertile Mississippi Delta land of east Arkansas and then to the neighboring states, the STFU soon aroused the enmity of local planters. For these planters, the interracial cooperation evidenced in the union activities, reminiscent of the Populist movement in the late nineteenth century, was ominous enough, but the STFU's open and close identification with the Socialist Party—primarily through the interest of the party leader Norman Thomas—exasperated the white establishment and prompted them to identify the union as part of a Communist plot.[1] While joining the STFU gave many black tenant farmers hope, it was also a risky business because, as one Arkansas sharecropper complained, "De landlord is landlord, de politicians is landlord, de judge is landlord, de shurf is landlord, ever'body is landlord."[2]

Another southern interracial enterprise was the Providence Cooperative Farm in the Mississippi Delta section of Holmes County, Mississippi. The farm was a brainchild of Sam H. Franklin Jr., A. Eugene Cox, and some other young and idealistic white Christian Socialists who were influenced and given moral support by Reinhold Niebuhr, the distinguished theologian at Union Theological Seminary in New York City.[3] Since its inception in 1938, the Providence Cooperative Farm (originally established as the Delta Cooperative Farm in Boliver County in 1936 with the involvement of the STFU) had annoyed the local whites with its forthright commitment to being "loyal to the principle of inter-racial justice" and its racially nondiscriminating practices on the farm, such as "giving titles of respect to black and white alike." Because of their simple decency, brotherhood, and benevolence, the white residents on Providence were "frequently charged by the neighboring planters and others in the white establishment with being communist."[4] By1956, the social and economic pressures exerted by the local white posses on the farm leaders proved unbearable, and the Providence director Cox, his family, and his associates were forced to abandon the interracial enterprise in the summer of 1956.[5] Those at the top of the white-supremacist hierarchy feared that any genuine interracial cooperative effort carried out by such organizations as the STFU and the Providence Cooperative Farm were "inspired by Communists" with a hidden agenda to dismantle racial segregation, which was integral to the social and economic status quo.[6]

Meanwhile, Communists did seek to make inroads in the South. In 1930, the Communist Party of the United States of America (CPUSA) proceeded to organize the southern states, creating three major organizational districts centered in Birmingham, Alabama; New Orleans, Louisiana; and Winston-Salem, North Carolina. The party established its southern headquarters in Birmingham because the city had a large number of black industrial workers and because the surrounding rural farming economy was sustained by economically and socially disadvantaged white sharecroppers.[7] Thus, it may not have been mere coincidence that Birmingham would soon become the birthplace of one of the most remarkable, as well as the most red-baited, interracial enterprises of the 1930s—the Southern Conference for Human Welfare (SCHW).

Organized principally by southern supporters of President Roosevelt and his New Deal programs, the SCHW sought to unite diverse social reformers—both black and white—in the South to seek solutions to the region's pressing economic problems. Frank Porter Graham, president of the University of North Carolina, served as the founding chair of the SCHW, which welcomed the federal government's programs to eliminate poverty, supported the labor union movement, campaigned against the administration of poll tax, and criticized racial discrimination.[8] When the SCHW's organizational meeting was held in Birmingham on November 20, 1938—"the largest assemblage of Southern progressives" since the Reconstruction era, with more than one thousand people taking part—President Roosevelt sent a congratulatory message to the gathered delegates. "If you steer a true course and keep everlastingly at it," Roosevelt stated, "the South will long be thankful for this day."[9] Among the delegates attending the founding meeting was the president's wife, Eleanor Roosevelt.[10]

The SCHW did not hesitate to organize a number of interracial meetings and conferences in the Jim Crow South and allied itself with the Congress of Industrial Organizations (CIO), which aroused white southerners' suspicions. Worse still, the SCHW did not vigorously purge professed Communists from its membership, though only a handful of them actually ever joined the interracial organization.[11] Its organizational policies quickly made the SCHW vulnerable to a mounting number of exaggerated charges by southern segregationists that the group was infested with Communist influences. Instead of being "thankful" for the creation of the SCHW, as President Roosevelt optimistically predicted, segregationists viewed the interracial organization as a gathering threat to their southern way of life.

Meanwhile, in the nation's capital, southern lawmakers and their sympathizers were equally eager to document the Communist Party's attempt to win black southerners' support for "revolutionizing" the United States. On May 26, 1938, only six months before the SCHW's inception, Congress created the House Special Committee on Un-American Activities.[12] Appointed as its chair was Martin Dies Jr., who, as a Democratic representative of the hill country of East Texas, had served in the House since 1931. Coupled with his unconcealed racism, Dies's suspicion of "big cities, big capital, big labor, big government, foreigners, and foreign ideologies" had eventually convinced him that subversive elements were infiltrating the government, the press, the labor, and the inceptive civil rights movement in the United States.[13] With a congressional appropriation of twenty-five thousand dollars at its disposal, in August 1938, the seven-member House committee, which would soon be referred to as the Dies Committee, began its initial round of hearings in Washington, D.C. Dies promised that his committee would conduct a "fearless investigation" to reveal "the extent, character, and objects" of subversive and un-American propaganda activities in the nation.[14] By the end of 1938, the Dies Committee had subpoenaed more than one hundred witnesses over a period of just four months and devoted considerable time and resources to the investigation of Nazi and fascist activities in the United States and their "intolerant ideologies . . . transplanted to our shores."[15]

During 1939, however, the Dies Committee had increasingly revealed its anti-Communist tendencies. In 1940, Dies published one of the most militantly anti-Communist books of the day, *The Trojan Horse in America.* "Moscow has long considered the Negroes of the United States as excellent potential recruits for the Communist Party," Dies asserted, "[and] it has envisaged an unusual opportunity to create racial hatred between the white and Negro citizens of the United States."[16] Five years later, the Dies-chaired House committee, which had been appropriated a total of $652,500 during its almost seven-year existence, would be transformed into a more powerful standing committee with the blessing of Representative John E. Rankin from Mississippi, one of the most rabid and outspoken southern racial reactionaries. With the expiration date of his committee close at hand, Dies wrote to his House colleagues in November 1944, asking them to give their careful consideration to "what disposition should be made of the files" accumulated by the committee—"the most complete files in the United States on subversive organizations and individuals," Dies boasted. "It is my opinion," he wrote, "that these files should be . . . actively maintained" and placed "under the jurisdiction of one of the standing committees of the House."[17]

Dies's passionate plea eventually bore fruit. On January 3, 1945, the first day of the first session of the new Seventy-Ninth Congress, Mississippi representative Rankin succeeded in getting an eleven-vote majority to reorganize and strengthen the Dies Committee, which had become defunct only a few hours earlier, as the House Un-American Activities Committee (HUAC)—the lower chamber's new standing committee. "The vote showed that the members of Congress are in favor of having a Vigilante Committee," Rankin triumphantly asserted two weeks later when interviewed on a CBS radio program, "[and] I took up this fight where he [Dies] left off."[18] At the helm of the new HUAC was Democratic representative Edward J. Hart from New Jersey, who would soon be succeeded as chair by another Democrat, Georgia representative John S. Wood. Later, when Republicans gained control of the House in the 1946 midterm elections, New Jersey representative J. Parnell Thomas, a former member of the Dies Committee, was appointed as its chair. Rankin, who then chaired the powerful House Veterans' Affairs Committee, could have taken the chairmanship of the HUAC as well. Instead, however, the Mississippi representative chose to sit on the HUAC as a regular member, from which position he could better promote his agenda of racism and anti-Semitism, manipulating a majority coalition of southern Democrats and conservative Republicans in the House.[19]

In 1947, the New York–based Civil Rights Congress (CRC)—one of the most vital civil rights organizations in the pre-*Brown* era—sarcastically noted that "Rankin and his committeemen" had behaved like "true vigilantes" since the HUAC's inception, "knowing no law but their own prejudices."[20] As if to substantiate this observation, in the same year, the SCHW—like virtually every other group seeking social and racial reforms in the South—became a target of the red-baiting House committee. Charging that the SCHW was "perhaps the most deviously camouflaged Communist-front organization," the HUAC's hastily gathered report of June 1947 charged that the organization's "professed interest in southern welfare is simply an expedient for larger aims serving the Soviet Union" and its subservient CPUSA. Even though the accusation was groundless, this de facto "guilty" charge by the government, along with southern segregationists' concerted efforts to label the interracial organization as "red," led to the SCHW's demise in 1948.[21] Although the group's educational arm—the New Orleans–based Southern Conference Educational Fund (SCEF)—survived and took the mantle of the SCHW for the time being, it would also soon be victimized by a series of congressional and southern states' probes as an "adjunct" to the SCHW—the CPUSA's "transmission belt," as it was identified by proponents of massive resistance.[22]

By the time the SCHW disbanded in 1948, the presumption that social and racial reformers concealed sinister ulterior motives behind their benign facades had become an "accepted gospel" in the South, prompting the region's white supremacists to claim that these liberal crusaders were promoting and spreading not only unsouthern, but also un-American, ideas.[23] At the same time, southern segregationists' hostility toward the probable increase of black civil rights activities and toward the comprehensive civil rights program being advanced by the federal government—or by the national Democratic Party, to be more precise—became increasingly evident by the late 1940s. The most immediate cause of this hostility was the 1947 report issued by the President's Committee on Civil Rights and the subsequent actions taken by President Harry S. Truman.

President Truman, who had come to realize that America's domestic racism posed a major stumbling block to the nation's reputation overseas and that his own electoral strategy for the upcoming 1948 presidential election required northern black votes, appointed the President's Committee on Civil Rights in December 1946. Assisting the president and the work of his committee was the National Association for the Advancement of Colored People (NAACP), a group destined to become the white South's principal enemy and probably the most red-baited civil rights organization during the following two decades. Besides Frank Porter Graham, who had served as the founding chair of the SCHW, the fifteen-member President's Committee included Channing H. Tobias, a member of the board of trustees of the NAACP.[24]

In October 1947, the President's Committee on Civil Rights released its report entitled *To Secure These Rights.* Determining that racial segregation was "inconsistent with the fundamental equalitarianism of the American way of life," the committee listed a total of thirty-five recommendations for both congressional and administrative actions in its report—the enactment of an anti–poll tax law, the prohibition of segregation in interstate transportation facilities, and the renewal of the Fair Employment Practice Committee (FEPC) originally created under the Roosevelt administration, among others—to protect the civil rights of black Americans and to begin eliminating racial segregation from American life. "There is no adequate defense of segregation," the committee report concluded definitively.[25] Observing that the title of his committee's report was taken from the Declaration of Independence, President Truman issued a statement praising the committee's work: "I hope this Committee has given us as broad a document as that—an American charter of human freedom in our time," adding that "the need for such a charter was never greater than at this moment."[26]

President Truman's words and conviction in support of a comprehensive civil rights program enraged most southern Democrats. Their worst nightmare, however, was yet to come. On July 12, 1948, despite vehement southern protest, the Democratic National Convention adopted its strongest and most forthright civil rights plank ever and commended Truman for his "courageous stand" on the issue when the convention met in Philadelphia—the City of Brotherly Love.[27] Although they were severely bruised, southern Democrats were in no mood for compromise. On July 17, only a few days after the Democratic National Convention adjourned, a disgruntled group of some six thousand delegates from thirteen southern states gathered in Birmingham—the birthplace of the SCHW—and began their rump convention. Before long, the hastily convened meeting formed the States' Rights Democratic Party, or the Dixiecrat Party, and elected South Carolina governor J. Strom Thurmond as the new party's presidential hopeful and Mississippi governor Fielding L. Wright as the nominee for vice president.[28]

The platform adopted by the Dixiecrats in Birmingham, a document of barely a thousand words, forcefully presented the case for laissez-faire economics as well as states' rights, stressing the importance of such concepts as home rule, police power, and local self-government. Furthermore, equating the "totalitarian government" of President Truman and the national Democratic Party with a Communist form of government, and thus playing on the larger Cold War rhetoric, the Dixiecrats resolved to defend the "American way of life," denouncing the racial egalitarianism advanced by what they described as "Federal fiat," which would sooner or later destroy their cherished "southern way of life."[29] Though they completely failed to recognize—or were unwilling to admit—the great discrepancy between the American and southern ways of life, the southern segregationists in the Dixiecrat revolt handily combined the volatile issues of states' rights ideology, racial segregation, and anticommunism.

Further, the proponents of the Dixiecrat movement were eager to articulate their opposition to Truman's proposed civil rights program in terms of what they conveniently identified as its anti-American and pro-Communist features. For instance, they asserted that the FEPC, "patterned after a Soviet law authored by Joseph Stalin" during the 1920s, offered tangible evidence that Communist influences had infiltrated the federal government. According to Mississippi governor Wright, the nation's central government was in decline, becoming a "remote, distant, mysterious" government "beyond the comprehension of the people themselves." South Carolina governor Strom Thurmond—one of the "deepest-dyed conservatives" of the white South, with a "passionate devotion to the Southern way of life"—elaborated. He charged that the newly proposed FEPC provisions would result in inviting Communist "agents and saboteurs" to "every tool and die room, every machine shop and every industrial plant" in the South.[30] Summing up, Mississippi circuit court judge Thomas P. "Tom" Brady, one of the state delegates to the Democratic National Convention, offered the following analysis: "The platform of the present National

Democratic Party more closely approximates the Russian philosophy of government than it represents the principals [*sic*] of the true Democratic Party." Brady's invocation of the Red Menace also provides a glimpse of his consistently racist posture. The Truman administration's "Anti-Segregation Bill is the rock which finally splits the Democratic river," he wrote, "and there is also no power on earth which can prevent or deter us from our sacred responsibility of purging OUR party of these mongrelizing forces, which have like termites secretly eaten into our foundations." After all, for the Dixiecrat insurgents, almost any course of action that could conceivably invite "federal interference undermining state sovereignty and individual freedom" as well as racial integrity deserved to be "denounced as 'un-American' and 'Communistic.'"[31]

In the presidential election on November 2, 1948, the States' Rights Democratic Party received 1,169,134 out of 48,692,442 popular votes and 39 out of 531 electoral votes. The party carried only four of the five Deep South states—Alabama, Louisiana, Mississippi, and South Carolina—and failed to win in Georgia. About 87 percent of Mississippi voters cast their votes for the Dixiecrat ticket, which was the highest percentage among the four southern states, followed by Alabama's 80 percent.[32] Despite the southern revolt's dismal failure to garner substantial nationwide electoral support, the region's segregationists, as Thurmond defiantly declared at the Dixiecrat convention in Birmingham, had only "just begun to fight" to perpetuate the white South's racial and racist orthodoxy by whatever means necessary. (In late August 1957, Thurmond, as a U.S. senator from South Carolina, would launch a twenty-four-hour, one-man filibuster in opposition to the enactment of the Civil Rights Bill of 1957 on the Senate floor, setting a record in congressional history.) "The South's racial problem is a national problem, and the solutions are of national interest," *Life* magazine editorialized eight months after the election, reflecting the view of the Truman administration. But these progressive-minded words were anathema to the Dixiecrat malcontents.[33]

Essentially, the 1948 Dixiecrat movement laid a solid foundation for the germination of a peculiar ideology in the Democratic "Solid South"—an ideology that combined segregationist and racist views, the proposition of states' rights and state sovereignty, and anti-Communist consensus. This popular ideology became the basis for white southerners' organized and all-out massive resistance to the civil rights movement. More important, their experiences in waging the Dixiecrat revolt taught southern segregationists to perfect their blending of race-baiting with red-baiting, a strategy that would be employed throughout the South in the wake of the U.S. Supreme Court's epoch-making school desegregation ruling in May 1954.

Following the highly publicized Army-McCarthy hearings that lasted from April to June 1954 and the subsequent censure of Joseph R. McCarthy by the U.S. Senate in December 1954, the demise of the personal influence exerted by the Wisconsin senator—the flagship of red-baiting forces on the national political scene—had become evident to any eye. When the *New York Times* reported the Supreme Court's landmark school desegregation decision on May 18, 1954, a bold-lettered headline reading "McCarthy Hearing off a Week as Eisenhower Bars Report" also appeared on the newspaper's front page. The article described President Dwight D. Eisenhower's disdain for McCarthy's most recent harangues in the protracted Army hearings—the "damn business on the Hill," as the president called it—in which the senator had been exploring disloyalty within the U.S. Army, exposing his abusive tactics, and inviting a backlash against his crumbling crusade.[34] Although Senator McCarthy was once vilified by Eisenhower's predecessor, Truman, as "one of the worst demagogues that we ever had" in the national arena, the fire-breathing senator, in carrying out his blazing crusade, cautiously refrained from pandering to crude prejudices that could have easily met with ready acceptance in the South—namely, white supremacy and anti-Semitism.[35] Furthermore, McCarthy's religious and political affiliations—Catholicism and Republicanism—made him somewhat less popular in the South than in the rest of the nation, limiting enthusiasm for his cause in the region.[36]

Nonetheless, the political and social phenomena referred to as McCarthyism certainly encompassed far more than McCarthy's actions as a politician and an anti-Communist. Even after the Wisconsin senator's disappearance from the national political arena, McCarthyism's unsavory legacies—the self-serving use and abuse of hearsay and insinuation, the deliberate indifference to hard evidence, and the strident cries of "Communist conspiracy" used to impugn the legitimacy of adversaries—outlived their original inventor and remained a part of the national political scene. In the South, McCarthyism most often took a racial—and racist—form, and southern segregationists perpetuated its legacy in their response to the civil rights movement. Historically obsessed by a long succession of what they perceived as outside agitators and meddlers ("abolitionists, marauding blue-coats, Carpetbaggers," labor union leaders and now, civil rights activists) and troubled with fears of the unknown, white southerners were especially susceptible to a particular form of anti-Communist hysteria—racially loaded and southern-flavored McCarthyism.[37]

Only after the nation's most visible and vicious anti-Communist crusader was finally discredited and had faded away into oblivion, however, did southern politicians, officials, and the general citizenry eagerly begin to employ Cold War rhetoric in promoting their segregationist cause, crafting a philosophy based on conformity to defend the white South's racial status quo. Consequently, while the rest of the nation was struggling to move away from the fanatical Red Scare of the mid-1950s, a homebred and homegrown McCarthyism began to take hold in "the besieged and paranoid South."[38] In employing and orchestrating inflammatory southern red-baiting, the architects and practitioners of segregationist orthodoxy hoped that they had found a silver bullet that would infuse the hearts and minds of their fellow white southerners with a passion for their cause. The white South's aroused fervor to make its resistance "massive" came to a head when the Supreme Court announced its fateful school desegregation decision.

On Monday, May 17, 1954, in its *Brown v. Board of Education* ruling, the Supreme Court unanimously outlawed legally imposed racial segregation in public schools.[39] For the vast majority of white southerners, the day that the desegregation decision was rendered would be remembered as "Black Monday"—a phrase that was originally coined by U.S. representative John Bell Williams from Mississippi, a future governor of the state—and that "was to stick as a Southern epithet."[40] Resenting—even despising—the voice of American conscience raised by the nation's highest tribunal, some white southerners asserted that racial segregation was God-ordained.[41] Others resurrected a seemingly more sophisticated theory of states' rights constitutionalism to defy the Supreme Court decree and to combat the intensifying civil rights movement in the South. As Will D. Campbell, a Baptist minister and a civil rights activist, once noted, following the *Brown* ruling, "words seldom heard before became commonplace: states' rights, interposition, nullification, massive resistance, miscegenation, amalgamation."[42]

More important, southern white leadership continued to emphatically insist that black southerners' crusades for social justice and simple human dignity were nothing more than a foreign scheme directed and dominated by nefarious outside agitators, race-mixers, and, worse, outright subversives and card-carrying Communists. Although some leaders and supporters of the civil rights movement were indeed committed Communists or were at least inclined to utilize Communist ideologies to accomplish their causes, the vast majority of the leaders and participants in the movement worked within the boundaries of the American democratic system. To be sure, the white South's equating the region's civil rights struggle with the worldwide "Communist conspiracy" arose from a strong sense of powerlessness felt by ordinary white citizens. They perceived the federal government's attempts to regulate time-honored race relations and private rights of association as "invasions" by the centralized and "Communistic" bureaucracy and courts that represented a "dangerous slide toward communism."[43]

Although Mississippi representative Williams was the first to coin the phrase "Black Monday," it was Mississippi circuit court judge Tom Brady, a future associate justice of the state's supreme court, who popularized the term in the South. In the immediate aftermath of the *Brown* decision, Brady, who had walked out of the 1948 Democratic National Convention as one of the Mississippi delegates six years earlier, delivered an inflammatory address entitled "Black Monday" before the Greenwood, Mississippi, chapter of the Sons of the American Revolution. Almost instantly, his crude anti-*Brown* rhetoric gained great popularity among segregationists in Mississippi and other southern states. Eventually, Brady expanded his address into a book published in his own hometown of Brookhaven.[44]

Dedicating his *Black Monday* to "those Americans who firmly believe socialism and communism are lethal 'messes of porridge' for which our sacred birthright shall not be sold," Brady played up the alleged Communist influences lurking behind the *Brown* decree and the civil rights movement, dexterously intermingling Black Monday, white fears, and Red Menace. "'Black Monday' ranks in importance with July 4th, 1776, the date upon which our Declaration of Independence was signed," the Mississippi judge asserted, "[because] May 17th, 1954, is the date upon which the declaration of socialistic doctrine was officially proclaimed throughout this nation."[45] On the back cover of his book, Brady proclaimed to his fellow white southerners: "Lest We Forget . . . Integration of the races and the destruction of White America is one of Communistic Russia's objectives."[46]

Clearly, white southerners' grassroots involvement—such as Brady's defiance of the Supreme Court's *Brown* decision and the official sanctions given to that defiance by the respective southern state governments—proved indispensable in moving the South's massive resistance forward. It was equally true, however, that southern representatives and their sympathizers—both Democrats and Republicans—on Capitol Hill were critical to the region's resistance movement because of their eagerness—and resources—to "supplement the work of state officials," in the words of the political historian Dewey W. Grantham.[47] These national lawmakers' words and deeds added much-needed respectability to the southern states' resistance by cloaking the recalcitrant movement in the guise of fighting the "Communist conspiracy" and thus upholding Americanism. In this respect, the very existence of the HUAC and its counterpart in the Senate, the Senate Internal Security Subcommittee (SISS), greatly contributed to establishing a national climate of fear of the alien ideology of communism, as well as identifying the noble cause of anticommunism with the defense of racial segregation and discrimination in the South. The SISS, authorized to study and investigate broadly defined subversive activities in the nation, had been created under the Senate Judiciary Committee in late December 1950.

During the Eighty-Third Congress, from 1953 to 1955, despite the fact that the HUAC was handsomely funded, receiving approximately $575,000 in operational funds—more than any investigative committee in the House had ever been granted—it nevertheless operated in the shadow of Senator McCarthy and his well-publicized farcical plays.[48] But the Wisconsin senator's eventual political demise in 1954, which coincided with the Supreme Court's *Brown* decision, breathed "new life" into the HUAC, as well as the SISS. Having languished in the shadow of McCarthyism and realized that reckless inquisition into Communist subversion in the federal government could backfire, these congressional investigating committees, working closely with each other, began to prey instead on racial moderates and liberals and their nongovernmental institutions in the South.[49] The invigoration of the HUAC and the SISS as keepers of a segregationist anti-Communist undertaking lifted the curtain on the "Great Southern Commie Hunt," and its troubling effects began to engulf the South.[50]

Seven months after *Brown*, in late December 1954, the HUAC released a sixteen-page report entitled *The American Negro in the Communist Party*, in which the committee reiterated an assertion similar to the one that it had made in June 1947—that one of the major goals of the CPUSA was the "infiltration and control of the Negro population" in the South.[51] While the House committee established itself as what the civil rights advocate Anne M. Braden called a "Bulwark of Segregation," U.S. senator James O. Eastland from Mississippi wielded the scepter in the SISS.[52] Eastland—one of the most powerful archsegregationists and the Senate's counterpart of Mississippi representative John Rankin, who had played a pivotal role in making the HUAC a standing committee—was definitely a "logical custodian of the union" between segregationist enterprises and anti-Communist thoughts.[53] Indeed, the Mississippi senator was once referred to, with only slight exaggeration, as the man who "could be standing right in the middle of the worst Mississippi flood ever known and he'd say the niggers caused it, helped out by some communists."[54]

On January 29, 1954, the SISS chair, Republican senator William E. Jenner from Indiana, announced that the New Orleans–based SCEF—the surviving educational arm of the now defunct SCHW—would soon be the subject of the SISS's three-day hearings to be conducted by Senator Eastland. Accordingly, on March 17, exactly two months before the Supreme Court announced its *Brown* ruling, the Mississippi senator marched into New Orleans with the investigative tools generated by the 1947 HUAC report regarding the SCHW, while restlessly awaiting the outcome of the impending school segregation case. Eastland's sole purpose in doing so was to crack down on the SCEF, whose mission, as its executive director, James A. Dombrowski, once explained, was to "eliminate, through education, . . . all forms of racial discrimination and segregation" in the South.[55] Duly including the SCEF executive director in his investigative enemy list, the Mississippi senator was determined to carry forward the torch of the blatant hatred passed on by his predecessor, Senator Theodore G. Bilbo. While ranting that "the nigger is only 150 years from the jungles of Africa, where it was his great delight to cut him up some fried nigger steak for breakfast," Bilbo once castigated the SCHW—the SCEF's parent organization—as an "un-American, negro social equality, communistic, mongrel outfit," identifying the group as the South's "Number One Enemy."[56]

Besides Dombrowski, those ruthlessly interrogated and summarily accused of being "Reds" at the SISS's New Orleans hearings included Myles F. Horton, director of the Highlander Folk School in Monteagle, Tennessee. According to Eastland, Highlander was a "freakish, mongrelized, and basically Communist" interracial enterprise.[57] Another target of the New Orleans inquisitions was Virginia Foster Durr of Montgomery, a longtime activist for civil rights and social justice who would play a vital role in organizing the Alabama capital's yearlong Montgomery Bus Boycott the following year. Eastland's questioning sought to connect Durr's early civil rights activities with the CPUSA and was focused on her kinship with the Supreme Court justice Hugo L. Black, Durr's brother-in-law. Durr later noted that few people in her hometown really believed that she was a sinister Communist, but, she added, "the fact that we are against segregation is blazoned forth to all the Southern world, and in the minds of most Southerners that is tantamount to being subversive if not actually insane."[58] "In the South," Aubrey W. Williams, the president of the SCEF who was also hauled up before the SISS hearings, wryly reminded himself, "we have no liberals—only conservatives and radicals."[59] As for Senator Eastland, there was no middle ground: one was either a dyed-in-the-wool segregationist or a treacherous integrationist. His venomous hatred of proponents of racial moderation and his intense determination to defend the white South from them were without peer. Eastland undoubtedly prided himself on his role as the guardian of his beloved "Southland." As *Time* magazine reported, the Mississippi senator was destined to become "the authentic voice" of the white South, presenting himself as the tireless "spiritual leader of Southern resistance to school desegregation" and black southerners' civil rights struggle.[60]

Senator Eastland's well-publicized "Great Southern Commie Hunt" notwithstanding, the nation's High Court finally rendered what the journalist Richard Kluger has termed "simple justice" in the 1954 school desegregation ruling.[61] But for the Mississippi senator and the vast majority of his fellow white southerners, this was not "simple," but "sordid," justice imposed by the federal tyranny. Only ten days after the Supreme Court announced its *Brown* decision, Eastland, in a speech delivered on the Senate floor, vehemently charged that the Court had been "indoctrinated and brainwashed by left-wing pressure groups" in outlawing racial segregation in the South, while accusing five of the Court's nine justices by name. The senator's foremost target was Justice Black, Durr's brother-in-law, who had been presented with the first Thomas Jefferson Award for his distinguished service to the nation by the SCHW, which, according to Eastland, was a "notorious Communist-front organization." It was a "mockery of law," Eastland declared, "[if] a man who sits on the highest tribunal of our country and interprets the laws of this free Nation" espoused "the cause of our greatest enemy." Seeing no contradiction in the perpetuation of racial segregation and discrimination in his "free Nation" and beloved South, the Mississippi senator proclaimed in his May 27, 1954, speech: "Mr. President, let me make this very clear: The South will retain segregation."[62] In its 1954 report, the Eastland-dominated SISS reached the unanimous conclusion that the defunct SCHW had been "conceived, financed, and set up by the Communist Party in 1938 as a mass organization to promote Communism throughout the Southern States," and that its remaining organ, the SCEF, should be accounted for being equally "Red" and guilty.[63]

After the Democrats regained control of Congress in the November 1954 midterm elections, the SISS chairmanship eventually fell to Senator Eastland in 1955. Following the first anniversary of the school desegregation decision, on May 25, the Mississippi senator again stood on the Senate floor, this time contending that his "provisional investigation" of the sociological and psychological authorities on which the Supreme Court had heavily relied in issuing its *Brown* ruling revealed their unsavory connections with the "worldwide Communist conspiracy" to a "shocking degree." That said, Eastland, swearing to fight the desegregation decree, submitted a Senate resolution declaring that "it is the sense of the Senate" that its Judiciary Committee "should proceed . . . to investigate the extent and degree of participation by individuals and groups identified with the Communist conspiracy . . . in the formation of the 'modern scientific authority'" which the Court had consulted in deciding *Brown*.[64]

On May 31, 1955, only a week after Eastland fired his verbal salvos against the nation's highest tribunal, the Supreme Court issued the implementation decree of its 1954 *Brown* ruling, contrary to the Mississippi senator's prediction that the Court's enforcement edict to end school segregation was likely to be issued "within three or four years."[65] Before the Supreme Court handed down the implementation ruling, which would later be referred to as *Brown II,* the Court had held oral arguments on how to carry out the original *Brown* decree. Though the Supreme Court invited all states that would be affected by the *Brown* ruling to participate in the hearings, only six states—Arkansas, Florida, Maryland, North Carolina, Oklahoma, and Texas—accepted its invitation. Aside from South Carolina, which had already been involved in the original *Brown* case, no other Deep South states accepted the invitation because "such participation might imply an obligation to comply" with the Court's decree and because they deemed it "futile to debate implementing a decision which was not recognized as valid in the first place."[66] Admitting that implementation of the *Brown* ruling would "require solution of varied local school problems," the Supreme Court's unanimous opinion in *Brown II* concluded that legally imposed racial segregation in public schools should be eliminated "with all deliberate speed."[67]

The Supreme Court demonstrated legal inconsistency in handing down the first and second *Brown* decisions. While the Court declared in the first *Brown* ruling that black schoolchildren had the right to attend racially nonsegregated public schools under the Fourteenth Amendment to the U.S. Constitution, it virtually "denied these same children a full and instant implementation of this constitutional right" in issuing *Brown II*.[68] This contradiction was succinctly acknowledged in the brief phrase, "with all deliberate speed." As a result, the Supreme Court ended up suggesting a public policy of gradualism in dismantling segregation in the schools. In addition and more important, the Court's pronouncement that there would be a phased approach to school desegregation had the unintended result of granting southern segregationists—including, obviously, Senator Eastland—ample time to organize themselves against what they by then had customarily referred to as "federal encroachment" on their cherished and segregated southern way of life.

Following the Supreme Court's *Brown II* ruling, Eastland continued to emphasize his grand theme of the "Communist conspiracy."[69] In Eastland's view, the federal government and particularly its judicial branch were dangerously influenced by "left-wing pressure groups" represented by the NAACP, and therefore the *Brown* decisions and other antisegregation rulings by the Supreme Court were natural consequences of "left-wing brainwashing" suffered by the Court's justices.[70] In March 1956, while still serving as the SISS chair, Eastland was chosen to chair the powerful Senate Judiciary Committee over the vehement protest of the NAACP. "The Senate of the United States," the civil rights organization lamented, "has just voted to put an accessory to murder and treason in its most powerful judicial position." The quotation refers to the August 1955 murder of Emmett L. Till in the Mississippi Delta county of Tallahatchie, a gruesome racial incident that had helped spread Mississippi's racist notoriety across the nation.[71] Once accepting the chairmanship of the Senate Judiciary Committee, Eastland did not fall short of the NAACP's dark expectations. As the senator himself once boasted, by the end of 1956, Eastland had "put a special pocket in [his] pants" where he dutifully kept a host of civil rights–related bills to prevent their passage in Congress.[72]

Whether fully intended or not, the segregationist anti-Communist postures and activities of the HUAC and Senator Eastland's SISS encouraged southern segregationists to openly tie their regional parochialism to Americanism. Ironically, given the prodigious amount of undeserved prestige enjoyed by these congressional witch-hunting committees, the American South at large and particularly its Deep South states were destined to become somewhat akin—although on a much smaller scale—to the Soviet Union in their negation of liberty and justice, as well as in their suppression of dissent. In this regard, it was no surprise that Eastland's home county in the "Deepest" South state—Sunflower County, Mississippi, where the senator owned a 2,000-acre plantation—played the leading role in oppressing dissenters from the region's racial norms, giving birth to the South's most recalcitrant white-supremacist private organization in the wake of the *Brown* decision.[73]

On July 11, 1954, less than two months after the Supreme Court handed down the *Brown* decision, fourteen white Mississippians met at the home of David H. Hawkins, manager of a cotton compress company, in the Mississippi Delta town of Indianola, Sunflower County. Robert B. Patterson, a young cotton and cattle farmer from nearby Holly Ridge, was instrumental in organizing this gathering.[74] Predicating that racial integration would "utterly destroy everything that [he] valued," Patterson, whose own daughter was about to enter a local white-only public school, had vowed to lay down his life to "prevent mongrelization" and "defeat this Communistic disease that is being thrust" upon the white South.[75] More concretely, the purpose of the meeting was to "set out to organize a pressure group that would be a counterbalance" to the "Communistic" NAACP.[76] The founders of this "counterbalance" to the civil rights organization initially pondered naming their new group the Sons of the White Camellia as a composite of the names of two Reconstruction-era white secret organizations in the occupied South—the Sons of Midnight and the Knights of White Camellia. In the end, however, they decided to adopt a somewhat more benign name—the Citizens' Council—and asked Judge Tom Brady, author of *Black Monday,* to assist them in writing the charter and by-laws of the new white-supremacist organization.[77] Like Senator Eastland, Brady recognized no middle ground on the issue of race. For the Mississippi judge, racial liberalism in the South was a malignant tumor gradually eroding the region's precious heritage, and even a racial moderate was someone "who is going to let a little sewage in the door."[78]

In no time, the Citizens' Council became the most vocal and widespread private organization dedicated to the segregationist cause and anti-*Brown* enterprises not only in Mississippi, but also in the entire South. Assuming the role of the defender of the southern way of life, the group used the terms "states' rights" and "racial integrity" on its organizational emblem. Assisting Patterson in his efforts to make the Citizens' Council the authentic voice of the white South and eventually becoming the chief architect of the entire Citizens' Council movement was William J. Simmons of Jackson, the capital of Mississippi. A student of French literature with a gentlemanly demeanor, Simmons was instrumental in organizing the influential Jackson Citizens' Council in the spring of 1955 and later served as the all-powerful administrator of the Citizens' Councils of America, de-voting his full-time services to the anti–civil rights resistance movement.[79]

Along with its strident cry of "states' rights," the Citizens' Council, from its very inception, also invoked the Red Menace to defend the white South's "racial integrity." "If you realize that . . . Communistic influences . . . stand behind every effort to invade States' Rights and force integration and mis-cegenation on the people of the South," then, according to a publication issued by the Jackson Citizens' Council, the sensible response was to join the group and be counted.[80] To the segregationist organization, submission to the "unconstitutional, destructive forces" of racial integration meant bowing to the malignant powers of "mongrelization, communism and atheism." The group argued that while segregation embodied American-ism, state sovereignty, and the survival of white race, integration, on the other hand, represented "darkness, regimentation, totalitarianism, com-munism and destruction."[81] By propagating this simplistic dichotomy, the Citizens' Council reminded white southerners that they were engaged in a grave moral conflict in which only one side could survive and no middle ground could exist.

In the early spring of 1955, when the Jackson Citizens' Council was es-tablished with much fanfare, W. Hodding Carter Jr., editor and publisher of the *Greenville Delta Democrat-Times* in Leflore County, Mississippi, wrote an article for *Look* magazine criticizing the Citizens' Council and equating it with the clandestine Ku Klux Klan. Carter, whose editorials had repeatedly attacked Senator McCarthy and his unsavory Communist witch-hunting since 1950, was by no means an ardent integrationist. He was, however, a voice of reason and conscience, arguing that all Missis-sippians, regardless of their color, were entitled to respect, fairness, equal opportunities, and justice.[82] Soon after the advance copies of Carter's article entitled "A Wave of Terror Threatens the South" became available in Mississippi, Patterson, one of the original founders of the Citizens' Council, angrily responded. "Citizens familiar with Carter's writings," he blasted, "know his intolerance toward the determination of white people to stay white."[83]

Opening fire at Carter in support of the Citizens' Council stalwart was Tom Ethridge, a staff writer of the *Jackson Clarion-Ledger,* who interpreted the Greenville editor's stance on racial justice as a "gradual surrender to creeping integration." Ethridge even saw Communist conspiracy behind Carter's writings. "Mr. Carter's article should delight the Communists," he asserted, "who seize every available propaganda weapon in exaggerating alleged racial tensions" in the South.[84] Carter continued to fight back with his pen. Despite his efforts, however, the clouds of the clandestine Citizens' Council were growing larger and darker, beginning to engulf Mississippi and casting doubt on the aphorism "the pen is mightier than the sword." For his unabated advocacy of simple decency and justice for black Mississippians and black southerners at large, Carter, through the rest of the decade, would continue to be the target of segregationists' wrath and their concerted red-baiting schemes.

While the Mississippi-bred Citizens' Council's self-proclaimed function as a racial arbiter and identifier of internal subversion became evident, on February 1, 1956, the Virginia state legislature adopted a so-called interposition resolution, in which the state asserted that the U.S. Constitution was a compact among the states and that each state could block actions of the federal government that adversely affected its interests and general well-being. More specifically, the resolution condemned the Supreme Court's 1954 *Brown* ruling and its implementation order of 1955 for having usurped Virginia's inherent right to maintain racially separated public school systems.[85] The next day, Alabama followed Virginia's lead, and on February 14, South Carolina also promulgated its own interposition resolution.[86] Then, a fateful statement was issued in the nation's capital by U.S. senator Harry F. Byrd Sr. from Virginia, who had earlier exhibited his aversion to the Truman-initiated federal civil rights program, describing it as an utter assault on "the dignity of Southern traditions and institutions."[87] Stressing the importance of unified southern support for interposition resolutions in his declaration, Byrd called for "massive resistance" in the South on February 25. The words "massive resistance" denoted southern segregationists' organized and all-out resistance to the implementation of the Supreme Court's school desegregation decrees and to the subsequently intensifying civil rights movement in the region.[88] Inspired and heartened by the Virginia senator's clarion call, Mississippi and Georgia adopted their interposition resolutions on February 29 and March 9, respectively.[89] By late spring of 1957, following Virginia and the four Deep South states, three other southern states—Louisiana (May 1956), Arkansas (November 1956), and Florida (May 1957)—had officially declared their opposition to *Brown*.[90]

The southern representatives in Congress lent further respectability to the defiant legislative actions taken by their home states. On March 12, 1956, nineteen senators and eighty-two representatives from the eleven former Confederate states approved and signed the "Southern Manifesto," formally entitled the "Declaration of Constitutional Principles." In this document, those 101 southern lawmakers pledged to "use all lawful means to bring about a reversal" of the *Brown* rulings.[91] Work on the manifesto had begun in early February, only a week after the Virginia legislature adopted its interposition resolution. On February 9, with the initiative taken by U.S. senator Walter F. George from Georgia, the powerful chair of the Senate Foreign Relations Committee, an informal three-member committee was organized to draft a "resolution or statement on the Supreme Court segregation issue as the Committee deems wise." The drafting committee was composed of Senators Richard B. Russell Jr. from Georgia, John C. Stennis from Mississippi, and Samuel J. "Sam" Ervin Jr. from North Carolina. Senator George designated his fellow Georgia senator, Russell, as the committee chair, who would oversee the final drafting of the "Southern Manifesto."[92] Certainly the drafters and signers of the manifesto made every effort to employ resistance rhetoric in their declaration. A careful reading of the "Southern Manifesto," however, reveals the southern lawmakers' illogical assertion that the "unwarranted exercise of power by the Court" and the impending "revolutionary changes" in the South's public school systems were the result of devilish handiworks of "outside agitators," "outside meddlers," and "troublemakers." Anticommunism was clearly playing an important role in the southern segregationists' massive resistance movement.[93]

By the end of 1956, when an overwhelming mood of defiance toward federal "judicial tyranny" took hold of the southern political scene—in some cases, even before the announcement of the *Brown* decision in May 1954—four of the five Deep South states (South Carolina, Georgia, Mississippi, and Louisiana, in that order) had been fully equipped with their administrative commissions and legislative committees to protect their public schools from racial integration and to resist the foreseeable civil rights crusade. Though their names varied, these tax-supported official organs were bound together by common interests and purposes—defending the South's cherished segregated way of life, devising legal means to circumvent the Supreme Court's desegregation rulings, propagandizing the vindication of states' rights constitutionalism and racial separation, and suppressing and suffocating dissenters and deviators from the region's prescribed racial norms. The first such strategy-mapping segregationist committee was created by South Carolina in April 1951—three years prior to *Brown*—when the state legislature organized the South Carolina School Committee, also called the Gressette Committee after its chair,

Senator L. Marion Gressette of Calhoun County.[94] Georgia then followed its neighboring state to establish the benign-sounding Georgia Commission on Education in December 1953.[95]

Meanwhile, the Mississippi state legislature appointed a provisional study committee called the Legal Educational Advisory Committee (LEAC) in April 1954. In the name of preserving and promoting "the best interests of both races and the public welfare," the twenty-five-member advisory committee was vested with authority to draft a host of segregationist laws to maintain racially separated schools in Mississippi.[96] Louisiana joined other Deep South states in the immediate aftermath of the May 1954 *Brown* ruling by organizing the Louisiana Joint Legislative Committee, chaired by an all-powerful state senator, William M. "Willie" Rainach. Under Rainach's leadership, Louisiana would soon become the birthplace of segregationist anti-Communist probes in the South.[97] Furthermore, following Senator Byrd's appeal for massive resistance in February 1956 and kindled by the issuance of their own interposition resolution, the Mississippi lawmakers created a tax-supported "permanent authority for maintenance of racial segregation" in accordance with the recommendation made by the fading LEAC.[98] On March 29, 1956, with the blessing of Governor James P. Coleman, the state established the Mississippi State Sovereignty Commission as an executive agency to "do and perform any and all acts . . . to protect the sovereignty of the State of Mississippi . . . from encroachment thereon by the Federal Government."[99] Almost immediately, the Mississippi State Sovereignty Commission became the most active and virulent anti-*Brown* and anti–civil rights official agency in the region, bearing the blazing torch of the white South's all-out massive resistance.

In July 1954, two months after the Supreme Court's *Brown* decision, Louisiana state senator Rainach, chair of the segregationist joint legislative committee, unequivocally proclaimed that "the chips are down, the lines are drawn" in his fight against the implementation of the school desegregation decree.[100] Armed with their "paranoid style in southern politics"—to paraphrase the words of the historian Richard Hofstadter—Rainach and his fellow southern segregationists stood ready to defend their region's racial rubric, letting the chips fall where they may.[101]

CHAPTER 1

CRYING ALOUD AND SPARING NOT

Myers G. Lowman, J. B. Matthews, and the Politics

of Insecurity

In the wake of the Supreme Court's 1954 *Brown* decision and the demise of the political influence exerted by Wisconsin senator Joseph McCarthy, some "professional" anti-Communists in the North began to recognize a promising opportunity in exporting their knowledge and expertise to southern segregationists. For the South's racist ideologues, these anti-Communist crusaders from the North became valued allies in carrying out the region's massive resistance under the guise of domestic anticommunism. Southern segregationists and professional northern anti-Communists shared a common cause, a common demeanor, and common adversaries whom they were committed to defeat and silence. Their analyses of the Communist-influenced international conspiracy stemmed from a mixture of paranoia, political expediency, and financial pragmatism, and they branded their enemies broadly and conveniently as "subversives." To be sure, as the British civil rights historian Adam Fairclough has accurately noted, the absolute line between "responsible" anticommunism and "irresponsible" racial and racist red-baiting in the South was almost impossible to draw.[1] And further blurring that line was the involvement of the northern anti-Communist crusaders in the region's resistance movement. Ultimately, as the Cold War historian Michael J. Heale has pointed out, anticommunism was indeed a "protean creature"—a versatile tool to suppress enemies, encompassing different regions and localities within the United States.[2] There was no doubt, though, that anticommunism's subtle versatility made it useful to southern segregationists.

Among the northern messiahs involved in the white South's segregationist cause were former members and sympathizers of the Communist

Party of the United States of America (CPUSA) who, for various reasons, had converted to the cause of anticommunism, rendering their aid as researchers, investigators, and witnesses to congressional investigative committees such as the House Un-American Activities Committee (HUAC) and the Senate Internal Security Subcommittee (SISS). Others lending support to southern segregationists were nationally known leaders of extremely conservative religious organizations in the North. God-denying communism and God-fearing religion were naturally viewed as bitter antagonists, and "subversion in the sanctuary" was regarded by anti-Communist religious groups as the "most deadly and insidious menace" facing the country.[3]

Edgar C. Bundy's Church League of America in Wheaton, Illinois, was one of the oldest and most influential right-wing religious organizations. Formed during the latter half of the 1930s in opposition to President Franklin Roosevelt's New Deal policies, the league, under the charismatic leadership of Bundy, an ordained minister for the Southern Baptist Convention, proudly claimed that it possessed the largest private collection of research files on America's domestic subversion. And Carl McIntire of Collingswood, New Jersey, a minister of the Presbyterian Church, founded his own church federation—the American Council of Christian Churches—in the early 1940s. In 1958, McIntire set up a subsidiary of his federation called the Twentieth Century Reformation Hour to broadcast his extreme anti-Communist views. Besides Bundy and McIntire, Frederick C. Schwartz, a native of Brisbane, Australia, whom McIntire had brought to the United States, organized the Christian Anti-Communism Crusade as a "nonprofit Christian organization" in Iowa in 1953. In 1958, its headquarters was moved to Long Beach, California, and Schwartz conducted a series of seminars billed as "schools of anti-Communism."[4]

Though their names varied, these and other organizations skillfully combined religious enthusiasm with their fanatical anti-Communist ideology, attracting not only religious-minded followers, but also secular anti-Communists. Portraying themselves as patriots and wrapping themselves in the anti-Communist flag, the vast majority of these religious anti-Communist crusaders argued that social and racial liberalism was, at best, an obstacle to the cause of anti-communism and, at worst, a betrayal of the American and Christian creeds. As religiously affiliated anti-Communist vigilante groups—both large and small, prominent and obscure—sprang up across the country in the early 1950s, Ralph Lord Roy, an ordained Methodist minister and an author, observed that those whom he termed "apostles of discord" had joined forces with secular anti-Communists to "replace apostles of prophetic Christianity with those faithful to the *status quo.*"[5]

Bundy, McIntire, Schwartz, and other religious anti-Communist crusaders were all involved to varying degrees in assisting southern segregationists in their defense of the South's racial status quo. However, the person upon whom the South's white supremacists—particularly those in the three Deep South states of Georgia, Louisiana, and Mississippi—would eventually depend as their most valued northern messiah appeared in Cincinnati, Ohio. His name was Myers G. Lowman, an obscure Methodist layman who would rise to national prominence for his collaboration in the white South's racist cause. Born in Cresson, Pennsylvania, on March 29, 1904, Lowman was the president of Mason and Lowman, Inc., an air-conditioning and refrigeration company in Cincinnati. Married to Dorothy Dawson, who was also originally from Cresson, Lowman had three children. While serving as a member of the board of managers of the Sons of the American Revolution's Cincinnati chapter, he claimed to be an active member of the Westwood Methodist Church (presently the Westwood United Methodist Church) and was also involved in the Wesley Foundation in his adopted city. In the fall of 1951, Lowman became the executive secretary of a Cincinnati-based Methodist laymen's anti-Communist group called the Circuit Riders, Inc.[6]

The origin of the Circuit Riders can actually be traced back to the South—to Houston, Texas, to be precise—where an extreme anti-Communist movement organized and led by the local Methodists began to engulf the city in the early 1950s. As well as Dallas, where the oil tycoon and billionaire Haroldson Lafayette "H. L." Hunt Jr.—a close friend of Senator McCarthy—launched his anti-Communist foundation called Facts Forum, Houston served as a vital center for Texas's organized Red Scare, which influenced the city's public school desegregation and led to the rise of the Texas Republican Party in the traditionally Democratic state.[7] The immediate cause that aroused the Methodist McCarthyites in Houston was an article written by Stanley High that appeared in *Reader's Digest* in February 1950—the same month that McCarthy became a national anti-Communist celebrity with his resounding Wheeling, West Virginia, speech in which the senator sensationally "revealed" the existence of "Communists in the State Department."[8] Entitling his article "Methodism's Pink Fringe," High, who had served as a roving editor of the popular magazine since the 1940s, launched a scathing assault on the Methodist Federation for Social Action (MFSA) and its approximately five thousand members.[9] The organizational purposes of the MFSA, High claimed, were to "discredit America at home and abroad, to condemn the American economic system as unchristian, and to . . . give aid and comfort to the Communists." High also reminded his readers—particularly those who argued that the MFSA was an unofficial Methodist agency—that the organization's national headquarters had been housed in the official Methodist Building in New York City for more than three decades.[10]

Despite the fact that the Methodist Church at large was virtually free of any systematic Communist infiltration, it had often been denounced by a host of conservatives and anti-Communists as harboring the "Methodist Reds."[11] Since the early twentieth century, the Methodist Church, by adopting its denominational Social Creed in 1908, had taken a progressive stand in favor of "equal rights and complete justice for all men in all stations of life" and rectifying America's "social ills." While advocating, among other causes, abolition of child labor, factory safety, and an "equitable division of the products of industry," the church had produced nationally prominent leaders in the area of social and economic reforms, many of whom were imbued with Christian Socialism.[12]

On December 3, 1907, the predecessor of the MFSA—the object of High's excoriation—was founded as the Methodist Federation for Social Service in Washington, D.C., to direct the Methodist Church's attention to social justice and conscience. Given a "semi-official" status by the 1908 General Conference of the Methodist Church, the federation had greatly influenced the church's denominational policy and provided a vital forum for the development of Methodist positions on social and economic issues.[13] Indeed, it was the federation that successfully secured the adoption of the Methodist Church's Social Creed at the 1908 General Conference.[14] For almost four decades after its inception, the federation was led by its executive secretary, Harry F. Ward, a prominent Methodist minister and a left-wing activist. Ward also served as a professor at Union Theological Seminary in New York City, the chair of the American League against War and Fascism, and the founding chair of the American Civil Liberties Union. During the Great Depression, when the federation advocated that the American economic system should be based on "social-economic planning" to "develop a society without class or group discriminations," conservatives began to see the federation members as misguided "Methodist Reds."[15] A concerted red-baiting campaign against the federation was launched in 1935 by the anti-Communist Hearst newspapers, in which the Methodist group was branded as the "Marxist Federation for Social

Strife."[16] The following year, when Methodist laymen responded to the Hearst-initiated red-baiting attacks by organizing the Methodist League against Communism, Fascism, and Unpatriotic Pacifism, the General Conference of the Methodist Church instructed the federation to add the word "unofficial" to the group's letterhead.[17] Daring to swim against the current, the federation members continued to call for "the right to unionize and full civil rights for communists and Blacks."[18]

In 1948, following World War II, the federation's name was changed to the Methodist Federation for Social Action (MFSA). After Ward was succeeded by his former student at Union Theological Seminary, Jack R. McMichael, who had taken the helm of the federation in 1945, the MFSA came under further intense scrutiny because radical conservatives suspected the organization of fomenting communism "under the guise of religion."[19] With the coming of anti-Communist hysteria of McCarthyism and on the strength of the 1948 report issued by the California Joint Legislative Fact-Finding Committee on Un-American Activities (also known as the Tenney Committee, named after California state senator Jack B. Tenney), the HUAC would declare in the spring of 1951 that the MFSA was one of the most "conspicuous fronts for Communist activity in the field of relief, assistance, and welfare work," including the Methodist organization in its "subversive organization" list.[20] For southern segregationists in general and Houston's white Methodists in particular, the most disturbing and deplorable aspect of this was the MFSA's explicitly declared aim to achieve "racial equality and brotherhood."[21]

To those familiar with High's personal background, his provocative attack against the MFSA was both enigmatic and ironic. A Methodist minister's son and a graduate of the Boston University School of Theology, High was once a candidate for the ministry of the Methodist Church. In his younger days, he was a close associate of Frank Mason North, one of the Methodist Episcopal clergy who founded the Methodist Federation for Social Service in 1907. Dedicating his 1923 book entitled *The Revolt of Youth* to North, High, while never embracing communism, deplored the "greed of American capitalism." He later became a speechwriter for President Roosevelt. After leaving this position and converting to Presbyterianism, High became a freelance writer and eventually an editor of *Reader's Digest,* specializing, for reasons best known to himself, in "identifying communists and persons with communist leanings in the churches."[22]

Immediately after High's article sent shock waves throughout Methodism, Houston's Methodist McCarthyites, led by Clarence Lohman, an affluent attorney for an oil company and a lay member of the city's St. Luke's Methodist Church, began to organize for action against the MFSA.[23] On June 2, 1950, the Texas Annual Conference of the Methodist Church adopted a memorial crafted and submitted to the conference by the Houston anti-Communists. Condemning the MFSA for using the Methodist Church to spread "socialist and communist teachings," the memorial demanded that the federation drop the word "Methodist" from its organizational name. It also urged Methodists to be "vigilant" and to look into "the background and beliefs of writers, speakers, teachers, and Church leaders" in order to "make our Church literature and all teachings conform to the views and beliefs of Methodism."[24]

Following this first victory in his efforts to crack down on the MFSA, Lohman then penned a guest editorial entitled "Socialism and Communism and the Methodist Church" for the November 2, 1950, issue of the *Christian Advocate,* the official organ of the Methodist Church, in which he sharply condemned the MFSA. The group's "official pronouncements and the utterances of its leaders," Lohman asserted, "can leave no reasonable doubt as to a definite purpose to bring about a Socialist or Communist state." "The great Methodist Church . . . needs to protect itself from these forces by positive affirmations and forthright action," the Houston attorney concluded.[25] In the same issue of the *Christian Advocate,* Francis J. McConnell of the MFSA defended his group, stating that "the official position of the federation regarding Communism is clear and unequivocal." The Methodist bishop insisted that the MFSA had vowed that it did not "front for Communism or any other 'ism.'"[26]

Still unconvinced, a vocal group of some thirty Methodist laymen in Houston, spearheaded by Lohman and others, organized the Committee for the Preservation of Methodism on December 19, 1950, as the city's first Red Scare–era anti-Communist group. The members of this newly created committee, whom Lohman described as "solid men to fight Communism in the churches," were mostly lawyers, bankers, and businesspeople.[27] As respected citizens in their communities, many of them belonged to Houston's wealthiest Methodist church—St. Paul's Methodist Church—but five other churches in the city, such as Lohman's St. Luke's Methodist Church and the First Methodist Church, were also represented by the committee members. Those who gathered at the Houston committee's organizational meeting resolved that they would take all actions "as shall be necessary and proper to effectuate the objectives" of the memorial adopted by the 1950 Texas Annual Conference of the Methodist Church—to support bishops and other leaders who opposed the Communist influences in the Methodist Church, to force the MFSA to drop the word "Methodist" from its name, and to oust the MFSA's national headquarters from the Methodist Building in New York City.[28] "Our job is much like McCarthy's," Lohman said in explaining his group's purpose. The committee's vested responsibility, he noted, was "to cleanse the churches as McCarthy is cleansing the government."[29]

For the chairmanship of the Committee for the Preservation of Methodism, Ewing Werlein, an attorney and a former school board president of the Houston Independent School District, was chosen. Werlein, whose father had once served as a pastor at Houston's First Methodist Church, was the dean of Houston Law School—a private night school—from 1927 to 1945, teaching many of the city's future judges. Describing himself as a "conservative conservative" and referring to the National Association for the Advancement of Colored People (NAACP) as the "National Association for the Agitation of Colored People," Werlein argued that communism and the Communist-influenced black civil rights movement posed an immediate threat to the local churches and schools.[30] Besides Lohman, other active members of the Houston committee included Hines H. Baker Sr., president of Humble Oil and Refining Company. A member of St. Luke's Methodist Church, Baker was a future vice president of Standard Oil Company in New Jersey.[31]

Four months after its inception, in late April 1951, Lohman's Committee for the Preservation of Methodism issued a booklet entitled *Is There a Pink Fringe in the Methodist Church?* as its first significant organizational project. Borrowing High's "Pink Fringe" label, the booklet tried to discredit bishops and ministers who supported the MFSA. Eventually, the Houston committee printed and distributed nationally fifty thousand copies of the anti-MFSA material.[32] The committee members were also busy monitoring every aspect of their church activities—looking into the contents of sermons delivered by local ministers and trying to censor "undesirable" material used at Sunday schools. Lohman, a member of St. Luke's Methodist Church, was a frequent visitor to the city's other Methodist churches, keeping his watchful eye on their ministers and congregations.[33]

Since the creation of the Committee for the Preservation of Methodism, Lohman had envisaged that Houston's localized anti-MFSA and anti-Communist movement should be expanded into a national one. In the fall of 1951, Lohman called a national meeting to discuss how concerned Methodists could most effectively oppose "all efforts to propagate Socialism and Communism and all other anti-American teachings in the Methodist

Church."[34] Responding to Lohman's invitation, thirty-three Methodists from sixteen states met at the Palmer House Hotel in Chicago for three days, September 28 to 30. Immediately following this meeting, on October 1, those who had gathered in Chicago announced the organization of the Circuit Riders, reviving the name formerly used to describe itinerant pioneer Methodist preachers who spread their faith in the sparsely settled areas of the country.[35] In an open letter addressed to "The Members of the Methodist Church," the founders of the Circuit Riders explained that their new national organization would serve as a "platform" whereby all Methodists, insofar as they elected to oppose "the use of our Church for the propagation of socialistic theories and trends," could be united. They also announced that the Circuit Riders' national office would be located in Cincinnati, and that Lowman, as executive secretary, would oversee the day-to-day business of their newly formed anti-Communist organization.[36]

The Circuit Riders elected William C. Perkins of Maryland as their founding president. Assisting Perkins was Clarence Lohman of Houston, who became the group's vice president. Perkins would soon be succeeded by John C. Satterfield, a prominent and segregationist attorney in Yazoo City, Mississippi. In November 1953, Lohman would become the president of the Circuit Riders, replacing Satterfield.[37] Satterfield was a future president of the Mississippi State Bar Association and the American Bar Association. As a rabid states' righter and an ardent anti-Communist, he would later become a major figure in southern segregationists' desperate efforts to defeat the 1963 civil rights bill then pending in Congress in collaboration with his friends, Senator James Eastland from Mississippi and Mississippi governor Ross R. Barnett.[38] Satterfield's presence at the Circuit Riders' founding meeting in Chicago lent much-needed respectability to the fledgling enterprise.

Another notable southern segregationist among the founders of the Circuit Riders, though much less prominent than Satterfield, was Blake Craft of Clayton, Georgia, a Methodist minister and publisher of *One Methodist Voice*. Seeing evil and red in alleged modernism within American Methodism, Craft would launch his poorly edited monthly tabloid in 1952 for those who believed in "evangelical Methodism, Americanism, and the peculiar heritages and cherished traditions of the Southland." Craft, whose understanding of the South's "peculiar heritages and cherished traditions" revolved around the upkeep of racial segregation and discrimination, once categorically listed the "Preservation of the Integrity of the Races" as one of his aims. While developing and proliferating his theology of white supremacy, Craft described the MFSA as "the 'pinkish leech' that becomes more red as it sucks the blood of our freedom." Like Satterfield, Craft was a close personal friend of his native state's chief executive, Georgia governor Herman E. Talmadge, who would author *You and Segregation* in 1955 in defense of the white South's racist practices.[39] The involvement of such racists as Satterfield and Craft in the founding of the Circuit Riders marked the germination of the intricate relations that would later be cultivated between southern segregationists and northern messiahs.

A few days after the founding of the Circuit Riders, Jack McMichael, executive secretary of the MFSA, issued a statement from its New York City headquarters, noting the birth of the Cincinnati-based group. "We certainly feel the Circuit Riders should have freedom to ride, or to travel any circuits they please," the MFSA's restrained statement read, "[and] free discussion and criticism are healthy for the church."[40] Meanwhile, in an editorial appearing in the October 18, 1951, issue of the *Christian Advocate,* the Methodist Church's official publication expressed a greater concern about the inception of the new laymen's organization. The publication urged the Circuit Riders to "avoid entangling alliances" with some "well-financed right-wing groups . . . campaigning across the country."[41] Ignoring the *Christian Advocate*'s advice, however, the Circuit Riders began to cultivate relations with various reactionary organizations and individuals, as well as opportunity-grabbing southern segregationists.

With a minimum of interference from either the president or the board of directors, the Circuit Riders' daily operation was executed almost exclusively by Lowman. Largely because the Circuit Riders had evolved from the anti-MFSA Committee for the Preservation of Methodism in Houston, it was quite natural for the national Methodist anti-Communist organization to set as its original aim the discrediting of the MFSA and its leaders. More broadly, however, the purposes of the Circuit Riders, as Lowman explained, were to "expose and oppose use of church facilities, personnel, programs, and publications for Socialistic, pro-Communistic, and other anti-American activities" and to support "those bishops and other leaders in the church field" whose messages were "spiritual, moral, and patriotic."[42]

Soon after the inception of the Circuit Riders, Lowman successfully prodded U.S. representative John S. Wood from Georgia, chair of the HUAC, into compiling and issuing a damaging report on the MFSA. Lowman specifically asked the HUAC chair to make the report public in time for the opening of the planned April 1952 General Conference of the Methodist

Church to be held in San Francisco, hoping that the conference, as the Methodist Church's national governing body, would be compelled to take action against the MFSA.[43] Heeding Lowman's request, on February 17, 1952, the HUAC issued its hurriedly compiled eighty-eight-page report on the MFSA. Entitled *Review of the Methodist Federation for Social Action,* this "careful . . . review" was largely composed of previously published and often ideologically slanted newspaper and magazine articles.[44] Reiterating the House committee's earlier assertion that the MFSA was one of the most "conspicuous fronts for Communist activity" in the United States, the *Review* labeled the Methodist group as a "tool of the Communist Party."[45]

During a short period between February and April 1952, more than twenty-five thousand copies of the HUAC publication were widely distributed among the nation's Methodists. Of these twenty-five thousand copies, the Circuit Riders was entrusted by the House committee with mailing out ten thousand.[46] Despite its dubious credibility, the HUAC report would turn out to have serious impact on the delegates to the 1952 General Conference of the Methodist Church. Besides the House committee's report, also issued and disseminated among the Methodist conference delegates for the purpose of discrediting the MFSA was the Circuit Riders' own booklet entitled *Information Concerning the Methodist Federation for Social Action.* Lowman had prepared four thousand copies of the twenty-four-page booklet in time for the opening of the Methodist conference.[47]

The concerted attacks launched by the Circuit Riders and the HUAC eventually bore fruit: the 1952 General Conference of the Methodist Church, meeting in San Francisco in late April, adopted a resolution to officially request the MFSA to "remove the word 'Methodist' from its name," as well as approving the previous action taken by the church's Board of Publications in asking the federation to "terminate its occupancy of quarters in the Methodist Building" in New York City.[48] The MFSA's executive secretary, Jack McMichael, was in no mood to retreat. Lamenting that the delegates to the Methodist conference were swayed by the hysterical anti-Communist rhetoric in the May 1952 issue of the *Social Questions Bulletin,* the federation's official organ, McMichael protested that the recently adopted resolution had failed to mention the Circuit Riders by name and to indicate the fact that the Cincinnati group had a hand in enacting "thought control which would make our freedom-loving founder John Wesley turn over in his grave." Notably, McMichael also raised the race issue, observing that eight out of ten federation critics at the Methodist conference were white southerners, and that no "single Negro speaker had been heard" during the debate on the MFSA's fate.[49] As the *Social Questions Bulletin*'s April 1953 issue reported, the MFSA overwhelmingly voted not to remove its national office from the Methodist Building and to refuse to drop the word "Methodist" from its name.[50]

In the face of the MFSA's uncompromising position, the Circuit Riders' "Three Musketeers"—Satterfield as its president, Lohman as vice president, and Lowman—sent a joint open letter to their fellow Methodists throughout the nation. The MFSA's "defiance" of the 1952 General Conference of the Methodist Church, they asserted, raised the question of whether the federation was "loyal to The Methodist Church or, as has been alleged, owes its first allegiance to another organization"—namely, the CPUSA.[51] In response, the MFSA insisted that the Circuit Riders' report on the federation contained "faulty and untrue misrepresentation of Methodists" that had been "gleaned from the unsupported files" of the HUAC. While criticizing Lowman for "threatening to destroy cherished Methodist liberty of opinion as proclaimed by John Wesley," the MFSA eventually bowed to the Methodist conference's demand at the end of June 1953, removing its headquarters from the Methodist Building. The federation remained determined, however, to retain the word "Methodist" in its organization's title.[52]

Six months after the 1952 General Conference of the Methodist Church adjourned, the Circuit Riders held a triumphant meeting, trumpeting its success in discrediting the MFSA. Billed as the Circuit Riders' first "national conference," the meeting was held at the Netherland Plaza Hotel in Cincinnati on October 26, 1952.[53] The featured speaker at this gathering was Joseph Zack Kornfeder of Detroit, Michigan, a former member of the Communist Party's International Secretariat. In an address entitled "Communist Deception in the Churches," Kornfeder told the audience exactly what it wanted to hear—that the MFSA was a "Communist front." Though the MFSA's true intent was "cleverly sugarcoated with religious shibboleths," the former Communist asserted, its officialdom had been occupied by those who were "none other than conscious and disciplined Communist[s]." He also identified Ward as one of the federation's leading agitators. "A Communist is an atheist so when he poses as a churchman he practices deception," Kornfeder explained in his well-received speech.[54]

As in the case of many other self-described "disillusioned" and "betrayed" former Communist members and sympathizers, Kornfeder had led a checkered life. A native of Slovakia and a tailor by profession, Kornfeder immigrated to the United States in 1917, and two years later, he joined the

CPUSA when it was organized. After being trained in "political warfare" at the Lenin School in Moscow from 1927 to 1930, Kornfeder was sent to Columbia and Venezuela as the "Comintern delegate to South America." In 1934, he broke with the Communist Party because of "the police-state atmosphere" he found in the Soviet Union.[55] Finding a well of valuable expertise and a trusted ally in Kornfeder, the Circuit Riders' executive secretary would increasingly rely on the former Communist, particularly when Lowman began to associate with segregationist defenders of racial status quo in the South.

In early 1953, the Circuit Riders, "organized and operated exclusively for educational purposes," was designated as a tax-exempt entity by the Office of Commissioner of Internal Revenue at the Department of Treasury.[56] During the following summer, Lowman was afforded an opportunity to make a name for himself as a credible anti-Communist fighter when he testified for three hours before the Ohio Un-American Activities Commission as an "expert witness."[57] The commission had been established in June 1951, inspired by an anti-Communist media campaign waged by the *Cincinnati Enquirer*.[58] Lowman's August 14, 1953, appearance before the Ohio Un-American Activities Commission served as a much-needed display of the commission's necessity and usefulness. As for Lowman, testifying before the commission offered a grand opportunity to establish himself as a reliable source of information beyond the circle of Methodist anti-Communists. Less than two months later, his aspiration was fulfilled. In early October, when the Columbus-based Ohio Coalition of Patriotic Societies held its anti-Communist seminar in Canton, Lowman was invited to address the group. The two-day seminar, attended by some four hundred people, was financially sponsored by the Ohio branches of the American Legion, the Daughters of the American Revolution (DAR), and a Connecticut-born anti-Communist group called the Minute Women of the U.S.A.[59] Publicized as a "Seminar on Socialism and Communism," the event was held at the American Legion auditorium in Canton from October 3 to 4.[60]

The Ohio Coalition of Patriotic Societies had been founded in 1947 under the leadership of William E. Warner, a professor of industrial vocational education at Ohio State University, as a "coordinating nucleus of some 150 patriotic groups" in Ohio.[61] In turn, the Ohio coalition was also part of its parent organization, the American Coalition of Patriotic Societies, which oversaw more than one hundred civic and patriotic groups throughout the United States.[62] Organized officially in 1929, the Washington, D.C.–based coalition had evolved out of an earlier informal coalition known as the

Citizens' Committee on Immigration Legislation, which was originally created for the purpose of "defending" the restrictive Immigration Act of 1924.[63] One of the aims of the American Coalition of Patriotic Societies, according to its constitution, was to "expose and combat the political and economic fallacies of socialism and communism" and thereby, to "keep America American."[64]

On the first day of the Canton seminar organized by the Ohio Coalition of Patriotic Societies, Lowman gave a speech entitled "Propriety of Congressional Investigations," praising another featured speaker, Republican senator William Jenner from Indiana. Jenner, who chaired the SISS and was one of the "most vociferous supporters" of Senator McCarthy in Congress, as the *New York Times* put it, talked about the "Interlocking Subversion in Government Departments." Besides Lowman and Jenner, other invited speakers included Benjamin Gitlow, the CPUSA candidate for vice president in 1924 and 1928 who, after breaking with the party in 1929, had become a popular anti-Communist writer and lecturer; Kornfeder, whose speech entitled "Communist Deception in the Churches" addressed the same topic as the talk he had offered at the October 1952 national conference of the Circuit Riders; and E. Merrill Root, an English professor at Earlham College in Richmond, Indiana, who specialized in detecting "subversive writings" in public school textbooks and "subversion in higher education."[65] Lowman's continued association with Kornfeder and his contact with Root at this Canton seminar would prove to be essential assets in fostering his future fraternization with the South's massive resisters.

When the Circuit Riders was organized in the fall of 1951, no one could have predicted that this Ohio-based anti-MFSA and anti-Communist group would soon be one of the most indispensable allies to southern segregationists' racist cause. Despite the fact that the Circuit Riders attracted the energetic support of such white supremacists as John Satterfield of Mississippi and Blake Craft of Georgia, neither the Circuit Riders as an organization nor its executive secretary, Lowman, as an individual ever officially and publicly endorsed racial segregation and discrimination in the South. Nor did Lowman and his group engage in anti-Semitism. Lowman himself probably did not suspect how his future crusade for what he once termed "God and the United States" would come to consume him.[66] Within only a few years, however, a collaborative and mutually expedient association between Lowman and the South's segregationist politicians and officials would be forged and solidified with the involvement of another Methodist in the North.

While Lowman undoubtedly possessed plenty of unabashed zeal to crack down on his enemies and those who disagreed with him, to make his accusations both acceptable and credible among his fellow Methodists and beyond religious circles, he needed to secure a reliable source of information. Eventually, Lowman found this in Joseph Brown "J. B." Matthews of New York City, a highly regarded professional anti-Communist information compiler of the era. And, indeed, what would make Lowman stand out among other religious anti-Communist crusaders in his future association with southern segregationists was his constant professional and personal relations with Matthews, whose eventful life adequately reflected what his own book's title described as an "odyssey of a fellow traveler."[67]

Matthews's "odyssey" had literally taken him from being "listed on the letterhead of several leftist organizations" during the 1920s to "searching out leftist letterheads" in order to viciously brand those listed there as Communists and fellow travelers beginning in the late 1930s.[68] It was, in fact, none other than Matthews who had provided High with the information on the MFSA that High used in preparing his controversial article criticizing the federation in the February 1950 issue of the *Reader's Digest*. "I'm collecting a lot of stuff for you on the MFSA," Matthews wrote to High in late 1949.[69] High's article, "Methodism's Pink Fringe," soon prompted Lohman to establish the Committee for the Preservation of Methodism in Houston, which in turn eventually led to the organization of the Lowman-led Circuit Riders.

Ten years senior to Lowman, Matthews was born on June 28, 1894, in Hopkinsville, Kentucky.[70] A great-great grandson of a Revolutionary War colonel, he was an "American of old stock," to use the words of George E. Sokolsky, one of Matthews's most trusted "comrades" in the anti-Communist circles.[71] At the age of twenty-one, immediately after graduating from Asbury College in Wilmore, Kentucky, in 1915, Matthews set off for Batavia in Java (presently Jakarta in Indonesia) as a Methodist missionary.[72] Two years later, while still serving in Java, Matthews married a Kentuckian and his first wife, Grace Doswell Ison, with whom he would eventually have four children.[73] On his return to the United States in 1921, Matthews continued his higher education.[74] His extensive academic training was centered on the fields of theology and Oriental languages. Educated at Drew University (bachelor of divinity) in New Jersey, Union Theological Seminary (master of sacred theology), Columbia University (M.A.), and finally the School of Oriental Languages at the University of

Vienna (Ph.D.) in Austria, Matthews was proficient in Arabic, Aramaic, Hebrew, Malay, Persian, Sanskrit, and Sundanese.[75]

While Matthews established himself as a noted specialist in Oriental languages, he became "imbued" with pacifism and racial justice. "My introduction to radicalism was via the religion of the social gospel," Matthews later reflected, "[and] interracialism and pacifism became the dominant features of my brand of the social gospel."[76] In 1924, around the same time he was appointed to teach Hebrew and religious history at Scarritt College—a Methodist institution in Nashville, Tennessee—Matthews's faith in the Methodist Church as an almighty "panacea for the world's ills" began to waver.[77] While, on the political side, Matthews worked for the campaign of the Progressive Party's presidential hopeful, Robert M. La Follette, he "took an advanced position on the question of race relations in the South," advocating "bold and radical experimentation in eliminating race prejudice."[78] Having realized that his opposition to racial segregation and discrimination did not sit well with the southern institution, Matthews resigned from Scarritt College in 1927.[79] After leaving the college, Matthews remained in Nashville and found a teaching position at Fisk University, a historically black educational institution. Matthews then moved to Washington, D.C., to join the faculty of Howard University, another traditionally black school, teaching Greek and Hebrew there for one year.[80]

In the summer of 1929, only a few months before the Great Depression began to plague the nation, Matthews was invited to become one of the two executive secretaries of the Fellowship of Reconciliation (FOR) with a monthly salary of eight hundred dollars.[81] The FOR was originally organized in the United Kingdom in 1914 at the outset of World War II and was extended to the United States the following year. Headquartered in Nyack, New York, the FOR was the nation's most influential pacifist organization, devoting itself to a "movement of Christian protest against war."[82] While spreading the idea of pacifism and pushing for social reforms, the FOR also aimed to improve the South's race relations. In 1942, led by such black pacifists as James Farmer and Bayard Rustin, both of whom were the FOR's field secretaries, the Congress of Racial Equality (CORE) would be organized as a nonviolent protest group against racial segregation and discrimination. In 1947, following the end of World War II, apprehensive about a surge of white-on-black racial violence in the South, the FOR, in association with the CORE activists, would launch what it billed as the "Journey of Reconciliation"—or the "First Freedom Ride." (The more dramatic "Freedom Ride" would take place in 1961, when an initial group of nine blacks and nine whites challenged racial segregation practiced in the South's interstate bus transportation systems.)[83]

No sooner had Matthews taken the helm of the FOR, to which he would end up devoting four years, than he joined and became a dues-paying member of the Socialist Party of America in New York in November 1929. "My pacifism gradually shifted from a religious to a political basis," Matthews later recalled, "[and] it seems that I had a finger in almost everything radical." He once prided himself on the fact that he had "made more speeches for the Socialist Party and its candidates for office . . . than any other member of that party, excepting only Norman Thomas," for and with whom Matthews had worked zealously. Thomas, who had edited the *World Tomorrow* as the FOR's official publication, was the Socialist Party's presidential candidate in 1928, 1932, and 1936 after the 1926 death of Eugene V. "Gene" Debs.[84]

Following his extensive fact-finding travel within the Soviet Union during the summer of 1932, Matthews was ready to become what he described as a "full-fledged fellow traveler," radicalizing himself to be "not only a Marxist but a confirmed exponent of the united front" for the American Communist movement. Thereafter, helping "the pitifully weak leftist groups to combine their resources in order to make a real Marxist impression upon the American scene" became Matthews's avowed mission.[85] When, in September 1933, the American League against War and Fascism held its organizational meeting, which was largely attended by the members of the CPUSA and other Communist-front organizations, Matthews was chosen as the league's founding national chair.[86] The irony of circumstances in this episode is that when Matthews resigned from the league's chairmanship, he was succeeded by Harry Ward of Union Theological Seminary—the executive secretary of the Methodist Federation for Social Service (later the MFSA) and a bitter foe of the Circuit Riders and Lowman.[87] It would soon become obvious that the anti-Communist frenzy to be created and sustained by Matthews did not excuse Ward, either.

Although Matthews never became a member of the CPUSA, he was deeply involved, either as an officer, a member, or a contributor, in a host of its front groups, working for more than sixty organizations and publications that advocated pacifism, antifascism, racial equality, and labor solidarity.[88] By 1936, however, Matthews—who had created a "one-man front coalition, a microcosmic red network" in the United States—had become disillusioned with radical politics.[89] His abrupt change of heart stemmed from a rather strange situation. In 1934, after resigning from the American League against War and Fascism, Matthews became the vice president of Consumers' Research, Inc., in Washington, New Jersey, with a salary of four thousand dollars a year. As a public service organization, Consumers' Research had been established to assist the economically hard-pressed public by making comparative ratings of consumer goods.[90] In partnership with Ruth E. Shallcross, Matthews coauthored a book with a strong pro-labor discourse in 1935 under the auspices of Consumers' Research. In their *Partners in Plunder: The Cost of Business Dictatorship,* Matthews and Shallcross asserted that business and government collaborated as "partners in the plunder" of the American public, and they criticized almost every aspect of the nation's business culture.[91] Soon after the book's publication, Matthews divorced his Kentucky sweetheart and first wife, Grace, and married Ruth Shallcross in 1936. Matthews's second marriage would produce a son, but it would not last long.[92]

When *Partners in Plunder* came out, no one would have been likely to imagine that Matthews would soon undergo a metamorphosis, turning against labor, but that was exactly what happened. During the summer and fall of 1935, Consumers' Research was in turmoil due to a prolonged labor strike, which was reinforced by some CPUSA-affiliated employees. Finding himself on the other side of the table from the striking employees, Matthews, as the vice president, eventually took a pro-business stand, trying to smash the picket lines. Matthews immediately paid dearly for his strike-fighting posture, for it brought him a host of bitter denouncements by his longtime associates.[93] The *Daily Worker,* the CPUSA's official newspaper published in New York City, even proposed to hold a "mass trial" of Matthews in October 1935 and encouraged its readers to openly criticize the "vicious opportunism of J. B. Matthews, his betrayal of labor, union-smashing, red-baiting and armed attacks on peaceful pickets."[94] With his radical friends falling away and ostracized from his left-leaning lecture circuit, Matthews not only turned away from the Left, but also began to turn on the Left. Denouncing the labor strike as a "Communist conspiracy," Matthews criticized those strikers for exploiting "consumer issues on behalf of Soviet interests."[95]

In his 1938 apologia, *Odyssey of a Fellow Traveler,* Matthews explained that his book revolved around "the story of how one American thinks he became, by gradual stages, a fellow traveler of the communists" and "why he turned back eventually to reconstruct a political faith for which there is no better word than Americanism." But in his short autobiography, he failed to offer any concrete explanation as to when and why exactly he had become disillusioned with radicalism. "I cannot name the precise day on which I became a socialist or the precise day on which I ceased to be one," he wrote.[96] Nevertheless, it can be safely surmised that his involvement in the Consumers' Research labor incident and the subsequent attacks on him by many of his trusted friends, coupled with his marital and other domestic problems, ultimately pushed Matthews in the completely opposite direction. Regarding himself as an "innocent victim of a Communist plot," Matthews, to use his own words, had reached "the deep conviction" that "radicalism in general and communism in particular" reflected "the most complete illusion ever born in the human brain."[97] Having realized that he was, after all, a "political and economic conservative," Matthews converted to the Right.[98]

Matthews could not have executed this about-face—from being one of the most radical fellow travelers to one of the most influential anti-Communist crusaders—without his association with the anti-Communist newspaper columnist George Sokolsky of New York and the Texas representative Martin Dies. In fact, Matthews even dedicated his *Odyssey of a Fellow Traveler* to the Texan, reminding its readers that "America owes Martin Dies . . . a debt of everlasting gratitude."[99] In 1938, Sokolsky was called upon by a representative of the newly created House Special Committee on Un-American Activities (or the Dies Committee), whom Sokolsky would later identify as "Stephen Birmingham, a detective." On behalf of the Dies Committee, the representative asked Sokolsky to confer with the committee members and to discuss "the nature of Communist penetration" in the United States. During this meeting, Sokolsky's visitor confessed that the House committee members and its staff "were not adequately informed on the subject" and thus had not been able to "evaluate the data that came before them." Sokolsky told the committee representative that he "could not be their man," instead recommending Matthews as an "excellent authority" on the subject of "Communist penetration."[100]

Like Matthews, Sokolsky proved to be a political and ideological chameleon. Born in 1893 in Utica, New York, as the son of a Russian rabbi who had immigrated to the United States, Sokolsky graduated from the Columbia University School of Journalism. Attracted by the Russian Revolution, he went to Russia in 1917 at the age of nineteen to observe it firsthand. Living in Petrograd (later Leningrad), Sokolsky worked as an editor for an English-language newspaper, the *Russian Daily News*. Four years later, however, Sokolsky "became disillusioned with the revolution" and went to China, where he worked as a special correspondent for such newspapers as the *St. Louis Post-Dispatch* and the *London Daily Express*. After fourteen years in China, Sokolsky returned to the United States in 1935 not only as an expert on Asian affairs but also as an advocate of the influential National Association of Manufacturers. Coming home with an avowed pro-business and pro-capitalist posture, Sokolsky fought with his pen against what he perceived as the evils of the New Deal, regularly contributing articles to the *New York Herald Tribune*.[101]

As Sokolsky's name gradually became synonymous with the word "anticommunism," William Randolph Hearst's Hearst Corporation in New York inaugurated its new policy, recruiting an army of reporters, columnists, editors, and commentators whose "specialty was anti-Communist warnings, diatribes, and rumors."[102] "Pride of place for witch-hunting histrionics" definitely belonged to the Hearst media, in which columnists like Howard Rushmore of the *New York Journal-American* fanned the anti-Communist hysteria with vindictiveness and venom.[103] Affectionately called the "high priest" of American anticommunism by his friends, Sokolsky became one of the most popular columnists for the Hearst press.[104] In due course, Matthews, too, would be enlisted into the ranks of the Hearst columnists.

In the early summer of 1938, Sokolsky introduced Matthews to U.S. representative Joseph "Joe" Starnes from Alabama, a member of the incipient Dies Committee. After discussing what Matthews later described as "plans for a fresh attack upon our unrelenting foe" with the Alabama representative and on the strength of Sokolsky's recommendation, Matthews got acquainted with Dies and was invited to testify before the House Special Committee on Un-American Activities.[105] Accordingly, on August 20, 1938, Matthews was afforded his life-altering grand opportunity to establish himself as an "unrelenting foe" of American communism by appearing before the Dies Committee. Matthews's public testimony lasted for two full days until August 22, while he spent more than ten hours before the committee's closed executive session.[106]

Introducing himself to the House committee as the one who had "associated more prominently . . . with the Communist Party's so-called 'innocents' clubs'" than "any other person in this country," Matthews submitted his "intimate and extensive knowledge of the 'united front'" during his testimony. Matthews described how the Communist Party, in an effort to extend its influence beyond its enrolled membership, relied upon the tactic known as the "united front." The Communist Party organizers, he explained, utilized the wide range of interests espoused by these "fronts" to lure "millions of innocent but dangerously gullible Americans" to "radicalize their thought and action."[107] After reading aloud the long roll of his own misdeeds, Matthews put into the record the names of his old friends and former colleagues, whom he disdainfully labeled as "dupes, stooges, and decoys" lured into the "front" organizations by the Communists.[108] Matthews even implied that the ten-year-old actress Shirley Temple had been duped into unwittingly working for the Communist interests. "They have found dangerous radicals there, led by little Shirley Temple," Harold L. Ickes, who served as secretary of the interior under the Roosevelt administration, later joked: "Imagine the great committee raiding her nursery and seizing her dolls as evidence!"[109] Matthews, in concluding his protracted testimony before the Dies Committee, reiterated what he had written in *Odyssey of a Fellow Traveler,* expressing his deep conviction that "present-day radicalism in general and communism in particular" were "the most complete illusion ever born in the human brain."[110]

His witness's absurd utterances about Shirley Temple notwithstanding, Dies, impressed by Matthews's "intimate and extensive knowledge" of the Communist maneuvering, decided to appoint Matthews as his committee's director of research and counsel.[111] Prizing Matthews "for his delusions, for his simplifications, and, most especially, for his supply of names" and offering him an annual salary of $7,200, the House committee would cling to Matthews until 1945.[112] Styling himself as not only Dies's "most fertile source of 'information,'" but also the committee chair's "hand and . . . brain" and "*alter ego,*" Matthews—"the darling of the nightshirt fringe," as one contemporary observer described him—provided the incipient Dies Committee with its raison d'être.[113] "My first job was to build up a file," Matthews once recollected, "[and] I started from scratch with five copies of the *Daily Worker.*"[114] Thereafter, Matthews tirelessly cross-indexed thousands of names, creating a vast collection of Communist publications and documents in the United States for his new employer. Having recognized the progress that the Dies Committee was making thanks to Matthews's hard work, Congress soon increased its appropriation for the committee from $25,000 to $100,000, and this great leap in appropriation in turn enabled Matthews to keep building up his filing system.[115]

For six and a half years, from the summer of 1938 to the early 1945, Matthews, as the Dies Committee's research director and counsel, "examined" approximately four hundred witnesses—both friendly and unfriendly—at the committee's public hearings and six hundred more during its executive sessions.[116] Ironically, one of those "unfriendly" witnesses grilled by Matthews before the Dies Committee was Harry Ward, executive secretary of the Methodist Federation for Social Service and Matthews's successor as the national chair of the American League against War and Fascism. With the unsparing inquisitions launched by Matthews, who had earlier identified the Ward-led federation as being "entirely in accord with the Communist Party," the committee brought down the American League against War and Fascism, concluding that "the credulous Ward had been a puppet hardly aware of the strings that made him dance to Moscow's tune."[117]

Built upon Matthews's restless investigative work was the Dies Committee's magnum opus, *Appendix IX*. Issued in 1944 as the committee's last official publication and containing 2,100 pages of material, the index to *Appendix IX* (previously, the Dies Committee had published eight different "appendixes") listed some twenty-two thousand individuals alleged to have been Communists and "fellow travelers" between 1930 and 1944. Seven thousand sets of *Appendix IX*, which was divided into seven volumes, were printed and distributed.[118] When the publication came out, Matthews expressed delight in his own "monumental" achievement. In his January 3, 1945, letter to George Sokolsky, Matthews wrote: "By this time you should have received a copy of our 'monumental' index to Appendix IX. . . . Well, even if I have to say it myself, the completed volumes of Appendix IX are the most significant contribution ever made to the subject of communism."[119] Matthews's boasting proved prescient because *Appendix IX* quickly became not only a "bible for intelligence and security officers" but also "the most important single asset of the dossier trade, a 'documentary' treasure" within the nation's anti-Communist circles.[120]

As Dies later admitted, Matthews was a "pillar of strength" for his committee's day-to-day business.[121] Nicknamed "Doc" by Dies, Matthews virtually ghostwrote *The Trojan Horse in America,* which was published under Dies's name in 1940.[122] For his "services in revising" the book (the Texas representative was careful enough not to use the words "writing" or "ghostwriting"), Matthews received a four-hundred-dollar check from Dies and was given 1.5 percent royalties on the book.[123] Furthermore, not only did Matthews dedicate his 1938 *Odyssey of a Fellow Traveler* to Dies and ghostwrite the Texas representative's anti-Communist book two years later, but he even named one of his sons for Dies. When a son was born on December 23, 1940, during his second marriage, Matthews named him Martin in honor of his close associate and friend.[124]

In the 1944 election, Dies decided not to run for Congress, and after his committee was transformed into a standing committee as the HUAC in early 1945, Matthews left the congressional committee and began to make a living as a professional anti-Communist researcher, writer, and lecturer. Leaving the nation's capital for New York City, he became a consultant to the anti-Communist Hearst newspapers, bringing with him the vast number of files on Communists and "fellow travelers" that he had assembled for the Dies Committee. While providing ammunition from his valued files for the red-baiting Hearst columnists, Matthews gradually began to gather around himself a flock of former Communists.[125] In his private life, after divorcing his second wife, the former Ruth Shallcross, Matthews married another "Ruth" in 1949—Ruth Inglis—and their marriage would last until his death. Holding a doctoral degree from Bryn Mawr College in Pennsylvania, Ruth I. Matthews was a well-educated liberal-turned-conservative woman who would soon become Matthews's indispensable partner in his anti-Communist work.[126]

One of the proudest moments in Matthews's life came on February 13, 1953, when a testimonial dinner was held in his honor at New York's Waldorf-Astoria Hotel. The black-tie, $12.50-per-plate dinner was organized by the "Dr. J. B. Matthews Dinner Committee" chaired by George Sokolsky.[127] Two distinguished guests, Senator Joseph McCarthy—the man of the hour—and Martin Dies, were scheduled to honor Matthews by addressing the vivacious gathering of, as Matthews later expressed it, "more anti-Communist experts than ever got under one ceiling before."[128] Indeed, the list of the dinner attendees read like a who's-who of America's domestic anti-Communist enterprise. Among the 280 guests, besides McCarthy and Dies, were: Benjamin Gitlow, an organizer of the CPUSA who had switched his allegiance in 1929; Benjamin Mandel, a former CPUSA member who had joined the research staff of the HUAC and was then serving as the research director of the SISS; Howard Rushmore, an ex-Communist who was the Hearst organization's *New York Journal-American* columnist and Senator McCarthy's speech writer; and Stanley High, a Presbyterian layman whose February 1950 *Reader's Digest* article entitled "Methodism's Pink Fringe" had eventually led to the organization of the Circuit Riders.[129]

Following the invocation offered by Benjamin Schultz, a rabbi and the executive director of the American Jewish League against Communism in New York, Senator McCarthy gave a speech in praise of Matthews. Calling Matthews "the real dean of fighters for America," McCarthy thanked him and expressed admiration for his "encyclopedic knowledge" about communism. "The work of J. B. Matthews may not be written large in the history books," the Wisconsin senator concluded, "[but] he stands among the few heroes of the greatest battle in American history—the battle to keep America American."[130] McCarthy, who was handily reelected to the Senate in1952, had just assumed the chairmanship of the Senate Permanent Subcommittee on Investigations in order to further nourish his anti-Communist crusade. The other featured guest, Dies, who had retired from Congress in 1944 but had been reelected to the House in 1952, could not attend the dinner due to flu. A message from Dies read by Sokolsky hailed Matthews as "the best-informed man in America on Communism and Communists," lauding his "great contribution . . . to the cause of freedom and democracy."[131]

The nation's other prominent anti-Communists who were unable to attend also sent their regrets and regards. Hearst, Matthews's employer at the Hearst Corporation, wired his regret that he could not "show in person to pay tribute to the first and greatest of the red-hot red baiters." Meanwhile, the newly elected vice president of the United States and a former member of the HUAC, Richard M. Nixon, asked Sokolsky to read a message to the dinner guests, in which Nixon extended to Matthews his "commendation and appreciation for his many years of outstanding service in the anti-Communist field."[132] "I cannot tell you how deeply I appreciate the message which your letter to George Sokolsky conveyed to me," Matthews later wrote to the vice president; "George read it to the dinner guests who packed the Sert Room at the Waldorf."[133]

In early 1953, around the same time that Matthews won the thunderous applause of his fellow anti-Communists, Harold H. Velde took the HUAC's helm. In February 1952, Velde had been invited by the Matthews family to spend a night at their New York City residence, and ever since then, Matthews and Velde had been close friends.[134] A Republican representative from Illinois and a member of the First Methodist Church in his hometown of Pekin, Velde, during the 1950 congressional session, had opposed legislation for establishing mobile library services in the nation's rural areas, stating that "the basis of communism and socialistic influence is education of the people."[135] No sooner had he become the HUAC chair than Velde made a public pronouncement on March 9, 1953, that it was "entirely possible" that his committee would extend its investigative arms into the "church field." For the other House committee members, Velde's announcement came as a bolt from the blue. Unprepared for and unwilling to strike back at mounting criticism aimed at their committee and its chair, they tried to disassociate themselves from Velde's idea.[136]

Not everyone, though, was disturbed by the implications of Velde's pronouncement. To be sure, some heartily welcomed the HUAC chair's boldness, and among those who did were the Circuit Riders' officials. Only a few days after Velde publicly suggested his interest in probing into the religious field (the Illinois representative was also a former special agent of the Federal Bureau of Investigation [FBI]), the Circuit Riders' president, John Satterfield, and its executive secretary, Myers Lowman, sent a cheering joint telegram to the HUAC chair, renewing their request previously made in 1952 for a "formal investigation and hearing of Jack R. McMichael and Harry F. Ward" of the MFSA by the House committee. "There is urgent need," Lowman and Satterfield assured Velde, "for public record of propaganda and infiltration methods used by alleged procommunists, communists, and/or collaborators approaching the religious field."[137] "The chairman of the House Un-American Activities Committee, who stirred up a storm by suggesting an investigation of churchmen[,] got a little moral support in Cincinnati yesterday," the *Cincinnati Enquirer* reported on March 13.[138] A month later, on April 16, Lowman wired another lengthy telegram to Velde and his House committee members. "I thank God publicly and privately for Velde," Lowman wrote, for having not "deviated from devotion to expose Soviet Communism, extreme socialism and other un-American activities." "Continue to expose Communists, pro-Communists, extreme socialists and their apologists wherever you find them," Lowman concluded.[139]

Heartened by his fellow Methodists of the Circuit Riders, in early May 1953, Velde acted on his previous intention to investigate the nation's religious field. Now convinced that "hardened and well-trained Communists" were planted among American clergy, the HUAC chair vowed that his committee would take charge of finding alleged Communists whether they were "in over-alls or in sanctified cloth." Making these remarks in a speech delivered before the American Jewish League against Communism on May 7, Velde declared: "I sincerely believe that there are individuals who have been planted in the clergy."[140] True to his own vow and to the delight of Lowman, in late July, Velde subpoenaed Jack McMichael to appear before his House committee in Washington, D.C. McMichael, a native of Georgia who took the helm of the MFSA as its executive secretary in 1945, had just resigned from the position and moved to northern California to serve as the pastor at the Upper Lake Methodist Church in Lakeport.[141]

By the time the Velde-chaired HUAC held the public session in which McMichael was expected to appear, the former MFSA executive secretary had already been "identified" as a member of the CPUSA and its various "front" organizations, including the MFSA, by the House committee's "friendly" witnesses during its closed executive hearings. For the occasion, Velde lined up two black former Communists, Manning Johnson and Leonard Patterson, as well as Martha N. Edmiston, a former undercover FBI informant.[142] Both the HUAC and the SISS had earlier employed these three as the investigative committees' cooperative witnesses, who would soon render their "expertise" to the South's state-operated "little HUACs" as well. During his public testimony before the HUAC, McMichael categorically denied the allegations made by Johnson, Patterson, and Edmiston. Observing that one of those committee-hired professional witnesses had inadvertently included the FBI in a list of organizations with which the Methodist pastor was accused of being associated, McMichael mischievously told the committee in his Georgia drawl: "I have never been a member of that." When the committee counsel, Robert L. Kunzig, humorlessly shouted at McMichael, instructing him to show more respect to the congressional body, McMichael replied without missing a beat: "I used to sell boiled peanuts as a little boy. I can speak as loudly as you."[143]

Looking sulky, Velde pounded his wooden gavel for silence "with as much effect as if he were commanding the sun not to rise." Trying to compose himself, Velde announced to McMichael that he would allow him "two minutes to make any derogatory statements" that he might want to make regarding the House committee.[144] "God is my judge," McMichael defiantly told Velde, "[but] not the Un-American Activities Committee." As soon as McMichael finished his testimony, his "guilt by suspicion" was pronounced by the committee chair. "There can be no question in any one's mind," Velde's posthearing statement read, "that there is considerable evidence that perjury has been committed during the course of this hearing."[145] Thus, Velde's initially rather offhanded utterance about the HUAC's possible investigation of the nation's religious field eventually led his House committee to take a high-handed stand on American clergy, causing considerable public outcry. At about the same time, Matthews, the HUAC chair's friend and associate, also became the focus of public flak in the other wing of the Capitol Building.

In mid-June 1953, Matthews was invited by McCarthy, chair of the Senate Permanent Subcommittee on Investigations, to fill in the subcommittee's executive directorship with an annual salary of $11,646 "upon the recommendation of every intelligence agency in Washington."[146] Earlier in 1952, when the Wisconsin senator published his book entitled *McCarthyism: The Fight for America,* it was largely ghostwritten by his chief staffer, Jean F. Kerr, who would soon marry the senator in September 1953. Collaborating with Kerr in this ghostwriting project were McCarthy's trusted friends, Matthews and his third wife, Ruth.[147] As the senator's close associate, Matthews "regularly advised McCarthy on where and how to find targets for his anti-Communist campaigns" and "introduced him to the esoterica of Communist conspiracy theories."[148] Matthews's devotion to the McCarthyist cause made the Wisconsin senator once proclaim that Matthews was a "star spangled American."[149]

Created under the Senate Government Operations Committee, the Senate Permanent Subcommittee on Investigations was originally organized to investigate inefficiency, mismanagement, and corruption in the federal government. But under the chairmanship of Senator McCarthy, who also chaired the Senate Government Operations Committee, its main focus shifted to investigating alleged subversive infiltrations in the Departments of State and Defense, as well as other government agencies such as the Voice of America.[150] Only about a week after Matthews was appointed as the executive director of the subcommittee, his article entitled "Reds and Our Churches," which Matthews had authored in defense of the HUAC chair Harold Velde, was printed in the July 1953 issue of the *American Mercury.*[151] Making its first appearance in 1924 as a journal of quality literature and thoughtful political commentary under the editorship of H. L. Mencken, the *American Mercury* had once been a "magazine of some distinction." However, when, in the summer of 1952, it was sold to J. Russell Maguire, a millionaire whose fortune had been made by oil and munitions, the magazine became a "conservative version of the *Reader's Digest,*" supporting Senator McCarthy's actions and viewpoints, espousing states' rights ideology, and calling for the abolition of the United Nations.[152]

The first sentence—and opening salvo—of Matthews's *American Mercury* article was quite an attention-getter: "The largest single group supporting the Communist apparatus in the United States today is composed of Protestant clergymen." He then asserted that during the previous two decades, "the Communist Party has enlisted the support of at least seven thousand Protestant clergymen," naming Harry Ward, Jack McMichael, and others as "top pro-Soviet propagandists."[153] "One clergyman is worth more to the Communist cause than a whole carload of garment workers in New York City," Matthews added.[154] As Ruth Young Watt, who had served as the chief clerk of the Senate subcommittee from 1948 to 1979, once recalled, Matthews's article "stirred up the biggest hornets' nest you ever saw" within the subcommittee.[155]

Swift and intense public outcries against Matthews and his July 1953 *American Mercury* article ensued. A Hasbrouck Heights, New Jersey, resident wrote to Matthews in early July: "In heaven's name just what are you, McCarthy and the rest of your ilk trying to do this democracy?" Matthews even heard from one of his old friends from his days with the FOR during the late 1920s and early 1930s. "I hope you did not sell your soul for a mess of pottage," the writer penned: "It astonishes me that anyone holding the views which you then held could work with men like Velde and McCarthy. Have you lost all faith in the social and spiritual principles of the Nazarene?" "If like McCarthy you prefer his form of fascism, preach it," Matthews's former associate advised, "but do not misname it Americanism—it has nothing to do with the American way of life." Meanwhile, a Methodist minister in Lewistown, Pennsylvania, sent his letter to Matthews in care of the "Committee of McCarthyism": "I resent with every drop of blood in my body this false accusation" because "it is a pure, filthy, intentional lie." And finally, signing his letter with a closing phrase reading "A Clergyman (and proud of it)," the pastor at the First Baptist Church in New Franklin, Missouri, criticized Matthews for having written an "irresponsible, ill-conceived and un-American" article. "I shall publicly ask my congregation this Sunday to join me in prayer for you," the Baptist minister informed Matthews, "[and] I trust you will join us in praying for yourself."[156]

Despite the fact that Matthews maintained that he could name those seven thousand Protestant clergy who comprised "the biggest single group supporting the Communist apparatus in America," the Senate subcommittee's executive director submitted his resignation to his boss, Joseph McCarthy, on July 2, 1953, in order to subdue the public fury.[157] Five days later, the subcommittee held a two-hour closed session to discuss Matthews's fate. There, three Democratic members—Senators Henry M. Jackson from Washington, John L. McClellan from Arkansas, and William Stuart Symington from Missouri—denounced Matthews's *American Mercury* article as a "shocking and unwarranted attack" against American clergy and demanded "the immediate removal" of the executive director. Even a Republican member of the subcommittee, Senator Charles E. Potter from Michigan, condemned Matthews's article. McCarthy did not budge in the face of these concerted protests from the subcommittee members and refused to accept Matthews's resignation.[158]

Mounting pressures coming from outside of the subcommittee, however, finally compelled the mulish Wisconsin senator to accept Matthews's resignation on July 9, 1953. The deciding factor that probably induced McCarthy to retreat from his recalcitrant position was President Dwight Eisenhower's telegram addressed to the leaders of the National Conference of Christians and Jews. Previously, the leaders of the influential religious group had sent a telegram to the president condemning Matthews's charges as "unjustifiable and deplorable." Concurring with them in their outpourings of concern, Eisenhower responded to the religious leaders in his publicized telegram, pronouncing that "irresponsible attacks that sweepingly condemn the whole of any group of citizens are alien to America" and "portray contempt for the principles of freedom and decency."[159] Some, of course, held different views. Protesting the president's statement, David A. Witts—a successful Dallas attorney and rancher who had worked for the FBI—sent a sarcastic letter to Eisenhower, with a copy mailed to Matthews. "The Kremlin should congratulate you," the Texan wrote, "on purging America's best informed and most capable anti-communist."[160]

Although Matthews submitted his resignation as the executive director and McCarthy quite reluctantly accepted it, Matthews remained unrepentant. In a statement released to the press on July 9, 1953, he insisted that the contents of his *American Mercury* article were "completely factual and fully documented" and requested "the opportunity to document and verify this" before the Senate subcommittee.[161] When the McCarthy-chaired subcommittee did not grant his request, Matthews sought an appearance before the HUAC chaired by Representative Velde. The House committee announced on July 20 that it had decided by a vote of six to three to grant Matthews his request. As this divided vote indicated, however, Matthews had become a controversial figure even at the HUAC, and his promised appearance before it never took place.[162] In the end, although Matthews "lasted only 17 days" on the McCarthy subcommittee before he virtually quit it on July 2, he was proud of his association with the congressional body. "Joe McCarthy begged me for six months to go down to Washington and take over his entire operation," Matthews wrote to his friend in early August, "[and] I was the big boss of the whole operation." "In the 17 days I was running the McCarthy committee, I put through one $1000 raise and two $500 raises for three of my 27 investigators," he boasted.[163]

Matthews eventually lost his federal paychecks, but the *American Mercury* incident further fortified his reputation, rather than diminishing it, as the nation's most indefatigable chronicler of Communist and subversive activities in the United States. As *Time* magazine succinctly reported soon after Matthews parted from the McCarthy subcommittee, "few Americans have held a Red hunting license longer or beat the bushes harder than J. B. Matthews."[164] Within the circles of prominent red-baiters and red-beaters, Matthews came to be often referred to as "Mr. Anti-Communist"—an appellation coined by John T. Flynn of Bayside, New York, a frequent contributor to the *American Mercury* who coauthored a series of articles entitled "Communists and the New Deal" with Matthews for the conservative periodical in 1953.[165] Revering Matthews as "the best informed man on the subject of Communist" in the nation, those red-baiters compared his "insight into the murky depths of Red intrigue" to an "X-ray searching out the untruths of Marxist philosophy."[166]

With his firsthand experiences in and encyclopedic knowledge of the American Left, Matthews accumulated a vast collection of research files consisting of letterheads, circulars, mailing lists, and even dinner programs of those organizations alleged to be either Communist or Communist-front enterprises.[167] Matthews "indexed, cross-indexed and recorded on file cards" thousands of names of individuals and organizations that he deemed to be seeking the destruction of the American way of life.[168] "I have to some extent been what you might call a squirrel," Matthews reflected in the late 1950s, "[for] I have stored documents, rarely if ever, destroying one without the thought as to whether it would be useful or not."[169] During the height of the McCarthy era, microphones and manila folders had been the anti-Communist extremists' greatest tools. But when the most virulent phase of McCarthyism subsided and the microphones were put away, those folders and their keepers survived, and Matthews and his manila folders endured as well.[170]

In his writings, speeches, and testimonies, Matthews studiously followed his established pattern: first presenting his targets' names and then listing their alleged "communist front" records. The process involved very little effort on his part to analyze and interpret those records, thereby virtually leaving his readers and listeners to assume that the greater the number of assumed Communist and pro-Communist organizations to which a person belonged, "the more notorious the individual in question."[171] In this respect, it cannot be substantiated by examining his personal papers whether or not Matthews himself was aware that his own research files were sought after and used to defile rather than uphold America's democratic system. There was one thing, however, that Matthews definitely understood well: that his anti-Communist manila folders could be used as a "source of personal political power and financial gain."[172] "To me the letterhead of a Communist front is a nugget. And I make a good living at it," Matthews once told the *Newsday* columnist J. Murray Kempton, who cynically ranked Matthews among "the odd new entrepreneurs to whom the letterhead of a dead subversive organization is at once a weapon and a commodity."[173] Echoing this observation, Matthews's own son, Martin S. Matthews, has cautioned historians not to assume that his father was involved in the anti-Communist crusade "purely for ideological reasons" and added that he "did derive status and financial reward" from his anti-Communist crusade.[174] Matthews's manila folders and yellowed documents filed in those folders represented his bread and butter.

Indeed, Matthews made a small fortune from his information-filled manila folders, allowing him and his third wife, the former Ruth Inglis, to live in a luxurious Manhattan penthouse apartment that one of Matthews's close associates, Benjamin Mandel, once affectionately called a "redbaiters' center."[175] "Our penthouse," Matthews proudly wrote to another anti-Communist comrade, "gives the most striking view of mid-town Manhattan to be had anywhere."[176] For his "clients" residing within New York City, to whom all "reports" were made by telephone, Matthews charged one thousand dollars per month as a "retainer's fee" with the provision that there was "no limit as to the number of name-checks" made for them. Meanwhile, as Matthews explained to William Simmons, administrator of the segregationist Association of Citizens' Councils of Mississippi, Matthews asked two hundred dollars a month from his out-of-town clients for his written reports on up to ten name-checks.[177] Matthews's close friends were often exempted from paying these service fees. For instance, when the Hearst columnist George Sokolsky—Matthews's anti-Communist colleague who had first introduced him to Texas representative Dies—asked him to run a check on a union leader in the early 1950s, Matthews wrote back: "The charge for this is an autographed photo of George Ephraim Sokolsky to be framed and hung in our study."[178]

By the time Matthews's June 1953 *American Mercury* article raised a confusing clamor among the American general public, Matthews had established himself as a "man long considered the eminence grise of the anticommunist crusade," in the words of the Cold War historian Ellen Schrecker.[179] Soon after the ensuing controversy leading to Matthews's resignation from the McCarthy subcommittee, the Circuit Riders' executive secretary, Myers Lowman, who had cheered on Representative Velde over the HUAC's investigations in the religious field, found an irresistible and formidable ally in Matthews. After all, Lowman and Matthews shared mutual concerns and common enemies. Aside from the fact that they were both Methodists, both men saw that the "pinkos in the pulpit" and "Social Gospel left wingers"—so often decried in the Citizens' Council's literature—were trying to dominate and direct American Protestantism.[180]

Neither the voluminous J. B. Matthews Papers at Duke University nor the equally extensive Myers G. Lowman Papers at Stanford University clearly attests as to exactly when and how the relationship between Matthews and Lowman began. It can be reasonably surmised, however, that one of their first opportunities to meet in person occurred at the October 1953 anti-Communist seminar sponsored by the Ohio Coalition of Patriotic Societies. Along with Lowman, Joseph Kornfeder, and Merrill Root, another guest speaker featured at this "Seminar on Socialism and Communism" was, indeed, Matthews. He addressed the group on the topic of "Reds and Our Churches," exactly the same title as that of his controversial article in the June 1953 issue of the *American Mercury*.[181]

By the fall of 1953, only a few months after the *American Mercury* ran Matthews's provocative piece, Lowman had begun to rely on Matthews for his unparalleled knowledge of and exhaustive research about the American Left. Beginning with his October 15, 1953, letter to Matthews, Lowman never failed to address his new anti-Communist ally as "Dear J. B." in their ensuing exchange of a countless letters. In the years to come, Lowman and his wife, Dorothy, would be counted among the Matthews family's favorite guests at the latter's Manhattan penthouse, and Matthews was even a special guest at the Lowmans' daughter's wedding.[182] For Lowman, Matthews towered as "the greatest authority on Communist-front enterprises in the United States," and his association with Matthews made Lowman proud to be "part of one of the most exhaustive researchers [*sic*] into Communistic activity in connection with religion ever made."[183] In his battle against "socialism and Communism in Protestant religion in the U.S. and particularly in The Methodist Church," Lowman increasingly came to recognize Matthews as the lifeline for his anti-Communist operation.[184]

Lowman's relationship with Matthews was by no means one-sided. While Lowman valued and made use of Matthews's information and knowledge, Matthews, too, benefited from his association with Lowman not only financially, but also in terms of Lowman's publicity and public relations skills, thereby further promoting himself as the nation's most reliable expert on anticommunism. In November 1954, Lowman visited the nation's capital to confer with the HUAC's incoming chair, Democratic representative Francis E. Walter from Pennsylvania. Reminding Walter that the Communist "exploitation of the facilities of religion and educa-tion" represented "the greatest security risk in America today," Lowman strongly suggested that the House committee's incoming chair get ac-quainted with Matthews. "I regard him as the best informed and . . . [he has] the most documentation regarding the Communist front," Lowman wrote to Walter after their meeting. At the same time, Lowman also recom-mended that the HUAC consider hiring Joseph Kornfeder and Manning Johnson—both former Communists—as the congressional committee's primary researcher and investigator, respectively. "I am proud," Lowman concluded his letter to the incoming chair, "to regard myself as one of your confidantes."[185] Thereafter, the HUAC continued to provide a forum for Lowman. In July 1955, Lowman wrote to one of the Ohio delegates to Congress, Republican representative Gordon H. Scherer, who served on the HUAC, with explosive, almost frightening emotion: "Again and again, again and again, again and again, I want to say, God save the United States."[186]

In the spring of 1955, Lowman concocted an idea to assemble a set of "complete card file[s]" on 1,350 Methodist ministers whom the Circuit Riders suspected of being "affiliated with Communist-Front enterprises." For his project, Lowman asked Matthews to provide him with information on each one of these individual ministers and paid Matthews the hand-some sum of two thousand dollars in research fees. This task of compiling what Lowman called "Who's Who in Left Wing Methodism" turned out to be the first major cooperative effort between Lowman and Matthews to weed out those whom they perceived as the Communist-influenced clergy and church leaders.[187] "We want to get as much work done as we can with only the Methodists fighting us, and then pick up the others when we no longer can ward off the idea of other organized groups being our formal opponents," Lowman wrote to Matthews in May.[188] By the following month, Lowman, with the help of Matthews, had "identified" 8,391 clergymen who, he claimed, were "connected with from one to one hundred each of the Communist-front enterprises." Among those whom Lowman named as "fronters" were approximately 1,800 Methodist ministers.[189] By March 1956, the grand total increased to 8,491, including 2,109 leaders of the American Methodist Church.[190] The results of this extensive collaborative research between Lowman and Matthews were published by the Circuit

Riders in a series with the dubious title "A Compilation of Public Records." By the summer of 1960, the series that began with a publication entitled *2109 Methodist Ministers* would include the titles *1411 Protestant Episcopal Rectors, 614 Presbyterian Church U.S.A., Clergymen*, and *660 Baptist Clergymen.* "Without statistician Myers Lowman," one observer noted in 1963, "the Riders might well be short-Circuited." Behind Lowman's "statistical talent," to be sure, was Matthews as the primary information provider.[191]

Meanwhile, in late 1955, Lowman included the National Council of Churches in his list of enemies, blaming the ecumenical organization composed of the nation's principal Protestant religious establishments for practicing and proliferating "pro-Communistic" programs.[192] Because of its progressive and liberal views on racial integration, labor unions, and the recognition of Communist China (particularly after 1959), the National Council of Churches was labeled as "socialistic" by a host of right-wing individuals and groups, as well as southern segregationists such as Mississippi senator James Eastland.[193] Lowman's investigative interest in the National Council of Churches stemmed from the fact that the Methodist Church was the largest denomination within the ecumenical group, and he believed that "the leftwing Methodists," as a "dominant element" in the council, had much to do with devising the group's "pro-Communistic" activities.[194] In Lowman's world, those "socialistic" reformers associated with the National Council of Churches were the most sinister creatures because they "neutralize the people against a firm stand in opposition to the world domination plot of the Soviets."[195] In this connection, the following short epigrammatic fable, composed by Lowman and entitled "Who's Running with the Ducks?," concisely sums up his simplistic view and exemplifies the discourse of the vast majority of the South's white supremacists of the day:

> There are those with web-feet like a duck and feathers like a duck and who make a noise like a duck and mess up the yard like a duck who say "we are not ducks," whenever they see the duck-counters at work.
>
> There is little suspicion that many of these "we are not ducks" are favorable to World Soviet Communism—they just run with the ducks when the corn of "peace" or "brotherly love" or "co-existence" is scattered to attract their attention and unwitting quacking aid.[196]

Though the investigative focus of the Lowman-led Circuit Riders extended out to cover other Protestant denominations, its original adversary, the MFSA, remained vulnerable to assaults from Lowman. During the summer of 1957, when the MFSA celebrated its fiftieth anniversary by holding a special conference at the Dodge Hotel in Washington, D.C., Lowman asked Matthews to have someone infiltrate the gathering. In response, Matthews sent his wife, Ruth, to the conference on July 17, who later prepared seven pages of "confidential notes" on the meeting. On the first day of the conference, L. F. Worley of the MFSA addressed the gathered audience with a speech entitled "On the Mary-Go-Around [*sic*] in Washington and with the Circuit Riders" that was highly critical of Lowman. Ruth Matthews noted that Worley blasted Lowman as being a "low man on the totem pole." At the end of Worley's address, someone from the audience asked if Senator Eastland, chair of the SISS, was Methodist. Ruth reported that when someone else in the audience answered affirmatively to the question, a follow-up inquiry was made by another participant: "Is Eastland a tool of the Circuit Riders?"[197]

Immediately following the MFSA's fiftieth-anniversary conference, the Circuit Riders published a report entitled *Fifty Years of Un-Methodist Propaganda* in July 1957. Written by Lowman, the report denounced the MFSA as one of the Communists' most "deceitful Trojan-Horse or front organizations." The report went on to assert that the federation had "from its beginning represented a red fringe among Methodist clergymen" and that Ward, founding executive secretary of the Methodist Federation for Social Service, had been "undoubtedly one of the most effective propagandists for Communism in the entire history of the Soviet conspiracy in the United States."[198] Lowman's aversion to the federation and its successive executive secretaries—Harry Ward and Jack McMichael—was immeasurable.

As David B. Sageser, one of Lowman's former colleagues at the Wesley Foundation in Cincinnati, recollected years later, Lowman might have begun his anti-Communist crusade "with the best intentions." Gradually, however, he became "misled" by his own "obsession" with his seemingly noble cause and, like Matthews, blinded by his desire for personal fame and financial gain.[199] Once he found his enemies, his zeal to crack down on them was unparalleled. Since the inception of his Circuit Riders, Lowman had proceeded to branch out into a wider field in search of adversaries, going far beyond the Methodist Church into Protestantism in general by the mid-1950s. And in no time, his investigative arms would also be extended to the intensifying civil rights movement in the South. Along with his own ardor and fanaticism, what Lowman needed and depended upon in this new endeavor was Matthews and his manila folders. Closely collaborating with one another and acting as "Tweedledum and Tweedledee," Lowman and Matthews would soon deeply involve themselves in protecting southern segregationists' vested interests—their racial and racist norms—under the ostensibly honorable banner of American anticommunism.

CHAPTER 2

"COMMUNISM AND INTEGRATION ARE INSEPARABLE"

Louisiana as the Harbinger of Segregationist Anti-Communist Inquisitions in the South

In late 1955, the Circuit Riders' Myers Lowman was honored by the New York–based Joint Committee against Communism for his "research and exposure of Communist-front records showing the exploitation of 8,391 American clergymen."[1] Presenting Lowman, who had flown to New York City for the occasion, with a plaque recognizing his achievement was Benjamin Schultz, national director of the committee. Having served as the rabbi at Temple Emanu-El of Yonkers in New York from 1935 to 1947, Schultz founded the American Jewish League against Communism in 1948, holding its executive directorship.[2] Created as a "non-profit educational organization," the league was intended to ferret out "all Communist activity in Jewish life, wherever it may be."[3] Included in its board of directors was George Sokolsky, J. B. Matthews's close associate, who would later serve as the board chair.[4]

When the Joint Committee against Communism announced that it would honor Lowman, Matthews penned a congratulatory letter to his friend. "In my 20 years of exclusive attention to the subject of subversion," he wrote, "I have never known anyone who surpasses you in the indefatigable energy with which you perform." "The Methodist Church—and the entire religious world—owes you much. Francis Asbury would be proud of the modern circuit riders," Matthews noted.[5] Republican representative Gordon Scherer from Ohio, Lowman's fellow Cincinnatian and a member of the House Un-American Activities Committee (HUAC), also echoed Matthews in writing to Lowman: "The honor was well deserved. It's long overdue."[6]

To be sure, Matthews and Scherer were not the only ones who noted Lowman's "indefatigable energy" for suppressing views and visions deemed unconventional—whether they were religious, social, political, or racial. Southern segregationists, too, would soon begin recognizing Lowman as their "indefatigable" northern messiah who was capable of helping them in their determined massive resistance campaign in the name of America's anti-Communist commitment. For proponents of massive resistance, there were obvious advantages to securing the knowledge and expertise of a person like Lowman who could skillfully and with the appearance of authority depict black southerners' freedom struggle as Communist-tainted.

Lowman became interested in probing into the civil rights field in the spring of 1956, when Matthews suggested that Lowman "do something about" Rosa Parks, who had "initiated all of this trouble down in Alabama." By then, the yearlong Montgomery Bus Boycott in the state's capital city—a major milestone in the civil rights movement that was ignited by Parks, led by Martin Luther King Jr., and carried out by the Montgomery Improvement Association—had been in progress for four months, since December 1955. Matthews also directed Lowman's attention to the Highlander Folk School in Monteagle, Tennessee, where Parks had been "trained" for the ongoing bus boycott. Calling Highlander a "Communist institution," Matthews informed Lowman that the school's director, Myles Horton, had been a student of Harry Ward—the founding executive secretary of the Methodist Federation for Social Service (later the Methodist Federation for Social Action [MFSA]). "You see," Matthews reminded Lowman in concluding his April 11 letter, "Ward's long arm reaches out and out and out."[7]

Prodded by Matthews and beginning to see the Reds and their sympathizers behind the South's racial strife, Lowman proceeded to establish a liaison with Georgia attorney general J. Eugene Cook.[8] As the attorney general of the Deep South state where the second-oldest anti-integration state agency—the Georgia Commission on Education—was organized even before the Supreme Court's 1954 *Brown* decision, Cook, by early 1956, had already become instrumental in waging Georgia's grand campaign to link the National Association for the Advancement of Colored People (NAACP) with the Communist Party of the United States of America (CPUSA). In the fall of 1955, Cook delivered a provocative address entitled "The Ugly Truth about the NAACP" before the Peace Officers' Association of Georgia. His speech was then printed by the segregationist Association of Citizens' Councils of Mississippi as a little booklet destined to become "one of the most quoted documents in the war against the NAACP" among southern segregationists.[9] Having added Cook's name to the Circuit Riders' mailing list, Lowman suggested to the Georgia attorney general that "the Communist-connected people" at the Highlander Folk School located in Georgia's neighboring state be "the subject of studies to reflect the origin of many of your problems."[10] Cook heeded Lowman's advice. Soon thereafter, in addition to the NAACP, Tennessee's Highlander would also fall prey to Georgia segregationists.

Among the nation's civil rights groups, the NAACP was most vulnerable to irresponsible racial and racist red-baiting, despite its repeated assertion that it was neither a Communist-led nor a Communist-dominated organization. At its forty-first annual convention held in June 1950 in Boston, the NAACP adopted a strong anti-Communist resolution and instructed its national board of directors to take bold actions to repudiate Communist influences at its local branches.[11] In the following year, Herbert Hill, labor secretary of the national NAACP, declared in the *Crisis*, the organization's publication, that the CPUSA was an "Enemy of Negro Equality."[12] Even the HUAC, after finding that the vast majority of the NAACP members were not "hoodwinked" by "false messiahs," recognized that the civil rights group was a "non-Communist organization" in late 1954.[13] Indeed, there was no credible evidence that large-scale Communist infiltration ever took place within the NAACP. Out of approximately 1,500 local branches nationwide, only a dozen local units at the most were alleged to have been affected by Communist infiltration. Furthermore, all of these incidents involved branches either in the North or on the West Coast, while those located in the South "remained completely unaffected."[14] Nevertheless, the NAACP could not escape from the charge, leveled primarily by southern white racists, that it was nothing but a disguised instrument of the Communist conspiracy.

By early 1957, the nation's prominent civil rights organizations and notably the NAACP had evidently become major targets of Lowman's anti-Communist investigations and exposés. At Lowman's request, Matthews compiled "Communist-front enterprise activity records" on the national NAACP leaders, for which the Circuit Riders paid Matthews two hundred dollars.[15] When, in February 1957, Lowman asked Matthews to provide him with the records of W. E. B. Du Bois, one of America's most renowned black leaders and a founder of the NAACP in 1909, Matthews gave Lowman a little lecture. "You don't know what you're asking," Matthews wrote back. "The record of DuBois [*sic*] is the longest in the entire history of the Communist movement in the United States." That said, Matthews, who had in fact accumulated more than four hundred information cards on Du Bois, let Lowman know that making a "tabulation of his pro-Communist record" would "require the de-coding" of each of those information cards and cost the Circuit Riders five hundred dollars. Lowman eventually gave up on the project due to the lack of money.[16] During the same month, however, Lowman asked and received from Matthews sets of compiled records on Walter F. White, who had served as the NAACP's executive secretary from 1931 to 1955, and James Dombrowski, executive director of the New Orleans–based Southern Conference Educational Fund (SCEF).[17] Subsequently, by the end of 1957, Lowman and Matthews in collaboration had made background checks on all 162 names that appeared on the national headquarters' letterhead of the NAACP.[18] "Even if the NAACP is not *technically* a Communist front," Matthews wrote to Lowman in December 1957, "it is the nearest thing to a front in the United States."[19]

The Southern Regional Council (SRC) in Atlanta, Georgia, was another civil rights organization on which Lowman piled up his investigative dossiers.[20] Created as the interwar-year Commission on Interracial Cooperation in 1919, the SRC was chartered as a nonprofit and nonpolitical civil rights group in Georgia in 1944. A brainchild of the sociologist Howard W. Odum at the University of North Carolina in Chapel Hill, the SRC initially carried out its mission to make "separate but equal"—the constitutional doctrine established in the Supreme Court's 1896 *Plessy v. Ferguson* decision—more equal for black southerners, preferring to work within the framework of racial separation rather than openly opposing the region's established racial practices. In December 1951, however, the SRC adopted a new policy that called for taking a stronger antisegregation position in order to rectify the South's racial discrimination.[21] Lowman found the SRC's use of the Wesley Memorial Building in Atlanta as its headquarters particularly upsetting. In April 1957, a meeting was arranged between Lowman and four members of the Wesley Memorial Building board of trustees in the Georgia capital. During the conference, Lowman presented "the records of Communist related affiliations" of the SRC officials and tried to persuade the board members to evict the SRC from the building. When no action that Lowman deemed satisfactory was taken by the board members and its chair, he wrote to Arthur J. Moore, a Methodist bishop in Atlanta and one of the SRC's five incorporators when it was legally created in early 1944. "It was obvious to me," Lowman complained, that "the chairman was more friendly to Southern Regional Council then [*sic*] to Circuit Riders, Inc."[22]

Lowman also spent a considerable amount of time investigating the Dombrowski-directed SCEF, the offshoot of the now defunct Southern Conference for Human Welfare (SCHW). The SCEF, according to Lowman, deserved to be ranked as one of the most sinister and Communist-tainted civil rights organizations because it had "exploited the race problem" and "the race grievance through the South as effectively as any other groups in America" for the Communist cause.[23] Lowman's interest in the civil rights field also extended to the Swedish economist Gunnar Myrdal, who had published a monumental analysis of black-and-white race relations in the United States, *An American Dilemma,* in 1944. Myrdal's book was one of the seven sociology and psychology works on which Chief Justice Earl Warren relied in declaring that "separate educational facilities are inherently unequal" when the Supreme Court dealt with the 1954 *Brown* case.[24]

The joint campaign waged by Lowman, Matthews, and Georgia attorney general Eugene Cook to link the South's civil rights movement with the "Communist conspiracy" became discernible in a public forum in the early spring of 1957. That forum was provided by the segregationist Joint Legislative Committee in Louisiana, where the first public bus boycott in modern civil rights history—the eight-day-long Baton Rouge Bus Boycott—had taken place in June 1953. With Lowman's involvement in and collaboration with Louisiana's segregationist forces as a major turning point, the influence of his Ohio-based anti-Communist cottage industry began to expand into the South. Inventing a paranoid version of the three Rs—Religion, the Reds, and Race—Lowman would throw his energies into orchestrating a variety of anti-integrationist and anti-Communist enterprises sought after by the white South's "little HUACs." Beginning with Louisiana, his relationship with the region's massive resisters would become more and more conspicuous in other southern states as well—namely Georgia, Florida, Arkansas, and Mississippi.[25]

When the Supreme Court announced its *Brown* decision on May 17, 1954, Louisiana was the sole southern state in which the legislature was in regular session, enabling it to mobilize the first state-sponsored resistance to the school desegregation ruling.[26] Taking charge of Louisiana's official and organized defiance as one of the state's most ardent spokespersons for white supremacy was William M. Rainach, a state senator from Summerfield in Claiborne Parish, whose parish seat was located in Homer. A vital center for the region's cotton production dotted with rich oil and gas fields, Claiborne Parish had one of the highest percentages of nonwhites in Louisiana (approximately 52 percent), somewhat resembling Sunflower

County in Mississippi—the home county of Senator James Eastland and the birthplace of the segregationist Citizens' Council.[27] In spite of his humble beginning, Rainach attended George Washington University in Washington, D.C., studying business administration. Having returned home at the age of twenty-five, Rainach organized the Claiborne Electric Cooperative, Inc., in 1939. As a rural electrification enterprise, the Claiborne Electric Cooperative brought the first electricity to farms and houses in north Louisiana, serving more than sixteen thousand users. On the strength of his success in the electrification project, Rainach was elected as a Louisiana state representative in 1939, and he was reelected to the House in 1943. Rainach then successfully ran for the state Senate and took office in 1948—the year of the Dixiecrat revolt. Incited by the southern Democrats' uproar over the national Democratic Party's civil rights programs, Rainach, as a state senator, began to transform himself into a guardian of white supremacy—or a "minister plenipotentiary in the segregationist cause," as he was once labeled—in Louisiana.[28]

On May 20, 1954, only three days after the Supreme Court rendered its *Brown* decree, the Louisiana state legislature struck back defiantly to safeguard the state's racial segregation by introducing House Concurrent Resolution № 22.[29] Sponsored by State Representative E. W. Gravolet Jr. of Point a la Hache in Plaquemines Parish, the House resolution recognized that "the abolition of the present system of segregation in the public schools would be intolerable to the great majority of the citizens . . . in Louisiana and contrary to their own wishes and interests." On this premise, the state legislature committed itself to furnishing "ways and means whereby our existing social order shall be preserved, and our institutions and ways of life . . . shall be maintained."[30] Following the adoption of this resolution on May 26, another resolution—House Concurrent Resolution № 27—was offered and passed to implement the resolve expressed in the legislators' former resolution, creating the Louisiana Joint Legislative Committee on June 11.[31]

Directed and empowered to "carry out the purposes of House Concurrent Resolution No. 22"—and thus charged with "providing ways and means of maintaining the institution of segregation" in the state's public schools—the Louisiana Joint Legislative Committee was chaired by State Senator Rainach, and it would soon become known as the Joint Legislative Committee on Segregation.[32] Even though the committee's official name did not include the words "on Segregation," by early 1960, Rainach had begun to add these words to the title in his official correspondence with other committee members.[33] With an initial annual appropriation of fifteen thousand dollars and equipped with subpoena power, the Rainach-chaired legislative committee not only "served as the nucleus" of Louisiana's official voices of all-out defiance, but also "became the final arbiter of racial orthodoxy" in the state.[34] The ten-member Louisiana Joint Legislative Committee was composed of five state senators and five state representatives. State Representative Gravolet, who had sponsored House Concurrent Resolution № 22, was appointed as the committee vice chair.[35]

Besides Gravolet, Senator Rainach's other right-hand man in the Louisiana House was Representative John S. Garrett, a member of the Louisiana Joint Legislative Committee who, according to one newspaper account, could "roar like a ruptured steam boiler when things get rough." As a dedicated segregationist, Garrett, a future Louisiana House Speaker, had succeeded Rainach as the state representative from Claiborne Parish in 1948.[36] Claiborne Parish's third major contributor to the state's massive resistance led by the Joint Legislative Committee was William M. Shaw, an attorney from Homer whom Rainach appointed as the general counsel of his committee.[37] Aiding Shaw in his segregationist undertaking was Louisiana state district attorney Leander H. Perez Sr. of Plaquemines Parish, the home parish of Representative Gravolet. In fact, Perez had helped Rainach draft the House resolution to organize the Louisiana Joint Legislative Committee.[38] Soon after its inception, in early August 1954, Shaw, as the legislative committee's general counsel, invited Perez to help the committee in its "fight to preserve segregation in Louisiana."[39]

As the all-powerful district attorney and political boss of Plaquemines Parish situated along the Mississippi River, Perez—who was often referred to as "Judge Perez" because he had served as the district judge covering Plaquemines and St. Bernard Parishes—was, without doubt, one of the most implacable segregationist ideologues in the South. While Mississippi House Speaker Walter Sillers Jr. praised Perez as "one of the most outspoken men in Louisiana on the segregation issue," *Time* magazine described him as "the symbol of Louisiana racism," with "cold blue eyes, a cunning legal mind and a fanatic's zeal."[40] In the wake of the High Court's *Brown* ruling in 1954, Perez, at a testimonial dinner held to celebrate his thirty-fifth anniversary as an elected Louisiana state official, solemnly declared an unconditional war against integrationists and pledged that he would devote "the rest of his life to the principle of segregation of the races." Dismissing the sociological and psychological works upon which the Supreme Court had relied in arriving at the *Brown* decision as "Communist trash," Perez pronounced that the desegregation ruling, rendered by "nine dishonest stooges [*sic*]," was evidence of "the pro-Communist penetration of the highest court in the land."[41] Perez, whom the journalist Robert Sherrill has sarcastically labeled "The Swamp's Gift to Dixie," once insisted that he "could smell" the Communist-concocted "Black Belt conspiracy" when the *Brown* decision was announced. A Catholic, "Judge Perez" would later be excommunicated from the Catholic Church by the Archbishop of New Orleans, Joseph F. Rummel, for "hindering his order to desegregate" the city's parochial schools.[42]

On July 20, 1954, a little over a month after the organizational meeting of the Louisiana Joint Legislative Committee, Rainach delivered an inflammatory address before the Louisiana Farm Bureau convention in Alexandria, in which the state senator revealed his segregationist anti-Communist discourse. Warning the audience to be mindful of what he referred to as the "sinister conspiracy" devised by "communistic, universal, totalitarian" forces, Rainach told them that the "astounding Supreme Court decision on segregation" was an "example of what length these sinister conspirators can go to gain through the Court." "The chips are down, the lines are drawn, the time has come to stand and be counted," Rainach concluded: "I know not what others may do, but my own course is clear."[43] Having set his "own course," Rainach appeared on a statewide television program accompanied by his legislative committee members and General Counsel Shaw. On the program, the fire-breathing state senator reserved his biting strictures for one of his natural foes—"the carpetbag NAACP"—and linked the civil rights organization with what he perceived as the domestic Communist advancement, where "racial hatred" was being promoted.[44]

While firmly establishing himself as the leader of Louisiana's official resistance to desegregation, Rainach also realized the importance of a grassroots movement mobilized against the NAACP-led civil rights struggle. In the fall of 1954, he organized the state's first Citizens' Council chapter in his home parish of Claiborne.[45] And later, when the statewide Association of Citizens' Councils of Louisiana was formed at the Virginia Hotel in Monroe on December 13, 1955, Rainach became its founding president. Elected as the executive secretary of the newly created statewide segregationist private group was William Shaw, general counsel of the Louisiana Joint Legislative Committee.[46] Observing that "the Communist conspiracy is skillfully using supporters of integration . . . to accomplish the planned destruction of the South," the Association of Citizens' Councils of Louisiana vowed to protect and preserve "our historical Southern social traditions."[47]

Then, only two weeks after the statewide Citizens' Council organization was created in Louisiana through the efforts of State Senator Rainach and his Joint Legislative Committee, yet another segregationist group determined to resist the civil rights movement came into existence. Headquartered in Louisiana, the South-wide group would soon become a vital financial patron of the state's segregationist anti-Communist inquisitions. Organized officially on December 28, 1955, at the Peabody Hotel in Memphis, Tennessee, the Federation for Constitutional Government attracted a host of noted politicians and officials from the Deep South states.[48] In addition to U.S. senators James Eastland from Mississippi and Strom Thurmond from South Carolina, the founding members of the federation included such segregationist dignitaries as U.S. representative John Bell Williams from Mississippi, former Mississippi governor Fielding Wright, Mississippi House Speaker Walter Sillers, Georgia governor S. Marvin Griffin, and Georgia attorney general Eugene Cook.[49] Although the federation was the brainchild of Senator Eastland and Mississippians, therefore, were somewhat overrepresented, the contributions of Louisiana's segregationists to its formation should not go unnoticed.[50] Elected as the chair of the federation's executive committee was John U. Barr of New Orleans, a member of the board of directors of the National Association of Manufacturers who had also been a prominent leader of the 1948 Dixiecrat movement in Louisiana.[51] Also sitting on the executive committee was, among others, General Counsel Shaw of the Louisiana Joint Legislative Committee.[52] Serving on the federation's advisory committee was the Louisiana committee's chair, State Senator Rainach.[53]

In its statement of purpose, the Federation for Constitutional Government, without directly mentioning the Supreme Court's *Brown* ruling, pledged that it would seek "in every honorable and legitimate way" to "counteract the effects and consequences . . . of decisions of the Federal Courts and the United States Supreme Court" that, in the federation's understanding, had "wrongfully abrogated" part of the United States Constitution and particularly, its Tenth Amendment. Despite the fact that the federation armed itself with a seemingly noble set of organizational purposes sustained by the states' rights ideology, its racial and racist thinking and willingness to link integration with communism were obvious. "The great distinction between the communist takeover in Russia and the communist design for the conquest of America is Russia remained white, though communist," the federation once wrote to its members and sympathizers, "whereas, the United States faces not only the danger of communization but mongrelization as well." "The menace of the negro in America is incalculable," the federation's open letter proclaimed.[54] Settling its headquarters in the American Bank Building in downtown New Orleans, where State District Attorney Perez had his law office, the Federation for Constitutional Government gave its unqualified support to the Louisiana Joint Legislative Committee.[55]

Following the creation of the Federation for Constitutional Government, in the spring of 1956, Rainach and his Joint Legislative Committee triumphed over their principal enemy in Louisiana—the state NAACP. Based on the research conducted by General Counsel Shaw, the legislative committee had prompted Louisiana attorney general Jack P. F. Gremillion to demand that the state NAACP comply with what Rainach termed the "Membership List Law," a 1924 statute originally intended to curb the activities of the state's Ku Klux Klan (KKK) organizations during the height of nativism.[56] Resurrecting the antiquated law, the Louisiana Joint Legislative Committee aimed, at this time, to cripple the civil rights organization. On April 24, 1956, in the face of the state NAACP's refusal to submit its membership list, Attorney General Gremillion succeeded in securing a state district court injunction that prohibited the civil rights group from "doing any business or holding any meetings in the State of Louisiana."[57]

Previously, in September 1954—just four months after the Supreme Court issued its fateful school desegregation ruling—Rainach had vowed that he and his fellow white Louisianans "must pass from the defensive to the offensive in our fight to restore to the states the powers in education that have been usurped by this Supreme Court in order to curry favor with the NAACP."[58] In keeping with this self-imposed pledge, Rainach undertook the full-scale offensive in early 1957. Prompted by the March 1954 hearings on the SCEF held by the Eastland-led Senate Internal Security Subcommittee (SISS) in New Orleans and imitating the February 1957 hearings conducted by the HUAC on "Communist activities" in the Crescent City, Rainach and his Louisiana Joint Legislative Committee decided to hold their own segregationist anti-Communist hearings for four days, from March 6 to 9, 1957.[59]

Even though Rainach was determined to "uproot influences from outside the state" that he believed were responsible for what the state senator perceived as racial unrest in his beloved Louisiana, there remained a major obstacle in his way.[60] The problem that Rainach was required to address by fair means or foul sprang from the troublesome fact that his Joint Legislative Committee did not have its own investigators and that General Counsel Shaw was far from being well versed in "uprooting outside influences" affecting the state's race relations. In other words, the state senator was in dire need of securing reliable resources and cooperative services provided by out-of-the committee experts who could make the planned hearings both authentic and authoritative. Before long, Rainach found such an expert in Myers Lowman, the Circuit Riders' executive secretary, who readily agreed to line up professional "friendly" witnesses coming from the North for Louisiana's pro-segregation committee.

A political biographer of Rainach has indicated that Lowman was originally recommended and introduced to the Rainach-chaired Louisiana Joint Legislative Committee by Senator Eastland from Mississippi.[61] Though this observation cannot be fully substantiated by examining the Rainach Papers housed at Louisiana State University in Shreveport, it is entirely possible that that was exactly what happened. By the time Rainach and his legislative committee began to contemplate holding their anti-integration and anti–civil rights hearings, Eastland was already well aware of Lowman and his anti-Communist zeal. In early 1956, soon after the Eastland-chaired SISS designated the MFSA—the primary enemy of Lowman and his Circuit Riders—as one of the most devious "religious fronts" operated by the CPUSA, Lowman praised Eastland and his Senate subcommittee in writing and asked the Mississippi senator to grant him an opportunity to testify before the SISS as what Lowman himself termed a "friendly witness."[62]

Another possibility, of course, is that Lowman was introduced to Louisiana's segregationists by Georgia attorney general Eugene Cook. Cook, after all, was the first southern official with whom Lowman had established a working liaison when he ventured into the civil rights field in the spring of 1956.[63] And as a matter of fact, the Georgia attorney general would attend the March 1957 hearings held by the Louisiana Joint Legislative Committee as an invited observer—perhaps indicating that it was he who recommended Lowman to the Louisiana committee.[64] Be that as it may, Lowman definitely played no small part in the success of the Rainach-led committee hearings by orchestrating a parade of carefully selected "friendly" witnesses on behalf of Louisiana's segregationists. "One of the gentlemen I came in contact with was Myers Loman [*sic*] from Cincinnati, Ohio, who had made quite a study of it," Rainach reminisced in a 1977 oral history. "He volunteered to get me witnesses," Rainach recollected, "if I would hold a committee to testify authoritatively on the Communist background . . . [and] he had the most comprehensive library in the United States on subversion."[65]

The grand preparation for the March 1957 hearings of the Louisiana Joint Legislative Committee began on December 18, 1956—only a couple of days before the triumphant ending of the yearlong Montgomery Bus Boycott—when Lowman, by invitation, visited Louisiana to confer with a few of the legislative committee members and its general counsel. Those who represented the state's segregationist committee and attended this strategic meeting with Lowman in Shreveport were Chairman Rainach, State Representatives John Garrett and Ford E. Stinson of Benton, Bossier Parish (Stinson would later call one of the Supreme Court's antisegregation rulings a "claptrap"), and General Counsel Shaw. Also present at the conference was State District Attorney Perez. Heartened by Lowman, who promised that he would provide necessary witnesses for the legislative committee during the conference, the Louisiana massive resisters decided to go on with their plan to hold the committee hearings, in which an "official investigation . . . into influences that are disturbing the peace and tranquility between the segments of population in Louisiana" would be conducted.[66]

Rainach wasted no time. On December 30, 1956, Rainach consulted over the phone with two prominent Mississippi segregationists—William Simmons, the kingpin of the Citizens' Council movement, and Circuit Court Judge Tom Brady, author of *Black Monday*—about his plan to hold the committee hearings.[67] Having received encouraging responses from Simmons and Brady, Rainach then dispatched General Counsel Shaw to Jackson, Mississippi, on January 2, 1957, to have him seek further advice from Simmons.[68] After returning to Louisiana, Shaw immediately took a three-day trip to the North on behalf of the legislative committee from January 4 to 6. His first order of business was to confer with Lowman in Cincinnati. Following this meeting, Shaw, accompanied by Lowman, visited Detroit to "interview" Joseph Kornfeder as one of the "prospective witnesses for the proposed hearings."[69] Lowman's partnership with Kornfeder—a former leader of the CPUSA—in the anti-Communist field had been forged in October 1952, when the Circuit Riders held its first "national conference" in Cincinnati, where Kornfeder was asked to address the meeting as its featured speaker.[70]

As Rainach and Shaw carefully crafted their plan for the Louisiana committee hearings, their dependence on Lowman increased. In late January 1957, Lowman again visited Rainach in Louisiana to prepare for the committee hearings.[71] While in Louisiana, Lowman also paid a visit to Perez at the latter's law office in the American Bank Building in New Orleans.[72] By then, Perez had promised Rainach that the "financing" of Lowman's expenditures was "coming from a Tax Exempt Foundation" in New Orleans, indicating, though without mentioning the name of the "foundation," that the expenses involving Lowman's services rendered for the legislative committee hearings would be provided by the pro-segregation Federation for Constitutional Government.[73] A month later, when the Louisiana Joint Legislative Committee met at the Bentley Hotel in Alexandria on February 24, Lowman was invited to attend the meeting and was officially introduced to the whole committee. At that meeting, Rainach revealed that he and Shaw had gone ahead and "advanced $665 of their own personal funds" to Lowman for "his use in arranging advance plane reservations for prospective witnesses to appear before the Committee in Baton Rouge." No objection was made among the gathered committee members, and by a unanimous vote, the segregationist committee officially decided to hold the planned hearings in March with Lowman's help.[74]

Presented to the whole legislative committee for the first time, Lowman addressed the committee members on "the influences causing disturbances between segments of the population" in Louisiana and "traced these influences from their origin to the present date." According to the February 24, 1957, meeting minutes of the Louisiana Joint Legislative Committee, Lowman then outlined "the manner in which the existence of these influences would be established publicly at the proposed hearings" through "testimony of witnesses and the introduction of documentary evidence."[75] As for the "prospective witnesses" scheduled to appear before the committee's March hearings, Lowman's final selections were Joseph Kornfeder, whom General Counsel Shaw had previously interviewed, and the HUAC's favorite professional witnesses—namely, Manning Johnson, Leonard Patterson, and Martha Edmiston. Johnson, Patterson, and Edmiston had all been lined up by Chairman Harold Velde as "friendly" witnesses when the House committee subpoenaed and grilled the former MFSA executive secretary Jack McMichael—one of the Circuit Riders' foremost enemies—in July 1953.[76] Meanwhile, the bulk of Lowman's "documentary evidence" had been provided to him by his close associate, Matthews, who would assist Lowman from behind the scenes.[77]

To be sure, Matthews, like Lowman, was neither segregationist nor racist—nor was he anti-Semitic. Why, then, any discerning observer might ask, did Matthews give aid and comfort to segregationists engaged in the South's massive resistance, when he knew that they were desperately trying to link the domestic Communist menace to the civil rights movement on the strength of the documentation and testimonies provided by him? "I can't give you . . . a factual answer as to why my father supported southern segregationists," Matthews's son, Martin Matthews, replied when asked this question more than four decades after his father's death, "[but] I believe that his support was limited to anti-Communist activities and that he did not appreciate their segregationist/racist activities." In the opinion of Martin Matthews, his father always "felt that the anti-Communist aspects were of such importance that they out-weighed the segregationist/racist aspects." "I know," he added, "my father worked with people in his anti-Communist work who he did not otherwise appreciate."[78] In the final analysis, though, regardless of whether J. B. Matthews sincerely embraced anticommunism, it is irrefutable that he ended up supporting southern segregationists in their battles against racial integration and the civil rights movement.

On February 27, 1957, three days after the Louisiana Joint Legislative Committee met in Alexandria, Rainach mailed summonses to the four out-of-state witnesses whom Lowman had orchestrated for him—Kornfeder of Detroit; Manning Johnson of New York City; Leonard Patterson of Jamaica, New York; and Martha Edmiston of Waynesville, Ohio. Rainach attached a cover letter to each summons inviting the witnesses to testify before the Louisiana committee "in accordance with our previous verbal communication," indicating unquestionably that they would appear before the committee as "friendly" witnesses.[79] Furthermore, those letters and summonses instructed the witnesses to be in Baton Rouge by March 6, even though the public hearings were to commence on March 7, so that the witnesses could take part in the committee's closed executive session, during which a "rehearsal for the public testimony" was expected to take place under Lowman's guidance.[80]

With the advanced money tendered privately by Rainach and Shaw, Lowman and Kornfeder flew together from Cincinnati to New Orleans on March 3, 1957.[81] A few days before he left Cincinnati, Lowman had verified in writing to Matthews that any last-minute documentation and information that Matthews might funnel for the use of Lowman and his witnesses should be sent to him at the Heidelberg Hotel in Baton Rouge "via *Air Mail, Special Delivery.*"[82] "Hearings limited to subversive influences in the race controversy are scheduled at Baton Rouge, Louisiana, Thursday, March 7, 1957," Lowman announced to the Circuit Riders' officers and contributors on March 2, the day before he left Cincinnati for Baton Rouge. He added that "sensational and important exposures and identifications not heretofore published are expected to be included in the testimony" at the planned hearings.[83] Thanks to Lowman, the Louisiana hearings would soon set a seminal example to segregationists in other southern states, who were determined to persecute any deviators—individuals and organizations alike—from the region's racial and racist orthodoxy.

The Louisiana Joint Legislative Committee's long-awaited public hearings on "Subversion in Racial Unrest" finally came off on March 7, 1957, at the State Capitol Building in Baton Rouge. Besides Lowman, those who attended the hearings by invitation included Georgia attorney general Eugene Cook.[84] Also observing the hearings were some of the members of the Mississippi General Legislative Investigating Committee, who would hold their own similar pro-segregation and anti-Communist public hearings in a few years.[85] "We are gathered here today on a very serious occasion," State Senator Rainach—Louisiana's segregationist dynamo—solemnly declared at the outset of his opening statement as the chair of the legislative committee. Reminding his fellow committee members and the audience that Louisianans were in the midst of "what is perhaps the second most serious crisis that the State of Louisiana has undergone in its entire history"—the first of which was obviously "the War Between the States" and the following Reconstruction—Rainach explained that the purpose of the public hearings was to expose "the influences . . . that are paving the way for a serious destruction of the peace and tranquility that normally exist between the races" in Louisiana.[86] Having pronounced his intention, Rainach then turned the hearings over to the committee's general counsel, William Shaw, who was to call and question the first witness.

During the legislative committee's three-day public hearings, in addition to the four out-of-state witnesses arranged by Lowman, three more witnesses were called up to testify for the committee, all of whom were Rainach's close friends and associates in Louisiana. The order in which these witnesses appeared during the hearings was a calculated and "intentional progression" staged by Lowman and Rainach.[87] Instead of being presented as a hodgepodge of various testimonies, the hearings were planned to reflect a general order, where each of the witnesses was expected to play a particular role. Kicking off the hearings as a prelude to the appearance of the Lowman-arranged witnesses, W. Guy Banister, assistant superintendent of the New Orleans Police Department and a former special agent of the Federal Bureau of Investigation (FBI) for twenty years, took the witness stand. He was the same Banister who would later be depicted in Oliver Stone's 1991 blockbuster, *JFK,* in which New Orleans district attorney Jim Garrison implicated Banister in the conspiratorial assassination of President John F. Kennedy in November 1963.[88] Banister believed with an astonishing certitude that racial integration in public schools and the ongoing civil rights movement were part and parcel of a devious plan formulated by Joseph Stalin and his Communist Party to create racial dissension in the South. As instructed by Rainach and Lowman, however, Banister largely confined his testimony to outlining the Communist intention to "dominate the world" and the threat it posed to the United States. "Communism exploits every complaint of the people made against the government or government officials," Banister asserted at one point during his testimony.[89] In his thinking, black southerners' freedom movement could not possibly be an exception to this generalization.

Banister delivered his little lecture faultlessly, much to Rainach's satisfaction. Unknown to the committee chair, however, Banister's reputation as a law enforcement officer was in jeopardy. On March 4, 1957, only three days before he delivered his testimony, Banister had been suspended from the New Orleans Police Department after being accused of public drunkenness and pulling his gun in a bar in the city's French Quarter.[90] Despite his questionable character, Banister, whose "obsession with communism approached paranoia," as one keen observer of Louisiana's modern history has noted, passably served as the outrider for the hearings' procession.[91] On the strength of his appearance before the segregationist committee in Louisiana, Banister would be invited to testify by the similar anti-integration legislative committee that would be created in Arkansas for the purpose of linking the civil rights movement, and more specifically the September 1957 Little Rock desegregation crisis, with the domestic Communist menace.[92]

Following Banister's historical analysis of Communist ideology and appearing as the last witness on the first day of the hearings was Joseph Kornfeder of Detroit, a former leader of the CPUSA who had broken with the party in 1934. Claiming to have known Stalin personally when he was "trained" at the Lenin School in Moscow to master "political warfare" during the late 1920s, Kornfeder revealed that one of Stalin's "orders" had been to "penetrate this country and to use as their principal agents the colored people." Asked by General Counsel Shaw where the NAACP stood on "that particular strategy," Kornfeder replied that he was not aware of any "recent effort of the N.A.A.C.P. uniting with Communist Negro fronts, but there's been plenty of that in the past." "The Communists produce the agitation," he hastened to add, "and the N.A.A.C.P. produces the organization."[93]

Testifying before Louisiana's segregationist committee on the second day of its public hearings were two black former CPUSA members: Leonard Patterson of Jamaica, New York, and Manning Johnson of New York City. Patterson, a native of North Carolina and a leader of the Young Communist League, joined the CPUSA in 1930, and he was sent, like Kornfeder, to the Lenin School from 1931 to 1932. But after realizing in 1937 that "the Communist Party did not have at heart the interest of Negro people," he left the party.[94] Patterson was expected to testify at the hearings to the effect that "the Communist Party was only interested in promoting among the Negro people a national liberationary movement" that would aid the party in its efforts to "overthrow the American Government." At the end of his testimony, a committee member, State Representative L. D. "Buddy" Napper of Ruston, Lincoln Parish, asked Patterson if he believed that "the Negro race has been and is presently being exploited as an ally" of the CPUSA for "world domination." "Absolutely right," Patterson flatly answered and then added that the Communist Party intended to "win the Negro for selfish ends."[95]

The second witness of the day was Manning Johnson, who had been coached by Lowman and Rainach to squarely link the Communist menace with the civil rights movement in the South. A native of Washington, D.C., Johnson had joined the CPUSA in 1930, believing that the party "would aid in bettering race relations." Six years later, in 1936, he was elected to the party's national committee—or its central executive committee—the CPUSA's highest governing body. But in 1940, Johnson "became fed up with Communism and decided to abandon it" because he had come to realize that the CPUSA was simply using black people "as a cat's paw and as an expendable."[96] Soon thereafter, Johnson, beginning with the FBI, undertook to cooperate with the federal government at large in its efforts to investigate the Communists and joined in a regular pack of professional "expert" witnesses working particularly for the HUAC.

Regardless of the fact that Johnson had once been investigated for perjury by the Department of Justice, the Louisiana committee welcomed him as its hearings' "star witness" and enthusiastically embraced his words.[97]

Chairman Rainach praised Johnson as a "national authority on the influences bringing about a sudden upsurge of disturbances between the races" in the South, and Johnson's testimony did not disappoint him.[98] "I have been studying very carefully the developments in Montgomery, Alabama," Johnson said, "[and] I'm not saying that Rev. King is a Communist." After this disclaimer, though, he lambasted the leader of the Montgomery Bus Boycott: "Rev. King has none of the qualifications, nor the wisdom, nor the experience required to give leadership to the Negro in the south in this period." According to Johnson, King was not only "playing around with the lives and the hopes and the aspirations of his people," but also spreading "the idea that all white people in the south hate him and are out to destroy him," thus fomenting a "psychosis of hate" among black southerners. And this "psychosis of hate," he asserted, could easily be "molded and fashioned" by the Communists "into instruments of rebellion."[99]

While denouncing King as a "dastardly misleader" who was ushering black southerners down "the road to bloodshed and violence," Johnson also pinned the Communist label on such civil rights organizations as the NAACP, the SRC in Atlanta, and the New Orleans–based SCEF.[100] Readily agreeing with State Representative Napper that the NAACP had been and was "being exploited" as a formidable ally for the Communist Party in its efforts "toward world domination" and that the "Communist Trojan Horse is stabled today" within the civil rights organization, Johnson finally asserted what Rainach, Napper, and the other committee members wanted to hear—that the NAACP was "nothing more than a vehicle of the Communist Party" and that "the Communists are colonizing for the purpose of inciting racial rebellion" in the South.[101] In Johnson's analysis, "the heavy hand of Communism" was and had always been behind the forces stirring up racial strife among black and white southerners. And those malignant forces, according to Johnson, were represented by the NAACP—the "National Association for the Agitation of Colored People," as he once styled it.[102] Also music to the ears of Louisiana segregationists were Johnson's extemporaneous malicious remarks about Eleanor Roosevelt: "Someone should muzzle her and put her in a cage," he told the committee.[103]

Well pleased with Johnson's testimony, Rainach was in a jubilant mood. In concluding the second day of the public hearings, Rainach told the committee members and the audience that the Louisiana Joint Legislative Committee was "in a small way making history." It was doing so because, insofar as he could determine, "this is the first time in the United States that a hearing has been conducted for the sole purpose of inquiring into the *racial aspects* of the subversion problem in this country."[104] At the end of the day, thanks to Johnson, Rainach was now fully convinced that, as the *Shreveport Journal* had suggested earlier, "the CP in NAACP means Communist Party" and that the civil rights organization should be renamed the "National Association for the Advancement of the Communist Party."[105] Obviously, not everyone was impressed by Johnson's testimony. Baltimore's *Afro-American,* for instance, labeled Johnson as an "enemy of colored man" and a "defamer of colored people" and condemned him for allowing Louisiana's segregationists to use him as a "tool of white supremacy."[106]

On March 9, 1957—the third and final day of the hearings conducted by the Louisiana Joint Legislative Committee—Lowman's fellow Ohioan and the only white female witness, Martha Edmiston of Waynesville, was called to the stand. Rainach and Lowman hoped that, on the heels of Johnson, who had linked the domestic Communist threat to the civil rights movement, Edmiston, a newspaper reporter for the *Middletown Journal,* would demonstrate how and to what extent those whom she alleged to be the Communists had been involved in and were "manipulating" public school desegregation in the South. Just before the United States entered World War II, from 1940 to 1941, Martha and her husband, John J. "Ed" Edmiston—a native of Columbus, Ohio, and the *Dayton Journal Herald*'s financial writer—had been members of the CPUSA, while voluntarily working as the FBI's undercover agents.[107]

Almost a decade after they were both expelled from the CPUSA as "proven FBI spies" in December 1941, Martha and John Edmiston testified before the HUAC in Washington, D.C.[108] Talking about their experiences as secret FBI operatives before the House committee for two days on July 12 and 13, 1950, they ended up naming some one hundred persons during their appearance whom they alleged to have been "Red party members in Ohio."[109] Two and a half years later, in January 1953, Lowman cemented his association with the Edmistons when he induced them to provide an affidavit—which was recorded by a Cincinnati notary public—in which they testified that one of the foes of Lowman and his Circuit Riders, the MFSA executive secretary Jack McMichael, had a hand in the CPUSA's various front organizations.[110] To be sure, that affidavit was duly forwarded by Lowman to the HUAC, where the committee chair, Harold Velde, gathered Martha Edmiston, Manning Johnson, and Leonard Patterson together during the House committee's July 1953 hearings to have them implicate McMichael in Communist activities.[111]

The focal point of Martha Edmiston's testimony before the Louisiana Joint Legislative Committee revolved around Lee Lorch, a white Jewish mathematician and longtime civil rights activist who had worked for the humanitarian cause together with his wife, Grace. In fact, by the time the Louisiana committee hearings were convened in March 1957, Lee Lorch's name was not unknown to either the HUAC or the many southern red-baiters who desperately tried to equate integrationists with subversives. In 1946, Lorch, a promising young mathematician, began his academic career at the City College of New York. Just three years later, however, he was "dropped" from the faculty "without explanation" when the college administration found out that he and his wife had been actively involved in an effort to desegregate the housing complex in which they lived in New York City's Lower East Side.[112] Although Lorch soon found another teaching position at Pennsylvania State University, his continuing activities related to housing desegregation once again cost him his job, and his appointment at Penn State lasted for only one academic year.[113]

In April 1950, three months after Lorch was dismissed from Penn State, the HUAC held its hearings on "Communist Activities in the Cincinnati, Ohio, Area." The Edmistons dealt Lorch an additional blow when, during their testimony before the House committee, they identified Lorch as a member of the CPUSA when he was a graduate student at the University of Cincinnati (and indeed, he had once been affiliated with the Communist Party).[114] Lorch and his family then moved to the South, where Lorch became the chair of the mathematics department at a historically black institution—Fisk University in Nashville, Tennessee. In 1954, when the Supreme Court handed down its *Brown* decision, Lee and Grace Lorch submitted an application to the Nashville School Board to enroll their ten-year-old daughter, Alice, in the school nearest to their home—all-black Pearl Elementary School—to "set an example of peaceful compliance" with *Brown* "by showing that white families were also interested in ending segregation."[115] Accordingly, on June 10, the city's school board held a hearing on the matter, ultimately rejecting the Lorches' application. Lee Lorch, who then served as the vice president of the Tennessee branch of the NAACP, took the floor following the board's decision and defiantly told the board members: "I believe the action you have just taken is illegal and without effect."[116]

The *Nashville Tennessean* widely reported on this incident, and before long, Lee Lorch was subpoenaed by the HUAC. On September 15, 1954, four months after the *Brown* ruling, Lorch was steamrollered into appearing before the Velde-chaired House committee in Dayton, which was purportedly holding its hearings to investigate "Communist infiltration" in the Ohio city. Lorch, however, had never before set foot in Dayton, which makes one wonder why he was hauled up before the committee on this particular occasion.[117] The answer can be found in a behind-the-scenes maneuver by Lowman. "At my suggestion," Lowman revealed to Clarence Lohman, president of the Circuit Riders, the day after Lorch's testimony, "the [HUAC] . . . included about two hours of examination of Dr. Lee Lorch."[118]

During the hostile questioning by the committee counsel and members, Lorch, while responding that he was no longer affiliated with the CPUSA, steadfastly refused to discuss his political views. Instead, he voiced his contempt for the House committee, telling its members that they were engaged in a "smear and diversion, a fishing expedition devoid of legislative purpose."[119] Lorch's defiance earned him the inevitable fate of those who dared to defy the HUAC. Two months later, on November 18, 1954, Lorch was cited for contempt of Congress after a unanimous vote of the committee.[120] It was sheer irony that those who sat on the HUAC should brand Lorch "un-American" for his support of the nation's Supreme Court. The contempt charge against Lorch was dropped in a few years, but Lorch himself was also dropped from the Fisk faculty by the university's predominantly white board of trustees.[121] Moving out of Nashville in September 1955, Lorch accepted the chairmanship of the mathematics department at Philander Smith College, a historically black institution in Little Rock, Arkansas, not knowing that his new hometown would soon become a major battle ground in the civil rights movement over the desegregation of the city's Central High School.[122] The 1957 Little Rock desegregation crisis would, once again, make the Lorch family—particularly Grace Lorch—a target of southern segregationists.

On February 26, 1957, shortly before the Louisiana Joint Legislative Committee convened its hearings, at the behest of Lowman, Matthews prepared a "compilation of Communist related activities connected with the name Lee Lorch" for the use of Lowman and Martha Edmiston, both of whom were then already scheduled to participate in the pro-segregation inquiries in Baton Rouge.[123] With that document in hand, Edmiston testified before the Louisiana committee, repeating her previous assertion made before the HUAC that Lorch was a "Communist and a Communist courier." Asked by General Counsel Shaw if Lorch was the same "white professor at Fisk University" who had dared to "demand entrance for his white children into a Negro school," Edmiston replied that the Lorches' unsuccessful attempt to enroll their daughter in the segregated all-black school was "another form of agitation" favored by the Communists.[124] Looking back, in a 2007 interview, on his 1954 appearance before the HUAC, Lee Lorch reminisced that a few years before he was subpoenaed by the congressional committee, "someone told them that I had been a member of the Communist Party," implying that that "someone" was Martha and John Edminston.[125] The Edmistons continued to dog Lorch at the 1957 Louisiana committee hearings.

Following Martha Edmiston, who had just demonstrated the Communists' involvement in school desegregation in the South, Sergeant Hubert J. Badeaux, agent in charge of the New Orleans Police Department's Division of Intelligence Affairs and one of Banister's subordinates, finally brought "this problem" of the Communist threat in relation to school integration "even closer to the State of Louisiana." The Communist Party existed not only in Louisiana as a state, but also "in this very city where we are having this hearing," Badeaux reminded the committee members at the outset of his testimony. Asked by General Counsel Shaw "what the target of Communist penetrations might be" in Louisiana, Badeaux jumped at the opportunity to implicate the NAACP for involvement in the Communist menace to the state. The civil rights organization, he asserted, had "thousands of documents which support the idea of Communist penetration" that would "convince even the most skeptical person of the extent of influence of the Communist Party" within the NAACP.[126]

Badeaux, who had testified before the HUAC in New Orleans just three weeks earlier, also cited the state NAACP's refusal to submit its membership list to the Louisiana authority during the previous year (in accordance with the 1924 anti-KKK act) as a clear indication that the civil rights group was not "dedicated to rooting out subversion" in the state, adding: "Now, of course, as an Intelligence Officer I don't care what the N.A.A.C.P. or the Ku Klux Klan . . . does politically, socially, or otherwise, except where it affects internal security of the government, the state, and the community." While Badeaux may well have been unconcerned about what the white-supremacist group was up to, he certainly had a vested interest in persecuting the civil rights organization's political and social activities in the state. At the end of Badeaux's protracted testimony, General Counsel Shaw asked the witness if he, as an intelligence officer, had any recommendations to the Louisiana Joint Legislative Committee "as to what might be done to help minimize this threat" to the state. Badeaux replied that the segregationist committee should "exert some effort or give some thought to the organization of a Central Intelligence Agency on a state level." Badeaux's testimony clearly impressed the committee members as Shaw requested that Badeaux attend the committee's executive session to be held at the close of the public hearings.[127]

Making a brief appearance before the Louisiana Joint Legislative Committee as the very last witness during its three-day hearings was Leander Perez, one of the ringmasters of the farce orchestrated by Lowman and Louisiana segregationists. Reminding the committee that those who dared to "take an active and effective part against Communists" tended to be ridiculed and "smeared," the all-powerful state district attorney praised the other witnesses for their courage in offering "valuable testimony against the Communist conspiracy against the South." Their collective testimony, Perez proclaimed, clearly revealed the extent of the "Communist Policy for the Negroes of the South."[128]

At the end of his committee's hearings on March 9, 1957, Chairman Rainach offered his "preliminary conclusions"—conclusions at which he had arrived long before the state inquisitions commenced. As an official voice of Louisiana representing 2.5 million people, including 880,000 blacks, Rainach, unsurprisingly, concluded that the recent "racial uprisings" against the white-supremacist "existing order" should be attributed to "the Communist Conspiracy," and that those Communist activities, "through . . . such organizations . . . as the NAACP," were "the prime cause of [the] racial unrest" undermining the nation, the South, and "particularly, in our own case, the State of Louisiana." Promising that his legislative committee would "make its finding and experiences in this field available to the other states in the South," Rainach banged the gavel and ordered the committee into an executive session.[129]

Lowman, Banister, Badeaux, and Perez were present in the closed session of the Louisiana Joint Legislative Committee that immediately followed the public hearings. Rainach told his committee members that without Lowman's assistance, "it would have been impossible to achieve the far-reaching results obtained in the hearings just concluded." By a motion of State Representative John Garrett—Rainach's right-hand man—the committee unanimously resolved to authorize Rainach to compose an "appropriate resolution to be forwarded to Mr. Lowman, which would express the official appreciation of the Committee and the State of Louisiana, for his splendid services."[130] It was also decided during the executive session to prepare four other resolutions as testimonials to be mailed to the four out-of-state witnesses whose appearances Lowman had arranged—Joseph Kornfeder, Leonard Patterson, Manning Johnson, and Martha Edmiston. Each of the resolutions was to express Louisiana's "official appreciation" to the witnesses for their help "in establishing that Communism is a prime cause of racial unrest" and "in pioneering the exposure of Communist strategy and development among the negroes . . . as the principal instrument by which the International Communist Conspiracy plans to destroy" the government of Louisiana and its cherished "social order."[131]

Proud to have received Louisiana's "official appreciation," one of the recipients of the committee's testimonials, Leonard Patterson, wrote back to Rainach: "Sir Iwant to theik youCommittee Members for the Resolution you passed on my behalf, I am verry happy that I could help you all some in the fight against communist stirring up racial strife. I think your beloved State taken a great step foward in combatting Communism and it,s methods of promoting Racial Strife[.]"[132] If Rainach had had an opportunity to examine any of Patterson's writing prior to the opening of the Louisiana committee hearings, he might have balked at Lowman's suggestion that Patterson serve as one of the "expert" witnesses. In the meantime, Louisiana's segregationist hearings on "Subversion in Racial Unrest" bolstered Manning Johnson's reputation as a trusted black warrior for the white South's racial orthodoxy among the region's defenders of segregation. Until Johnson's death in July 1959, as other southern states such as Georgia and Arkansas decided to hold their own pro-segregation and anti-Communist public hearings, Johnson would remain one of the most popular "friendly" witnesses appearing and testifying before the HUAC's more racist versions in the South.[133]

Satisfied with his segregationist committee's public hearings, Rainach, acting on Badeaux's suggestion to create a "Central Intelligence Agency on a state level," asked the state legislature to consider the formation of a tax-supported "statewide Red-hunting group."[134] His wish was granted in the early summer of 1960 with the organization of the Louisiana Joint Legislative Committee on Un-American Activities. Meanwhile, State Representative John Garrett, Rainach's sworn ally in his fight against racial integration, later boasted that the Louisiana committee hearings had proven an irrefutable truth. "Communism and integration," he proclaimed in a ringing voice, "are inseparable," adding: "Integration is the southern expression of the communist movement."[135] For Rainach, Garrett, and many other Louisiana segregationists, the civil rights movement and racial integration in the South were, to quote a June 1951 speech by Joseph McCarthy, nothing but "the product of a great conspiracy" devised by the Communists to capture the allegiance of black southerners—the "conspiracy on a scale so immense" and the "conspiracy of infamy" so red and black.[136]

No sooner had the Louisiana Joint Legislative Committee hearings ended with self-congratulatory fanfare than the extensively disseminated publicity for the tax-supported inquisitions brought inquiries from legislative committees and executive agencies of other southern states, all of which were exploring the possibilities of holding hearings similar to Louisiana's. In a March 16, 1957, letter to Roy V. Harris of Augusta, a member of the Georgia Commission on Education and a political kingpin in the state, Rainach informed him that a transcript of his committee hearings would be on its way to Georgia attorney general Eugene Cook, who had attended the hearings in Baton Rouge as an invited observer. "I hope," the Louisiana state senator urged, "that Georgia likewise can get an investigation underway."[137] On the same day, Rainach also wrote to Truman Veran "T. V." Williams Jr., executive secretary of Georgia's segregationist commission that he "trust[ed] that the State of Georgia will similarly inquire into the causes of racial unrest within the near future."[138]

Meanwhile, noting that the Florida Legislative Investigation Committee had earlier indicated that "they plan action similar to ours," Rainach offered his help to the segregationist body in Florida by "placing your Committee in touch with a source who can furnish witnesses and documentary evidence."[139] The "source" to which Rainach referred is evidently meant to be Myers Lowman of the Circuit Riders. Furthermore, Rainach advised Stanton A. Hall, a Mississippi state senator and the chair of the Mississippi General Legislative Investigating Committee, whose representatives had also attended the Louisiana committee hearings, to "take similar action."[140] A little later, Rainach had Leander Perez mail copies of the still-unedited hearing transcript to some Mississippi officials, including Attorney General Joe T. Patterson and Assistant Attorney General Dugas Shands, as well as Senator Eastland at his Washington, D.C., office.[141]

As Rainach referred Lowman to the segregationist authorities of other southern states, his own dependence on the Circuit Riders' executive secretary further deepened. True to his promise that his legislative committee would officially "make its finding and experiences in this field available to the other states in the South," Rainach began to entertain the idea of publishing an official report based on the stenographic transcript of those testimonies given at the March 1957 public hearings.[142] Rainach asked Lowman to serve as the editor of the official report in late March.[143] "There are many minor corrections which should be made before this record is distributed to those who have asked for copies," Lowman informed Rainach on April 1, after glancing over the unedited transcript. Lowman then suggested that each of those who testified before the Louisiana Joint Legislative Committee be given an opportunity to take a look at his or her relevant portion of the transcript prior to Lowman's editing.[144] In accordance with Lowman's suggestion, Rainach asked in writing for the four out-of-state witnesses—Kornfeder, Patterson, Johnson, and Edmiston—to review the accuracy of their respective hearing transcripts. Conspicuously, in his correspondence with the two black witnesses, Patterson and Johnson, Rainach never used the courtesy title "Mr."[145]

Lowman revisited Louisiana in June 1957 to confer with Rainach by invitation.[146] "One of the nice parts of my work is meeting wholesome people like Mrs. Rainach and your friends," Lowman wrote the Louisiana state senator on July 2 after returning to Cincinnati.[147] Announcing the hearing transcript's upcoming release in book form, Rainach informed the publication's intended recipients and prospective purchasers on August 1 that the Louisiana Joint Legislative Committee hearings had abundantly revealed "the degree to which the Communist Party, USA, under directives from Moscow, has succeeded in creating racial tension" not only in Louisiana, but in the entire South.[148] In a two-day trip to Louisiana in mid-August, Lowman paid another visit to Rainach to discuss his editing project.[149] "Our mutual friend, Mr. Lowman, was here yesterday," Rainach informed Manning Johnson on August 19, letting the black witness know that he and Lowman had "finally agreed to publish the hearings in two parts, because of the great volume of testimony and evidence presented."[150]

Three months later, in mid-November 1957, the Louisiana Joint Legislative Committee issued the first part of its hearings' transcript and findings.[151] Entitled *Subversion in Racial Unrest*, the official report bore the rather sensational subtitle *An Outline of a Strategic Weapon to Destroy the Governments of Louisiana and the United States*.[152] The report, containing many of the Matthews-compiled lists and tabulations that had been duly entered as exhibits during the public hearings, was printed by the newspaper company in Rainach's hometown, the *Homer Guardian-Journal*.[153] Initially, the segregationist committee printed 2,500 copies of the official report. However, the high demand for the first part of the report later "made it necessary to purchase four hundred additional copies," as Rainach informed Louisiana's supervisor of public funds.[154] In March 1958, a year after the public hearings took place, the second and last part of *Subversion in Racial Unrest* was released. Mailing two hundred complimentary copies of the volume to Lowman, Rainach praised Lowman for his "outstanding contribution" to making the report's publication possible and pompously asserted that "history will establish their significance as a pivot upon which the course of this country will have turned."[155] Orders from the general public cost $1.50 for a two-volume set, and even the Central Intelligence Agency (CIA) showed interest in obtaining and reviewing the Louisiana committee report.[156]

By the time Louisiana's segregationist committee completed its official report, Rainach's conviction that communism and racial integration were inseparable had become—in the words of State Representative John Garrett—"downright evident."[157] "The Communist conspiracy originating with Joseph Stalin is . . . [the] guiding influence behind the move to integrate the public schools of the South," Rainach thus wrote to Mark R. Hawes, chief counsel of the equally segregationist Florida Legislative Investigation Committee, on March 14, 1958.[158] For Rainach, it was apparent that the most sinister dupe of what he termed the "Communist conspiracy" was the NAACP. On March 10, just a few days earlier, the Louisiana Joint Legislative Committee, prompted by its chair, had unanimously adopted a resolution noting the NAACP's "high degree of penetration by the Communist apparatus." "Official records show conclusively," the resolution entitled "The NAACP as a Communist Penetrated Organization" read, "that the Communist apparatus has registered a degree of success in penetrating the NAACP not paralleled in the case of any other organization of significant size in the United States."[159] Rainach dutifully mailed certified copies of the resolution to Representative Francis Walter, chair of the HUAC, and Senator James Eastland, chair of the SISS, for their "official review."[160]

In fact, the phrasing of the anti-NAACP resolution adopted by the Louisiana Joint Legislative Committee came mostly from Lowman, who had previously forwarded his "suggested wording" to Rainach on March 6, 1958.[161] Rainach slightly reworked Lowman's text before the resolution's final adoption by his committee members on March 10. Along with a certified copy of the resolution that he mailed to Lowman on April 3, Rainach included a letter revealing his opinion of a recent assessment of the NAACP by the FBI director J. Edgar Hoover. Referring to Hoover's recently published book, *Masters of Deceit*, Rainach complained that the FBI director "completely absolves the NAACP of serious Communist penetration and actually implies that its leadership, to the contrary, is militantly anti-

Communist." "I think it would be appropriate for this Committee to send Hoover a copy of this resolution also, along with copies of . . . *Subversion in Racial Unrest*," the Louisiana state senator concluded, "[for] he seems to have never heard of the latter."[162]

Not only the NAACP, but any organization that dared to insist on the legitimacy of the Fourteenth Amendment to the U.S. Constitution for the protection of black southerners—along with those who supported it—fell prey to Rainach and his segregationist committee. In the spring of 1958 as the opening of the state legislative session approached—following the publication of the second and last part of *Subversion in Racial Unrest* and the adoption of the anti-NAACP resolution by the Louisiana Joint Legislative Committee—the Louisiana branch of the American Civil Liberties Union (ACLU), backed by the New Orleans–based SCEF, launched a statewide petition drive on university and college campuses. In essence, the ACLU petition asked the legislature to defeat the school closing bill sponsored by Rainach committee, which was expected to be debated during the upcoming session. The school closure bill would authorize the governor to shut down the state's public schools in the face of federally mandated integration court orders. Among the total of some six hundred petitioners who supported the ACLU's petition drive, sixty-six employees at Louisiana State University (LSU) in Baton Rouge—fifty-seven faculty members, eight library staffers, and the director of LSU Press, Donald R. Ellegood—were included.[163] LSU English professor Waldo F. McNeir, who branded the anti-integration bill as "un-American" and "un-democratic," spearheaded the efforts to gather signatures for the petition.[164] A respected official of the inceptive Louisiana branch of the ACLU established only two years earlier, McNeir would soon assume its chairmanship.[165]

On June 9, shortly after the 1958 state legislative session commenced, four representatives of the ACLU petition drive, including McNeir and the SCEF executive director James Dombrowski, appeared before the House Committee on Education hearings, where the merits of the school closure bill were discussed. While testifying against the measure, McNeir and Dombrowski submitted the ACLU petition to the committee. The anti–school closing petition was then duly filed with State Senator Rainach.[166] With the petition now before him and "alarmed over the possibility" that LSU was "being used as a base of operation by individuals and organizations whose purposes and aims were hostile to the official policies" of Louisiana, Rainach decided to strike back.[167] At the behest of the state senator, the segregation-minded legislature, instead of defeating the school closure bill, hastily created the Louisiana Special Joint Legislative Committee to Investigate Louisiana State University.[168] The eleven-member special legislative committee was composed of five senators and six representatives. Among them, five members represented the Louisiana Joint Legislative Committee known as the Rainach Committee. Not only that, while Rainach became the special committee's chair, State Representative John Garrett served as its vice chair with William Shaw being appointed as the committee counsel.[169] Thus, the newly organized special legislative committee to investigate LSU was, in reality, the Rainach-chaired Louisiana Joint Legislative Committee.

In rapid succession, only two days after McNeir and Dombrowski presented their ACLU petition to the House Committee on Education, Rainach held the special legislative committee's public hearings in Baton Rouge on June 11, 1958, to "investigate whether LSU professors may be teaching contrary to the laws" of Louisiana and "to the way of life of our people." In their short opening statements, while Rainach made it clear that his special committee was "not going to burn down the barn to chase away the mice," Counsel Shaw reminded the committee members that there was a "small clique of professors" at LSU who had been "giving the state so much trouble."[170] Asked to appear before the special committee as the principal witness of the day was the LSU president, Troy H. Middleton, who had been a distinguished U.S. Army general in Europe during World War II. Born and educated in Mississippi, Middleton, who was appointed as the president in 1951, had repeatedly made it clear that LSU "preferred to maintain segregation" for as long as it could. At the same time, however, Middleton had also let it be known in 1956 that his university, as Louisiana's flagship institution of higher learning, "believes in law and order and . . . respects the decisions of the court . . . no matter how strongly it may disagree."[171] In fact, in January 1951, just before Middleton took the helm of LSU, the university's law school had admitted a black student under a court order. A little over two and a half years later, in the fall of 1953, as a result of litigation involving the staunch segregationist Leander Perez, LSU's undergraduate program was racially desegregated by Alexander Pierre Tureaud Jr., whose father was New Orleans's lead attorney for the NAACP.[172] Testifying before the special legislative committee created for the sole purpose of investigating his university, President Middleton, with a prepared statement in hand, insisted that LSU had "advocated segregation" and "refused admission to Negroes . . . and admitted them only at court orders." "To my knowledge," he went on, "no member of the

LSU faculty is teaching integration." And on the issue of "Communistic leanings" allegedly espoused by some faculty members, the president vehemently denied that "any teacher is a Communist or has taught their philosophy." "We would not permit the teaching of communism or integration," Middleton concluded.[173]

In spite of the LSU president's best efforts to assure the special investigating committee that no subversive activities and teaching were taking place on his university campus, Rainach, not quite fully convinced, indicated at the end of the June 11, 1958, hearings that his committee would summon the LSU petition signers as witnesses and hold "further hearings." Wishing to conduct a thorough background check on them before they were subpoenaed, Rainach—who had told Lowman in the previous summer that he hoped their mutual association would be further strengthened "during the months and years ahead"—turned to Lowman for his assistance.[174] "Your L.S.U. situation shows symptom of needing some records," Lowman warned Rainach in writing on June 12, the day after LSU president Middleton appeared before the public hearings conducted by the Louisiana Special Joint Legislative Committee to Investigate Louisiana State University.[175] The following day, after conferring with Lowman on the phone, the state senator mailed him a copy of the ACLU petition bearing the names of those six hundred signers, a list of the LSU faculty who had signed the petition, and LSU's most recent school catalogue. Rainach then asked Lowman to examine these mailed items and to inform him of "any subversive activity record" on the petitioners, instructing him to "give priority to LSU parties."[176] In accordance with the agreement made with Rainach, Lowman began, with Matthews's help, to investigate the possible "subversive" backgrounds of the LSU petitioners. Rainach's efforts availed him little, however. Finally, with no incriminating evidence on the LSU petition signers forthcoming from Lowman and despite Rainach's zealous efforts to shield his beloved state's "internal security" from enemies within, the special investigating committee "did not 'grill' the Professors or carry out their threats to 'clean out the pinkos at LSU,'" in the words of one of the LSU petitioners.[177]

Around the same time that the ACLU's Louisiana branch launched its petition drive, Rainach unsuccessfully sought to hold a set of legislative hearings on "subversion in higher education," modeled after his own March 1957 "Subversion in Racial Unrest" public hearings. The state senator believed that higher education, besides religion and the labor movement, was one of the "major sources from which the Communist assaults are launched" on racial segregation. In February 1958, Rainach informed Leander Perez that Lowman was ready to provide witnesses and documentary evidence for such hearings at a cost of five thousand dollars, hoping that the pro-segregation Federation for Constitutional Government in New Orleans would once again finance the expenses of Lowman and his professional witnesses.[178] In the end, such extravagant funds proved unavailable, but Rainach continued to mail the catalogues of Louisiana's colleges and universities to Lowman for examination.[179]

Rainach kept in contact with Lowman during 1959. While the NAACP remained the primary investigative target of the Rainach-chaired Louisiana Joint Legislative Committee, at Lowman's urging, the committee also began to keep tabs on other civil rights groups in the state, most notably the New Orleans–headquartered SCEF. On January 2, 1959, Lowman suggested to Rainach that they hold a conference in New Orleans "in connection with security risk situations in Louisiana" endangered by the SCEF. "I should think your Committee should start preparing for a second series of hearings," Lowman urged Rainach, adding that "my services would be available in return for two round-trip tickets."[180] Having discussed the probability of their SCEF probe with General Counsel Shaw and other members of his legislative committee, Rainach concurred with Lowman that the SCEF investigation should be made "by all means." "I will get back in touch with you about the middle of February," the state senator wrote in a January 21 letter to Lowman, "and we will go into the investigation in detail with you at that time."[181]

The New Orleans conference that Lowman suggested was eventually held on February 22, 1959. At the meeting attended by Rainach and his legislative committee members, Lowman agreed to run a background check on those who had appeared before the 1958 state legislature to oppose the Rainach committee's segregationist programs "under the direction of James A. Dombrowski," executive director of the SCEF. During this conference, Rainach also furnished Lowman with lists of officers of the Louisiana branch of the ACLU and the Louisiana Council on Human Relations, whose parent organization was the Atlanta-based SRC, for the purpose of ascertaining if any of these leaders could be identified as subversives.[182] Also at the New Orleans meeting, Rainach and Lowman explored the possibility of launching another round of public hearings "relative to extensive [Communist] influences in race . . . in the New Orleans area," primarily targeting the SCEF. The planned hearings were scheduled for April 1959, but because Rainach was then contemplating a run for governor, the time-consuming preparations for the hearings were put aside.[183]

On July 2, 1959, State Senator Rainach officially announced his candidacy for Louisiana governor. The announcement was made before an appreciative crowd assembled in the Claiborne Parish seat of Homer on the occasion of "Willie Rainach Day."[184] William Shaw of Homer, general counsel of the Louisiana Joint Legislative Committee, became the Rainach camp's campaign director.[185] During the first Democratic primary election in 1959, Rainach, the most militantly segregationist candidate among the five major contenders, emphasized his spotless record as a foe of racial integration, castigating the NAACP and criticizing the other candidates for being soft on segregation. "I got into this race to preserve peace between the races," Rainach liked to tell the crowds while on the stump. In his terminology, "peace between the races" required black Louisianans' acceptance of the state's racial and racist practices. Racial tranquility, Rainach asserted, was being endangered because white Louisianans and southerners as a whole foolishly "went to sleep and let the NAACP and the Communist Party bring pressure on the Supreme Court."[186]

In the first Democratic primary, Louisiana voters offered 278,956 votes to the Catholic New Orleans mayor deLesseps S. "Chap" Morrison, a moderate segregationist and a leader of the anti-Long faction within the state Democratic Party. The Long political machine had dominated Louisiana politics since the late 1920s, revolving around Louisiana governor and U.S. senator Huey P. Long Jr., and his younger brother, Earl K. Long, who was then serving as governor. In the first primary, the Long faction was represented by two candidates—former governor James A. Noe and former lieutenant governor William J. "Bill" Dodd—who finished fourth and fifth.[187] New Orleans mayor Morrison was followed by James H. "Jimmie" Davis of Shreveport, who garnered 213,551 votes. Davis, a country musician and a former Louisiana governor (1944–48), was often referred to as the "singing governor" and had been associated with several popular songs including "You Are My Sunshine." Rainach finished third with 17 percent of the total votes, obtaining 143,096 votes.[188]

Following the first primary, Davis, who had finished second, struck a deal with Rainach in preparation for the upcoming second and run-off primary to be held in January 1960. In return for Rainach's support in the second primary, Davis promised Rainach, who had decided not to seek reelection to the state Senate, the continued funding of his pet group—the Louisiana Joint Legislative Committee—with State Representative John

Garrett as its succeeding chair. Davis also promised the creation of the new Louisiana State Sovereignty Commission to be chaired by Rainach.[189] In the January 9, 1960, second Democratic primary, Davis beat Morrison with 54.1 percent of the total votes.[190] His final victory for the governorship was largely accounted for by Rainach's segregationist constituencies, including the Citizens' Council members.

Over the previous year, Rainach's health had gradually deteriorated, and at the close of his gubernatorial campaign, it finally failed. "I will be out of the picture temporarily while I am getting my business and other affairs in order," Rainach wrote to Roy Harris, one of his segregationist allies in Georgia, after the first Democratic primary, "but I by no means expect to drop my share of the South's load in this struggle" against the civil rights movement.[191] Expecting to chair the state's new segregationist agency, Rainach, in early February 1960, asked the then four-year-old Mississippi State Sovereignty Commission to help him organize a "Sovereignty Commission for the State of Louisiana."[192] He also sent a letter to David J. Mays, chair of the pro-segregation Virginia Commission on Constitutional Government in Richmond, asking Mays to provide him with a "copy of the law creating your Commission for our study in drafting an act" to establish the Louisiana State Sovereignty Commission.[193] "I am about recovered completely now, and am getting back into the fight," Rainach wrote to Lowman in the early spring of 1960.[194]

As promised, the Louisiana State Sovereignty Commission was created on June 17, 1960, under the new administration of Governor Davis.[195] The newly organized thirteen-member state agency—organized according to the template of the Mississippi State Sovereignty Commission—was charged with the responsibility of "exercising every legal means to preserve and protect for the State and its people those rights which are legally and traditionally theirs." As he had done for the Rainach Committee, Leander Perez drafted the bill that created the Louisiana State Sovereignty Commission.[196] All seemed to be in order, but there was one major problem. Instead of making the new state agency autonomous under the direction of Rainach, Governor Davis, over Rainach's adamant protest, placed the Louisiana State Sovereignty Commission under his administrative control, retracting his earlier promise to Rainach. Feeling betrayed and deeply disgruntled, Rainach declared that he would have nothing to do with the new commission if he were to be only a "figurehead." In the end, he refused to serve on the commission as a marionette of the new administration. After this incident, Rainach, who had led Louisiana's official fight against school desegregation and the civil rights movement for some six years, gradually sank into political oblivion.[197]

On June 14, 1960, during the same month that the Louisiana State Sovereignty Commission was born, the state legislature transformed the Rainach Committee—now without its namesake—into the new Louisiana Joint Legislative Committee on Un-American Activities.[198] Rainach had served as the chair of the Louisiana Joint Legislative Committee until May 9, when he departed from the state Senate. State Representative John Garrett succeeded Rainach as its chair, as previously promised by Governor Davis, and would serve in that capacity until the committee was officially disbanded in the fall of 1960.[199] Thus, on the heels of the November 1960 public school desegregation crisis in New Orleans—the very first Deep South city to desegregate its public schools in response to a federal court order—Louisiana equipped itself with two separate, but tightly interwoven, segregationist state organs: the State Sovereignty Commission as an executive agency to "fight for States' Rights against Federal encroachment" and to halt "creeping federalism" in the area of school integration; and the Joint Legislative Committee on Un-American Activities as a legislative body to "investigate, analyze and report on un-American or subversive activities" that were allegedly facilitating the civil rights movement.[200] Though superficially different in their expected functions, the commission and the committee were "more or less one in the same," serving, in essence, as Louisiana's chariot of segregation.[201]

Chaired by State Representative James H. Pfister of Orleans Parish—whose opposition to communism and racial integration was "unimpeachable"—the Louisiana Joint Legislative Committee on Un-American Activities kept its watchful eyes, as the Rainach Committee had done, on the SCEF, the SRC, the ACLU, and other civil rights–related organizations, designating them as the "subversive and communist front" groups working for the destruction of Louisiana's white supremacy-based society.[202] While LSU English professor Waldo McNeir, who had incurred Senator Rainach's wrath, became one of the initial investigative targets of the Joint Legislative Committee on Un-American Activities, the committee's persistent persecution was aimed at the SCEF and its executive director, James Dombrowski, whom the legislative committee once sarcastically called "our old friend."[203] In the course of its probe into the SCEF activities in New Orleans (code-named "Project No. 50"), Louisiana's un-American activities committee sought the assistance of Matthews—who had funneled a host of documentary evidence into the March 1957 Rainach Committee hearings through Lowman—and his wife, secretary, and research associate, Ruth Matthews. "As a result of consultation . . . with Mr. and Mrs. 'M,'" the committee's staff director wrote to Pfister on July 16, 1962, concealing the Matthewses' identity for security reasons best known to them, "we have come up with a list of approximately seventy names" who "were active in the Communist Party" and might have something to do with the SCEF activities.[204]

After conducting its intense investigation of the SCEF for some eleven months, the Pfister-chaired Joint Legislative Committee on Un-American Activities requested the Louisiana state troopers and the New Orleans Police Department to neutralize the civil rights organization. Accordingly, on the evening of October 4, 1963, the law enforcement authorities raided the SCEF office, confiscating a truckload of the group's records and office equipment. Dombrowski was arrested and charged with criminal conspiracy because, according to the legislative committee's allegation, he had been "willingly and knowingly participating in the management of a subversive organization" and "distributing and storing Communist political propaganda in Louisiana." The raid was "part of the general attack on the integration movement," Dombrowski charged, "[and] this is, of course, subversive to Louisiana legislators."[205]

In the end, State Senator Rainach's strident claim that his Louisiana Joint Legislative Committee had spearheaded the historic undertaking to attribute the civil rights movement to the "Communist conspiracy" in the South turned out to be accurate. The March 1957 public hearings conducted with much fanfare by the segregationist Louisiana committee became the shining example for those desperate to arrest the invading tides of racial justice. The initiative taken by Louisiana would prove an ominous harbinger of a series of inquisitions in other southern states that would attempt to link black southerners' quest for simple human dignity with the Communist movement—and thus to make integrationists and Communists appear to be "two names for the same creature."[206] And as Louisiana segregationists' rallying cry—"Communism and integration are inseparable"—galvanized the defiant spirit of racial conservatives and reactionaries in their southern sister states, the involvement of the Circuit Riders' Myers Lowman and his associate, J. B. Matthews, as northern messiahs in the white South's segregationist enterprises would intensify.

CHAPTER 3

WITH UNWISDOM, INJUSTICE, AND IMMODERATION

A Southern-Flavored McCarthyism in Georgia

Among the five Deep South states—Alabama, Georgia, Louisiana, Mississippi, and South Carolina—Georgia, the Peach State, was the one regarded as somewhat moderate with respect to public school desegregation and the civil rights movement in general. To explain Georgia's reputation as a "weak sister of the Deep South" in terms of the region's massive resistance, scholars and journalists have often cited "economic considerations rooted in the city of Atlanta."[1] It is true that Atlanta mayor William B. Hartsfield proudly heralded his beloved Georgia capital as a "city too busy to hate," and it is also true that, under the leadership of Hartsfield on August 30, 1961, the state achieved its first public school desegregation below the college and university level when nine black students entered four historically all-white high schools in Atlanta without any violence.[2] Both impressed and relieved, President John F. Kennedy, during his press conference held on the same day, congratulated Mayor Hartsfield and other state and city officials for their "responsible, law-abiding" response to racial desegregation. "Their efforts have borne fruit in the orderly manner in which desegregation was carried out—with dignity and without incident," the president said.[3] The "Wisdom, Justice, and Moderation" invoked on the Georgia state seal seemed to have prevailed.[4]

Nevertheless, though Georgia did not display the same degree of defiance as that seen in Louisiana, Mississippi and, particularly later in the 1960s, Alabama, the state's white officials and citizenry, for the most part, were no more inclined than those in the other Deep South states to let the institution of segregation crumble without a fight. And in Georgia, the birthplace of the twentieth century's resurrected Ku Klux Klan (KKK), the foundations for preserving the educational status quo and waging massive resistance in the future had been cemented even before the Supreme Court announced its *Brown* ruling in May 1954. Eugene "Gene" Talmadge, Georgia's segregationist four-time governor (elected in 1932, 1934, 1940, and 1946) who was often referred to as the "Wild Man from Sugar Creek," used to say, "The poor dirt farmer ain't got but three friends on this earth—God Almighty, Sears Roebuck, and Gene Talmadge."[5] One might also fairly say that, to paraphrase Talmadge's words, even with the influence exerted by the "city too busy to hate," Georgia's white politicians and officials didn't have but three principles—"racial integrity," states' rights, and a broadly and conveniently defined anticommunism—for preserving the state's segregated way of life and mantling their political expediencies. Thus, even in the relatively more moderate state of Georgia, home-brewed McCarthyism merged southern parochialism with Americanism. Contrary to Georgia's noble state motto, it was unwisdom, injustice, and immoderation that prevailed in the state politics of racial insecurity during the 1950s.

On December 10, 1953, five months before the Supreme Court nullified legally imposed racial segregation in public schools in its *Brown* decree, the state legislature created the Georgia Commission on Education as a new state agency. Composed of twenty-one members including Governor Herman Talmadge, who had succeeded his father, Eugene; Lieutenant Governor S. Marvin Griffin, a future governor; House Speaker Frederick B. "Fred" Hand Sr.; and Attorney General Eugene Cook, the commission was directed, according to the legislative resolution providing for its creation, to "formulate a plan or plans of legislation, prepare drafts of suggested laws, and recommend courses of action for consideration by the General Assembly," so that "the State may . . . continue to provide adequate education for all its citizens."[6] In reality, by creating the innocuously named Georgia Commission on Education, Georgia initiated its preparation for state action "in the event of an unfavorable ruling in the school segregation cases" then being considered by the nation's highest court.[7] Furnishing "adequate education"—especially to black Georgians—was put on the back burner. "Georgia will not be without a plan of decisive action in the event so dark an hour comes upon us in this enlightened age," Governor Talmadge pledged, "[and] I will not hesitate one second to act."[8] "We intend to maintain separate schools in Georgia one way or another, come what may," the governor declared on another occasion.[9] To Georgia's segregationist leaders, "adequate education for all its citizens" meant exactly two separate, distinct, and segregated educational systems—one for blacks and the other for whites.

Originally, the idea to create the Georgia Commission on Education was concocted by Charles J. Bloch, a Jewish white supremacist from Macon and one of the most prominent states' rights advocates and constitutional lawyers in the South, whom the British civil rights historian Clive Webb has designated as a "mastermind" of "the forces of massive resistance" in the Peach State and whom another observer called "the eminence grise of the Georgia legal establishment."[10] A native of Baton Rouge, Louisiana, Bloch became active in Georgia politics and was elected to the state House in 1927. There he befriended a future Georgia governor and U.S. senator from the state, Richard Russell, who then was waging his successful campaign to become the House Speaker.[11] In the years to come, Bloch became one of Senator Russell's most trusted and intimate political and personal friends.[12] The Macon lawyer entered the national political scene in the summer of 1948, when he delivered a nominating speech supporting the candidacy for president of Senator Russell, instead of Harry Truman, at the Democratic National Convention held in Philadelphia. Alluding to a famous line from William Jennings Bryan's "Cross of Gold" speech made before the 1896 Democratic convention ("You shall not crucify mankind upon a cross of gold!"), Bloch vowed defiantly: "You shall not be crucified on the cross of civil rights!"[13]

Though Russell's party candidacy did not go far, Bloch's passion and eloquence won him recognition among recalcitrant and retrogressive southern segregationists, inducing them to organize a party of their own, the Dixiecrat Party. Indeed, Bloch's slanted racial and racist views were often repellently virulent. Asserting that blacks and whites should not and could never be treated as equals, the constitutional lawyer compared blacks to farm animals in a letter to Russell: "It is true that there are laws to protect livestock. And there are customs, too. Hogs and pigs have their separate pens; chickens have their coops; cattle have their barns; horses and mules have their stables; and none of them eat with people."[14] Bloch was also convinced that black southerners would never have questioned their social and political status if the Communist-infested National Association for the Advancement of Colored People (NAACP) had not sowed discontent among them.[15] He would rather prefer, as he made clear in one of his speeches, "no schools" to "those run by Chief Justice Earl Warren and . . . other advisors of the NAACP."[16]

On December 23, 1952, almost a year before the creation of the Georgia Commission on Education and seventeen months prior to the *Brown* ruling, Bloch sent a memo to Herman Talmadge and offered the governor his draft of an executive proclamation to organize a new state agency for the purpose of fortifying Georgia against the impending onslaught of the civil rights movement. "The white people of Georgia," Bloch's proclamation read, "will never consent to the inter-mingling and the association which would ensue from white and negro children attending the same schools." It then provided that the governor would appoint a twelve-member committee, "in advance of any decision of the Supreme Court," to make a study of "this grave subject with the hope that our system of public schools . . . may be preserved" in Georgia.[17] Eventually, Bloch's appeal and suggestion to equip Georgia with an official segregationist agency in the face of the Supreme Court's desegregation ruling would be heeded by Governor Talmadge and other state officials. When the state organized the Georgia Commission on Education in late 1953, Bloch became a member of the new commission by virtue of his official capacity as the chair of the Georgia State Judicial Council.[18] Throughout the rest of the 1950s, Bloch continued to represent Georgia's official voice in massive resistance not only as an strong states' rights advocate, but also as a staunch anti-Communist, contending that the international and internal Communist conspiracy had been behind and agitating the civil rights movement.[19]

When the Georgia Commission on Education was organized under the chairmanship of Governor Talmadge, its day-to-day business responsibilities were shouldered by the commission's executive secretary, Durwood T. Pye, an attorney in Atlanta. Later, in the early spring of 1956, Pye would resign from the commission to serve as a Fulton County Superior Court judge.[20] Describing Pye as one of "the South's toughest judge[s] in civil rights cases," *Time* magazine once called him a "terrible-tempered, robe-twitching jurist whose boiling point is the lowest on the Atlanta bench."[21] Succeeding Pye as the segregationist commission's executive secretary would be T. V. Williams Jr., also an Atlanta attorney in his mid-twenties. (Williams Jr.'s father, T. V. Williams, was the state revenue commissioner and one of Marvin Griffin's close political allies.) He would take the five-hundred-dollar-per-month position in April 1956 at the request of Talmadge's successor and former lieutenant governor, Governor Griffin.[22]

Situated in the Agriculture Building in downtown Atlanta and with B. D. "Buck" Murphy, a leading Atlanta attorney, acting as its general counsel, the Georgia Commission on Education launched its initial task in 1954—a grand campaign to persuade the state's teachers and parents to approve a proposed constitutional amendment that would allow the state to abolish its public school systems if and when needed and to replace them with private schools. Earmarking some thirteen thousand dollars for disseminating a total of ninety thousand pieces of printed literature in favor of the constitutional amendment, Executive Secretary Pye, who saw the Communist enterprises at every corner of the school desegregation issues, was determined to preserve "Georgia's way of life." "The Communists and their dupes are on the march," he projected, "to destroy . . . all standards set by laws such as those providing for separate education."[23] The commission's endeavor eventually paid off, with the state's voters' narrowly approving the amendment on November 2, 1954.[24]

Six months earlier, in May 1954, the nation's High Court had rendered its *Brown* decision. Reacting to the ruling, Governor Talmadge once again vowed that integrated schools would never become reality in Georgia as long as he was the governor. "Georgia is going to resist mixing the races in the schools" even if it should be "the sole state in the nation to do so," he added.[25] Meanwhile, in his statement issued in the wake of *Brown*, Senator Richard Russell from Georgia denounced the decision as a "flagrant abuse of Judicial power" and pledged to find ways to reverse what he described as the socializing tendency of the Court.[26] On the heels of this school desegregation decree and in the midst of the confusion and resentment created by the ruling, Georgia's white voters elected Marvin Griffin, who had served as the lieutenant governor during the Talmadge administration, as their new governor in the September 8, 1954, Democratic primary.[27]

During his campaign, Griffin, who was blessed with the backing of the Talmadge supporters, let it be known that he would fight against the "meddlers, demagogues, race baiters and Communist[s]" who were out to destroy his beloved state's dual school systems, conveniently ignoring the fact that the segregationist campaign he was waging fully qualified him as a "demagogue" and "race baiter." "A vigorous campaign against these poisonous enemies of our people is in order," he said, presenting his discourse in the framework of the pro-segregation Cold War consensus.[28] Griffin also promised the state's voters that if elected, he would protect Georgia from "outside NAACP agitators and the Ohio-owned carpetbag Atlanta press," indicating that both of the major Atlanta dailies—the *Atlanta Journal* and the *Atlanta Constitution*—had been purchased by former Ohio governor James M. Cox in 1939 and 1950, respectively.[29] The future Georgia governor, in the meantime, would soon rely on another Ohioan—Myers

Lowman, executive secretary of the Cincinnati-based Circuit Riders—not as a "carpetbagger" but as a "collaborator" in the state-sponsored efforts to preserve discrimination and traditional racial practices in Georgia.

As governor, Griffin maintained his defiant posture on segregation issues. When the Supreme Court announced its implementation order of the original *Brown* decision—*Brown II*—on May 31, 1955, Griffin, who had been elected by billing himself as "the white man's candidate," was in no mood to retreat. Vowing to resist racial desegregation "come Hell or high water," he rejected the Court's implementation ruling. "No matter how much the Supreme Court seeks to sugarcoat its bitter pill of tyranny," Griffin exclaimed, "the people of Georgia and the South will not swallow it."[30] Echoing the defiance of his successor, former Governor Talmadge wrote to an out-of-state supporter in Gasport, New York, on June 7, 1955: "I frankly think that it will be another two generations before segregation is broken down in any of our elementary schools here in Georgia."[31]

To make his case, Talmadge took "it upon himself to write a bible for his disciples," penning an eighty-page analysis with the inflammatory title *You and Segregation* in 1955, in which he asserted that "Commie 'Experts,'" as well as "the left-wingers, the NAACP, the 'race-mixers' and a few misguided individuals," had successfully brainwashed the Supreme Court justices "in an effort to fool the citizens of Georgia into believing" that the state would have to integrate public schools. In the book's final chapter, entitled "A Plan of Action," Talmadge suggested that it was high time for Georgia to organize a pro-segregation and anti–civil rights statewide private group. Such an organization, he advised, "must be composed of outstanding citizens of integrity, patriotism and determination, pledged to the maintenance of harmonious race relations through the preservation of the traditional establishment of segregation in both public and private places" in Georgia. "We must organize as we have never before organized," Talmadge concluded, "[and] we must not, we shall not fail!"[32] Though the overall discourse in his book was unsophisticated, to say the least, part of Talmadge's plan would soon take shape with the foundation of the state's most vibrant private anti-integration organization, the States' Rights Council of Georgia, which, in essence, served as the state's version of the Citizens' Council that was then spreading across the South.

Officially organized on September 23, 1955—four months after the Supreme Court announced its desegregation implementation decree in *Brown II*—and headquartered at the William-Oliver Building in downtown Atlanta, the States' Rights Council of Georgia was dedicated to "the maintenance of harmonious race relations" in the state "through preservation of the traditional establishment of segregation in both public and private places." Notably, this wording, which appeared in the council's publication entitled *The Aims and Purposes of the States' Rights Council of Georgia, Inc.,* almost exactly duplicated language that appeared on the concluding page of Talmadge's book, confirming the fact that the appeal for organizing a statewide white-supremacist group made by the former governor in his *You and Segregation* had strongly influenced the creation of the States' Rights Council.[33] When the council held its "first grass roots meeting" in the southwest Georgia city of Americus on January 11, 1956, Talmadge was one of the featured speakers. "The meeting here today is the beginning of a great crusade," the former governor told some six hundred cheering attendees, "to let the world know, regardless of what the Supreme Court says . . . , that by the grace of God, Georgia will continue running its own affairs." Among the founders of the newly established private segregationist group were R. Carter Pittman, the council's president (prior to its official organization, Hugh G. Grant of Augusta, a one-time supporter of President Franklin Roosevelt and a former diplomat, had served the council as its founding president), and Roy Harris, who would succeed Pittman in 1958. Later, Bloch, who had been a member of the Georgia Commission on Education (whose creation in 1953 was largely attributed to him), would serve as the first vice president of the States' Rights Council of Georgia.[34]

Appointed as the States' Rights Council's executive director with an annual salary of ten thousand dollars was Georgia state representative William T. Bodenhamer of Ty Ty, Tift County. Equating the South's racial unrest with the threat of communism, Bodenhamer, the pastor of the Ty Ty Baptist Church by profession and a leader of the Georgia Baptist Convention, once declared: "The Communists planned over thirty years ago to inflame the Negro minority against the whites and to instill in the whites a guilt complex for their exploitation of the Negroes." Later, in the early spring of 1958, when the state representative announced his candidacy for the governorship (his bid was unsuccessful), William A. Lufburrow took up the council's executive directorship in place of Bodenhamer.[35]

Pittman, the venerated president of the Citizens' Council–like segregationist organization comprised of those whom Talmadge had called "outstanding citizens of integrity, patriotism and determination," was an eminent constitutional lawyer of Dalton, Georgia, on par with Bloch. A fiery states' righter, anti-Communist, and segregationist, Pittman, by the time he assumed the presidency of the States' Rights Council of Georgia, had already become well known in the state's legal circles for his vicious attacks on the Supreme Court's dependence on "non-legal, illegal, and inadmissible sociological materials to sustain judicial legislation based on false Marxist propaganda secretly supplied to the court by the NAACP" in announcing its *Brown* and *Brown II* decisions.[36] In the spring of 1958, Pittman would deliver an address before the annual banquet of the Demosthenian Literary Society, a historic debating society at the University of Georgia in Athens. In the address entitled "The Supreme Court Must Be Purged," Pittman argued that "no fair person" could possibly fail to suspect "that there are at least five members of the Court," including its chief justice, Earl Warren, "who have a fellow feeling for communists."[37]

Outshining even Pittman was Roy Harris of Augusta, the Georgia council's real power wielder, whose reach seemed to extend into every segregationist enterprise in the state. Harris was first elected to the Georgia state House in 1921, representing Jefferson County. After serving as a state senator for a short two-year period, he was reelected to the state House in 1933, where he came to wield considerable political influence as a four-term House Speaker. Both revered and feared, Harris had developed the reputation of being the "kingmaker" within the state's political circles. To the question, "What do you need to be elected governor of Georgia?" a contemporary popular saying would state: "Fifty thousand dollars and Roy Harris."[38] After he left the state House following his unexpected defeat in the 1946 election, Harris, to quote from his own reminiscences, elected to quit being a "public prostitute for nothing" and to devote the rest of his life to "preserving the separation of the races" in Georgia as a private citizen.[39]

True to his own resolve, the political "kingmaker" became known as "Mr. Segregation." His rabid opposition to racial integration and uncompromising support of ultraconservative values were abundantly revealed in the *Augusta Courier,* the newspaper that Harris edited for almost three decades after leaving state politics.[40] Just as Louisiana's Leander Perez reinforced the vitality of the pro-segregation Louisiana Joint Legislative Committee as one of the protagonists of the New Orleans–based Federation for Constitutional Government, Harris, who would also become the president of the Citizens' Councils of America in 1958, became the most influential official in the States' Rights Council movement, while galvanizing the Georgia Commission on Education with his virulent rhetoric.[41]

In late September 1955, less than four weeks after the founders of the States' Rights Council of Georgia celebrated the organization of their promising anti-*Brown* private group, Georgia's grand red-baiting campaign against the NAACP began in earnest as well. The leading figure in this state-sanctioned campaign was Georgia attorney general Eugene Cook, who, in the wake of the *Brown* ruling, had declared that he would maintain the segregated public school systems in the state "with every legal resources at my command as long as I am attorney general of Georgia."[42] On October 19, appearing before the fifty-fifth annual convention of the Peace Officers' Association of Georgia held in Atlanta, Cook delivered a lengthy address, determined to fully utilize the occasion "as the proper forum for revealing, for the first time, the authenticated details of the most ominous . . . threats to arise during our lifetime." One of those "most ominous threats," according to the attorney general, was nothing but "the misnamed National Association for the Advancement of Colored People and its fellow-traveling fronts" that had been forcing on the white South "the Communist-inspired doctrine of racial integration and amalgamation." "The ugly truth about the NAACP and its origin, aims and manipulators," Cook continued, "is so shocking as to stagger the imagination."[43]

During his fervid speech, Cook also claimed that his findings had been the result of "many weeks of intensive investigation" and "cooperative effort" rendered by the staffs of U.S. senator James Eastland from Mississippi, the recently seated and all-powerful chair of the Senate Internal Security Subcommittee (SISS), and a representative from Georgia, James C. Davis. On the basis of the "authenticated" evidence now in his hand, the attorney general insisted that "no other conclusion can be drawn but that the NAACP is being used as a front and tool by subversive elements" in America, having "allowed itself to become part and parcel of the Communist conspiracy," and that through its "nefarious activities," the civil rights organization was "fomenting strife and discord between the white and negro races in the South."[44]

Furthermore, aiding the NAACP in its racial agitation were some "'front' organizations on the Southern scene" such as the Atlanta-based Southern Regional Council (SRC) and the New Orleans–headquartered Southern Conference Educational Fund (SCEF), whose organizational purposes, as Cook explained, were to exploit and "dupe naïve do-gooders, fuzzy-minded intellectuals, misguided clergymen and radical journalists to be their pawns." Cook concluded that "the activities of the NAACP and its local fronts pose a serious threat" to the "way of life of our State" and "our traditional pattern of race relations."[45] The Georgia attorney general's speech would be printed by the Educational Fund of the Association of

Citizens' Councils of Mississippi in the immediate aftermath of the 1957 Little Rock desegregation ordeal in Arkansas. Entitled *The Ugly Truth about the NAACP*, it would become, as the civil rights activist Anne Braden observed, one of the most authoritative and frequently quoted segregationist publications "in the war against the NAACP" waged by the South's white supremacists, despite the civil rights group's swift and adamant protest against Cook's venomous discourse and the *Baltimore Afro-American*'s hopeful prediction that the segregationist "conspiracy publicly launched" by the Georgia attorney general was "another of the death throes of Dixieism." Unmindful of the black newspaper's editorial, Cook would continue to proclaim that the NAACP was "doing as much to damage race relations in the South as did the Ku Klux Klan."[46]

In the meantime, fully supported and enthusiastically embraced by the States' Rights Council and Attorney General Cook, the Georgia Commission on Education was invested with a public relations function in early 1957 at the request of Governor Griffin. When the commission was created in late 1953, it was only authorized "from time to time to print and distribute report of its findings and recommendations."[47] Now, with the blessing of the state legislature, Georgia's segregationist agency would be expected to aggressively combat "the distorted views" presented by "certain segments of the Northern press" and to offer Georgia's and the South's viewpoints relating to school segregation issues.[48] Accordingly, the Georgia commission organized its Advertising, or Publicity, Committee (the names were frequently used interchangeably within the commission) composed of four commission members, including Harris and Pittman, with the former serving as the committee chair.[49] In addition to its newly specified public relations function, the Georgia Commission on Education, under the chairmanship of Governor Griffin, was also invested with "the power to employ investigators, to hold hearings, and . . . to subpoena witnesses," remaking itself as the Georgia version of the House Un-American Activities Committee (HUAC).[50] The Georgia commission's Investigation Committee was comprised of three members. Governor Griffin and Harris sat on the new committee, and it was chaired by Attorney General Cook, the leading architect of the state's smear campaign against the NAACP, with whom the Ohio-based Circuit Riders' executive secretary, Myers Lowman, had established a connection in the spring of 1956.[51]

On August 3, 1958, while the liaison between Lowman and Louisiana state senator William Rainach, chair of the pro-segregation Louisiana Joint Legislative Committee, was kept intact, the Sunday *Atlanta Jour-*

nal-Constitution reported that Lowman had been employed as a "secret investigator" for the similarly segregationist Georgia Commission on Education.[52] Apparently, Lowman's relations with the Georgia commission began in early July 1957, only four months after he helped Rainach to launch Louisiana's March 1957 "Subversion in Racial Unrest" public hearings.[53] At this state-sponsored anti-integration and anti–civil rights hearings, Lowman got acquainted in person with Georgia attorney general Cook, who also attended the hearings as one of the invited out-of-state observers.[54] During the fall of 1957, the States' Rights Council of Georgia loaned two thousand dollars to T. V. Williams, executive secretary of the Georgia Commission on Education, helping the state agency to finance a project that was not yet publicly revealed. At the time, Williams also borrowed $2,500 from a bank for the same purpose with the endorsement given by the States' Rights Council.[55]

After almost a year, on August 1, 1958, the *Atlanta Journal* publicly revealed for the first time that a total of $4,500 had been used by the Georgia Commission on Education to pay a "mysterious undercover man 'named Lowman' who operates out of Cincinnati." The employment of this "mysterious" investigator, the daily noted, had been recommended and fully approved by the Georgia commission's Investigation Committee members—Governor Griffin, Attorney General Cook, and Harris.[56] On the following day, in a hurriedly issued statement, Governor Griffin acknowledged that the commission, with his "wholehearted approval," had indeed paid $4,500 to Lowman for his "services rendered for investigation and research" on behalf of the segregationist state agency. In defense of the state agency's action, the governor explained that Lowman had been recommended by segregationist leaders in Louisiana, and that "he did an excellent job for us on the Georgia Commission on Education and earned his money."[57]

Thus, though Lowman's association with the Georgia Commission on Education was brought to light in a rather awkward fashion, his involvement in Georgia's official segregationist projects had been predictable. After all, Attorney General Cook was the first influential southern official with whom Lowman had sought to establish a liaison. In addition, Lowman's usefulness for the South's segregationist cause is likely to have been well recognized by Roy Harris, the kingpin of the States' Rights Council of Georgia as well as a vital member of the Georgia commission, through the correspondence between the Augusta editor and Louisiana state senator William Rainach.[58] While, at Rainach's behest, still devoting considerable time to his editorial work on the transcript generated by the Louisiana Joint Legislative Committee's March 1957 hearings, Lowman also set about to strengthen his association with Attorney General Cook and Georgia's anti–civil rights agency as well.

On July 2, 1957, Executive Secretary Williams of the Georgia Commission on Education mailed Lowman a list of organizations and individuals, in which, Williams explained, the commission had "particular interest," asking Lowman to run a check on what the Georgia agency perceived as their subversive activities. At the top of the list came the NAACP, "the most ominous" threat to Georgia's segregated way of life, according to Attorney General Cook. The NAACP was followed on the list by the SRC and the SCEF, both of which had also been denounced by Cook during his September 1955 "The Ugly Truth about the NAACP" speech. Among those individuals about whom Williams sought information were Rosa Parks, the "instigator" of the 1955–56 Montgomery Bus Boycott in Alabama; and the founders of the Highlander Folk School in Monteagle, Tennessee.[59]

In response, Lowman provided the Georgia Commission on Education with the exhibits that had been introduced as evidence before the March 1957 public hearings conducted by the Louisiana Joint Legislative Committee. The exhibits, which had originally been compiled by Lowman's most trusted associate, J. B. Matthews of New York City, listed the "subversive" records of ten members of the national NAACP's board of directors, who were allegedly in "association with Communist fronts." Among those named in the documentary evidence were Eleanor Roosevelt and Benjamin E. Mays, president of Morehouse College, a historically black educational institution in Atlanta. Soon afterward, the Georgia commission's Advertising Committee, chaired by Harris, converted this information into a booklet, entitling it *Ten Directors of the N.A.A.C.P.*[60] The Advertising Committee printed fifty thousand copies of the booklet and widely distributed them among state officials and white-supremacist groups in the South.[61] Of those, five thousand copies were set aside and mailed to William Simmons of Jackson, Mississippi, administrator of the Citizens' Councils of America.[62]

Impressed by the well of information that Lowman could potentially furnish to Georgia's massive resisters, Executive Secretary Williams wasted no time in extending an invitation to Lowman to visit Atlanta. Conferring with Williams in July 1957 in the office of the Georgia Commission on Education, Lowman was assigned to investigate NAACP activities in Florida.

Later in the same month, Lowman was dispatched by the Georgia commission to various Florida cities including Miami Beach, Naples, and Tampa, where he gathered information on the NAACP and prompted the state and local officials, including those of the pro-segregation Florida Legislative Investigation Committee created in the previous year, into invigorating their investigations on the civil rights organization. Revisiting Atlanta in early August, Lowman reported back his findings to Williams and the Georgia commission members during their weekend three-day conference.[63]

When the Georgia commission's use of Lowman was unveiled a year later, in the summer of 1958, the *Atlanta Journal-Constitution,* dissatisfied with the seemingly secret affair that had consumed the state taxpayers' hard-earned money, editorialized: "Floridians, we believe, are perfectly capable of handling their own problems without the help of investigators from way up north in Georgia."[64] The Atlanta daily claimed that it was difficult to comprehend why the Georgia Commission on Education was so concerned about the racial situation in its neighboring state. Yet, the segregationist leaders in Georgia had legitimate cause for their expressed fear of "outside interference in Georgia's domestic affairs" surging from Florida, where the NAACP-backed and eventually successful Tallahassee Bus Boycott had been shaking the foundations of the Florida capital's longtime Jim Crow practices.[65]

Besides the NAACP, other prime targets of the Georgia commission's Investigation Committee, chaired by Attorney General Cook, included the SRC. The Atlanta-based civil rights organization had also been investigated by Lowman and his Methodist laymen's anti-Communist group—the Circuit Riders—since the early 1957 because of the SRC's use of the Wesley Memorial Building as its headquarters.[66] The SRC's board of directors, Lowman once noted, was "heavily weighted with people" whose pro-Communist affiliations were "longer than Joseph Stalin's left arm."[67] And there was no doubt in his mind that the SRC and what Lowman termed "other sputniks" such as the SCEF in New Orleans were "directed at white and Negro exploitation in the southern part of the United States."[68] Also attracting the keen attention of the segregationist commission in its own state's domestic sphere were the higher educational institutions in Georgia where, as Matthews warned Lowman, "the Communist-front apparatus has gained support" for their unsavory deeds.[69] At the request of the Georgia commission and with the assistance extended by Matthews, Lowman launched his probe into the state's colleges and universities, and compiled a list of those institutions, including Emory University in Atlanta and Mercer University in Macon, with faculty members who allegedly had "Communist affiliations."[70]

The Georgia commission's most thorough investigation and most vicious attack, however, were directed at the Highlander Folk School, located in another of Georgia's neighboring states, Tennessee. Both Lowman and his associate, Matthews, were largely responsible for sustaining the Georgia Commission on Education's tenacious persecution of Highlander. In August 1957, immediately following his return from Florida, where he had spent a few weeks as the Georgia commission's "secret investigator" of the NAACP activities, Lowman began his all-out investigation of the Highlander Folk School in collaboration with Matthews. Lowman informed Matthews that the Georgia Commission on Education was very "anxious to use" any information on Highlander, where some of those involved in the Montgomery Bus Boycott, such as Parks and Martin Luther King Jr., had attended its interracial activities.[71] Eventually, the information that Lowman and Matthews gathered on the Tennessee school was shared not only with Georgia's segregationist agency, but also with Richard Arens, the HUAC's chief counsel.[72] With their involvement in the Georgia commission's persecution of Highlander, the state agency's reliance on Lowman and Matthews further increased. For instance, when Matthews made a speech, at Lowman's invitation, before the Cincinnati chapter of the Sons of the American Revolution on September 9, 1957, representatives from the Georgia Commission on Education were among the audience. Lowman had sold more than four hundred tickets to those who wished to hear Matthews speak about the "threats to the Constitution" posed by the Supreme Court and its 1954 *Brown* ruling.[73]

Cofounded in 1932 by Myles Horton, Donald L. "Don" West, James Dombrowski, and others, Highlander Folk School in Monteagle, Tennessee, was a "community folk school in the Danish tradition" with emphasis on providing broadly defined adult education.[74] Horton, a native white Tennessean who became Highlander's founding director, had studied at Union Theological Seminary in New York City under the guidance of Harry Ward—one of the principal foes of Lowman, his Circuit Riders, and Matthews. Since its inception, Highlander's primary goal had been "to build a progressive labor movement" in the South in the wake of the 1929 Great Depression. To achieve its organizational objective, the Tennessee school supported labor strikes and organizing drives, as well as training activists "to take leadership in labor unions."[75]

In 1953, the Highlander Folk School altered its focus from the labor movement to the civil rights movement. In anticipation of the Supreme Court's school desegregation ruling, Highlander began to develop an interracial "experimental program" for fostering community leaders—both black and white—in the South "to implement the expected decision." Thereafter, from 1953 to 1957, Highlander held annual workshops on the theme of "The *Brown* Case and Public School Integration" to nourish the activists who would soon lead the region's civil rights struggle.[76] "Today we are concentrating the major part of our staff work on promoting a practical long-term program for bringing about an orderly transition from segregated to better schools for all children throughout the South," Horton wrote in February 1955, nine months after the nation's highest court outlawed legally imposed public school segregation.[77] Among those civil rights activists who benefited from Highlander's educational programs was Rosa Parks of Montgomery, Alabama. In the summer of 1955, four months before the Alabama capital's massive bus boycott began, Parks attended a two-week workshop entitled "The South Prepares to Carry Out the Supreme Court Decision Outlawing Segregation in Public Schools" at the Highlander Folk School. Then, while the Montgomery Bus Boycott was in progress, in early March 1956, Parks was invited by Highlander to participate in its planning conference on a series of public school desegregation workshops.[78] Not only Parks's association with the Highlander Folk School, but also the school's founders themselves, troubled and irritated southern segregationists.

Two months before the *Brown* decision, when the SISS held its hearings in New Orleans for the purpose of cracking down on the SCEF in March 1954, James Dombrowski, one of the cofounders of the Highlander Folk School and the executive director of the SCEF, was hauled up before the Senate subcommittee. Along with Dombrowski, Myles Horton, another cofounder and the director of Highlander, was among those who were interrogated and accused of "being subversive" during the hearings led by Mississippi senator Eastland.[79] When Horton was summoned to appear before the SISS on March 20, he declined to answer Eastland's questions, refusing to name names. Having lasted only a few minutes on the witness stand without being given a chance to read his six-page prepared statement, he was ejected by the U.S. marshal from the hearing room for "disorderly conduct."[80] "It was the only time I ever made the front page of the *New York Times*," Horton reminisced years later.[81]

Shortly after his return from New Orleans, Horton held an open forum at the Highlander Folk School, inviting some seventy residents and newspaper reporters from Grundy County, where the school was located. While denying categorically that he had ever been a member of the Communist Party of the United States of America (CPUSA), Horton sarcastically commented that the "hysteria spread by Eastland's committee . . . has substantially contributed to the fiction that the only dynamic force in the world is Communism." "De-segregation and integration of the public schools . . . would spectacularly refresh the democratic thesis everywhere," he told his audience, "[and] the inspiration of such an event would reach into the remotest corners of . . . Mississippi."[82] Regardless of whatever Horton had to say, for the Mississippi senator and the bulk of other southern segregationists, Highlander epitomized "freakish, mongrelized, and basically Communist" enterprises.[83]

Among Highlander's cofounders, the case of Don West was slightly different from those of the others in terms of his tangible Communist affiliation. Imbued with the Danish folk school philosophy, West, a native of Gilmer County, Georgia, played a vital role in establishing the experimental school with Horton and Dombrowski. After less than a year at Highlander, however, he left the school due to the differences of opinion that developed between him and Horton with regard to how best to achieve Highlander's "educational and social objectives."[84] Having returned to his native Georgia, West and his wife, Connie, subsequently established the Southern Folk School and Libraries in Kennesaw, Cobb County, as an outreach project intended to "educate farmers and industrial workers for the cooperative commonwealth." At the same time, West increasingly immersed himself in labor and union activities, promoting the CPUSA's cause in Georgia and North Carolina.[85] Though he had never been a card-carrying, dues-paying member of the CPUSA, West "worked very closely" with those whom he "knew to be communist."[86] Thus, when T. V. Williams, executive secretary of the Georgia Commission on Education, asked Lowman in July 1957 to run a background check on several organizations and individuals about which the commission had "particular interest" in obtaining information, it was no coincidence that West's name was conspicuously enumerated on Williams's list along with that of Rosa Parks in Montgomery.[87]

Georgia's white supremacists were especially troubled by the fact that a prominent supporter of the Tennessee school was Martin Luther King Jr., the emerging leader of the entire civil rights movement, whose Southern

Christian Leadership Conference (SCLC) was headquartered in Atlanta. Other influential supporters of Highlander's programs and projects included Frederick B. Routh, assistant director of state organizations at the SRC, another stronghold of the civil rights movement based in Atlanta.[88] For Georgia's massive resisters, each and every "Communistic" integrationist enterprise seemed to point to Highlander, where, as Lillian Smith—a nationally acclaimed, but regionally despised, civil and human rights activist—once affectionately noted, an interracial "family reunion of humanity" could thrive in the face of the white South's inhumane treatment of black southerners.[89]

On Labor Day weekend of 1957, for the four days from August 30 to September 2, the Highlander Folk School held a special workshop entitled "The South Thinking Ahead," celebrating the school's twenty-fifth anniversary. For the occasion, some 180 participants gathered at Highlander, including Martin Luther King Jr. and Rosa Parks.[90] The folk singer Pete Seeger, a sympathizer of the CPUSA, entertained the participants. He would soon be instrumental in renaming "We Will Overcome"—originally a union song adopted in the 1945 American Tobacco Company strike in Charleston, South Carolina—to "We Shall Overcome" and helping it to become one of the most popular songs of the civil rights era.[91] On September 2, the last day of Highlander's commemorative workshop, King delivered a speech in which he commended the Tennessee school for having "stood with dauntless courage and fearless determination," bringing "special greetings from the 50,000 Negro citizens of Montgomery."[92]

A few weeks before the Highlander Folk School celebrated its milestone, the Georgia Commission on Education, being "anxious to use" any damaging information regarding Highlander, began the first round of its offensive against the Tennessee school.[93] The Georgia commission, on the strength of the subpoena power conferred to it earlier in the year, floated the idea of holding its first closed-door hearing in the hope of linking Highlander with what it perceived as subversive activities. At the segregationist commission's request, Lowman recommended Manning Johnson to the commission members as the planned hearing's "friendly" witness. Johnson, a black former CPUSA member, had served as the "star witness" during the March 1957 Louisiana Joint Legislative Committee hearings on the recommendation of the Circuit Riders' executive secretary. Lowman also furnished the Georgia commission with the lists of public records of those to whom Johnson would refer during the forthcoming hearing in Atlanta. Most of the lists on individuals whom both Lowman and the commission recognized as Communist-influenced race agitators had originally been prepared by Matthews.[94]

Giving his statement before the hurriedly prepared closed hearing launched by the Georgia Commission on Education on August 10, 1957, Johnson asserted that southerners—both black and white—had been "confronted with one of the most dangerous conspiracies in the history of the world"—namely, the Communist-forged "well-organized international conspiracy" revolving around the civil rights movement. Among the leading vehicles of this grand "conspiracy," according to Johnson, were the Atlanta-based SRC and King, whom "the 'Commies' are building up . . . as the man of the hour in the South."[95] The Georgia commission, following this closed hearing, planned to hold a public hearing with Johnson serving as the witness. Unfortunately for the commission and Lowman, however, Johnson's inability to provide any useful information regarding Highlander's "subversive" activities dissuaded the segregationist agency from carrying out this scheme.[96] Instead of depending on Johnson, the Georgia Commission on Education, realizing that the Tennessee school would soon hold its twenty-fifth anniversary workshop, decided to dispatch a white employee of the state government to Monteagle to "cover" Highlander's activities.[97] In so doing, Georgia's massive resisters were determined to "find out whether that malignancy of the NAACP and Communism was leaking out over Georgia" through the interracial school in Tennessee.[98]

Entrusted with this task by the Georgia Commission on Education was Edwin H. "Ed" Friend Sr. A conservation officer of the Georgia Forestry Commission, Friend was known for his photographic skills. In fact, he had served as the official photographer of Governor Herman Talmadge and was then serving in the same capacity for Governor Griffin.[99] On August 29, 1957, the day before the kickoff of Highlander's commemorative workshop, Friend was "assigned a mission" by Williams, executive secretary of the segregationist commission, to "infiltrate" the school's gathering. In accordance with Williams's instructions, Friend drove up to the Highlander Folk School the next day and returned to Atlanta on September 2.[100] While he stayed at Highlander, Friend, accompanied by his wife, presented himself as a "free-lance writer" and a "commercial photographer."[101] Having convinced the other workshop attendees that he was genuinely interested in the civil rights movement, Friend stood in front of the Highlander Library's entrance and filmed the other workshop participants such as Horton, King, Parks, and Seeger. His 16-mm silent, color film contains a long scene depicting "integrated swimming" at a small lake on the school premises.[102] Several duplicate copies of the film were later made by the Georgia commission and distributed to, among others, the Citizens' Council's national headquarters in Jackson, Mississippi, and the Federal Bureau of Investigation (FBI).[103]

In addition to the 16-mm film, a particular still photograph taken by Friend fell into the hands of southern segregationists through the Georgia Commission on Education. The photograph, which would be massively reproduced, was taken at one of the seminars held during Highlander's anniversary gathering, and it showed, sitting together, Myles Horton, Martin Luther King Jr., Aubrey Williams of the SCEF, and Abner W. Berry, whom the Georgia commission and Roy Harris's *Augusta Courier* called the "'Four Horsemen' of racial agitation."[104] Among the "Four Horsemen," the only card-carrying CPUSA member was Berry, who had joined the Communist Party in 1929 and was subsequently elected to its national committee in 1934.[105] Though Berry would resign from the CPUSA later in 1957, his presence at the workshop proved damaging to Highlander's reputation, making somewhat credible segregationists' assertion that Horton, King, and others were "consorting with 'known Communists'" and that those Communists directed the civil rights movement through Highlander's programs. In a few years, Harris, chair of the Georgia commission's Advertising Committee and editor of his tabloid newspaper, would print Friend's photograph in a flier and distribute, as he later boasted, "a million copies" of it among the interested politicians, officials, and white supremacist organizations throughout the South.[106] Bearing the sensational title "Martin Luther King at Communist Training School," the flier encouraged its recipients: "JOIN THE AUGUSTA COURIER IN THE FIGHT FOR FREEDOM."[107]

On October 1, 1957, a month after Highlander's twenty-fifth anniversary workshop, the Georgia Commission on Education once again dispatched Friend to the Tennessee school. This time, Friend was asked to "procure a duplicate set of tape recordings" that had been made at the workshop. During a lunch at Highlander with Horton and Septima P. Clark, the school's education director, Friend learned that the original set of audiotapes generated at the gathering was in possession of a Cincinnati, Ohio, minister who had attended the workshop. Friend left Monteagle in haste and drove through the night to Cincinnati, eventually locating the minister and acquiring the tapes.[108]

Immediately following Friend's return to Atlanta, the Georgia Commission on Education held a meeting in the capital on October 4, 1957. There, the commission members heard a staff report on the Highlander Folk School given by Executive Secretary Williams with the avowed purpose of "letting the people see the close relationship between Communism and racial strife."[109] Among those present at the meeting were Governor Griffin, Lieutenant Governor Ernest S. Vandiver, Attorney General Eugene Cook, and Harris. It also attracted some keen observers dispatched by Georgia's neighboring states—Assistant Attorneys General John N. Baker and Joseph A. Malone from Alabama, who represented Alabama attorney general John M. Patterson, and Chief Counsel Mark Hawes of the Florida Legislative Investigation Committee.[110] Baker and Malone had been instructed by their superior, Patterson, to probe into subversive influences behind the Montgomery Bus Boycott and the two most visible and influential figures in the boycott movement—King and Parks. Meanwhile Hawes, representing Florida, expressed concern about what his segregationist committee perceived as subversive nature of the protracted Tallahassee Bus Boycott launched in May 1956.

Calling the meeting to order as the chair of the segregationist commission, Governor Griffin offered a brief statement at the outset. "It has been necessary that announcement of the purpose of this meeting be withheld for security reasons," he explained, "[for] until late last night there were undercover investigators in direct contact with the Highlander Folk School situation, and any disclosure might have placed them in futher [*sic*] jeopardy."[111] Though the governor hinted at the existence of "undercover investigators" in the plural form, Friend, who then testified before the commission, was actually the only one who had been "in direct contact" with Highlander. Following Friend's testimony, Williams introduced as "exhibits" a total of thirty-eight photographs taken by Friend at Highlander. Harris, who had looked forward to having an opportunity to brand the Tennessee school as a "Communist training school," eagerly helped the commission's executive secretary to mark the introduced pictures for identification.[112]

Among the photographs taken by Friend at Highlander and introduced as exhibits during the meeting were those depicting racially "mixed dancing and social activities" by the workshop participants, including Horton, King, Parks, Berry, Seeger, Aubrey Williams of the SCEF, and Routh of the SRC—a "most amazing assortment of persons," as Executive Secretary T. V. Williams noted sarcastically in his presentation.[113] For instance, Seeger, to borrow the words of the Georgia commission's executive secretary, had given his precious "time and talents to the support of Communist apparatuses at any meeting . . . held up at Highlander." Special words were also reserved for the SCEF president Aubrey Williams by the commission's executive secretary. "I think that it would be appropriate at this time to state," T. V. Williams told the commission members, "that few people have done so much to stir racial agitation and create tension and strife in the South than has Aubrey Williams." When the subject of T. V. Williams's presentation shifted to the Atlanta-headquartered SRC, one of whose original incorporators had been Ralph E. McGill, the editor and publisher of the *Atlanta Constitution* and Georgia's leading voice for racial moderation, Harris suddenly chipped in: "Let's stop right there. . . . [W]e will pay our respects to Mr. McGill. We are going to say he is the worst enemy the white people of Georgia have had" since the Reconstruction days.[114]

Near the end of T. V. Williams's presentation, Governor Griffin asked him to state whether, in his opinion, the Highlander workshop had taken place as a "high level conference of the leaders" of racial agitations with a leaning toward supporting communism. "This included the leadership of every major race incident that has taken place in the South between the time of the Supreme Court decision in 1954 and the close of this meeting, September 2, 1957," the executive secretary replied. To the delight of Griffin and his fellow commissioners, Williams also offered his conclusion that the Highlander gathering was "honeycombed with individuals of Communist activities and identifications."[115] Praising both Friend and Williams for having presented the "amazing factual compilation" before the commission, Governor Griffin concluded the meeting with his promise that the Georgia Commission on Education would continue to make "reports to the people" on the Highlander Folk School where, as he saw it, the unsavory alliance between communism and the civil rights movement had been forged. As Benjamin Mays, one of the most outspoken black critics of segregation and the president of Morehouse College in Atlanta from 1940 to 1967, would later write in his autobiography, "anyone who attended a meeting where any Communists were present, no matter how few, was promptly accused of having 'Communist leanings.'"[116]

Meanwhile, asked by a newspaper reporter to comment on the findings revealed by Georgia's segregationist state agency, Horton pointed out that all of the discussions and activities taken place during the Highlander workshop were a matter of public record. "That's not much undercover, is it?" he scornfully asked.[117] Echoing the Highlander director was the *Atlanta Constitution* editor Ralph McGill, whom Harris had just branded as "the worst enemy" of "the white people of Georgia." Equating the Georgia Commission on Education with a "bush-league secret police," McGill lashed out at the segregationist agency's "Gestapo activities" and "far-fetched 'educational' propaganda." If, in fact, any "Communist meeting" had taken place at the Highlander Folk School, as the Georgia commission's "gum-shoe agents maintain," why on earth could "anyone who was willing to pay the registration fee" have been able to "get in at the Highlander School, make photographs, or attend the dance?," the *Atlanta Constitution* editor mischievously asked his readers. "That isn't in the Commie pattern," McGill observed.[118]

Neither hearing nor heeding what Horton and McGill had to say and not betraying his own resolve to keep the people of Georgia and the South informed on the matter of Highlander Folk School, Governor Griffin took an additional action. During the same month that the Georgia commission members heard T. V. Williams's "amazing factual compilation" about Highlander, the segregationist agency published a sensational piece of propaganda in October 1957, intending to further discredit the Tennessee school.[119] Entitled *Highlander Folk School: Communist Training School, Monteagle, Tennessee,* the four-page newspaper-size folder, which included some of the pictures that Ed Friend had taken at the school's anniversary workshop, charged that Highlander had been nothing but a hotbed of the Communist movement, fomenting racial troubles throughout the entire South.[120] Listing the Matthews-compiled and Lowman-provided "records of Communist Affiliations" of Don West, James Dombrowski, and Aubrey Williams in the folder, the Georgia Commission on Education asserted that those listed there represented "the nucleus of this Communist Training School."[121] Not only that, the commission publication insisted, many of the other participants in the Highlander workshop—Horton, King, and Parks included—were "specialists in inter-racial strife . . . in the company of many known Communists," and such a workshop was "the typical method whereby leadership training and tactics are furnished to the agitators."[122]

At the outset, the Georgia Commission on Education printed one hundred thousand copies of the Highlander Folk School folder at a cost of $2,975, which was financed by state taxpayers—including, of course, segregated black Georgians. Shortly, the printing of an additional one hundred thousand copies was authorized, and the bulk of these were mailed to state and federal officials and lawmakers, educators, ministers, and civic leaders.[123] Officers of various segregationist and white-supremacist organizations also received the Highlander folder. While William Rainach, chair of the Louisiana Joint Legislative Committee, received three thousand copies of the publication, the Georgia commission mailed, by request, a total of five thousand copies to Robert Patterson, secretary of the Association of Citizens' Councils of Mississippi.[124] "We will put them in good hands," Patterson promised T. V. Williams in early 1958.[125] Mississippi assistant attorney general Dugas Shands was equally pleased with the Georgia commission's "splendid work" in "uncovering" what he considered to be the evil deeds of the Tennessee school. "You gentlemen are doing a wonderful job in holding the line against those who are seeking to destroy States' Rights and the precepts of the South," Shands told commission members after he received the Highlander folder.[126] Later, when the Georgia commission met at Governor Griffin's office on January 3, 1958, it was unanimously decided that the state agency would print and mail three hundred thousand additional copies of the folder to "every post office box and rural box holder in Georgia."[127]

As Highlander hit the newspaper headlines throughout the South, Myles Horton, the director of the Tennessee school, was in no mood to retreat. In his December 14, 1957, interview with Jack Nelson, an investigative reporter of the McGill-edited *Atlanta Constitution,* Horton blasted Governor Griffin for having dispatched Friend as a "stoolpigeon" to his school, adding that the governor and his segregationist commission might have been responsible for "planting" Berry, a CPUSA member, at Highlander's workshop.[128] "Highlander did not and does not welcome enrollment of anyone with a totalitarian philosophy whether from the extreme right or from the extreme left," the school director replied to the charges levied by the Georgia Commission on Education, "[and] in these troubled times, nothing but more trouble can come from the White Citizens['] Councils' and the Communist Party's infiltration into groups earnestly seeking a democratic solution to our problems." Condemning the white-supremacist organization, as well as the CPUSA, as "morally bankrupt" and having "nothing to offer" toward the betterment of the South's race relations, Horton emphasized that what Highlander and the South really needed was a group of people "who do their own thinking."[129]

Proudly proclaiming itself the guardian of "the Georgia way of life," the Georgia Commission on Education, as defiant as ever, continued to mail out numerous copies of its sensational Highlander folder. Aside from segregationist politicians and officials in the South, ordinary white citizens in and out of the region encouraged the commission with positive responses. The Highlander folder "confirms my own suspicions of Communist direction of the racial conflict in the United States," a Sarasota, Florida, resident wrote. Meanwhile, from Providence, Rhode Island, a former elder-general of the National Society of the Sons and Daughters of the Pilgrims wrote to Williams. "Where so many white Americans have been gullible enough to accept the teachings of Communism," he observed, "we can hardly blame the ignorant Negro for being coaxed into this vicious unAmerican [*sic*] type of false-economics and pseudo-democracy."[130]

At Lowman's suggestion, the Georgia Commission on Education also set aside a large quantity of the Highlander folders intended to be delivered into the hands of ministers and other church leaders throughout the nation. Lowman's scheme somewhat backfired, however, for the Georgia commission's publication induced far more critical comments than congratulatory remarks. Most southern ministers who received the Highlander folders probably either simply ignored them or did not dare to voice their opinions. Granted, some southern ministers were courageous enough to denounce the segregationist commission. "I have no affiliation whatsoever with the Communist party, nor do I desire to be affiliated," James S. Clinefelter, a pastor in Miami, Florida, wrote to Executive Secretary Williams: "In like manner I do not desire any affiliation with the Georgia Commission on Education." The Highlander folder, he observed, only confirmed the Georgia agency's strategy of "defin[ing] a Communist as anyone in disagreement with you." Thomas R. Miller, rector at St. Christopher's Episcopal Church in Lubbock, Texas, also asked the Georgia commission not to send him "any further mailings from your organization!" "I shall endevour [*sic*] to love even you, but I have absolutely no interest in your publications," he added.[131]

One of the strongest protests among southern ministers came from the pastor at the Church of the Advent in Marion, South Carolina. "It is a sin and a disgrace to have the State of Georgia represented by such a publication," Ralph E. Cousins Jr., a native of Elberton, Georgia, wrote to Williams: "Communism is bad, but your brand of Facism [*sic*] is not the answer. . . . We all have to pay for our sins against our neighbors, but I dislike very much the possibility of having to pay for yours." The Georgia commission's executive secretary, as the official records of the state agency attest, seldom bothered to write back to ministers who voiced their disagreements with the commission. But Cousins's accusation that the Georgia commission was promoting fascism infuriated Williams into responding. "I fail to see that there is any possibility of your having to pay for my sins," the executive secretary replied, "[and] if the dissemination of truth is a sin in your church, then it is fortunate I am not a member."[132]

All of the protest letters penned by southern white ministers and church leaders testified to the fact that, regardless of what the majority of segregationists might believe, the seemingly solid white South was, in actuality, neither solid nor monolithic. In the meantime, from outside of the South, much harsher responses decrying the Georgia commission's "hate campaigns" bombarded the commission office in Atlanta.[133] "My reaction to the paper is that it is purely a smokescreen, hiding the major issue of segregation behind the cry of Communism," Pastor James Cosbey Jr. at the Church of Holy Spirit in Mattapan, Massachusetts, observed. "As a Christian clergyman," Cosbey offered, "I shall have prayers in church this Sunday, praying that God may open the eyes of the blind to the dignity of all his children." Finding the contents of the Highlander folder to be "salacious and subversive of the US Government and the decisions of the Supreme Court," Enrico C. S. Molnar, rector at St. Timothy's Episcopal Church in Compton, California, pondered: "I thought integration was the law of the land, and not a Communist tactic as you allege."[134]

Others did not hesitate to call the Georgia commission members a posse of "violent race haters." "I want to state as strongly as possible," J. Robert Zimmerman at the Cathedral Church of the Nativity in Bethlehem, Pennsylvania, wrote in haste, "that I resent getting a copy of your filty [*sic*] smear sheet"—"the most despicable thing I have ever seen." "As for Communism, is it not abundantly [*sic*] clear to you that the only people who ar [*sic*] really helping the worldwide communist cause are violent race haters such as yourself?," the minister asked. Addressing his letter to "the Un-American Governor of Georgia," Alvin V. P. Hart at the Protestant Chaplaincy of Bellevue Hospital in New York City vowed that he was not going to be "fooled by the Nazi southerners' attempt to call both Christianity and Democracy Communism." "I am ashamed," Hart concluded, "that you are citizens of the same country of which I am a citizen." Even from Lowman's hometown of Cincinnati, Ohio, Thomas I. Spitler at St. James Episcopal Church mailed back the Highlander folder to the Georgia commission, simply offering a one-word response—"Nuts!"—on the attached memo sheet.[135]

The Highlander Folk School, too, continued to fight back. In February 1958, John B. Thompson, chair of the Guarantors for Highlander who was one of the school's founders and a white Presbyterian minister, wrote to Highlander's financial contributors. "As you well know, there are two Souths," he observed: "There is the soul-sick South of the Ku Klux Klan, of the White Citizens['] Councils who try to bolster segregation with bogus-anthropology and illiterate religion, [and] of Gov. Griffin who identifies desegregation with communism." "But," Thompson continued, "there is also the South of Martin Luther King and Rosa Parks."[136] Siding emphatically with the old "soul-sick South" and trying desperately to contain the emergence of the other and new South, the Georgia Commission on Education would continue to represent the state's "unwisdom, injustice, and immoderation" until its eventual demise in the fall of 1959, when it was converted into the new Governor's Commission on Constitutional Government under the administration of Governor Ernest Vandiver, Griffin's successor.[137]

As 1957 neared its end, Lowman evaluated the Circuit Riders' activities and achievements in his working paper dated December 6. "During 1957 the greatest effort in subversion in the United States is in the race field with the religious exploitation feature as the glaringly outstanding phenomenon," the document read, bearing the capitalized words "NOT FOR PUBLICATION, DISTRIBUTION, OR RELEASE."[138] "Each time the Communist Party secretly develops a new plan or program to exploit a major complaint of man, the Communist corn of propaganda is skillfully scattered," he further observed on December 23, warning that "the Communist corn" had been seeded "in the fields of race incitation and race tension." "Those white and Negro people" in the South should be "looking up often enough to see who is placing the corn of propaganda before them," Lowman concluded, "[and] every kernel should be examined."[139] And indeed, each and every "kernel" was going to be thoroughly examined by confused, but ever recalcitrant, southern segregationists in the unsettled aftermath of the September 1957 Little Rock desegregation crisis in Arkansas—the very crisis that brought about a major turning point in segregationists' overall massive resistance strategy.

CHAPTER 4

"A PEACEFUL PEOPLE HAVE BEEN TORN ASUNDER BY THE COMMUNIST CONSPIRACY"

The Little Rock Desegregation Crisis in Arkansas as a Turning Point in Massive Resistance

In several respects, the 1957 Little Rock, Arkansas, desegregation crisis was one of the defining moments in America's civil rights movement. With the values of American democracy at stake in a Cold War environment, federal troops, for the first time since Reconstruction, used their might to protect black civil rights in the South, demonstrating the federal government's resolve to bolster the "American way of life" in the face of southern defiance. Not only was the Little Rock crisis the first dramatic confrontation between a southern state and the federal government over school desegregation, but it also represented a pivotal turning point in white southerners' resistance movement to the civil rights crusade. After the Little Rock incident, the architects and practitioners of the South's massive resistance realized that their strategy of employing the revived theory of states' rights constitutionalism—or the doctrine of interposition—could no longer be counted upon to preserve the region's racial segregation.

One of the central figures in the Little Rock desegregation ordeal, who eventually ended up siding with the proponents of massive resistance, was Arkansas governor Orval E. Faubus. Elected as governor of the Peripheral South state six months after the Supreme Court announced its May 1954 *Brown* decision, Faubus had never been a fanatic segregationist prior to the showdown at Central High School, where the capital city's token desegregation process, devised by the Little Rock School Board, was to start in the fall of 1957 "with all deliberate speed." In fact, Faubus, the son of a known Socialist, John Samuel "Sam" Faubus, and a racial moderate in the South's contemporary standard, was an unlikely villain in the drama that unfolded over the desegregation of the city's all-white Central High School.[1] By the same token, the city of Little Rock was also an unlikely place for an all-out state-federal confrontation over public school desegregation. Though it may not have been a genuinely progressive southern city, Little Rock nevertheless showed a much greater degree of racial tolerance than did many cities in the Deep South states. Little Rock's relative racial moderation, for instance, was evidenced in April 1956 in its voluntary abolition of segregated seating on the city's public bus transportation system.[2]

During the summer of 1957, as the planned date for the desegregation of Central High School approached, white Arkansans' anti-integration sentiment surged. On August 22, the Capital Citizens' Council of Little Rock held a fund-raising rally and demanded that Governor Faubus protect the city's segregated school system. Invited to address the rally as featured guest speakers were Georgia governor Marvin Griffin, chair of the segregationist Georgia Commission on Education, and Roy Harris, mastermind of the equally recalcitrant States' Rights Council of Georgia, who "pushed him [Faubus] around" and delivered the "coup de grace" to the Arkansas governor's noncommittal posture on school desegregation, to borrow the words of Harry S. Ashmore, editor of the *Arkansas Gazette*.[3] Sensing that he was being forced to follow the destructive path of defiance by the die-hard segregationists who encircled him, Faubus turned to President Dwight Eisenhower's administration for assistance.

Responding to the Arkansas governor's plea, the Eisenhower administration decided, even if reluctantly, to send Arthur B. Caldwell, assistant to Assistant Attorney General Warren R. Olney III of the Department of Justice, to Little Rock to talk with Faubus on August 28, 1957. During this presumably secret conference with the federal government's representative, Governor Faubus expressed his fear of racial violence erupting over the forthcoming desegregation of Central High School and asked Caldwell whether he would be able to count on any federal assistance if the city of Little Rock fell into racial turmoil. The only answer that Caldwell was authorized to convey to the Arkansas governor was that President Eisenhower did not want his administration to get involved in local desegregation matters.[4] Two days after the conference in Little Rock, the Eisenhower administration issued a report on the supposedly confidential meeting to the press.[5] Feeling betrayed by the White House's unexpected disclosure of his secret meeting with the Eisenhower administration's delegate, the embittered Arkansas governor stiffened his attitude toward the federal government, declaring that it was "cramming integration down our throats."[6] After all, even in the Peripheral South state of Arkansas, any sort of "consorting with the federal government on racial issues" could deliver a death blow to the political ambitions of state officials.[7]

On September 2, 1957, the day before the planned desegregation of Central High School, Arkansas governor Faubus, justifying his actions with the theory of states' rights constitutionalism, became "the first southern politician to do more than talk about resistance."[8] After much hesitation, he threw down the gauntlet against the federal government by sending the Arkansas National Guard to Central High School, so that the "public peace will be preserved" in Little Rock. Those national guardsmen deployed at the high school would "act not as segregationists or integrationists," Faubus explained in his televised speech.[9] Faubus's overriding intention to halt the desegregation process at Central High, however, was obvious. The original desegregation date had gone by, and on September 4, the National Guard acted on the governor's orders and turned away the nine black students—the Little Rock Nine—who were to desegregate Central High School.[10]

As disturbing words and photographs documenting the incident proliferated in the nation's dailies, emotions ran high among segregationists throughout the South. Two weeks after the failure of the Little Rock Nine's initial attempt to enter Central High School, the Greater New Orleans Citizens' Council in Louisiana organized a rally to fire up the Arkansas segregationists at the Crescent City's municipal auditorium. Along with State Senator William Rainach, chair of the Louisiana Joint Legislative Committee and president of the Association of Citizens' Councils of Louisiana, the boisterous rally featured such vocal and volatile speakers as District Attorney Leander Perez of St. Bernard and Plaquemines Parishes and William Simmons from Mississippi, administrator of the Citizens' Councils of America. As a delegate from Arkansas, L. D. Foreman, pastor at Antioch Missionary Baptist Church who served as the "chaplain" of the Capital Citizens' Council of Little Rock, also appeared on the platform. But the words of Roy Harris from Georgia were what set the tone for the defiant gathering. The "race war" waged in Little Rock was "being engineered by Communists, Socialists, the pinks and the punks," he shouted into a microphone, "who have wormed their way into influential places in this nation."[11]

In the midst of the chaos and confusion, Governor Faubus visited Newport, Rhode Island, to confer with President Eisenhower face to face on the Little Rock situation. However, this September 14, 1957, meeting did not result in any practical and mutually satisfying solutions for breaking their legal and political impasse.[12] Finally, the task to resolve the deadlock and to render justice would be shouldered by the federal judiciary. On September 20, Judge Ronald N. Davies of the U.S. District Court for the Eastern District of Arkansas (Davies was then sitting in Little Rock on a temporary basis, serving as a visiting judge from North Dakota) enjoined the Arkansas governor "from obstructing or preventing" the desegregation process at Central High School "by use of the National Guard."[13] Facing the court order, Faubus went on statewide television and radio to speak to his fellow Arkansans. While he lashed out at Davies, stating that the judge's decision was both "unwarranted and biased," the governor nevertheless complied with the federal court injunction and voluntarily withdrew the National Guard from Central High School.[14] Having ended his seventeen-day military encounter with the federal authority—but having been unable to come up with any realistic way to balance Arkansas's "state's rights" with the Little Rock Nine's "civil rights"—Faubus hurriedly left Little Rock to attend the Southern Governors' Conference in Sea Island, Georgia. "He was reflecting the fears and the wishes . . . of a lot of his people," Judge Davies recollected years later, and the governor's sudden absence from Arkansas's capital at this crucial juncture inevitably created a leadership vacuum in Little Rock.[15]

With the removal of the National Guard, the desegregation process at Central High School resumed on September 23, 1957. Under the leadership of the Capital Citizens' Council of Little Rock and the recently organized pro-segregation Mothers' League of Central High School, bellicose white mobs surrounded the school. When the news came out that all nine black students had finally entered the high school, mob violence broke out. Faced with the worsening situation and in the absence of Governor Faubus, Mayor Woodrow Wilson Mann of Little Rock sent a telegram to President Eisenhower on the following morning and asked for federal military intervention. Thus, to protect the constitutional rights of nine courageous black students, Eisenhower, in the end, was compelled to federalize almost ten thousand men and women of the Arkansas National Guard and to dispatch some twelve hundred troops of the U.S. Army to Little Rock.[16] Faces twisted with fear and hatred continued to surround Central High School, which the American Institute of Architects had once designated as the "most beautiful high school" in the United States.[17]

Having crossed the Rubicon, President Eisenhower was now compelled to explain his course of action to the American people on nationwide television. In his address of September 24, 1957, Eisenhower offered three main justifications for his actions in Little Rock—the importance of "law and order" ("Mob rule cannot be allowed to override the decisions of the courts"); what the historian Mary L. Dudziak has termed a "Cold War imperative" ("Our enemies are gloating over this incident and using it everywhere to misrepresent our nation"); and the need to appease the white South. In an attempt to quell further rebellion from white Arkansans and southerners, the president appealed to their sense of decency. "The decision of the Supreme Court . . . affects the South more seriously than it does other sections of the country," Eisenhower said, "[but] from intimate personal knowledge, I know that the overwhelming majority of the people in the South . . . are of good will, united in their efforts to preserve and respect the law even when they disagree with it."[18]

As strange as it may seem, these very three pillars espoused by Eisenhower—to which John F. Kennedy would cling during the first two years of his presidency—were also adopted and used by the white South in a completely different fashion. In order to defend their social, political, and economic status and privilege, all of which were inextricably connected with race and caste in southern societies, white leaders and elites often appealed to "law and order." While portraying civil rights leaders, activists, and demonstrators as troublemakers, instigators, and lawbreakers, white southerners tended to regard those who were committed to the movement as grave violators and usurpers of local racial autonomy. Also, southern white leaders based their defense of racial segregation on their self-proclaimed decency and honor—a sense of honor that stemmed from picturing themselves as noble paternalists. In reality, however, they degraded their fellow black southerners as second-class citizens or less. In addition, southern whites obviously had their own Cold War imperative, contending that their black subordinates' civil rights struggle must have been part and parcel of a nefarious enterprise that, as Harris claimed, was "being engineered by Communists, Socialists, and the pinks and the punks."[19]

Unfortunately for President Eisenhower, his claim that he had "intimate personal knowledge" of the white South was soon proved to be unfounded. The moment after the president finished his nationwide address, Senator James Eastland told a group of reporters in Forest, Mississippi, that Eisenhower's use of federal troops in Little Rock had made "Reconstruction II official." "This is an attempt by an armed force to destroy the social order of the South," Eastland asserted, adding that, "nothing like this was ever attempted [even] in Russia." In the meantime, "hav[ing] just listened to the president's address" with "anger," a white mother of two young daughters (and a native of Arkansas) wrote to Eisenhower from Beaumont, Texas, where Texas representative Martin Dies had been raised. "I question you, Mr. President, about knowing the feelings of the people of the southern states," she vented her emotion, "[and] I say you do not know how closely you have struck in the homes of the southern people. You do not know how many tempers you have stirred in the southern states."[20]

On the following day, the *Jackson Daily News* in Senator Eastland's home state ran the shortest editorial that ever appeared on its front page: "TO THE PRESIDENT: (an editorial) NUTS!" Other Mississippi newspaper editors offered a few more words. "Maybe it is high time President Eisenhower abdicated, fired his cabinet, disbanded the Congress and set up an absolute monarchy," wrote William H. "Billy" Hight, editor of the weekly *Winston County Journal* in Louisville. And that "absolute monarchy" in Washington, D.C., Hight went on, was to be constituted "with [U.S. attorney general Herbert W.] Brownell on the throne and the members of the Supreme Court as chore boys." (Attorney General Brownell had filed an *amicus curiae* brief in the 1954 *Brown* case in support of public school desegregation.)[21] On September 26, 1957, two days after President Eisenhower dispatched the federal troops to Little Rock, Governor Faubus once again went on statewide television and radio to remind Arkansans that their beloved state was now "occupied territory" due to "the cleverly conceived plans" concocted by the federal government to carry out "the military occupation of Arkansas." "In the name of God whom we all revere; in the name of liberty we hold so dear; in the name of decency which we all cherish," Faubus asked, "what is happening in America?"[22]

This mournful statement by the Arkansas governor made it clear to southern segregationists that their massive resistance was on the horns of a dilemma. In the end, the Little Rock desegregation crisis taught white southerners that the federal executive branch had now joined forces, even if reluctantly, with the judicial branch to implement the *Brown* decisions and uphold the "American way of life" above the "southern way of life." And more important, for the first time since the Supreme Court's desegregation rulings, southern segregationists began to realize that the doctrine of interposition and strident invocations of "states' rights" would no longer suffice to sustain their all-white schools. The day after Arkansas became, in Governor Faubus's words, an "occupied territory," Senator Eastland addressed a Citizens' Council rally in the Mississippi Delta town of Belzoni. At the gathering, the officers of the segregationist organization symbolically wore black armbands, "mourning the death of states' rights."[23] In the late fall of 1957, as if to commemorate the regrettable passing of states' rights, the Association of Citizens' Councils of Mississippi produced a large number of rubber stamps bearing the words "Remember Little Rock." The stamps became popular among southern segregationists and could be obtained from the association's headquarters in Greenwood for two dollars each.[24] Meanwhile, an anonymous white Arkansan who identified himself only as "A Patriot" composed a poem entitled "The Battle between Ike and Faubus." After denouncing President Eisenhower as a race mixer and revering Governor Faubus as one who had stood tall to "uphold the rights of our dear 'Southland,'" the poem ended with the following verses: "Old Ike had won and felt mighty nippy. But God help their souls when they try 'MISSISSIPPI.'"[25] In the fall of 1962, during the Kennedy administration, the ominous prediction made by the Arkansas "Patriot" would prove to be more than just bluster.

In the wake of the Little Rock desegregation crisis (by which Arkansas became one of only four former Confederate states, along with Tennessee, Texas, and North Carolina, to admit a handful of black students into white public schools), Governor Faubus's public utterances and political behavior increasingly became characterized by a "blend of coded white supremacy and McCarthyism." And under the reign of Faubus, the "Three 'R's" in Arkansas seemed to stand for "Race Hate," "Rights Denial," and "Red Propaganda Boost" as a political cartoon appeared in the *Minneapolis Star* had suggested earlier.[26] To be sure, invoking McCarthyism to combat school desegregation and the civil rights movement was by no means limited to the Arkansas governor. After the Central High debacle, the white South's defiance "had to take different forms to be effective."[27] With the notable exception of some of the most ardent and defiant political leaders in Mississippi and Alabama (and, to a lesser extent, Virginia) who would continue to cling to the doctrine of interposition, southern segregationist ideologues increasingly relied on the use and abuse of anti-Communist rhetoric to defend and disguise their racial and racist practices. As it became ever more apparent, on the heels of the 1957 Little Rock confrontation, that states' rights ideology had lost its efficacy as a weapon in massive resistance, southern segregationists turned to strident cries of "Communist conspiracy" in their efforts to quash the civil rights movement. Following in Louisiana's footsteps, only after the Little Rock desegregation ordeal did other southern states—including Arkansas—earnestly begin to deploy anti-Communist rhetoric in their battle against desegregation.

Just less than a year after the Little Rock incident, on the eve of the August 1958 special legislative session, the Arkansas state legislature organized a special education committee, climbing on the bandwagon to desperately equate the Red Menace with black southerners' civil rights movement. Created on August 15 by House Resolution № 28, whose author was State Representative Paul Van Dalsem of Perry County, the Special Education Committee of the Arkansas Legislative Council was authorized to conduct public hearings to "determine if there is any subversion present" in Arkansas, which was "designedly creating and fomenting strife and racial unrest."[28] The thirteen-member Special Education Committee was composed of six state senators and seven state representatives with Representative Van Dalsem becoming its chair. State Senator Charles F. "Rip" Smith of West Memphis, who had served on the segregationist Arkansas State Sovereignty Commission (organized in February 1957), was chosen as the new committee's vice chair. Ready to allow "anything short of violence" to prevent the state's wholesale school desegregation, Senator Smith declared that "the time has come for the state to use all of its resources . . . to protect our way of life."[29] Meanwhile, Arkansas attorney general Bruce Bennett, one of the state's most recalcitrant segregationists, was instructed to exercise his subpoena power to secure "witnesses, documents and papers that may be of value" in conducting the expected committee hearings.[30]

Following the establishment of the Special Education Committee of the Arkansas Legislative Council, Faubus, who had just handily won the Democratic gubernatorial primary and thus had been elected to the two-year term governorship for the third time (with 68.8 percent of the total vote), called the extraordinary session of the state legislature to "address the race issue."[31] Convened on August 26, 1958, the special legislative session produced more than a dozen segregationist measures to add to the state's massive resistance arsenal. One of these newly enacted laws empowered Governor Faubus, in the event of federally forced integration, to shut down the affected public schools with the provision that the governor's action would need to be approved by the voters of the relevant communities within thirty days.[32] Also included in the Faubus-sanctioned segregationist bills was a legislative package aimed at the National Association for the Advancement of Colored People (NAACP)—the driving force of the efforts to integrate Central High School. Crafted by Attorney

General Bennett, the anti-NAACP legislative package, as its author would later publicly proclaim, was "designed to harass" and "to keep the enemies of America busy." In the eyes of the attorney general, anyone who was soft on segregation was a Communist who, as another Arkansas segregationist put it, was "too well paid off by [the] NAACP."[33]

On September 12, 1958, as if to subdue the mutinous posture evident during Arkansas's special legislative session, the nation's highest tribunal made another fateful legal decision. Previously, the U.S. District Court for the Eastern District of Arkansas had granted the Little Rock School Board a thirty-month delay in further integrating Central High School on the grounds of continued "conditions of chaos, bedlam, and turmoil" in the city.[34] In deciding *Cooper v. Aaron* and thus reversing the district court ruling, the Supreme Court held firmly that the constitutional rights of black schoolchildren could "neither be nullified openly and directly by state legislators or state executive officials nor nullified indirectly by them by evasive schemes for segregation."[35] Giving a "solemn warning" to Arkansas "as to the folly of Massive Resistance" backed by the doctrine of interposition, the Court made it clear that no state official could "war against the Constitution."[36]

Governor Faubus, who had steadily strengthened his ties with the state's segregationist camps, refused to retreat, and he immediately signed a proclamation closing Little Rock's four public high schools and called for a referendum on his action.[37] On September 27, 1958, the Little Rock voters sanctioned the governor's die-hard stand, inaugurating what would become known as the city's "Lost Year." During this year, the state (and the majority of the city's voters) deprived Little Rock's high school students—both black and white—of educational opportunity in the name of preserving Arkansas's segregated way of life. Not until August 12, 1959, did the Little Rock high schools reopen their doors.[38] After the results of the referendum were reported, Faubus duly reminded his fellow Arkansans that the Supreme Court, in issuing its 1954 *Brown* decision, had already been influenced by the authorities who "had been cited for pro-Communist activity" by congressional investigating committees. Now, in the face of the Court's *Cooper* decision, he raised the question as to "how high in the government the Communists had penetrated."[39]

Covering the flank of Governor Faubus was the equally defiant state attorney general. In the wake of the Little Rock school closure, Bennett announced his "Southern Plan for Peace" program, which aimed to restore "peaceful harmony between the white and Negro races" damaged by the recent Little Rock incident. Although it might have sounded harmless or even benign, the "plan" fell far short of advocating racial reconciliation or racial integration. The crux of the attorney general's "Southern Plan for Peace" lay instead in his determination to use criminal prosecution, economic pressure, intimidation, and other methods to crack down on the NAACP and other civil rights organizations. Sending the outline of his newly devised "plan" to lawmakers and officials in Arkansas's southern sister states, the attorney general asserted that the NAACP had been "at the heart of our racial problems" and that the only way for the white South to restore "peaceful harmony"—a euphemism for complete racial segregation—was to "neutralize" the NAACP. As Bennett succinctly put it: "No NAACP, no NAACP-inspired law suits, no federal court integration orders, no more Little Rocks."[40] The attorney general, who had begun to contemplate a run in the 1960 gubernatorial election, was determined to publicize and execute his "Southern Plan for Peace" during the expected public hearings to be held by the Special Education Committee of the Arkansas Legislative Council.[41]

At long last, fifteen months after the Little Rock desegregation crisis and after four months of preparation beginning in August 1958, the Special Education Committee of the Arkansas Legislative Council was ready to hold its hearings to "determine if there is any subversion present" in the state, which had suffered what the Arkansas segregationists considered a disturbing setback in its overall massive resistance strategy.[42] As a matter of fact, exposing the existence of subversive elements in the dishonorable Central High School ordeal was a grave matter of honor for most of these bruised segregationists. Coming to the aid of the Arkansas segregationists in their efforts to settle an old score with the integrationist forces was, once again, an unlikely messiah from the North—Myers Lowman, executive secretary of the Circuit Riders in Cincinnati. At the behest of the Special Education Committee, Lowman, who by then had orchestrated both of the public and closed hearings held by the Louisiana Joint Legislative Committee and the Georgia Commission on Education, promised to provide the Arkansas committee with three out-of-state "friendly" witnesses—J. B. Matthews of New York City; Manning Johnson, also of New York City; and Guy Banister of New Orleans.[43]

Precisely when and how Lowman's association with the Arkansas segregationists began cannot be fully determined, but as his personal papers housed at Stanford University attest, only a month after the Little Rock desegregation crisis, Lowman sent a letter from Tampa, Florida, to Leon B.

Catlett in Little Rock, a lawyer and a close friend of Arkansas governor Faubus.[44] Lowman was then investigating the NAACP activities in Tampa as a "secret investigator" of the Georgia Commission on Education.[45] Attached to Lowman's December 11, 1957, letter addressed to Catlett were a Matthews-prepared tabulation entitled "February 26, 1957 compilation of Communist related activities connected with the name Lee Lorch" and an information sheet regarding Lorch's wife, Grace. The Lorches, now residents of Little Rock, had been identified as "Communist" and "Communist courier[s]" by Martha Edmiston—on the strength of the same compilation prepared by Matthews—during the Louisiana Joint Legislative Committee's "Subversion in Racial Unrest" hearings nine months earlier.[46] Matthews would update his report on the Lorches in March 1958, six months after the Little Rock desegregation crisis, for the use of Lowman and the Special Education Committee of the Arkansas Legislative Council.[47]

Noting the white couple's involvement in the Arkansas State Conference of the NAACP, the civil rights organization's Little Rock chapter, and thus the Central High School desegregation, Lowman advised, in concluding his letter to Catlett, that Arkansas officials further scrutinize the Lorches' subversive records.[48] It is possible that Catlett forwarded Lowman's letter to his friend, Governor Faubus, and that it then fell into the hands of Attorney General Bennett. In mid-June 1958, two months before the attorney general and the legislative leaders organized the Special Education Committee of the Arkansas Legislative Council, Lowman visited Little Rock, apparently to hold a meeting with them and draw up a plan for the forthcoming public hearings of the Special Education Committee.[49]

From December 16 to 18, 1958, the Special Education Committee of the Arkansas Legislative Council held its hearings in the House chamber of the State Capitol Building, deploying those "friendly" witnesses provided by Lowman. For the occasion, Little Rock's NBC-affiliated television station, KARK, broadcast the hearings live "as a public service."[50] The Arkansas committee hearings commenced on December 16 with the opening statement made by Attorney General Bennett, who was to conduct the bulk of the previously charted questioning of the summoned witnesses. Despite the fact that "nowhere has so much peace and progress been enjoyed between the white and black people as that in the South," the attorney general reminded the committee members, "We are probably in the second most serious crisis that our State has undergone in its entire . . . history." Bennett then promised the state's citizens that during the ensuing hearings, it would be shown "beyond a doubt" that the "most serious crisis"—meaning "the race agitation"—in both Arkansas and the South was being propelled by a "communist conspiracy." In the attorney general's world, Little Rock and other Arkansas communities were programmed as "segments in the international scheme of the Russian Kremlin," where "communists, pro-communists, fellow travelers, [and] dupes" had been deployed to create confusion and turmoil.[51] And Bennett was determined to prove it beyond a shadow of a doubt.

Following his opening statement, Attorney General Bennett called his first witness, J. L. "Bex" Shaver, a former Arkansas lieutenant governor and the legislative secretary to Governor Faubus. Bennett hoped that Shaver's testimony before the Special Education Committee would prove that Arkansas had been troubled with radicals since the Great Depression. Most of the former lieutenant governor's testimony concerned the then already defunct Commonwealth College in Mena, Polk County.[52] And, in-deed, the college, along with the Southern Tenant Farmers' Union (STFU) organized in 1934, was one of "the most prominent examples" of southern radicalism in Arkansas during the 1920s and 1930s.[53] Established in 1923 as a residential labor school, Commonwealth College was originally located in Vernon Parish, Louisiana. Two years later, the faculty moved the small institution to Arkansas. Because of its open espousal of Socialist ideas and interracialism, however, the secluded school soon became the object of a witch-hunt conducted by the Arkansas Department of the American Legion, which pronounced in the summer of 1926 that the school was "heavily endowed by the 'Reds.'" This charge prompted the Federal Bureau of Investigation (FBI) to conduct probes on the college, and much later (after it became defunct), Commonwealth was included on the U.S. attor-ney general's list of subversive organizations considered to be manipulated by the Communist Party of the United States of America (CPUSA).[54]

As the influence of the STFU grew and as Commonwealth College's involvement with and support of the biracial union activities increased, segregationist spokespersons representing the Black Belt of East Arkan-sas in the state legislature became restless. In February 1935, when the Arkansas legislature created a five-member special legislative committee to investigate Commonwealth, Shaver, then a House member, served on the committee. The investigating committee reasoned that because "per-sistent rumors recur" to the effect that the college "permits the teaching of un-American doctrines," it was obligated to determine if Commonwealth College had been "used for the teaching of atheism, free love, and com-munism." The pro-segregation special legislative committee, in less than no time, not only found that these "persistent rumors" were true, but also ascertained that the college was advocating "complete social equality of blacks and whites."[55] Due to the Arkansas legislature's 1935 investigation, the college leadership's alleged Communist sympathies, and, finally, a state court order, Commonwealth College was forced to close its doors in 1940.[56]

After Shaver's lengthy testimony, which consumed seventy pages of the hearing transcript, Attorney General Bennett asserted that Arkansas, beyond question, had been infested by "subversive" elements whose primary objective was "creating racial unrest" since "at least 1925," when Commonwealth College was settled in the state, unmistakably implying that, as Louisiana state representative John Garrett had declared earlier, "Communism and integration are inseparable."[57] Notably, no troublesome remarks about Governor Faubus, who had briefly attended the college—a "discredited Communist-controlled institution"—in his younger days, were made by either the governor's legislative secretary or the attorney general.[58]

Having charted the course that he wished the Arkansas committee to follow, Attorney General Bennett, on the second day of the hearings, began his grand assault on his adversaries on December 17, 1958. Obviously, for the attorney general, one of the most vexing civil rights groups was the NAACP—his mortal enemy—whose legal maneuvering had brought about what Bennett somewhat mildly termed "the difficulty" in Little Rock—the Central High School desegregation crisis.[59] Other than the NAACP, Bennett's main organizational targets included the New York City–based Fund for the Republic; the Southern Regional Council (SRC) in Atlanta; the Arkansas Council on Human Relations (ACHR); the New Orleans–based Southern Conference Educational Fund (SCEF); and the Highlander Folk School in Monteagle, Tennessee. By exposing what the attorney general believed to be the true intent and the subversive nature of these organizations, Bennett hoped to discredit prominent civil rights advocates in Arkansas who had been giving aid and comfort to his enemy groups.[60]

Daisy Bates, president of the Arkansas State Conference of the NAACP who had served as a physical protector and a spiritual mentor of the Little Rock Nine, along with her husband, L. C. Bates, whose newspaper business (the weekly *Arkansas State Press*) would be forced to shut down in 1959, became natural prey to the attorney general. Another individual who faced Bennett's wrath was Harry Ashmore, who, as the editor of the *Arkansas Gazette,* had consistently opposed Governor Faubus's defiant stand during the Little Rock desegregation crisis. In addition, Ashmore had joined the board of directors of the Fund for the Republic, whose financial support was essential to the operation of the SRC, of which he was also a board member. The Atlanta-based SRC in turn donated a considerable amount of money to the ACHR, one of whose founders and incorporators was, again, the *Arkansas Gazette* editor.[61]

Neither were Lee and Grace Lorch excused by Attorney General Bennett. The name of Lee Lorch, who had joined the faculty of Philander Smith College, a historically black institution in Little Rock, as the chair of its mathematics department in the fall of 1955, had been well known to the pro-segregation House Un-American Activities Committee (HUAC) and the segregationist-controlled Senate Internal Security Subcommittee (SISS) since the early 1950s.[62] But it was when the Lorches unsuccessfully tried to enroll their daughter in an all-black elementary school in Nashville, Tennessee, less than a month after the Supreme Court's *Brown* decision that the southern states undertook in earnest their concerted efforts to red-bait him, beginning with Louisiana's Joint Legislative Committee.[63] To make matters worse for the white couple, Lee's wife, Grace, happened to be the one who came to the aid of Elizabeth Eckford, one of the Little Rock Nine, during the Little Rock crisis. On the day of her first attempt to enter Central High School, Eckford came alone to the school and was immediately surrounded by an angry mob. Feeling helpless, Eckford sat at a nearby bus stop.[64] As Grace comforted the frightened young girl, she told the encircling mob, "Six months from now, you will hang your heads in shame."[65]

Grace Lorch would pay a high price for this brave act. About a month after the Little Rock showdown, the Eastland-chaired SISS held its two-day hearings in Memphis, Tennessee, to throw the book at her. On October 29, 1957, she was duly hauled up before the congressional committee.[66] In the face of humiliating questioning and venomous verbal salvos fired by Robert J. Morris, the Senate subcommittee's chief counsel and a future president of the University of Dallas in Texas, Grace, realizing that she was dealing with a group of relentless sharks, repeatedly offered (on a total of six different occasions during her brief appearance before the subcommittee) a one-sentence response: "I am here under protest, and have been deprived against my will of my constitutional rights."[67]

Soft-pedaling and trying to charm his hostile witness, Senator William Jenner from Indiana, a Republican lawmaker and Eastland's predecessor as the SISS chair, asked Grace Lorch to cooperate with the subcommittee and "be enough of a lady" to answer his questions. But when she once again fired back with her now familiar statement, Jenner's patience ran out. "You are a troublemaker, aren't you?" the Indiana senator shouted into a microphone, pounding the table with his clenched fist: "You came in here yesterday just as a Communist functionary to attract attention and attract the press of this Nation, saying this committee was down here to investigate you because you had protected some colored girl over at Little Rock." "This committee at this time is not interested in integration in any sense of the word," Jenner said, attempting to spin the Little Rock incident as a matter of national security, "but we are interested in protecting this country against the Communist conspiracy that is out to overthrow and destroy this country." "Your statement you are reading there, would you like to file it for the record?," Subcommittee Chair Eastland chipped in, abruptly and impatiently asking Grace if she was a Communist. Setting aside her prepared statement, Grace answered: "We all know well what Mr. Eastland means by communism."[68]

Having been verbally abused, shouted down, and denounced as a "troublemaker" by the indignant Indiana senator, Grace Lorch neverthe-less stood firm in her protest against the SISS and its all-powerful chair, Eastland, who had taken the helm of the Senate Judiciary Committee during the previous year. "The only subversive activities I know about are the ones that Sen. Eastland and the rest of his crowd are engaging in," she observed, "and we've had a good case of them in Little Rock." Echoing Grace, the CPUSA-published *Daily Worker* editorialized the day after her appearance before the congressional committee: "James O. Eastland . . . is again dragging the name of the U.S. through the muck of racism. He has carried his caravan to Memphis to investigate 'Communism' in the South and will seek to put a 'subversive' tag on those Americans who refuse to honor his code of white supremacy." In the meantime, the *Washington Post* had something to say about the Indiana senator's ungraceful treatment of Grace. "Mr. Jenner seems to think," the daily editorialized, "that ordinary Christian kindness, if it is exhibited by a white person to a colored person, is Communist."[69]

Eastland was certainly determined to protect "his code of white su-premacy" by whatever means necessary, including the strident, if ground-less, cry of Communist-infested "subversive activities." Coming back to the nation's capital from the SISS's two-day hearings in Memphis, the Missis-sippi senator announced that his subcommittee had detected a "conspiracy in the Midsouth area" and that "there have been extraordinary security measures undertaken by the Communists to protect their identity and activities."[70] A month later, in releasing printed copies of the testimony taken during the SISS's Memphis hearings, Senators Eastland and Jenner, referring to Grace Lorch, asserted that "the Communist network in the South includes housewives."[71]

Meanwhile, in line with the groundwork laid down by Arkansas attorney general Bennett, who had implied during his opening statement that the purpose of the public hearings held by the Special Education Committee of the Arkansas Legislative Council would not be "fact-finding" but, rather, "fact-confirming," three more witnesses appeared on December 17 and 18, 1958. All of them—J. B. Matthews, Manning Johnson, and Guy Banister—were "friendly" witnesses previously recommended to the Special Education Committee by Lowman. Johnson, a black former CPUSA member and a "veteran" witness for the white South's racist cause, testified on December 18, the final day of the committee hearings. As an "expert" witness who had appeared before the Louisiana Joint Legislative Committee hearings in 1957 and had also assisted the Georgia Commission on Education, Johnson told the Arkansas committee members that "the NAACP and the Communist[s] are responsible for the racial turmoil and strife" and were using "Little Rock as a place where they can make a test battle." "The Reds are going to do all their devilish work in and through the NAACP," he continued, and the civil rights organization offered one of the most desirable fronts for the Communists operating in the South "because it has kept its skirts clean while wearing dirty underwear."[72]

Banister of New Orleans, a former FBI special agent who had also appeared before Louisiana's segregationist committee, followed Johnson to testify on December 18, 1958. He was fired from the New Orleans Police Department only a few months after his March 1957 appearance before the Louisiana committee and had subsequently opened a private detective agency called Guy Banister Associates in New Orleans.[73] Banister, whose assigned task for the Arkansas hearings was to demonize the Atlanta-based SRC, asserted that the real objective of the civil rights organization and its subsidiaries, including the ACHR in Little Rock, was to "create friction between the races." And "communism thrives" on that very friction, he concluded. Later, a few years prior to his death in 1964, Banister would begin to publish a fervently segregationist periodical entitled *Louisiana Intelligence Digest,* devoting himself to "the exposure of the operations of the Socialist and Communist organizations" in his native state and labeling the entire civil rights movement as "communist-inspired."[74]

Arkansas attorney general Bennett's "star witness" during the three-day hearings was Matthews, Lowman's most trusted ally, who had flown from New York City for the occasion. In the immediate aftermath of the September 1957 Little Rock desegregation crisis, Matthews prepared a fifty-one-page report entitled *Communists, Negroes, and Integration* for John A. Clements, public relations counsel at New York's Hearst Corporation.[75] Previously, both Clements and Matthews had worked for Richard Nixon, then a U.S. representative and a member of the HUAC, in his successful 1950 campaign to seat himself as a U.S. senator from California.[76] In the report's introduction, Matthews claimed that the Communists were "at work, with their customary fanatical dedication, in stirring up trouble in the field of public school integration in the South," and that they had relied "chiefly upon the support which they are able to command from misguided Southern liberals."[77] In late October 1957, only a month after the Little Rock incident, Clements sent an internal memorandum to President Richard E. Berlin of the Hearst Corporation, revealing his idea to widely distribute Matthews's report on "the Communist Party's efforts to capitalize on the segregation issue in the South" to an "awful lot of newspapers" throughout the nation. "I am sure it is the most comprehensive one ever prepared" on the subject, Clements wrote to Berlin, asking the Hearst president's permission to mail advance copies of the Matthews report to some of the nation's most influential anti-Communist crusaders.[78]

Clements's list of the prospective recipients of Matthews's report included U.S. senators James Eastland from Mississippi, Herman Talmadge from Georgia, and Harry Byrd from Virginia, as well as FBI director J. Edgar Hoover.[79] One of the actual recipients, Senator Eastland, wrote back to Clements with enthusiasm: "From my own intimate knowledge of the conspiracy, I can testify that this is a careful and accurate documentation."[80] This authoritative endorsement of the Matthews report by the powerful Mississippi senator, who now chaired both the Senate Judiciary Committee and its SISS, assured that the document would eventually fall into the hands of most of the segregationist leaders in the South, including Arkansas attorney general Bennett. Then, in February 1958, less than five months after the Little Rock desegregation crisis and ten months before Arkansas's Special Education Committee hearings, Matthews's encyclopedic knowledge of the American Left and his cooperative posture toward the white South were first officially tested and proved among southern segregationists. The Florida Legislative Investigation Committee invited him to testify at its public hearings in Tallahassee, where Matthews pointed out that the NAACP had "been the prime target of Communist penetration for the past thirty years."[81] Like Florida, Arkansas had been a source of

Matthews's paychecks before Attorney General Bennett embarked on his hunt for subversives with segregationist zeal. Among Arkansas's early financial contributors to Matthews was all-white Harding College, a Church of Christ educational institution in Searcy.

In 1948, George S. Benson, one of Harding's first graduates who had assumed the presidency of his alma mater twelve years earlier, inaugurated the National Education Program (NEP) on campus with a budget of thirty-two thousand dollars from the college funds.[82] Since his return to the United States in 1936 from a decade of "spreading the Gospel" in China, Benson had been deeply concerned that "Americans had lost their desire for freedom and their faith in their own destiny." "Once proud America," he wrote, was "losing its great heritage," and this conviction led him to founding the NEP as an anti-Communist and patriotic project.[83] President Benson quickly converted the "Harding-NEP complex" into a big anti-Communist enterprise (bringing an average of $1 million per year to the campus) that became, in the words of contemporary observers, "the academic seat of America's Radical Right."[84]

To "bring about a better public understanding of the American Way of Life" and "immunize our people to Communist infiltration and propaganda," the president of the Arkansas college and his pet project handled speaking engagements and produced pamphlets, printed "educational" materials, radio programs, and even motion pictures with an antilabor and anti–civil rights tint.[85] While Benson, in 1952 alone, had 144 speaking engagements in thirty-two states, the NEP's radio program *Land of the Free* was broadcast on 368 stations as of late 1953.[86] Around the same time, the NEP launched its *American Adventure* film series. The motion picture series consisted of ten individual episodes dealing with such topics as "The Structure of the American Way of Life," "A Look at Communism," and "Responsibilities of American Citizenship." These 16-mm, black-and-white films were available to the general public for purchase at seventy-five dollars each.[87] Later, the NEP produced a three-part movie series called the *War We Are In*. The second film in the series, entitled "Communism versus Capitalism," featured a lecture in which Benson talked about how the Communists had planned to destroy the cherished American way of life. One of the most ominous methods employed by the Communists to achieve their ultimate objective in the United States, according to President Benson, was to "work with the colored, join them in any problem they have, be their friend under all circumstances, make the Communist Party appear to be the party of the colored."[88]

Besides these audiovisual and other types of products that, as the NEP's booklet proclaimed, were intended to serve as "the tools with which you can become a civilian soldier in the war which atheistic Communism and its twin, Socialism, are waging against the free world," the Harding-NEP complex's most influential project was its Freedom Forum.[89] Officially inaugurated in 1949 and regularly held on the Harding campus and sometimes off campus, the Freedom Forum was billed by the NEP as "the Cradle of Education on the American Way of Life."[90] The Freedom Forum, in essence, offered a stage for "the nation's foremost authorities on the American way of life and its enemies" to talk about the virtue of American capitalism, the nation's socialistic trends, and the Communist menace before Harding College's student body and faculty members, as well as interested local citizens.[91] The success of the Freedom Forum owed much to Glenn A. "Bud" Green, the NEP's executive director (later associate director under President Benson after 1954) and a journalist by profession, who had served as the publicity director for the State of Arkansas for a total of seven years under three different governors.[92]

The mutually beneficial relationship between Harding College and Matthews, whom the NEP's executive director Green revered as a leading figure in "the great fraternity of anti-Communist fighters," began in the spring of 1951, almost eight years prior to Matthews's appearance before the public hearings conducted by the Special Education Committee of the Arkansas Legislative Council.[93] In early March, Green asked Matthews to help the NEP in compiling a "file documenting the records and affiliations" of some newspaper reporters and magazine writers who had "directed their fire at Dr. Benson."[94] Pleased with Matthews's thorough work, the NEP's executive director then invited Matthews to appear at the tenth Harding College Freedom Forum scheduled to be held in Detroit, Michigan, in September 1951. Green wanted Matthews to give a lecture on "the dangers accruing from infiltration into the various media of communications" made by the Communists, offering him an honorarium of two hundred dollars and travel expenses.[95] In extending this invitation to Matthews, the executive director explained to him that the grand objectives of the Freedom Forum rested upon "maintaining . . . basic American principles" and "exposing Communism and Socialism wherever it is found."[96] Having been "greatly interested in the activities of Harding College and President Benson for many years," Matthews eagerly accepted Green's invitation.[97]

Soon afterward, Executive Director Green again invited Matthews to appear on the Freedom Forum program, this time at Harding's Searcy campus in May 1952.[98] Nine months later, on February 13, 1953, when a testimonial dinner in honor of Matthews was held at New York's Waldorf-Astoria Hotel, the president of Harding College, Benson, was among the 280 invited guests selected by George Sokolsky, Matthews's trusted ally in their anti-Communist crusade.[99] On that occasion, Benson presented Matthews a congratulatory scroll prepared and signed by Harding's faculty members and students, as well as prominent citizens in Searcy, "with more than 500 names on it."[100] Matthews penned a lengthy thank-you note to President Benson on February 22: "Your generous tribute still rings in my ears. One of the most delightful surprises of my life was to hear George Sokolsky introduce you. . . . I do not know of any greater honor that could come to any man than to have the certificate of confidence which you brought from more than five hundred members of Harding College's faculty and student body. I shall cherish it to the end of my days." "Harding College stands like Benson's Beacon in a stormy spiritually uncertain academic sea," Matthews concluded, "[and] May God bless you and your noble band of teachers and students."[101]

By the time President Benson was invited to attend Matthews's testimonial gathering in February 1953 and thus was included in Matthews's and the Hearst Cooperation's anti-Communist sanctuary, the mutual trust and respect between Matthews and the Harding-NEP complex had become unshakable. Having become one of the NEP's most trusted and valued lecturers, Matthews once again traveled to Searcy to speak before the October 1953 Freedom Forum. To meet the NEP's expectation that he would deliver what Executive Director Green termed "the traditional Matthews talk," Matthews gave his lecture on the topic "What John Q. Citizen Can Do about Communism" at Harding College.[102] On October 23, after being introduced to the appreciative audience by President Benson as the keeper of "the finest files on subversive activities in this country," Matthews asked the Freedom Forum attendees to take heed of the danger stemming from "the Communist-front apparatus." This apparatus—"the outer fringe of the Communist conspiracy"—concealed the CPUSA's real objectives, he cautioned, "under idealistic-sounding slogans such as 'peace,' 'democracy,' 'civil liberties.'" All such phrases represented "perfect word traps for the gullible, 'liberal' suckers," Matthews asserted.[103] He also praised his former boss in the U.S. Senate, Joseph McCarthy, from whose committee (the Senate Permanent Subcommittee on Investigations) he had been recently compelled to resign: "Only one man, in my personal acquaintance, comes directly to grips with the question, uncompromising, with sufficient intellectual and physical stamina to take the gaff, and that's Joe McCarthy." "This country can be proud that it has produced a man of such unflagging energy," Matthews said of the Wisconsin senator.[104] As the registration fee for this October 1953 Freedom Forum, the NEP collected $115 from each conferee. Meanwhile, Matthews pocketed the usual two-hundred-dollar honorarium for providing his talk and expertise.[105]

In the meantime, Matthews developed his relationship with James D. "J. D." Bales, Harding's Bible professor and the NEP's "research analyst" on communism.[106] As a professor in the Bible Department, Bales offered a class, among others, on "Christianity and Communism" from which he was "determined to turn out a well-indoctrinated group of young preachers on the subject of communism."[107] The Bible professor, who eagerly put himself at Matthews's "disposal" for "chauffeuring" him whenever Matthews visited Arkansas, soon became a frequent visitor to Matthews's New York City penthouse.[108] The depth of their friendship can be measured, for instance, by the fact that when the Matthewses held a private gathering on New Year's Eve (which happened to be the birthday of his wife, Ruth) of 1958, Bales was invited to their penthouse party as the featured guest.[109] "He is an engrossingly charming personality with the first-rate mind," Matthews once wrote of Bales to the NEP's executive director, Glenn Green, "and he has made a deep impression upon some of my friends here."[110] Matthews's third and, probably last, visit to the Harding campus was made possible in early May 1957, only four months prior to the Little Rock incident, when Bales invited him to speak before the college's "students and friends."[111] Thereafter, Matthews asserted that the friendship and mutual respect forged between him and Bales would last "to the end of my days."[112] In fact, two months after Matthews passed away in July 1966, Bales would officiate at Matthews's graveside service in Lexington, Kentucky.[113]

The Harding-NEP complex's reliance on Matthews also extended to the political arena when, in the summer of 1954, a hotly contested gubernatorial election dominated Arkansas's political scene. Disgusted by the outcome of the recent Democratic primary, where the incumbent Governor Francis A. Cherry was defeated by a narrow margin, Executive Director Green of the NEP wrote to Matthews asking for assistance. "I was working with our excellent Governor Cherry, trying to assist him in his campaign for a second term," Green explained, "against a Socialist by the name of Orval Faubus who was trying to hide his Leftwing background." To help the Cherry camp's campaign with its strategy of raising the issue of Faubus's connection with Commonwealth College, Green and his NEP had gathered "the documentation on Orval Faubus' attendance" at the college and "his election to president of the student body." But with Faubus's triumph in the Democratic primary, Green was now inclined to support the candidacy of Republican Pratt C. Remmel, mayor of Little Rock. In search of more damaging information on Faubus that he could turn over to the Republican candidate's camp, Green solicited Matthews's help, asking him if he had "run across the name Faubus anywhere in files" and could "still track down any Socialist Party connection with the Faubuses." "I still have a keen interest in blocking a Truman-Roosevelt Socialist from becoming Governor of Arkansas," concluded Green, who had carefully avoided using the Harding College letterhead.[114]

By an odd twist of fate brought about by the Little Rock desegregation crisis, however, after the fall of 1957, Harding College became Governor Faubus's pro-segregation ally. Less than two months after the Central High School incident, the overwhelming majority of Harding's all-white students circulated a petition on campus asking the college's administration and board of trustees to end "the de facto policy of racial segregation" at the school. The petition was drawn up by the student body president, William K. Floyd, and was submitted to Harding's officials on November 10, 1957. "Deeply concerned about the problem of racial discrimination," the petitioners (a total of 946 signers out of the entire student body of 986) stated that they were "ready to accept as members of the Harding community all . . . qualified applicants, without regard to arbitrary distinctions such as color" and committed themselves to "treat such individuals with the . . . dignity appropriate to human beings created in the image of God." Both perplexed and outraged, President Benson made a special announcement during the daily chapel service, denouncing the petition drive as utterly "improper" and insisting that "the signatures were not an accurate expression of student feeling."[115] "The redbirds, the bluebirds, the blackbirds, they don't mix and mingle together, young people!," the president admonished the gathered students, adding that "Negroes in America have more cars than the people in Russia" as if to thereby justify black southerners' and black Americans' disadvantaged plight.[116] It would take six more years for Harding College to make a token integration of its student body. Having been influenced in part by a decision made by Abilene Christian College in Abilene, Texas—one of the three major southern Church of Christ–affiliated institutions of higher learning, along with Harding and David Lipscomb College in Nashville, Tennessee—to admit two black students to its undergraduate programs in 1962, Harding College finally took a similar step in 1963.[117] Just like Governor Faubus, as one observer has mentioned, Benson "failed to read"—or more accurately, refused to read—"the signs of the times and move with them" with perspicacious conviction.[118]

On December 17, 1958—the second day of the public hearings conducted by the segregationist Special Education Committee of the Arkansas Legislative Council—Matthews took the witness stand in Little Rock, fifty miles southwest of Searcy, where Harding College was situated. He was expected to confirm Attorney General Bennett's zealous and obsessive belief in "guilt by association"—the assertion that anyone or any organization that had anything to do with the civil rights struggle in Arkansas and the South should automatically be labeled as subversive. Following the attorney general's introduction of Matthews as "the outstanding authority on Communism and the Communist Apparatus" who possessed "the largest library on Communism in America today," Matthews was sworn in before the committee members as well as Green, now the associate director of the NEP at Harding College, who had driven to Little Rock from Searcy for the occasion.[119] Sitting close to Matthews was Ruth—his wife, secretary, and associate.[120] Attorney General Bennett, who would take the witness stand twice during the day, also sat at Matthews's side.[121]

After Bennett's introduction identifying him as an anti-Communist expert with "the largest library on Communism" in the nation, Matthews could not help boasting a bit. "I know the [H]ouse Committee has published the names of some 800 Communist and Communist-front organizations and these 800 are a mere fraction of the total number of Communist-front organizations in the United States," he said, "[but] in my own files, I have records which indicate there are at least 25,000 Communist-front organizations that have been set up in this country since the beginning of the Soviet Revolution."[122] Then, as the Arkansas attorney general expected, Matthews testified during the televised public hearings presided over by State Senator Charles Smith, the committee's vice chair, that the then-defunct Southern Conference for Human Welfare (SCHW) was "the first major thrust of the communists in the South" and that its successor—the SCEF—was as evil as its parent group.[123] He asserted that as "the vanguard of the pro-Communist integration forces," the SCEF had served "as a bridge between the Communist Party on the one hand and misguided Southern Liberals on the other hand." Choice words were reserved for the NAACP as well. Matthews explained to the committee members that, although the civil rights organization was not originally set up as such, "throughout the years[,] the Communists have so heavily infiltrated the NAACP" that "it has become a more effective agency for the Communist line than some of the Communist front organizations."[124] Eager to neutralize the NAACP, Bennett must have been elated by Matthews's utterances.

Besides these civil rights groups, Matthews went on, the various state Councils on Human Relations, including the one in Arkansas, and their parent organization, the SRC in Atlanta, had all been "infiltrated by communists and/or communist sympathizers."[125] Specifically asked by Attorney General Bennett to describe the objective of the ACHR, Matthews responded that its real purpose was "to promote the line of activities" approved and supported by "the Communist apparatus." During Matthews's testimony, the Arkansas committee also viewed the silent film taken by Ed Friend, who had been dispatched by the Georgia Commission on Education to spy on the Highlander Folk School's twenty-fifth anniversary workshop in the fall of 1957. Just before the film's showing, Bennett asked Matthews if, in his opinion, the Tennessee school had been "used for Communist purposes." "Yes, indeed," Matthews crisply replied.[126]

Furthermore, Matthews singled out Grace Lorch as a person on the blacklist who had been "engaged in Communist activities in the South."[127] Even after Grace's appearance at the SISS's Memphis hearings in October 1957, the Senate subcommittee continued to keep tabs on her. During the spring of 1958, the subcommittee's research director, Benjamin Mandel, gathered further information on Grace from the authorities in Boston and the Commonwealth of Massachusetts, where she used to reside—the Bureau of Criminal Investigation at the Boston Police Department and the Division of Subversive Activities at the Massachusetts Department of Public Safety. Mandel then turned some of the collected information over to his friend, Matthews, who, like Mandel, had once "found a home in Congress."[128] Reminding the segregationist committee members that Grace Lorch had "suddenly appeared to put on her act" in the midst of the mob surrounding Central High School during the desegregation crisis, Matthews observed that "Communists do not just happen to be in the neighborhood when trouble is brewing." "They are present by design and under instructions from their Communist Party masters," he elaborated.[129] Finally, after pointing out that Daisy Bates, L. C. Bates, and Harry Ashmore were all involved in three of the Bennett-designated enemy organizations—namely, the Fund for the Republic, the SRC, and the SCEF—Matthews concluded his testimony with what the attorney general had looked forward to hearing—that the Bates pair and Ashmore were "not worthy of the public confidence and leadership" in Arkansas.[130] For thus making Bennett's day, Matthews received, in payment for his "services," $960 of the Arkansas taxpayers' money.[131]

On December 18, 1958, after all of the witnesses had been heard and excused, Attorney General Bennett wound up by demanding that the ACHR either "disband or tell what they are doing." Branding the interracial council as a "hotbed of all those involved" in the integration movement in Arkansas, Bennett threatened to subpoena the group's records. Following the public hearings, the Arkansas committee went into an executive session. Coming out of the closed meeting, State Representative Paul Van Dalsem, the committee's chair, proudly told the gathered reporters that the public hearings had "definitely succeeded" in proving Communist infiltration in Arkansas. Meanwhile, the committee vice chair, State Senator Charles Smith, concurred with Van Dalsem, stating that he was fully "convinced" that the CPUSA was behind racial unrest in the state.[132]

Later, in issuing a summary of its public hearings, the Special Education Committee of the Arkansas Legislative Council self-servingly concluded that the Little Rock incident "was not something that just happened overnight." Rather, the committee explained, it was a deliberately planned and calculated scheme, with "the international communist conspiracy of world domination" being "squarely behind the entire shocking episode." "We feel that the people of the world are entitled to know," the segregationist committee concluded, "that a peaceful people have been torn asunder by the communist conspiracy."[133] In the eyes of Arkansas's massive resisters, "the Supreme Court, the president . . . and the NAACP" had all completed their transformation into "wicked communist agents bent on destroying southern traditions." (Interestingly, C. N. King, a black Baptist minister in Kentucky, "turned the tables on" Arkansas's segregationists by equating their defiance of the Court's *Brown* decisions with a communist plot. "Perhaps, and it could be possible," the minister asserted in late 1957, "that behind . . . the leaders of the White Citizens' Councils may be Communist money. It is a certainty that by their divisive tactic and defiance of established courts, they are playing into the hands of Communism.")[134]

In sum, the 1957 Little Rock crisis and its aftermath—during which Arkansas governor Faubus and his segregationist allies had "misunderstood the past, miscalculated the present and ignored the future," according to Harry Ashmore—certainly emerged as an important milestone in America's civil rights movement, demonstrating that the New South, like the Old South, continued to look upon the accommodation of black southerners as the region's "greatest single social problem."[135] At the same time, the desegregation ordeal—while marking the effective end of the use of the doctrine of interposition as a tactic with which to defend segregation— ended up exerting a great influence on the architects and practitioners of the white South's massive resistance, leading them to cling onto their conveniently molded anti-Communist thoughts and discourse in defense of the region's gradually crumbling segregated way of life. And in this transitional process, both Lowman and Matthews played no small role.

J. B. Matthews (*right*) examining collected "Communist evidence" with Democratic representative Martin Dies Jr. from Texas (*center*), chair of the House Special Committee on Un-American Activities (the Dies Committee), in Washington, D.C., on August 22, 1938. Standing with them is Democratic representative Joseph "Joe" Starnes from Alabama, a segregationist member of the House committee. (Library of Congress, Prints and Photographs Division, Harris and Ewing Photographs Collection, LC-DIG-hec-24990)

J. B. Matthews (*left*) and Myers G. Lowman in September 1957. This photograph, apparently taken at Lowman's home in Cincinnati, Ohio, bears Lowman's inscription on its back, which reads: "The Most (Matthews) and the More (Lowman) Divisive Methodists." (J. B. Matthews Papers, David M. Rubenstein Rare Book and Manuscript Library, Duke University.)

State Senator William M. "Willie" Rainach (*left*), chair of the Louisiana Joint Legislative Committee (the Rainach Committee), posing during the Shreveport Chamber of Commerce Goodwill Tour in Marksville, Louisiana, on April 23, 1959. Sitting with Rainach are Governor Earl K. Long (*center*), and former (1944–48) and future (1960–64) Governor James H. "Jimmie" Davis. (Henry Langston McEachern Photographic Collection, Noel Memorial Library, LSU–Shreveport Archives and Special Collections)

Myles F. Horton (*second from left*), Rosa Parks (*third from left*), and Septima P. Clark (*center*) taking a break during the Highlander Folk School's twenty-fifth anniversary workshop in Monteagle, Tennessee, on August 31, 1957. (Nashville Public Library, Special Collections Division, *Nashville Banner* Archives)

Arkansas governor Orval E. Faubus addressing the participants of a pro-segregation rally held in front of the State Capitol Building in Little Rock on August 12, 1959. (Library of Congress, Prints and Photographs Division, *U.S. News and World Report* Magazine Photograph Collection, LC-DIG-ppmsca-03120)

Arkansas attorney general Bruce Bennett presenting his analysis on the Highlander Folk School's "subversive" nature before the Tennessee General Assembly Special Investigating Committee in Nashville on March 4, 1959. (Wisconsin Historical Society, Archives Division, Highlander Research and Education Center Records, WHS-53011)

Ernest Salley, identified as an employee of the Florida state government, playing an audio tape that he had recorded as an "undercover investigator" for the Florida Legislative Investigation Committee (the Johns Committee). Listening to the tape with Salley in this February 10, 1961, photograph is Mark R. Hawes, chief counsel of the segregationist legislative committee. (Florida Photographic Collection, RC21815. Courtesy of the State Archives of Florida)

The morning after the nightmarish riots engulfed the University of Mississippi campus, James H. Meredith, whom Mississippi governor Ross R. Barnett blamed for being backed by the National Association for the Advancement of Colored People as a "communist front," heads for his class—American history—as the university's first black student on October 1, 1962. Escorting Meredith are James P. McShane, chief of the Executive Office of the U.S. Marshals (*left*), and Attorney John Doar from the Civil Rights Division of the Department of Justice. (Library of Congress, Prints and Photographs Division, *U.S. News and World Report* Magazine Photograph Collection, LC-DIG-ppmsca-04292)

CHAPTER 5

"RUN 'EM OUT, BOYS, RUN 'EM OUT"

Webs of Suspicion, Suppression, and Suffocation in Tennessee and Florida

In 1959, the cry of "Communist conspiracy" did not abate in Arkansas—the state where the first dramatic state-federal confrontation over public school desegregation had taken place. Besides providing impetus to the civil rights and integrationist forces, the outcome of the September 1957 Little Rock desegregation ordeal also taught the South's massive resisters that the use of states' rights ideology to defend segregated schools was both impractical and ineffective. Even after the pro-segregation Special Education Committee of Arkansas Legislative Council adjourned its three-day public hearings in December 1958, the committee's self-serving finding that "the international communist conspiracy" was to blame for Little Rock's "shocking episode" continued to resonate among Arkansas's white supremacists.[1]

Two months after the Special Education Committee concluded its hearings, Arkansas attorney general Bruce Bennett, who had held center stage in the segregationist committee's farcical play, implied in a February 16, 1959, speech that both the National Association for the Advancement of Colored People (NAACP) and the *Arkansas Gazette,* edited by Harry Ashmore, were serving as agents of a grand conspiracy devised and led by the Communist Party of the United States of America (CPUSA) in its effort to set up a "Black Republic" in the South's "Red Future."[2] In addition, as he had done during the August 1958 special legislative session, Bennett again introduced fifteen new segregationist bills into the 1959 state legislature in early February. Aiming to further neutralize the NAACP, the attorney general's legislative package was "designed to harass" and "to keep the enemies of America busy."[3]

On February 17, 1959, the day after Attorney General Bennett made his inflammatory speech, Representative Thomas Dale Alford from Arkansas took the House floor in the nation's capital to speak on "subversive activity in the South."[4] Previously, in November 1958, when the incumbent governor Orval Faubus was elected to his third term as Arkansas's chief executive, the militant segregationist write-in candidate Alford—an ophthalmologist who had sat on the Little Rock School Board—defeated Representative Lawrence Brooks Hays, an eight-term incumbent and a racial moderate, "riding the wave of popularity he had built through his segregationist position," to borrow the words of Alford's grandson.[5] Alford and his wife would write a racist "inside story" of the Little Rock mayhem entitled *The Case of the Sleeping People* in 1959, and their book would be duly included in the "recommended literature" designated by the Citizens' Councils of America.[6]

While prefacing his speech with the statement that he was "certainly not one of those individuals who looks under the bed at night to ascertain whether a Communist is hiding there," Representative Alford presented his argument on the House floor that "racial agitation is a major weapon of the Communist party." "The South, both white and colored, was happy with the evolutionary method of progress," Alford asserted, "but illegal and military enforcement of destruction of age-old social customs with overnight speed has played into the hands of the Communist Party." It had been recently and abundantly revealed, the Arkansas representative continued, that Grace Lorch, who was "'befriending and comforting' a young Negro girl" during the Central High School crisis, was a "Communist functionary." Having joined the camp of Arkansas attorney general Bennett and other segregationist anti-Communists, Alford proceeded to denounce Lorch: "Her yeoman service to the Communist apparatus was so great that she was sent to Arkansas . . . to help create racial incidents in my state." Alford also took aim at Ashmore, editor of the *Arkansas Gazette*. In the mind of the Arkansas representative, Ashmore was nothing but a "renegade journalist" who had "profited quite materially in the capitalistic line by writing detrimental articles about his native Southland."[7]

Despite these defiant postures taken by Attorney General Bennett and Representative Alford, in the spring of 1959, voices against the continuation of die-hard massive resistance in Little Rock began to be heard from the capital city's business circles. In March, the Little Rock Chamber of Commerce issued a statement, urging Governor Faubus to reopen Little Rock's high schools, including Central High School, which had been closed during the previous year to avoid desegregation. "The decision of the Supreme Court of the United States, however much we dislike it, is the declared law and is binding upon us," the statement proclaimed.[8] In the face of the emergence of an open-school movement represented by the "embattled ladies" of the Women's Emergency Committee to Open Our Schools (organized in September 1958 during the school closure controversy) in Little Rock and supported by the city's influential business leaders, who had raised doubts about the wisdom of continued defiance, Faubus and his segregationist cohorts now found themselves in serious straits.[9] Then the federal judiciary dealt the final and fatal blow, smashing any remnants of the validity of the interposition doctrine embraced by Faubus and other Arkansas segregationist officials. On June 18, 1959, a three-judge federal district court passed judgment that Arkansas's school-closing scheme was unconstitutional, ordering the Little Rock School Board to reopen the closed high schools.[10]

In accordance with this federal court order, eleven months after the city's uneasy "Lost Year" commenced and nineteen days ahead of initial schedule, the Little Rock public high schools reopened their doors with limited desegregation at Central High School and Hall High School on August 12, 1959.[11] With the basis of Arkansas's legal efforts to perpetuate racial segregation in its public schools having now completely crumbled, two hundred segregationists held a rally in front of the State Capitol Building, protesting the inevitable. Dutifully greeting the gathered recalcitrant whites was Governor Faubus. "I see no reason for you to be beaten over the head today, or to be jailed," the governor cautioned the crowd, "[and] that should be faced only as a last resort, and when there is much to be gained."[12] Or perhaps Faubus was cautioning himself, trying to come to terms with the hard fact that there wouldn't be "much to be gained" by prolonging the state's opposition to public school desegregation. After guardedly advising the rally's participants not to carry out any "rambunctious protest," Governor Faubus hurried back to his office.[13]

Similarly, the gathered protesters could do little to stem the tide of the capital city's long-postponed school desegregation except to show their utmost contempt and defiance by waving a host of placards that proclaimed with bold letters: "RACE MIXING IS COMMUNISM." Leaving the Capitol Building behind, the protesters began their march to Central High School, singing to the tune of "Dixie" as loud as they could: "In Arkansas, in the state of cotton / Federal courts are good and rotten / Look away, look away, look away, Dixieland!" Before long, however, the marchers were met and turned away by the city's police force. Leading the police was Chief Gene Smith, who made it clear that he and his subordinates were "not going to stand for any foolishness."[14]

In July 1959, one month before Arkansas's segregationists were forced to realize that they could not forever stem the tide of the changing world, two Tennessee writers, Wilma Dykeman and James Stokely, described the contemporary South as a "no-man's land of uncertainty and suspicion"—as a land infested with white fears that their long-cherished racial practices were about to crumble away.[15] In this "no-man's land" of Arkansas, segregationist pressures mounted against Lee and Grace Lorch, prime targets of Attorney General Bennett during the December 1958 public hearings held by the Special Education Committee of the Arkansas Legislative Council. Soon after Grace's appearance before the Memphis hearings conducted by the Senate Internal Security Subcommittee (SISS) in late October 1957, a burning cross was dumped on the Lorch family's lawn, and dynamite was planted under their garage door. As for Grace's husband, Lee, he was compelled to resign from Philander Smith College in Little Rock. Having been driven from four higher educational institutions (the City College of New York, Pennsylvania State University, Fisk University, and Philander Smith); hauled up before the House Un-American Activities Committee (HUAC) and the SISS; denounced on the floors of Congress as well as southern state legislatures; and ostracized by the Little Rock community, Lee and Grace Lorch moved to Middletown, Connecticut, in 1958, where Lee briefly taught at Wesleyan University.[16]

In the fall of 1959, the Lorches left their native country for Canada, and Lee secured a teaching position at the University of Alberta in Edmonton.[17] But even after their self-exile, the persecution of Lee and Grace Lorch by the Arkansas segregationists and their northern messiahs continued. Within a month after the Lorch family settled in Edmonton, Myers Lowman, the executive secretary of the Circuit Riders in Cincinnati who had arranged three "friendly" witnesses for the Arkansas committee's December 1958 hearings, tried to destroy the Lorches' credibility in their newly adopted country. In late November 1959, Lowman, with the consent of Arkansas attorney general Bennett, contacted an officer of the Royal Canadian Mounted Police in Alberta who was identified only as "Mr. Bingham" and mailed him a volume of "exhibits related to the Communist affiliations" of Lee and Grace Lorch that had been compiled by Lowman's trusted associate, J. B. Matthews of New York City. "In the United States," the Circuit Riders' executive secretary wrote to the Canadian law enforcement officer, "the two major programs of the Communist Party are race incitation and an effort to stop nuclear tests."[18] On October 28, 1974, fifteen years after the Lorch family found their new home in Canada, Grace passed away—almost exactly seventeen years after her appearance before the SISS hearings on October 29, 1957, at which she was branded as a traitor to the white South. "I would have paid a higher price living with my conscience if I hadn't done [what I did]" to help promote racial justice, Lee reflected years later.[19]

Although massive resistance in Arkansas eventually tumbled down, it took almost two decades after the Supreme Court's 1954 *Brown* ruling for Little Rock to desegregate all grades of its public schools.[20] As the civil rights historian David L. Chappell has quite accurately observed, the "very determination and viciousness" of the resistance movement "imposed too high a cost on southern society."[21] And in this respect, "the long shadow of Little Rock," to borrow the title of the memoir written by the civil rights activist Daisy Bates, certainly left its dark traces, and the 1957 desegregation crisis itself and what happened in its aftermath in Arkansas had much to do with explaining why the price of defiance was so immeasurably high.[22]

Before the dawn of the 1960s, however, Arkansas attorney general Bruce Bennett, while patting himself on the back for what he considered to be the success of the Special Education Committee's public hearings held in late 1958, remained determined to expand his segregationist "Southern Plan for Peace" program into Arkansas's sister states in the South. Aside from the NAACP, Bennett's overarching concern was the Highlander Folk School in Tennessee, whose civil rights–related activities and interracial programs had been intensely investigated by the segregationist Georgia Commission on Education since the summer of 1957. The Arkansas attorney general was convinced that in order to eliminate the NAACP from his beloved state, he must go deeper—to uproot and dry up the NAACP's allied institutions such as Highlander. Calling the school a "gathering place for Communists and fellow travelers," he was resolved to see to it that the Highlander Folk School in Monteagle—a "public nuisance" to not only Tennessee but also Arkansas—would be shut down.[23] In a speech in early 1959, Bennett officially warned the Tennessee state legislature of what he regarded as subversive activities at Highlander. "I would gladly come to Tennessee if invited," he proclaimed, volunteering his services to the Volunteer State's segregationists, "to lend whatever help I could to close Highlander."[24]

Encouraged and assisted by the Arkansas attorney general, in late January 1959, two Tennessee state representatives—Shelby A. Rhinehart of Spencer and Harry Lee Senter of Bristol—introduced a House resolution for the purpose of appointing a special joint legislative committee to investigate the Highlander Folk School and its involvement in "activities subversive to and contrary to the form of good government."[25] Senter declared that the proposed investigation of Highlander would "show the world" that Tennessee was not "going to let the left-wingers, the Communists, the do-gooders, and the one-worlders take over" the state. Lending his unconditional support to the House resolution in the Senate was State Senator David Barton Dement Jr. of Murfreesboro, who argued that the school in Monteagle was a "finishing school for Communists" that advocated "the intermingling of the races."[26] On February 12, with the blessing of the newly elected governor, Earl Buford Ellington, and the appropriation of five thousand dollars, the five-member Tennessee General Assembly Special Investigating Committee was formed to inquire into "the alleged subversive activities" at Highlander.[27] Composed of two state senators and three state representatives, the membership of the newly created Special Investigating Committee included Senators Dement and Lawrence T. Hughes of Arlington, and Representatives Senter, J. Alan Hanover of Memphis, and Z. Cartter Patten Jr. of Chattanooga. While Senator Dement was elected as the committee chair, serving as its vice chair was Representative Senter.[28] In addition, State District Attorney J. H. McCartt of Wartburg agreed to contribute his services as the investigating committee's counsel.[29]

As the Tennessee lawmakers busied themselves launching their frontal attack on the Highlander Folk School, the state's most conspicuous white-supremacist organization—the Tennessee Federation for Constitutional Government—rose to the occasion, pledging its unconditional support to the legislature. And in truth, not betraying the high expectations placed by the state's segregationists, the federation played a major role in assisting the legislative maneuvers to red-bait Highlander. Following the organization of the Tennessee General Assembly Special Investigating Committee, the federation issued a statement jointly signed by its some fifty officers and leaders. The statement, composed by Donald G. Davidson, chair of the private anti-*Brown* and anti–civil rights group, asserted that the officials of the federation "heartily commend and support" the state legislature's "thorough investigation" of Highlander in "the interest of the public welfare" of Tennesseans.[30] Davidson, a leading poet and a professor of English at Vanderbilt University in Nashville, was one of the twelve southerners who had penned *I'll Take My Stand: The South and the Agrarian Tradition* in 1930 in defense of a "Southern way of life against what may be called the American or prevailing way."[31]

Embodying a "Snopesean [referring to the fictitious "Snopes clan" depicted in William Faulkner's novels] perversion of the aristocratic agrarian tradition," the Vanderbilt professor, in the words of Ralph McGill of the *Atlanta Constitution,* "put on armor and rode out to challenge the snorting bulldozer dragon" and longed for the South's "agrarian tradition" and hence, the region's paternalistic and segregated black-and-white race relations. (It is somewhat ironic that Davidson's middle name—Grady—was bestowed in honor of Henry W. Grady, "the greatest of New South boosters" and the personification of what came to be called the New South Creed, which promised modernization and industrialization for the region in the late nineteenth century.)[32] When, in 1948, South Carolina governor Strom Thurmond ran for the presidency as the Dixiecrat Party's candidate, Davidson lent his support to Thurmond, successfully getting the South Carolina governor placed on the Tennessee ballot. Canvassing his colleagues and friends on and off the campus of Vanderbilt University for their backing before the November election, Davidson enthusiastically wrote to an acquaintance: "This is the first time in my life that I have had a chance to vote for a real Southerner, a decent and intelligent Southerner, who is brave enough to express views that I can accept."[33]

On June 30, 1955, in response to *Brown II*—the U.S. Supreme Court's implementation decree for the 1954 *Brown* ruling—that had been issued a month earlier, Davidson and a small group of his followers in Nashville organized the Tennessee Federation for Constitutional Government. Davidson was then chosen as the chair of Tennessee's most respectable pro-segregation group "composed of members of upstanding character."[34] Included among those of "upstanding character" who were "instrumental in founding" the new anti-*Brown* organization was Jack Kershaw, who served as the federation's vice chair under Davidson. A native of Missouri and a graduate of Vanderbilt, he was one of the most colorful, seasoned, and iconic American white supremacists of the twentieth century. An attorney as well as a talented sculptor, Kershaw would later represent James Earl Ray following Ray's conviction for the 1968 assassination of Martin Luther King Jr. in Memphis.[35] In late December 1955, six months after the establishment of Tennessee's federation, a host of southern segregationist politicians and officials gathered in Memphis and formed the New

Orleans–based Federation for Constitutional Government as a South-wide anti-*Brown* resistance organization. Serving as the model for this relatively short-lived regionwide federation was the Davidson-chaired Tennessee Federation for Constitutional Government. Launched prior to the birth of the Federation for Constitutional Government, which was closely associated with the segregationist Louisiana Joint Legislative Committee, the Tennessee Federation for Constitutional Government would outlive the South-wide federation.[36] While the Federation for Constitutional Government was active, Davidson's pet group became "loosely affiliated" with it, and the Vanderbilt poet also numbered among its members.[37]

In Davidson's "unregenerate" world, black southerners' civil rights struggle was "nauseating and terrifying." To his mind, the civil rights movement would eventually rob the South of its purity of white blood— the very "foundation of civilized order" of the region. The integrationist forces, composed of both blacks and whites and shamelessly ravaging the South's "civilized order," must have been "duped and manipulated" into deeds that resulted in "demeaning and punishing southern whites."[38] As his group's name suggested, Davidson's prime line of defense against racial integration consisted of states' rights constitutionalism and strict constitutional interpretations. But Davidson, a strong supporter of U.S. senator Joseph McCarthy, was also convinced that there were "socialist and communist influences" squarely behind the South's integrationist and civil rights movement propelled by "the NAACP and other intruders."[39] Increasingly, saving the white South's segregated "civilized order" became his obsessive mission.

Davidson's resolve to serve as an "intellectual" defender of Tennessee's and the South's segregated way of life was first tested in the late summer of 1956, when the efforts to desegregate a public school in Clinton, the seat of Anderson County near Knoxville, attracted national attention. In compliance with the Supreme Court's *Brown* and *Brown II* rulings, the local school board, in a token gesture, had previously decided to admit twelve black students (known as the "Clinton Twelve") who were to desegregate the traditionally all-white Clinton High School. On Monday, August 27, ten of the Clinton Twelve made history by joining some 750 whites to attend classes at Clinton High. Although Governor Frank G. Clement, Ellington's predecessor, was compelled to dispatch the Tennessee National Guard (six hundred troops with seven M41 Walker Bulldog light tanks) to the city to quell some demonstrations staged by white protesters, the desegregation of Clinton High School became a fait accompli, achieving the very first racial desegregation of a public high school not only in Tennessee, but also in the entire South.[40]

Meanwhile, the Davidson-chaired Tennessee Federation for Constitutional Government was busy trying to obtain a state court injunction to stall the Clinton High desegregation. However, in September 1956, the Tennessee State Supreme Court unanimously dismissed the federation's claim and declared, in the words of Chief Justice Albert Bramlett "A. B." Neil Sr., that "the question is fully foreclosed by the United States Supreme Court."[41] A year later, while the Central High School desegregation crisis was under way in Little Rock, Arkansas, some previously all-white elementary schools in Nashville were also desegregated by brave first-graders in September 1957.[42] One of the white demonstrators who gathered on the streets in Tennessee's capital to protest against the desegregation carried a sign proclaiming: "Communists Infiltrated Our Churches. Now It Integrates Our Schools."[43] "Well, we failed utterly," said Jack Kershaw, vice chair of the Tennessee Federation for Constitutional Government, resentfully acknowledging his group's powerlessness in the desegregation incidents in Clinton and Nashville.[44]

Thus, almost three decades after the publication of *I'll Take My Stand*, Davidson once again took his stand in 1959. This time, instead of resisting modern technology and industrialization, he sought to check the invading tide of racial and social change. And, as if to settle an old score with the state's integrationist forces for his dishonorable defeat in the 1956 Clinton High School desegregation incident, the poet was determined to join forces with the legislative Special Investigating Committee, fighting against what he regarded as the Communist-influenced Highlander Folk School. The legislative action, he hoped, could "finally get to the root of the troubles" at Highlander—a "seat of agitation and subversion." "The Tennessee Legislature has the right and duty to inquire," the February 1959 joint statement prepared by Davidson concluded, "whether there is a connection between . . . Highlander . . . and the disorders and incitements to disorder occurring at Clinton, Nashville, Little Rock, Atlanta, Montgomery, and other places" in the South. According to Davidson, the time had come for the state's massive resisters to determine if the Highlander Folk School and its officials should be subjected to "prosecution for creating a public nuisance and constituting a threat to the peace and tranquility of Tennessee."[45]

One of the signers of the joint statement issued by Davidson and his Tennessee Federation for Constitutional Government was a graduate of Vanderbilt University in his early thirties, Richard J. Burrow Jr. of Milan, Gibson County. A member of the federation's board of advisors and a regular contributor to the Citizens' Councils of America's official monthly publication, the *Citizens' Council,* Burrow was also active in the Anti-Subversive Committee of the Tennessee Department of the American Legion. On February 18, 1959, only a few days before the official inquiry into the Highlander Folk School was launched by the Tennessee General Assembly Special Investigating Committee, Burrow sent a telegram to Donald I. Sweany Jr., a research specialist at the American Legion's National Americanism Commission in Washington, D.C. (and a former staff member of the HUAC), asking his friend to "draft ten or more questions for counsel to ask [the Highlander director] Myles Horton."[46] In response to Burrow's request, Sweany, also a friend of the Matthewses, composed a set of twenty-three questions, which included such hackneyed inquiries as, "Are you now or have you ever been a member of the Communist Party?" and "Are you a believer in Marxist-Leninist ideology?" One of the other questions reflected the Legionnaire's mentality: "In the case of shooting war between the Soviet Union and the United States, would you wholeheartedly support the defense of our country against the threat of international Communism?" Expressing hope that his question list would produce "satisfactory as well as fruitful" results during the planned hearings to be conducted by the Tennessee legislature, Sweany asked Burrow to "continue forwarding us newsclippings on this important subject to our Washington office."[47] The National Americanism Commission of the American Legion, through its periodical, *Firing Line,* would soon brand the Highlander Folk School as a "notorious" and "undesirable" "interracial institution."[48] In the meantime, the Burrow-concocted and Sweany-compiled list of questions intended for the Highlander director was duly forwarded to the legislative Special Investigating Committee.

On February 21, 1959, the Tennessee General Assembly Special Investigating Committee met in a closed session held in Tracy City, the county seat of Grundy near Monteagle, where the Highlander Folk School was located. Following this gathering, the legislative committee held its preliminary public hearings at the Grundy County High School Auditorium on February 26 with two hundred spectators attending. Assisted by the agents deployed by W. E. "Bud" Hopton, director of the Tennessee Bureau of Criminal Identification, the committee members also visited Highlander's "grounds and buildings and examined the library."[49] During the Tracy City hearings, the committee summoned a total of some twenty witnesses, including May Justus as Highlander's unpaid secretary-treasurer, hoping to expose the school's affiliation with "Communist front" groups.[50] As "friendly" witnesses, some "respected" local citizens—a county judge, a county school superintendent, and a newspaper editor, among others—were also asked to appear before the committee. Sharing their appraisals of the interracial school, all of them told the committee members that Highlander's officers and staff had been involved in "some sort of communistic activity."[51] After meeting twice in Tracy City, the Special Investigating Committee then set the stage for its full-scale assault on the Highlander Folk School. On March 4, the segregationist committee commenced its two-day public hearings—which Reinhold Niebuhr, Horton's mentor, described as "shocking political blackmail"—at the War Memorial Auditorium in Nashville.[52]

For his part, Arkansas attorney general Bruce Bennett was now ready and eager to launch a frontal attack on the Highlander Folk School in collusion with the Tennessee state legislature. J. B. Matthews did not attend the Tennessee hearings as a "friendly" witness as he had done in Arkansas. But Bennett—representing Matthews—marched into Nashville in high spirits, armed with the derogatory information on Highlander generated and distributed by Matthews and Myers Lowman, as well as the biased findings about the school proliferated by the pro-segregation Georgia Commission on Education.[53] Also in the arsenal of the Arkansas attorney general and Counsel McCartt of the Special Investigating Committee was the list of proposed questions provided by Burrow of the Tennessee Federation for Constitutional Government, which dutifully sent its "representatives" to Nashville to have them observe the hearings. The first and principal witness subpoenaed by the Tennessee General Assembly Special Investigating Committee on March 4, 1959, was Myles Horton, director of the Highlander Folk School. Grilled by Committee Counsel McCartt for almost five hours on the stand, Horton steadfastly denied that either he or his school was pro-Communist or subversive in any way. During most of the questioning, Arkansas attorney general Bennett sat beside McCartt and offered suggestions in low whispers. When the committee members took over the interrogation, Bennett started moving around behind the committee table, feeding questions to them. At one point, when the committee's vice chair, State Representative Senter, ran out of questions, he had "his memory jogged" by the Arkansas attorney general.[54]

Also on hand during the Nashville hearings was Ed Friend from Atlanta, who had worked for the Georgia Commission on Education. During

Horton's testimony, the committee showed the silent film that Friend had taken when he "infiltrated" Highlander's twenty-fifth anniversary gathering in the late summer of 1957. When a scene depicting blacks and whites swimming together appeared on the screen, Friend told the committee members that it was his belief that any institution permitting such an activity in Tennessee was unquestionably subversive of "Southern tradition."[55] Committee Counsel McCartt also entered some still photographs taken by Friend at Highlander as exhibits. Asked by McCartt to explain the nature of one of those photographs, which seemed to depict a black man and a white woman embracing, Horton replied that it was a square dance step. To convince the segregationist committee, the Highlander director even had to use the committee counsel as his "partner" to demonstrate the dance step. The most dramatic moment during the March 4, 1959, hearings came when Horton and his attorney refused to allow the committee to enter the original charter of Highlander as an exhibit. When Horton insisted that a certified copy of the charter be submitted, the committee chair, State Senator Dement, instructed Sergeant Joe Williams of the Tennessee State Highway Patrol, who was serving as the committee's sergeant at arms, to forcibly take the original charter from Horton.[56] As the civil rights activist Anne Braden would later observe, Tennessee's legislative "circus" was ostentatiously continued in the name of inquiring into "the alleged subversive activities" at the Highlander Folk School.[57]

Following Horton's testimony, Bennett used a blackboard to present his analysis of Highlander's "subversive" nature and influences and its interlocking relations with what the Arkansas attorney general called "known Communists or fellow-travelers."[58] As he revealed his "evidence" to the segregationist committee, Bennett wrote Horton's name in the center of the blackboard. The Arkansas attorney general then studded the blackboard with a host of names of known civil rights activists and drew radiating lines to connect Horton's name with those of the other movement leaders, showing that all the names led back to the Highlander director. According to his analysis of the "Communist-directed southern conspiracy," the Highlander Folk School and its director were "flying in formation with a lot of people" and organizations whose individual and collective aims were "the destruction of these United States as we know them."[59] After Bennett's presentation, Committee Chairman Dement incisively asked Horton: "Will you deny that you're not the center of the Communist network in the South?" Horton initially refused to make any comment, but when Dement rephrased his question, asking Horton what he thought the Bennett presentation had proved, the Highlander director quipped: "It proves that you can write a name and write other names and draw lines between them."[60]

Arkansas attorney general Bennett at last saw his glorious moment come round. When asked by State Representative Senter, the committee's vice chair, if it was his indubitable opinion that the Highlander Folk School was "Communist-dominated," Bennett replied decidedly: "Yes, sir." After his presentation, greeting and shaking hands with the pro-segregation committee members before returning to Little Rock, Bennett issued marching orders to his fellow segregationists in Tennessee: "Run 'em out, boys, run 'em out. That's the main thing."[61] Horton was not so readily excused by the investigating committee, and his testimony continued on the following day.[62] The *Nashville Tennessean,* which had condemned the Special Investigating Committee for putting up a witch-hunting "smoke screen" to "harass and intimidate the institution because of its candid advocacy of integration," editorialized on the two-day Nashville hearings: "[The] two-act drama . . . had some interesting casting . . . in which the so-called 'villains' outperformed the so-called 'heroes.' . . . [But it] was pretty much the dud of advance predictions."[63]

On March 6, 1959, just one day after it concluded its Nashville hearings, the Tennessee General Assembly Special Investigating Committee submitted a fourteen-page report on its investigative findings to the state legislature. The committee, under pressure to produce before the legislature's scheduled adjournment in mid-March, composed its report so hurriedly that misspellings of the witnesses' names and even those of the committee members abounded. As had already happened in Louisiana, Georgia, and Arkansas, Tennessee's segregationist committee reported that it "found" what they had long before determined to be the case—that a great deal of "competent" circumstantial evidences was unfolded before the committee during its hearings, and that, in turn, led the committee members to the unquestionable conclusion that the Highlander Folk School was indeed a "meeting place" for those who had been shamelessly aided and comforted by the Communists.[64]

Named specifically by the Special Investigating Committee as "known Communists or fellow-travelers" who had been associated with Highlander were, among others, Don West, James Dombrowski, Aubrey Williams, Martin Luther King Jr., Abner Berry, and Pete Seeger. "It is significant," the committee report added, "that no witness other than Myles Horton had ever seen the American flag fly over this 'School' in the twenty-six years of its existence." Thanks to Arkansas attorney general Bennett and the cooperation rendered by the state's citizens, the Tennessee segregationist committee jubilantly asserted that the "existence [of] a very questionable activity on the part of the Administration of the Highlander Folk School and its members" was now brought to light.[65] And finally, in accordance with these findings, the Special Investigating Committee recommended to the state legislature that it pass a resolution which, in essence, would direct State District Attorney Albert F. "Ab" Sloan to find a way to revoke the state charter of the Highlander Folk School and, thus, to "run 'em out," as Bennett had advised.[66]

Heeding the recommendation made by the Tennessee General Assembly Special Investigating Committee, the state legislature wasted no time in adopting the suggested resolution on March 13, 1959, just a week after the segregationist committee issued its Highlander report.[67] "The State Legislative Investigation instigated by Atty. Genl. Bruce Bennet [*sic*] of Arkansas," Horton wrote to his friends and supporters in Tennessee, "spectacularly failed to prove that Highlander's stand on integration was subversive."[68] Despite Horton's optimism, the embattled Highlander Folk School was raided by the Tennessee authorities the very same month.[69]

On the evening of July 31, 1959, while Horton was in Germany attending an international conference on adult education, a posse of local and state law enforcement officers converged on Highlander. Directed by State District Attorney Sloan and reinforced by Grundy County Sheriff Elston Clay and Kenneth Shelton from the Tennessee Bureau of Criminal Identification, the authorities "discovered" a trifling amount of liquor at Horton's home and confiscated it. Because Grundy was a dry county—and even though Horton's house, as his private property, was not covered by the search warrant—they summarily arrested Septima Clark, the school's education director, who then happened to be conducting a racially integrated workshop, on the cooked-up charge of "possessing whiskey." A few school staff members who dared to ask the law enforcement officers if Clark could call an attorney were also apprehended for interfering with the officers, resisting arrest and, finally, "public drunkenness."[70] "The members of the legislative committee gave me information mostly on integration and communism," Sloan conceded soon after the raid, "[but] I wasn't satisfied I could be successful at that."[71]

In other words, the state district attorney himself was not fully convinced that the charge of "Communist conspiracy" leveled against Highlander by the Tennessee General Assembly Special Investigating Committee was adequate legal justification to raid the school. Nevertheless, the Highlander director was indicted on the bogus charge of the illegal sale of alcohol on the school premises and for being in violation of Tennessee's antiquated 1901 segregation statute. Oddly enough, the latter charge was later dropped. On February 16, 1960, Horton was found guilty of the former charge by a state court, which led the State of Tennessee to successfully revoke Highlander's charter. The school director appealed his case to the Tennessee State Supreme Court and then to the U.S. Supreme Court, but his efforts were of no avail. In early November 1961, soon after the nation's highest tribunal decided that no constitutional question justifying its intervention was involved, the Tennessee government confiscated the Highlander Folk School's land, buildings, and other property valued at $136,000 and sold them at a public auction. "There is not generally much good news from the Supreme Court for the South. But we can be pleased with the jurists' decision," a Birmingham, Alabama, daily editorialized with a tinge of sarcasm on October 10, 1961, the day after the Court declined to review the Highlander case.[72]

In late 1961, the Highlander Folk School was reborn as the Highlander Research and Education Center in Knoxville, demonstrating Horton's resolve that segregationists "could padlock the school but not the idea" embodied in Highlander.[73] The state's die-hard segregationists, however, continued to persecute the school. During 1963, for instance, the Nashville Citizens' Council, as a "public service," dutifully distributed a number of reproduced copies of an article entitled "Martin Luther King at Communist Training School," which was taken from the June 17, 1963, issue of the *Augusta Courier*, published and edited by Roy Harris, one of Georgia's most able and formidable architects of massive resistance.[74] "We were betrayers," Horton recollected years later. "We were white people who were betraying the white people. We were Southerners who were betraying the Southerners. . . . We were worse than the Communists."[75] Trespasses against southern segregation committed by white southerners were deemed an unforgivable sin. On another occasion, the Highlander director reflected: "They called us Communists, but they misunderstood. We've always been pursuing something much more radical than communism. What we've been after from the very beginning is democracy."[76]

Besides Arkansas and Tennessee, Florida—the Sunshine State—was the only Peripheral South state, in which a pro-segregation "little HUAC"— the Florida Legislative Investigation Committee—was organized for the purpose of discrediting the state's and the South's civil rights movement by raising the specter of an anti-Communist menace. Though the Florida committee's original aim—to suppress dissent regarding the state's segregated way of life—was to be drastically altered to weeding out homosexuals from Florida's higher educational institutions, the legislative committee, which would end up leaving an indelible stain on the state's reputation, also benefited from the assistance provided by Myers Lowman of the Circuit Riders in Cincinnati and J. B. Matthews of New York City.

Florida's tax-supported "little HUAC" was created on the heels of and in direct response to the NAACP-instigated, and ultimately successful, Tallahassee Bus Boycott—the third such boycott to take place in the South. It was preceded by the short-lived but inspiring 1953 Baton Rouge Bus Boycott and the better-organized and more successful 1955–56 Montgomery Bus Boycott. In late May 1956, nearly five months after Rosa Parks courageously initiated the Montgomery Bus Boycott in the Alabama capital, black citizens in Tallahassee began to attack one of "the most visible and humiliating symbols of racism in the city," challenging the segregated seating policy being enforced by the Florida capital's public transit authority.[77] Originated by two female students at Florida Agricultural and Mechanical University (FAMU), Carrie Patterson and Wilhemina Jakes, the organized bus boycott was launched with the assistance of Charles Kenzie "C. K." Steele, pastor at the Bethel Missionary Baptist Church and acting president of the Tallahassee chapter of the NAACP.[78]

Eager to probe into the role played by the NAACP in the Tallahassee Bus Boycott, State Senator Charley E. Johns prodded the state legislature to establish a new investigation committee. Johns was then one of the key figures of the so-called "Pork Chop Gang," a political label coined by James Clendenin of the *Tampa Tribune* to describe a group comprised of approximately twenty conservative and pro-segregation state senators from rural northern Florida.[79] Representing the Florida Panhandle, where the "sense of place, kinship, tradition, and ties to the land" was as strong as that manifested in Florida's two neighboring Deep South states of Georgia and Alabama, the "Pork Choppers" wielded disproportionate political power in the state legislature, affording themselves "the best cut of the hog."[80] And reigning over the state's "sleepy, rural, Old South" communities, to borrow the expression of the political scientist V. O. Key Jr., the members of the Pork Chop Gang worked to protect their constituencies' vested interests—whether economic, social, or racial.[81]

Johns—a native of Starke in Bradford County and a onetime railroad conductor—entered state politics as a member of the House in 1935. After serving in that capacity for two years, he was first elected to the state Senate in 1937 and later became the president of the legislative body in the spring of 1953. When Governor Daniel T. "Dan" McCarty passed away in September 1953, Johns assumed the duties of governorship. In the following year, he ran in a special election in a bid to complete the rest of the late governor's term but was defeated by Thomas LeRoy Collins, a state senator from Tallahassee and a relative racial moderate. Having served as Florida's acting governor for fifteen months, Johns left the office in January 1955 and returned to his seat in the state Senate.[82] A commanding speaker, he was gifted in impressing his audiences both inside and outside of the state legislature. "Listening to him make a point that was important to him," as one of Johns's former legislative colleagues has put it, "was like being in a country church and hearing an energized preacher denounce the devil and all he stands for."[83]

A month after the Tallahassee Bus Boycott commenced, some two hundred segregationists, meeting in the state capital, formed the Association of Citizens' Councils of Florida in late June 1956 to defend white Floridians' "racial integrity."[84] Meanwhile, the Florida state legislature, led by Johns, undertook to neutralize the NAACP in the state. Backed by his fellow Pork Choppers, State Senator Johns introduced Senate Bill № 38 on July 25 during the 1956 special legislative session, aiming to form a legislative investigation committee. Johns's bill summarily passed the thirty-five-member Senate with only one dissenting vote. On August 1, the House concurred with the upper legislative body on the bill.[85] The result of this legislative maneuvering was the birth of the Florida Legislative Investigation Committee, whose prescribed duty was to investigate "all organizations . . . [that] would be inimical to the well-being" of the Florida citizens.[86] In the name of preserving "the peace and dignity of the state," the newly organized legislative committee—the Johns Committee, as it was often called—would evolve into the final arbiter of race relations and civil liberties in the Sunshine State.[87]

Purporting to be the state's authentic defender of racial orthodoxy, the Florida Legislative Investigation Committee was composed of seven members—three legislators from the Senate and four from the House. For about eighteen months—from its inception until early 1958—the investigation committee was chaired by State Representative Henry W. Land of Orange County, with State Senator Johns functioning as the committee's wire-puller. The Florida committee employed a Tampa attorney, Mark Hawes, as its chief counsel. In addition, leading the committee's investigative activities was its chief investigator, Remus J. Strickland, a former chief of the Tallahassee Vice Squad.[88] As if to proclaim the segregationist committee's loftiness and dignity, its members adopted a set of "rules and regulations" governing their own conduct of committee business. While a strict policy of "neat dress" was imposed upon the members, counsels, and investigators of the legislative committee—reminiscent of the Federal Bureau of Investigation (FBI) director J. Edgar Hoover's stringent dress code requiring his agents to wear suits, ties, and white shirts—the guidelines also reminded them that "rumor, hearsay, . . . side remarks" could only be "destructive to all concerned." "This committee is neither an accusing nor a trial body," the members wrote, "but rather is an investigative arm of the state legislature."[89] The committee's actions, however, quickly began to deviate from its noble code of conduct.

The members of the Florida Legislative Investigation Committee soon assumed the role of the Sunshine State's "Cold Warriors," who were determined, in a Cold War environment, to suppress what they perceived as the Communist-influenced NAACP in the state. Steered by State Representative Land as its founding chair, Florida's pro-segregation committee began to accumulate files and records disclosing, as it asserted, that "the Communist party, its fronts and apparatus and other subversive organization" had been joining forces with each other to "agitate . . . ill-will between the races." Regarded by the investigation committee as the chief threat to peaceful relations between black Floridians and white ones, the NAACP functioned as the committee's principal enemy, even though the bill creating the Florida committee did not single out the civil rights organization by name.[90] In February 1957, the legislative committee, aiming to cripple the NAACP's credibility, launched the first in a series of segregationist anti-Communist public hearings.[91]

The Florida Legislative Investigation Committee initially focused on those associated with the Tallahassee Bus Boycott. Two of the first people summoned by the committee were Carrie Patterson and Wilhemina Jakes, the boycott's originators. Interrogated by Chief Investigator Strickland and asked to confess that a "Communist organization or the NAACP had put them up" to defying the segregated seating arrangement, both of them vehemently refuted the pro-segregation committee's conspiracy theory. Emmitt W. Bashful, a political science professor at FAMU, was another uncooperative witness who was forced to appear before the committee. Serving as the faculty sponsor for the NAACP's university branch, Bashful was among some twenty FAMU faculty and staff members actively involved in the bus boycott.[92] In the end, unable to uncover any evidence that the boycott was part of a plot orchestrated by "the Communist-influenced NAACP," Strickland and Chief Counsel Hawes filed their report on the matter with the committee, admitting that "the boycott movement appears to have been spontaneously started and does not appear to have been either carefully planned or executed" by any Communist-related forces. They also added, with apparent frustration, that the boycott was staged and carried out "with the NAACP having relatively little to do with it."[93]

Stymied in its efforts to discredit the Tallahassee Bus Boycott but determined nonetheless to make a connection between the NAACP and subversive activities (any activities intending to topple the state's racial norms were "subversive" in the committee's book) in the Sunshine State, the Florida Legislative Investigation Committee shifted its attention to Miami, where the largest and probably the most active branch of the NAACP in the state was located.[94] Initiating a six-year witch-hunt in 1957 to "show a definite tie-up between the Communist movement and the NAACP" in the city, the segregationist committee tried to tar and feather the civil rights group's Miami branch, which had filed a public school integration lawsuit during the previous year.[95] Miami, as one of the country's leading tourist and wintering destinations with a cosmopolitan population, was often thought to be "more northern and less southern" and more liberal, or at least more progressive, than the rest of the South.[96] In reality, however, Miami had been a hotbed of both white-supremacist activities contrived by the Ku Klux Klan (KKK) and strong anti-Semitism since the late 1930s.[97]

Serving as the president of the NAACP's Miami branch was Theodore R. Gibson, an Episcopal priest and the city's preeminent black civil rights activist. In 1954, the year of the Supreme Court's *Brown* decision, Gibson took the helm of the Miami NAACP and transformed his branch into a "forceful voice for racial justice."[98] Two years later, in 1956, under his leadership, the Miami branch successfully led the city's bus integration fight and filed a school desegregation suit, in which Gibson's own son numbered among the plaintiffs.[99] As "the symbol of the militant integration movement" in southern Florida, Gibson stood in the forefront of the legal battle to desegregate the Jim Crow city of Miami.[100] For this very reason, Gibson, along with his colleagues at the Miami NAACP, would be repeatedly hauled up before the segregationist Florida Legislative Investigation Committee under the guise of protecting Floridians' "well-being."[101]

When the 1957 regular session of the state legislature convened, the Florida Legislative Investigation Committee, having been established as an interim committee, was authorized to function for two more years. With this extension of the pro-segregation committee's life, State Senator Johns was selected to replace State Representative Land as its chair.[102] Around the same time, the association between Myers Lowman and Florida's segregationist committee became apparent. Lowman, then on a mission assigned by the Georgia Commission on Education, visited Florida on several occasions for six months beginning in July 1957. Assisted by the Florida committee, the Circuit Riders' executive secretary investigated the NAACP activities in the Sunshine State as a "secret investigator" of Georgia's pro-segregation state agency.[103] Lowman's perceived expertise in the fight against communism and his accommodation of the anti–civil rights movement soon became widely known among Florida's massive resisters. At the behest of Johns and his legislative committee, Lowman recommended J. B. Matthews as a "friendly" witness to assist the committee in its frantic efforts to pin down and manacle the state's NAACP organizations.[104]

Through Lowman's public relations skills and salesmanship, Matthews was afforded a grand opportunity by the Florida Legislative Investigation Committee in February 1958, where his encyclopedic knowledge of the American Left and cooperative bearing toward the white South were officially and publicly tested and appraised among southern segregationists for the first time. On February 10—five months after the Little Rock desegregation crisis and ten months prior to his appearance before Arkansas's Special Education Committee hearings—the Johns-chaired Florida committee invited Matthews to testify at its public hearings held in Tallahassee.[105] Before Matthews was sworn in as the day's witness, Johns offered a brief opening statement, explaining the purpose of the gathering. "We shall attempt," the committee chair remarked solemnly, "to determine the degree of influence that the Communist Party has succeeded in exerting on the actions of individuals and organizations presently active in Florida in the field of racial relations."[106]

Following this formality, State Senator Johns implied that the primary purpose of his committee's hearings was to be "fact-confirming"—an assertion that Arkansas attorney general Bruce Bennett would repeat ten months later. Matthews then testified to the effect that the Communists and their influences had inspired every major racial incident in the South—including the Florida capital's bus boycott—since the Supreme Court's *Brown* ruling.[107] Without wasting much time, Matthews cut to the chase and denounced the Florida committee's mortal enemy—the NAACP. The civil rights organization, according to Matthews, had been "the prime target of Communist penetration for the past thirty years." The "degree of success in penetrating the top leadership" of the NAACP by the CPUSA, he added, had been both "extraordinary and unparalleled."[108] Having testified to exactly what State Senator Johns wished to hear, Matthews submitted to the Florida Legislative Investigation Committee a ninety-nine-page list of alleged Communist citations of 145 national leaders of the NAACP.[109] Exhibiting his satisfaction, Johns expressed his unstinting gratitude to Matthews. His investigation committee, the chair duly mentioned, was "extremely fortunate" to have Matthews as a witness—a "man whom this Committee firmly believes to be the leading authority on the subject of Communism."[110]

Although Matthews's February 1958 testimony before the Florida Legislative Investigation Committee did not present solid evidence that any NAACP branches in the state had been infiltrated by the CPUSA, his guilt-by-association condemnation of the national NAACP had an immediate effect on the segregationist committee's witch-hunting strategy. About two weeks after Matthews appeared before the Florida committee in Tallahassee, the committee held its three-day public hearings in Miami from February 26 to 28. While announcing that his committee had accumulated, with the assistance of Matthews and Lowman, the names of some 150 "past and present" members of the CPUSA in Florida, Chief Counsel Hawes let it be known that the investigation committee's overarching intent was to crack down on the Miami NAACP and its parent organization, the Florida State Conference of the NAACP.[111]

During the first two days of what the *Miami Herald* termed the "frequently-riotous" hearings held at the Dade County Courthouse, more than a dozen of those subpoenaed "unfriendly" witnesses were cited for contempt. Among those who were cited was Theodore Gibson, president of the NAACP's Miami chapter. Appearing before the pro-segregation committee, Gibson denounced the legislative body, refused to produce his chapter's membership records, and walked out of the hearings. The white secretary of the Miami NAACP was another uncooperative witness. Ruth Willis Perry, a librarian and a native of New York, repeatedly refused to answer any questions put by Chief Counsel Hawes. State Representative William C. "Cliff" Herrell of Miami Springs, sitting with Johns, lost his temper in the face of Perry's defiance. "Anyone refusing to answer questions of this committee which is attempting to improve conditions in this state," Herrell shouted at her, "is not fit to be a citizen of the state of Florida."[112]

In the meantime, Matthews's appearance before the Florida Legislative Investigation Committee not only lent impetus to the state's anti–civil rights committee, but also spurred on southern segregationists as a whole to renewed efforts to red-bait the NAACP under the disguised banner of national security. For instance, the Georgia Commission on Education published Matthews's testimony in the form of two-volume report entitled *Communism and the NAACP* soon after he appeared at the Florida committee's Tallahassee hearings.[113] Although the civil rights organization was not a "Communist front" per se, the report read, a "special word concerning the NAACP is necessary." The report noted that "it must be observed that the NAACP has been a prime objective of Communist penetration" in the United States.[114] Chaired by Roy Harris, the Advertising Committee of the Georgia Commission on Education printed and widely distributed a total of 100,000 sets (50,000 sets initially and later 50,000 additional sets) of *Communism and the NAACP.*[115]

While the contents of Matthews's testimony taken before the Florida Legislative Investigation Committee were added to southern segregationists' canons, State Senator Johns, despite his expressed satisfaction with Matthews's appearance, was deeply troubled in private. If Matthews—the nation's "Mr. Anti-Communist," as John Flynn had called him—was unable to offer solid evidence linking the state's NAACP organizations with Communist conspiracy, Johns began to ponder, how could his segregationist committee legitimately continue to red-bait them?[116] Johns was also annoyed by Gibson's unabated defiance of the investigation committee. In November 1959, the president of the Miami NAACP was subpoenaed by the committee for the second time. The committee members and the chief counsel were keen to determine whether fourteen individuals, whom they had previously identified as Communists or Communist sympathizers, were members of the Miami branch of the civil rights group. But Gibson again flatly refused to comply with the investigation committee's demand to submit his chapter's membership records. Gibson's steadfast defiance of the committee earned him a conviction for contempt of the committee, and he was sentenced to six months in prison and fined $1,200. Robert L. Carter, an attorney of the national NAACP's Legal Defense Fund, would eventually bring a case against the Florida committee and fight for Gibson all the way to the U.S. Supreme Court.[117]

Although the Florida Legislative Investigation Committee failed to link the Florida NAACP with communism, it nevertheless continued to pour its energy and resources into probing what it believed to be the Communist-infiltrated civil rights movement in the state. Accordingly, Johns turned his committee's investigative attention to filtering out Communists and subversives from Florida's tax-supported higher institutions of learning. Insisting that integrationists were using these educational institutions as their bases for facilitating racial unrest in the state, Johns proclaimed that his legislative committee was resolved to purge "Red influences among the faculty" and get rid of "any Communist professors teaching in university."[118] In the fall of 1958, Chief Investigator Strickland turned to Matthews for help in carrying out this new mandate and had Matthews "run a close security check" on a number of professors at the University of Florida in Gainesville and other schools.[119]

The Florida Legislative Investigation Committee—Chief Investigator Strickland, Chief Counsel Hawes, and Chairman Johns, to be more precise—also requested Lowman's help. Asked by the committee to provide information on "certain faculty members of the educational systems" in Florida, Lowman funneled into the hands of the investigation committee lists of what he deemed the pro-Communist affiliations of professors teaching at the state's tax-supported universities.[120] Furthermore, the Florida committee subscribed to and relied upon a vast number of the Circuit Riders' publications put out by Lowman, which the committee praised as both "very informative" and "constantly fighting the Red movement" in the South. In preparing his typed report entitled "Report of Organizations, Publications and Findings Pertaining to Communists and Racial Agitation in the State of Florida," Strickland strongly recommended that other southern state agencies "assigned to the duties of exposing" the civil rights movement "in the field of Communism and Racial Agitation" subscribe to and carefully study the Circuit Riders' literature.[121]

During the 1959 regular session of the state legislature, the life of the Florida Legislative Investigation Committee was extended for another two-year period for the second time since its inception in 1956. State Representative William G. O'Neill of Marion County became the chair of the investigation committee, replacing State Senator Johns, who nevertheless continued to serve as the committee's real power broker.[122] When O'Neill took the helm of the committee, however, Florida's officially sanctioned massive resistance to the civil rights struggle, sustained by the investigation committee under the seemingly noble guise of anticommunism, suddenly took a strange turn. Having realized that his legislative committee was unable to demonstrate the existence of Communist conspiracy arising from either the state's NAACP organizations or the academic communities in Florida, Johns found another holy crusade just for his pet committee. The state senator's newfound mission was to weed out homosexuals and those labeled "immoral" among the faculty members and student bodies on the campuses of the University of Florida in Gainesville, Florida State University in Tallahassee, and later, the 1960-established University of South Florida in Tampa.[123] "We got rid of seventeen of them [homosexual faculty members] at the University of Florida and did not scratch the surface," Johns once recounted.[124] During the 1961 regular session, as if to confer the investigation committee with ex post facto approval, the state legislature not only extended the committee's life for two more years, but also broadened its organizational purpose. Through this imprudent legislative action, the Johns Committee was officially authorized to conduct investigations of "the extent of infiltration into agencies supported by state funds by practicing homosexuals."[125]

Like the similar state-sponsored segregationist anti-Communist groups that sprang up in other southern states, the Florida Legislative Investigation Committee was both a product and a barometer of the times, reflecting white Floridians' fears that their state was evolving in ways they could no longer control. In the end, by combing the state in search of integrationists, Communists, and homosexuals—all of whom were regarded as "inimical" to "the peace and dignity" of Florida—and by espousing "the apparent theory that the three were essentially the same," State Senator Johns and his committee exhibited the Florida segregationists' "bizarre novelty" and "political immorality."[126] At the height of the state's twisted version of McCarthyism, an anonymous Floridian wrote lyrics intended to ridicule Johns and his pet committee. Set to the tune of "Santa Claus Is Coming to Town," the lyrics read:

> You better watch out,
> You better not cry,
> You better be good, I'm telling you why,
> Charley Johns is coming to town.
>
> He's making a list,
> Checking it twice,
> Gonna find out who's
> Naughty and nice,
> Charley J. is coming to town.[127]

When Charley Johns "came to town" as the Sunshine State's Santa Claus, he was by no means empty-handed. He came carrying a big sack filled with surprises—insinuating documents rife with rumors, gratuitous investigative "findings," and coerced "confessions" made by frightened and involuntary informants—capable of destroying the lives of those whom the Johns Committee designated as "deviators" in terms of racial norms and sexual practices.

In the spring of 1963, more than three years after the Dade County School Board finally admitted a handful of black pupils to the formerly all-white Orchard Villa Elementary School in Miami in the fall of 1959, the U.S. Supreme Court reversed Gibson's contempt conviction.[128] On Monday, March 25, 1963, the nation's High Court found that forcing Gibson to disclose the Miami NAACP's membership records did not constitute Florida's "compelling and subordinating governmental interest" because the state had failed to prove the existence of a "substantial connection" between the Miami branch of the civil rights organization and any Communist or subversive activities.[129] While Roy Wilkins, executive secretary of the national NAACP, jubilantly noted that the Court's decision "underscored once more the Americanism of the NAACP," the ruling symbolized another "Black Monday" for the state's massive resisters.[130] Thus, Florida's official efforts to sustain what the historian John Egerton has termed "anticommunist white supremacy" in the Sunshine State eventually petered out.[131] In the process, however, as was also demonstrated in Tennessee, both the oppressed and the oppressors found themselves entangled in invisible and formidable webs of suspicion, suppression, and suffocation.

CHAPTER 6

"WE MUST IDENTIFY THE TRAITORS
IN OUR MIDST"

Red Hearings, Red Herrings, and Red Machiavellianism

in Mississippi

Only a year after the 1948 Dixiecrat revolt shook the national Democratic Party, revealing the depth and intensity of the white South's animosity toward the civil rights programs promoted by the national party, the political scientist V. O. Key offered the following somewhat caustic observation about Mississippi—the Magnolia State—in his *Southern Politics in State and Nation:*

> Northerners, provincials that they are, regard the South as one large Mississippi. Southerners, with their eye for distinction, place Mississippi in a class by itself. North Carolinians, with their faith that the future holds hope, consider Mississippi to be the last vestige of a dead and despairing civilization. Virginia, with its comparatively dignified politics, would, if it deigned to notice, rank Mississippi as a backward culture, with a ruling class both unskilled and neglectful of its duties. And every other southern state finds some reason to fall back on the soul-satisfying exclamation, "Thank God for Mississippi!"[1]

Though Key hastened to acknowledge that Mississippi "only manifests in accentuated form the darker political strains that run throughout the South," as if to warrant the distinction he observed, the state certainly exemplified, in terms of its culture and politics, the very essence of the South that W. J. Cash once described as being "not quite a nation within a nation, but the next thing to it."[2] Concerning the South's massive resistance, no state fought harder than Mississippi to thwart the racial integration process after the Supreme Court's 1954 school desegregation ruling.

The Magnolia State, founded on "the rock of racial discrimination," was destined to become the South's last citadel of racial segregation and discrimination, presenting "the greatest resistance to the progress of African Americans in the entire South."[3] Within the state government as well as the private sphere, and even on the floors of the U.S. Congress, Mississippi's political leaders and officials vehemently vowed to resist what Key had termed "external intervention" in the Mississippi way of life.[4] Those who dared to differ and even distance themselves from this cherished and segregated way of life were summarily labeled renegades—traitors who had "either sold out for cash" or had "been . . . Communist all the time," to quote the 1964 reminiscences of Frank E. Smith, a racially moderate former U.S. representative from Mississippi. "To understand the world, you must first understand a place like Mississippi," William Faulkner once said. And to fully measure the volatile substance of all-out massive resistance in the South, one needs to comprehend the venomous nature of the white establishment's ardor to defend their racial and racist practices in the Magnolia State.[5]

During the 1956 state legislative session—the first regular session held after the Supreme Court's 1955 *Brown II* decree—along with the segregationist bills devised by the Legal Educational Advisory Committee (LEAC), the Mississippi legislature was flooded with introduced resolutions, ranging from one that commended U.S. senator James Eastland for "his outspoken and unrelenting fight against the Communist Party and all un-American and subversive activities" (House Concurrent Resolution No 8) to one that praised State Circuit Court Judge Tom Brady, author of *Black Monday*, for "his invaluable services in promotion of the preservation of segregation in Mississippi and the South" (Senate Concurrent Resolution No 144).[6] However, the legislature's strongest determination to defend Mississippi against the "illegal encroachment" of the federal government—more specifically, the Supreme Court's *Brown* decisions—was expressed in its adoption of the interposition resolution (Senate Concurrent Resolution No 125) on February 29, 1956.

Introduced by the entire forty-nine-member Senate, Mississippi's interposition resolution explained that the state had "at no time, through the Fourteenth Amendment to the Constitution of the United States . . . delegated to the Federal Government its right to educate and nurture its youth and its power and right of control over its schools, colleges, educational and other public institutions and facilities." Noting further that a "question of contested power has arisen" between Mississippi and the federal government, it declared that the state possessed the rightful authority to "interpose for arresting the progress of the evil" being inflicted by the federal government. Finally, the resolution asserted the state's "firm intention to take all appropriate measures honorably and constitutionally available" to "void this illegal encroachment" upon the rights reserved to Mississippi.[7]

Inspired by state's official declaration of its right to refuse to recognize the validity of the Supreme Court's desegregation rulings, Mississippi's lawmakers now turned to organizing, in place of the LEAC, a permanent tax-supported agency to implement the resolve expressed in the interposition resolution—to "take all appropriate measures" for the purpose of perpetuating Mississippi's racial segregation and discrimination. Accordingly, exactly a month after the adoption of the interposition resolution, the state created the twelve-member Mississippi State Sovereignty Commission on March 29, 1956, as an executive agency authorized to "do and perform any and all acts . . . to protect the sovereignty of the State of Mississippi . . . from encroachment thereon by the Federal Government."[8]

In reality, though, the Mississippi State Sovereignty Commission, for all the pompous language describing its purpose, was expected to "maintain segregation in the State of Mississippi" and to pulverize "any . . . organization which is attempting to advocate integration," as the state agency would soon publicly acknowledge.[9] Standing out as the Mississippi commission's primary target among those organizations advocating racial integration was none other than the Mississippi State Conference of the National Association for the Advancement of Colored People (NAACP). Employing its investigators and mobilizing a number of black informants as its "eyes and ears" in the state's black communities, the Mississippi State Sovereignty Commission spied on NAACP meetings and the civil rights group's field secretary in Mississippi, Medgar W. Evers, who would be brutally gunned down by a white supremacist, Byron De La Beckwith, in June 1963.[10]

In the wake of the dramatic federal-state confrontation that occurred in the fall 1957 Central High School desegregation crisis in Little Rock, Arkansas, the Mississippi legislature moved quickly to strengthen the state's power to keep Mississippi's segregated way of life intact. Among the segregationist measures introduced into and passed by the 1958 regular legislative session was Senate Concurrent Resolution № 127, prepared by State Senator George M. Yarbrough, a future member of the Mississippi State Sovereignty Commission under Governor Ross Barnett's administration. Intended to cripple the formidable foe of the state's segregationist policies—the NAACP—the resolution, introduced on February 12, requested that the Mississippi State Sovereignty Commission intensify its investigations on the activities of the civil rights organization.[11]

During the floor debate in the Senate, however, an amendment to the Yarbrough resolution was offered and subsequently approved, changing the investigative authority from the two-year-old Mississippi State Sovereignty Commission to the Mississippi General Legislative Investigating Committee, which was about to become another state arbitrator of racial orthodoxy and the other wheel of Mississippi's chariot of segregation.[12] Created in 1946 by the state legislature, the Mississippi General Legislative Investigating Committee possessed broad authority, just as Senator Joseph McCarthy's Senate Permanent Subcommittee on Investigations did in Congress. The Mississippi legislative committee was charged with "the duty to conduct investigation of state offices, departments, agencies, institutions and instrumentalities, and of the administration and enforcement of laws," and it had, until then, virtually confined its probes to determining if there was any graft or corruption within these governmental entities.[13]

The final version of the anti-NAACP resolution sought by State Senator Yarbrough eventually requested "the General Legislative Investigating Committee to investigate the activities of the NAACP," whose leaders and members were "known to have been affiliated with various Communists and Communist-front organizations" that threatened "our traditional American way of life."[14] On March 19, 1958, two weeks after the legislature adopted its anti-NAACP resolution, thirty-five senators led by Yarbrough introduced a follow-up bill to give effect to the resolution. Aiming to curtail the NAACP activities in Mississippi, but without mentioning the organization by name, Senate Bill № 1973 would "authorize and empower the Secretary of State to require an investigation by the attorney general or the General Legislative Investigating Committee of certain organizations." These "certain organizations" were those that had a "national or state officer" who also belonged to any organization listed as a "subversive or communist-front group" by the U.S. attorney general, the House Un-American Activities Committee (HUAC), or the Senator Eastland–headed Senate Internal Security Subcommittee (SISS). The anti-NAACP bill would further authorize the Mississippi secretary of state to "require any officer or director or member" of the aforementioned "certain organizations" to file with his office a "full, complete, and true list of the names and addresses of all officers and members" of their respective groups. In the following month, the Senate bill was unanimously passed by the state legislature, and Governor James Coleman signed it into law on May 8.[15]

The change in the authority over the NAACP investigation from the Mississippi State Sovereignty Commission to the Mississippi General Legislative Investigating Committee that occurred during the deliberation of the anti-NAACP resolution in the legislature was partially prompted by the dissatisfaction expressed by some rabidly segregationist legislators, who claimed that the State Sovereignty Commission—Mississippi's segregation watchdog—had not been vigorous enough in investigating the civil rights organization.[16] In fact, though the Governor Coleman–chaired State Sovereignty Commission, by 1959, would have "gone into every county in Mississippi to determine just where NAACP chapters are located, who the negro agitators might be, and where the potential trouble spots in the state might be," the details of the state agency's investigative activities were largely unknown to the majority of the state's lawmakers, let alone the general public, reflecting the governor's low-key approach to the commission's investigative operations.[17] The change of the investigative authority probing the state NAACP was also influenced by the fact that the General Legislative Investigating Committee had been mandated, by the 1950 Mississippi legislature, to "make a study of un-American activities and report its findings" to the legislative body during the quickening period of national McCarthyism.[18] More important, the General Legislative Investigating Committee, not the State Sovereignty Commission, was the one that had first initiated Mississippi's all-out assault on the civil rights organization by establishing a liaison with one of the most prominent professional anti-Communists in the North—namely, J. B. Matthews of New York City, the nation's "Mr. Anti-Communist."[19]

A year earlier, when the Louisiana Joint Legislative Committee had launched the South's first "Subversion in Racial Unrest" hearings in March 1957, the Mississippi General Legislative Investigating Committee, then chaired by State Senator Stanton Hall, had dispatched some of its members to Baton Rouge to observe the public hearings.[20] The segregationist hearings, concocted by State Senator William Rainach as the Louisiana committee chair, were virtually orchestrated by the Cincinnati-based Circuit Riders' executive secretary, Myers Lowman, and the Rainach Committee made ample use of the documentary evidence compiled by Lowman's anti-Communist ally, J. B. Matthews. Soon afterwards, when the Louisiana committee began editing the hearing transcript—with Lowman serving as the chief editor—Rainach urged the Mississippi committee chair to "take similar action" in the Magnolia State, using public hearings to cripple the NAACP's reputation and activities.[21] Less than six months after the Louisiana committee's public hearings, the working relationship between the Mississippi General Legislative Investigating Committee and Matthews was forged.

In the summer of 1957, the new chair of the Mississippi General Legislative Investigating Committee, State Representative Russell L. Fox, mailed Matthews a package of the state's university and college catalogues, asking him to "find information" on the faculty members of those higher educational institutions and to determine if any of them were associated with the NAACP and other civil rights organizations. The Fox-chaired legislative committee was particularly interested in any new findings on the state's black college presidents, including those at Jackson State College and Alcorn Agricultural and Mechanical College.[22] Thereafter, Matthews's association with the Mississippi legislative committee would continue, culminating in his appearance before the committee as a "friendly" witness when it held its anti–civil rights public hearings in November 1959. Thus, while the Mississippi State Sovereignty Commission secretly deployed its own investigators and paid black informants as the segregationist agency's "eyes and ears" to snoop into the NAACP activities within the state, the General Legislative Investigating Committee, assisted by Matthews and Lowman, sought to crack down on the civil rights group by publicly revealing what Georgia attorney general Eugene Cook had called the NAACP's "ugly truth."[23]

Mississippi provided Lowman with an ideal setting for his role as a nationally recognized leader of Methodist laymen's anti-Communist movement. On December 14, 1954, seven months after the Supreme Court issued its initial *Brown* decision, 275 Methodist ministers and laymen from the denomination's all-white Southeastern Jurisdiction (covering Alabama, Florida, Georgia, Mississippi, South Carolina, and Tennessee) gathered at Highlands Methodist Church in Birmingham, Alabama, to take "effective measures . . . to restrain the efforts of those who are determined to break down all racial lines in the Methodist Church." What was born out of this Birmingham meeting was the Association of Methodist Ministers and Laymen.[24] Under this umbrella organization, its Alabama chapter became the center of the association's pro-segregation and anti-Communist activities. Composed of five standing committees overseeing organization, publication, circulation, finance, and women's activities, the Montgomery-based Alabama Association of Methodist Ministers and Laymen served as the

nucleus of the Methodist church's anti-*Brown* and anti–civil rights enterprises in the South.[25]

As in Alabama, the Association of Methodist Ministers and Laymen
attracted substantial support in Mississippi. In March 1955, three months
after the Birmingham gathering, at which the parent association was organized, some two hundred white Mississippi Methodists met in Jackson
to form the Mississippi Association of Methodist Ministers and Laymen.[26]
According to its periodical literature entitled *Information Bulletin,* the
Jackson-based association, which had no official relationship to the Methodist Church's Mississippi Conference, served as a "volunteer organization
resolved to respect and maintain racial customs in churches, schools,
[the Methodist] conferences and jurisdictions."[27] Thus, having become
the "Citizens' Council of the Methodist Church," the Mississippi Association of Methodist Ministers and Laymen also dedicated itself to curbing
the "teaching of integration, socialism, and communism in the Methodist church literature," placing racial integration and communism in the
same class.[28] The Mississippi group was composed of some of the most
prominent and vocal segregationists that the state could offer, including
John Satterfield, a Yazoo City attorney who had served as a president of
the Lowman-directed Circuit Riders, and Ellis W. Wright, president of the
Jackson Citizens' Council.[29] In January 1959, when Lowman's association
with Mississippi's white supremacists became evident, Hugh N. Clayton, a
distinguished lawyer in New Albany and a member of the Mississippi State
Sovereignty Commission, took the helm of the Mississippi Association of
Methodist Ministers and Laymen as its president.[30]

In the wake of the 1959 gubernatorial election, in which Ross Barnett, a
Jackson attorney, won the day with his vocal racist pronouncements, Mississippi, led by the General Legislative Investigating Committee, decided
to hold its own public hearings modeled after those previously conducted
by the Louisiana Joint Legislative Committee in March 1957; the Special
Education Committee of the Arkansas Legislative Council in December
1958; the Tennessee General Assembly Special Investigating Committee
from February to March 1959; and the Florida Legislative Investigation
Committee during the latter half of the 1950s. By launching their own "Red
hearings" and thus joining Arkansas attorney general Bruce Bennett's
"Southern Plan for Peace" program as the region's last state before the
dawn of the 1960s, Mississippi segregationists were eager to identify any
manifestation of Communist conspiracy lurking behind the civil rights
movement. And in so doing and by drawing "Red herrings" across the

track, the massive resisters in Mississippi were determined to thin out the "magnolias in pink" in order to protect the lily-white magnolias—the embodiment of white Mississippians and their racial customs—from the Red Menace. "We must identify the traitors in our midst," Barnett would soon vow, "[and] we must eliminate the cowards from our front lines."[31]

While the Mississippi General Legislative Investigating Committee busied itself with holding its segregationist anti-Communist hearings in late 1959, its chairmanship was assumed by State Senator H. B. Mayes McGehee. The legislative committee's former chair, State Representative Russell Fox, who had cultivated the committee's relationship with Matthews during the summer of 1957, was designated as the vice chair under McGehee. In addition, Mississippi assistant attorney general Dugas Shands, who had previously been associated with both the Louisiana Joint Legislative Committee and the Georgia Commission on Education, was assigned to the legislative committee as its counsel by his superior, Attorney General Joe Patterson, to expedite the proceedings of the anti-NAACP and anti–civil rights hearings to be held in the name of exposing subversive activities in Mississippi.[32] Assisting Shands at the hearings was State Senator-Elect Frank D. Barber, a future member of the Mississippi General Legislative Investigating Committee.[33] Shands and Barber had been well acquainted with each other in Washington, D.C., where both worked for U.S. senator James Eastland. While Barber served as a legislative assistant to the all-powerful Mississippi senator, Shands was the general counsel for the SISS—Eastland's segregationist stronghold.[34] As the Magnolia State's assistant attorney general and anti–civil rights strategist, Shands would defend Mississippi's Board of Trustees of State Institutions of Higher Learning in the early 1960s when James H. Meredith, represented by Attorney Constance Baker Motley of the NAACP, sought admission to the all-white University of Mississippi.[35]

On the afternoon of November 17, 1959, seizing a grand opportunity to connect the civil rights movement to the domestic Communist menace, Chairman McGehee announced that his Mississippi General Legislative Investigating Committee would hold what Wilson F. Minor, the *New Orleans Times-Picayune*'s Jackson correspondent, called Mississippi's "surprise hearing" on the following day. Asked by the gathered reporters about the public hearings' prime objective, McGehee declined to make public, for "security reasons," the names of the witnesses expected to appear before the committee.[36] Although the committee chair's announcement came rather unexpectedly, preparations for the November hearings had been under way since the late summer of 1959. By the time McGehee revealed his committee's scheme to hold its "surprise hearing," all of the "friendly" witnesses for the legislative committee had already been lined up.

The Mississippi legislative committee's star witness was none other than J. B. Matthews, who was expected to fly from New York and give his testimony on the first day of the planned two-day hearings. The arrangement for Matthews's testimony before the legislative committee was made by Myers Lowman of the Circuit Riders, who served as Matthews's conduit as he had done in arranging Matthews's appearance before the Florida Legislative Investigation Committee and the Special Education Committee of the Arkansas Legislative Council in February and December 1958. "I suppose it is confidential, but it looks as though we may be coming to Mississippi in November," Matthews's wife, Ruth, wrote to William Simmons, administrator of the Citizens' Councils of America and one of the Magnolia State's segregationist kingpins, in October 1959: "You probably know about it or, if not, can guess [why we are coming]."[37]

Besides Matthews as the sole out-of-state witness, two white Mississippians had been invited to take the stand as "friendly" witnesses. One of them was Zack J. Van Landingham, chief investigator of the Mississippi State Sovereignty Commission. A former agent of the Federal Bureau of Investigation (FBI) who had served at one time as an administrative assistant to Director J. Edgar Hoover, Van Landingham was instrumental in devising a filing system for the segregation watchdog agency's accumulating investigative records. He organized the commission files using a classification system consisting of thirteen subject categories, including "Informants," "Integration Organizations," "Race Agitators," "School Integration," and "Subversion."[38] By the early summer of 1959, the State Sovereignty Commission, thanks to Van Landingham's initiative, had also created some four thousand index cards "cataloguing information in several hundred files." Among those files were a number of investigative reports identifying the "NAACP agitators" in Mississippi.[39]

Two months before the Mississippi legislative committee's public hearings, Van Landingham was invited by Chairman McGehee to attend the committee's executive meeting held on September 15, 1959. At the meeting, the State Sovereignty Commission's investigator was informed that the General Legislative Investigating Committee had "for sometime been working on a project" to organize its public hearings similar to those which had "been held in Louisiana, Arkansas, and other Southern States" to demonstrate "the tie-in between Communism and the NAACP."[40] On November 13, just five days before the planned hearings were to commence, the McGehee-chaired legislative committee, which had been "securing information from the files" of the Mississippi State Sovereignty Commission, officially asked Van Landingham to testify before the committee. Assistant Attorney General Shands, who was expected to direct the hearings, courteously assured the State Sovereignty Commission investigator that "no question would be asked which would 'put either me [Van Landingham] or the Sovereignty Commission on the spot.'"[41] Along with Van Landingham, another former FBI special agent—John D. Sullivan—had been standing by to appear before the legislative committee. The operator of the Delta Investigative Bureau (later the Delta Detective Agency) in Vicksburg, Sullivan would soon be hired by the State Sovereignty Commission as one of its private eyes.[42]

True to the short advance notice given on the previous day, Chairman McGehee of the Mississippi General Legislative Investigating Committee opened its rarely held public hearings on November 18, 1959, in the House of Representatives chamber in Jackson. Before taking testimony, McGehee revealed to the gathered audience and the press what they had already surmised—that the purpose of his committee's two-day hearings would be to "determine to what extent, if any, un-American or subversive activities have been and are now conducted within the State of Mississippi."[43] Listening attentively to the committee chair's opening statement was Matthews. He was accompanied by his wife and "secretary," Ruth Matthews, who was also under subpoena.[44] In the audience to assist the Matthewses was Lowman, who, two weeks earlier, had been the featured speaker at a public dinner in the Mississippi capital. The dinner, held at the King Edward Hotel on November 3, was sponsored by the National Defense Council of the Mississippi Society of the Daughters of the American Revolution (DAR), and tickets for the gathering were sold to the interested general public for $3.75 per plate. "Communists headquartered at key points in the South have aimed a death blow at Mississippi," Lowman asserted in a fiery speech perhaps intended to serve as the outrider for the committee hearings' procession.[45] A group of women representing the National Defense Council of Mississippi's DAR, led by its chair, Mrs. Harry A. Alexander (Edna Whitfield Alexander) of Grenada, was dutifully present in the House chamber to hear Matthews's testimony.[46]

Furthermore, sitting next to Lowman in the audience was the bigwig of the entire Citizens' Council movement, William Simmons of Jackson.[47] The association between Simmons and Matthews had been forged four years earlier through the intercession of Lee R. Pennington, director of the National Americanism Commission of the American Legion in Washington, D.C.[48] "We in the South are now distressed and concerned about the agitation by Communist-fronters and fellow travelers among the good Negroes," Simmons wrote to Matthews on September 6, 1955, three months after the nation's highest court announced its *Brown II* ruling. The immediate cause of this deplorable situation, according to Simmons, was the Supreme Court's *Brown* decisions. He contended that these desegregation rulings had "given the subversives a powerful weapon with which to disrupt the South, and which they are not slow to use." Simmons further explained to Matthews that his group had endeavored to "handle this complex and difficult situation fairly and peaceably" but that it was being "hampered by the lack of expert knowledge on the personal backgrounds of many of the radical leaders." Soliciting Matthews's assistance in advancing the Citizens' Council's cause, Simmons then asked Matthews if he "could in good conscience work with us in exposing the records of the agitators who are raising so much racket about 'civil rights' but who are interested in the Southern Negro only as a tool."[49]

A week later, on September 12, 1955, Matthews wrote back to Simmons, thanking him for what Matthews considered to be a "very thoughtful and intelligent letter." Apparently impressed by Simmons's correspondence, which demonstrated to Matthews that Simmons was "not one of the so-called 'crackpot fringe,'" Matthews agreed to offer his services to the Simmons-led segregationist organization. The relationship between the Citizens' Council and Matthews, however, should be "strictly confidential," Matthews reminded the Council administrator, adding, "This is for our mutual protection."[50] Thereafter, immediately following the Louisiana Joint Legislative Committee's pioneering "Subversion in Racial Unrest" hearings held in March 1957, Simmons visited the Matthewses in New York City for the first time, accompanied by the Circuit Riders' executive secretary, Lowman.[51]

The triangular association among Matthews, Lowman, and Simmons was molded with Simmons's visit to the Matthewses' residence, where Simmons was thoroughly impressed with "the vast amount of painstaking research" conducted by Matthews.[52] "We greatly appreciate Myers' [Myers Lowman's] bringing you to see us," Matthews cordially replied to Simmons's thank-you letter on March 24, 1957.[53] Six months passed, and in early September 1957 when the Little Rock desegregation crisis was making headlines, Simmons and his wife, Becky, flew to Cincinnati to spend some time with the Lowmans, where Matthews also joined them.[54] Subsequently, when Matthews appeared before the Florida Legislative Investigation Committee's public hearings on February 10, 1958, Simmons flew from Jackson to Tallahassee so that he and Lowman could observe Matthews's testimony together.[55] "You did a tremendous job for the Florida hearing," Simmons later commended Matthews.[56]

On November 18, 1959, measuring up to the high expectations of Lowman, Simmons, Chairman McGehee, and his Mississippi General Legislative Investigating Committee, Matthews took the witness stand for an hour and a half.[57] "The full force of the organizing genius of the Communist Party and its members is being brought to bear upon this question of integration," Matthews, now the most trusted anti-Communist witness among the southern segregationist circles both in name and reality, authoritatively began his testimony:

> This is not because the Communists themselves desire to recognize the social relationships of the whites and Negroes of the United States. On the contrary, the offensive which the Communists have launched against the social relationships of the Southern community is based upon a desire to create trouble. The Communists[,] to put it in a colloquial sort of way, are experts at fishing in troubled waters.
>
> The Communists are aware that they have an issue handed them on a silver platter by the Supreme Court's decision of May 17, 1954, an issue on which they can agitate until Doom's day.[58]

One of the most notable and notorious "experts at fishing in troubled waters," according to Matthews, was Grace Lorch, who had come to the rescue of a black student, Elizabeth Eckford, during the September 1957 Little Rock desegregation crisis. "Well, now, there's absolutely no risk in stating that Grace Lorch was planted by the Communists on that street corner for the express purpose of creating an incident—an incident of any kind that would get a headline," Matthews mentioned, essentially repeating the testimony that he had given almost a year earlier at the public hearings held by the Special Education Committee of the Arkansas Legislative Council. "She was not there for the protection of the little girl" or for the cause of the civil rights movement, he added.[59]

Matthews then asserted that "the organizing genius" for deceiving black southerners, as well as white liberals and moderates, of the Communist Party of the United States of America (CPUSA) was clearly demonstrated by the thriving status that the "two major propaganda groups"—"one, an infiltrated group, and the other, a Communist front"—had been enjoying. Both of these groups, he claimed, were "dedicated to the achievement of so-called integration in the South." While Matthews identified the Atlanta-headquartered Southern Regional Council (SRC) as a Communist-infiltrated organization, he condemned the New Orleans–based Southern Conference Educational Fund (SCEF), an often red-baited civil rights group, as a Communist front serving as an "out-and-out instrument of the Communist apparatus," and "creat[ing] social chaos in the South" by pushing for racial integration.[60] And the SCEF's stigmatized executive director, James Dombrowski, had been "one of the shrewdest Communist operators in the nation," Matthews testified.[61] Furthermore, Matthews reminded Chairman McGehee and his Mississippi General Legislative Investigating Committee members that the SRC and the SCEF were "characterized by interlocking personnel" and that, among those who were involved in these two civil rights organizations, two white Mississippians—Hodding Carter, editor and publisher of the *Greenville Delta Democrat-Times,* and Adam Daniel "A. D." Beittel, the racially moderate white president of Tougaloo College near Jackson, a traditionally black institution—were "particularly noted."[62] Matthews then suggested that the Mississippi's anti-integration red-baiting committee keep tabs on Carter in particular, because the Greenville journalist, as Matthews saw it, must have been unquestionably "Communist[-]tainted."[63]

Having thus properly designated the SRC, the SCEF, Carter, Beittel, and nine other state citizens as white Mississippians' natural foes, Matthews turned his attention to the NAACP.[64] Categorizing the civil rights organization as a "Communist-infiltrated" group, he declared loud and clear: "I will say that considering the general run of infiltrated organizations, I know of no other in the United States that has been so heavily infiltrated as the NAACP, infiltrated with Communists and the Communist influences."[65] Referring to the NAACP's publicly avowed resolve to purge itself of Communist influences, Matthews told the Mississippi pro-segregation committee that he would "challenge them on the grounds of hypocrisy."[66] The CPUSA and its followers and sympathizers, he asserted, had used the NAACP as their major weapon in "propagandizing integration in the South."[67]

Following Matthews's detailed, but now somewhat hackneyed, testimony, Zack Van Landingham, the chief investigator of the Mississippi State Sovereignty Commission, and John Sullivan made their brief appearances before the Mississippi General Legislative Investigating Committee on the second and final day of the public hearings.[68] Taking the stand with pride on November 19, 1959, as the day's principal "friendly" witness, Van Landingham testified to the effect that the State Sovereignty Commission's investigative dossiers abundantly revealed that those representing what Matthews had just designated as the Communist-infiltrated organizations had "addressed Mississippi Negroes on many occasions in recent years."[69] While referring to and occasionally holding up a copy of the Georgia Commission on Education's 1958 report, *Communism and the NAACP,* which was composed of Matthews's February 1958 testimony before the Florida Legislative Investigation Committee in Tallahassee, the State Sovereignty Commission investigator told the Mississippi legislative committee that the NAACP had held "at least a dozen meetings in Mississippi since 1956" where the principal speakers were "leaders and officials of Communist-front organizations."[70] Among those speakers, Van Landingham emphasized, was Martin Luther King Jr., who had attended a "Communist training school" in Monteagle, Tennessee—a designation that the Georgia Commission on Education had given to the Highlander Folk School.[71]

Although the Mississippi General Legislative Investigating Committee viewed the public hearings as successful in exposing the alleged Communist influences on the civil rights movement in the Magnolia State, the ramifications of the hearings ran deep and wide. Aaron E. Henry, president of the Mississippi State Conference of the NAACP, sarcastically praised the legislative committee for its "thorough job of trying to sell Communism to the Negroes of Mississippi" because its recent public hearings "gave to Communism more credit for espousing the cause of justice and freedom than it did to Democracy." "The desire of the Mississippi Negro to be free will not be stopped," he proclaimed, "by any smear tactics of a Legislative Investigating Committee" employed "under the banner of patriotism" and "no matter how effective the activity" of the McGehee-chaired committee, the State Sovereignty Commission, the Citizens' Council, and their northern messiahs to "try to stir us into the Communist Camp."[72] It was "hell enough being black" in Mississippi "without being black and red at the same time," Henry recollected years later.[73]

Meanwhile, just a day after Matthews gave his testimony before the Mississippi General Legislative Investigating Committee, Carter—a "flaming liberal" who was "unfit to live in a decent white society," according to Mississippi House Speaker Walter Sillers—fired back, issuing a front-page statement in his *Greenville Delta Democrat-Times.* "Of the organizations named by professional anti-Communist J. B. Matthews, the only one to which I belonged was the Southern Regional Council," he explained, "[and] I belonged to it openly and believe it a worthwhile inter-racial organization in these unhappy times." The only matter that became evident during Matthews's "paid testimony," Carter maintained, was the fact that the invited New Yorker was nothing but a "damned liar" who reminded him of "what is found in wet places beneath a rotted log." "And this goes for those who hired him," Carter added, referring to the segregationist legislative committee.[74]

While Carter fought back by aiming his signature satirical invective at Mississippi's die-hard segregationists and their northern allies, a group of twenty-five political and civic leaders in Washington County (its county seat was Greenville) issued a jointly signed statement on November 21, 1959, in reference to Matthews's testimony before the legislative committee. "We wish to express our belief in the good citizenship, honesty and patriotism of our fellow citizen Hodding Carter," the statement began. "We have not always agreed with him," it went on, "but we recognize his right to differ as well as our own." Sensing that such a "right to differ" was being threatened in Mississippi, the signers condemned Matthews and the pro-segregation committee for their "smear techniques in which a man's good name can be dragged in the mud" and warned that "the recent hearings in Jackson" should not "set a pattern for the future." Among those who signed the statement was State Representative Joseph E. Wroten of Greenville, an influential Methodist layman who was destined to become one of a handful of legislative dissenters to the Magnolia State's massive resistance policies carried out under Governor Barnett's administration. Obviously, the moderate argument advanced by the Washington County leaders was far from being acceptable to some quarters. For instance, C. C. Smith of Dumas, Tippah County, whom Governor James Coleman had once called an "extremist for segregation," wrote to the editor of the *Jackson State Times* to refute the contention made by the Carter supporters. "Whether he [Carter] be a fronter or a backer, or actually a card-carrier [of the CPUSA]," Smith penned, "is beside the point." But as long as Carter dared to support black Mississippians' civil rights advancement, "he is anti-Mississippi and a thorough-bred South hater, and that's enough to put him in a category objectionable to decent Christian ladies and gentlemen in our parts," Smith concluded.[75]

In its preliminary report submitted to the governor and the legislature following the November 1959 public hearings, the Mississippi General Legislative Investigating Committee concluded that the state had been, beyond any doubt, invaded by "persons identified as members of the Communist

Party" or "Communist apparatus," who were not only "un-American" in their character, but also "detrimental to the peace, tranquility and preservation of order." The destructive forces threatening to upset that "order"— the state's cherished racial and racist order—would, if not contained, lead to "the ultimate overthrow of the government of the State of Mississippi," the preliminary report read.[76] Subsequently, Mississippi's investigating committee, just as the Rainach-chaired Louisiana Joint Legislative Committee had done a few years earlier, asked Lowman to edit the transcript of its public hearings. In accordance with their agreement, Lowman spent a week in Jackson in July 1960 conferring with the legislative committee members. "In Mississippi last week," Lowman wrote to Matthews on August 5, "I was informed that approval had been given to the printing of approximately 385 pages of print covering the Mississippi hearings." By testifying before the Mississippi committee, "you added so much information for public record purposes," Lowman wrote appreciatively.[77] It would take another one and a half years for the legislative committee to issue the Lowman-edited final report on its pro-segregation anti-Communist public hearings. Submitted to the 1962 state legislature, the committee report determined that "the Communist Party and the Communist conspiracy" had been present "within the State of Mississippi to pit race against race and to agitate, stir up and foment trouble between the races."[78]

Thus, with the 1960s just around the corner, Mississippi, as the white South's most promising citadel of racial segregation and discrimination, climbed on the bandwagon already occupied by the Louisiana Joint Legislative Committee, the Georgia Commission on Education, the Special Education Committee of the Arkansas Legislative Council, the Tennessee General Assembly Special Investigating Committee, and the Florida Legislative Investigation Committee. And, despite State Representative Wroten's appeal that the November 1959 anti–civil rights hearings should not "set a pattern" for the Magnolia State's immediate future, the Mississippi General Legislative Investigating Committee, in rapid succession, embarked on an inquiry into and an attack on what the state's white supremacists deemed to be undesirable textbooks used in public schools.[79]

United under the banner of seeming patriotism and assisted by a professional book-banning authority imported from the North, the Mississippi General Legislative Investigating Committee served as the final arbiter of the state's textbook censorship. By conferring the unsavory task on the legislative committee, Mississippi's massive resisters hoped to keep the state's white schools pure and white. In this respect, the state's conservative women—determined to wage a fierce battle for the South's righteousness in their own right—represented the major force behind Mississippi's racist book-banning scheme. Most of these women activists were members of the National Defense Council of the Mississippi Society of the DAR, chaired by Mrs. Alexander, which proudly sponsored Lowman's November 1959 speaking engagement held at the King Edward Hotel in downtown Jackson.[80]

In the late 1950s, urged by the National Defense Committee of the DAR's National Society headquartered in Washington, D.C., the group's chapters throughout the nation had begun to review textbooks used in their respective communities and to send reports on the matter to the national headquarters.[81] Among the southern states, the DAR proved most successful in Mississippi (and in Texas as well) in carrying out its often disingenuous book-burning campaigns, in which the organization's members obtained the backing of other conservative, patriotic, and segregationist organizations—the American Legion and the Citizens' Council, for instance—and of supportive state legislators and officials.[82] Terms such as "Americanism" and the "American way of life" became their watchwords of the day, but these loaded slogans were intended to debilitate the intensifying civil rights movement and thus to preserve the "southern," instead of "American," way of life.

Despite fragmentary historical accounts, the pivotal roles that conservative Mississippi women played with their efforts on behalf of both national security and preserving racial integrity should not pass unnoticed. Eager to defend Mississippi's racial status quo from what she perceived as the Communist-tainted civil rights movement, Mrs. Alexander's sister— Lorayne W. Westbrook of Jackson—for instance, once wrote to Director Albert N. Jones of the Mississippi State Sovereignty Commission, offering her "services" to the state's segregation watchdog agency to "help in any way possible." "These are critical times," Westbrook reminded the commission director, "and we all need to put our shoulder to the wheel."[83] For their part, she and her sister were more than ready to assist the state's massive resisters to "seek out our enemies and make them show their colors" in their beloved state of Mississippi.[84] To be sure, in making their enemies "show their colors," Mississippi's conservative women were also resolved to protect the almost mythological "Pure, White, Southern Womanhood" from "the Communist goal of amalgamation," as G. T. Gillespie, prosegregation president emeritus of Belhaven College in Jackson, observed in the wake of the 1954 *Brown* ruling.[85]

As a prelude to the Magnolia State's wholesale textbook censorship sanctioned by the Mississippi General Legislative Investigating Committee in late 1959, the state's conservative women, with Alexander and her DAR organization taking the lead, had successfully won some of the state's most rabid segregationist politicians over to their side in an effort to curb what they suspected as the "subversion of Southernism" on the campus of the University of Mississippi in Oxford, or Ole Miss—the state's flagship university.[86] A chain of events that would culminate in the legislative committee's textbook investigation in November 1959 had begun a year earlier. On November 18, 1958, State Representative Edwin Wilburn Hooker Sr. submitted a thirty-six-page allegation criticizing Ole Miss to the Board of Trustees of State Institutions of Higher Learning. Assisting Hooker in bringing these accusations against their alma mater was a former state representative, Hillery Edwin "Ed" White. Hooker was to become the most ardent segregationist among the Mississippi State Sovereignty Commission members when Ross Barnett assumed the governorship in 1960. In presenting his case to the board, Hooker asserted that he had detected some surreptitious activities on the campus of the University of Mississippi intended to subvert "our civilization here in Mississippi."[87] Hooker and White accused some Ole Miss faculty members of "teaching integration, subversion and apostasy, or desertion of religious faith."[88] For Hooker, the ideal Mississippi civilization consisted of such "keystone principles" as a belief in God, the accuracy of the Bible, the sovereignty of the state, and, most vitally, "the inalienable right to preserve the identity of the white race."[89]

Those whom Hooker and White named as apostates from the white-dominated Mississippi civilization included Professor James W. Silver in the History Department and Russell H. Barrett, an associate professor of political science. While Silver was suspected to be one of the renegade "pinkos" on the faculty, Barrett was indicted for having invited "undesirables" to speak at the university whose views were favorable to "Leftwing, radical and integrationist elements."[90] Later, in the aftermath of the 1962 desegregation ordeal at the University of Mississippi, where James Meredith became the first black student enrolled in the all-white institution, both professors would condemn in writing—Silver in his *Mississippi: The Closed Society* and Barrett in *Integration at Ole Miss*—Mississippi's white leadership for having created a calamity on the Ole Miss campus over the desegregation crisis.[91] Because of their unrelenting courage and sense of justice, both of them, and particularly Silver, would have to endure persistent state-sponsored persecution. Besides Professors Silver and Barrett, Hooker and White also had something to say about the university library at Ole Miss. Many books purchased by the library during the summer of 1956, they contended, were written by "biased" authors with a "slant in favor of integration." Furthermore, they found that the library had subscribed to the *New South,* a monthly publication of the SRC in Atlanta that would soon be publicly labeled as a Communist-infiltrated organization by Matthews during the November 1959 legislative investigating committee hearings in Mississippi.[92] In response to the allegations made by Hooker and White against the University of Mississippi, the Board of Trustees of State Institutions of Higher Learning created its Special Committee on Charges of Apostasy headed by Charles D. Fair, a board member and an attorney in Louisville.[93]

Complying with the request made by the board's special committee, the University of Mississippi then prepared a fifty-eight-page written reply to the accusations. While the university recognized "the principle of racial segregation in Mississippi," it vehemently defended the concept of academic freedom. If the faculty and students at Ole Miss were deprived of the freedom to freely discuss and investigate both old and new ideas, the university maintained, the institution itself would, sooner or later, become a "tool for the perpetuation of a closed and static society"—a society "characterized by the thought control so familiar to us as the technique of the Nazis and the Communists." Mississippi could not and should not afford to exist, the reply concluded, "as a closed society."[94] Unsatisfied with their alma mater's refutation, Hooker and White decided to make public their charges against Ole Miss in late July 1959, expecting that their revelation would prompt the Board of Trustees of State Institutions of Higher Learning to take decisive action.[95] A month later, on August 27, the board's special committee dismissed the bulk of the allegations made against the University of Mississippi as "groundless."[96] At the same time, however, the special committee's final ruling admitted that "there is evidence that there have been some tactlessness and imprudence on the part of a very few of the faculty and staff."[97]

Four days after the Board of Trustees of State Institutions of Higher Learning found that most of the accusations made against Ole Miss were "without foundation in fact," Hooker and White called on the board in Jackson on August 31, 1959. There, they demanded that the board be more explicit as to which of the total of twenty-six complaints they had made against the university and its faculty members were deemed to be

"groundless." "The people," they insisted, "would appreciate the board going further than a general denial."[98] The board, however, proved equally
uncompromising, sticking to its position on the matter and reiterating
that the named professors were "merely imprudent."[99] On October 26, only
three weeks before State Senator McGehee announced that his Mississippi
General Legislative Investigating Committee would launch a "surprise
hearing" involving Matthews, former State Representative White, following his speech made before the National Defense Council of the Mississippi
Society of the DAR, expressed his wish that his conviction that Ole Miss
"teaches integration and subversion" would "get into the legislature," but
he declined to "inject the charges himself."[100] After some twists and turns,
the grand task of weeding out "integration and subversion" teachings from
not only the Ole Miss campus but also the state's public school textbooks
fell on the shoulders of Mississippi's conservative women—more specifically, the members of the state DAR organization.

Immediately following the adjournment of the two-day public hearings
conducted by the McGehee-chaired Mississippi General Legislative Investigating Committee in November 1959, the state DAR's National Defense
Council, chaired by Mrs. Alexander, classed a total of forty-four textbooks
used in the state's public schools as advocating, or at least acquiescing in,
racial integration, subversion, and "one-worldism."[101] The conservative
women's group then prevailed on the legislative committee to secure the
services of a professional northern book-banner for establishing "the
depravity of Mississippi textbooks," while the committee trimmed the
DAR's list to twenty-seven books.[102] Hired by Mississippi's segregationist committee was E. Merrill Root, a poet and an English professor at
Earlham College in Richmond, Indiana, a liberal arts college founded
by the Religious Society of Friends (Quakers). Root, as the legislative
committee's report later revealed, was "confidentially recommended . . .
by an unimpeachable source" as an "expert in the field of public school
textbooks and subversive writings."[103] The "unimpeachable source" who
suggested that the pro-segregation committee rely on the Earlham College
professor in its battle against what the state's massive resisters saw as the
union of communism and the civil rights movement was none other than
J. B. Matthews, though the committee never mentioned him by name.

Root's association with Matthews dated back to late 1952, when he was
introduced to the New Yorker by Eugene Lyons, the Russia-born editor of
the conservative magazine *American Mercury* who, as a former Communist
sympathizer, had authored a number of books exposing Stalin's reign of

terror in the Soviet Union. "I have long known you as a brave and brilliant fighter in the same cause, a fighter who goes deeper and wider than I, and whom I admire and applaud," Root wrote to Matthews on December 14. Root, who had just embarked on writing the first of his two influential books in the field of anticommunism—*Collectivism on the Campus: The Battle for the Mind in American Colleges,* to be published in 1955—then asked Matthews for "accurate, full, unimpeachable evidence" concerning some university and college professors allegedly connected with "various [Communist] fronts" in the past.[104] Soon afterward, Root visited Matthews in New York City for the first time and obtained "a lot of information and guidance" from Matthews in preparation for writing his book.[105] "I cannot do my work unless I have a chance to fortify my files with your knowledge and guidance," Root wrote to Matthews in July 1953.[106]

After the face-to-face meeting between Matthews and Root during the summer of 1953 and as their mutual respect further developed, Root customarily ended his correspondence addressed to Matthews with "Admiringly yours." In return, Matthews cordially responded with the words "Fraternally yours."[107] "As you know, the life of a radical conservative is both lonely and dangerous," Root wrote to Matthews in November 1958, exactly a year before Matthews recommended the Earlham College professor to the Mississippi General Legislative Investigating Committee, "[but] to have you as a friend helps to strengthen me against such things."[108] In the meantime, Myers Lowman's partnership with Root had begun in early October 1953, when they both attended an anti-Communist seminar sponsored by the Ohio Coalition of Patriotic Societies as guest speakers.[109] At the same seminar, Matthews was also featured as an invited speaker.[110] With Matthews's assistance, Root published *Collectivism on the Campus* in 1955 as his full-scale public warning that Communist and leftist successes were rampant in American colleges and universities, conflating the meanings of "collectivism" and communism. In no time, the Citizens' Council included Root's work in its "Books Worth Reading" list.[111] Three years later, in 1958, following the theme and style of his first book, Root published *Brainwashing in the High Schools: An Examination of Eleven American History Textbooks.*[112]

In accordance with the request made by the Mississippi General Legislative Investigating Committee, Root spent two weeks in November 1959 examining the previously named twenty-seven public school textbooks that the Mississippi DAR and others had identified as propagating "un-American teachings," "the breaking down of the segregation laws," and "race-mixing."[113] Pocketing four hundred dollars from Mississippi for his services, Root labeled twelve of the books "satisfactory," twelve "unsatisfactory," and three "mediocre."[114] Among the textbooks that he branded as "unsatisfactory" were: *United States History,* for its failure to "prepare students to understand the political facts of life in relation to Communism in the world, . . . 'liberal' collectivism at home, . . . [and] the role of true conservatism in the American story"; and *Economic Problems of Today,* because its authors "evidently believe in the welfare state." Furthermore, while asserting that *Men's Achievements through the Ages* virtually ignored "the grim truth of our mortal struggle with communism today," Root concluded that *Geography and World Affairs* would leave students "in a pink political fog."[115] In response to Root's assessments, the legislative committee issued a forty-eight-page report recommending to the state's new governor, Ross Barnett, and the state legislature that the fifteen textbooks Root classified as either "unsatisfactory" or "mediocre" be further scrutinized by the Mississippi State Textbook Rating and Purchasing Board. If and when the board found no legitimate reason for retaining them, "all such textbooks should be eliminated from further use," the legislative committee concluded.[116] After working for Mississippi's segregationist committee as an expert on subversive textbooks and "tiptoe[ing] around the race issue," Root began his new career as an associate editor of a conservative magazine, *American Opinion,* put out by the Robert W. Welch Jr.–led John Birch Society in Belmont, Massachusetts.[117]

Following the issuance of the legislative committee report virtually comprised of Root's findings, the 1960 Mississippi legislative session took up a DAR-backed bill for the purpose of eliminating "subversive material" from the state's public schools. Among those who enthusiastically supported the enactment of the textbook censorship bill was Governor Barnett, a Citizens' Council stalwart and admirer of the DAR. If the state legislature failed to act favorably on the bill, the governor declared, it would "hamper our efforts to clean up our public school textbooks and give our children the instruction[al] material they must have if they are to be properly informed of the Southern . . . way of life."[118] Eventually, the textbook censorship bill became law, and Governor Barnett emerged from the 1960 state legislative session being empowered to share, with State Superintendent of Education Jack M. Tubb, appointive power for the eight subject-by-subject textbook screening committees placed under the Textbook Rating and Purchasing Board.[119]

After Barnett left the governor's office in early 1964, Mississippi state treasurer William F. Winter, a progressive-minded future governor of the Magnolia State who, as a state representative, had opposed the creation of the Mississippi State Sovereignty Commission, would make an address before a Phi Delta Kappa meeting held in Jackson.[120] "We have recently seen the spectacle," Winter told the gathered professional educators, "of self-styled experts on textbooks going around over our state peddling the myth that patriotic educators who have devoted their lives to the education of our children have somehow become either subversives or dupes." Criticizing Root, Alexander, and the Mississippi Society of the DAR without naming them, the racially moderate state treasurer reminded the audience that Mississippians should not "equate all differences of opinions with subversion" in the name of "patriotism or freedom or some other worthy cause that really have had nothing to do with either patriotism or freedom" and in truth "have been inconsistent with the real meaning of both."[121] Unfortunately, though, the vast majority of the state's political leaders in the late 1950s were not quite ready to embrace Winter's calm judgment. On the contrary, Matthews's appearance before the Mississippi General Legislative Investigating Committee and the concurrently orchestrated textbook censorship scheme—an alarming thought-control stratagem assisted by Root—only resulted in fortifying the segregationist ardor espoused by the state's white supremacists under the guise of anticommunism. In their frantic effort to keep Mississippi's closed society closed by whatever means necessary, the state's segregationist forces were convinced that they had found a trusted accomplice in Matthews.

Matthews, too, seemed to enjoy the mutually beneficial associations forged between him and the Magnolia State's massive resisters. In the wake of the traitor-hunting hearings carried out by the Mississippi General Legislative Investigating Committee, J. B. and Ruth Matthews promised Simmons and his Citizens' Council that they, along with Lowman, would continue to cooperate with Mississippi's pro-segregation officials to keep tabs on Carter and those others who had been identified by Matthews as "Communist-tainted" during the legislative committee hearings.[122] Thanking her new Mississippi friends—Simmons and his wife—in a Christmas card for their hospitality in Jackson, Ruth also alluded to the progress of her husband's Parkinson's disease, from which he had been suffering for some time: "Next time we hope we can stay longer and really visit—and we're haping [*sic*] there will be a 'next time' of some kind."[123] As it turned out, the November 1959 trip to Jackson proved to be Matthews's last visit to Mississippi. In addition to his physical hardships, unknown to most of his associates in Mississippi, Matthews was then also being challenged by a devastating family tragedy that had occurred in the spring of 1959.

On April 11, 1959, J. B. Matthews Jr., a forty-year-old aeronautical engineer working for the recently created Federal Aviation Agency, clubbed his three teenage children to death with a baseball bat while injuring his wife, Helen. Matthews Jr., who was the son of Matthews and his first wife, Grace, then killed himself, cutting his throat with a kitchen knife.[124] Five weeks after this nightmarish incident, Matthews wrote to President George Benson at Harding College in Searcy, Arkansas—a source of Matthews's paychecks since 1951—and declined Benson's invitation to appear on the college's Freedom Forum program. "The awful tragedy of my son's and my three grandchildren's deaths has overwhelmed me," Matthews confessed.[125] The murder and suicide case of Matthews Jr. was eventually closed with his motive never discovered.[126] The sudden and tragic loss of his first son and three beloved grandchildren certainly did not help Matthews's deteriorating health. "Much as I would love to accept your invitation, I am afraid that there are too many uncertainties in my life at the present time," Matthews wrote to President Benson on May 18, 1959, "[for] my Parkinson's disease has developed some complications which have not been cleared up."[127] A year later, in late May 1960, Matthews wrote to his nineteen-year-old son, Martin, and Martin's mother, Ruth Shallcross, who was Matthews's second wife. "My Parkinson's does not get any better," he vented his frustration, "[and] I have not had shoes on since the day—April 1959—I went to Joe's [Matthews Jr.'s] funeral in Arlington."[128] Matthews's health was gradually but steadily deteriorating.

Nevertheless, Matthews managed to travel to Jackson in November 1959 to give his testimony before the Mississippi General Legislative Investigating Committee with his third wife, Ruth, sitting next to him as his secretary and caretaker. After his appearance before the Magnolia State's segregationist committee, however, it became more evident that his Parkinson's disease would prevent Matthews from taking trips to the South. And Matthews's misfortune soon drove Lowman—who, until then, had played a role as the behind-the-scene sales representative of Matthews's anti-Communist and anti–civil rights "services" rendered in southern states—to fill his sworn friend's shoes in funneling much-needed and sought-after information to southern audiences.

While Lowman seemed to have positioned himself as a nationally recognized "authority on subversion" in religion and race relations, by the time he fully expanded his investigations into racial matters in the South, his inflated guilt-by-association tactics of accusing anyone who disagreed with him had begun to backfire.[129] Among the first to criticize Lowman were the nation's lawmakers in Washington, D.C. It all began in mid-January 1959, when Lowman wrote to the entire U.S. House of Representatives, asking them to defeat a recently introduced resolution prepared by Representative James Roosevelt, a Democratic lawmaker from California and a son of former president Franklin Roosevelt. Representative Roosevelt's resolution was intended to abolish the fourteen-year-old HUAC and to transfer part of its investigative powers to the House Judiciary Committee chaired by Emanuel Celler from New York. "You are urged to do *all in your power* to defeat the Roosevelt Resolution," Lowman, who had enjoyed cordial relations with the successive chairs of the HUAC since the days when Representative John Wood from Georgia took the committee's helm in the early 1950s, prodded the lawmakers.[130] The trouble arose, however, when Lowman openly questioned the integrity and loyalty of Celler, a respected Jewish Democrat. While discredited by many southern segregationists as a liberal "New York holy roller," Celler was known to have been a vocal opponent of Senator McCarthy and to have spoken out against the HUAC's high-handedness and imprudence.[131] Attached to Lowman's open letter to each member of the House was a six-page list of "the Communist and Communist-front enterprises" with which, he claimed, the chair of the House Judiciary Committee had been "affiliated."[132] "As you will see from the enclosed record of Congressman Emanuel Celler," Lowman wrote, "to put him in charge of investigating the Communist apparatus in this country would be like putting the wolf in charge of the sheep."[133]

Eventually, Representative Roosevelt's resolution was killed in the House Rules Committee, and very few House members actually took the time to respond to Lowman.[134] However, Lowman's irresponsible accusations against the House Judiciary Committee chair did not go unnoticed by some influential members of the legislative body. Among those who did respond to Lowman was James Claude "Jim" Wright Jr., a Texas Democrat like House Speaker Samuel T. "Sam" Rayburn and a future Speaker himself. While asserting that the HUAC should continue to function as it had done and admitting that he and Celler had sometimes disagreed, Representative Wright admonished Lowman that his unwarranted attack on the Judiciary Committee chair "was not only ridiculous, but was actually harmful" to the nation's anti-Communist cause. "Intemperate remarks and bitter accusations against men who disagree with us," Wright warned the Circuit Riders' executive secretary, were not only undemocratic, but also contemptible.[135]

As indications appeared that Lowman was losing credibility even among southern Democrats in the nation's capital, he also began to encounter severe criticisms from Protestant church leaders. "At the risk of being listed later" on one of Lowman's "pro-communist" tabulations, Hugh F. Miller, pastor at the First Baptist Church in Brockport, New York, for instance, penned a protest note to the executive secretary of the Methodist laymen's anti-Communist group in May 1959. Describing Lowman as a "supreme judge of opinion, theological, social, and political" who persistently condemned those who did not agree with him with a paranoid fervor, the Baptist minister concluded: "This constitutes a threat to American freedom and I want to register the most rigorous protest that I can."[136] Lowman immediately forwarded Miller's letter to the Matthewses in New York City, asking them to run a thorough background check on his new enemy. To Lowman's disappointment, however, Ruth Matthews did not find "any adverse record" on the Baptist pastor, whom Matthews's wife dismissed as a "compulsive correspondent."[137]

In the meantime, the pastor at the Northridge Presbyterian Church in Dallas, Texas, W. Walter Johnson, directed even harsher words at Lowman. Denouncing the Circuit Riders' publications as "extremely distasteful," Johnson wrote to Lowman that it was beyond his comprehension "how in the name of Christ anyone with talents enough to compile all of this insidious information" could possibly "justify the use of his time before God in such an anti-Christian undertaking." After reminding Lowman that Christ himself was "known as one of the most extreme radicals in his day," the Presbyterian minister ended his letter with evident sarcasm: "I am surprised to find that you have not included His name among those you are condemning." Incensed, Lowman responded to Johnson: "Your letter [should] be repulsed, rejected and denounced as one of the most stupid [letters] received by me during the past ten years devoted to anti-Socialist and anti-Communist work."[138] Echoing the Dallas minister, the New York–based Religious Freedom Committee condemned Lowman as a bigot who shamelessly ran "his own private Un-American Activities Committee."[139]

Aside from the Baptist and Presbyterian circles, Lowman's own Methodist Church also began to take note of his arrogant excesses. In early May 1960 in Denver, Colorado, the General Conference of the Methodist Church overwhelmingly adopted a resolution entitled "Attacks upon Churches and Churchmen" that strongly criticized the Circuit Riders. "We regret," the resolution read, "that any Methodists contribute either money or leadership to such organizations as [the] Circuit Riders, Inc., which utilize the 'guilt by association' and 'fellow-traveler' approaches as they stir up unjustified suspicion and develop unfounded fears."[140] In addition, a memorial entitled "Concerning Myers G. Lowman, Methodist Executive Director [*sic*] of the Circuit Riders, Inc.," was submitted during the church conference, which was specifically aimed at Lowman.[141]

Lowman's reaction to these official measures taken by his own church was swift and venomous. "We have never stated which ministers were innocent dupes and which ones made a career out of being duped, or which were known to be conscious collaborators with the Communist apparatus," Lowman spat out angrily when asked by a newspaper reporter about the adopted resolution, stressing that he had been merely "compiling records" on those suspicious clergymen.[142] He also wasted no time in launching a malicious personal attack on the person who had presented the Lowman memorial to the Methodist Church's General Conference—James Dombrowski, executive director of the SCEF in New Orleans and Lowman's, as well as the white South's, mortal enemy.[143]

Despite Lowman's waning credibility, Mississippi's massive resisters—both men and women—continued to cling to him, hoping that he would be instrumental in assisting them to somehow reverse the surging tide of racial justice by doing exactly what the 1960 General Conference of the Methodist Church decried—"stir[ring] up unjustified suspicion and develop[ing] unfounded fears."[144] As the self-proclaimed last citadel of racial injustice, Mississippi, with the wholesale mobilization of the state's elected officials, vowed to live up to its own resolve. While it was true that the white South had been compelled to retreat from some individual battles on the civil rights front and that Little Rock might have been taken over by an abominable "Communist conspiracy," the majority of white Mississippians still hoped to win the ongoing war against what they perceived as the Communist-infested black civil rights crusade. And at just the right moment, Ross Barnett—the personification of Mississippi's politics of defiance—ascended to power as the state's chief executive.

On January 19, 1960, only two months after the Mississippi General Legislative Investigating Committee held its public hearings that attempted to conflate the civil rights movement with domestic communism, Barnett took his oath of office as the state's fifty-third governor. "You know and I know," he pledged in his inaugural address, "that we will maintain segregation in Mississippi at all costs."[145] As James Coleman, Barnett's predecessor, had promised in his own inaugural address four years previously, "the separation of the races in Mississippi" was still "intact" when Barnett took his official oath.[146] And the new governor, too, was determined to keep intact what he once referred to as "Mississippi's fine traditions."[147] As if to fortify Barnett's resolution, no sooner had the 1960 state legislature been convened than the lawmakers flooded the legislative body with scores of bills designed to further strengthen Mississippi's racist maneuvering. While these legal measures were added to the state's arsenal in its battle to maintain the Mississippi way of life, the legislature also appropriated the handsome sum of $350,000 for the pro-segregation Mississippi State Sovereignty Commission for the fiscal biennium beginning on July 1, 1960. The new biennial appropriation was more than double the allocation given to the state agency during the preceding two-year period under the Coleman administration.[148]

Heartened by the governor's renewed resolve and the lawmakers' vigor, Mississippi's conservative and segregationist women were also on the move. On May 28, 1960, only a week after Governor Barnett called the first meeting of the Mississippi State Sovereignty Commission under his administration, some thirty Magnolia State "ladies" attended a luncheon organized by Sara C. McCorkle of Grenada for the purpose of organizing Mississippi's concerned women to wage an "all[-]out fight against the Communist Conspiracy" in their beloved state and to protect "our American way of life."[149] In late December 1957, McCorkle had been appointed by the Association of Citizens' Councils of Mississippi to the directorship of the segregationist group's women's activities. As a past state president of the American Legion Auxiliary and a mother of four daughters, McCorkle, while serving as the women's activities director, tirelessly encouraged all "Southern ladies" to contribute to the South's "struggle for states' rights and racial integrity"—the two principal organizational mottoes espoused by the Citizens' Council.[150]

In January 1958, McCorkle had also assumed the directorship of the Citizens' Council's youth activities division.[151] Under her direction, the division soon inaugurated its annual statewide essay contest for high school students to "assist our young people to develop into informed, patriotic, American citizens." The McCorkle-crafted "Rules Governing Contest" provided four essay topics from which students could choose, and one of these topics was "Subversion in Racial Unrest"—the exact title of the 1957–58 two-volume report issued by the Louisiana Joint Legislative Committee. The Association of Citizens' Councils of Mississippi even suggested that prospective contestants consult a pro-segregation discourse, *The Ugly Truth about the NAACP*—a publication of Mississippi's statewide council organization, whose original form was the 1955 address made by Georgia attorney general Eugene Cook. *Black Monday*, which had been authored by State Circuit Court Judge Tom Brady in the wake of the Supreme Court's 1954 *Brown* decision, was also strongly recommended to those who wished to take part in the essay contest.[152]

Responding to McCorkle's call to rally Mississippi's conservative women to the defense of their segregated way of life, a host of prominent figures active in the state's massive resistance establishment attended the luncheon held in Jackson in late May 1960. Among those present were: Mrs. Harry Alexander, chair of the National Defense Council of the Mississippi DAR; Mary D. Cain, editor and publisher of the weekly *Summit Sun* in Pike County and an unsuccessful gubernatorial contender in the 1951 and 1955 elections; Naomi Scrivner, research clerk for the Barnett-chaired Mississippi State Sovereignty Commission; and Mrs. Andrew Hopkins, wife of one of the commission investigators.[153] Cain was known to be one of the most prominent national leaders of the Minute Women of the U.S.A.—a Connecticut-based anti-Communist group—and she had been quite vocal in defense of the South's racial segregation.[154]

At their May 1960 meeting, the Mississippi women unanimously decided that four committees—the Youth, Public Relations, Education, and Church Committees—would be established. Having provisionally named their group the Independent Women's Organization and selected McCorkle as its secretary, they agreed to meet again later in the year.[155] Six months later, on December 8, the Independent Women's Organization met for the second time at the War Memorial Building in downtown Jackson. The meeting's first order of business was to decide on the group's official name. Two names—the "Mississippi Women Alerted" and the "Mississippi Women for God and Country"—were submitted for consideration, but the final selection of the official name was deferred until the organization's next planned meeting in mid-December. On behalf of the newly established group's Education Committee, Scrivner, the research clerk of the Mississippi State Sovereignty Commission, announced that at the forthcoming meeting, a plan would be considered to bring a nationally known "authority on subversion in America" into the state to educate its citizens.[156]

On December 14, 1960, eighteen women attended their group's third meeting, at which House Speaker Walter Sillers of the Mississippi state legislature—an all-powerful guardian of racial segregation who had once castigated the Supreme Court justices as "a cheap bunch of politicos"—gave a "very fine Americanism address." Sillers's speech was followed by brief remarks by some of the state's political dignitaries such as State Senator George Yarbrough, the Senate president pro tempore who had sponsored the anti-NAACP resolution during the 1958 state legislature; State Representative Wilburn Hooker, a hard-line member of the Mississippi State Sovereignty Commission and the instigator of the "subversion" probes on the University of Mississippi and its faculty; and State Representative Russell Fox, a former chair of the Mississippi General Legislative Investigating Committee. During this third meeting, Scrivner suggested the "Paul Revere Ladies" as their organization's official name, and her idea was unanimously approved.[157] For the occasion, Scrivner had even prepared the Paul Revere Ladies' "statement of belief and action" in the form of a poem entitled "Battle Cry":

> Our rights have been seized!
> We must spread the alarm
> Throughout every . . . Village and Farm.
> Conscienceless tyrants usurped the code,
> We're now in greater danger than when Paul Revere rode.
>
> The hour is late! There is no time to spare!
> The enemy is upon us. . . .
> Washington has been taken, Little Rock has been occupied.
> The battle of New Orleans is raging. . . .[158]

"We must stand, and fight, or die," the poem concluded. Referring to the school desegregation crises in Little Rock and New Orleans, the "statement of belief and action" abundantly revealed the Paul Revere Ladies' determination to preserve Mississippi's racial status quo. Impressed by Scrivner's leadership, the Paul Revere Ladies then promptly selected her as its chair "with a unanimous vote of confidence." While Scrivner's "Battle Cry" reverberated through Jackson's War Memorial Building, Alexander announced the Education Committee's plan to bring Myers Lowman into Mississippi for a series of speaking engagements on the condition that the Mississippi State Sovereignty Commission would be willing to cover the expenses of the event. Following her announcement, Alexander circulated a petition prepared by House Speaker Sillers's sister, Florence Sillers Ogden, requesting financial help from the state's segregation watchdog agency.[159] Like her brother, Ogden was a firm believer that the Supreme Court's *Brown* rulings had been "absolutely . . . inspired by the Communists."[160] The petition was immediately signed by all eighteen participants at the meeting.[161]

While the Revolutionary War hero Paul Revere rode on horseback from Boston to Lexington in 1775 to warn his fellow American colonists of an impending British military advance, in the early 1960s, the Magnolia State's Paul Revere Ladies were eager to alert their fellow white Mississippians to the dangers of communism and to expose its exploitation of racial unrest. On December 15, 1960, the day after the official establishment of the Paul Revere Ladies, Scrivner, Alexander, and McCorkle visited the Mississippi State Sovereignty Commission office to submit the petition prepared by the sister of the Mississippi House Speaker, who was also an ex-officio member of the State Sovereignty Commission.[162] The petition was accompanied by a list of the names of the women who belonged to the Grenada Citizens' Council, of which both Alexander and McCorkle were members, to show those council women's support given to the cause espoused by the Paul Revere Ladies.[163]

Calling the segregationist state agency's attention to "the importance of alerting our Mississippi people, by every means possible, to our National threat" of communism and to related threats to Mississippi's racial practices, the representatives of the Paul Revere Ladies presented their request to the Mississippi State Sovereignty Commission for the funds to invite Lowman to the state. With the enthusiastic support of House Speaker Sillers—a "Delta Baron," as James Coleman had once called him—and Governor Barnett, the state agency decided on the spot that it would set aside three thousand dollars to cover Lowman's expenses on a two-week speaking tour.[164] On January 4, 1961, about two weeks before Lowman's planned visit to Mississippi, the Paul Revere Ladies once again met at the War Memorial Building in Jackson to finalize Lowman's tour schedule, and they divided his speaking engagements into two separate tours—one in January and the other in February.[165]

The Paul Revere Ladies meticulously organized Lowman's first speaking tour in Mississippi, which lasted from January 16 to 22, 1961.[166] The tour kicked off on January 16 with a three-dollar-per-plate luncheon meeting to welcome Lowman at the King Edward Hotel in Jackson, where Lowman had once spoken before the National Defense Council of the DAR's Mississippi Society in November 1959.[167] The luncheon guests included Governor Barnett, Lieutenant Governor Paul B. Johnson Jr., House Speaker Sillers, and Jackson mayor Allen C. Thompson.[168] Prior to the luncheon, Lowman held a press conference at the Jackson hotel. "Communists don't want integration to work," Lowman told the gathered newspaper reporters. Rather, he said, Communists' involvement in the civil rights movement was "one of the most successful formulas for division of the people they have ever found." Echoing Matthews's contention in the November 1959 public hearings of the Mississippi General Legislative Investigating Committee, Lowman called the NAACP the most seriously Communist-infiltrated organization in the nation.[169] On the evening of January 16, following the press conference and the luncheon at the King Edward Hotel, Lowman was featured at the "Operation Survival" patriotic rally held in the auditorium of the Woolfolk State Office Building in downtown Jackson. There, a jam-packed crowd that included state legislators, department heads, the State Sovereignty Commission members, the Paul Revere Ladies, and the general public attentively listened to their northern messiah's anti-Communist and pro-segregation message.[170]

Lowman's tightly scheduled January 1961 speaking tour, whose overall theme was billed as "Subversion Challenges Sovereignty," included a number of public meetings in Mississippi's major cities, as well as campus lectures held at Mississippi Southern College (later the University of Southern Mississippi) and William Carey College, both in Hattiesburg, and Belhaven College in Jackson.[171] In her interim report on the tour to the Mississippi State Sovereignty Commission, the chair of the Paul Revere Ladies, Naomi Scrivner, commended the segregationist agency for sponsoring a tour that would "alert the people to our extremely dangerous situation" and "advise them on ways to combat the enemy and protect our sovereignty." "Little time should be lost in fortifying the people . . . in their fight against Godless communism," Scrivner wrote.[172]

Having found in Lowman a well of "authoritative information" to carry out their battle against communism—and their crusade for preserving white Mississippians' racial norms—the Paul Revere Ladies and the Mississippi State Sovereignty Commission again invited the Cincinnatian to their state from February 19 to 28, 1961, for his second series of speaking engagements. At the request of the Paul Revere Ladies, who hoped that Lowman's program would reach every institution of higher learning in Mississippi, most of his February appearances were held at state universities and colleges.[173] Accompanied by Scrivner and Alexander, and with the State Sovereignty Commission investigator Virgil S. Downing acting as the chauffeur, Lowman visited such institutions as the University of Mississippi in Oxford, Mississippi State University in Starkville, Delta State College in Cleveland, Mississippi State College for Women in Columbus, Hinds Junior College in Raymond, Decatur Junior College in Decatur, Meridian Junior College in Meridian, and Sunflower Junior College in Moorhead.[174]

Heeding House Speaker Sillers's advice, the Paul Revere Ladies also scheduled Lowman to appear before the student bodies at three black colleges—Mississippi Vocational College in Itta Bena, Alcorn Agricultural and Mechanical College in Alcorn, and Jackson State College in the state capital—to "inform and alert" young black Mississippians "to the inroads being made by the international Communist conspiracy."[175] With the cooperation of its black president, James H. White, whom the Mississippi State Sovereignty Commission had once called one of the state's "fine, level-headed negro citizens who are actively opposed to the NAACP," Mississippi Vocational College politely welcomed Lowman.[176] The other two black presidents, John D. Boyd at Alcorn College and Jacob L. Reddix at Jackson College, were also highly regarded by Mississippi's segregationist officials for their cooperative postures.[177] Although it was then unknown to the Paul Revere Ladies and the State Sovereignty Commission, President Boyd later reported to the state agency that when Lowman addressed the faculty and the student body at his college in February 1961, the "topic of his speech was so controversial that it almost created a riot at the college." In order for him to "get the student body and the faculty quieted down," Boyd confessed in the fall of 1963, he quietly told Lowman that "things were getting beyond his [Boyd's] control" and that "it would be better for him [Lowman] to leave the campus."[178]

Lowman also encountered some hostile receptions at the all-white University of Mississippi. On February 20, 1961, the Circuit Riders' executive secretary spoke at Fulton Chapel on the university campus and implicated Hodding Carter in helping blacks and Communists make inroads into Mississippi, just as Matthews had done during his appearance before the Mississippi General Legislative Investigating Committee.[179] Among the audience was the history professor James Silver, one of the faculty members targeted by State Representative Wilburn Hooker in his unabashed crusade to cleanse Ole Miss of racial "subversion." Together with some of his students who were "grouped around him," Silver, as Scrivner would later angrily describe, "plunged into a vicious verbal attack" on Lowman and "continued to interrupt" the meeting until it was closed. "Here we had an incident," the chair of the Paul Revere Ladies reported the disturbance to her employer, the Mississippi State Sovereignty Commission, "where a College Professor who is an employee of the State of Mississippi was leading a demonstration against an authority whom a branch of the state government had brought in" for the vital purpose of alerting "the student body to the peril in which this nation stands."[180] "I didn't like his innuendo and his cheap platform tricks," Silver later wrote to the editor of the *Jackson State Times*.[181]

After this Ole Miss incident, Lowman "included me among his Reds," Silver subsequently recollected in his memoir, *Running Scared*.[182] A few days after Lowman left the Magnolia State for home, the Mississippi Historical Society held its annual meeting in Clinton. On March 3, 1961, as the president of the society, Silver delivered his presidential address and devoted more than half of his talk to denouncing Lowman, who, as Silver claimed, had put his name on the Circuit Riders' list of "suspected Communists." "I have been called a Communist before by some pretty good local demagogues," Silver said, "but hiring someone from Ohio and then charging me taxes for him to come down here and accuse me is worse."[183] Thanks partially to Lowman, but largely to his own implied attack on the Mississippi State Sovereignty Commission made during the presidential address, Silver's name was prominently included in the segregationist agency's investigative dossiers. Later, in the wake of the September 1962 desegregation crisis at the University of Mississippi, the history professor would become the object of persistent persecution by the State Sovereignty Commission.[184]

In the meantime, unknown to Lowman, no sooner had the Circuit Riders' executive secretary completed his second speaking tour in Mississippi than his credibility as what the Mississippi State Sovereignty Commission called an "internationally recognized anti-Communist" suddenly fell under suspicion.[185] On February 28, 1961—the day Lowman left Mississippi—State Representative Horace H. Harned Jr., a future State Sovereignty Commission member, dropped an unexpected bombshell. Harned, who would later reminisce that "anti-communism has long been high on my [political] agenda," notified Director Albert Jones of the State Sovereignty Commission that a reliable rumor existed that Lowman himself had been "connected with a Communist front organization," indicating that Mississippi's massive resistance establishment, including the state's segregation watchdog agency, might be swimming with sharks.[186] Faced with this bolt from the blue, the disconcerted commission director immediately asked U.S. representative John Bell Williams from Mississippi in Washington, D.C., to run a check on Lowman. At the behest of Williams, Republican representative Gordon Scherer from Ohio, chair of the HUAC, did some research on his committee's records. On March 2, Scherer sent a telegram to the State Sovereignty Commission director, stating that the rumor reported by Harned was "ABSOLUTELY UNTRUE."[187] Still perturbed, Jones also conferred with William Simmons in Jackson, who claimed to have personally met Director Hoover of the FBI in Washington, D.C., accompanied by Lowman. Simmons, the driving force of the entire Citizens' Council movement, assured Jones that Lowman had been "leading his tireless efforts in oppressing Communism and Communist front organizations in every field," including that of race relations.[188] The whole incident, in essence, provided eloquent testimony to the presence of a distrust-filled police-state mentality, where boundless suspicion not only oppressed Mississippi's black citizens, but also haunted even the state's segregationist oppressors.

Once the rumor could be dismissed as untrue and the Mississippi State Sovereignty Commission heaved a deep sigh of relief, the segregationist state agency met with criticism from a different quarter. The state auditor's office issued reports indicating that the State Sovereignty Commission had generously paid Lowman a total of $3,824—$2,470 for his January 1961 tour and $1,354 for his February 1961 speaking engagements—derived from the state's taxpayers' money.[189] As Wilson Minor, Jackson correspondent for the *New Orleans Times-Picayune,* sarcastically observed, the state's level-headed white citizenry began to realize that those "self-styled experts on Communism subversion" such as Matthews, Root, and Lowman had now apparently found Mississippi to be a "happy hunting ground to pick up nice fees for their services."[190] In the face of vocal criticism by the press, House Speaker Sillers (whose nickname, ironically, had been "Red" in his college days because of his red hair) continued to defend Lowman's credibility and the importance of his Mississippi tours. Sillers, in fact, had privately run a background check on Lowman with the help of U.S. senator Eastland's office prior to the segregationist agency's decision to finance the Cincinnatian's speaking tours.[191] "We've spent $80 billion in Europe since the war to fight Communism, and President Kennedy has asked Congress for $800 million to fight Communism in Latin America," the all-powerful House Speaker said, "but when we put out a little money to alert our people here at home, people set up a howl."[192]

Undaunted, the Mississippi State Sovereignty Commission sponsored Lowman's third set of speaking engagements in April 1961 in cooperation with the Paul Revere Ladies. This time, however, his tour lasted for only three days, from April 18 to 20.[193] In order to minimize any further criticism of its making free use of the state taxpayers' money, the State Sovereignty Commission purchased eight hundred dollars' worth of "literature" from Lowman's Circuit Riders instead of paying him directly.[194] While in Mississippi, Lowman conducted a series of public seminars at William Carey College, Holmes County Junior College in Goodman, and an American Legion post in Clarksdale.[195] During his talk before the veterans' organization on April 20, 1961, Lowman once again, as he had done at the University of Mississippi in February, attacked Hodding Carter of the *Greenville Delta Democrat-Times*. Just like the *New Orleans Times-Picayune*'s Wilson Minor, Carter had criticized the State Sovereignty Commission for using taxpayers' money to subsidize Lowman's malicious public addresses throughout the state. Among other white Mississippians whom Lowman cast as deplorable "Red sympathizers" during his appearance before the American Legion was State Representative Joseph Wroten.[196]

Wroten, as a Mississippi House member from Washington County, had time and time again defended "the good citizenship, honesty and patriotism" of his fellow Greenville citizen Hodding Carter. While protesting the state's reckless massive resistance policies in the legislature, Wroten, who then was also in charge of the Board of Christian Social Concerns of the North Mississippi Conference of the Methodist Church, had crossed swords with Lowman.[197] During the previous month, in March 1961, the board had criticized Mississippi's official support of northern "anti-communist" campaigners, charging that they had waged "smear attacks" against the mainstream church organizations, including the Methodist Church, and some of their faithful ministers by branding them as being "sympathetic toward Communism." In a statement issued by Wroten as the board chair in March, the North Mississippi Methodist Conference's Board of Christian Social Concerns made "specific reference" to the state "subsidies paid in connection with recent speaking tours" made by Lowman, whom Wroten would remember as a "renegade member of the same [C]hurch of which I'm a member."[198] "We register our protest against any and all state subsidies used for such purposes," Wroten's statement decried.[199]

Notably, some of Mississippi's Methodist ministers, despite their racial beliefs and aversion to the civil rights movement, squarely sided with Wroten and his Board of Christian Social Concerns. One of them was John W. Moore, pastor at the First Methodist Church in Brookhaven. A committed segregationist and a "next[-]door neighbor" of Tom Brady—the state circuit court judge who wrote *Black Monday*—Moore had been given "the privilege of opening" Brady's court "with prayer."[200] On Sunday morning, June 4, 1961, Moore, who regarded himself as "an American, a Southerner, and a Mississippian" as well as "a segregationist" by conviction, delivered an address before his congregation. Acknowledging at the beginning of his address—which consisted of a single-spaced, twelve-page typescript— that it might well "stretch the meaning of the word 'Sermon,'" the pastor nevertheless "felt obliged to speak" on the subject of "Communism in the Methodist Church."[201]

Early in his address, Moore made a forthright confession: "It is humiliating to me that for the past half-dozen years I have not given a sufficiently positive leadership to my people in the matter of their understanding and appreciation of the Methodist Church and its relationship to national and world events." "As a result of that failure," the Methodist minister stated, "some of my people have fallen victim to the insidious propaganda of the 'Apostles of Discord'" composed of "small groups of malicious men whose consciences seem plagued" with bigotry and hatred. Typifying these "Apostles of Discord" was J. B. Matthews of New York City, by whom, Moore asserted, both the Mississippi state legislature and its General Legislative Investigating Committee had been "duped." The pastor blamed Matthews for having spread his irresponsible "prevarication" among Mississippians and suggested that one of the nation's most respected anti-Communists was not only a "false witness," but also a "mountebank" and a "charlatan."[202]

In addition, Moore insightfully identified Lowman as a trusted and indispensable ally of Matthews—"this persistent prevaricator," as the Methodist minister referred to Matthews. Lowman, according to Moore, was "another irresponsible promoter of hate." Moore reminded his congregation that by inviting northern anti-Communists like Lowman to their state, Mississippians were "dealing with hate mongers who have no sense of decency or honor." For this, the pastor asserted, the Mississippi State Sovereignty Commission was equally to be blamed, since "it is a sobering fact that your tax money has been spent to bring such a man . . . into the State."[203] Moore's address also dealt with the issue of integration and anticommunism, and criticized the state's political leadership for "venting the hatred of little minds for everything" that they could not control:

> Let it be understood that they who seek to relate integration to communism imagine a vain thing. The tendency to call everything we dislike by the name "communism" is an indication of weakness on our part. Not many white people in the south [*sic*] like the NAACP. That is a matter of freedom;

each man is entitled to like or dislike whatever he will or not. But the fact of our likes or dislikes does not alter the thing liked or disliked. Disliking the NAACP doesn't make the NAACP communist.[204]

"Ignorance speaks with a loud voice in our land and the loud voice of ignorance is heard with gladness by many people," Moore concluded, asserting that those people "ought to hear that voice with embarrassment and shame."[205]

Lowman was quick to respond to the courageous dissenting voices that were beginning to be raised by the Brookhaven Methodist minister and others. Two weeks after he completed his third speaking tour in Mississippi, Lowman composed an open letter entitled "The Right to Know" and mailed copies of it to the state's newspaper editors in early May 1961. Both "the favorable publicity . . . [and] the adverse criticism" of his recent Mississippi tours, Lowman wrote, had brought the subject of Communist menace in the civil rights movement "to the attention of thousands of Mississippians." "The general criticism and smear efforts against the conservatives" such as Matthews and himself had been "so persistent and consistent," Lowman continued, that they had created a lamentable situation in which "Joe and Mary America at the cross-roads seem better informed regarding what is pro-Communist and anti-United States than do many of the persons in church, education, journalism, entertainment and government."[206]

Lowman also mailed his May 1961 statement to Mississippi governor Ross Barnett. On May 17, the seventh anniversary of the Supreme Court's 1954 *Brown* decree, the governor responded to Lowman, thanking him and informing him that he had read the statement "with a great deal of interest."[207] Perhaps Lowman's letter reawakened Barnett to the imperative that, as he had proclaimed earlier, "the traitors in our midst" be identified and "the cowards from our front lines" be eliminated.[208] For the keepers of Mississippi's "closed society," Lowman's involvement in the state's massive resistance had become all the more imperative in the absence of Matthews.

CHAPTER 7

"THIS IS A PART OF THE WORLD COMMUNIST CONSPIRACY"

The White South's Desperate Stand against the
Civil and Voting Rights Acts

For the black civil rights struggle in Mississippi, 1961—the same year in which the influence of Myers Lowman on the state's segregationist power structure and its entourage became apparent—turned out to be both crucial and crucifying. On March 27, three weeks before Lowman visited Mississippi for his third state-sponsored speaking tour, the capital city of Jackson witnessed a "study-in" launched by nine students from historically black Tougaloo College, which Mississippi lieutenant governor Carroll Gartin would refer to as a haven for "queers, quacks, quirks, political agitators and possibly some communists." The "Tougaloo Nine," as they were soon to be called, were members of the youth council of the National Association for the Advancement of Colored People (NAACP) operated on the college campus, and they tried to desegregate the Jackson Public Library, which served only whites, located in the heart of the city. For their peaceful direct-action protest, the black students were summarily arrested and jailed by the Jackson Police Department on charges of "breach of the peace."[1] The Mississippi State Sovereignty Commission's relentless investigation of Tougaloo and its white president, A. D. Beittel, would quickly ensue. (Beittel was on J. B. Matthews's enemy list when Matthews testified before the segregationist anti-Communist hearings held by the Mississippi General Legislative Investigating Committee in November 1959.)[2] Although the Tougaloo Nine's courageous civil disobedience seemed to be a single incident rather than part of any larger plan, it did serve as a critical prelude to the capital city's full-scale civil rights activism two years later—the 1963

Jackson movement, in which the well-organized sit-in demonstrations at Woolworth's segregated lunch counter were carried out.[3]

The "crucible of race," in the words of the southern historian Joel Williamson, continued to overshadow Mississippi's civil rights movement.[4] In the spring of 1961, President John F. Kennedy came face to face with his administration's first constitutional crisis over black civil rights. Determined to make racial desegregation in interstate travel facilities a reality, the racially integrated Freedom Riders, organized by James Farmer, who served as the national director of the Congress of Racial Equality (CORE), headed for Mississippi. Before the Freedom Riders reached the Magnolia State, however, they had received violent "welcomes" from the local white mobs at Anniston, Birmingham, and Montgomery in Alabama, and these racial incidents suddenly became the center of national and even international press coverage. As Attorney General Robert F. Kennedy, the president's younger brother, tried to move the Freedom Riders out of Alabama as quickly as possible, he pleaded with them to allow a "cooling-off" period. Dismayed and outraged, Farmer told a reporter: "We have been cooling off for 100 years [since the Emancipation Proclamation was issued]. If we got any cooler we'd be in a deep freeze."[5]

Finding themselves in serious straits, President Kennedy and his attorney general secretly struck a deal with Mississippi governor Ross Barnett. Their veiled agreement was first mediated by former Mississippi governor James Coleman and then by the all-powerful chair of the Senate Judiciary Committee, Senator James Eastland from Mississippi.[6] Though the matchup was a rather "bizarre combination" of the nation's youthful reform-minded politicians and one of the South's most ultraconservative and rabid segregationists, the Kennedys and Eastland understood each other.[7] As a result of this Kennedy-Eastland agreement, the president and the attorney general decided that they would not enforce the Supreme Court's 1960 *Boynton v. Virginia* ruling, which would have granted the Freedom Riders their constitutional rights to use any public facilities at the Jackson bus terminal.[8] In return for the Kennedy administration's half-hearted concession, Governor Barnett promised that he would make sure that no violence would be used against the Freedom Riders. On May 24, 1961, the first group of Freedom Riders wheeled into Jackson on two buses. By the end of the day, twenty-seven of them, including CORE's Farmer, had been arrested for "breach of the peace," as in the case of the Tougaloo Nine. They were first held at the Hinds County Jail and then were transferred by vans to the notorious maximum-security Mississippi

State Penitentiary in Parchman, Sunflower County—the home county of Eastland, who denounced the Freedom Riders as "Communist agitator[s]" on the Senate floor on May 25.[9]

Although the president and the attorney general did manage to avoid bloodshed in Mississippi by giving in to the state's segregationist laws, they instead ended up putting the Freedom Riders at the mercy of the local police and judges. Thereafter, the Freedom Riders continued to pour into Jackson, and by the end of the summer of 1961, approximately 430 participants had been arrested. Among them, some 300 freedom fighters were sent to the Mississippi State Penitentiary, a destination that the Nobel laureate William Faulkner, in one of his novels, associated with "doom."[10] At least this time, Mississippi's state sovereignty and Barnett's personal honor had been preserved. In late June 1961, Erle E. Johnston Jr., the public relations director and a future overall director of the Mississippi State Sovereignty Commission, confidently told the audience during his speech before a Rotary Club meeting in Pocatello, Idaho, that the "self-styled freedom riders" had miserably failed "in their efforts to embarrass Mississippi or to provoke violence." "Instead," he continued, "they brought many representatives of news media into Mississippi who were able to learn first-hand how the two races work and live in harmony" in the state's segregated and closed society. The Freedom Riders had "actually done the state a service," Johnston noted.[11]

Behind Johnston's seemingly sanguine remarks, however, Mississippi's segregationist forces had been busy "tar-brushing" the Freedom Riders with the "subversive" label with a helping hand from Myers Lowman of the Circuit Riders.[12] When the Freedom Riders first flocked to Jackson in late May 1961, Lowman asked Naomi Scrivner, the Mississippi State Sovereignty Commission's research clerk and chair of the Paul Revere Ladies, to send pictures of and information about the Freedom Riders to him for the purpose of determining their "subversive affiliations."[13] In response, the State Sovereignty Commission compiled a nine-page list of the Freedom Riders who had "invaded" Mississippi from May 24 to July 6, 1961.[14] "I am grateful," Scrivner once proudly wrote to the members of the state's segregation watchdog agency, "for the privilege of being one of your servants in this lofty undertaking."[15] As one Alabama journalist accurately observed, the State Sovereignty Commission under the Barnett administration was increasingly emerging as a "sort of un-Mississippi activities Committee."[16]

On June 29, 1961, about a month after Mississippi received the first wave of the Freedom Riders, the state's public safety commissioner, T. B. Birdsong, held a press conference at the Mississippi State Highway Patrol headquarters in Jackson. Birdsong asserted that a group of his investigators, headed by Gwin Cole at the State Highway Patrol's Identification Bureau, had determined that the apparently endless assaults by the Freedom Riders on Mississippi's social and racial norms were "directed, inspired and planned by known Communists." And some of the participants, the public safety commissioner added, were definitely "pawns in the hands of Communist powers that be."[17] Though Birdsong emphasized that the incriminating information on the "Communist-directed" Freedom Riders had been "secured through our own efforts from our own sources," the Mississippi State Sovereignty Commission had much to do with the Birdsong investigation.[18] In fact, the bulk of the information that the public safety commissioner revealed to the press and the public was, both directly and indirectly, provided by the State Sovereignty Commission, which, in turn, had been assisted by Lowman through what the agency called "Mrs. Scrivner's project." Additionally, Lowman's friend in the Sunshine State, Chief Investigator Remus Strickland of the Florida Legislative Investigation Committee, was also a vital source of information that Mississippi officials gathered on the Freedom Riders.[19]

Immediately following Birdsong's press conference, Field Secretary Gordon Carey at the CORE headquarters in New York vehemently refuted the Mississippi public safety commissioner's charge, calling it another "smear campaign" waged by Mississippi with the obvious intent to discredit the civil rights movement. Birdsong's accusation, Carey said, was "so ridiculous as to merit no reply." "However," he went on, "because the reputation of scores of imprisoned Freedom Riders is at stake, the Congress of Racial Equality feels compelled to answer briefly." "The Freedom Riders have no connection whatsoever with the Communist party in this nation or any other. They [The Freedom Rides] are taking place because the aspirations of the American Negro have been so long denied and stifled by un-American states such as Mississippi," Carey asserted.[20]

While CORE's field secretary was concerned about the reputations of the incarcerated Freedom Riders at the Mississippi State Penitentiary, others were worried about the Freedom Riders' safety. Minnesota attorney general Walter F. Mondale, a future vice president of the United States, sent a telegram to his counterpart in Mississippi, Joe Patterson, asking him to investigate a report that six Minnesota Freedom Riders were being mistreated at the state penitentiary—also known as "Parchman Farm." Denying the allegation, State Penitentiary Superintendent Jesse Fred Jones—a fervent states' righter and a Citizens' Council stalwart, as well as a former Mississippi state senator chairing the upper House's Penitentiary Committee—responded defiantly: "If they the riders [*sic*] show no respect for the customs and laws of Mississippi, I'm not going to turn the prison into a country club."[21] "We are still having a lot of fun with the 'freedom riders,'" the Citizens' Council leader William Simmons in Jackson wrote to Ruth Matthews, who, by then, had taken over most of her ailing husband's correspondence. Simmons made no effort to conceal his antipathy for the Freedom Riders:

> We keep hearing that several thousand will make the assault on our big-oted ways during the month of July. That is interesting, because the demand for cotton-choppers on the 21,000-acre prison farm in the delta will be at its peak just about then.
>
> If they keep up through August into the fall, there might be a host of well qualified cotton pickers turning up at northern colleges during the winter.[22]

Responding to Simmons's "amazing letter," Ruth Matthews asked the mastermind of the Citizens' Council movement to "make a list of the 'freedom riders'" and "run a carbon for us." "We have no immediate need for it," she added, "but it might be interesting."[23] Two weeks after this correspondence between Simmons and Ruth Matthews, the Citizens' Councils of America, headquartered in Jackson, issued a press release on July 12, 1961, announcing that some four hundred radio stations in forty-two states were now broadcasting the segregationist group's three-part special *Citizens' Council Forum* program concerning the Freedom Riders' "invasion of Mississippi."[24] Having been initiated in April 1957 as the Citizens' Council's publicity and educational tool to "acquaint the public with the serious problems affecting states' rights and race relations, and with steps being taken to meet them," the *Citizens' Council Forum* series consisted of fifteen-minute telecasts and five-minute radio broadcasts.[25] Appearing on these programs, conservative and segregationist southern politicians and officials, as well as some "experts" in various fields, advanced their views on states' rights and constitutional government while detailing "the world-wide Communist conspiracy" in the civil rights movement, the black race's intellectual inferiority, and the "vice" of interracial dating and marriages.

Featured in the special *Citizens' Council Forum* broadcasts in the early summer of 1961 were U.S. representative John Bell Williams from Mississippi, Mississippi attorney general Joe Patterson, and Grady Gilmore, public relations director of the Mississippi State Highway Patrol. Patterson, for his part, bluntly stated that "there is not a bit of doubt in the world" that Communist influences had been behind the integrationist scheme carried out by the Freedom Riders. "The Communists have endorsed the program," the attorney general pointed out, "and it is in direct keeping with their plan of activity in the South, to go in and create chaos, confusion, strife and discontent among the races." On another broadcast, Gilmore predicted that "in a very short time, we will be able to expose many more of these so-called 'freedom riders' as either sympathetic towards Communism or as out-and-out Communists." "We are interested in only one thing," the State Highway Patrol official flatly explained in his interview, and that was "to get to the bottom of this, and to expose these people who are trying to destroy our way of life."[26]

In the midst of the concerted red-baiting of the Freedom Riders orchestrated by the Mississippi State Sovereignty Commission, the Mississippi State Highway Patrol, and the Citizens' Council, Lowman paid a visit to Mississippi in October 1961, following his January, February, and April speaking tours in the state. Two months earlier, on August 1, the *Jackson Daily News* reported that "plans for an anti-communism seminar to be held in Mississippi" had recently been discussed at a meeting of the Paul Revere Ladies. The proposal to hold the seminar in the Magnolia State had apparently been prompted by the report made at the group's gathering by Mrs. Harry Alexander, who had just returned from Montana. In that western state, Alexander had addressed a seminar sponsored by a patriotic organization called the Montanans for Better Citizenship on her favorite topic, "Subversion in Textbooks." Alexander, who had shared the Montana seminar platform with Lowman, suggested that the Paul Revere Ladies once again rely upon Lowman's expertise, and they eventually decided to offer him financial support of their own.[27]

In spite of the fact that the state's tax money was no longer being funneled into the Circuit Riders, it was obvious that not everyone was pleased with Lowman's October 1961 appearance in Mississippi. "Myers Lowman, the Pied Piper of the lunatic right wing, was in Mississippi only long enough to play a short rendition of his old tune last week," Hodding Carter editorialized in his *Greenville Delta Democrat-Times* on November 1, lamenting that Mississippi had become the stronghold for Lowman's "one-man character assassination crusade."[28] On November 8, a week after the publication of Carter's editorial, the National Defense Council of the Mississippi Society of the Daughters of the American Revolution (DAR) held a round-table conference at Mississippi College in Clinton, located near Jackson. Through Alexander's efforts as the National Defense Council chair, Lowman was again invited to come to Mississippi to attend the conference as a "distinguished" guest speaker. Sharing the podium with U.S. representative John Bell Williams from Mississippi, Lowman talked about the four "important subjects vital to the interest" of patriotic Mississippians—"Textbook Survey," "Federal Aid to Education," "Patriotic Education," and one of his mortal enemies, the National Council of Churches.[29] Thereafter, Lowman and Alexander would maintain a steady association. For instance, when the Circuit Riders launched its own series of seminars billed as "Socialist-Communist Exploitation of Youth" in the summer of 1963, Alexander, advertised as the Cincinnati group's "Consultant—Lecturer," was slated to be an invited speaker.[30]

At the time that Lowman made his fourth and fifth visits to Mississippi in the fall and winter of 1961, the Paul Revere Ladies—the original organizer of his anti-Communist and anti–civil rights speaking tours in the state—was about to evolve into an organization called Patriotic American Youth. In late 1961, Sara McCorkle, whose May 1960 call to organize Mississippi's conservative women for the purpose of fortifying the state's racial norms had led to the creation of the Paul Revere Ladies, was deeply involved in founding the new Jackson-based reactionary group. The stated purposes of Patriotic American Youth included to "develop our students into informed and active leaders" who then would "be able to give other students and the public the truth regarding the Communist conspiracy to dominate the World," the United States, the South, and Mississippi, as well as the black civil rights movement.[31] McCorkle became the executive director of the Mississippi's newly established anti-Communist youth group, and under her leadership, Patriotic American Youth began publishing its monthly (later, quarterly) bulletin called *Pay Day* in November 1961. Furthermore, a list of the group's "advisory board" members read like Mississippi's "segregationist who's who." Besides McCorkle, the board harbored State Circuit Court Judge Tom Brady; State Representative Wilburn Hooker, a rabid massive resister and a member of the Mississippi State Sovereignty Commission; William D. McCain, president of Mississippi Southern College; and others.[32] With the enthusiastic support of Governor

Barnett, House Speaker Walter Sillers, and Representative Hooker, the State Sovereignty Commission granted $2,500 to the group as a donation in the late spring of 1962.[33]

Meanwhile, on June 9, 1962, the North Mississippi Methodist Conference, supplementing and reinforcing the March 1961 action taken by its Board of Christian Social Concerns to protest Lowman's "smear attacks," adopted an official resolution condemning as "false and irresponsible" the Cincinnatian's indiscreet and ruthless charges against the Methodist Church and some of its ministers.[34] Enraged, Lowman released a statement through Mississippi's dailies, issuing a standing challenge to "debate any members of the Mississippi Methodist Conference" on the subject that he termed "Communists Exploit the Churches."[35] The young pastor at the Caswell Springs Methodist Church in Pascagoula, O. Gerald Trigg, accepted Lowman's invitation to debate.[36] In accepting the challenge, Trigg mentioned that he regretted "that such a debate will offer Lowman another opportunity to pull out his files of nebulous charges calculated to sow seeds of suspicion." "But," the pastor hastened to add, "allowing his challenge to Mississippi Methodists to stand unchecked would be taken by some as proof of guilt."[37] Lowman and Trigg thus were scheduled to debate at the King Edward Hotel in Jackson on July 30, 1962.[38]

The debate attracted a lively and partisan audience of four hundred, including a host of Citizens' Council members. Lowman asserted at the outset that Mississippi had been "one of the most Communist-exploited states in the nation" and accused Trigg of having refused to denounce the New Orleans–based Southern Conference Educational Fund (SCEF). Trigg responded that the "Church of Jesus Christ faces its greatest threat from Communism," as well as "those un-intelligent anti-Communists who seek to divide by accusation." He then charged that Lowman, by sowing the seeds of suspicion among Mississippians, had "played into the hands of Communism." "To be that stupid, you have to work at it," the Methodist minister said.[39] Immediately following the explosive Jackson debate, Lowman warned Mississippians that "ignorance of Communist tactics including the use of non-Communists is one of the greatest internal security risks" in the state and concluded that the clergymen represented by the Pascagoula pastor—the "Trigg type," as he disdainfully labeled them— "often throws rocks at the person who sounded the fire-alarm rather than put out the fire and help apprehend the arsonists."[40] Observing Lowman's almost obsessive interest in Mississippi's internal affairs, the *Madison County Herald* in Canton editorialized critically that the state's "fair capital city" had become "the real fertile [place] . . . for the self-styled crusaders and communist hunters":

> Although Jackson is far from the center of national affairs, it is being recognized as a mecca for those who have communistic warning to voice at a price. It must indeed be a lush field in the minds of those who are looking for appreciative audiences that will listen and cheer any speaker who says he has vital information about the Reds and has the answer to their aggression and efforts to take over this wonderful country of ours.[41]

The main reason why those "self-styled crusaders and communist hunters" such as Lowman were busy "flocking to Jackson," the Canton paper noted, was that "they have been informed that the picking is good down this way."[42] And to be sure, Lowman's highly visible visit to Mississippi in July 1962—his sixth trip to the state since January 1961—was not to be his last.

While Lowman's involvement in Mississippi's racial affairs deepened, the state once again became a major battlefield for black civil rights. Only a day after Kennedy's inauguration in January 1961, in keeping with the idealistic words of the young president's inaugural address, James Meredith, a twenty-seven-year-old black veteran of the U.S. Air Force, set out to do what he could do for his country and his home state of Mississippi. A native of Attala County, Meredith had served in the Air Force for almost a decade from 1951 to 1960 to "preserve and protect the rights and privileges of democracy" that he himself "didn't in fact enjoy." When he got out of the military service and came back to Mississippi, where racial segregation and discrimination remained intact, Meredith was determined to do everything he could to right the wrongs for himself and his fellow black southerners. And soon, breaking down the high wall of one of the most conspicuous symbols of the state's white supremacy—the all-white University of Mississippi, or Ole Miss—became his "absolute conscious decision."[43]

On September 29, 1962, in the face of the defiance of Mississippi governor Ross Barnett, who elected to repeat Arkansas governor Orval Faubus's 1957 performance "with some Mississippi variations," President Kennedy reluctantly federalized the Barnett-commanded Mississippi National Guard and authorized Secretary of the Army Cyrus R. Vance to call out troops for the purpose of sending them to the University of Mississippi if it became necessary to protect Meredith's admission to the all-white institution. Earlier in the day, William Rainach—no longer a Louisiana state senator but still a prime mover in Louisiana's Citizens' Council move-ment—had driven onto the Ole Miss campus. Holding an impromptu news conference, Rainach told the gathered reporters that he had advised Barnett that there were ten thousand men in Louisiana who were eager and "ready to come to Mississippi and place themselves" under Barnett's command to keep Meredith from entering the University of Mississippi. Meanwhile, as President Dwight Eisenhower had done five years earlier during the Little Rock desegregation crisis, President Kennedy addressed the nation on television to explain his course of actions and, more impor-tant, to try to prevent riots on the Ole Miss campus over Meredith's regis-tration. Reminiscent of Eisenhower's 1957 speech, Kennedy's September 30 nationwide address emphasized the gravity of "law and order," the presi-dent's constitutional duty, and the Cold War imperative, appealing to white Mississippians' "sense of honor."[44] In constructing the Ole Miss crisis as a "legal contest" and a "problem of enforcement" rather than addressing the desegregation issue as the nation's most urgent moral dilemma, Kennedy made exactly the same mistake that Eisenhower had made.[45] Despite his best intentions, by the time Kennedy began his address, campus riots had already flared up at the University of Mississippi. To subdue the rioting that would result in two deaths, the Kennedy administration dispatched more than twenty thousand federal troops to Oxford.[46] "We lacked," Spe-cial Assistant Edwin O. Guthman would later admit to Attorney General Robert Kennedy, "a sense of Southern history."[47]

On the morning of October 1, 1962, Meredith—whom Governor Barnett labeled "one little boy . . . backed by the NAACP which is a communist front"—officially became the first black student to enroll at the University of Mississippi. Prior to Meredith's desegregation of Ole Miss, no public school in the state—neither its elementary and secondary schools, nor colleges and universities—had been racially integrated, though there had been a few unsuccessful attempts to break down the wall of segrega-tion in the state's institutions of higher education. (Clyde Kennard's 1959 failed endeavor to enroll at all-white Mississippi Southern College—where William McCain served as president—undoubtedly reflected the efforts of the state's segregationist power structure.)[48] As Nicholas deBelleville Katzenbach and Harrison Jay Goldin, who assisted with Meredith's en-rollment as the Department of Justice's deputy attorney general and as one of the department's attorneys respectively, looked back years later, the Ole Miss crisis "showed people that you are going to have to obey the law even if it takes twenty-two thousand soldiers" to "protect a single citizen."[49] Meanwhile, at the White House, President Kennedy wearily asked his younger brother, Attorney General Robert Kennedy, if there would be "any more like this one coming up soon." The attorney general replied that the president "could look forward to losing at least one more state's electoral votes" if he decided to run in the 1964 presidential election.[50] True to Robert Kennedy's prediction, Mississippi's neighboring state, Alabama, as "the Heart of Dixie," would become the next major battleground for black civil rights.

On January 14, 1963, four months after the University of Mississippi desegregation ordeal, George C. Wallace, the newly inaugurated forty-three-year-old governor of Alabama, set out to make himself a renewed symbol of southern defiance in the state capital of Montgomery. In so doing, Wallace—formerly a racially moderate Alabama circuit court judge—made Arkansas governor Faubus "seem like an admirer of the N.A.A.C.P.," as one news reporter observed. "Let us rise to the call of freedom-loving blood that is in us and send out answer to the tyranny that clanks its chains upon the South," Wallace proclaimed in his inaugural address. "In the name of the greatest people that have ever trod this earth," he proclaimed, "I draw the line in the dust and toss the gauntlet before the feet of tyranny . . . and I say . . . segregation today . . . segregation tomorrow . . . [and] segregation forever."[51] Wallace, during his gubernatorial campaign in the previous year, had made it clear that if the federal government forced his state to desegregate its public universities, he would defy such "illegal" orders "to the point of standing in the schoolhouse door."[52] Since the debacle of the University of Mississippi desegregation crisis, southern segregationists had been desperately searching for someone or something to cling to, and in January 1963, they found their "someone" in Alabama governor Wallace and their "something" in his unyielding defiant posture. In no time, Wallace became the most conspicuous personification of Alabama's official state motto, "Audemus Jura Nostra Defendere" (We Dare Defend Our Rights)—in this case, their presumed right to maintain segregation in the state's public educational institutions.

Three months had passed since Wallace's inauguration when, in the spring of 1963, one of the most violent and racist incidents of the modern civil rights movement exploded in Birmingham, Alabama, where Martin Luther King Jr. had been invited to lead nonviolent demonstrations against the city's racial practices. Public Safety Commissioner T. Eugene "Bull" Connor's ferocious use of police dogs and fire hoses to disperse the demonstrators on May 3 brought national and international attention to the Alabama city's civil rights campaign, as well as to the angry faces of southern defiance. While making Birmingham a major battlefield for civil rights, Governor Wallace took the opportunity to appear before the Alabama state legislature on May 7. Reiterating his previous pledge that he would maintain racial segregation by fair means or foul, Wallace insisted that the "troubles in Birmingham stem from a long history of outside agitation planned and directed by members" of the Communist Party of the United States of America (CPUSA) and "their fellow-travelers." The time was ripe for Alabama, Governor Wallace noted, to strike out at the Communist-riddled civil rights "troubles."[53] Aroused by their governor, the legislators interrupted Wallace more than twenty times "with tumultuous applause."[54] Wallace expressed himself ready to do everything possible within his command to "keep the nigger communists from taking over" his beloved state.[55]

Two weeks later, on May 21, 1963, state legislators created the Alabama Legislative Commission to Preserve the Peace—more succinctly referred to as the Alabama Peace Commission.[56] As a legislative body designed to help the governor keep his segregationist pledge, the incongruously named commission was authorized to exercise the powers and duties to "study, investigate, analyze and interrogate persons, groups and organizations" that were "engaged in activities of an unlawful nature against the sovereignty of the State of Alabama" and thus were "detrimental to the peace and dignity" of the state.[57] Comprised of five legislators (two state senators and three state representatives), the Alabama Peace Commission was chaired by State Representative John H. Hawkins Jr. of Birmingham, who had been recommended to Governor Wallace by Albert J. "Al" Lingo, head of the recently renamed Alabama State Troopers (changed from the Alabama State Highway Patrol) and a native of the governor's home county of Barbour.[58] Assisting Hawkins as the commission's vice chair was State Senator James S. "Jimmy" Clark, a future Alabama House Speaker.[59]

A "prophet of impending doom at the hands of the Communists," Representative Hawkins, who also served as the chair of the Subversive Activities Committee of the Alabama American Legion, warned his fellow white Alabamians that "Communist subversion" in the nation and specifically in the South was "in large measure directed through minority groups."[60] Martin Luther King Jr.'s "rise to prominence" through the nationally publicized 1955–56 Montgomery Bus Boycott and his advocacy of "Social Revolution," according to the Alabama Peace Commission chair, were "part and parcel of the Communist operation in America." Determined to expose "the entire scope of the subversive apparatus" threatening Alabama, the Wallace-sanctioned legislative commission would soon equip itself with C. Edwin "Ed" Strickland, a former newspaper reporter who would serve the commission as its staff director, in early 1964.[61] Prior to his appointment to the Alabama Peace Commission, Strickland, in the immediate wake of the fall 1962 University of Mississippi desegregation crisis, had written a fierce letter of protest to Attorney General Robert Kennedy, criticizing the Kennedy administration's "mewling approach" to "appease the Red-ridden" NAACP and other "left-wing minority groups to the extent of invading a sovereign state" of Mississippi by deploying "more troops than we currently have in Laos and West Berlin combined." Any measure of token desegregation might be forced and accomplished with the presence of federal troops in the South, but, he warned the attorney general, "you are fighting windmills and trying to sweep back the tide" of the white South's resistance movement "with bloom." Strickland signed his biting protest letter, "A disgusted American."[62] After assuming the directorship of the Alabama Peace Commission, Strickland, a devoted and loyal servant of George Wallace, reminded the governor that "we are with you in any course you decide is best for Alabama."[63]

By the time the Alabama Legislative Commission to Preserve the Peace was created in May 1963, a federal district court had ruled that the all-white University of Alabama in Tuscaloosa must admit two twenty-year-old black students—Vivian J. Malone and James A. Hood. Unlike the flamboyant Mississippi governor Ross Barnett, Wallace was a shrewd and calculating politician. Having learned a crucial lesson from his neighboring state's desegregation debacle, the Alabama governor understood how far he could take his defiance of the federal government. At the same time, however, Wallace would not simply retreat from the impending federal "tyranny" without a fight to defend his beloved state—"the last stronghold of the Anglo-Saxon civilization," as the governor called it in the wake of the University of Mississippi ordeal. Thus, Wallace needed a little farcical show at the schoolhouse door to prove to his fellow white Alabamians and the world that he would abandon his campaign pledge only when faced with the formidable might of federal troops. True to his vow, on June 11, 1963, Governor Wallace stood in front of the door of Foster Auditorium on the University of Alabama campus, physically blocking the enrollment of Malone and Hood in defiance of the federal court order and denouncing the Kennedy administration's "unwelcomed, unwanted, unwarranted and force-induced intrusion" on "the peace and dignity" of his state.[64]

In response, President Kennedy issued an executive order to federalize the Alabama National Guard. Three hours after the confrontation broke out, Henry V. Graham, the commanding general of the National Guard, strode to the door of the auditorium and informed Wallace, his "former" commander-in-chief: "It is my sad duty to ask you to step aside." The Alabama governor subsequently backed down, saying, before he left center stage, that he could not "fight bayonets with my bare hands." Malone and Hood registered without violence.[65]

While the day of Alabama's bloodless desegregation incident marked the inevitable receding of its state-supported massive resistance, it also served as the belated beginning of the Kennedy administration's full-fledged commitment to the cause of black Americans' civil rights. The 1961 Freedom Ride incident, the 1962 Ole Miss crisis, the recent white violence against the nonviolent protesters in Birmingham, and Governor Wallace's defiant stand "in the schoolhouse door" had all shown President Kennedy "how stubborn, savage, [and] deeply rooted" the South's racial problems were.[66] Heaving a sigh of relief and, at the same time, realizing that the University of Alabama incident offered an important and appropriate moment, the president addressed the country on national television on the subject of its most pressing domestic issue—civil rights. With the text of an unfinished speech in hand, Kennedy revealed his plan to ask Congress to enact sweeping civil rights legislation to "make a commitment . . . to the proposition that race has no place in American life or law."[67] As promised, on June 19, 1963, only eight days after his historic address, President Kennedy sent a package of civil rights legislation to Congress. In a special message to the nation's lawmakers, the president insisted that the legislation would be needed "not merely for reasons of economic efficiency, world diplomacy and domestic tranquility—but, above all, because it is right." In conclusion, Kennedy directed a few carefully chosen words to southern lawmakers: "I . . . ask every member of Congress to set aside sectional and political ties, and to look at this issue from the viewpoint of the Nation. I ask you to look into your hearts . . . for the one plain, proud and priceless quality that unites us all as Americans: a sense of justice."[68]

President Kennedy's impassioned appeal notwithstanding, neither the southern politicians in Congress nor most of their white constituents and allies were yet ready to set aside their sectional ties and abandon their cherished and segregated southern way of life. On July 1, 1963, the Senate Commerce Committee opened its hearings in the nation's capital on the Kennedy administration's proposed civil rights legislation, dealing specifically with the bill's public accommodations section.[69] As a whole, the Senate Commerce Committee, composed of seventeen members and chaired by Warren G. Magnuson, a Democratic senator from Washington, was sympathetic to the public accommodations section included in the legislation, especially when compared with the other Senate committee that was conducting hearings on the civil rights bill—Eastland's Judiciary Committee. Of these seventeen lawmakers, there were five Republicans, none of whom was from the former Confederate states. In addition, the committee's twelve Democrats included only two southern senators. One of them was Strom Thurmond from South Carolina, the 1948 presidential candidate of the States' Rights Democratic, or Dixiecrat, Party, who would soon switch his allegiance to the Republican Party. Thurmond's defense of and clinging to racial segregation, however, was somewhat mitigated and balanced by the presence of the other southern senator, Ralph W. Yarborough of Texas, who was known to be a racially moderate and reform-minded lawmaker.[70]

During its twenty-two-day hearings, the Senate Commerce Committee, until the hearings' adjournment on August 2, 1963, gathered testimony from almost eighty witnesses, including half of the nation's governors.[71] Vocal opposition to the civil rights bill was voiced by such architects and keepers of the white South's massive resistance as Mississippi governor Ross Barnett, Alabama governor George Wallace, and Arkansas attorney general Bruce Bennett, whose "Southern Plan for Peace" program had aimed to crack down on the NAACP and other civil rights organizations in the aftermath of the 1957 Little Rock desegregation crisis.[72] Joining these proponents of southern segregation in opposition to the bill was James J. Kilpatrick, the editor of the pro-segregation *Richmond News Leaders* in Virginia and an acclaimed states' righter, whom *Time* magazine once called "one of the most gifted and eloquent spokesmen for the Old South." Kilpatrick's 1957 work, *The Sovereign States: Notes of a Citizen of Virginia*, and his 1962 analysis entitled *The Southern Case for School Segregation* had by then become essential reference works for the white South's defenders of racial status quo.[73] Allying himself with Virginia's illustrious states' righter was William Loeb III, the archconservative publisher of the *Manchester Union Leader* in New Hampshire, who also testified during the committee hearings.[74]

On July 12, 1963, appearing before the Senate Commerce Committee, Mississippi governor Barnett was determined to seize the opportunity to let the world know that black southerners' quest for racial justice, the resulting civil rights movement, and now the federal government's proposition to support the movement by enacting Kennedy's civil rights legislation were all the results of nefarious Communist enterprises. "I am convinced that this is a part of the world Communist conspiracy to divide and conquer our country from within," Barnett told the committee members, indicating that the proposed civil rights legislation, or what the Mississippi governor termed the "White Slave Bill," reflected the CPUSA's ominous "drive to mobilize both colored and white for the overthrow of our government." And if the country was to survive as a "Constitutional Republic of Sovereign States," he went on, the civil rights bill must be defeated in Congress. "The decision is yours. May God have mercy on your souls!," Barnett remarked, concluding his prepared statement with what Edwin King, a noted white civil rights activist in Mississippi who had served as the chaplain of Tougaloo College, once called a "frightening kind of sincerity."[75]

Unconvinced by Barnett's allegation that the civil rights movement was part and parcel of "the world Communist conspiracy," Senator A. S. Mike Monroney, a Democrat from Oklahoma, asked the Mississippi governor what evidence he had that black southerners' civil rights struggle was Communist-inspired, rather than being an earnest protest by "American citizens seeking rights they are entitled to." In response, Barnett told the committee that Martin Luther King Jr. was a leader of the Communist "agitators" and ostentatiously pulled a flier out of his briefcase.[76] The flier was the one that Roy Harris, who served as the chair of the segregationist Georgia Commission on Education's Advertising Committee, had recently produced, claiming to have distributed "a million copies" of it among the South's politicians, officials, and white-supremacist groups.[77] Sensationally entitled *Martin Luther King at Communist Training School,* the flier contained a photograph taken at the Highlander Folk School in Monteagle, Tennessee, in 1957 on the occasion of the school's twenty-fifth anniversary.[78] Taken by Ed Friend as the Georgia commission's white informant, the photo depicted Martin Luther King Jr. allegedly "consorting with 'known Communists'" while listening to, as Barnett claimed, "a Communist lecture." Another Democratic senator, Philip A. Hart from Michigan, challenged the Mississippi governor, informing him that Hart was "for civil rights" and that he "would walk with Martin Luther King." "[And] I hope that doesn't make me [a] suspect," the Michigan senator quipped.[79] Following Hart's remarks, when Senator Monroney further questioned the accuracy of the characterization of King and the others shown in the photograph as communists, Barnett was forced to respond evasively that he had not checked the allegation with the Federal Bureau of Investigation (FBI). The Mississippi governor then suggested that the Senate Commerce Committee make inquiries at the bureau on his behalf, concluding his three-hour testimony.[80]

Three days after Barnett's testimony, on July 15, 1963, Governor Wallace got his chance to launch a tirade before the Senate Commerce Committee in opposition to the proposed civil rights bill. As if to take vengeance on the Kennedy administration for the University of Alabama's desegregation incident that had occurred in the previous month, Wallace—the personification of Alabama's racial injustice—berated the administration and its congressional allies. The governor, acting as though he were a "one-man army at war with the Federal government," was back in the game. "As a loyal American and as a loyal Southern Governor, who has never belonged to or associated with any subversive element," he railed, "I resent the fawning and pawing over such people as Martin Luther King and his pro-Communist friends and associates."[81] In concluding his harangue, Wallace stated that the bulk of those involved in the South's integration movement were the nation's "enemies":

> Gentlemen . . . before leaving I have a request I would like to make. I have charged here today that there are Communist influences in the integration movement. From the mountain of evidence available everyone should realize that they are true. . . . Why don't you do something about it? Don't sweep this matter under the rug—let's expose these enemies . . . of both black and white in this country—bring them out in the open.[82]

When asked by a Senate Commerce Committee member to substantiate his assertion that communism was indeed behind the entire civil rights movement, Wallace—as Mississippi governor Barnett had done three days earlier—held up the Highlander Folk School flier as part of what he termed "the mountain of evidence."[83] In the meantime, a Democratic member of the committee, Senator Edward L. Bartlett from Alaska, asked Wallace a question: If it were discovered that a southern segregationist governor had once been a "student leader" at a Communist-influenced school, Bartlett wanted to know, would the Alabama governor concur that it could be surmised that racial segregation might be a product of what Wallace identified as "Communist technique" during his own statement? Perturbed, the Alabama governor replied that he could not quite comprehend the senator's inquiry.[84] Thereupon, Bartlett told Wallace that he had been informed that Arkansas governor Orval Faubus had attended Commonwealth College in Mena, Arkansas, which was "not only affiliated with the Highlander Folk School but was also on the Attorney General's list."[85] Senator Bartlett thus deployed Governor Wallace's own theory of Communist conspiracy to see if it could be applied "in the other direction." Refusing to respond to the senator's argument, Wallace set his lips and spat out, "Faubus is no Communist." Vowing that the white people in the South would "take the lead . . . in an all-out effort to defeat" the proposed civil rights legislation, the Alabama governor added angrily: "No part of the Civil Rights Act of 1963 is acceptable." Continuing his testimony on the following day, Wallace let it be known before the Senate committee that he "would not make any effort to help enforce" the civil rights bill if Congress enacted it and "would just go ahead and be governor of Alabama."[86]

On July 16, 1963, following Wallace's second appearance before the Senate Commerce Committee, Faubus's segregationist comrade in Arkansas, Attorney General Bruce Bennett, testified before the committee. Bennett, who had just been reelected to the attorney general's office, had been instrumental in staging the December 1958 public hearings conducted by the Special Education Committee of the Arkansas Legislative Council, where J. B. Matthews was invited to give his testimony for the pro-segregation committee to "determine if there is any subversion present" in the state.[87] After reviewing some racial incidents that had occurred in Arkansas, including the 1957 Little Rock desegregation crisis, Attorney General Bennett told the Senate Commerce Committee members that these racial disturbances in his state had been "deliberately planned" by the CPUSA "as a part of the directive handed down by Moscow."[88] On the following day, July 17, during President Kennedy's White House news conference, a reporter, referring to the recent testimony by Governors Barnett and Wallace and Arkansas attorney general Bennett before the Senate committee, asked Kennedy whether the nation was once again "entering into a period of McCarthyism." "We have no evidence that any of the leaders of the civil rights movements [*sic*] in the United States are Communism [*sic*] . . . [and] that the demonstrations are Communist-inspired," the president replied. Kennedy then added: "I think it is a convenient scapegoat to suggest that all the difficulties are Communist[-directed]."[89] Echoing his elder brother, Attorney General Robert Kennedy notified the Senate Commerce Committee on July 25 that "based on all available information from the FBI and other sources," the federal government had "no evidence that any of the top leaders of the major civil rights groups are Communists, or Communist-controlled." "This is true as to Dr. Martin Luther King Jr., about whom particular accusations were made," the nation's attorney general added.[90]

Responding to the Kennedy administration's pronouncement that Martin Luther King Jr. and other civil rights leaders had nothing to do with the Communist menace, Governor Barnett dispatched one of his most trusted and rabidly segregationist members of the Mississippi State Sovereignty Commission to Washington, D.C., near the end of the public hearings being conducted by the Senate Commerce Committee.[91] Appearing before the committee on July 31, 1963, Mississippi state senator John C. McLaurin, who was then making an unsuccessful bid for the state's attorney generalship, charged that the statement issued by Attorney General Robert Kennedy was "the most brazen cover-up job ever perpetrated on the American people." The younger Kennedy must be, McLaurin asserted, either "deliberately white-washing the negro leadership with which he is in daily contact" or "the most ignorant Attorney General this nation has ever had."[92] While citing Matthews's testimony made before the Florida Legislative Investigation Committee in February 1958, which had been compiled in *Communism and the NAACP* published by the Georgia Commission on Education, McLaurin wrapped up his testimony before the congressional committee by disclosing his and southern massive resisters' true intention in merging their racist views with anticommunism: "Gentlemen, I am sure that the Communists have a major part in the negro demonstrations that are underway in our Nation. . . . We in Mississippi and in many parts of the South do not want integration!"[93]

As if to reflect McLaurin's resolve, just before the Senate Commerce Committee opened its public hearings with regard to the proposed civil rights bill on July 1, 1963, Mississippi had spearheaded what Alabama governor Wallace would soon term the South's "all-out effort to defeat" the legislation during his congressional testimony.[94] After the fall 1962 Ole Miss desegregation crisis, Mississippi had been eager to wage another battle against the Kennedy administration, and the Mississippi-led white South's major offensive was entrusted to John Satterfield—a noted segregationist attorney in Yazoo City, Mississippi, and a former president of the Mississippi State Bar Association as well as of the American Bar Association. As a Methodist, an anti-Communist, and a states' righter, he had also served as the president of the Lowman-propelled Circuit Riders in Cincinnati during the 1950s.[95] In late June 1963, Satterfield, along with Erle Johnston, who was the newly appointed director of the Mississippi

State Sovereignty Commission, attended a series of meetings in Washington, D.C., to "lay plans for an organized effort to defeat the new Kennedy civil rights program." "It was apparent from these meetings," Johnston later reported to Governor Barnett and the other commission members, "that we in the South now have new and important allies, who never before seemed seriously concerned with . . . the federal government's determination to take over private enterprise."[96]

Despite Johnston's slightly exaggerated report to the Mississippi State Sovereignty Commission, those who attended the Washington gatherings in late June 1963 represented a parade of impressive figures. For example, at one unpublicized meeting arranged by Satterfield, the attendees included high-ranking representatives of such nationally influential organizations as the Chambers of Commerce of the United States, the National Association of Manufacturers, the National Association of Real Estate Boards, the National Association of Home Builders, and the Council of State Government. While in the nation's capital, Satterfield and Johnston also conferred with Senator James Eastland and Hugh V. White Jr. of Richmond, Virginia, a former executive director of the pro-segregation Virginia Commission on Constitutional Government. "It was a thrill for me," Johnston wrote in his report on his Washington trip with Satterfield, "to see how the gentlemen at these meetings looked to Mississippi for leadership and expressed such confidence in Mr. Satterfield."[97]

As a result of the meetings held in the nation's capital, in July 1963, while the Senate Commerce Committee was busy taking testimony on the merits of the proposed civil rights legislation, Satterfield set out to organize a group in Washington, D.C., that would soon become known as the Coordinating Committee for Fundamental American Freedoms, or the Satterfield Committee. As an educational and lobbying organization, the Satterfield Committee's sole purpose was set to prevent the passage of what the group detestably called "the Kennedy bill" in Congress.[98] Heading the committee as its chair was William Loeb, publisher of the *Manchester Union Leader,* who appeared before the Senate Commerce Committee in opposition to the Civil Rights Bill of 1963.[99] An ardent anti-Communist and an admirer of Senator Joseph McCarthy, Loeb began his association with Matthews in the summer of 1954.[100] In addition, James Kilpatrick, editor of Virginia's *Richmond News Leader* who also testified before the Senate Commerce Committee, was chosen as vice chair of the new anti–civil rights group.[101] Another Virginian, John J. Synon, founder of a Richmond-based conservative organization called the Patrick Henry Club, who had won

Satterfield's confidence with an "impressive record in conservative public relations," was appointed as the committee's full-time director.[102] As for Satterfield—the man *Time* magazine would call "the most prominent segregationist lawyer in the country" in the late 1960s—he became his group's secretary-treasurer and subsequently set up the committee's headquarters in a luxurious $637-a-month suite at the Carroll Arms Hotel, located only a block away from Capitol Hill.[103]

From its inception, Satterfield and the other officials of the Coordinating Committee for Fundamental American Freedoms hoped that their new Washington, D.C.–based organization would help create a genuine nationwide movement to defeat the civil rights bill. But in reality, bent on denying any of those "fundamental American freedoms" to black southerners, the Satterfield Committee showed itself to be just another coordinated and desperate endeavor—like the Mississippi-born Citizens' Councils of America and the Federation for Constitutional Government based in New Orleans—to preserve its "fundamental southern segregationism and injustice" despite the committee's appeal to and support given by the North and other regions of the nation. Thus, as the citadel of the South's racial segregation and discrimination, it was almost natural that Mississippi became the most vigorous supporter of the anti–civil rights bill project envisioned by the Satterfield Committee. For the nine-month period from July 1963 to the end of March 1964, Satterfield's group would spend $343,200 for its activities. And, indeed, out of this total amount, the financial contributions made by or funneled through the Barnett-chaired and Johnston-directed Mississippi State Sovereignty Commission amounted to some $262,600.[104]

Meanwhile, Governor Wallace's Alabama—Mississippi's trusted ally in waging its last-ditch fight to prevent the passage of the comprehensive federal civil rights legislation—was restless as well. No sooner had Wallace returned home from the nation's capital, where he had testified against the enactment of the civil rights bill, than the state legislature created the Alabama State Sovereignty Commission at the behest of the governor in the summer of 1963.[105] Alabama thus became the last southern state to establish a state sovereignty commission, following in the footsteps of Mississippi, Arkansas, and Louisiana in that order. Maintaining that the creation of the new executive agency, to be placed directly under him, was justified by a "clear need to investigate communist infiltration" into the civil rights movement in Alabama, Wallace pressed home the absolute necessity of equipping his state with a set of twin commissions—the Alabama Legislative Commission to Preserve the Peace and the Alabama State

Sovereignty Commission as the two wheels of the state's chariot of segregation—to launch white Alabamians' counteroffensive against the "federal juggernaut" that the governor believed was promoting civil rights.[106]

With a biennial appropriation of $100,000 by the state legislature, the newly established Alabama State Sovereignty Commission—whose template could easily be traced to the Mississippi State Sovereignty Commission—was composed of eight members, including Wallace as its ex-officio chair.[107] And to "add a patina of legality to the unsupportable challenge to federal supremacy," the governor made sure that the bulk of his commission members were appointed by the Alabama State Bar Association.[108] Eli H. Howell, a forty-eight-year-old lawyer and a former analyst at the Alabama State Legislative Reference Service, took the commission's $10,000-per-year executive secretary position.[109] Though the Alabama State Sovereignty Commission would not fully and officially function until January 3, 1964, when the agency's first organizational meeting was held, and despite its relative inactivity in comparison with the Mississippi counterpart, the birth of the State Sovereignty Commission clearly demonstrated Governor Wallace's and his fellow massive resisters' unrelenting resolve to leave no stone unturned in their fight to perpetuate Alabama's segregated way of life.[110]

Besides the official actions taken by Mississippi and Alabama, the semi-official Jackson-based segregationist organization Citizens' Councils of America, directed by William Simmons, also attempted to mobilize the South's massive resisters to bury the Civil Rights Act of 1963. By fully utilizing its "public affairs program," where what the pro-segregation group termed "the AMERICAN Viewpoint with a SOUTHERN Accent" was presented, the Citizens' Councils of America and its devoted guru, Simmons, were in no mood to sit idly by.[111] Two leaders of the Coordinating Committee for Fundamental American Freedoms—Satterfield of Mississippi and Synon of Virginia—appeared on the organization's *Citizens' Council Forum* broadcasts, criticizing the civil rights legislation and what they perceived as the frightening "extension of federal power brought on by the act."[112] Myers Lowman was also featured on the telecasts on five separate occasions during 1963. Appearing with U.S. representative John Bell Williams from Mississippi on one occasion, Lowman, having by then become one of the *Citizens' Council Forum*'s favorite guests, discussed the Communist infiltration into the civil rights movement and Martin Luther King Jr.'s "communistic" activities.[113]

While the grand scheme concocted by the Coordinating Committee for

Fundamental American Freedoms to shelve the civil rights bill in Congress developed in the nation's capital, Mississippi was about to experience the most traumatic summer in its recent history—"the long, hot summer" of 1964—with a thousand civil rights activists descending on the state. A new phase of Mississippi's civil rights movement had begun in 1962, when a statewide coalition composed of several civil rights organizations—the Council of Federated Organizations (COFO)—was formed under the leadership of Robert P. Moses of the Student Nonviolent Coordinating Committee (SNCC) and CORE's David Dennis. Realizing that black Mississippians would not be able to enjoy true "freedom" as long as their political participation was suppressed, the COFO leaders began to focus on conducting voter registration campaigns in Mississippi. While the civil rights movement in the state during the latter half of the 1950s had been largely "based in the cities, dominated by the NAACP, and centered around the small black middle class," the movement's new leadership in the 1960s saw the importance of embracing Mississippi's ordinary black citizens and "the rural poor" as "their natural constituency."[114] The establishment of the COFO and its vigorous black enfranchisement drives were largely funded by the Voter Education Project created under the auspices of the Southern Regional Council (SRC), which had been on Lowman's enemy list since early 1957.[115] In late 1963, the COFO organizers developed a statewide summer project for 1964—the Mississippi Freedom Summer Project—in which a thousand predominantly northern and white college students would join a cadre of black freedom fighters in Mississippi.[116]

As the COFO staff members, most of whom were derived from the SNCC, were getting ready for the Mississippi Freedom Summer Project, the Mississippi State Sovereignty Commission—directed by Johnston and now chaired by Governor Paul Johnson as Barnett's successor—was busy preparing to defend the state from "the anticipated invasion of students from other states."[117] Johnson, as the lieutenant governor, had "stood tall" with Barnett to block James Meredith's admission to Ole Miss in the fall of 1962.[118] Beginning in January 1964, all of the three State Sovereignty Commission investigators—Virgil Downing, Andrew L. "Andy" Hopkins, and Tom I. Scarbrough—set out to make a "personal visit to each sheriff" in each of the state's eighty-two counties in an attempt to acquaint them with the state's segregation laws.[119] During a two-hour conference with the law enforcement and other elected officials of Lafayette County held in Oxford (where Ole Miss was located) on May 1, 1964, for instance, Investigator Scarbrough, a former commissioner of the state's public safety whom Director Johnston valued as his most trusted investigator, observed that the "city and county officials are very much concerned about what is in store for their city, county, and state this summer."[120] After pointing out to the meeting's participants that the state officials, with former Governor Barnett being at the head of the list, had "been telling the rest of the country for five or six years" that the Communists were "the main force behind all of the racial unrest and civil rights agitation," Scarbrough then advised the group that those who would take part in the Mississippi Freedom Summer Project were most likely "communists, sex perverts, odd balls, and do-gooders."[121]

White Mississippians' animosity and resentment toward the Mississippi Freedom Summer Project reached its boiling point, as the hot and steamy summer of 1964 approached. Summing up their indignation and echoing the thinking of Investigator Scarbrough of the Mississippi State Sovereignty Commission, the *Meridian Star,* in an editorial entitled "God Help the USA," warned its readers to prepare themselves for an ordeal to be caused by "outside agitators": "The student volunteers—the beatniks, the wild-eyed left wing nuts, the unshaven and unwashed trash, and the just plain stupid or ignorant or misled—go on meddling and muddling with things about which they know nothing and which concern them not."[122] By the early summer, as the Freedom Summer Project participant Sue Thrasher recalled, Mississippi had "had its armor up" against these unwelcome outsiders.[123] As a means of reeducating white Mississippians about the vice of the "Communist activities" in the civil rights movement and, more specifically, of the incoming summer workers, Mississippi's massive resisters once again relied on the expertise of one of their trusted northern messiahs, Myers Lowman, who had last visited the state in July 1962.[124]

Under the sponsorship of the Mississippi Association of Methodist Ministers and Laymen—a relatively small but vocal segregationist group in Jackson—Lowman came to Mississippi in June 1964 and traveled around the state for two weeks, visiting such cities as Greenwood, Meridian, and Vicksburg.[125] On June 12, at a prearranged press conference held at the Jackson Airport, Eugene Carson Blake, the Presbyterian Church's stated clerk and a former president of the National Council of Churches (earlier, he had convinced the ecumenical organization to create its Commission on Religion and Race), outlined the role that the council would play in the Mississippi Freedom Summer Project.[126] When he discovered that Blake would be holding a press conference, Lowman, who was then on his way to a speaking engagement in Greenwood, made a brief appearance at the airport just as Blake finished talking. Castigating the National Council of Churches—one of Lowman's mortal enemies since the organization of his Circuit Riders in the early 1950s—Lowman warned before the gathered reporters that white Mississippians "should not believe anything that Carson Blake says." Seizing the opportunity, the Circuit Riders' executive secretary explained that the reason he had come to Mississippi was to "tell the people the other side of coin." White Mississippians, Lowman said, must not "swallow any of this" planned invasion concocted by the Freedom Summer Project.[127]

During his two-week stay in Mississippi, Lowman continued to fire verbal salvos at the National Council of Churches and individual church leaders including Blake, and to blame them with cutting remarks for their involvement in the Mississippi Freedom Summer Project.[128] Speaking before an appreciative audience of one hundred people at the Lamar Hotel in Meridian on June 18, 1964, he claimed that the impending "summer invasion" of Mississippi by northern college students would be conducted "under the façade, the umbrella, of the National Council of Churches," whether or not "those invaders belong to CORE, SNCC, or the NAACP."[129] Lowman's aversion to the church council was also amply revealed when he spoke at the Vicksburg Hotel on the evening of June 24, where he charged that the real purpose behind the "invasion" of Mississippi supported by the National Council of Churches was to "encourage the eventual sending of troops to the state by the federal government" when violence erupted, as had happened in the Ole Miss riots in the fall of 1962.[130] In seeming confirmation of Lowman's analysis, by the time he spoke in Vicksburg, three young civil rights workers from CORE's Meridian office—Michael H. Schwerner, Andrew Goodman, and James E. Chaney—had mysteriously disappeared in Neshoba County, Mississippi.

Since the spring of the fateful year of 1964, reflecting the surging revival of Ku Klux Klan (KKK) activities in Mississippi, cross burning on weekends had been reported in such cities as Brookhaven (Judge Tom Brady's hometown), McComb, and Natchez. A total of twelve crosses were simultaneously burned in Neshoba County alone on the night of April 5.[131] On June 16, two days before Lowman spoke in Meridian, the Mount Zion Methodist Church, a black church located in Longdale in the eastern part of Neshoba County, received a Klan-inspired baptism in kerosene and was burned to the ground. The church had been previously designated as a "Freedom School" site by the COFO. Five days after the Mount Zion

Methodist Church was destroyed and only three days prior to Lowman's speaking engagement in Vicksburg, on June 21, Schwerner and Goodman, white volunteers from New York, and Chaney, a black civil rights activist from Meridian, drove to Philadelphia, the seat of Neshoba County, to investigate the burning of the black church. No one expected that their short drive to Neshoba County would be a one-way journey. That afternoon, Chaney, who was driving a Ford station wagon, was stopped and then arrested, ostensibly for speeding, by Neshoba County Deputy Sheriff Cecil R. Price. Both Schwerner and Goodman, in the meantime, were placed in custody for what the deputy sheriff outwardly called "investigation." The three young men were immediately taken to the county jail in Philadelphia by Price and were released late in the evening. Outside the county jail, however, a posse of Klansmen from Neshoba County and neighboring Lauderdale County was eagerly waiting to get rid of Chaney and the two "nigger-lover[s]" for good. Within an hour, after a high-speed car chase, the posse had brutally murdered Schwerner, Goodman, and Chaney.[132]

On June 23, 1964, two days after the Klansmen killed the three civil rights workers, President Lyndon B. Johnson, in an eight-minute telephone conversation with Senator Eastland from Mississippi, expressed his concern about the missing young men, not knowing that they were already dead. "Jim, we've got three kids missing down there. What can I do about it?," the president asked. "I don't think there's a damn thing [to do] about it," the Mississippi senator flatly replied, expressing his belief that the disappearance of Schwerner, Goodman, and Chaney was a "publicity stunt" orchestrated by the Communist-infiltrated civil rights forces. "There's not a Ku Klux Klan in that area. There's not a Citizens' Council in that area. There's no organized white man in that area. So that's why I think it's a publicity stunt," Eastland answered authoritatively.[133] A month later, on July 22, the whereabouts of Schwerner, Goodman, and Chaney remained unknown. When Eastland stood on the Senate floor to speak about "Communist infiltration into the so-called civil rights movement" on that day, he maintained that "there is a conspiracy to thrust violence" upon the people of his native state. "Many people in our State assert that there is just as much evidence, as of today, that they are voluntarily missing as there is that they have been abducted," the Mississippi senator asserted.[134]

The *Jackson Clarion-Ledger* sided with Senator Eastland, editorializing on August 3, 1964, that if the three civil rights activists had been murdered, "it is by no means the first case of such disposition by Communists of their dupes to insure their silence." "However," the editorialist hastened to add, "the careful absence of clues makes it seem likely that they are quartered in Cuba or another Communist area awaiting their next task." "There is no reason to believe them seriously harmed by citizens of the most law-abiding state of the union," the editorial concluded.[135] On the next day, however, the self-serving observations made by Eastland and the Mississippi newspaper proved to be both inaccurate and imprudent. Forty-four days after the disappearance of Schwerner, Goodman, and Chaney, the FBI finally discovered their decomposed bodies in an earthen dam in Neshoba County.[136] "Red Machiavellianism," as one critic of Senator Eastland and his ilk had predicted only three days prior to the bodies' discovery, "is to be the rug under which segregationist sins will be swept."[137]

While the search for the three civil rights workers was still being conducted in Mississippi, the Civil Rights Act of 1964—what Senator Eastland had once described as a "hydra-headed monster"—passed Congress and was signed into law by President Johnson on July 2. The legislation's enactment dealt a fatal blow to the already crumbling walls of racial segregation in Mississippi and the entire South.[138] Despite the efforts made by the Coordinating Committee for Fundamental American Freedoms, which had been organized to oppose what John Satterfield termed "civil wrongs" under the guise of "civil rights," President Johnson's determination to "honor President Kennedy's memory" with "the earliest possible passage of the civil rights bill" won the day.[139]

As Mississippi's eventful "long, hot summer" of 1964 proceeded, Lowman, following his June visit, revisited the state in the middle of July to speak in the capital city of Jackson. The northern volunteers taking part in the Mississippi Freedom Summer Project, the Cincinnatian declared, were composed of "social misfits in their own communities."[140] Lowman also contended that Mississippi was duty bound to get rid of these northern "social misfits," as well as those renegades in the race field at home who might offer helping hands to the project workers. One of Lowman's and the Mississippi segregationists' primary adversaries at home was James Silver at the University of Mississippi, whom Lowman had included "among his Reds" when Silver confronted Lowman during the latter's February 1961 red-baiting speaking tour in Mississippi.[141]

In the wake of the fall 1962 University of Mississippi desegregation ordeal, some forty professors resigned from the school in protest against the state's and the university's handling of the crisis.[142] Among those who remained at the university, Silver had been the most vocal critic of the Barnett administration's defiant and self-destructive posture. "No man ever went into public office as ignorant as he did," the history professor would say of Barnett when his governorship ended in early 1964, "and no man ever stayed in office for four years and is coming out as ignorant as he is."[143] On November 7, 1963, Silver was scheduled to deliver his presidential address at the annual meeting of the Southern Historical Association in Asheville, North Carolina. Incorporating the words used in the University of Mississippi's 1959 response ("Mississippi cannot exist as a closed society") to the state's die-hard segregationists' allegations that the school was "teaching integration, subversion and apostasy," the Ole Miss professor entitled his presidential address "Mississippi: The Closed Society."[144] In the address, Silver relentlessly criticized the cultural, mental, and intellectual restrictiveness of Mississippi society and described how the state's reckless commitment to the doctrine of white supremacy had inevitably led to the 1962 University of Mississippi riots.

The day after Silver delivered his provocative address, Mississippi governor Barnett, asked by a newspaper reporter for his comments on the Ole Miss professor's speech, responded: "Old Silver's liable to say anything. I wouldn't waste words on that man."[145] While the governor would waste few words on Silver, the Barnett-chaired Mississippi State Sovereignty Commission, in collaboration with the Board of Trustees of State Institutions of Higher Learning, would invest ample time and energy in the effort to rid the state of him. On December 2, 1963, less than a month after Silver's address had infuriated Mississippi's white supremacists, Director Erle Johnston of the State Sovereignty Commission wrote a letter to the chair of the board of trustees, Thomas J. Tubb, questioning "the propriety or wisdom of retaining" on the state's payrolls a professor who, according to Johnston, "so flagrantly demonstrates disloyalty" to both the University of Mississippi and the state. Displaying his indignation that Silver's recent remarks and behavior were "not in accord with . . . the programs of the Sovereignty Commission" to preserve and protect the state's and the South's racial segregation, the commission director asked the board's chair to find a way to "relieve" Silver of his duties at Ole Miss. As one reporter for the *Memphis Commercial Appeal* in Tennessee put it, Mississippi's segregationist forces were all over the history professor "like gnats on a running sore" in their fight to keep their "closed society" closed.[146]

Then, in the early summer of 1964, when Mississippi began to witness the inflow of the Freedom Summer Project volunteers, Silver published a book that was an expanded version of the address he had delivered before the Southern Historical Association. The publication date of *Mississippi:*

The Closed Society happened to coincide with the nationally publicized disappearance of the three civil rights workers in Neshoba County in late June, and the book quickly became a best-seller. "The inspiration for Negro demands," the embattled Ole Miss professor lamented in his book, "becomes the Communist Manifesto, not the Declaration of Independence" in Mississippi, and "shotgun blasts fired into Negro homes become an NAACP plot."[147] Subsequently, Silver—one of the last "breathing, practicing example[s] of academic freedom in Mississippi," as he was once described—was granted a leave of absence from the University of Mississippi to accept a visiting professorship at the University of Notre Dame in Indiana before the Board of Trustees of State Institutions of Higher Learning made its final resolution against him. In the late summer of 1964, Silver self-exiled from Mississippi, officially leaving Ole Miss, where he had taught—and had been taunted by the state's white supremacists for "selling out to the Communists"—for twenty-eight years.[148]

Along with Mississippi's massive resisters, the die-hard segregationists at the helm of their proud "Heart of Dixie" also closed ranks during the spring of 1964 in the face of the foreseeable passage of the civil rights bill in Congress. Fortifying the Alabama segregationists in their opposition to the civil rights legislation was a set of the state's recently created twin agencies, the Legislative Commission to Preserve the Peace and the State Sovereignty Commission, both organized in 1963 with Governor Wallace's blessing. In March 1964, the Alabama Peace Commission issued a report that voiced its aversion to the civil rights bill, proclaiming that a "careful reading" of the legislation then under debate in Congress made the 1928 Communist Party platform, where "full racial, political and social equality for the Negro Race" was sought, "seem most conservative."[149] Even after the passage of the Civil Rights Act of 1964 in early July, the Alabama Peace Commission's insistence that the "Communists have been assuming leadership roles in the civil rights movement" did not abate. The Communists, as the commission's October report entitled *Communists in Civil Rights* asserted, were the ones who had been "promoting violence, racial hatred and widespread law violations" in Alabama and the South. The legislative commission's ten-page report, filled with outrage against the newly enacted comprehensive civil rights legislation, further stated that the evidence provided by such "outstanding authorities" on communism in America as Senator Eastland "clearly supports the charge" that the recent Mississippi Freedom Summer Project was "Communist-dominated."[150]

In the early spring of 1965, Alabama witnessed another hate-filled racial incident in Selma. Following the epoch-making passage of the Civil Rights Act of 1964, Martin Luther King Jr. and his Southern Christian Leadership Conference (SCLS) selected Selma—where only 1 percent of the city's some fifteen thousand black residents was registered to vote—to dramatize the need for more federal legislation to protect black voter registration in the South. Although their efforts, in the end, would bear fruit in the form of the Voting Rights Act of 1965, which President Lyndon Johnson would sign into law on August 6, the events in Selma displayed to the world the ugly and desperate faces of southern defiance enacted by the sworn opponents of the region's Second Reconstruction. On Sunday, March 7, some six hundred participants began an orderly march, leaving Selma and heading for the state capital of Montgomery. As they were about to cross the Edmund Pettus Bridge at the edge of Selma, an armed posse of the Alabama State Troopers mercilessly clubbed and kicked the fleeing marchers. The term "Bloody Sunday" was later used to describe the day's tragic events. Following this nationally publicized incident, Governor Wallace failed to issue a single word of public apology, thus seeming to condone the state troopers' violent tactics. In response to the Alabama governor's apparent disregard of the marchers' safety, President Johnson would later call Wallace a "no good son of a bitch."[151]

Meanwhile, on March 18, 1965, standing on the Senate floor in the nation's capital, Mississippi senator Eastland defended Alabama's indefensible deeds, alleging that the "magnifying racial tensions" and accompanying "violence and bloodshed" in Selma were "all in furtherance of the Communist objective of weakening this Nation internally to advance the day of the projected Communist takeover."[152] Three days later, on March 21, a group of eight thousand marchers—whose right to demonstrate was backed by a court order issued by Judge Frank M. Johnson Jr. of the U.S. District Court for the Middle District of Alabama—set out to walk the fifty miles from Selma to Montgomery. Five days after the marchers arrived at the Alabama capital on March 25, the newly elected U.S. representative William L. Dickinson from Alabama took the House floor in Washington, D.C., to castigate the civil rights forces. Dickinson, whose congressional district included Montgomery, was one of the white South's Republican lawmakers who had been politically benefited from the surge of the Republican Party in the 1964 presidential election with Barry M. Goldwater's electoral sweep in the region.[153] Speaking for an hour and readily concurring with Senator Eastland, Dickinson contended that the "Communist Party and the Communist apparatus" were "the undergirding structure for all of the racial troubles in Alabama." Dickinson's baseless and ruthless attacks against those who had taken part in the voting rights march knew no bounds. According to the Alabama representative, "drunkenness and sex orgies" among the marchers, which were deliberately encouraged by the Communists and Communist sympathizers, were "the order of the day" during the Selma-to-Montgomery march.[154]

In the immediate wake of the historic civil rights march, the Eastland-chaired Senate Judiciary Committee held hearings on the merits of the voting rights bill in late March 1965. Appearing before the congressional committee as the official representative of Louisiana governor John J. McKeithen, Leander Perez—one of the most rabid segregationists in Louisiana who had closely associated with State Senator William Rainach in vitalizing the Louisiana Joint Legislative Committee's segregationist witch-hunting activities—testified on March 30 in opposition to the bill and created a "minor spectacle." While inserting some 250 pages of testimony and documents, including the entire Soviet constitution, into the records, Perez rattled on for hours about his belief that if black southerners were granted the right to vote, the next thing to emerge would be a "Communist-directed governmental authority in the entire territory of the Black Belt."[155] During Perez's tirade, Senator Everett M. Dirksen from Illinois, Republican Senate minority leader and one of the voting rights legislation's chief architects, barely managed to control his temper. But when Perez began to charge that "there is a Communist plan" behind the voting rights bill and insisted that the bill was part of a "Black Belt Communist conspiracy . . . laid out by Stalin," the Illinois senator's patience finally wore thin. "That is about as stupid a statement as has ever been uttered in this committee room," Dirksen admonished his witness.[156] As if to console his bruised segregationist ally from Louisiana, who had once been referred to as the "swampland Caesar," Senator Eastland graciously congratulated Perez on offering his committee a "very fine statement."[157]

Before the enactment of the voting rights legislation in Congress, Alabama—the last of the Deep South states to establish the tax-supported segregationist commissions—vainly tried to prevent the bill's passage. During the March 1965 Selma-to-Montgomery march, the Alabama Legislative Commission to Preserve the Peace, in close cooperation with the Alabama State Sovereignty Commission and the governor's office, filmed the historic march.[158] With its staff director, Remus Strickland, coordinating this filmmaking, the Alabama Peace Commission intended to "document Communist infiltration, direction and control of the march."[159] Subsequently, in the early summer, at the behest of the Alabama Peace Commission, the State Sovereignty Commission offered some $35,000 to Keitz and Herndon, Inc., a motion-picture production firm in Dallas, Texas, to make a documentary featuring various scenes previously filmed by the Peace Commission.[160] The result was a fifty-eight-minute, 16-mm film narrated by Leland Childs of the Birmingham radio station WCRT.[161] In what would be the Alabama segregationists' last major publicity and propaganda stunt, the poorly produced film, entitled *We Shall Overcome,* cunningly imitated the words that President Johnson had used during his eloquent congressional message delivered on March 15, in which Johnson resolved to protect black southerners' voting rights.

Alabama's officially sanctioned segregationist documentary alleged that the Communists and their allies had directed the entire Selma-to-Montgomery march and concluded with the following words: "We've viewed the red hand of Communism at work in this movement."[162] When *We Shall Overcome* was completed, the Alabama Legislative Commission to Preserve the Peace made an annotated list of the individuals and organizations depicted and mentioned in the film "with a compilation of affiliations showing affinity with Communism and Communist causes."[163] During the ensuing months, the Wallace-endorsed documentary film and the accompanying list of subversives tabulated by the Alabama Peace Commission became indispensable sources of information among the members of the Citizens' Council, as well as other conservative and pro-segregation groups, across "the Heart of Dixie."[164]

Even as the successive enactment of the civil and voting rights acts in the mid-1960s seemed to sound the death knell of the white South's massive resistance, the region's white supremacists, particularly those in Mississippi and Alabama, refused to fade gently away. "Martin Luther King, Jr., is most probably not a member of the Communist Party, U.S.A., nor of any identified Communist splinter party," the Alabama Legislative Commission to Preserve the Peace finally admitted in its 1965 report to the state legislature, "but the ten-year history of his rise to prominence through advocating Social Revolution is part and parcel of the Communist operation in America during that same period."[165] The contention that "the red hand of Communism" had been and was at work in the civil rights movement—a shrewd and unscrupulous assertion espoused by southern segregationists—would ultimately die a slow death in the white South.

"NO LIE CAN LIVE FOREVER"

From Massive Resistance to Massive Fallacy

Even after the white South's massive resisters met their waterloo in the face of the enactment of the Civil Rights Act of 1964 and the Voting Rights Act of 1965, Myers Lowman, the executive secretary of the Cincinnati-based Circuit Riders who had been deeply involved in the region's segregationist cause and enterprises, continued to funnel his anti-Communist propaganda with a discernible anti–civil rights slant to appreciative southern audiences. On March 15, 1966, seven months after the Voting Rights Act became the nation's law, Lowman made a speech in Pascagoula, Mississippi, accusing the leadership of the National Council of Churches of "persistent association with the violent radical left" and portraying the civil rights struggle as synonymous with the anti–Vietnam War movement that was then gaining national momentum.[1] Following his appearance in Mississippi—probably his last visit to the Magnolia State—Lowman went to Pensacola, Florida, to address a conservative group. There, Lowman asserted that the National Council of Churches had been "lending its umbrella of respectability" to the various civil rights organizations that, in turn, were still shamelessly "preaching violent revolution . . . in Mississippi" and elsewhere in the South.[2]

Just a few months later, on July 16, 1966, J. B. Matthews of New York City, whose Parkinson's disease, according to his third wife, Ruth, had become "considerably worse" in early May, died at the Columbia-Presbyterian Medical Center at the age of seventy-two. Three days after Matthews's death, a funeral service was held for him in New York City. At Matthews's own request, one of his longtime anti-Communist allies, Carl McIntire, the pastor at the Bible Presbyterian Church in Collingswood, New Jersey, and the director of the *Twentieth Century Reformation Hour* radio broadcast, officiated at the funeral. During the service, a daughter of James Bales, a Bible professor at Harding College in Searcy, Arkansas, who had been a close friend and admirer of Matthews's since the early 1950s, sang the deceased's favorite hymn.[3] Matthews's death put an end to what he had called his eventful "odyssey" from being a "fellow traveler" to becoming the nation's "Mr. Anti-Communist." He was buried on September 22 in the Lexington Cemetery in his native state of Kentucky, near the grave of the famed nineteenth-century politician and orator Henry Clay.[4] Conducting the burial service was Bales, who had offered his time and friendship to Ruth Matthews.[5] Following Matthews's passing, Bales strengthened his association with Billy James Hargis's Christian Crusade in Tulsa, Oklahoma, as if to fill the void created by the death of his anti-Communist mentor and comrade. (A colorful and controversial anti-Communist fighter and segregationist, Hargis—whose enemy list included President John F. Kennedy, Attorney General Robert F. Kennedy, Martin Luther King Jr., and the National Council of Churches—was often referred to as a "bawl and jump" preacher by his fellow Oklahomans.) In 1967, Bales would publish a book critical of Martin Luther King Jr. Entitling it *The Martin Luther King Story: A Study in Apostasy, Agitation, and Anarchy,* Bales contended that King's "contribution to anarchy" and "cooperation with Communists" had resulted in a "defeat for freedom and victory for communism" within the United States.[6]

After his appearance before the Mississippi General Legislative Investigating Committee in November 1959, Matthews's health had forced him to stop making trips to the South, where he had made speeches and testified before the region's segregationist audiences and state agencies. In 1964, two years before his death, Matthews had officially left the Hearst organization—his anti-Communist base of operations since the late 1930s—and begun to contemplate offering for sale, with a price tag of some $150,000, a substantial portion of his spectacularly large collection of anti-Communist files.[7] In 1965, less than a year before Matthews's passing, Edgar Bundy's Church League of America in Wheaton, Illinois, announced that the anti-Communist league's Research Department would be "the future repository" of Matthews's "famous files." At the same time, Matthews was also hired as the Church League's "consultant," and what Bundy proudly described as a means of "instantaneous communication by teletype" was established between the league's Wheaton office and Matthews's New York City penthouse.[8]

On September 11, 1967, fifteen months after Matthews's death, the Church League of America held the groundbreaking ceremonies for the

J. B. Matthews Memorial Research Library, to be adjoined to the league's headquarters, in Ruth Matthews's presence. In inviting John Clements, the Hearst Corporation's public relations counsel, to the ceremonies, Bundy wrote to Clements that he considered the new library to be "the finest and modern private research facility on communism and national security" in the entire nation.[9] Soon after the ceremonies, Bundy publicized the league's official acquisition of Matthews's "massive files on communism" in his open letter addressed to "Every Dedicated Anti-Communist" and noted that the merger of "the Matthews files with our own" would give birth to his organization's "Project Anti-Communist."[10]

Explaining further that these combined files would be "the world's most complete reference source on *all* leftists and their groups, apart from the FBI files—which, of course, are not open to the public," Bundy asked for donations for the library that would bear Matthews's name. Those who contributed twenty-five dollars or more, Bundy promised, would be entitled to receive six customized reports from the league's "Project Anti-Communist" on "any person or organization." In the end, Bundy succeeded in raising $108,000 for the "maximum-security library, plus equipment," as well as an additional $100,000 for hiring a staff to "collate the data." The Matthews Memorial Research Library was completed on June 10, 1968, and the duty to oversee the new staff of twenty-five fell to Ruth Matthews.[11] By the winter of 1967, Ruth, following in her late husband's footsteps, had established herself as a reliable anti-Communist researcher and become one of the featured contributors to the league's *News and Views,* a "monthly documented summary of current subversive activity." Other contributing writers included E. Merrill Root, who had collaborated with Mississippi's segregationists through J. B. Matthews's veiled mediation.[12]

While the Illinois-based Church League of America acquired the bulk of Matthews's anti-Communist files and documents, his death spelled the end of Myers Lowman's anti-Communist enterprise. For the Circuit Riders' executive secretary, it had taken two—Matthews and himself—to tango since the mid-1950s. Aside from losing his indispensable ally, Lowman found himself in financial trouble. In January 1965, the Cincinnati district office of the Internal Revenue Service (IRS) notified Lowman that it no longer regarded the Circuit Riders as an "educational" organization and deprived it of the "tax deductibility privileges" that the Methodist anti-Communist group had enjoyed since 1953.[13] Lowman told a *Cincinnati Enquirer* reporter that he believed the action taken by the IRS had resulted from the hostile criticism recently voiced by U.S. representative John William Wright Patman from Texas—a consistent supporter of the social and racial reforms advocated by Presidents Harry Truman, John F. Kennedy, and Lyndon Johnson—of the tax-exempt status of a total of twenty-four ultraconservative anti-Communist organizations including the Circuit Riders.[14]

Battling down to the wire, Lowman announced to the Circuit Riders' contributors in August 1966, a month after Matthews's death, that the organization's scope of activities would be "broadened to meet today's realities." "Current activities and programs of the left, *New Left* and related groups make it imperative for us," Lowman's announcement read, "to identify todays [*sic*] *revolution* aimed toward youth education." He also lamented that young Americans—both black and white, and particularly those in the South—were alarmingly "separated, diverted, detached from home, parents, church, God and country." To rectify this situation, Lowman revealed that his Circuit Riders would retain the services of Mrs. Harry Alexander—chair of the National Defense Council of the Mississippi Society of the Daughters of the American Revolution (DAR), who had been one of Lowman's trusted associates in Mississippi since the early 1960s—as the group's director of education and pledged to support her program to "stop disarming of the United States on a spiritual, moral and patriotic basis."[15] Despite Lowman's resolve to save American youth from being trapped in a maze of unspiritual, immoral, and unpatriotic "revolutionary" thought, the influence that he and his Circuit Riders had once exerted among the anti-Communist and segregationist circles was clearly on the wane. And ironically, it was one of Lowman's old friends who would deliver the final blow to the Circuit Riders.

On March 30, 1967, David Sageser of Columbus, Ohio, a former president of the Council of Churches of Greater Cincinnati who had served as the pastor at the Clifton Methodist Church, filed a libel suit at the Hamilton County Common Pleas Court against Lowman and the Circuit Riders. Asking for a total of $100,001—$100,000 for punitive damage and $1 for personal damage—Sageser maintained that for the previous fifteen years, Lowman had propagated malicious lies against him and the Council of Churches of Greater Cincinnati composed of 350 member churches. What prompted Sageser to take legal action had actually happened eleven months earlier, when Lowman circulated a memorandum at the Westwood Methodist Church in Cincinnati on the evening of April 25, 1966, in which he alleged that Sageser was "a liar and an associate of Communists."[16] On that evening, President Sageser and Executive Director Richard Isler of the Council of Churches of Greater Cincinnati met with the members of the Westwood Methodist Church's Commission on Christian Social Concern to discuss the city's race relations in general and some other issues concerning its public school desegregation. In the memorandum addressed to the church commission, Lowman observed that both Sageser and Isler had revealed "little information related to [the] Greater Cincinnati Council of Churches['] meddling with and complicating school matters" in the city.[17] By then, controversies regarding public school desegregation had no longer been confined to the South, and, in this respect, Cincinnati was no exception. The city had, in fact, already witnessed its first school desegregation litigation in 1963, when some forty-five plaintiffs filed a class-action lawsuit against the Cincinnati Board of Education.[18]

Back in the early 1950s, Sageser and Lowman had worked together for the Wesley Foundation in Cincinnati, which served as a citywide Methodist organization engaged in ministry to college students at the University of Cincinnati and other institutions of higher learning. Soon after Sageser became the first full-time director of the Wesley Foundation in September 1950, Lowman was brought into the foundation's board of directors. In 1954, Sageser left Cincinnati temporarily to take up a position as the executive director of the Department of Campus Christian Life for the National Council of Churches. Then, around the same time, the National Council of Churches became one of Lowman's and his Circuit Riders' major investigative targets, and Lowman became convinced that his friend, Sageser, had been "corrupted by 'Communist' friends." Following his return to Cincinnati, Sageser assumed the presidency of the Council of Churches of Greater Cincinnati in the early 1960s. In that capacity, Sageser was involved in the Martin Luther King Jr.–led March on Washington in August 1963, and under his leadership, the Council of Churches of Greater Cincinnati organized a similar march in the city during the fall of the same year. At the same time, Sageser also served on the City of Cincinnati's advisory committee, created to find a way to achieve peaceful desegregation of the city's public schools.[19]

As the involvement by the Council of Churches of Greater Cincinnati in the fields of civil rights and school desegregation grew deeper, Lowman became, in Sageser's words, further "obsessed" with Sageser and his church council. Lowman even established a special telephone call-in line incongruously named "Let Freedom Ring," where interested local callers could listen to recorded weekly diatribes against the "Communist conspiracy" allegedly concocted by the Council of Churches of Greater Cincinnati. When Sageser finally publicly denounced Lowman's vicious attacks on him and his church congregation, describing Lowman as being "of doubtful mental stability," Lowman sued Sageser for damages in the amount of $1,050,000. In response, Sageser, with the help of Charles P. Taft, a local attorney and a son of former President William Howard Taft, countersued Lowman in late March 1967 for $100,001. Sageser withdrew his claim when Lowman's legal action was dismissed by the court.[20]

Feeling that his legal skirmish with Sageser had jeopardized his standing in the Cincinnati Methodist community, Lowman decided to move to Buena Park in Orange County, California. Exactly when Lowman moved to the West Coast is unknown, but he had become a resident of California by the fall of 1968.[21] Located in the middle of a densely populated area stretching from Los Angeles to San Diego, Orange County had a reputation as an "enclave of right-wing voting power" and a "WASP bastion" when Lowman moved there. The county, as one observer noted in the early 1970s, was the California version of "the solid South"—but with Republican rather than Democratic domination—where the influence of the John Birch Society flourished.[22] Thus, it was an ideal place for Lowman to make a fresh start in propagating his conservative points of view as the Circuit Riders' executive secretary. Besides that, Orange County had produced someone whom Lowman could look up to—U.S. representative James B. Utt, a Santa Ana attorney and a Republican lawmaker elected to Congress in 1952.

Since Matthews's death in July 1966, Lowman had been in dire need of a reliable information provider who could take over the former role of his deceased friend. Lowman soon found a replacement for Matthews in Representative Utt, who was once described as one of "the most flamboyant examples of the political excesses of Orange County." Through the good offices of Utt and aided by his administrative assistant, Robert A. Geier, Lowman continued to familiarize himself with congressional reports and other documents related to the activities of such civil rights and anti–Vietnam War organizations as the Student Nonviolent Coordinating Committee (SNCC) and the Students for a Democratic Society (SDS).[23] As an outspoken conservative, as well as an ardent advocate of removing the United States from the United Nations, Utt had caused a commotion in 1963 when he made the outlandish statement that a "large contingent of barefooted Africans" might be gathering and training somewhere in Georgia.[24] Identifying the unlikely military maneuver in the Deep South state as "Operation Water Moccasin," Utt further implied that the contingent's presence in Georgia could be part of a military exercise being secretly conducted by the Communist-trained United Nations forces, whose ultimate goal would be to take over the entire United States. During the 1964 presidential election, Utt threw his unconditional support behind a fellow Republican, U.S. senator Barry Goldwater from Arizona, a vigorous opponent of the 1964 Civil Rights Act. And, due at least partly to Utt's endorsement of the Republican hopeful, Orange County became one of only two California counties that went for Goldwater.[25]

Having voted against the Civil Rights Act of 1964 and the Voting Rights Act of 1965, Utt was known to be anything but a friend of black southerners' civil rights struggle. A month after the disappearance of three civil rights workers—Michael Schwerner, Andrew Goodman, and James Chaney—and while they were still missing in Neshoba County, Mississippi, the California representative, standing on the floor of the U.S. House on July 28, 1964, asserted, as U.S. senator James Eastland had insisted six days earlier, that "the sinister work of forces alien to America" had brought forth the Mississippi Freedom Summer Project and that "the invasion of Mississippi, by expeditionary forces from other States, was carefully planned by the Communist conspiracy." "The cunning Communists have been able to entice fine Americans to do their work," he observed, "but the guiding hand is still the Communist conspiracy."[26] While Utt's anti-Communist and pro-segregation remarks were enthusiastically embraced by Mississippi's dailies and massive resisters, they did not go unnoticed by Alabama's segregationists. The Alabama Legislative Commission to Preserve the Peace, in its October 1964 report entitled *Communists in Civil Rights,* praised Utt as one of the "outstanding authorities" on American communism and its nefarious schemes for promoting the South's civil rights movement. The Alabama Peace Commission then concluded that Utt's investigation "clearly supports the charge that the civil rights movement in Mississippi"—and more specifically, the recent Mississippi Freedom Summer Project—had been "Communist-dominated."[27]

Aside from the presence of U.S. representative Utt, there seemed to be another vital reason why Lowman moved to California. Buena Park, a city located in the northwestern part of Orange County, provided him with an employment opportunity at the Americanism Educational League situated on Walter Knott's famed 150-acre family entertainment complex—Knott's Berry Farm.[28] From a humble beginning on a small farm in San Bernardino where he was born in 1889, Knott leased ten acres of farmland in Buena Park in 1920, setting up a berry stand on a road traveled by beachgoers. He subsequently began to specialize in cultivating the newly developed boysenberry and successfully introduced it to the market. An ambitious entrepreneur, Knott added a family restaurant on his farm during the Great Depression, where berry pies baked by his wife, Cordelia, drew special praise. After World War II, Knott expanded his restaurant business into a multimillion-dollar amusement park operation.[29] On his Knott's Berry Farm, he also established a conservative Methodist church, the Church of the Reflections, for his father, who was an evangelical Methodist preacher.[30]

In addition to being an accomplished businessperson and devout Methodist, Knott played a "pivotal role in fostering the grassroots conservative revival"—a side of him that was little known to the bulk of visitors to his amusement enterprise.[31] With his business success, Knott increasingly devoted his time and resources to fighting against what he perceived as "creeping socialism" infesting the nation.[32] While serving on the advisory board of Billy James Hargis's anti-Communist Christian Crusade, he eventually launched his own pro-laissez-faire and anti-Communist pet projects in the early 1960s—the California Free Enterprise Association and the Americanism Educational League, both of which were based at the Freedom Center, a converted farmhouse on Knott's Berry Farm.[33] The Freedom Center, serving as the conning tower of Knott's projects, took up the task of providing speakers and motion pictures for civic, patriotic, and religious organizations in the nearby communities. One of the films in great demand was *Communism on the Map,* a 1960 product of the National Education Program (NEP) operated on the Harding College campus in Arkansas—one of Matthews's sources of income in the South. For some time, Knott's Freedom Center served as "the West Coast distribution center" for NEP-produced films, pamphlets, and other material.[34]

The Americanism Educational League on Knott's Berry Farm was often referred to as the "Walter Knott Branch" because the actual headquarters of the league was situated in Los Angeles (during the 1950s, it was located in Inglewood, California). The patriotic anti-Communist group also claimed to maintain a small office in Washington, D.C., staffed by a "legal counsel." Originally founded in January 1927 as a "public service organization" by John R. Lechner, a native of Austria and a Baptist minister, who assumed its executive directorship, the league had served as Lechner's personal soapbox, from which he crusaded against any "isms" that were not Americanism and to some extent, racism. During World War II, Lechner was one of "the most energetic" individual campaigners in support of the continued exclusion of Japanese Americans from California, spreading virulent anti-Japanese American rhetoric and hysteria.[35]

Neither the archival documents located in the Myers Lowman Papers and the Circuit Riders Records nor the administrative files left at the present-day Americanism Educational League attest to the precise circumstances under which Lowman found a position with the league. However, it can be reasonably assumed that he attained the position through Ruth Matthews, for both she and her late husband had been closely associated with the league's executive director, William E. Fort Jr.[36] Lowman's precise work title and responsibilities at the Americanism Educational League are also a matter of conjecture, but a piece of audiovisual material included in the Lowman Papers suggests that he was most likely put in charge of the league's anti-Communist lecture series.[37] Furthermore, it is unclear exactly when the Lowman-led Circuit Riders was terminated, though the Circuit Riders Records reveal that Lowman continued to issue and distribute his group's literature as late as 1970, the same year in which Lowman's relationship with U.S. representative James Utt came to an abrupt end. The conservative lawmaker who, as one newspaper account sarcastically reported, had represented "the John Birch territory around Disneyland and Knott's Berry Farm" in Congress, unexpectedly died of a heart attack in Bethesda, Maryland. Three years later, on May 18, 1973, Lowman passed away in Orange County at the age of sixty-nine.[38]

In the meantime, during the period between J. B. Matthews's death in 1966 and Myers Lowman's passing in 1973—and even prior to these years—virtually all of the standing commissions and committees established by Alabama, Florida, Georgia, Louisiana, and Mississippi to wage their officially sanctioned and publicly supported massive resistance to the civil rights movement either had become defunct or were on their deathbeds. Having played a vital role in the white South's efforts to discredit the Highlander Folk School in Tennessee and its director, Myles Horton, by invoking the Red Menace, the Georgia Commission on Education—the state's guardian of racial segregation and architect of a homegrown McCarthyism for some six years—was transformed into the new Governor's Commission on Constitutional Government on October 7, 1959, at the behest of Governor Ernest Vandiver.[39] Several months before Vandiver organized his governor's commission, one of the state's segregationist icons, Roy Harris, made an unsuccessful attempt to create a legislative investigating committee separate from the five-year-old Georgia Commission on Education. Drafted by Harris, a pivotal member of the Georgia

Commission on Education, and expected to be introduced to the state legislature, the resolution to organize the legislative investigating committee provided that the new investigative body would be responsible for determining whether "a great deal of agitation and unrest" occurring in Georgia and the South was "connected with or influenced by members of, or affiliates of, or fellow travelers of any of the Communist front organizations or the Communist Party in this country." Harris's plan called for the five-member legislative investigating committee to be authorized to employ investigators and research clerks, to hold public and closed hearings, and to issue subpoenas "relative to the cause of unrest and turmoil" upsetting Georgia's traditional and cherished race relations.[40]

In February 1959, Harris forwarded his draft of the resolution to William O. Brooks, the key administrative assistant to the then newly elected governor Vandiver on "the segregation and massive resistance question."[41] "I am not sure that such a committee is . . . [absolutely] necessary," Harris wrote to Brooks, not fully realizing that the governor was contemplating abolishing the Georgia Commission on Education. "But we never know and if we had such and picked the right members and lay quietly," he added, "it could be used to good advantage in times of crisis."[42] In the end, Vandiver did not give the nod to Harris's plan. Instead, the governor terminated the Georgia Commission on Education and replaced it with the Governor's Commission on Constitutional Government composed of twenty members, including Harris as a prominent "citizen member." The newly created state agency was expected to "provide for the prevention of encroachment by the Federal Government on the functions, powers, and rights" of Georgia and was designed to serve as the state's version of the pro-segregation Virginia Commission on Constitutional Government.[43] Despite the high expectations of the state's massive resisters, however, the governor's commission never became as active as the Georgia Commission on Education had been, and the torch of the persecution of Highlander—a "Communist Training School," as the Georgia commission had labeled it—was passed to Arkansas attorney general Bruce Bennett, who had served as the mainstay of the Special Education Committee of the Arkansas Legislative Council and later assisted the Tennessee General Assembly Special Investigating Committee. The Governor's Commission on Constitutional Government in Georgia was eventually abolished in the early 1970s.[44]

Almost exactly a year before Matthews died, in June 1965, Florida's pro-segregation and anti-Communist organ—the Florida Legislative Investigation Committee, or the Johns Committee—drew its last breath. Although the Supreme Court's 1963 *Gibson* ruling, which declared that Florida's segregationist committee had failed to reveal any "substantial connection" between the National Association for the Advancement of Colored People (NAACP) and the Communist activities in the state, seemed to sound the death knell of the state's massive resistance forces, State Senator Charley Johns and his like-minded lawmakers refused to let the legislative investigation committee die.[45] Two years after it was officially authorized to conduct probes into "the extent of infiltration into agencies supported by state funds by practicing homosexuals," the Johns Committee was put under the chairmanship of State Representative Richard O. Mitchell of Tallahassee in 1963. During that year's legislative session, the investigation committee, as its last anti-Communist hurrah, made a sweeping attack on the University of South Florida, accusing the state-supported institution of "being soft on Communist teachings" and of using subversion-tainted "intellectual garbage" in its classes.[46] With an appropriation of $155,000 from the state legislature, the reorganized Florida Legislative Investigation Committee was determined to abide by a "deeper dedication to securing the State of Florida against the thrusts and parries" waged and manipulated by "those who would . . . weaken the structure of our government and the moral forces which sustain it."[47] By then, the committee chief investigator, Remus Strickland, as his expenditure vouchers indicated, had traveled some eighty thousand miles all over the state in search of what the Florida committee branded as "subversives"—racial troublemakers, Communists, and "sexual perverts."[48]

Finally, however, it was not the 1963 *Gibson* ruling that dealt the fatal blow to the Florida Legislative Investigation Committee. Ironically, the committee itself eventually brought about its own ruin in the following year. In January 1964, the Johns Committee published a scurrilous booklet on "the nature and extent of homosexuality in Florida."[49] Popularly known as the "Purple Pamphlet," *Homosexuality and Citizenship in Florida* was intended to prepare the state's youths to repel "the temptation of homosexuality lurking today in the vicinity of nearly every institution of learning."[50] Containing excessively graphic photographs depicting homosexual activities, the booklet—a "well documented report," as the committee boasted "with pride"—was widely distributed among educators and civic organizations throughout Florida.[51] In spite of the Johns Committee's self-serving praise of its own handiwork, an overwhelming public outcry, led by the American Civil Liberties Union (ACLU) of Florida, against the "Purple Pamphlet" and its compiler soon ensued. Calling the pamphlet a "pornographic booklet," the *Miami News* editorialized in March that "the latest outrage perpetrated" by the investigation committee should put "this outfit out of business once and for all." Even a state official in Dade County labeled the booklet "obscene."[52] Senator Johns resigned from the committee on September 30, 1964, after having spearheaded Florida's reign of terror for nine years. On June 30, 1965, the controversial Florida Legislative Investigation Committee was dissolved, five weeks before the historic Voting Rights Act took effect. When it was terminated, the investigation committee, having combed the state for its "homosexual integrationist Communists," left behind it almost 4,300 sets of documents detailing one of the most sordid episodes in modern Florida history.[53] "I don't get no love out of hurting people," Johns recollected in 1972, "[and] if we saved one boy from being made a homosexual, it was justified."[54]

Between the late 1960s and the mid-1970s, even those segregationist state agencies established in three "deepest" states of the Deep South—Louisiana, Mississippi, and Alabama—also went into permanent eclipse. On June 30, 1969, exactly four years after the Florida Legislative Investigation Committee was disbanded—and nine years after it was brought to life with the stroke of a pen of the state's "singing governor," James "Jimmie" Davis—the Louisiana State Sovereignty Commission ceased functioning. By the time the 1964 Civil Rights Act became the law of the land, the Louisiana state legislature had enacted some 130 segregationist measures (more than any other Deep South state), most of which were either devised or drafted by the Louisiana Joint Legislative Committee chaired by State Senator William Rainach from 1954 to 1960 and, later, by the State Sovereignty Commission.[55] In 1969, Louisiana's other segregationist organ—the Louisiana Joint Legislative Committee on Un-American Activities—was also dissolved. During the mid-1960s, the Louisiana version of the House Un-American Activities Committee (HUAC), chaired by State Senator Jesse M. Knowles and vice-chaired by State Representative Ford Stinson (Stinson had previously sat on the Rainach Committee), even kept tabs on the state's Ku Klux Klan (KKK) organization, whose violent confrontations with the Deacons for Defense and Justice—an armed self-defense black organization that originated as a "community protection" group in Jonesboro, Louisiana, in the summer of 1964—had frequently been registered in the state and troubled the comparatively racially moderate governor John McKeithen (in comparison with his predecessor, Davis).[56] In issuing its ninety-page investigative report, the Joint Legislative Committee on Un-American Activities eventually cleared the KKK of any wrongdoing, absurdly concluding that the violence-prone organization was a mere "political-action group" with a "certain Halloween spirit" that was "common to most Americans."[57] Having given its tacit endorsement to the white-supremacist organization, the legislative committee added: "It is not the function of the Committee to criticize or praise the philosophy or orientation of any group . . . in regard to race relations."[58]

Outlasting its Louisiana counterpart for four years was the seventeen-year-old Mississippi State Sovereignty Commission—the most virulent tax-supported agency that the white South ever produced to resist black southerners' aspirations during the civil rights years and the template of the Louisiana and Alabama State Sovereignty Commissions, as well as the Arkansas State Sovereignty Commission. Having outlived its usefulness by 1968, the Mississippi commission, in its final days, poured its resources into investigating and cracking down on what it regarded as "new subversives"—black nationalists, anti–Vietnam War demonstrators, and campus radicals—reflecting the volatile transformation of the nation's social and political trends in the late 1960s.[59] On June 30, 1973, Mississippi's segregation watchdog became defunct when Governor William L. Waller vetoed the appropriation bill, which had been introduced to the state legislature to continue to fund the agency. It would take four more years for the commission to be officially terminated by a legislative act passed during the 1977 state legislative session. By the time its death knell sounded, the Mississippi State Sovereignty Commission had spent more than $1,542,000 of the state's taxpayers' money to "protect the sovereignty" of Mississippi.[60] Years after the commission was disbanded, Erle Johnston, who had assumed the segregationist agency's directorship from 1963 to 1968, reminisced that the State Sovereignty Commission was "just one great big mirage" for most of Mississippi's white citizenry, who were desperate to cling onto anyone and anything to reverse the tide of the South's civil rights revolution. "But they were looking for a mirage," he added.[61]

As if to follow the fate of the Mississippi State Sovereignty Commission, the Alabama State Sovereignty Commission also faded away in 1973. When the last commission meeting was held on September 19, 1973, at the Downtowner Motel in Birmingham, only four members were present, barely making a quorum. Not even Governor George Wallace, an ex-officio member and the commission's chair, attended this last meeting. The Alabama state legislature had earlier refused to appropriate further funds for the State Sovereignty Commission during the 1973 legislative session, and the last meeting's attending members reluctantly resolved that the commission "shall cease active operations" as of September 30, after generating more than sixteen thousand official documents.[62] There had also been growing sentiment among state legislators since 1969 to terminate the other wheel of Alabama's segregationist chariot—the Alabama Legislative Commission to Preserve the Peace.[63] In addition, the ACLU brought a suit in 1969 at the U.S. District Court for the Middle District of Alabama, aiming to enjoin the Alabama Peace Commission.[64] By the spring of 1971, the commission's staff director, Edwin Strickland, and two other office staff members—Secretary Mavis Hicks and Investigator R. Y. Ball—had become prepared to disband their Peace Commission. In fact, on March 22, 1971, Strickland, Hicks, and Ball had jointly asked the commission members "not to seek its continuation beyond the expiration of this budget year."[65] Taking due note of the staff members' wish, the House Appropriation Committee actually once refused to fund the Alabama Peace Commission during the 1971 state legislative session. But Wallace, who had just begun his second term as governor after a four-year interval (during part of that interval, Wallace's wife, the cancer-stricken Lurleen B. Wallace, took the helm of the state as her husband's surrogate governor), successfully exerted his pressure on the House members to reverse the Appropriation Committee's decision not to continue to fund the segregationist commission.[66]

In the fall of 1972, the government efficiency experts hired by the governor's Cost Control Survey Board determined that there were "too few personnel" at the Alabama Legislative Commission to Preserve the Peace to "effectively monitor statewide activities" of "unlawful nature . . . detrimental to the peace and dignity" of the state.[67] They then recommended that the Peace Commission be terminated and that its responsibilities be turned over to the Alabama Department of Public Safety. Backing up this recommendation was Alabama attorney general William J. Baxley, a future lieutenant governor of the state. The progressive-minded attorney general saw that the legislative commission was no longer performing its originally intended duties and had instead become a mere "political" arm of some politicians including Wallace. For Baxley, who would soon appoint the state's first black assistant attorney general, the Alabama Peace Commission's investigative function was "repugnant to the American way of life." "They're not spying on people who have broken laws," the attorney general observed, "[but] they're spying on people who have different political views than they do."[68] Despite the recommendations made by his own Cost Control Survey Board and Attorney General Baxley's outcry,

Governor Wallace was not yet ready to let his antiquated brainchild fade away. During its last days, the Peace Commission, which was expected to submit its biennial report to the state legislature, did not even have enough funds to print the report for distribution. With an abridged two-page report prepared by Staff Director Strickland on September 30, 1975, in which the legislative commission summarized its investigative findings on "organized crime" and "white-collar crime" in the state, the Alabama Legislative Commission to Preserve the Peace came to a miserable end after twelve years of existence, surviving the Alabama State Sovereignty Commission for two years.[69]

Although the 1975 termination of the Alabama Legislative Commission to Preserve the Peace signified the collapse of the last vestige of the white South's organized defiance to the civil rights movement in its public sphere, some of the region's die-hard segregationists could not yet find it in their hearts to accept the inevitable. Among those unreconstructed resisters was former Louisiana state senator William Rainach, whose Louisiana Joint Legislative Committee, assisted by both Myers Lowman and J. B. Matthews, had initiated the white South's first grand-scale anti-Communist inquisition with a discernible tinge of racism and segregationism in early 1957. Two decades later, in the summer of 1977, when asked if he still believed that a Communist conspiracy had been behind the entire civil rights movement, the former Louisiana state senator replied without hesitation: "Well, it was largely conceived and organized and directed by Communist conspiracy. . . . There is no question that the Civil Rights Movement was largely fostered by the Communist Party."[70]

On January 26, 1978, Rainach, who had been in ill health, committed suicide by shooting himself with a pistol. He was sixty-four years old.[71] Just two weeks prior to his death, Rainach was interviewed by a reporter from the *Shreveport Journal* about the righteousness of racial segregation, which he had fiercely defended ever since the Supreme Court's 1954 school desegregation ruling. He was still convinced, Rainach told the inquirer, that "segregation is not an antiquated idea, but a natural relation which occurs between the two races." "[And] when you try to do away with these natural laws," he concluded, "you disrupt society."[72] In essence, Rainach was repeating the unaltered resolve that he had articulated before the Louisiana Farm Bureau convention in July 1954, two months after the *Brown* decision was announced. There, Rainach proclaimed that "our American way of life" and "our Southern institutions" were what he believed in with all his heart. "I shall continue to believe in these things," he promised, "until the day I die."[73] Though Rainach certainly lived up to his own promise, he was never able to understand the great discrepancy between upholding the American way of life and perpetuating the white South's racial and racist institutions. His rigidly held "racial principles" somehow remained perfectly compatible with his "patriotic commitments."[74]

To be sure, Rainach was not an exception. Others continued to assert, even until the end of the 1970s, that the civil rights movement had been, in large part, directed by international and domestic Communist conspiracy. In a June 1979 oral history interview, William Simmons—the kingpin of the pro-segregation Citizens' Council movement and an influential ally of Matthews's and Lowman's in Mississippi—still clung to what he had advocated for the previous quarter century. "My feeling is that they [the Communists and their sympathizers] saw it [the civil rights movement] as a handy device to create turmoil," Simmons mentioned, "and as the saying goes, the Communists always like to fish in troubled waters."[75] A decade later, in June 1989 and twenty-five years after the passage of the 1964 Civil Rights Act, the headquarters of the once all-powerful Citizens' Council in Jackson, Mississippi, finally closed its doors. Robert Patterson, one of the driving forces of the Council movement since its 1954 inception, explained the reason for the segregationist group's closure: "Our program was based on legality. Every law supporting segregation has been struck down by the courts. . . . We had no program left."[76]

By the early 1980s, southern conservatism in general and its accompanying covert expression of racism had no longer found expression in the region's traditional and once "predominant Democratic ideology." Instead, the legacy of the southern Democrats' race-baiting and red-baiting would be inherited by the emerging southern Republicans—the latter-day "Stars of the New Confederacy," to use the subtitle of Robert Sherrill's work.[77] As the collapse of the erstwhile formidable and Democrat-reigned Solid South advanced, more and more conservative southern whites—politicians, public office holders, and voters alike—began to identify themselves with the growing Republican Party in the South, a party that owed very little to President Abraham Lincoln, but much to U.S. senator Barry Goldwater from Arizona and President Richard Nixon, and even more to President Ronald W. Reagan.[78] With his ringing endorsement of states' rights, Reagan even chose, over his staff's objection, to kick off his 1980 presidential campaign at a nationally little known, but locally loved, annual county fair in Neshoba County, Mississippi—the very place where the three Mississippi Freedom Summer Project volunteers had been brutally murdered by the local KKK hoodlums in the scorching summer of 1964 under the banner of "states' rights," "anti-Communism," and "racial integrity."[79] "I talked about the Supreme Court usurpation of power, I talked about the big central government. . . . Isn't that what Reagan got elected on?" George Wallace asked in 1986. In keeping with his gubernatorial campaign pledge, Wallace, during the 1960s, had "stood up for Alabama" against the federal government's "tyranny."[80] His observation was right on target. "The Old South is gone," but "the New South is still opposed to government regulation of our lives," uttered Wallace, the four-time Alabama governor and four-time candidate for president of the United States.[81]

One of the Republicans coming to power as a heavyweight in southern politics after the region's Second Reconstruction became a fait accompli was U.S. senator Jesse A. Helms Jr. from North Carolina. A former conservative radio commentator, Helms changed his political party affiliation from Democrat to Republican in 1970, and two years later, he became the first North Carolina Republican elected to the Senate since the Reconstruction days following the Civil War.[82] On October 3, 1983, Senator Helms launched his opposition to the bill making the late Martin Luther King Jr.'s birthday a federal holiday. Embarking on a filibuster on the Senate floor while distributing copies of a three hundred-page document among the Senate members that detailed King's alleged Communist connections, he "picked up the [J. Edgar] Hooverite anti-King line" and castigated the deceased civil rights icon as a practitioner of "action-oriented Marxism," whose ideas were "not compatible with the concepts of this country."[83]

Despite his admission that "there is no evidence that King was a member of the Communist Party," Helms nevertheless asserted that King's "associations with persons close to the Party," his "political allies in the Kennedy Administration," and his overall "views of American society" all suggested that "King may have had an explicit but clandestine relationship with the Communist Party" with "the totalitarian goals and ideology of Communism" in his mind.[84] "What a shame that the supporters of this holiday were not willing to submit to a full examination of all the facts about Dr. King[!]," the senator later wrote in his memoir. As far as Helms was concerned, "the glorification of Martin Luther King, Jr.," was nothing but un-American. Both praised by his supporters and despised by his opponents for his calculated charms as a "southern gentleman," Helms, when he encountered Democratic senator Carol Moseley Braun from Illinois—the very first black woman ever elected to the U.S. Senate—in an elevator at the Capitol ten years after his unsuccessful attempt to bury the King holiday bill, mischievously told Republican senator Orrin G. Hatch from Utah, a future chair of the Senate Judiciary Committee, who then happened to be with him: "Watch me make her cry. I'm going to make her cry. I'm going to sing 'Dixie' until she cries." He then abruptly proceeded to serenade his black colleague with "Dixie" ("I wish I was in the land of cotton. Old times there are not forgotten. . . ."). Apparently, the North Carolina senator's attempt to make the Illinois senator cry proved unsuccessful, but he made his racist point literally—and perhaps quite annoyingly—"loud and clear."[85]

While King, as the most renowned national civil rights leader, was not allowed to rest in peace even after his death in April 1968, some of the South's comparatively obscure, but nevertheless spirited, proponents of black civil rights were free at last. Among them was Eugene Cox, a former white director of the interracial Providence Cooperative Farm in Holmes County, Mississippi. In December 1992, Cox passed away in Memphis, Tennessee, thirty-six years after he and his family were forced to disband Providence and leave Mississippi under the pressure exerted by the witch-hunting local Citizens' Council members. In the eyes of the Holmes County white supremacists, Cox was guilty of subverting the "American Way of Life."[86] But his only "wrongdoing" was his unwavering belief and tireless advocacy that "segregation was inconsistent with Christianity."[87] When Cox died, he was survived by his wife, Lindsey, who had also worked on the Providence Cooperative Farm as a medical missionary. "The people involved can no longer hurt my husband," Lindsey wrote upon Eugene's death.[88]

By the time Senator Helms made his hullabaloo in Congress over the bill establishing the King holiday, the white South's officially sanctioned and all-out resistance movement to school desegregation and other facets of the civil rights movement had virtually ceased. Even though the politics of coded racism and racial prejudice in much subtler forms would replace it during and after the 1980s at a calculated risk of substantially alienating now enfranchised and empowered black voters (as to be manifested, for instance, by the rather impressive political advance made by Republican Louisiana state representative David E. Duke, a former Grand Wizard of the Knights of the Ku Klux Klan), the segregationist South's massive resistance, effectuated and sustained by southern-flavored anticommunism, proved to be a massive fallacy in the end because, as the nineteenth-century poet and journalist William Cullen Bryant once wrote, "Truth crushed to earth shall rise again."[89] On March 25, 1965, three years prior to his untimely death, Martin Luther King Jr.—having just led the historic Selma-to-Montgomery march where Alabama's die-hard massive resisters claimed to have witnessed "the red hand of Communism at work"—stood before the Alabama State Capitol.[90] Invoking Bryant's words, King reminded those who had gathered that what America as a nation must embrace was a "society at peace with itself." But how long would it take for Americans to bring about such a society? It would not take too long, he encouraged his audience, "because no lie can live forever" and because the time had also come for the white South to be at peace with itself.[91]

In 1949, six years before King propelled himself into the South's surging civil rights movement as a charismatic leader, V. O. Key predicted, in the closing pages of *Southern Politics in State and Nation,* that "until greater emancipation of the white from the Negro" was accomplished, "the southern political and economic system will labor under formidable handicaps."[92] King understood what Key had meant in his scholarly observation. And when King, fresh from his Montgomery Bus Boycott experiences, launched the Atlanta-based Southern Christian Leadership Conference (SCLC) in early 1957 as a "distinctly southern" civil rights organization, his immediate goal was to redeem the twisted and hatred-filled soul of the segregationist South—to paraphrase the SCLC's official motto, "To Redeem the Soul of America"—with the power of agape as "redemptive love toward all men" including his racist adversaries.[93] Unfortunately, the vast majority of white southerners refused to be redeemed but chose to resist, leading their beloved region into a quagmire as one of the most tragic flaws in the making of the modern South. This tragedy resided in the fact that the white South, instead of boldly confronting the region's appalling racial problems, ended up "dr[awing] within itself," to borrow the phrase of the southern historian David R. Goldfield.[94]

In other words, white southerners in general, as the Georgia author and social critic Lillian E. Smith has stated, elected to shut themselves "away from so many good, creative, honest, deeply human things in life" and "feared the lighting of one candle that might push back the darkness and show what was really there." And when southern blacks' civil rights struggle became one bright candle to reveal the region's racial injustice, their white counterparts were eager only to restore the very same darkness that afflicted the South (or the darkness that "smothered the goodness" in white southerners, as Smith has described on another occasion)—a homeland of not only whites but also blacks.[95] Thus, by willingly refusing to face up to reality, the white South became a land of fear, rage, and desperation, being able neither to emancipate itself from the self-imposed spell of racism nor to come to reasonable grips with black southerners' earnest quest for simple human dignity. And when professional anti-communism and its diabolic schemes finally found themselves to be no longer persuasive to anyone but the region's most rabid segregationists, the white South belatedly realized that it was not the outside influence of communism but "the inner functioning of democracy" that had ushered forth black southerners' civil rights crusade, acknowledging—or at least introducing itself to—the Mississippi laureate William Faulkner's follow-ing perceptive words penned in late 1955.[96]

> We accept insult and contumely and risk of violence because we will not sit quietly by and see our native land, the South, not just Mississippi but all the South, wreck and ruin itself twice in less than a hundred years, over the Negro question.
>
> We speak now against the day when our Southern people who will resist to the last these inevitable changes in social relations, will, when they have been forced to accept what they at one time might have accepted with dignity and goodwill, will say, "Why didn't someone tell us this before? Tell us this in time?"[97]

History testifies that in his imprudent and persistent pursuit of those whom he labeled as his mortal enemies, Senator Joseph McCarthy lost not only his political prominence but also his "sense of decency."[98] In the same fashion, by committing themselves to perpetuating the white South's undemocratic cause, both Myers Lowman and J. B. Matthews, not only as the nation's most illustrious—and controversial—anti-Communists but also as the most conspicuous northern messiahs for the region's massive resisters, ended up throwing themselves into a dark pit of insanity—an insanity that induced them to "use a shotgun instead of a rifle" in their ef-forts and to "hit many innocent people and tarnish many good reputations in the process," as one influential southern Presbyterian leader lamented in the early 1960s.[99] And yet, the modern American South's uniquely un-American experience that emerged during the turbulent civil rights era was largely attributable to the architects and practitioners of the southern version of McCarthyism, for they were the ones who turned a blind eye to the long-standing promise of democracy for every American citizen. By using anticommunism to attempt to perpetuate racist oppression—and by "crying aloud and sparing not"—southern segregationists, at the end of the day, lost their sense of decency as well.

ABBREVIATIONS AND SHORTENED REFERENCES USED IN NOTES

ACHR Records	Arkansas Council on Human Relations Records, University of Arkansas
ALCPP	Alabama Legislative Commission to Preserve the Peace
ALCPP Records	Alabama Legislative Commission to Preserve the Peace Records (microfilm), Alabama Department of Archives and History
ASSC	Alabama State Sovereignty Commission
ASSC Records	Alabama State Sovereignty Commission Records (microfilm), Alabama Department of Archives and History
Barrett Collection	Russell H. Barrett Collection, University of Mississippi
Bloch Papers	Charles J. Bloch Papers, Washington Memorial Library
Blossom Papers	Virgil T. Blossom Papers, University of Arkansas
Broadside Collection	Broadside Collection, University of Georgia
CA Collection	*The Christian Advocate* Collection, Ohio Wesleyan University
CC Collection (MSU)	Citizens' Council Collection, Mississippi State University
CC Collection (UM)	Citizens' Council Collection, University of Mississippi
CC/CR Collection	Citizens' Council/Civil Rights Collection, University of Southern Mississippi
Cox Collection	A. Eugene Cox Collection, Mississippi State University
Cox Papers	Earnest S. Cox Papers, Duke University
CPL	Cincinnati Public Library
CR Records	Circuit Riders, Inc., Records, University of Oregon
DPCF Papers	Delta and Providence Cooperative Farms Papers, University of North Carolina
Faulkner Papers	L. E. Faulkner Papers, University of Southern Mississippi
FC Collection:	Freedom Center Collection, California State University

FF	*Facts on Film* (microfilm), Southern Education Reporting Service, Nashville, Tenn.
FLIC	Florida Legislative Investigation Committee
FLIC Records:	Florida Legislative Investigation Committee Records, Florida State Archives (presently State Archives of Florida)
FR Archives	Fund for the Republic Archives, Princeton University
Garman Papers	W. O. H. Garman Papers, Bob Jones University
GCE	Georgia Commission on Education
GCE Records	Records of the Georgia Commission on Education, Georgia Archives
Godwin Collection	Godwin Advertising Agency Collection, Mississippi State University
Hagerty Papers	James C. Hagerty Papers, Dwight D. Eisenhower Presidential Library
Johnson Papers	Paul B. Johnson Family Papers, University of Southern Mississippi
Johnston Papers	Erle E. Johnston Jr. Papers, University of Southern Mississippi
Levy Collection	Charles Levy Civil Rights Collection, Texas A&M University
LJLC	Louisiana Joint Legislative Committee
LJLCUA	Louisiana Joint Legislative Committee on Un-American Activities
LJLCUA Records	Louisiana Joint Legislative Committee on Un-American Activities Records, Louisiana State Archives
LLMV Collection	Louisiana and Lower Mississippi Valley Collections, Louisiana State University
Lowman Papers	Myers G. Lowman Papers, Stanford University
LSSC	Louisiana State Sovereignty Commission
Marshall Papers	Burke Marshall Personal Papers, John F. Kennedy Presidential Library
Matthews Papers	J. B. Matthews Papers, Duke University
Matusow Archive	Harvey Matusow Archive, University of Sussex
McCain Collection	William D. McCain Pamphlet Collection, University of Southern Mississippi
McCain Library	William D. McCain Library and Archives, University of Southern Mississippi
McIlhenny Papers	George N. McIlhenny Papers, Mississippi State University
MDAH	Archives and Library Division, Mississippi Department of Archives and History
MFSA Records	Records of the Methodist Federation for Social Action, Drew University

MGLIC	Mississippi General Legislative Investigating Committee
Minor Papers	Wilson F. "Bill" Minor Papers, Mississippi State University
MSSC	Mississippi State Sovereignty Commission
MSSC Records	Records of the Mississippi State Sovereignty Commission, Mississippi Department of Archives and History
NR Records	*The National Republic* Records (microfilm), Stanford University
Perez Papers	Leander H. Perez Papers, New Orleans Public Library
Rainach Papers	William M. Rainach Papers, Louisiana State University in Shreveport
Reynard Papers	Charles A. Reynard–Marian Reynard Baun Papers, Louisiana State University
Root Papers	E. Merrill Root Papers, University of Oregon
Russell Collection	Richard B. Russell Jr. Collection, University of Georgia
Satterfield Collection	John C. Satterfield/American Bar Association Collection, University of Mississippi
SECALC	Special Education Committee of the Arkansas Legislative Council
SI Collection	Social Issues Collection, University of Notre Dame
Sillers Papers	Walter Sillers Jr. Papers, Delta State University
SLL	State Library of Louisiana
Sokolsky Papers	George E. Sokolsky Papers, Stanford University
Talmadge Collection	Herman E. Talmadge Collection, University of Georgia
TGASIC	Tennessee General Assembly Special Investigating Committee
TGASIC Records	Records of the 81st Tennessee General Assembly Special Investigating Committee, Tennessee State Library and Archives
Toler Papers	Kenneth Toler Papers, Mississippi State University
Touchstone Papers	Ned Touchstone Papers, Louisiana State University in Shreveport
Vandiver Papers	S. Ernest Vandiver Jr. Papers, University of Georgia
Welch Papers	Nut Welch Papers, Birmingham Civil Rights Institute
WHC Files	White House Central Files (Records as President), Dwight D. Eisenhower Presidential Library
WHS Files	White House Special Files, Richard M. Nixon Presidential Library

NOTES

PREFACE

1. Blake, *Children of the Movement*, 119.
2. Dykeman and Stokely, "McCarthyism under the Magnolias," 6.
3. *Brown v. Board of Education*, 347 U.S. 483 (1954); Paul M. Gaston, "Foreword by Way of Memoir," in *The Moderates' Dilemma*, ed. Lassiter and Lewis, ix.
4. Martin, *The Deep South Says "Never*," 85, 132; Smith, *How Race Is Made*, 132; *Sarasota (Fla.) Herald-Tribune*, Mar. 9, 1954; Boyle, *The Desegregated Heart*, 237.
5. Boyle, *The Desegregated Heart*, 236–37.
6. Lubin, *Romance and Rights*, 67; Chappell, "Religious Ideas of the Segregationists," 237–62.
7. Katagiri, *The Mississippi State Sovereignty Commission*.
8. Cook, *Sweet Land of Liberty?*, 95.
9. Woodward, *The Burden of Southern History*; Paul D. Escott, "The Special Place of History," in *The South for New Southerners*, ed. Escott and Goldfield, 4–5.
10. Bartley, *The Rise of Massive Resistance*; McMillen, *The Citizens' Council*.
11. Schrecker, "Archival Sources for the Study of McCarthyism," 207.
12. Lewis, *The White South and the Red Menace*; Woods, *Black Struggle, Red Scare*; Woods, "The Cold War and the Struggle for Civil Rights," 13–17.
13. Dunbar, "The Changing Mind of the South," 13.
14. Matthew D. Lassiter, "De Jure/De Facto Segregation: The Long Shadow of a National Myth," in *The Myth of Southern Exceptionalism*, ed. Lassiter and Crespino, 28.
15. Jacoway, *Turn Away Thy Son*, 299.
16. Lewis, *The White South and the Red Menace*, 166.
17. Klehr et al., *The Soviet World of American Communism*, 1.
18. "The Self-Bound Gulliver."
19. Franklin, "The Great Confrontation," 20; Franklin, *Race and History*, 365.
20. *Jackson (Miss.) Daily News*, June 10, 1958; Bartley, *The Rise of Massive Resistance*, 187; Fosl, *Subversive Southerner*, 201; Baer, *Resistance to Public School Desegregation*, 177; Record, "The Red-Tagging of Negro Protest," 325–33. "The red-tagging of Negro protest fills a gaping hole in Southern logic," Record observed in 1957, criticizing the white South's "Communist-plot theory of desegregation": "It purports to rescue a cherished Southern axiom from the reaches of cold fact. The white Southerner has long insisted that he *understands* Deep-South

colored folk and *knows* them to be happy with their lot. Now he is confronted on every side with demands, by Negroes themselves, that the basic pattern of Southern life be changed. But if Negroes are happy as they are, why are they protesting? Here there appears an embarrassing break in the Southerner's chain of reasoning. Communism supplies the missing link" (see "Looking and Listening: Red-Tagging," 622).

21. Faulkner, *Requiem for a Nun*, 92.

22. Halberstam, "An Address by David Halberstam," 163.

INTRODUCTION

1. Grubbs, *Cry from the Cotton*, 28; Dyson, "The Southern Tenant Farmers['] Union and Depression Politics," 230–31; Gilmore, *Defying Dixie*, 212; Danny Duncan Collum, "The Tupelo Solution," in *American Crisis, Southern Solutions*, ed. Dunbar, 113; Michael K. Honey, "Operation Dixie, the Red Scare, and the Defeat of Southern Labor Organizing," in *American Labor and the Cold War*, ed. Cherny et al., 216. See also Cobb, *The Most Southern Place on Earth*, 201.

2. Peter Coclanis and Bryant Simon, "Exit, Voice, and Loyalty: African American Strategies for Day-to-Day Existence/Resistance in the Early-Twentieth-Century Rural South," in *African American Life in the Rural South*, ed. Hurt, 200.

3. Egerton, *Speak Now against the Day*, 127; Fred C. Smith, "Cooperative Farming in Mississippi," *Mississippi History Now*, Mississippi Historical Society, Jackson, http://mshistory.k12.ms.us/articles/219/cooperative-farming-in-mississippi.

4. Smith, "Cooperative Farming in Mississippi"; K'Meyer, *Interracialism and Christian Community in the Postwar South*, 20; Delta Cooperative Farm, "Foundation Principles of the Delta Cooperative Farm, Hillhouse, Mississippi," May 1936, folder 5, DPCF Papers; Sam H. Franklin Jr., "Cooperative Farming in Mississippi: Some Reflections," typescript, n.d. [1988], 2, in the author's possession by courtesy of the late Lindsey H. Cox, Memphis, Tenn.

5. Wilburn Hooker [Mississippi state representative] to Albert Jones [MSSC director], July 2, 1960, record nos. 2–54–1–26–1–1–1 to 2–1–1, p. 1–1–1, MSSC Records; Dunbar, *Against the Grain*, 243–45; Cobb, *The Most Southern Place on Earth*, 223–24; Campbell, *Providence*, 10, 19; Silver, *Mississippi*, 37; Smith, *Congressman from Mississippi*, 265; Bryan, *These Few Also Paid a Price*, 72–75; Sperry, "Caught 'Between Our Moral and Material Selves,'" Ph.D. diss., 561–70, 596–97, 608–9, 618–19.

6. Asch, *The Senator and the Sharecropper*, 137–38.

7. Tindall, *The Emergence of the New South*, 377–78, 507–8; Klehr, *The Heyday of American Communism*, 273; Ottanelli, *The Communist Party of the United States*, 39; Egerton, *Speak Now against the Day*, 457–58; Rogers et al., *Alabama*, 484; Solomon, *The Cry Was Unity*, 112, 119.

8. Charles H. Martin, "The Rise and Fall of Popular Front Liberalism in the South: The Southern Conference for Human Welfare, 1938–1948," in vol. 3 of *Perspectives on the American South*, ed. Cobb and Wilson, 120; Klibaner, "The Travail of Southern Radicals," 179; Sullivan, *Days of Hope*, 6.

9. Susan M. Glisson, "Lucy Randolph Mason: 'The Rest of Us,'" in *The Human Tradition in the Civil Rights Movement*, ed. Glisson, 115; Sullivan, *Days of Hope*, 6; SECALC, untitled transcript of J. B. Matthews's testimony, n.d. [Dec. 17, 1958], 13, folder: "Matthews, John [*sic*, Joseph] B.," box 3, CR Records.

10. William H. Chafe, "Race in America: The Ultimate Test of Liberalism," in *The Achievement of American Liberalism,* ed. Chafe, 163; Pamela Tyler, "'Blood on Your Hands': White Southerners' Criticism of Eleanor Roosevelt during World War II," in *Before* Brown, ed. Feldman, 100.

11. Reed, *Simple Decency and Common Sense,* 65–98; Egerton, *Speak Now against the Day,* 444; Grantham, *The South in Modern America,* 164.

12. Martin Dies to "Dear Colleague," Nov. 17, 1944, 1, folder 2, box 506, Matthews Papers.

13. Woods, *Black Struggle, Red Scare,* 26; Payton, "That Man from Texas," 16, *CA* Collection.

14. National Broadcasting Company, "Address of Representative Martin Dies of Texas Made on the National Radio Forum Arranged by the Washington Evening Star and Broadcast over the National Broadcasting Company's Blue Network at 9:30 P.M., EST," press release, Aug. 29, 1938, 1, 4; "Dies Committee Investigation," 1, both in folder: "Investigation (Dies), 1938–39," box 25, Lowman Papers.

15. National Broadcasting Company, "Un-American Activities in the United States: Address of Congressman Martin Dies of Texas, Broadcast December 13, at 8:00 P.M., over the National Broadcasting Company," press release, Dec. 13, 1938, 1, folder: "Dies (Investigation), Clippings, etc.," box 25, Lowman Papers.

16. Dies, *The Trojan Horse in America,* 118.

17. Dies to "Dear Colleague," Nov. 17, 1944, 1–2. See also "Un-American Activities," 30.

18. John E. Rankin to L. E. Faulkner [president, Mississippi Central Railroad Company], Aug. 30, 1950, 1, folder 6, box 21, Faulkner Papers; Civil Rights Congress, *America's "Thought Police,"* 4, folder 6, box 166, Matthews Papers.

19. Goodman, *The Committee,* 167–89, 497; Haynes, *Red Scare or Red Menace?,* 69–70.

20. Civil Rights Congress, *America's "Thought Police,"* 4.

21. U.S. Congress, House, Committee on Un-American Activities, *Southern Conference for Human Welfare,* 13, 17; Clark, "An Analysis of the Relationship between Anti-Communism and Segregationist Thought in the Deep South," Ph.D. diss., 23; Patricia Sullivan, "Southern Reformers, the New Deal and the Movement's Foundation," in *New Directions in Civil Rights Studies,* ed. Robinson and Sullivan, 98–99.

22. U.S. Congress, Senate, Committee on the Judiciary, Subcommittee to Investigate the Administration of the Internal Security Act and Other Internal Security Laws, *Subversive Influence in Southern Conference Educational Fund, Inc.,* n.p. [reproduction], folder: "Lowman, Myers G., 1962," box 671, Matthews Papers.

23. Sarah Hart Brown, "Communism, Anti-Communism, and Massive Resistance: The Civil Rights Congress in Southern Perspective," in *Before* Brown, ed. Feldman, 171.

24. President's Committee on Civil Rights, *To Secure These Rights,* viii, xii.

25. Ibid., 151–73, 166.

26. Harry S. Truman, "Statement by the President Making Public a Report by the Civil Rights Committee," Oct. 29, 1947, American Presidency Project, University of California at Santa Barbara, www.presidency.ucsb.edu/ws/index.php?pid=12780.

27. McGuiness, ed., *National Party Conventions,* 99.

28. Frederickson, *The Dixiecrat Revolt and the End of the Solid South,* 134–40.

29. McGuiness, ed., *National Party Conventions,* 99–100.

30. Frederickson, *The Dixiecrat Revolt and the End of the Solid South,* 148, 171–72; "Nation: The Senator from South Carolina." See also Barnard, *Dixiecrats and Democrats,* 116.

31. Brady, *The South at Bay,* n.p. [p. 9]; Perman, *The Southern Political Tradition,* 55. See also Hall, "The Long Civil Rights Movement and the Political Use of the Past," 1250.

32. Goldinger, ed., *Presidential Elections since 1789,* 131, 204.

33. "The South of V. O. Key," in *The American South Comes of Age* series, videocassette; Washington-Williams and Stadiem, *Dear Senator,* 175; "The South Awakens," 32.

34. *New York Times,* May 18, 1954; James C. Hagerty [White House press secretary to Eisenhower], "Monday, May 17, 1954: Breakfast at the White House at 7:15," memo, 1, box 1, Hagerty Papers.

35. Gallen, ed., *The Quotable Truman,* 15.

36. Hero, *The Southerner and World Affairs,* 428; Heale, *American Anticommunism,* 176.

37. Killian, *White Southerners,* 83. See also Record, "The Red-Tagging of Negro Protest," 325–33; and "Looking and Listening: Red-Tagging," 622.

38. Perman, *Pursuit of Unity,* 282. See also Kruse, "The Paradox of Massive Resistance," 1009.

39. *Brown v. Board of Education,* 347 U.S. 483 (1954).

40. U.S. House, Representative John Bell Williams of Mississippi speaking on the U.S. Supreme Court's *Brown* decision, 83d Cong., 2d sess., *Congressional Record* (May 19, 1954), 6857; Carter, *The South Strikes Back,* 26.

41. As Martin Luther King Jr. abundantly demonstrated, the rhetoric of the civil rights movement was often based on biblical writings and made frequent use of the oral conventions of religious speech. But only recently have the important roles of religion and churches in the civil rights movement, as well as in the white South's massive resistance to the movement, begun to receive serious attention by historians and theologians. For some superb treatments of this subject matter, see Findlay, *Church People in the Struggle;* Marsh, *God's Long Summer;* Chappell, *A Stone of Hope;* Collins, *When the Church Bell Rang Racist;* Manis, *Southern Civil Religions in Conflict;* and Harvey, *Moses, Jesus, and the Trickster in the Evangelical South* (particularly chap. 3, "Suffering Saint: Jesus in the South").

42. Campbell, *Providence,* 4–5.

43. Horowitz, "White Southerners' Alienation and Civil Rights," 175.

44. Brady, "Interview with the Honorable Thomas P. Brady," 24–25, 39–40; McMillen, *The Citizens' Council,* 17.

45. Brady, *Black Monday,* n.p. [dedication and foreword].

46. Brady, *Black Monday,* reprint ed., n.p. [back cover].

47. Grantham, *The Life and Death of the Solid South,* 143.

48. Goodman, *The Committee,* 345.

49. Brown, "Congressional Anti-Communism and the Segregationist South," 786, 790–91.

50. Salmond, "The Great Southern Commie Hunt," 433–52.

51. U.S. Congress, House, Committee on Un-American Activities, *The American Negro in the Communist Party,* 1.

52. Braden, *House Un-American Activities Committee,* 24.

53. Fried, *Nightmare in Red,* 176.

54. Mooney, *LBJ,* 49–50; Finley, *Delaying the Dream,* 76.

55. Adams, *James A. Dombrowski,* 222–23; Zellner, "Red Roadshow," 32, 38; James Dombrowski to "Dear Friend," n.d., folder: "Lowman, Myers G., 1962," box 671, Matthews Papers.

56. "Political Notes: Prince of the Peckerwoods"; Brown, *Standing against Dragons,* 14; Egerton, "Homegrown Progressives," 9–10.

57. Branch, *Parting the Waters,* 122.

58. Sullivan, ed., *Freedom Writer,* 30, 67; Sokol, *There Goes My Everything,* 40; Garrow, ed., *The Montgomery Bus Boycott and the Women Who Started It,* 104. See also Williams, "Grace and Guts," 35.

59. Williams, "Huey, Lyndon, and Southern Radicalism," 272. For further details on the March 1954 SISS hearings to investigate the SCEF, see Durr, *Outside the Magic Circle,* 254–73; Kilbaner, *Conscience of a Troubled South,* 73–100; Reed, *Simple Decency and Common Sense,* 158–59; and Brown, *Standing against Dragons,* 115–39.

60. "The South: The Authentic Voice."

61. Kluger, *Simple Justice.*

62. U.S. Senate, Senator James O. Eastland of Mississippi speaking on the Supreme Court, segregation, and the South, 83d Cong., 2d sess., *Congressional Record* (May 27, 1954), 7253–55; *Jackson (Miss.) Daily News,* May 27, 1954.

63. U.S. Congress, Senate, Committee on the Judiciary, Subcommittee to Investigate the Administration of the Internal Security Act and Other Internal Security Laws, *Subversive Influence in Southern Conference Educational Fund, Inc.,* n.p.

64. U.S. Senate, Senator James O. Eastland of Mississippi speaking on the investigation of certain matters relating to the Supreme Court decision in the so-called school integration cases, 84th Cong., 1st sess., *Congressional Record* (May 25, 1955), 6963–64.

65. *Jackson Daily News,* July 19, 1954.

66. Bartley, *The Rise of Massive Resistance,* 59, 75.

67. *Brown v. Board of Education,* 349 U.S. 294 (1955).

68. Kelly and Harbison, *The American Constitution,* 863–64.

69. See, for instance, *Jackson Daily News,* Dec. 27, 1955; "The Congress: The New Chairman"; and Patrick Henry Group, *Is the Supreme Court Pro-Communist?,* folder 14, box 3, CC/CR Collection.

70. *New York Times,* Jan. 30, 1956.

71. *Jackson Daily News,* Mar. 3, 1956. See also "The Congress: The New Chairman." In late August 1955, the severely mutilated body of Till, a fourteen-year-old black youth from Chicago, was found in the Tallahatchie River. In the early hours of August 28, Roy Bryant, a local store owner, and his half brother, J. W. Milam, kidnapped Till, brutally beat him, shot him in the head, and threw his body into the river. Till was murdered for having allegedly whistled at a white woman—Bryant's wife. On September 19, the murder trial of Bryant and Milam began in the Tallahatchie County seat of Sumner—"A Good Place to Raise a Boy," as the town officials billed their small and closely knit rural community. County Sheriff Harold Clarence Strider, who was also a local plantation owner, told a news reporter with contempt and in his heavy southern drawl, "We never have any trouble until some of our southern niggers go up North, and the NAACP talks to them, and they come back home." Strider blamed the civil rights organization for fanning racial troubles in his beloved South, "[and] if they keep their noses and mouths out of our business, we would be able to do more when we enforce the laws of Tallahatchie County in Mississippi." Testifying in the trial for the defense, Strider speculated that the "NAACP had plotted Till's so-called killing, and that Till himself was living happily" in the North. Outside of the courthouse, a well-dressed and middle-aged local white woman was interviewed by a television reporter. "I'm almost convinced," the woman proclaimed in her high-pitched voice, "that the very beginning of this [incident] was [staged] by a communistic front," implying that the discovery of and the furor over the slain body alleged to

be Till's were part of a well-orchestrated Communist plot. In the end, after deliberating for only sixty-seven minutes, the all-white and all-male jury delivered justice in the Mississippi style of the 1950s, acquitting Bryant and Milam of the charges for their deeds, which the local whites considered as "self-defense" in the service of undefiled southern womanhood. "If we hadn't stopped [the deliberation] to drink pop," one juror later explained, "it wouldn't have taken that long" (see *The Murder of Emmett Till,* videocassette; and Whitfield, *A Death in the Delta,* 41–42, 44).

72. "Mississippi Group Backs Equalization Building Plans," 7; *Segregation and the South,* videocassette; Fund for the Republic, "Segregation and the South," documentary film script, 1957, 17, folder 4, box 112, FR Archives; Johnston, interview by Cal Adams, videocassette.

73. Fairclough, *Better Day Coming,* 261.

74. W. F. Minor, "The Citizens' Councils: An Incredible Decade of Defiance," typescript, n.d., folder: "Citizens' Council," box 2, Minor Papers; McMillen, *The Citizens' Council,* 18–23.

75. Martin, *The Deep South Says "Never,"* 3; Luce, "The Mississippi White Citizens['] Council," master's thesis, 17; Raines, *My Soul Is Rested,* 297–98.

76. Simmons, "An Oral History with Mr. William J. Simmons," 44–46.

77. Brady, "Interview with the Honorable Thomas P. Brady," 25. See also Routh and Anthony, "Southern Resistance Forces," 50.

78. *Jackson (Miss.) State Times,* Dec. 9, 1958.

79. Simmons, "An Oral History with Mr. William J. Simmons," 9–10, 44; McMillen, *The Citizens' Council,* 122.

80. Jackson Citizens' Council, *The Eight Ifs and Your Answer!,* n.p., folder: "Simmons, W. J., 1954–1963 and n.d.," box 680, Matthews Papers.

81. Patterson, *The Citizens' Council—A History,* 5–6, folder 10, CC Collection (MSU).

82. Wroten, "An Oral History with Mr. Joseph E. Wroten," 12–14. The entire transcript of the author's interview with Wroten can be read online at Civil Rights in Mississippi Digital Archive, McCain Library, http://digilib.usm.edu/cdm/compoundobject/collection/coh/id/8019.

83. Carter, "A Wave of Terror Threatens the South," 32–36; Waldron, *Hodding Carter,* 244.

84. Ethridge, "Mississippi Notebook: Moderation Is Futile," 2; Waldron, *Hodding Carter,* 244.

85. *Acts and Joint Resolutions of the General Assembly of the Commonwealth of Virginia,* 1956, regular sess., 1213–15.

86. Vanderbilt University School of Law, ed., vol. 1 of *Race Relations Law Reporter,* 437; Johnston, "Communism vs. Segregation," 22.

87. Dickson, *Sustaining Southern Identity,* 201. See also Leuchtenburg, *The White House Looks South,* 219–20.

88. *New York Times,* Feb. 26, 1956; Heinemann, *Harry Byrd of Virginia,* 334.

89. *Laws of the State of Mississippi,* 1956, regular sess., 744; "Joint Resolution of the Georgia General Assembly: Interposition Resolution, Mar. 9, 1956," GeorgiaInfo, GALILEO (Georgia Library Learning Online) and the University of Georgia Libraries, http://georgiainfo.galileo.usg.edu/interpos.htm.

90. Vanderbilt University School of Law, ed., vol. 1 of *Race Relations Law Reporter,* 591–92, 753–55, 948–53, 1116–17; Colburn and Scher, "Aftermath of the *Brown* Decision," 62–81.

91. Vanderbilt University School of Law, ed., vol. 1 of *Race Relations Law Reporter,* 436.

92. Walter F. George to Richard B. Russell, Feb. 9, 1956, folder 9, box 27, series III, Russell Collection; Fite, *Richard B. Russell, Jr.,* 333.

93. Vanderbilt University School of Law, ed., vol. 1 of *Race Relations Law Reporter,* 436; Lewis, *The White South and the Red Menace,* 43.

94. Bartley, *The Rise of Massive Resistance,* 45.

95. Georgia State Law Department, comp. and ed., *Compilation of Georgia Laws and Opinions of the Attorney General Relating to Segregation of the Races,* 46–48, in both folder 3, box 22, subseries A, series I, Vandiver Papers; and box 3 (item no. 64), Levy Collection; Roche, *Restructured Resistance,* 18–20.

96. *Laws of the State of Mississippi,* 1954, regular sess., 585–87; William J. Simmons [former administrator, Citizens' Councils of America] to Erle E. Johnston Jr. [former MSSC director], Nov. 25, 1987, folder 9, box 2, Johnston Papers; Bolton, *The Hardest Deal of All,* 61–66.

97. Fairclough, *Race and Democracy,* 170; McCarrick, "Louisiana's Official Resistance to Desegregation," Ph.D. diss., 40; Stowe, "Willie Rainach and the Defense of Segregation in Louisiana," Ph.D. diss., 29.

98. *Memphis Commercial Appeal,* Sept. 22, 1955; "Mississippi LEAC Presents Six-Point Plan to Retain School Segregation," 4–5; "Mississippi Leaders 'Divided' on Proposal for Nullification," 6–7.

99. *Laws of the State of Mississippi,* 1956, regular sess., 520–24. For more details on the creation of the Mississippi State Sovereignty Commission, see Katagiri, *The Mississippi State Sovereignty Commission,* 5–8.

100. W. M. Rainach, untitled speech before the Louisiana Farm Bureau convention, Alexandria, July 20, 1954, 5, folder 442, box 38, Rainach Papers.

101. Hofstadter, *The Paranoid Style in American Politics and Other Essays.*

CHAPTER ONE

1. Fairclough, *Race and Democracy,* 137. See also Lowndes, *From the New Deal to the New Right,* 5–6.

2. Michael J. Heale, "Beyond the 'Age of McCarthy': Anticommunism and the Historians," in *The State of U.S. History,* ed. Stokes, 131.

3. Roy, *Communism and the Churches,* 3.

4. Forster and Epstein, *Danger on the Right,* 47–51, 99–101, 144–45; Powers, *Not without Honor,* 294; Heale, *American Anticommunism,* 171; Diamond, *Roads to Dominion,* 101; Marty, *Under God, Indivisible,* 366–71; Twentieth Century Reformation Hour, *Who Is Carl McIntire?,* 5–6; Carter, "The Rise of Conservatism since World War II," 12.

5. Roy, *Apostles of Discord,* 228.

6. M. G. Lowman, "An Address by Benjamin Gitlow," letter to the Circuit Riders' contributors, n.d. [Sept. 1953], folder 5, box 83; "Myers G. Lowman," biographical notes, n.d. [1959], folder: "Lowman, Myers G., 1959," box 671; "Myers G. Lowman," biographical notes, n.d. [1954?], folder: "Lohman, Clarence, 1953–1954," box 718, all in Matthews Papers; *Johnstown (Pa.) Tribune-Democrat,* n.d. [1955], box 90, Lowman Papers; *Cincinnati (Ohio) Times-Star,* Mar. 20, 1953; *Indianapolis (Ind.) Star,* Aug. 21, 1953; Stephen L. Bennett [senior and coordinating pastor, Westwood United Methodist Church, Cincinnati, Ohio], "Re: Myers G. Lowman," e-mail to the author, Aug. 24, 2003.

7. Carleton, *Red Scare!,* 84, 135–36; Kellar, *Make Haste Slowly,* 47–63; Oshinsky, *A Conspiracy So Immense,* 303; Phillips, *White Metropolis,* 134, 161; Davidson, *Race and Class in*

Texas Politics, 199, 209–12. On Hunt's Facts Forum, see Hendershot, *What's Fair on the Air?,* 26–64.

8. Fried, ed., *McCarthyism,* 78.

9. John K. Finger, "Circuit Riders: A Message to Methodists about Circuit Riders, Inc.," open letter, Mar. 1954, folder: "MFSA and Circuit Riders," MFSA Records; Stanley High to J. B. Matthews, Dec. 13, 1949, folder: "High, Stanley, 1949–1950 and n.d.," box 665, Matthews Papers.

10. High, "Methodism's Pink Fringe," 134–38; Carleton, *Red Scare!,* 106; Roy, *Communism and the Churches,* 304.

11. Heale, *American Anti-Communism,* 118.

12. Norwood, *The Story of American Methodism,* 392. See also Dorrien, *The Making of American Liberal Theology,* 29.

13. Ward, *A Year Book of the Church and Social Service in the United States,* 45–46; George D. McClain, "Pioneering Social Gospel Radicalism: An Overview of the History of the Methodist Federation for Social Action," in *Perspectives on American Methodism,* ed. Richey et al., 372; Wilson, *Biases and Blind Spots,* online ed., Concerned Methodists, Officers and Directors of Concerned Methodists, Inc., Fayetteville, N.C., www.cmpage.org/biases/chapter2.html.

14. McClain, "Pioneering Social Gospel Radicalism," 372; Ward, *A Year Book of the Church and Social Service in the United States,* 46.

15. Powers, *Not without Honor,* 35; "Who We Are: History," Methodist Federation for Social Action, Washington, D.C., www.mfsaweb.org/whoweare/A0300.html; McEllhenney, *Two Hundred Years of United Methodism,* online ed., Story of United Methodism in America, Drew University, Madison, N.J., http://depts.drew.edu/lib/books/200Years/part4/075.htm; Heale, *American Anticommunism,* 118.

16. Rossinow, "The Radicalization of the Social Gospel," 91.

17. Heale, *American Anticommunism,* 118; Carleton, *Red Scare!,* 104.

18. "Methodist Federation for Social Action History Highlights: 1907–2007," MFSA History, Methodist Federation for Social Action California-Pacific Chapter, n.p., www.cal-pacmfsa. org/MFSA_Year_By_Year.php. On the Methodist Federation for Social Service, see King, "The Emergence of Social Gospel Radicalism," 436–49.

19. Rossinow, "The Radicalization of the Social Gospel," 97; Wilson, *Biases and Blind Spots;* Heale, *American Anticommunism,* 188.

20. U.S. Congress, House, Committee on Un-American Activities, *Guide to Subversive Organizations and Publications,* 75.

21. *St. Louis (Mo.) Post-Dispatch,* Nov. 11, 1952.

22. Roy, *Communism and the Churches,* 303–4; High, *The Revolt of Youth;* Wilson, *Biases and Blind Spots.*

23. Finger, "Circuit Riders."

24. Committee for the Preservation of Methodism, *Is There a Pink Fringe in the Methodist Church?,* 2–3, item 74, box 1, SI Collection; Carleton, *Red Scare!,* 108.

25. Finger, "Circuit Riders"; Lohman, "Socialism and Communism and the Methodist Church," 4, *CA* Collection.

26. "Federation Speaks for Itself," 31, *CA* Collection.

27. *Daily Worker (N.Y.),* Feb. 14, 1954.

28. Committee for the Preservation of Methodism, *Is There a Pink Fringe in the Methodist Church?,* n.p.; Finger, "Circuit Riders"; Carleton, *Red Scare!,* 103, 108–9; Olsen, "Teaching Americanism," 259. See also Nickerson, *Mothers of Conservatism,* 87.

29. *Daily Worker,* Feb. 14, 1954.

30. *Houston (Tex.) Post,* Nov. 4, 1953; Carleton, *Red Scare!,* 162–63; Kellar, *Make Haste Slowly,* 82.

31. *Daily Worker,* Feb. 14, 1954; Irvin M. May Jr., "Baker, Hines Holt, Sr.," *Handbook of Texas Online,* Texas State Historical Association, Austin, www.tsha.utexas.edu/handbook/online/articles/BB/fbaba.html. To be sure, even in the face of the feverish atmosphere created by some of his own congregation, Lawrence Durwood Fleming, founding pastor at St. Luke's Methodist Church since 1945, served as a voice of reason among the Houston Methodists. Believing that McCarthyism was an "affront to God" and "the integrity of the church," Fleming was "crucial to providing a moderating voice among leaders in the denomination" (see *Houston [Tex.] Chronicle,* Jan. 27, 2007; and Tom Pace [senior pastor, St. Luke's United Methodist Church, Houston, Tex.], e-mail to the author, Aug. 30, 2011).

32. Committee for the Preservation of Methodism, *Is There a Pink Fringe in the Methodist Church?;* Finger, "Circuit Riders"; Wilson, *Biases and Blind Spots; Daily Worker,* Feb. 14, 1954; Carleton, *Red Scare!,* 109; Roy, *Apostles of Discord,* 327.

33. Carleton, *Red Scare!,* 151; Deckman, *School Board Battles,* 8.

34. Circuit Riders, *Principles and Purposes,* n.p., folder 5, box 83, Matthews Papers.

35. *Cincinnati (Ohio) Enquirer,* Oct. 2, 1951; "Group against 'Isms,'" 14, *CA* Collection; Department of Christian Social Relations of the National Council of the Protestant Episcopal Church, "Sowing Dissension in the Churches: A Report on Some of the Individuals and Groups Engaged in Attacks on the Leadership of the Churches," typed report, n.d. [Mar. 1962], 15–16, folder 7, box 83, Matthews Papers.

36. William C. Perkins, Clarence Lohman, M. G. Lowman et al., to "The Members of the Methodist Church," n.d. [1951], folder: "Circuit Riders Literature (1950–57)," box 1, CR Records.

37. Ibid.; John C. Satterfield and M. G. Lowman to Harold H. Velde [HUAC chair], Western Union telegram [confirmation copy], Mar. 12, 1953, folder 5, box 83, Matthews Papers; *Houston Post,* Nov. 3, 1953.

38. Katagiri, *The Mississippi State Sovereignty Commission,* 122–25, 150–52; Morris, *Yazoo,* 72.

39. Roy, *Apostles of Discord,* 140, 334–35; Talmadge, *You and Segregation.* Some issues of Craft's *One Methodist Voice* are contained in folder: "Craft, Blake, 1953–1954," box 656, Matthews Papers.

40. "Group against 'Isms,'" 14.

41. "Circuit-Riding Methodists," 11, *CA* Collection.

42. Lowman, *Citizens' Council Forum,* reel no. 27, videocassette.

43. Finger, "Circuit Riders."

44. U.S. Congress, House, Committee on Un-American Activities, *Review of the Methodist Federation for Social Action;* Payton, "Federation Review," 16, *CA* Collection; Clyde R. Miller [MFSA member] to John S. Wood, Apr. 17, 1952, 1, folder: "MFSA and Circuit Riders," MFSA Records; Roy, *Communism and the Churches,* 309.

45. Committee on Un-American Activities, *Guide to Subversive Organizations and Publications,* 75; Circuit Riders, *Fifty Years of Un-Methodist Propaganda,* 2, folder: "Circuit Riders," Garman Papers. Following in the HUAC's footsteps, in late 1955, the SISS also designated the MFSA as one of the most notorious "religious fronts" formed by the Communist Party in issuing a report entitled *The Communist Party of the United States of America: What It Is, How It Works—A Handbook for Americans* (see U.S. Congress, Senate, Committee on the Judiciary, Subcommittee to Investigate the Administration of the Internal Security Act and

Other Internal Security Laws, *The Communist Party of the United States of America,* 91; and M. G. Lowman to James O. Eastland, Feb. 15, 1956, folder: "MFSA [Methodist Federation for Social Action]," box 52, Lowman Papers).

46. Finger, "Circuit Riders"; National Americanism Commission of the American Legion, untitled article, *Firing Line,* Oct. 15, 1952, n.p. [p. 1], folder: "Circuit Riders Literature (1950–57)," box 1, CR Records.

47. Circuit Riders, *Information Concerning the Methodist Federation for Social Action,* folder: "Circuit Riders," Garman Papers; National Americanism Commission of the American Legion, untitled article, n.p. [p. 1]; Methodist Federation for Social Action, "Memorial to General Conference in 1956," draft attached to the Apr. 28, 1955, letter from Mark A. Chamberlin [federation membership secretary] to "Dear Brothers and Sisters," folder: "Miscellaneous," box 88, Lowman Papers.

48. Circuit Riders, *Fifty Years of Un-Methodist Propaganda,* 3; Wilson, *Biases and Blind Spots;* Roy, *Communism and the Churches,* 304.

49. Roy, *Communism and the Churches,* 311.

50. John C. Satterfield, Clarence Lohman, and M. G. Lowman to "The Delegates to the 1952 General Conference and Other Methodists," n.d. [1953], folder: "Circuit Riders Literature (1950–57)," box 1, CR Records.

51. Ibid.

52. Methodist Federation for Social Action, "Memorial to General Conference in 1956"; Circuit Riders, *Fifty Years of Un-Methodist Propaganda,* 3.

53. M. G. Lowman, "Notice of Annual Meeting," Sept. 25, 1952; Circuit Riders, "Invitation to Hear 'Communism in Religion,'" Oct. 6, 1952, both in folder: "Circuit Riders Literature (1950–57)," box 1, CR Records.

54. Myers G. Lowman to Joseph Kornfeder, Feb. 22, 1957, folder: "Kornfeder, Joseph," box 45; Kornfeder, "Communist Deception in the Churches," speech, Oct. 26, 1952, 10, folder: "Speeches, Statements, Resolutions, etc.," box 77, both in Lowman Papers.

55. Roy, *Communism and the Churches,* 235; Fried, *The Russians Are Coming!,* 70.

56. Norman A. Sugarman [assistant commissioner, Office of Commissioner of Internal Revenue] to Circuit Riders, Jan. 6, 1953, folder 5, box 83, Matthews Papers.

57. *Cincinnati Enquirer,* Aug. 15, 1953; *Cincinnati Times-Star,* Aug. 15, 1953; *Indianapolis Star,* Aug. 21, 1953.

58. Caute, *The Great Fear,* 80.

59. Ohio Coalition of Patriotic Societies, "Financial Statement, Canton Seminar, 3–4 October 1953," n.d., folder: "Circuit Riders, Inc.—Correspondence," box 14, Lowman Papers.

60. Ohio Coalition of Patriotic Societies, "Seminar on Socialism and Communism," program, n.d. [Oct. 1953], box 87, Lowman Papers.

61. William E. Warner to W. O. H. Garman [vice president, American Council of Christian Churches, Wilkinsburg, Penn.], Feb. 25, 1954, folder: "Ohio Coalition of Patriotic Societies," Garman Papers.

62. American Coalition of Patriotic Societies, "Proposed List of Organizations to Be Invited to Cooperate with the American Coalition," typed list, n.d., box 89, Lowman Papers; American Coalition of Patriotic Societies, "Societies Cooperating with the American Coalition," typed list, Nov. 8, 1949, folder: "Ohio Coalition of Patriotic Societies," Garman Papers.

63. American Coalition, *The American Coalition,* 1, 3, 6, folder: "American Coalition," box 1, CR Records; Powers, *Not without Honor,* 79–80.

64. American Coalition, *The American Coalition*, 3.

65. Ohio Coalition of Patriotic Societies, "Seminar on Socialism and Communism"; Ohio Coalition of Patriotic Societies, "Speakers Budget, Canton Seminar, 3–4 October 1953," n.d., folder: "Circuit Riders, Inc.—Correspondence," box 14; Ohio Coalition of Patriotic Societies, "Your Speakers and Staff," program, n.d. [Oct. 1953], box 87, both in Lowman Papers; *New York Times*, Dec. 3, 1954.

66. Lowman, *Citizens' Council Forum*, reel no. 96, videocassette.

67. Matthews, *Odyssey of a Fellow Traveler*. Matthews's book can be read online at American Deception, n.p., www.americandeception.com/index.php?page=usercat&catid=28.

68. Gregory L. Williams, "Biographies: J. B. Matthews," *Inventory to the Records of Consumers' Research, Inc., 1910–1983*, online inventory, Jan. 1995, Special Collections and University Archives, Rutgers University Libraries, Rutgers University, New Brunswick, N.J., www2.scc.rutgers.edu/ead/manuscripts/consumers_introf.html.

69. J. B. Matthews to Stanley High, n.d. [1949]; High to Matthews, Dec. 13, 1949, both in folder: "High, Stanley, 1949–1950 and n.d.," box 665, Matthews Papers.

70. FLIC, "Transcript of Testimony [of Joseph Brown Matthews]," Feb. 10, 1958, 6, folders 13 and 14, box 4, FLIC Records.

71. Williams, "Biographies: J. B. Matthews"; *New York Journal-American*, July 9, 1953. Regarding the association between Matthews and Sokolsky, see also Pizzitola, *Hearst over Hollywood*, 359.

72. Matthews, *Odyssey of a Fellow Traveler*, 52; "Uncheckable Charge."

73. Wiener, "J. B. Matthews," 2, folder 2, box 132, reel no. 147, *NR* Records; "Biographical Note," *Inventory of the J. B. Matthews Papers, 1862–1986*, online inventory, Rare Book, Manuscript, and Special Collections Library, Duke University, Durham, N.C., http://library.duke.edu/digitalcollections/rbmscl/matthews/inv; Williams, "Biographies: J. B. Matthews."

74. Matthews, *The "United Front" Exposed*, 2, folder: "Investigation (Dies), 1938–39," box 25, Lowman Papers.

75. Ibid.; Joseph Brown Matthews to the School of Oriental Languages [University of Vienna, Austria], Oct. 4, 1965; Church League of America, "Biographical Note: J. B. Matthews," typescript, n.d. [1965?], n.p. [p. 1], both in folder: "Biographical, 1963–1967," box 696, Matthews Papers; *New York Journal-American*, July 9, 1953.

76. Matthews, *Odyssey of a Fellow Traveler*, 56–57, 59, 61; Goodman, *The Committee*, 36.

77. Wiener, "J. B. Matthews," 3.

78. Matthews, *Odyssey of a Fellow Traveler*, 57, 59.

79. Ibid., 64; Dawson, "From Fellow Traveler to Anticommunist," 285.

80. Matthews, *The "United Front" Exposed*, 3.

81. Matthews, *Odyssey of a Fellow Traveler*, 69; Wiener, "J. B. Matthews," 3.

82. Fellowship of Reconciliation, *That Men May Live*, n.p., folder: "Fellowship for [*sic*] Reconciliation," box 2, CR Records.

83. James Peck, "Freedom Rides, 1947 and 1961," in *Nonviolent Direct Action*, ed. Hare and Blumberg, 49–75.

84. FLIC, "Transcript of Testimony [of Joseph Brown Matthews]," 7; Matthews, *Odyssey of a Fellow Traveler*, 69, 77–78, 95; Horton, *The Long Haul*, 38.

85. Matthews, *Odyssey of a Fellow Traveler*, 91, 96–97.

86. Matthews, *The "United Front" Exposed*, 4; Lichtman, "J. B. Matthews and the 'Counter-Subversives,'" 6; Powers, *Not without Honor*, 120.

87. Matthews, *Odyssey of a Fellow Traveler,* 178; Bell, *Marxian Socialism in the United States,* 147–48.

88. Matthews, *Odyssey of a Fellow Traveler,* 72–76; Wiener, "J. B. Matthews," 2; *New York Journal-American,* July 9, 1953; Church League of America, "Biographical Note: J. B. Matthews"; Goodman, *The Committee,* 37.

89. Powers, *Not without Honor,* 104.

90. Wiener, "J. B. Matthews," 3; Dawson, "From Fellow Traveler to Anticommunist," 290.

91. Matthews and Shallcross, *Partners in Plunder;* Wiener, "J. B. Matthews," 3; Dawson, "From Fellow Traveler to Anticommunist," 291.

92. "Biographical Note," *Inventory of the J. B. Matthews Papers;* Williams, "Biographies: J. B. Matthews."

93. Wiener, "J. B. Matthews," 3; Lichtman, "J. B. Matthews and the 'Counter-Subversives,'" 6.

94. Roy, *Communism and the Churches,* 250.

95. Kempton, *Part of Our Time,* 166; Dawson, "From Fellow Traveler to Anticommunist," 292.

96. Matthews, *Odyssey of a Fellow Traveler,* 16–17, 183–84.

97. Ibid., 184, 269; Roy, *Communism and the Churches,* 250.

98. Goodman, *The Committee,* 41.

99. Matthews, *Odyssey of a Fellow Traveler,* 274.

100. *New York Journal-American,* July 9, 1953; Rushmore, "Mr. Anti-Communist," 83, folder 4, box 18, Archive I: Un-American Activities (1950–55), Matusow Archive.

101. "The Man in the Middle."

102. Nasaw, *The Chief,* 588.

103. Caute, *The Great Fear,* 446–47.

104. "The Man in the Middle."

105. Ceplair, *Anti-Communism in Twentieth-Century America,* 26–27; J. B. Matthews to George E. Sokolsky, Western Union telegram [draft], n.d. [Feb. 13, 1962], folder: "Sokolsky, George, 1954–1964 and n.d.," box 681, Matthews Papers; Sokolsky to Matthews, July 7, 1938, folder 1, box 87, Sokolsky Papers.

106. Alwood, *Dark Days in the Newsroom,* 25–26; Rushmore, "Mr. Anti-Communist," 83; Kempton, *Part of Our Time,* 168.

107. Matthews, *The "United Front" Exposed,* 5, 25.

108. Kempton, *Part of Our Time,* 171.

109. J. B. Matthews to Martin Dies, May 11, 1954; "The Administration Won't Sneer 'One-Man Gestapo' as Martin Dies Heads Back to Washington," 23, both in folder: "Dies, Martin, Oct. 1939–Aug. 1952," box 657, Matthews Papers. See also Ogden, *The Dies Committee,* 64.

110. Matthews, *The "United Front" Exposed,* 30. On the contents of Matthews's August 1938 testimony before the Dies Committee, see also Matthews, *Doctor Matthews' Amazing Statement before the Dies' Committee Investigating Un-American Activities,* folder: "Investigation (Dies), 1938–39," box 25, Lowman Papers.

111. FLIC, "Transcript of Testimony [of Joseph Brown Matthews]," 7.

112. Wiener, "J. B. Matthews," 2; Goodman, *The Committee,* 35, 42.

113. Bentley, ed., *Thirty Years of Treason,* 727; Wiener, "J. B. Matthews," 2; Carl McIntire, "J. B. Matthews" [introduction], in Matthews, *Communism in Our Churches,* 3, folder: "Pamphlets," box 5, CR Records.

114. Rushmore, "Mr. Anti-Communist," 84.

115. Wiener, "J. B. Matthews," 2.

116. Rushmore, "Mr. Anti-Communist," 85.

117. Duke, *In the Trenches with Jesus and Marx,* 179; Powers, *Not without Honor,* 161.

118. Lichtman, "J. B. Matthews and the 'Counter-Subversives,'" 7–8; Carleton, *Red Scare!,* 130.

119. J. B. Matthews to George Sokolsky, Jan. 3, 1945, folder 2, box 87, Sokolsky Papers.

120. Caute, *The Great Fear,* 572; Donner, *The Age of Surveillance,* 421.

121. Martin Dies, "Congressman Martin Dies['s] Message," n.d. [Feb. 1953], 2, folder: "Testimonial Dinner, 1952–1953," box 700, Matthews Papers.

122. Kempton, *Part of Our Time,* 172; Goodman, *The Committee,* 35; Egerton, *Speak Now against the Day,* 653; Dies, *Trojan Horse in America.*

123. Martin Dies to J. B. Matthews, Oct. 2, 1940, folder: "Dies, Martin, Oct. 1939–Aug. 1952," box 657, Matthews Papers.

124. Rushmore, "Mr. Anti-Communist," 85; Martin Shallcross Matthews, "Resume," n.d. [May 1970], folder: "Matthews, Martin: Correspondence from, 1952–1970," box 698, Matthews Papers.

125. Lichtman, "J. B. Matthews and the 'Counter-Subversives,'" 3, 9; Nasaw, *The Chief,* 588; Roy, *Communism and the Churches,* 251.

126. Helen Hope Shallcross Hogue [formerly Mrs. J. B. Matthews Jr.] to "A Dear Friend and His Son, a Living Relative," July 17, 1966, 3, folder: "Letters from Family, 1966–1967," box 708, Matthews Papers; Lichtman and Cohen, *Deadly Farce,* 75.

127. George E. Sokolsky to "Dear Frined," n.d., folder 4, box 18, Archive I: Un-American Activities (1950–55), Matusow Archive.

128. "Testimonial Dinner to Dr. J. B. Matthews by His Friends, Sert Room, Waldorf-Astoria," program, Feb. 13, 1953, n.p.; J. B. Matthews to Benjamin Schultz [executive director, American Jewish League against Communism, New York], Feb. 23, 1953, both in folder: "Testimonial Dinner, 1952–1953," box 700, Matthews Papers.

129. "Dr. J. B. Matthews Dinner Guest List," n.d. [Feb. 1953], folder 4, box 18, Archive I: Un-American Activities (1950–55), Matusow Archive; Caute, *The Great Fear,* 227.

130. "Testimonial Dinner to Dr. J. B. Matthews by His Friends," n.p.; Joseph R. McCarthy, "Eulogy of J. B. Matthews by Senator Joseph R. McCarthy: At Testimonial Dinner in Honor of Matthews, Held at the Waldorf-Astoria Hotel, New York City, February 13, 1953," typescript, folder: "Matthews, J. B.," box 49, Lowman Papers.

131. "The Administration Won't Sneer 'One-Man Gestapo' as Martin Dies Heads Back to Washington," 23; Dies, "Congressman Martin Dies['s] Message," 1–2.

132. Lichtman, "J. B. Matthews and the 'Counter-Subversives,'" 22; Lichtman and Cohen, *Deadly Farce,* 76.

133. J. B. Matthews to Richard M. Nixon, Feb. 22, 1953, folder: "Testimonial Dinner, 1952–1953," box 700, Matthews Papers.

134. Harold H. Velde to Mr. and Mrs. J. B. Matthews, Feb. 24, 1952, folder: "Velde, Harold H., 1952 and n.d.," box 682, Matthews Papers.

135. Finger, "Circuit Riders"; Braden, *House Un-American Activities Committee,* 20.

136. Goodman, *The Committee,* 332.

137. Satterfield and Lowman to Velde, Western Union telegram, Mar. 12, 1953.

138. *Cincinnati Enquirer,* Mar. 13, 1953.

139. M. G. Lowman to Harold H. Velde, Western Union telegram [confirmation copy], Apr. 16, 1953, folder: "Methodist Federation for Social Action," box 3, CR Records.

140. *Cincinnati (Ohio) Post,* May 7, 1953.

141. *Santa Rosa (Calif.) Press Democrat,* Apr. 12, 1954; *Lake County (Lakeport, Calif.) Bee,* Apr. 16, 1954; Goodman, *The Committee,* 341–42.

142. U.S. Congress, House, Committee on Un-American Activities, *Annual Report of the Committee on Un-American Activities for the Year 1953,* 97–98; Buckley, *The Committee and Its Critics,* 302; Weigand, "The Red Menace, the Feminine Mystique, and the Ohio Un-American Activities Commission," 83.

143. Goodman, *The Committee,* 342.

144. Ibid., 343.

145. *Cincinnati Enquirer,* Aug. 1, 1953.

146. U.S. Congress, Senate, Committee on Governmental Affairs, *Executive Sessions of the Senate Permanent Subcommittee on Investigations of the Committee on Government Operations,* xxvii–xxviii; *New York Herald,* July 8, 1953; *New York Daily News,* July 8, 1953.

147. McCarthy, *McCarthyism;* Herman, *Joseph McCarthy,* 14.

148. Herman, *Joseph McCarthy,* 163. See also Evans, *Blacklisted by History,* 492.

149. Williams, "Biographies: J. B. Matthews."

150. Wehrkamp, comp., *Reference Information Paper 107.*

151. Matthews, "Reds and Our Churches."

152. Lichtman, "J. B. Matthews and the 'Counter-Subversives,'" 25; Justin Raimondo, untitled article, Oct. 30, 2000, Behind the Headlines, Antiwar.Com, Redwood City, Calif., www.antiwar.com/justin/j103000.html. See also "The Press: Blowup at the Mercury."

153. Matthews, "Reds and Our Churches," 3; Bentley, ed., *Thirty Years of Treason,* 728.

154. Matthews, *Some Facts about the Communist Apparatus,* 14.

155. Watt, "Ruth Young Watt," recorded interview, 115.

156. Howard V. Hansen to J. B. Mathews [*sic*], July 3, 1953; Robert Gray Taylor to Mathews [*sic*], July 3, 1953; Edward Z. Utts to Matthews, July 6, 1953; Denzil Albin to Matthews, July 10, 1953, all in folder: "Clergy Incident, July 1953," box 696, Matthews Papers.

157. "Three Democrat Senators Refuse to Aid McCarthy," unidentifiable newspaper, July 12, 1953, folder 4, box 18, Archive I: Un-American Activities (1950–55), Matusow Archive; *New York Daily News,* July 8, 1953.

158. "Uncheckable Charge"; *New York Daily News,* July 8, 1953; Goodman, *The Committee,* 336. See also Kaufman, *Henry M. Jackson,* 76–77.

159. Nutt, "For Truth and Liberty"; Dawson, "From Fellow Traveler to Anticommunist," 301–2; "Inquiries: Joe Stubs Toe," 29. See also Crosby, *God, Church, and Flag,* 126–28.

160. David A. Witts to Dwight D. Eisenhower, July 10, 1953, folder: "Clergy Incident, July 1953," box 696, Matthews Papers; "Deaths: David A. Witts."

161. J. B. Matthews, "Statement of Dr. J. B. Matthews," press release, July 9, 1953, folder: "Matthews Quits McCarthy Committee, 1953–1960," box 698, Matthews Papers.

162. Lichtman, "J. B. Matthews and the 'Counter-Subversives,'" 27; Roy, *Communism and the Churches,* 260–61.

163. J. B. Matthews to Glenn A. Green [executive director, National Education Program, Harding College, Searcy, Ark.], Aug. 8, 1953, folder: "Harding College: National Education Program, 1951–1963," box 663, Matthews Papers.

164. "Uncheckable Charge."

165. McIntire, "J. B. Matthews," 3; John T. Flynn to J. B. Matthews, Mar. 27, 1953, folder: "Flynn, John T., 1947–1964 and n.d.," box 661; Flynn, "Communists and the New Deal, Part

II," folder 14, box 220; Matthews, "Communists and the New Deal, Part III," folder 14, box 220, all in Matthews Papers. On Flynn's checkered career, see Raimondo, "John T. Flynn."

166. Rushmore, "Mr. Anti-Communist," 79.

167. Lichtman and Cohen, "Harvey Matusow, the FBI, and the Justice Department," 55.

168. Lichtman, "J. B. Matthews and the 'Counter-Subversives,'" 2.

169. MGLIC, *A Report to the 1962 Regular Session of the Mississippi State Legislature,* 13, box 72, Rainach Papers.

170. Fried, *Nightmare in Red,* 188.

171. Roy, *Communism and the Churches,* 251.

172. Lichtman and Cohen, *Deadly Farce,* 52.

173. Kempton, *Part of Our Time,* 4, 175.

174. Lichtman, "J. B. Matthews and the 'Counter-Subversives,'" 3; Robert M. Lichtman [attorney and historian, San Francisco], e-mail to the author, Sept. 25, 2007; Martin S. Matthews [Langley, Wash.], e-mail to the author, Jan. 13, 2008.

175. Rothbard, *The Betrayal of the American Right,* 150; Benjamin Mandel to J. B. Matthews, Oct. 17 or 18 [?], 1950, folder: "Correspondence between Matthews and Mandel, 1950–1953," box 692, Matthews Papers.

176. J. B. Matthews to Glenn A. Green, Sept. 15, 1951, folder: "Harding College: National Education Program, 1951–1963," box 663, Matthews Papers.

177. J. B. Matthews to W. J. Simmons, Sept. 6, 1955, folder: "Simmons, W. J., 1954–1963 and n.d.," box 680, Matthews Papers.

178. J. B. Matthews to George E. Sokolsky, Aug. 6, 1951, folder: "Sokolsky, George, 1931–1953," box 681, Matthews Papers.

179. Schrecker, "Archival Sources for the Study of McCarthyism," 203. See also Schrecker, *Many Are the Crimes,* 44.

180. McMillen, *The Citizens' Council,* 178.

181. Ohio Coalition of Patriotic Societies, "Seminar on Socialism and Communism."

182. M. G. Lowman to J. B. Matthews, Oct. 15, 1953, folder 5, box 83; Lowman to Matthews, Oct. 23, 1953, folder 5, box 83; Mr. and Mrs. Myers G. Lowman to Matthews, wedding invitation, n.d. [Nov. 1956], folder: "Lowman, Myers G., 1951–1956," box 670, all in Matthews Papers.

183. Circuit Riders, untitled press release, June 2, 1955, box 87, Lowman Papers; *Houston Post,* Nov. 3, 1953.

184. M. G. Lowman to J. B. Matthews, Feb. 18, 1954, 1, folder: "Lohman, Clarence, 1953–1954," box 718, Matthews Papers.

185. M. G. Lowman to Francis E. Walter, Nov. 22, 1954, folder: "Circuit Riders, July 1950–Apr. 1955," box 655, Matthews Papers.

186. M. G. Lowman to Gordon H. Scherer, July 20, 1955, 2, folder 6, box 83, Matthews Papers.

187. M. G. Lowman to J. B. Matthews, May 4, 1955, folder: "Circuit Riders, May–Dec. 1955 and n.d.," box 655, Matthews Papers.

188. M. G. Lowman to J. B. Matthews, May 20, 1955, folder 6, box 83, Matthews Papers.

189. Circuit Riders, untitled press release, June 2, 1955.

190. J. B. Matthews to M. G. Lowman, Mar. 9, 1956; Matthews to Lowman, Apr. 10, 1956; Circuit Riders, untitled press release, Aug. 1956, all in folder: "Lowman, Myers G., 1951–1956," box 670, Matthews Papers.

191. Circuit Riders to Lee Pennington [National Americanism Commission, American Legion, Washington, D.C.], book order form, n.d. [Dec. 1959], folder 6, box 83; J. B. Matthews to M. G. Lowman, June 16, 1960, folder: "Lowman, Myers G., 1960," box 671; Circuit Riders, "660 Baptist Clergymen," book order form attached to an August 1960 memo from Lowman to Matthews, folder: "Lowman, Myers G., 1960," box 671, all in Matthews Papers; Cain, *They'd Rather Be Right,* 206.

192. M. G. Lowman to J. B. Matthews, Nov. 16, 1955, folder 6, box 83, Matthews Papers.

193. Findlay, *Church People in the Struggle,* 28; "The Congress: The New Chairman."

194. Circuit Riders, *Recognize Red China?,* n.p. [preface], CPL.

195. Circuit Riders, untitled press release, June 2, 1955.

196. Myers G. Lowman, "Who's Running with the Ducks?," typescript, May 1956, folder: "Lowman, Myers G., 1951–1956," box 670, Matthews Papers.

197. Ruth Matthews, "Confidential Notes Taken July 17, 1957, at the 50th Anniversary Conference of the Methodist Federation for Social Action Held at the Dodge Hotel, 20 E. Street, N.W., Washington, D.C.," n.d. [1957], 6–7, folder: "Circuit Riders, Inc.—Correspondence," box 14, Lowman Papers.

198. Circuit Riders, *Fifty Years of Un-Methodist Propaganda,* 1, 2, 5.

199. David B. Sageser [Fort Myers, Fla.], "Myers G. Lowman: A Personal Recollection," e-mail to the author, Sept. 19, 2003.

CHAPTER TWO

1. *Cincinnati (Ohio) Times-Star,* n.d. [1955], folder: "Circuit Riders, Inc.—Correspondence," box 14; *Johnstown (Pa.) Tribune-Democrat,* n.d. [1955], box 90, both in Lowman Papers.

2. Lottie E. Schultz [wife of Benjamin Schultz] to J. B. Matthews, Apr. 19, 1955; Benjamin Schultz to Matthews, Dec. 10, 1953, both in folder: "Schultz, Rabbi Benjamin, 1946–1964," box 680, Matthews Papers.

3. "Rabbi Benjamin Schultz," biographical sketch, n.d., folder: "Schultz, Rabbi Benjamin, 1946–1964," box 680, Matthews Papers; Powers, *Not without Honor,* 229.

4. Benjamin Schultz to Matthews, Dec. 10, 1953; Lottie Schultz to Matthews, Apr. 19, 1955.

5. J. B. Matthews to M. G. Lowman, Oct. 2, 1955, folder: "Circuit Riders, Inc.—Correspondence," box 14, Lowman Papers. Sent by John Wesley as a missionary to colonial America in 1771, Asbury became the founding bishop of American Methodism and promoted the circuit rider system. He himself delivered some sixteen thousand sermons as he traveled for more than 270,000 miles (see Robert Simpson, "The Circuit-Riders in Early American Methodism," History Note Series, General Commission on Archives and History of the United Methodist Church, Drew University Methodist Library, Drew University, Madison, N.J., www.gcah.org/Circuit_Riders.html).

6. Gordon H. Scherer to Myers G. Lowman, Nov. 15, 1955, folder: "Circuit Riders, Inc.—Correspondence," box 14, Lowman Papers.

7. J. B. Matthews to M. G. Lowman, Apr. 11, 1956, folder: "Lowman, Myers G., 1951–1956," box 670, Matthews Papers.

8. M. G. Lowman to Eugene Cook, Apr. 12, 1956, folder: "Lowman, Myers G., 1951–1956," box 670, Matthews Papers. "In 1955 I undertook to conduct a series of hearings before several State Investigating Committees re: Subversion of Race Grievances by C.P.U.S.A.," Lowman's

1967 handwritten memo reads, "[and] Eugene Cook, Attorney General of Georgia, was approached first" (see M. G. Lowman, "A Privileged Record of Race . . . [illegible] . . . in [the] South," handwritten notes, June 21, 1967, folder: "Georgia Commission on Education," box 95, Lowman Papers).

9. Cook, *The Ugly Truth about the NAACP,* in both folder: "Association of Citizens' Councils: Folder 1," box 26, Cox Papers; and folder 24, box 2, McCain Collection; Braden, *House Un-American Activities Committee,* 28.

10. M. G. Lowman to Eugene Cook, Apr. 19, 1956, folder: "Lowman, Myers G., 1951–1956," box 670, Matthews Papers.

11. Record, *Race and Radicalism,* 164–65; White, *A Man Called White,* 344–45; Wilkins and Matthews, *Standing Fast,* 210; Fairclough, *Race and Democracy,* 143; Carol Anderson, "Bleached Souls and Red Negroes: The NAACP and Black Communists in the Early Cold War, 1948–1952," in *Window on Freedom,* ed. Plummer, 93, 107; Klarman, *From Jim Crow to Civil Rights,* 191; Sullivan, *Lift Every Voice,* 370.

12. Hill, "The Communist Party."

13. U.S. Congress, House, Committee on Un-American Activities, *The American Negro in the Communist Party,* 1, 13; Whitfield, *The Culture of the Cold War,* 22.

14. Berg, "Black Civil Rights and Liberal Anticommunism," 89–90. See also Berg, *"The Ticket to Freedom,"* 116–39.

15. M. G. Lowman to J. B. Matthews, Jan. 16, 1957, folder: "Lowman, Myers G., 1957," box 671, Matthews Papers.

16. M. G. Lowman to J. B. Matthews, Feb. 11, 1957; Matthews to Lowman, Feb. 14, 1957; Lowman to Matthews, Feb. 18, 1957, all in folder: "Lowman, Myers G., 1957," box 671, Matthews Papers. Later in 1961, Du Bois would become an official member of the CPUSA two years prior to his death, and this fact definitely did not help the NAACP's endeavor to dispel its pro-Communist reputation that lingered among white southerners at large (see Du Bois, *The Souls of Black Folk,* n.p. [biographical sketch]).

17. J. B. Matthews to M. G. Lowman, Feb. 26, 1957; Matthews to Lowman, Feb. 27, 1957, both in folder: "Lowman, Myers G., 1957," box 671, Matthews Papers.

18. M. G. Lowman, "In the Periphery," typescript, Dec. 23, 1957, 2, folder: "Lowman, Myers G., 1957"; J. B. Matthews to Lowman, Jan. 7, 1958, folder: "Lowman, Myers G., 1958," both in box 671, Matthews Papers.

19. J. B. Matthews to M. G. Lowman, Dec. 5, 1957, folder: "Lowman, Myers G., 1957," box 671, Matthews Papers.

20. M. G. Lowman to Arthur J. Moore [Methodist bishop, Atlanta, Ga.], Mar. 14, 1957; Lowman to Carl McIntire [founder, American Council of Christian Churches, Collingswood, N.J.], Apr. 9, 1957; Lowman to Moore, Dec. 27, 1957, all in folder: "Lowman, Myers G., 1957," box 671, Matthews Papers.

21. Williamson, *The Crucible of Race,* 485–86; Cunnigen, "Men and Women of Goodwill," Ph.D. diss., 76–83; *Plessy v. Ferguson,* 163 U.S. 537 (1896); Southern Regional Council, "A Statement of Policy and Aims," Dec. 12, 1951, folder 10, Welch Papers.

22. Egerton, *Speak Now against the Day,* 311; Dunbar, *Against the Grain,* 252; M. G. Lowman to Arthur J. Moore, May 17, 1957, folder: "Investigation, 1957," box 22, GCE Records.

23. Lowman, *Citizens' Council Forum,* reel no. 96, videocassette.

24. Myrdal, *An American Dilemma; Brown v. Board of Education,* 347 U.S. 483 (1954).

25. Lowman, "A Privileged Record of Race . . . [illegible] . . . in [the] South."

26. Rainach, "An Interview with William M. Rainach," June 28, 1977, 19; *Baltimore Afro-American,* July 13, 1954; Quin, "The Dominance of the Shadow in Southern Race Relations," 15.

27. McMillen, *The Citizens' Council,* 61.

28. Rainach, "An Interview with William M. Rainach," June 28, 1977, 2–3, 11, 13–14, 16; *Shreveport (La.) Times,* Jan. 27, 1978; Havard and Steamer, "Louisiana Secedes," 141.

29. McCarrick, "Louisiana's Official Resistance to Desegregation," Ph.D. diss., 27.

30. House of Representatives of the State of Louisiana, "House Concurrent Resolution Number 22," May 26, 1954, folder 441, box 38; LJLC, *Biennial Report, 1954–1956,* 1, box 72, both in Rainach Papers; Quin, "The Dominance of the Shadow in Southern Race Relations," 15–16.

31. House of Representatives of the State of Louisiana, "House Concurrent Resolution Number 22"; William M. Rainach, untitled typescript prepared for submission to the Louisiana Board of Liquidation of State Debt, Sept. 16, 1954, n.p. [p. 1], folder 442, box 38, Rainach Papers; Quin, "The Dominance of the Shadow in Southern Race Relations," 16.

32. LJLC, *Biennial Report, 1954–1956,* 1; W. M. Rainach to Allison R. Kolb [secretary, Louisiana Board of Liquidation of State Debt, Baton Rouge], Aug. 25, 1954, 1, folder 339, box 29, Rainach Papers; Rainach, "An Interview with William M. Rainach," June 28, 1977, 19.

33. See, for instance, W. M. Rainach to W. M. Shaw [LJLC general counsel], Western Union telegram, Apr. 18, 1960, folder 107, box 11, Rainach Papers.

34. Rainach, "An Interview with William M. Rainach," Aug. 19, 1977, 3; Rainach to Kolb, Aug. 25, 1954, 2; Allison R. Kolb to W. M. Rainach, Oct. 5, 1954; Louisiana Board of Liquidation of State Debt, meeting minutes, Sept. 16, 1954, 6–7, both in folder 339, box 29, Rainach Papers; McCarrick, "Louisiana's Official Resistance to Desegregation," 40; Stowe, "Willie Rainach and the Defense of Segregation in Louisiana," Ph.D. diss., 29.

35. LJLC, meeting minutes, June 14, 1954, folder 441, box 38; LJLC, *Segregation Measures Passed by the Regular Session of the Louisiana Legislature, 1958,* n.p., box 72, both in Rainach Papers.

36. Rainach, "An Interview with William M. Rainach," June 28, 1977, 17; *Cape Girardeau Southeast Missourian,* Nov. 18, 1960; Cowan and McGuire, *Louisiana Governors,* 208.

37. Rainach, "An Interview with William M. Rainach," June 28, 1977, 24; McMillen, *The Citizens' Council,* 62.

38. Rainach, "An Interview with William M. Rainach," June 28, 1977, 20; Jeansonne, *Leander Perez,* 231.

39. W. M. Shaw to Leander H. Perez, Aug. 3, 1954, folder: "Segregation—Joint Legislative Committee, 1954," box 1, Perez Papers.

40. Vetter, *Fonville Winan's Louisiana,* 58–59; *New Orleans Times-Picayune,* Oct. 24, 2011; Walter Sillers to Roman Kelly [clerk, the Mississippi House of Representatives, Jackson], Mar. 3, 1956, folder 19, box 12, Sillers Papers; "National Affairs: Racist Leader."

41. Jeansonne, *Leander Perez,* 227–28. See also Parent, *Inside the Carnival,* 99–100; and *The Ends of the Earth,* videocassette.

42. Sherrill, *Gothic Politics in the Deep South,* 5; "A Kneeling Racist and an Upright Archbishop," 44.

43. W. M. Rainach, untitled speech before the Louisiana Farm Bureau convention, Alexandria, July 20, 1954, 2–3, 5, folder 442, box 38, Rainach Papers.

44. LJLC, "Transcript of Film Television Address by W. M. Rainach," Oct. 14, 1954, 3, folder 443, box 38, Rainach Papers; LSSC and LJLC, *Don't Be Brainwashed!*, n.p., vertical file (microfilm): "Louisiana State Sovereignty Commission," LLMV Collections.

45. Rainach, "An Interview with William M. Rainach," Aug. 19, 1977, 7.

46. Association of Citizens' Councils of Louisiana, untitled signed statement organizing the association, Dec. 13, 1955, folder 446, box 39, Rainach Papers; McCarrick, "Louisiana's Official Resistance to Desegregation," 40; Stowe, "Willie Rainach and the Defense of Segregation in Louisiana," 29.

47. Association of Citizens' Councils of Louisiana, *The Citizens' Councils,* n.p., folder: "Simmons, W. J., 1954–1963 and n.d.," box 680, Matthews Papers; *Shreveport Times,* Jan. 27, 1978.

48. John U. Barr [interim chair, Federation for Constitutional Government] to William M. Rainach, Dec. 19, 1955, folder 66, box 5, Touchstone Papers.

49. Dickerson, *Dixie's Dirty Secret,* 4.

50. John U. Barr to "Dear Fellow American," n.d. [1955]; Federation for Constitutional Government, "Resolution," typescript, Jan. 22, 1955; Federation for Constitutional Government, "Excerpts from Speech Made by Senator James O. Eastland," typescript, n.d. [1955], all in box 89, Lowman Papers; Federation for Constitutional Government, untitled press release, n.d. [Jan. 22, 1955]; W. M. Rainach to Barr, July 21, 1955, both in folder 66, box 5, Touchstone Papers.

51. Katagiri, *The Mississippi State Sovereignty Commission,* 288; Dickerson, *Dixie's Dirty Secret,* 4.

52. Drew L. Smith, "Russia, Communism and Race," newsletter of the Federation for Constitutional Government, n.d., n.p. [p. 1], folder: "Conservative: Literature," box 2, CR Records.

53. John U. Barr to William M. Rainach, Sept. 21, 1955, folder 66, box 5, Touchstone Papers.

54. Federation for Constitutional Government, "The Purpose of the Federation for Constitutional Government," n.d.; Federation for Constitutional Government, "Please Read the Message Below!," open letter, n.d., both in folder: "F-Fl," box 28, Cox Papers. See also Brown, "The Role of Elite Leadership in the Southern Defense of Segregation," 839–40.

55. John U. Barr to M. G. Lowman, Oct. 16, 1957, folder: "Miscellaneous," box 88, Lowman Papers; Dickerson, *Dixie's Dirty Secret,* 12.

56. LJLC, *Biennial Report, 1954–1956,* 6; Bartley, *The Rise of Massive Resistance,* 215.

57. Vanderbilt University School of Law, ed., vol. 1 of *Race Relations Law Reporter,* 571–76; LJLC, *Biennial Report, 1954–1956,* 6.

58. Rainach, untitled typescript prepared for submission to the Louisiana Board of Liquidation of State Debt, n.p. [p. 1].

59. U.S. Congress, Senate, Committee on the Judiciary, Subcommittee to Investigate the Administration of the Internal Security Act and Other Internal Security Laws, *Subversive Influence in Southern Conference Educational Fund, Inc.;* U.S. Congress, House, Committee on Un-American Activities, *Investigation of Communist Propaganda in the United States;* LJLC, *Subversion in Racial Unrest,* 2 vols., folder: "Circuit Riders, Inc.—Colored Question and Communism," box 95, Lowman Papers; *Baton Rouge (La.) Morning Advocate,* Mar. 3, 1957.

60. Bartley, *The Rise of Massive Resistance,* 187.

61. Stowe, "Willie Rainach and the Defense of Segregation in Louisiana," 153.

62. U.S. Congress, Senate, Committee on the Judiciary, Subcommittee to Investigate the Administration of the Internal Security Act and Other Internal Security Laws, *The Communist*

Party of the United States of America, 91; M. G. Lowman to James O Eastland, Feb. 15, 1956, folder: "MFSA (Methodist Federation for Social Action)," box 52, Lowman Papers.

63. Lowman to Cook, Apr. 12, 1956.

64. W. M. Rainach to T. V. Williams Jr. [GCE executive secretary], Mar. 16, 1957, folder: "Louisiana, Miscellaneous Correspondence," box 26, GCE Records.

65. Rainach, "An Interview with William M. Rainach," Oct. 7, 1977, 18.

66. Stowe, "Willie Rainach and the Defense of Segregation in Louisiana," 153; LJLC, meeting minutes, Feb. 24, 1957, 1, folder 128, box 13, Rainach Papers. On State Representative Stinson, see Peltason, *Fifty-Eight Lonely Men,* 235.

67. Stowe, "Willie Rainach and the Defense of Segregation in Louisiana," 153.

68. W. M. Shaw to LJLC, travel expenses report, Jan. 11, 1957, folder 341, box 30, Rainach Papers.

69. Ibid.; Stowe, "Willie Rainach and the Defense of Segregation in Louisiana," 153–54; LJLC, meeting minutes, Feb. 24, 1957, 1.

70. M. G. Lowman, "Notice of Annual Meeting," Sept. 25, 1952; Circuit Riders, "Invitation to Hear 'Communism in Religion,'" Oct. 6, 1952, both in folder: "Circuit Riders Literature (1950–57)," box 1, CR Records; Joseph Kornfeder, "Communist Deception in the Churches," speech, Oct. 26, 1952, folder: "Speeches, Statements, Resolutions, etc.," box 77, Lowman Papers.

71. W. M. Rainach to M. G. Lowman, Jan. 15, 1957, folder 86, box 8, Rainach Papers.

72. W. M. Rainach to M. G. Lowman, Jan. 26, 1957, folder 86, box 8, Rainach Papers.

73. W. M. Rainach to M. G. Lowman, Jan. 16, 1957, folder 86, box 8, Rainach Papers.

74. LJLC, meeting minutes, Feb. 24, 1957, 1; Western Union Telegraph Company, receipt, Feb. 20, 1957, folder 341, box 30, Rainach Papers; Stowe, "Willie Rainach and the Defense of Segregation in Louisiana," 154.

75. LJLC, meeting minutes, Feb. 24, 1957, 1.

76. Buckley, *The Committee and Its Critics,* 302; Roy, *Communism and the Churches,* 235.

77. M. G. Lowman to J. B. Matthews, Feb. 28, 1957, folder: "Lowman, Myers G., 1957," box 671, Matthews Papers.

78. Martin S. Matthews [Langley, Wash.], e-mail to the author, Jan. 13, 2008.

79. The copies of the summonses and their cover letters addressed to Kornfeder, Johnson, Patterson, and Edmiston are all located in folder 80, box 8, Rainach Papers.

80. Stowe, "Willie Rainach and the Defense of Segregation in Louisiana," 155.

81. Myers G. Lowman to Joseph Kornfeder, Feb. 22, 1957, folder: "Kornfeder, Joseph," box 45, Lowman Papers; Lowman to Matthews, Feb. 28, 1957.

82. Lowman to Matthews, Feb. 28, 1957.

83. M. G. Lowman, untitled typescript, Mar. 2, 1957, folder: "Lowman, Myers G., 1957," box 671, Matthews Papers.

84. Rainach to Williams, Mar. 16, 1957; *Baton Rouge Morning Advocate,* Mar. 11, 1957.

85. Stanton A. Hall [MGLIC chair] to W. M. Rainach, Mar. 1, 1957, folder 68, box 7; Rainach to Hall, Nov. 2, 1957, folder 68, box 7; Rainach to Joe T. Patterson [Mississippi attorney general], Nov. 2, 1957, folder 97, box 10, all in Rainach Papers.

86. LJLC, vol. 1 of *Subversion in Racial Unrest,* 1–2.

87. Stowe, "Willie Rainach and the Defense of Segregation in Louisiana," 158.

88. *JFK,* videocassettes.

89. LJLC, vol. 1 of *Subversion in Racial Unrest,* 12, 106.

90. A. J. Weberman, "Oswald in New Orleans: Part One," Coup d'Etat in America, n.p. www.ajweberman.com/nodules2/nodulec13.htm; Summers, *Not in Your Lifetime,* 225.

91. Fairclough, *Race and Democracy,* 202.

92. SECALC, "Hearing before the Special Education Committee of the Arkansas Legislative Council," summary, Dec. 16–18, 1958, 27–29, folder 46, box 5, ACHR Records.

93. LJLC, vol. 1 of *Subversion in Racial Unrest,* 18–20, 79–81, 106.

94. Ibid., 107–10, 117–19; Roy, *Communism and the Churches,* 236–37.

95. LJLC, vol. 1 of *Subversion in Racial Unrest,* 119, 135.

96. GCE, "Pre-Hearing Statement of Manning Johnson, Taken at 515 William-Oliver Building, Atlanta, Georgia, on Saturday, August 10, 1957, Commencing at 10:45 A.M.," transcript, 2–3, folder: "Circuit Riders," Garman Papers; Roy, *Communism and the Churches,* 237; Caute, *The Great Fear,* 129. See also Johnson, *Color, Communism and Common Sense.*

97. Fariello, ed., *Red Scare,* 471; *New Orleans Times-Picayune,* Mar. 7, 1957. See also Cook, *The Segregationists,* 298.

98. *New Orleans Times-Picayune,* Mar. 7, 1957.

99. LJLC, vol. 2 of *Subversion in Racial Unrest,* 203–204.

100. Ibid., 204; Braden, *House Un-American Activities Committee,* 26.

101. LJLC, vol. 2 of *Subversion in Racial Unrest,* 206, 214; *New Orleans Times-Picayune,* Mar. 9, 1957.

102. Johnson, *Color, Communism and Common Sense.*

103. LJLC, vol. 2 of *Subversion in Racial Unrest,* 201.

104. Ibid., 214.

105. Fairclough, *Race and Democracy,* 225.

106. *Baltimore Afro-American,* n.d. [Mar. 1957], folder 77, box 7, Rainach Papers.

107. LJLC, vol. 2 of *Subversion in Racial Unrest,* 216–17; *Dayton (Ohio) Journal Herald,* July 13, 1950; *Lebanon (Ohio) Western Star,* July 20, 1950; *Middletown (Ohio) Sunday News-Journal,* June 21, 1953; Weigand, "The Red Menace, the Feminine Mystique, and the Ohio Un-American Activities Commission," 83.

108. Martha N. Edmiston and John J. Edmiston, "Affidavit," taken before the Hamilton County, Ohio, notary public, Jan. 31, 1953, 7, box 87, Lowman Papers.

109. LJLC, vol. 2 of *Subversion in Racial Unrest,* 217; *Dayton Journal Herald,* July 13, 1950; *Lebanon Western Star,* July 20, 1950.

110. Edmiston and Edmiston, "Affidavit."

111. Buckley, *The Committee and Its Critics,* 302; Roy, *Communism and the Churches,* 235.

112. Fariello, ed., *Red Scare,* 491; *New York Times,* Nov. 21, 2010. On the City College of New York as "the site of the largest political purge of faculty" during the 1930s and the 1940s, see Smith, "The Dress Rehearsal for McCarthyism."

113. *New York Times,* Apr. 10, 1950.

114. U.S. Congress, House, Committee on Un-American Activities, *Hearings Regarding Communist Activities in the Cincinnati, Ohio, Area,* 2675, 2718; J. B. Matthews, "Lee and Grace Lorch," typescript, Mar. 10, 1958, 1, folder: "Lorch, Lee," box 47, Lowman Papers; Herzog, "A Life in Sum"; Stockley, *Daisy Bates,* 60, 161–62.

115. Lorch, telephone interview by Andy Barrie, www.cbc.ca/metromorning/media/20070109LLJAN09.ram, online Real Player audio; Fariello, ed., *Red Scare,* 493.

116. "From the *Nashville Tennessean,* June 11, 1954," typescript, n.d., folder: "Circuit Riders, Inc.—Correspondence," box 14, Lowman Papers.

117. Fariello, ed., *Red Scare,* 493.

118. Myers G. Lowman to Clarence Lohman, Sept. 16, 1954, box 89, Lowman Papers.

119. Herzog, "A Life in Sum"; Stockley, *Daisy Bates,* 60; U.S. Congress, House, Committee on Un-American Activities, *Investigation of Communist Activities in the Dayton, Ohio, Area,* 6953–77; *National Guardian (N.Y.),* Dec. 9, 1957.

120. *Cincinnati (Ohio) Enquirer,* Nov. 28, 1954.

121. "York Professor Honored for Civil Rights Activism"; Meier, *A White Scholar and the Black Community,* 16.

122. Georg G. Iggers [distinguished professor emeritus, Department of History, State University of New York at Buffalo], "Re: Lee Lorch," e-mail to the author, Sept. 14, 2007.

123. M. G. Lowman to Leon B. Catlett [attorney, Little Rock, Ark.], Dec. 11, 1957, 1, folder: "Circuit Riders, Inc.—Correspondence," box 14, Lowman Papers; LJLC, vol. 2 of *Subversion in Racial Unrest,* 247.

124. LJLC, vol. 2 of *Subversion in Racial Unrest,* 232–33.

125. Lorch, telephone interview by Andy Barrie.

126. LJLC, vol. 2 of *Subversion in Racial Unrest,* 215, 254–55.

127. U.S. Congress, House, Committee on Un-American Activities, *Investigation of Communist Propaganda in the United States,* 105–18; LJLC, vol. 2 of *Subversion in Racial Unrest,* 332–33, 336, 339.

128. LJLC, vol. 2 of *Subversion in Racial Unrest,* 340–41.

129. Ibid., 350; LJLC, vol. 1 of *Subversion in Racial Unrest,* 3.

130. LJLC, meeting minutes, Mar. 9, 1957, 1, folder 455, box 41; M. G. Lowman to LJLC, Mar. 28, 1957, folder 86, box 8, both in Rainach Papers.

131. LJLC, "Resolution: In Recognition of the Testimony of Joseph Z. Kornfeder," Mar. 9, 1957, folder 80, box 8; LJLC, "Resolution: In Recognition of the Testimony of Leonard Patterson," Mar. 9, 1957, folder 455, box 41; LJLC, "Resolution: In Recognition of the Testimony of Manning Johnson," Mar. 9, 1957, folder 455, box 41, all in Rainach Papers.

132. Leonard Patterson to LJLC, n.d. [Mar. 29, 1957], folder 97, box 10, Rainach Papers.

133. California Department of Public Health, "Certificate of Death [of Manning Johnson]," July 1959, folder: "Johnson, Manning," box 45, Lowman Papers.

134. *Baton Rouge Morning Advocate,* Mar. 11, 1957.

135. *Jackson (Miss.) Daily News,* June 10, 1958; Fosl, *Subversive Southerner,* 201. See also Bartley, *The Rise of Massive Resistance,* 187; and Baer, *Resistance to Public School Desegregation,* 177.

136. Powers, *Not without Honor,* 244; "Senator Joseph McCarthy: The History of George Catlett Marshall, 1951," Internet History Sourcebooks Project, ed. Paul Halsall, Fordham University, Bronx, N.Y., www.fordham.edu/halsall/mod/1951mccarthy-marshall.html.

137. W. M. Rainach to Roy V. Harris, Mar. 16, 1957, folder 69, box 7, Rainach Papers.

138. "Georgia: Wrong Target"; Rainach to Williams, Mar. 16, 1957.

139. Rainach to Harris, Mar. 16, 1957; Stowe, "Willie Rainach and the Defense of Segregation in Louisiana," 162.

140. Stowe, "Willie Rainach and the Defense of Segregation in Louisiana," 162.

141. Ibid., 162–63; M. G. Lowman to W. M. Rainach, Apr. 2, 1957, folder 86, box 8; Leander H. Perez to Rainach, memo, Apr. 30, 1957, folder 98, box 10; Rainach to Perez, May 1, 1957, folder 98, box 10, all in Rainach Papers.

142. LJLC, vol. 2 of *Subversion in Racial Unrest,* 350.

143. W. M. Rainach to M. G. Lowman, Mar. 27, 1957, folder 86, box 8, Rainach Papers; Lowman to W. Guy Banister, Jan. 20, 1959; Lowman to Manning Johnson, Jan. 20, 1959, both in folder: "Circuit Riders, Inc.—Correspondence," box 14, Lowman Papers.

144. M. G. Lowman to W. M. Rainach, Apr. 1, 1957, folder 86, box 8, Rainach Papers.

145. W. M. Rainach to Joseph Z. Kornfedder [*sic*], Apr. 13, 1957, folder 80, box 8; Rainach to Leonard Patterson, Apr. 13, 1957, folder 97, box 10; Rainach to Manning Johnson, Apr. 13, 1957, folder 77, box 7; Rainach to Martha Edmiston, Apr. 13, 1957, folder 54, box 5, all in Rainach Papers.

146. W. M. Rainach to M. G. Lowman, June 27, 1957; Lowman to Rainach, July 17, 1957, both in folder 86, box 8, Rainach Papers.

147. M. G. Lowman to W. M. Rainach, July 2, 1957, folder 86, box 8, Rainach Papers.

148. W. M. Rainach, untitled typescript, Aug. 1, 1957, vertical file (microfilm): "Louisiana—Legislature—Joint Committee on Segregation," LLMV Collections.

149. W. M. Rainach to M. G. Lowman, Aug. 19, 1957, folder 620, box 82; Lowman to Mr. and Mrs. W. M. Rainach, Aug. 22, 1957, folder 86, box 8, both in Rainach Papers.

150. W. M. Rainach to Manning Johnson, Aug. 19, 1957, folder 77, box 7, Rainach Papers.

151. W. M. Rainach to Martha Edmiston, Nov. 4, 1957, folder 54, box 5; Rainach to J. B. Lancaster [Louisiana supervisor of public funds], Jan. 8, 1958, 1, folder 341, box 30, both in Rainach Papers.

152. LJLC, vol. 1 of *Subversion in Racial Unrest.*

153. Rainach to Lancaster, Jan. 8, 1958, 1; W. M. Rainach to M. G. Lowman, Jan. 27, 1959, folder 86, box 8, Rainach Papers.

154. Rainach to Lancaster, Jan. 8, 1958, 1; Stowe, "Willie Rainach and the Defense of Segregation in Louisiana," 164.

155. LJLC, vol. 2 of *Subversion in Racial Unrest;* W. M. Rainach to M. G. Lowman, Mar. 14, 1958, box 90, Lowman Papers.

156. W. M. Rainach to Mildred Johnson [secretary, Warren County Citizens' Council, Vicksburg, Miss.], June 7, 1960, folder 77, box 7; Central Intelligence Agency to LJLC, "Request for Quotation," Nov. 5, 1958, folder 43, box 4; Rainach to Central Intelligence Agency, Nov. 19, 1958, folder 43, box 4, all in Rainach Papers.

157. *Jackson Daily News,* June 10, 1958; Fosl, *Subversive Southerner,* 201.

158. W. M. Rainach to Mark R. Hawes, Mar. 14, 1958, folder 69, box 7, Rainach Papers.

159. LJLC, "Citation of the NAACP as a Communist Penetrated Organization," Mar. 10, 1958, folder: "Lowman, Myers G., 1958," box 671, Matthews Papers. See also LJLC, "Resolution," Mar. 10, 1958, folder 86, box 8, Rainach Papers.

160. W. M. Rainach to Francis Walter, Apr. 28, 1958, folder: "Lowman, Myers G., 1958," box 671, Matthews Papers; Rainach to James O. Eastland, Apr. 28, 1958, folder 54, box 5, Rainach Papers.

161. M. G. Lowman to W. M. Rainach, Mar. 6, 1958, folder 86, box 8, Rainach Papers.

162. Hoover, *Masters of Deceit;* W. M. Rainach to M. G. Lowman, Apr. 3, 1958, folder 86, box 8, Rainach Papers.

163. LJLC, *Segregation Measures Passed by the Regular Session of the Louisiana Legislature, 1958,* 1, box 72, Rainach Papers; Louisiana Special Joint Legislative Committee to Investigate Louisiana State University [?], "List of LSU Faculty Members Who Signed a Statement Op-

posing the Proposed Legislation to Abolish the Public Schools in Louisiana . . . in Order to Maintain Segregation," n.d. [1958], folder 4, box 1, series III, subgroup 1, Reynard Papers; Stowe, "Willie Rainach and the Defense of Segregation in Louisiana," 241–51.

164. McCarrick, "Louisiana's Official Resistance to Desegregation," 71.

165. Louisiana Special Joint Legislative Committee to Investigate Louisiana State University, report, July 2, 1958, 1, folder 4, box 1, series III, subgroup 1, Reynard Papers; American Civil Liberties Union, *"Testing Whether That Nation,"* 24.

166. Untitled and unofficial transcript of the Louisiana Special Joint Legislative Committee to Investigate Louisiana State University hearings, June 11, 1958, 1–2, 7, folder 4, box 1, series III, subgroup 1, Reynard Papers; Louisiana Special Joint Legislative Committee to Investigate Louisiana State University, report, 1; W. M. Rainach to M. G. Lowman, Mar. 14, 1959, folder 86, box 8, Rainach Papers; McCarrick, "Louisiana's Official Resistance to Desegregation," 71–73.

167. Louisiana Special Joint Legislative Committee to Investigate Louisiana State University, report, 1.

168. Louisiana Special Joint Legislative Committee to Investigate Louisiana State University, meeting transcript, July 2, 1958, box 82, Rainach Papers.

169. W. M. Rainach to Emmett Asseff [executive director, Louisiana Legislative Council, Baton Rouge], Aug. 28, 1958, folder 128, box 13, Rainach Papers.

170. Untitled and unofficial transcript of the Louisiana Special Joint Legislative Committee to Investigate Louisiana State University hearings, 1.

171. "Unit History," Army ROTC, Department of Military Science and Leadership, Louisiana State University, Baton Rouge, http://appl003.lsu.edu/artsci/milscience.nsf/$Content/ Unit+History?OpenDocument; Valera T. Francis and Amy E. Wells, "On Opposite Sides of the Track: New Orleans' Urban Universities in Black and White," in *Historically Black Colleges and Universities,* ed. Gasman and Tudico, 126; "History Timeline—1947–1956: Building on the Beginnings," About the School of Social Work, School of Social Work, Louisiana State University, www.socialwork.lsu.edu/html/about/1947-56.html.

172. Hargrave, *LSU Law,* 151; Rogers, *Righteous Lives,* 81; Francis and Wells, "On Opposite Sides of the Track," 126; Fairclough, *Race and Democracy,* 65–68; Emanuel and Tureaud, *A More Noble Cause,* 138–42; Anderson, *Black, White, and Catholic,* 120; McKenzie, "The Desegregation of New Orleans Public and Roman Catholic Schools in New Orleans," master's thesis, 23, 25–26.

173. Associated Press wirephoto taken during Troy H. Middleton's testimony before the Louisiana Special Joint Legislative Committee to Investigate Louisiana State University in Baton Rouge, June 11, 1958, photo no. rwt41250stf-rwt, in the author's possession; untitled and unofficial transcript of the Louisiana Special Joint Legislative Committee to Investigate Louisiana State University hearings, 2–3. See also *New York Times,* June 12, 1958; and Bailey and Easson, *The Education of a Black Radical,* 39.

174. Rainach to Lowman, Aug. 19, 1957.

175. M. G. Lowman to William Rainach, June 12, 1958, folder 86, box 8, Rainach Papers.

176. W. M. Rainach to M. G. Lowman, June 13, 1958, folder 86, box 8, Rainach Papers; Stowe, "Willie Rainach and the Defense of Segregation in Louisiana," 251–52.

177. Charles A. Reynard, handwritten notes scribbled on Louisiana Special Joint Legislative Committee to Investigate Louisiana State University, report, 1. As a law professor at LSU, Reynard was one of the signers of the ACLU petition.

178. W. M. Rainach to Leander H. Perez, Feb. 12, 1958, 1, folder 98, box 10, Rainach Papers; Stowe, "Willie Rainach and the Defense of Segregation in Louisiana," 241.

179. Rainach to Lowman, June 13, 1958.

180. M. G. Lowman to W. J. [*sic*] Rainach, Jan. 2, 1959, folder 86, box 8, Rainach Papers.

181. W. M. Rainach to M. G. Lowman, Jan. 21, 1959, folder 86, box 8, Rainach Papers.

182. Rainach to Lowman, Mar. 14, 1959; Stowe, "Willie Rainach and the Defense of Segregation in Louisiana," 267–68.

183. W. M. Rainach to M. G. Lowman, Mar. 28, 1959, folder 86, box 8, Rainach Papers.

184. *Shreveport (La.) Journal,* Jan. 27, 1978; Stowe, "Willie Rainach and the Defense of Segregation in Louisiana," 271.

185. W. M. Rainach to W. M. Shaw, Oct. 13, 1959, folder 107, box 11, Rainach Papers.

186. Black, *Southern Governors and Civil Rights,* 189–90.

187. Ibid.; Bartley and Graham, comps., *Southern Elections,* 121–22.

188. Bartley and Graham, comps., *Southern Elections,* 121–22.

189. Rainach, "An Interview with William M. Rainach," Aug. 19, 1977, 25; "Louisiana: Jambalaya"; *Cape Girardeau Southeast Missourian,* Nov. 18, 1960; Louisiana State Advisory Committee to the United States Commission on Civil Rights, *The New Orleans School Crisis,* 3; McCarrick, "Louisiana's Official Resistance to Desegregation," 105; Jeansonne, "Racism and Longism in Louisiana," 262; Stowe, "Willie Rainach and the Defense of Segregation in Louisiana," 278–79.

190. Bartley and Graham, comps., *Southern Elections,* 122.

191. W. M. Rainach to Roy V. Harris, Dec. 21, 1959, folder 69, box 7, Rainach Papers.

192. W. M. Rainach to Maurice L. Malone [MSSC director], Feb. 1, 1960, record no. 99–95–0–15–1–1–1; Malone to Rainach, Feb. 3, 1960, record no. 99–95–0–16–1–1–1, both in MSSC Records.

193. W. M. Rainach to David J. Mays, Feb. 1, 1960, folder 90, box 9, Rainach Papers. Created in March 1958, six months after the September 1957 Little Rock desegregation crisis, the Virginia Commission on Constitutional Government functioned as Virginia's official "states' rights propaganda agency" and was assigned to "develop and promulgate information concerning the dual system of government, federal and state" established under the U.S. Constitution for the purpose of defending the state's racial segregation (see Lewis, "Virginia's Northern Strategy," 115–16; and Sweeney, ed., *Race, Reason, and Massive Resistance,* 215–29).

194. W. M. Rainach to M. G. Lowman, Mar. 4, 1960, folder 86, box 8, Rainach Papers.

195. Editorial, *Baton Rouge (La.) State-Times,* June 23, 1969.

196. Louisiana State Advisory Committee to the United States Commission on Civil Rights, *The New Orleans School Crisis,* 6; LSSC, *Fifty Sovereign States or Fifty Federal Districts?,* record nos. 3–16A-2–102–1–1–1 to 8–1–1, p. 3–1–1, MSSC Records; Jeansonne, *Leander Perez,* 235.

197. Rainach, "An Interview with William M. Rainach," Aug. 19, 1977, 25; McCarrick, "Louisiana's Official Resistance to Desegregation," 105–6; Stowe, "Willie Rainach and the Defense of Segregation in Louisiana," 279–81; McMillen, *The Citizens' Council,* 319.

198. Jerry P. Shinley, "Origins of Louisiana Un-American Activities Committee," JFK Online: JFK Assassination Resources Online, ed. David A. Reitzes, n.p., www.jfk-online.com/jpsorigluac.html.

199. J. B. Lancaster to Jimmie H. Davis and LJLC, Sept. 29, 1960, folder 128, box 13, Rainach Papers.

200. "The South: D-Day in New Orleans"; James H. Pfister [LJLCUA chair], untitled typescript, June 4, 1962, folder: "Joint Legislative Committee on Un-American Activities," LJLCUA Records; *New York Times,* Sept. 21, 1960. See also Rogers, *Righteous Lives,* 70; and

Prechter, "The Highest Type of Disloyalty," master's thesis, 30–31. Prechter's understanding and narrative that the Louisiana Joint Legislative Committee on Un-American Activities was "formed in the mid-1950s" are erroneous.

201. L. Malcolm Morris [assistant director, Louisiana State Archives, Baton Rouge], letter to the author, July 29, 1993.

202. Brown, "Redressing Southern 'Subversion,'" 307; LJLCUA, "Operations Plan: With Comments Justifying an Appropriation," typescript, n.d., n.p. [p. 2], folder: "Joint Legislative Committee on Un-American Activities," LJLCUA Records.

203. *Lake Charles (La.) American Press,* Dec. 16, 1960; *Jennings (La.) Daily News,* Dec. 19, 1960; Louisiana State Advisory Committee to the United States Commission on Civil Rights, *The New Orleans School Crisis,* 18; LJLCUA, *The Case of Dr. Waldo F. McNeir;* LJLCUA, *Activities of the Southern Conference Educational Fund, Inc., in Louisiana,* 3 vols., both at SLL; Patenaude, "Providing for the Common Defense," Ph.D. diss., 109–18; Jack N. Rogers [LJLCUA counsel] to "All Committee and Staff Members," "Current Operation," confidential memo, Nov. 1, 1962, folder: "Joint Legislative Committee on Un-American Activities," LJLCUA Records.

204. Frederick B. Alexander Jr. [LJLCUA staff director] to James H. Pfister, July 16, 1962, folder: "Rep. James H. Pfister," LJLCUA Records.

205. *St. Petersburg (Fla.) Evening Independent,* Oct. 5, 1963; *Toledo (Ohio) Blade,* Oct. 6, 1963.

206. Dunbar, *Against the Grain,* 252.

CHAPTER THREE

1. McMillen, *The Citizens' Council,* 73; Sanders, *Mighty Peculiar Elections,* 146. See also Cobb, *The Brown Decision, Jim Crow, and Southern Identity,* 30.

2. Alton Hornsby Jr., "A City That Was Too Busy to Hate: Atlanta Businessmen and Desegregation," in *Southern Businessmen and Desegregation,* ed. Jacoway and Colburn, 120; Goldfield, *Black, White, and Southern,* 112–14; Brown-Nagin, *Courage to Dissent,* 171, 324; "Education: Southern Milestones."

3. John F. Kennedy, "The President's News Conference of August 30, 1961," in *Public Papers of the Presidents of the United States: John F. Kennedy, 1961,* 572. See also Harmon, *Beneath the Image of the Civil Rights Movement and Race Relations,* 117.

4. "Georgia Symbols, State Mottos," Guide to Georgia Facts on the Web, SHG Resources: State Handbook and Guide, n.p., www.shgresources.com/ga/symbols/motto.

5. Anderson, *The Wild Man from Sugar Creek,* 226; Grantham, *The Life and Death of the Solid South,* 91; Ed Jackson and Charly Pou, comps., "This Day in Georgia History: December 21," GeorgiaInfo, GALILEO (Georgia Library Learning Online) and the University of Georgia Libraries, http://georgiainfo.galileo.usg.edu/tdgh-dec/dec21.htm.

6. Georgia State Law Department, comp. and ed., *Compilation of Georgia Laws and Opinions of the Attorney General Relating to Segregation of the Races,* 46–48, in both folder 3, box 22, subseries A, series I, Vandiver Papers; and box 3 (item no. 64), Levy Collection; "Joint Resolution of the Georgia General Assembly: Georgia Commission on Education Established, Dec. 10, 1953," GeorgiaInfo, http://georgiainfo.galileo.usg.edu/1953resn-4.h.; *Hapeville (Ga.) Statesman,* Jan. 7, 1954.

7. McMillen, *The Citizens' Council,* 73.

8. Herman Talmadge, "Why I Say the Constitution Upholds Segregation in Our Public Schools," speech draft, n.d., 4, folder 6, box 4, subseries A, series I, Talmadge Collection.

9. Talmadge, interview by Larry Lesueur and Kenneth Crawford, www.archive.org/download/longines-talmadge/longines-talmadge.mpeg, online MPEG movie.

10. Webb, "Charles Bloch," 271; Jenkins, *Blind Vengeance,* 73. On Bloch's constitutional discourse set against the Supreme Court's *Brown* rulings, see Bloch, *We Need Not Integrate to Educate;* Bloch, *States' Rights;* and Bloch, "The School Segregation Cases."

11. Manis, *Macon Black and White,* 163; Webb, *Fight against Fear,* 131.

12. Fite, *Richard B. Russell, Jr.,* 229–30, 240, 293, 475.

13. Nancy Lisenby, "Charles J. Bloch: A Short Biography," typescript, 1985, Bloch Papers; Webb, "Charles Bloch," 268–69; Webb, *Fight against Fear,* 130; Manis, *Macon Black and White,* 163–64.

14. "Notice!: To True Southern Democrats—Hear Hon. Charles Bloch of Macon, Georgia, Speak at the Court House, Griffin, Georgia, Tuesday, Oct. 26 [, 1948], 8 P.M., on the Issue of States['] Rights and the Candidacy of Strom Thurmond and Fielding Wright," broadside, item no. BRO 1948 N6, Broadside Collection; Webb, "Charles Bloch," 281; Manis, *Macon Black and White,* 163.

15. Webb, "Charles Bloch," 271–73, 281–82; Webb, *Fight against Fear,* 135–36.

16. Manis, *Macon Black and White,* 178.

17. Charles Bloch to "the Governor," memo, Dec. 23, 1952; Bloch, untitled draft of an executive proclamation, n.d., 1, both in folder 15, box 13, subseries B, series I, Talmadge Collection.

18. *Hapeville Statesman,* Jan. 7, 1954; GCE, meeting transcript, July 19, 1954, n,p., folder 5, box 13, subseries C, series II, Vandiver Papers.

19. Charles J. Bloch, untitled speech before the Civitan Club, Macon, Ga., Aug. 8, 1958, 7, folder 289, box 41, Bloch Papers.

20. GCE, meeting transcript, July 19, 1954, n.p.; Marvin Griffin [Georgia governor] to T. V. Williams Jr. [GCE executive secretary-to-be], Apr. 4, 1956, folder: "Hon. Marvin Griffin, Governor, 1956," box 21, GCE Records.

21. "Shoofly Pye"; "Long Reach of the Law."

22. Griffin to Williams, Apr. 4, 1956; T. V. Williams Jr. to Marvin Griffin, Apr. 6, 1956, folder: "Hon. Marvin Griffin, Governor, 1956," box 21, GCE Records; *Atlanta Journal,* Mar. 8, 1957; "Georgia: Wrong Target"; Brazeal, "Some Problems in the Desegregation of Higher Education in the 'Hard Core' States," 364; Kruse, "The Paradox of Massive Resistance," 1023; Roche, *Restructured Resistance,* 72.

23. Pratt, *We Shall Not Be Moved,* 49; Advertising Committee of the GCE, untitled memo, n.d., folder: "Advertising Committee, Roy V. Harris, Chairman, 1957," box 22, GCE Records; GCE, meeting transcript, July 19, 1954, n.p.; Heale, *McCarthy's Americans,* 246–47, 249; Bartley, *The Rise of Massive Resistance,* 54–55.

24. Bartley and Graham, comps., *Southern Elections,* 94.

25. Newman, "The Georgia Baptist Convention and Desegregation," 691; Manis, *Macon Black and White,* 171–72.

26. Richard B. Russell Jr., "Statement of Senator Richard B. Russell on Supreme Court Decision in School Segregation Cases," n.d. [May 1954], folder: "Ro-Se," box 30, Cox Papers.

27. Bartley and Graham, comps., *Southern Elections,* 93; Robert W. Dubay, "Marvin Griffin and the Politics of the Stump," in *Georgia Governors in an Age of Change,* ed. Henderson and Roberts, 105.

28. Dubay, "Marvin Griffin and the Politics of the Stump," 105; Heale, *McCarthy's Americans,* 249; Buchanan, *"Some of the People Who Ate My Barbecue Didn't Vote for Me,"* 95.

29. Black, *Southern Governors and Civil Rights,* 66; "Atlanta Journal, Atlanta Constitution to Combine," Write News, Oct. 17, 2001, Write News Archives, Writers Write, Inc., Dallas, Tex., www.writenews.com/2001/101701_atlanta_journal_constitution.htm.

30. Manis, *Macon Black and White,* 172–73.

31. Herman E. Talmadge to Mrs. Albert Genet, June 7, 1955, folder 6, box 4, subseries A, series I, Talmadge Collection.

32. *Harvard Crimson* [student newspaper, Harvard University, Cambridge, Mass.], Dec. 6, 1955; Talmadge, *You and Segregation,* 70, 76–77, 79.

33. McMillen, *The Citizens' Council,* 82; W. A. Lufburrow [executive director, States' Rights Council of Georgia] to Ernest Vandiver [Georgia governor], Oct. 26, 1959; States' Rights Council of Georgia, *The Aims and Purposes of the States' Rights Council of Georgia, Inc.,* n.p., both in folder 6, box 41, subseries A, series I, Vandiver Papers.

34. *Rome (Ga.) News Tribune,* Jan. 12, 1956; *Charleston (S.C.) News and Courier,* Sept. 4, 1955; Hugh G. Grant, letter to the editor, *Charleston News and Courier,* Feb. 7, 1963; McMillen, *The Citizens' Council,* 81, 83; Lufburrow to Vandiver, Oct. 26, 1959.

35. William T. Bodenhamer to "All Who Attended the Atlanta Conference," memo, Oct. 30, 1957, folder 91, box 7, Touchstone Papers; *Early County (Ga.) News,* May 29, 1958; editorial, *Atlanta Journal-Constitution,* June 24, 1958; McMillen, *The Citizens' Council,* 80, 84, 88; Williams, *From Mounds to Megachurches,* 111; Roche, *Restructured Resistance,* 72.

36. McMillen, *The Citizens' Council,* 83.

37. R. Carter Pittman, "The Supreme Court Must Be Purged," Selected Works of R. Carter Pittman, ed. Joel T. LaFevre, n.p., www.rcarterpittman.org/essays/judiciary/Supreme_Court_Must_Be_Purged.html.

38. "Roy V. Harris Papers: Biographical/Historical Note," Collections, Richard B. Russell Library for Political Research and Studies, University of Georgia, Athens, www.libs.uga.edu/russell/collections/rvharris/index.shtml; Chappell, "The Divided Mind of Southern Segregationists," 46. See also Talmadge, "Conversations with Senator Herman Talmadge."

39. Harris, "Politics #3 and #4," recorded reminiscences, 23.

40. *Houston (Tex.) Chronicle,* Sept. 9, 1960; "Roy V. Harris Papers"; Chappell, "The Divided Mind of Southern Segregationists," 47.

41. McMillen, *The Citizens' Council,* 121.

42. Unidentifiable newspaper, n.d. [1954], folder 9, box 27, series III, Russell Collection.

43. Cook, *The Ugly Truth about the NAACP,* 1, in both folder: "Association of Citizens' Councils: Folder 1," box 26, Cox Papers; and folder 24, box 2, McCain Collection; "Along the N.A.A.C.P. Battlefront: Attorney General Cook," 620; *New York Times,* Oct. 20, 1955.

44. Cook, *The Ugly Truth about the NAACP,* 1–2, 10.

45. Ibid., 2, 10–11.

46. Braden, *House Un-American Activities Committee,* 28; editorial, *Baltimore Afro-American,* Nov. 5, 1955; *Harvard Crimson,* Dec. 9, 1955. On October 19, 1955—the very same day the Georgian attorney general gave an address before the Peace Officers' Association of Georgia—the NAACP's executive secretary, Roy Wilkins, issued a statement, asserting that Cook's speech was "part of a conspiracy by some southern state officials to combat" the Supreme Court's school desegregation rulings by "charging the NAACP with being subversive." "It is he, not we, who are [*sic*] seeking to undermine the government of the United States" and "subverting the Constitution," Wilkins concluded (see "Along the N.A.A.C.P. Battlefront: Attorney General Cook," 620–21).

47. Georgia State Law Department, comp. and ed., *Compilation of Georgia Laws and Opinions of the Attorney General Relating to Segregation of the Races,* 48; "Joint Resolution of the Georgia General Assembly: Georgia Commission on Education Established."

48. "Joint Resolution of the Georgia General Assembly: Georgia Commission on Education, Feb. 15, 1957," GeorgiaInfo, http://georgiainfo.galileo.usg.edu/1957resn-4.htm.

49. Advertising Committee of the GCE, untitled memo, n.d.; R. Carter Pittman to Roy Harris, Apr. 14, 1958, folder 69, box 7, Rainach Papers.

50. Heale, *McCarthy's Americans,* 257.

51. *Atlanta Journal,* Aug. 1, 1958; M. G. Lowman to Eugene Cook, Apr. 12, 1956, folder: "Lowman, Myers G., 1951–1956," box 670, Matthews Papers.

52. *Atlanta Journal-Constitution,* Aug. 3, 1958.

53. M. G. Lowman to W. M. Rainach, July 17, 1957; Lowman to Rainach, July [*sic,* Aug.] 4, 1957, both in folder 86, box 8, Rainach Papers.

54. W. M. Rainach to T. V. Williams Jr., Mar. 16, 1957, folder: "Louisiana, Miscellaneous Correspondence," box 26, GCE Records.

55. Editorial, *Atlanta Journal-Constitution,* June 24, 1958; *Atlanta Journal,* Aug. 1, 1958; *Atlanta Journal-Constitution,* Aug. 3, 1958; Bartley, *The Rise of Massive Resistance,* 223.

56. *Atlanta Journal,* Aug. 1, 1958.

57. *Atlanta Journal-Constitution,* Aug. 3, 1958; Department of Christian Social Relations of the National Council of the Protestant Episcopal Church, "Sowing Dissention in the Churches: A Report on Some of the Individuals and Groups Engaged in Attacks on the Leadership of the Churches," typed report, n.d. [Mar. 1962], 16, folder 7, box 83, Matthews Papers; Nelson and Roberts, *The Censors and the Schools,* 154.

58. See, for instance, Roy V. Harris to W. M. Rainach, Jan. 15, 1957; Rainach to Harris, Mar. 16, 1957; and Harris to Rainach, Mar. 19, 1957, all in folder 69, box 7, Rainach Papers.

59. T. V. Williams Jr. to M. G. Lowman, July 2, 1957, folder: "Circuit Riders, Inc.—Correspondence," box 14, Lowman Papers.

60. GCE, *Ten Directors of the N.A.A.C.P.,* folder: "Literature Submitted to Georgia Education Commission, 1957," box 20, GCE Records.

61. Advertising Committee of the GCE, untitled memo, n.d.

62. Franklin Printing and Manufacturing Company [Atlanta, Ga.] to W. J. Simmons, Sept. 26, 1957, folder: "Highlander Folks [*sic*] School, 1957," box 22, GCE Records.

63. Lowman to Rainach, July 17, 1957; Lowman to Rainach, July [*sic,* Aug.] 4, 1957; Heale, *McCarthy's Americans,* 263.

64. Editorial, *Atlanta Journal-Constitution,* June 24, 1958.

65. Ibid.; Gregory B. Padgett, "The Tallahassee Bus Boycott," in *Sunbelt Revolution,* ed. Hyde, 190–209.

66. M. G. Lowman to Arthur J. Moore [Methodist bishop, Atlanta, Ga.], Mar. 14, 1957, folder: "Lowman, Myers G., 1957," box 671, Matthews Papers; Lowman to Moore, May 17, 1957, folder: "Investigation, 1957," box 22, GCE Records.

67. Circuit Riders, "63 Auburn Avenue, N.E., Atlanta, Georgia—An Umbrella of Respectability for Southern Regional Council," press release, Jan. 2, 1958, folder: "Lowman, Myers G., 1958," box 671, Matthews Papers.

68. Circuit Riders, "Names in the News, 1938–1958: A Few Methodists and Others United in United Fronts," newsletter, July 1958, folder: "Lowman, Myers G., 1958," box 671, Matthews Papers.

69. J. B. Matthews to M. G. Lowman, Sept. 14, 1957, folder: "Lowman, Myers G., 1957," box 671, Matthews Papers.

70. J. B. Matthews to M. G. Lowman, July 12, 1957; Lowman to Matthews, Aug. 19, 1957, both in folder: "Lowman, Myers G., 1957," box 671, Matthews Papers.

71. M. G. Lowman to J. B. Matthews, Aug. 23, 1957, folder: "Lowman, Myers G., 1957," box 671, Matthews Papers.

72. M. G. Lowman to Richard Arens, Oct. 17, 1957, folder: "Lowman, Myers G., 1957," box 671, Matthews Papers.

73. Lowman to Matthews, Aug. 19, 1957; Lowman to Matthews, Aug. 23, 1957; M. G. Lowman to J. B. Matthews, Sept. 10, 1957, folder: "Lowman, Myers G., 1957," box 671, Matthews Papers.

74. Lewis Sinclair [member, board of directors, Highlander Research and Education Center, New Market, Tenn.], letter to the author, May 8, 1998.

75. Hughes, "A New Agenda for the South," 243; "History—1930–1953: Beginnings and the Labor Years," Highlander's History, Highlander Research and Education Center, New Market, Tenn., www.highlandercenter.org/a-history.asp.

76. Myles Horton to "Dear Friend," May 24, 1958, folder 2, box 253, Matthews Papers; Hughes, "A New Agenda for the South," 244; "History—1953–1961: The Civil Rights Movement and the Citizenship Schools," Highlander's History, www.highlandercenter.org/a-history2.asp.

77. Highlander Folk School, "What's Happening Today in the South?," typescript, Feb. 12, 1955, folder 2, box 741, reel no. 678, *NR* Records.

78. Highlander Folk School, *The South Prepares to Carry Out the Supreme Court Decision Outlawing Segregation in Public Schools, July 24–August 6, 1955,* workshop pamphlet, n.d. [1955]; Highlander Folk School, "Mrs. Rosa Parks Reports on Montgomery, Ala., Bus Protest" recorded meeting transcript, n.d. [Mar. 1956], both in folder 1, box 253, Matthews Papers; Parks and Haskins, *Rosa Parks,* 101–7; Brinkley, *Rosa Parks,* 93–95.

79. Sullivan, ed., *Freedom Writer,* 30.

80. Horton, *The Long Haul,* 45; Zellner, "Red Roadshow," 56–57; *Atlanta Constitution,* Dec. 16, 1957; J. B. Matthews, "Communists, Negroes, and Integration," typed report, n.d. [1957], 18, folder: "What's Ahead for the American Negro under Desegregation, 1954–1955," box 722, Matthews Papers.

81. Jacobs, ed., *The Myles Horton Reader,* 125; *New York Times,* Mar. 21, 1954. See also *New York Times,* Mar. 23, 1954.

82. *Nashville (Tenn.) Banner,* Mar. 26, 1954.

83. Branch, *Parting the Waters,* 122.

84. Lorence, *A Hard Journey,* 34.

85. Ibid., 40; Solomon, *The Cry Was Unity,* 248.

86. West, "Interview with Don West," 68.

87. Williams to Lowman, July 2, 1957.

88. John Kirk, "Facilitating Change: The Arkansas Council on Human Relations, 1954–1964," paper delivered at the conference entitled "The Southern Regional Council and the Civil Rights Movement," University of Florida, Gainesville, Oct. 23–26, 2003, Southern Regional Council History Project, University of Florida, http://plaza.ufl.edu/wardb/Kirk.doc.

89. John B. Thompson [chair, Guarantors for Highlander] to "Dear Friend of Highlander," Feb. 20, 1958, folder 2, box 253, Matthews Papers.

90. Highlander Folk School, "The Human Aspects of the Integration Struggle," invitation letter to the twenty-fifth anniversary workshop, n.d. [1957], folder 1, box 253, Matthews Papers; *Birmingham (Ala.) Post-Herald,* Oct. 7, 1957.

91. *New York Sun,* Aug. 31, 2007; Raines, *My Soul Is Rested,* 397; Horton, *The Long Haul,* 158; Dunaway, *How Can I Keep from Singing?,* 273, 275.

92. Martin Luther King Jr., "The Look to the Future," recorded speech transcript, Sept. 2, 1957, n.p. [p. 1], folder 2, box 253, Matthews Papers; King, "'A Look to the Future,' Address Delivered at Highlander Folk School's Twenty-Fifth Anniversary Meeting," Sept. 2, 1957, in *Symbol of the Movement,* vol. 4 of *The Papers of Martin Luther King, Jr.,* ed. Carson et al., 270.

93. Lowman to Matthews, Aug. 23, 1957.

94. M. G. Lowman, "A Privileged Record of Race. . . [illegible]. . . in [the] South," handwritten memo, June 21, 1967, folder: "Georgia Commission on Education," box 95, Lowman Papers; *New Orleans Times-Picayune,* Mar. 7, 1957.

95. GCE, "Pre-Hearing Statement of Manning Johnson, Taken at 515 William-Oliver Building, Atlanta, Georgia, on Saturday, August 10, 1957, Commencing at 10:45 A.M.," transcript, 4, 10, 14, folder: "Circuit Riders," Garman Papers.

96. Lowman, "A Privileged Record of Race. . . [illegible]. . . in [the] South"; GCE, "Pre-Hearing Statement of Manning Johnson," 29.

97. Francis J. McNamara [HUAC staff director] to Prentiss Walker [U.S. representative from Mississippi], Apr. 5, 1965, record nos. 3–85–0–10–1–1–1 to 2–1–1, p. 1–1–1, MSSC Records.

98. Egerton, "The Trial of the Highlander Folk School," 86; Egerton, *Shades of Gray,* 67.

99. GCE, "Deposition of Edwin H. Friend, Sr., Taken in the Highlander Folk School Matter, at Room 220, 19 Hunter Street, Atlanta, Georgia, on Tuesday, October 8, 1957, Commencing at 11:00 A.M., before Louise Bickerstaff, Notary Public," transcript, 2, folder: "Georgia Commission on Education," box 95, Lowman Papers; "Ed Friend Visual Materials Collection: Biographical/Historical Note," Collections, Richard B. Russell Library for Political Research and Studies, www.libs.uga.edu/russell/collections/efriend/index.shtml.

100. GCE, "Meeting of the Georgia Commission on Education at Room 177, 244 Washington Street, S.W., Atlanta, Georgia, on September 30 [*sic,* October 4], 1957, Commencing at 10:00 A.M.," meeting minutes, 4, folder: "Georgia Commission on Education," box 95, Lowman Papers. Though the cover page of the Georgia commission's meeting minutes indicates that the meeting was held on Monday, September 30, 1957, by carefully examining the minutes' contents and further consulting some other primary source material, it is reasonable to construe that the commission meeting in fact took place on Friday, October 4, 1957. In this regard, see Mark Smith [GCE member] to T. V. Williams Jr., Sept. 27, 1957; S. Marvin Griffin, "Statement Opening the Meeting of the Georgia Commission on Education, October 4, 1957, Atlanta, Georgia," typescript, both in folder: "Georgia Commission on Education Meeting, Friday, October 4, 1957," box 22, GCE Records; *Atlanta Journal,* Oct. 4, 1957; and *Tampa (Fla.) Morning Tribune,* Oct. 5, 1957.

101. GCE, "Deposition of Edwin H. Friend, Sr., . . . Commencing at 11:00 A.M.," 3, 11. See also Anne Braden [SCEF field secretary] to Martin Luther King Jr., Sept. 23, 1959; and King to Braden, Oct. 7, 1959, both in *Threshold of a New Decade,* vol. 5 of *The Papers of Martin Luther King, Jr.,* ed. Carson et al., 291.

102. *Highlander—Segregation,* videocassette and 16-mm film. Owing to the innovative initiative taken by the Digital Library of Georgia based at the University of Georgia Libraries,

the Highlander film shot by Friend can also be viewed online at "Integration in All Respects," Digital Library of Georgia, University of Georgia Libraries, Athens, http://dlg.galileo.usg.edu/highlander.

103. Lowman, "A Privileged Record of Race. . . [illegible]. . . in [the] South."

104. Alert Americans Association [La.], "Martin Luther King at Communist Training School" [reprint of *Augusta (Ga.) Courier*, July 8, 1963], record no. 3–85–0–2–1–1–1, MSSC Records.

105. James Wrenn, "Berry, Abner Winston," in *Encyclopedia of the American Left*, ed. Buhle et al., 85.

106. Raines, *My Soul Is Rested*, 395.

107. Alert Americans Association, "Martin Luther King at Communist Training School."

108. GCE, "Deposition of Edwin H. Friend, Sr., Taken in the Highlander Folk School Matter, at Room 220, 19 Hunter Street, Atlanta, Georgia, on Tuesday, October 8, 1957, Commencing at 12:00 Noon, before Louise Bickerstaff, Notary Public," transcript, 2–4, folder: "Georgia Commission on Education," box 95, Lowman Papers.

109. *Tampa Morning Tribune*, Oct. 5, 1957.

110. GCE, "Meeting of the Georgia Commission on Education," 1, 3, 16.

111. Griffin, "Statement Opening the Meeting of the Georgia Commission on Education."

112. GCE, "Meeting of the Georgia Commission on Education," 5, 9.

113. Ibid., 9; *Atlanta Journal*, Oct. 4, 1957.

114. Clowse, *Ralph McGill*, 120–21; GCE, "Meeting of the Georgia Commission on Education," 11, 13, 18.

115. GCE, "Meeting of the Georgia Commission on Education," 21.

116. *Tampa Morning Tribune*, Oct. 5, 1957; Mays, *Born to Rebel*, 209.

117. *Tampa Morning Tribune*, Oct. 5, 1957.

118. Editorial, *Atlanta Constitution*, Oct. 31, 1957.

119. *Atlanta Journal-Constitution*, Dec. 15, 1957.

120. GCE, *Highlander Folk School*, folder: "Churches, 1958," box 28, GCE Records; Lowman and Williams, *Citizens' Council Forum*, reel no. 37, videocassette.

121. GCE, *Highlander Folk School*.

122. Editorial, *Maryville-Alcoa (Tenn.) Daily Times*, Dec. 16, 1957.

123. Roy V. Harris, untitled memo, Jan. 10, 1958, folder: "Advertising Committee, 1958, Roy V. Harris, Chairman," box 28, GCE Records.

124. M. A. Perry [Franklin Printing and Manufacturing Company] to W. M. Rainach, Oct. 18, 1957, folder: "Highlander Folks [*sic*] School, 1957," box 22, GCE Records; Robert B. Patterson to T. V. Williams Jr., Oct. 15, 1957; Williams to Patterson, Oct. 18, 1957; Patterson to Williams, Western Union telegram, Oct. 28, 1957; Patterson to Williams, Nov. 5, 1957, all in folder: "Citizens['] Council, Mississippi," box 22, GCE Records.

125. Robert B. Patterson to T. V. Williams Jr., Feb. 11, 1958, folder: "Mississippi, Miscellaneous Correspondence," box 26, GCE Records.

126. Dugas Shands to GCE, Oct. 17, 1957, 1, folder: "Mississippi, Miscellaneous Correspondence," box 26, GCE Records.

127. GCE, meeting minutes, Jan. 3, 1958, 2, folder: "Hugh G. Grant, Augusta, Ga.," box 28, GCE Records.

128. *Atlanta Journal-Constitution*, Dec. 15, 1957. See also Adams and Horton, *Unearthing Seeds of Fire*, 125–26.

129. Highlander Folk School, "National Leaders Answer Griffin's Attack on Highlander," statement, Dec. 18, 1957, 1–2, folder 1, box 253, Matthews Papers.

130. Louis F. Hoffman to T. V. Williams Jr., Feb. 20, 1958; Robert Lewis Weil to Williams, Feb. 25, 1958, both in folder: "Churches, 1958," box 28, GCE Records.

131. James S. Clinefelter to T. V. Williams Jr., Feb. 17, 1958; Thomas R. Miller to GCE, Feb. 13, 1958, both in folder: "Churches, 1958," box 28, GCE Records.

132. Ralph E. Cousins Jr. to T. V. Williams Jr., Feb. 10, 1958; Williams to Cousins, Feb. 11, 1958, both in folder: "Churches, 1958," box 28, GCE Records.

133. John A. Kirstein [pastor, Beulah Presbyterian Church, Fern Creek, Ky.] to Marvin Griffin, Feb. 18, 1958, folder: "Churches, 1958," box 28, GCE Records.

134. James Cosbey Jr. to T. V. Williams Jr., Feb. 18, 1958; Enrico C. S. Molnar to Williams, Feb. 15, 1958, both in folder: "Churches, 1958," box 28, GCE Records.

135. J. Robert Zimmerman to T. V. Williams Jr., Feb. 25, 1958; Alvin V. P. Hart to Marvin Griffen [*sic*], Feb. 13, 1958; Thomas I. Spitler to GCE, n.d. [1958], all in folder: "Churches, 1958," box 28, GCE Records.

136. Thompson to "Dear Friend of Highlander," Feb. 20, 1958.

137. Editorial, *Macon (Ga.) News,* Oct. 9, 1959; *Augusta (Ga.) Herald,* Oct. 10, 1959; Bartley, *The Rise of Massive Resistance,* 183; Henderson, *Ernest Vandiver,* 96.

138. M. G. Lowman, untitled working paper, Dec. 6, 1957, folder: "Lowman, Myers G., 1957," box 671, Matthews Papers.

139. M. G. Lowman, "In the Periphery," typescript, Dec. 23, 1957, 1, folder: "Lowman, Myers G., 1957," box 671, Matthews Papers.

CHAPTER FOUR

1. Reed, *Faubus,* 7, 25–40; Goldfield, *Black, White, and Southern,* 107. See also McMillen, "The White Citizens' Council and Resistance to School Desegregation in Arkansas," 134; and Chappell, "Diversity within a Racial Group," 184–85.

2. Record and Record, eds., *Little Rock, U.S.A.,* 18; Walker, *Remember Little Rock,* 58.

3. McMillen, *The Citizens' Council,* 272–73; Ashmore, "Interview with Harry Ashmore," 49–50.

4. Burk, *The Eisenhower Administration and Black Civil Rights,* 192; "Episode 2: Fighting Back (1957–62)," in *Eyes on the Prize* series, videocassette; Mayer, "With Much Deliberation and Some Speed," 48–76.

5. *New York Times,* Aug. 31, 1957; Olney, "Comment: A Government Lawyer Looks at Little Rock," 516–23.

6. *New York Times,* Sept. 1, 1957.

7. Bartley, *The Rise of Massive Resistance,* 263.

8. Tony A. Freyer, "The Past as Future: The Little Rock Crisis and the Constitution," in *Understanding the Little Rock Crisis,* ed. Jacoway and Williams, 148.

9. *Arkansas Gazette,* Sept. 3, 1957; Record and Record, eds., *Little Rock, U.S.A.,* 37.

10. *Arkansas Democrat,* Sept. 4, 1957.

11. *New Orleans States,* Sept. 18, 1957; *Arkansas Times,* Sept. 20, 2007; Foreman, "Interview with Gene Foreman," 25.

12. Faubus, interview by Mike Wallace, www.hrc.utexas.edu/multimedia/video/2008/wallace/faubus_orval.html, online video; *Arkansas Gazette,* Sept. 15, 1957.

13. Peltason, *Fifty-Eight Lonely Men,* 162, 173–74; "I'm Just One of a Couple of Hundred."

14. Peltason, *Fifty-Eight Lonely Men,* 174.

15. *New York Times,* Apr. 21, 1996.

16. Woodrow Wilson Mann to Dwight D. Eisenhower, Western Union telegram, Sept. 24, 1957, "Civil Rights: The Little Rock School Integration Crisis," Online Documents, Dwight D. Eisenhower Presidential Library, Abilene, Kans., www.eisenhower.archives.gov/research/online_documents/civil_rights_little_rock/1957_09_24_Mann_to_DDE.pdf.

17. Ernest Dumas, "Central High School: Symbol of Inequities Past and Present," 20 Arkansas Icons, Arkansas Business 20, Arkansas Business Publishing Group, Little Rock, www.arkansasbusiness.com/20/icon_article.asp?articleID=9.

18. Dudziak, "Desegregation as a Cold War Imperative," 61–120; White House, "Text of the Address by the President of the United States, Delivered from His Office at the White House, Tuesday, September 24, 1957, at 9:00 P.M., EDT," press release, 3–4, "Civil Rights: The Little Rock School Integration Crisis," Online Documents, Dwight D. Eisenhower Presidential Library, www.eisenhower.archives.gov/research/online_documents/civil_rights_little_rock/1957_09_24_Press_Release.pdf. See also Smith, *Eisenhower,* 728.

19. Gaines M. Foster, "Confess Ethical Lapse," commentary on the author's paper entitled "'Because It Is Right': President John F. Kennedy and His Rhetoric on Civil Rights during the South's Second Reconstruction," twenty-second Gulf South History and Humanities Conference of the Gulf South Historical Association, Pensacola Beach, Fla., Oct. 17, 2003, 4, in the author's possession by courtesy of Foster, Louisiana State University, Baton Rouge; *New Orleans States,* Sept. 18, 1957.

20. *Arkansas Gazette,* Sept. 25, 1957; Maxine G. Allison to Dwight D. Eisenhower, Sept. 23 [*sic,* 24], 1957, box 1, Bulk Mail, WHC Files.

21. Johnston, *Mississippi's Defiant Years,* 71, 75; William E. Leuchtenburg, "The White House and Black America," in *Have We Overcome?,* ed. Namorato, 123; Joseph Crespino, "Civilities and Civil Rights in Mississippi," in *Manners and Southern History,* ed. Ownby, 134.

22. *New York Times,* Sept. 27, 1957.

23. Johnston, *Mississippi's Defiant Years,* 71.

24. Robert B. Patterson [secretary, Association of Citizens' Councils of Mississippi] to T. V. Williams Jr. [GCE executive secretary], Nov. 15, 1957, folder: "Citizens['] Council, Mississippi," box 22, GCE Records.

25. "The Battle between Ike and Faubus," typed poem, n.d. [1957], folder: "Circuit Riders, Inc.—Correspondence," box 14, Lowman Papers.

26. Douglas, "The Rhetoric of Moderation," 131; Reed, *Faubus,* 260; Dudziak, *Cold War Civil Rights,* 124. See also Ashmore, *Civil Rights and Wrongs,* 132.

27. Anderson, *Little Rock,* 81. See also Smith, "The Southern Tradition Baying," *American Communication Journal,* American Communication Association, n.p., http://ac-journal.org/journal/2008/Summer/5CitizensCouncil.pdf.

28. SECALC, "Hearing before the Special Education Committee of the Arkansas Legislative Council," summary, Dec. 16–18, 1958, 1, folder 46, box 5, ACHR Records.

29. Ibid., n.p. [cover page]; "Act № 83: An Act Creating the [Arkansas] State Sovereignty Commission," Feb. 26, 1957, record nos. 3–16–1–12–1–1–1 to 6–1–1, MSSC Records; Jacoway, *Turn Away Thy Son,* 256.

30. SECALC, "Hearing before the Special Education Committee," summary, 1.

31. Bartley and Graham, comp., *Southern Elections,* 29; Woods, *Black Struggle, Red Scare,* 72.

32. Bartley, *The Rise of Massive Resistance,* 274; Elizabeth Jacoway, "Understanding the Past: The Challenge of Little Rock," in *Understanding the Little Rock Crisis,* ed. Jacoway and Williams, 11.

33. *Arkansas Gazette,* Feb. 5, 1959; Record and Record, eds., *Little Rock, U.S.A.,* 139; Jacoway, *Turn Away Thy Son,* 304; unsigned letter addressed to the Little Rock School Board by a Texarkana, Ark., resident, Sept. 17, 1958, n.p. [p. 3], folder 4, box 10, Blossom Papers.

34. Kelly and Harbison, *The American Constitution,* 867.

35. *Cooper v. Aaron,* 358 U.S. 1 (1958).

36. Ibid.; Wilhoit, *The Politics of Massive Resistance,* 170.

37. Jacoway, "Understanding the Past," 11.

38. Jack Schnedler, "What Happened after Central High Crisis?," Little Rock 1957, www.ardemgaz.com/prev/central/wcentral04.html; *The Lost Year,* DVD.

39. Record and Record, eds., *Little Rock, U.S.A.,* 123.

40. Bartley, *The Rise of Massive Resistance,* 213, 221; Jacoway, *Turn Away Thy Son,* 279.

41. Jacoway, *Turn Away Thy Son,* 299; Black, *Southern Governors and Civil Rights,* 348.

42. SECALC, "Hearing before the Special Education Committee," summary, 1.

43. M. G. Lowman, "A Privileged Record of Race . . . [illegible] . . . in [the] South," handwritten memo, June 21, 1967, folder: "Georgia Commission on Education," box 95, Lowman Papers.

44. M. G. Lowman to Leon B. Catlett, Dec. 11, 1957, folder: "Circuit Riders, Inc.—Correspondence," box 14, Lowman Papers; Reed, *Faubus,* 147.

45. *Atlanta Journal-Constitution,* Aug. 3, 1958.

46. Lowman to Catlett, Dec. 11, 1957; LJLC, vol. 2 of *Subversion in Racial Unrest,* 233.

47. J. B. Matthews, "Lee and Grace Lorch," typescript, Mar. 10, 1958, folder: "Lorch, Lee," box 47, Lowman Papers.

48. Lowman to Catlett, Dec. 11, 1957.

49. M. G. Lowman to William Rainach, June 12, 1958, folder 86, box 8, Rainach Papers.

50. SECALC, "Hearing before the Special Education Committee," summary, n.p. [cover page]; *Arkansas Gazette,* Dec. 19, 1958.

51. SECALC, "Hearing before the Special Education Committee," summary, 2–4, 8.

52. Ibid., 15–16; SECALC, "Hearing before the Special Education Committee of the Arkansas Legislative Council," partial transcript, Dec. 16–18, 1958, n.p. [pp. 13–83], folder: "Arkansas (Oversized)," box 1, CR Records.

53. Cobb and Grubbs, "Arkansas' Commonwealth College and the Southern Tenant Farmers' Union," 293.

54. Cobb, *Radical Education in the Rural South,* 15; *Commonwealth College Fortnightly,* Sept. 15, 1926; Schrecker, *The Age of McCarthyism,* 192. Excepting a few, all of the issues of the *Commonwealth College Fortnightly,* the college's biweekly paper published between 1926 and 1938, can be read online at "Commonwealth College Fortnightly," Commonwealth College Collections, Special Collections, David W. Mullins Library, University of Arkansas, Fayetteville, http://libinfo.uark.edu/specialcollections/commonwealth/fortnightly.asp.

55. "Commonwealth to Be 'Investigated,'" supplement to *Commonwealth College Fortnightly,* Feb. 15, 1935; Cobb, *Radical Education in the Rural South,* 148.

56. Kester, "Interview with Howard Kester," 35; SECALC, "Hearing before the Special Education Committee," summary, 16.

57. SECALC, "Hearing before the Special Education Committee," partial transcript, n.p. [pp. 13–83]; SECALC, "Hearing before the Special Education Committee," summary, 16; *Jackson (Miss.) Daily News*, June 10, 1958; Fosl, *Subversive Southerner*, 201.

58. Reed, *Faubus*, 75, 91; Woods, *Black Struggle, Red Scare*, 72; Iggers and Iggers, *Two Lives in Uncertain Times*, 81.

59. SECALC, "Hearing before the Special Education Committee," partial transcript, n.p. [p. 154].

60. Ibid., n.p. [pp. 171–72, 188]; SECALC, "Hearing before the Special Education Committee," summary, 9–12, 14–15.

61. SECALC, "Hearing before the Special Education Committee," summary, 9–12, 14–15; SECALC, "Hearing before the Special Education Committee," partial transcript, n.p. [pp. 168, 172–73, 187]; Ashmore, *Hearts and Minds*, 273–75; Ashmore, interview by Mike Wallace, www.hrc.utexas.edu/multimedia/video/2008/wallace/ashmore_harry.html, online video; Reed, *Beware of Limbo Dancers*, 28. As a financial beneficiary of the Ford Foundation with $15 million, the Fund for the Republic, since its inception in late 1952, had also been victimized by broadly defined McCarthyism on the national scene. By May 1956, the fund had given grants totaling $445,000 to the SRC in Atlanta. And with that money, the SRC had established twelve state affiliates, usually called the Councils on Human Relations, throughout the South (see Fund for the Republic, "The Fund for the Republic: Civil Liberties and Race Relations," bulletin, May 1956, n.p. [pp. 2–3], folder: "Fund for the Republic," box 40, Lowman Papers).

62. SECALC, "Hearing before the Special Education Committee," partial transcript, n.p. [pp. 169–71]; *Cincinnati (Ohio) Enquirer,* Nov. 28, 1954; Caute, *The Great Fear,* 418; Georg G. Iggers [distinguished professor emeritus, Department of History, State University of New York at Buffalo], e-mail to the author, Sept. 14, 2007.

63. "From the *Nashville Tennessean,* June 11, 1954," typescript, n.d., folder: "Circuit Riders, Inc.—Correspondence," box 14, Lowman Papers; Fariello, ed., *Red Scare,* 493; LJLC, vol. 2 of *Subversion in Racial Unrest,* 232–35.

64. Fariello, ed., *Red Scare,* 495; *Arkansas Democrat,* Sept. 4, 1957; Beals, *Warriors Don't Cry,* 49–50.

65. Bates, *The Long Shadow of Little Rock,* 70; Kirk, *Redefining the Color Line,* 117.

66. *New York Times,* Oct. 30, 1957; *Nashville (Tenn.) Banner,* Oct. 30, 1957; Associated Press wirephoto taken during Grace Lorch's testimony before the Senate Internal Security Subcommittee in Memphis, Tenn., Oct. 29, 1957, in the author's possession.

67. U.S. Congress, Senate, Committee on the Judiciary, Subcommittee to Investigate the Administration of the Internal Security Act and Other Internal Security Laws, *Communism in the Mid-South,* 79–81; *Washington Afro-American,* Nov. 5, 1957.

68. Committee on the Judiciary, Subcommittee to Investigate the Administration of the Internal Security Act and Other Internal Security Laws, *Communism in the Mid-South,* 80–81; *Washington Evening Star,* Oct. 31, 1957; Brown, *Standing against Dragons,* 163. Although the civil rights historian Elizabeth Jacoway has described that Grace Lorch was a "member of the Communist Party" in her book on the Little Rock desegregation crisis and Grif Stockley, an Arkansas historian, has "assumed" that "Grace had . . . been a member" of the CPUSA in his work on Daisy Bates, the evidences on which they based their assertion and assumption are inconclusive. In this respect, Roy Reed, a former reporter for the *Arkansas Gazette* and the author of an incisive biography of Arkansas governor Faubus, has been careful enough to call Grace "the so-called Communist." Despite the fact that Grace, along with her husband,

Lee (who had once been affiliated with the CPUSA), might have espoused Communist ideologies to some degree in putting her civil and human rights crusade into practice, there has been no definite and irrefutable evidence, at least to the author's knowledge, which indicates that Grace was indeed a card-carrying CPUSA member (see Jacoway, *Turn Away Thy Son*, 6; Stockley, *Daisy Bates*, 162; and Moseley, "Interview with Ray Moseley," 20).

69. Editorial, *Daily Worker (N.Y.)*, Oct. 29, 1957; Ogden, *My Father Said Yes*, 71–72.

70. *Washington Evening Star*, Oct. 31, 1957.

71. Senate Internal Security Subcommittee, untitled press release, Nov. 27, 1957, folder 13, box 490, Matthews Papers.

72. SECALC, "Hearing before the Special Education Committee," summary, 24–25.

73. David A. Reitzes, "Who Was Guy Banister?," JFK Online: JFK Assassination Resources Online, ed. David A. Reitzes, n.p., www.jfk-online.com/jfk100whoban.html.

74. SECALC, "Hearing before the Special Education Committee," summary, 28; Russo, *Live by the Sword*, 140; Hinckle and Turner, *Deadly Secrets*, 231.

75. J. B. Matthews, "Communists, Negroes, and Integration," typed report, n.d. [1957], folder: "What's Ahead for the American Negro under Desegregation, 1954–1955," box 722, Matthews Papers.

76. Pizzitola, *Hearst over Hollywood*, 425.

77. J. B. Matthews, "Introduction," attachment to his typed report entitled "Communist, Negroes, and Integration," n.d. [1957], folder: "Communist, Negroes, and Integration," box 714, Matthews Papers.

78. John A. Clements to Richard E. Berlin, memo, Oct. 24, 1957, folder: "Clements, John A., 1941–1962," box 696, Matthews Papers; Nasaw, *The Chief*, 588.

79. John A. Clements, untitled list of individuals, n.d. [Oct. 1957], folder: "Clements, John A., 1941–1962," box 696, Matthews Papers.

80. James O. Eastland to John A. Clements, Nov. 18, 1957, folder: "Clements, John A., 1941–1962," box 696, Matthews Papers.

81. FLIC, "Transcript of Testimony [of Joseph Brown Matthews]," Feb. 10, 1958, 37, folders 13 and 14, box 4, FLIC Records.

82. Forster and Epstein, *Danger on the Right*, 90.

83. Benson and Watson, *Missionary Experiences*, 103–5; National Education Program, *The Origin and Purpose of the National Education Program*, n.p., folder 1, box 405, Matthews Papers. See also "History," About Harding, Harding University, Searcy, Ark., www.harding.edu/about/history.html.

84. Coleman Yoakum, "George S. Benson, Pt. 2," May 23, 2011, Life after Death (to Self): Christ, Culture, and Community, Pontiac, Mich. [?], http://coleyoakum.wordpress.com/2011/05/23/george-s-benson-pt-2; Forster and Epstein, *Danger on the Right*, 87, 91. Since its inception until 1954, the NEP, according to a booklet published by the institution, had been a "division" of Harding College. Though the NEP became a separately incorporated entity from the college in 1954, Benson, while being president of Harding, had continued to serve as the NEP director (see National Education Program, *The Origin and Purpose of the National Education Program*, n.p.).

85. National Education Program, *The Origin and Purpose of the National Education Program*, n.p.; Forster and Epstein, *Danger on the Right*, 87–88; Heale, *American Anticommunism*, 171.

86. Matthews, *Some Facts about the Communist Apparatus*, n.p., box 91, Lowman Papers; Forster and Epstein, *Danger on the Right*, 88.

87. National Education Program, *The Origin and Purpose of the National Education Program,* n.p. The innovative endeavors made by the San Francisco–based Internet Archive make it possible for us to view the NEP-produced film entitled "Responsibilities of American Citizenship" online (see "Responsibilities of American Citizenship," www.archive.org/download/Responsi1955/Responsi1955.mpg, online MPEG movie).

88. National Education Program, *The Origin and Purpose of the National Education Program,* n.p. Each of the thirty-minute-long films in the *War We Are In* series featured different lectures given by President Benson, and they were also available to the general public for purchase at fifty dollars per part. The second part of the series, "Communism versus Capitalism," can be viewed at the Internet Archive (see "Communism versus Capitalism," www.archive.org/download/WarWeAre1962/WarWeAre1962.mpg, online MPEG movie).

89. National Education Program, *The Origin and Purpose of the National Education Program,* n.p.

90. Ibid.; Forster and Epstein, *Danger on the Right,* 97. See also Dochuk, *From Bible Belt to Sunbelt,* 132–33.

91. National Education Program, *The Origin and Purpose of the National Education Program,* n.p.

92. Ibid.; Glenn A. Green to J. B. Matthews, May 16, 1951; Green to Matthews, Nov. 22, 1955, both in folder: "Harding College: National Education Program, 1951–1963," box 663, Matthews Papers.

93. Glenn A. Green to George E. Sokolsky [columnist, *New York Herald Tribune*], Jan. 26, 1953, folder: "Testimonial Dinner, 1952–1953," box 700, Matthews Papers. See also Hicks, *"Sometimes in the Wrong, but Never in Doubt,"* 60–61.

94. Glenn A. Green to J. B. Matthews, Mar. 2, 1951, folder: "Harding College: National Education Program, 1951–1963," box 663, Matthews Papers.

95. Green to Matthews, May 16, 1951.

96. Glenn A. Green to J. B. Matthews, June 7, 1951, folder: "Harding College: National Education Program, 1951–1963," box 663, Matthews Papers.

97. J. B. Matthews to Glenn A. Green, Sept. 15, 1951, folder: "Harding College: National Education Program, 1951–1963," box 663, Matthews Papers.

98. Glenn A. Green to J. B. Matthews, Feb. 7, 1952, folder: "Harding College: National Education Program, 1951–1963," box 663, Matthews Papers.

99. George S. Benson to George E. Sokolsky, Jan. 19, 1953, folder: "Testimonial Dinner, 1952–1953," box 700, Matthews Papers; "Dr. J. B. Matthews Dinner Guest List," n.d. [Feb. 1953], 1, folder 4, box 18, Archive I: Un-American Activities (1950–55), Matusow Archive.

100. George S. Benson to J. B. Matthews, Feb. 18, 1953, folder: "Harding College: National Education Program, 1951–1963," box 663, Matthews Papers.

101. J. B. Matthews to George S. Benson, Feb. 22, 1953, folder: "Testimonial Dinner, 1952–1953," box 700, Matthews Papers.

102. Glenn A. Green to J. B. Matthews, Apr. 23, 1953; National Education Program, "An Invitation to the Harding College Freedom Forum: Seminar 14," *October 19–23, 1953,* pamphlet, n.d. [1953], n.p., both in folder: "Harding College: National Education Program, 1951–1963," box 663, Matthews Papers. See also Glenn A. Green to J. B. Matthews, July 13, 1953, folder: "Clergy Incident, July 1953," box 696, Matthews Papers.

103. Matthews, *Some Facts about the Communist Apparatus,* 2, 13.

104. Ibid., 9.

105. National Education Program, "An Invitation to the Harding College Freedom Forum," n.p.; Green to Matthews, Apr. 23, 1953.

106. National Education Program, *The Origin and Purpose of the National Education Program,* n.p.; Brown, "Powerful Voice against the Reds," 2–3; "Bales Family History Pages," Home Sweet Home Page, Bales Family website, n.p., www.jonbales.com/family.

107. J. D. Bales to J. B. Matthews, Oct. 24, 1956, folder: "Harding College: National Education Program, 1951–1963," box 663, Matthews Papers.

108. Glenn A. Green to J. B. Matthews, Sept. 24, 1953, folder: "Harding College: National Education Program, 1951–1963," box 663, Matthews Papers.

109. J. B. Matthews to Glenn Green, Dec. 31, 1958, folder: "Harding College: National Education Program, 1951–1963," box 663, Matthews Papers.

110. J. B. Matthews to Glenn A. Green, Aug. 8, 1953, folder: "Harding College: National Education Program, 1951–1963," box 663, Matthews Papers.

111. Clifton Ganus Jr. [vice president and dean of the School of American Studies, Harding College] to J. B. Matthews, Mar. 20, 1957, folder: "Harding College: National Education Program, 1951–1963," box 663; Matthews, "Big Government and Communism," speech draft, n.d. [May 7, 1957], folder: "Speech: Harding College, May 7, 1957," box 716, both in Matthews Papers.

112. Matthews to Benson, Feb. 22, 1953.

113. Ruth I. Matthews to Mary Kay [Ruth Matthews's personal friend?], Sept. 11, 1966, folder: "Biographical, 1963–1967," box 696; Ruth Matthews, "Burial Service for J. B.," typescript, n.d. [1966], folder: "Grave-Side Service for J. B. Matthews, 1966," box 708, both in Matthews Papers.

114. Glenn A. Green to J. B. Matthews, Sept. 4, 1954, folder: "Harding College: National Education Program, 1951–1963," box 663, Matthews Papers.

115. William K. Floyd, "Why I Could Not Be a Career Preacher," in *Voices of Concern,* ed. Meyers, 166–68; Crawford, "From Segregation to Independence," Ph.D. diss., 103.

116. Don Haymes, "Introduction to the Text [of William K. Floyd's "Why I Could Not Be a Career Preacher"]," Restoration Movement, ed. Hans Rollmann, Department of Religious Studies, Memorial University of Newfoundland, St. John's, Newfoundland and Labrador, Canada, www.mun.ca/rels/restmov/texts/race/haymes12.html; Crawford, "From Segregation to Independence," Ph.D. diss., 103; Floyd, "Why I Could Not Be a Career Preacher," 168.

117. Hughes and Roberts, *The Churches of Christ,* 134; Hughes, *Reviving the Ancient Faith,* 290–91; Colter Hettich, "First African-American Student Recalls Struggle," *Optimist* [student newspaper, Abilene Christian University, Abilene, Tex.], online ed., posted May 1, 2009, www.acuoptimist.com/2009/05/first-african-american-student-recalls-struggle; Key, "On the Periphery of the Civil Rights Movement."

118. Haymes, "Introduction to the Text [of William K. Floyd's "Why I Could Not Be a Career Preacher"]."

119. SECALC, untitled transcript of J. B. Matthews's testimony, n.d. [Dec. 17, 1958], 1, folder: "Matthews, John [*sic,* Joseph] B.," box 3, CR Records; Matthews to Green, Dec. 31, 1958.

120. Matthews to Green, Dec. 31, 1958; *Arkansas Gazette,* Dec. 19, 1958.

121. *Memphis Commercial Appeal,* Arkansas ed., Dec. 18, 1958.

122. SECALC, untitled transcript of J. B. Matthews's testimony, 3.

123. *Memphis Commercial Appeal,* Arkansas ed., Dec. 18, 1958; SECALC, "Hearing before the Special Education Committee," summary, 20.

124. SECALC, untitled transcript of J. B. Matthews's testimony, 16, 40.

125. SECALC, "Hearing before the Special Education Committee," summary, 20.

126. SECALC, untitled transcript of J. B. Matthews's testimony, 10, 34.

127. Ibid., 18.

128. Michael T. Clougherty [deputy superintendent, Bureau of Criminal Investigation, Boston Police Department] to Francis J. Hennessy [superintendent of police, Boston Police Department], "Attached Communication from Benjamin Mandel, Research Director, Internal Security Subcommittee, United States Senate, Washington, D.C., in Relation to Obtaining Police Record of Grace K. Lonergan, Alleged to Have a Communist Record," memo, Mar. 5, 1958; George D. Canty [sergeant, Division of Subversive Activities, Massachusetts Department of Public Safety] to Benjamin Mandel, Apr. 18, 1958, both in folder: "Lorch, Lee and Grace," box 3, CR Records; Schrecker, *The Age of McCarthyism,* 17.

129. SECALC, untitled transcript of J. B. Matthews's testimony, 19. See also Matthews, "Lee and Grace Lorch," 4.

130. SECALC, "Hearing before the Special Education Committee," summary, 23.

131. *Arkansas Gazette,* Dec. 19, 1958.

132. Ibid.

133. SECALC, "Hearing before the Special Education Committee," summary, 29, 32.

134. Pete Daniel, "Accidental Historian," in *Shapers of Southern History,* ed. Boles, 169; Manis, *Southern Civil Religions in Conflict,* 105.

135. Ashmore, "A Southern Challenge and Epitaph for Dixie," 129.

CHAPTER FIVE

1. SECALC, "Hearing before the Special Education Committee of the Arkansas Legislative Council," summary, Dec. 16–18, 1958, 32, folder 46, box 5, ACHR Records.

2. *Arkansas Gazette,* Feb. 17, 1959; Record and Record, eds., *Little Rock, U.S.A.,* 159.

3. *Arkansas Gazette,* Feb. 5, 1959; Record and Record, eds., *Little Rock, U.S.A.,* 139; Jacoway, *Turn Away Thy Son,* 304.

4. U.S. House, Representative Dale Alford of Arkansas, "Subversive Activity in the South," speech, 86th Cong., 1st sess., *Congressional Record* (Feb. 17, 1959), n.p. [reproduction], folder 2, box 128, Matthews Papers.

5. Reed, *Faubus,* 246–49; *Arkansas Democrat-Gazette,* Sept. 9, 2007.

6. Alford and Alford, *The Case of the Sleeping People;* "Recommended Literature Available from the Citizens' Council."

7. U.S. House, Representative Alford, "Subversive Activity in the South," n.p.

8. Muse, *Ten Years of Prelude,* 192.

9. Tony A. Freyer, "The Past as Future: The Little Rock Crisis and the Constitution," in *Understanding the Little Rock Crisis,* ed. Jacoway and Williams, 144; Brewer, *The Embattled Ladies of Little Rock.*

10. Kelly and Harbison, *The American Constitution,* 868.

11. Miller, *Fearless,* 48; "The Presidency: Little Rock's Finest."

12. "The Presidency: Little Rock's Finest."

13. "The 1957–58 School Year: History of Little Rock Public Schools Desegregation," Little Rock Central High Fortieth Anniversary, ed. Craig Rains, n.p., www.centralhigh57.org/1957-58.htm.

14. "The Presidency: Little Rock's Finest"; Abernathy, *Partners to History,* 40.

15. Dykeman and Stokely, "McCarthyism under the Magnolias," 6.

16. *Pittsburgh (Pa.) Courier,* Oct. 31, 1959; Georg G. Iggers [distinguished professor emeritus, Department of History, State University of New York at Buffalo], e-mail to the author, Sept. 14, 2007.

17. "York Professor Honored for Civil Rights Activism." Around the same time the Lorches left the United States for Canada, in October 1959, Ashmore also left the *Arkansas Gazette* and moved to California to join the Center for the Study of Democratic Institutions in Santa Barbara (see, Jacoway, *Turn Away Thy Son,* 353).

18. M. G. Lowman to "Mr. Bingham," Nov. 28, 1959, folder: "Lorch, Lee," box 47, Lowman Papers.

19. Fariello, ed., *Red Scare,* 496; *New York Times,* Nov. 21, 2010.

20. "The 1957–58 School Year."

21. Chappell, *Inside Agitators,* xxv.

22. Bates, *The Long Shadow of Little Rock.*

23. *Chattanooga (Tenn.) News-Free Press,* Jan. 20, 1959; Glen, *Highlander,* 222; *Baltimore Afro-American,* Oct. 10, 1959.

24. James B. Jones Jr., "Myles F. Horton, Tennessee's 'Radical Hillbilly': The Highlander Folk School and Education for Social Change in America, the South, and the Volunteer State," *Southern History,* ed. James B. Jones Jr., n.p. [Tenn.?], www.southernhistory.net/index.php?name=News&file=article&sid=10263.

25. E. Thomas Wood, "Nashville Now and Then: Surging Commerce and Suspected Commies," Mar. 7, 2008, *NashvillePost.Com,* NashvillePost.Com, Nashville, Tenn., www.nashvillepost.com/news/2008/3/7/nashville_now_and_then_surging_commerce_and_suspected_commies; Glen, *Highlander,* 222. See also J. Edgar Hoover [director, Federal Bureau of Investigation (FBI)] to unidentifiable special agents at the FBI's Savannah, Ga., and Knoxville, Tenn., offices, "Attention: SACs, Savannah and Knoxville," memo, n.d. [Mar. 12, 1959?], 3, "Highlander Folk School," Freedom of Information Act Electronic Reading Room, Federal Bureau of Investigation, Washington, D.C., http://foia.fbi.gov/hfschool/hfschool6a.pdf.

26. *Nashville Tennessean,* Feb. 5, 1959; Glen, *Highlander,* 222–23.

27. *Memphis Press-Scimitar,* Feb. 12, 1959; Highlander Research and Education Center, "Highlander News: The Story of Highlander—A Sermon by Kenneth Torquil MacLean," pamphlet, n.d. [1965], n.p., folder 6, box 253, Matthews Papers; TGASIC, "Committee Report," Mar. 6, 1959, 9, folder 2, box 303, reel no. 293, *NR* Records.

28. TGASIC, "Committee Report," 1; *Memphis Press-Scimitar,* Feb. 12, 1959; Glen, *Highlander,* 224.

29. An unidentifiable special agent at the FBI's Knoxville office to J. Edgar Hoover, "Highlander Folk School, Monteagle, Tennessee," memo, Feb. 21, 1959, "Highlander Folk School," Freedom of Information Act Electronic Reading Room, Federal Bureau of Investigation, http://foia.fbi.gov/hfschool/hfschool6a.pdf; Glen, *Highlander,* 224.

30. Donald Davidson, "Joint Statement of State Officers and Organization Leaders of the Tennessee Federation for Constitutional Government," press release, n.d. [Feb. 1959], 1, folder 2, box 253, Matthews Papers.

31. Twelve Southerners, *I'll Take My Stand,* ix.

32. Bartley, *The Rise of Massive Resistance,* 99–100; Williamson, *William Faulkner and Southern History,* 133; McGill, *The South and the Southerner,* 208; Hobson, *Tell about the South,* 207. See also Duck, *The Nation's Region,* 73.

33. Winchell, *Where No Flag Flies*, 290; Murphy, *The Rebuke of History*, 202.

34. Winchell, *Where No Flag Flies*, 290; McMillen, *The Citizens' Council*, 109; Davidson, "Joint Statement of State Officers and Organization Leaders of the Tennessee Federation for Constitutional Government," 1; Kershaw, recorded interview, 3; Lovett, *The Civil Rights Movement in Tennessee*, 38. See also Webb, *Rabble Rousers*, 56.

35. Kershaw, recorded interview, 2; Winchell, *Where No Flag Flies*, 290; *New York Times*, Sept. 24, 2010.

36. John U. Barr [interim chair, Federation for Constitutional Government] to William M. Rainach [LJLC chair], Dec. 19, 1955, folder 66, box 5, Touchstone Papers.

37. Murphy, *The Rebuke of History*, 202; Kershaw, recorded interview, 9. See also Benjamin Houston, "Donald Davidson and the Segregationist Intellect," in *Southern Character*, ed. Frank and Kilbride, 168.

38. Malvasi, *The Unregenerate South*, 207.

39. O'Brien, *The Idea of the American South*, 208; Daniel, *Lost Revolutions*, 200; Houston, "Donald Davidson and the Segregationist Intellect," 170. See also Schneider, *The Conservative Century*, 84.

40. Patterson, Brown v. Board of Education, 101–2; Irons, *Jim Crow's Children*, 178–79; "The Story of Desegregation in Clinton, Tennessee," Green McAdoo Cultural Center, Clinton, Tenn., www.greenmcadoo.org/story.html; Halberstam, "The White Citizens['] Councils"; *Washington Post*, Oct. 15, 2006.

41. Winchell, *Where No Flag Flies*, 293; Flood, "Chaos in Clinton," master's thesis, 51–52; Raimondi, "The Clinton 12 Chronicles," master's thesis, 41; Robert S. Griffin, "The Tale of John Kasper," n.p. [pp. 6–7], Writings, website for Robert S. Griffin, n.p., www.robertsgriffin.com/TaleKasper.pdf.

42. Lovett, *The Civil Rights Movement in Tennessee*, 55.

43. Egerton, "Walking into History."

44. Kershaw, recorded interview, 6.

45. Davidson, "Joint Statement of State Officers and Organization Leaders of the Tennessee Federation for Constitutional Government," 4–5.

46. "Richard Jackson Burrow, Jr.," May 1, 2012, Find a Grave, Salt Lake City, Utah, www.findagrave.com; McMillen, *The Citizens' Council*, 110; Richard Burrow Jr. to Donald I. Sweany Jr., Western Union telegram, Feb. 18, 1959, folder 2, box 253, Matthews Papers.

47. Donald I. Sweany Jr., "Proposed Questions—Witness: Myles Horton, Founder and Director, Highlander Folk School, Monteagle, Tennessee," typescript, n.d. [Feb. 1959], 1; Sweany to Richard Burrow Jr., Feb. 20, 1959, both in folder 2, box 253, Matthews Papers. The Sweany-crafted "Proposed Questions" is also located in folder 5, box 1, TGASIC Records.

48. "Investigations of Highlander," n.p., folder 6, box 143, Matthews Papers.

49. Ibid.; TGASIC, "Committee Report," 1–2; Oliver W. Jervis, "Highlander Folk School," speech delivered in Monteagle, Tenn., Feb. 25–26, 2006, 4–5, Education for Freedom 2007, Scribd, San Francisco and New York, www.scribd.com/doc/54287008/Education-for-Freedom-2007; *Chattanooga (Tenn.) Times*, Feb. 20, 1959. See also *Nashville Tennessean*, Feb. 27, 1959.

50. Jervis, "Highlander Folk School," 4–5; Loveland, "A Greater Fairness," 105, 107–8.

51. Jervis, "Highlander Folk School," 4–5; Glen, *Highlander*, 224.

52. TGASIC, "Committee Report," 2; Wood, "Nashville Now and Then."

53. At least two different versions of Matthews's reports on the Highlander Folk School, both of which were prepared immediately prior to the outbreak of the September 1957 Little

Rock desegregation crisis, were also provided to the FBI director Hoover through the Hearst Corporation in New York City (see J. B. Matthews, "Highlander Folk School," Aug. 6, 1957; and Matthews, ". . . [illegible] Communist Activities," Sept. 3, 1957, both at "Highlander Folk School," Freedom of Information Act Electronic Reading Room, Federal Bureau of Investigation, http://foia.fbi.gov/hfschool/hfschool5a.pdf).

54. *Nashville Tennessean,* Mar. 5, 1959.

55. Ibid.; Glen, *Highlander,* 228–29. See also *Nashville Banner,* Mar. 5, 1959.

56. *Nashville Tennessean,* Mar. 5, 1959.

57. Braden, *House Un-American Activities Committee,* 27; TGASIC, "Committee Report," 9.

58. *Nashville Tennessean,* Mar. 5, 1959; Horton, *The Long Haul,* 109; TGASIC, "Committee Report," 9.

59. Horton, *The Long Haul,* 108; Glen, *Highlander,* 229.

60. Horton, *The Long Haul,* 108.

61. *Nashville Tennessean,* Mar. 5, 1959.

62. TGASIC, "Committee Report," 2; *Memphis Commercial Appeal,* Mar. 6, 1959.

63. Glen, *Highlander,* 223; editorial, *Nashville Tennessean,* Mar. 7, 1959.

64. TGASIC, "Committee Report," 9; Glen, *Highlander,* 224.

65. TGASIC, "Committee Report," 10–11; *Charleston (S.C.) News and Courier,* Mar. 28, 1959.

66. TGASIC, "Committee Report," 12; *Nashville Tennessean,* Mar. 5, 1959.

67. "Investigations of Highlander," n.p.

68. Myles Horton to "Fellow Tennesseans," n.d. [1959], reproduced in the Sept. 11, 1959, memo from an unidentifiable special agent at the FBI's Knoxville office to the FBI director, "Subject: Highlander Folk School, Monteagle, Tennessee, Information Concerning," "Highlander Folk School," Freedom of Information Act Electronic Reading Room, Federal Bureau of Investigation, http://foia.fbi.gov/hfschool/hfschool6a.pdf.

69. Dykeman and Stokely, "McCarthyism under the Magnolias," 6.

70. Horton, *The Long Haul,* 110; Jones, "Myles F. Horton, Tennessee's 'Radical Hillbilly'"; "The Highlander Folk School: A Photographic History," MetaScholar: An Emory University Digital Library Research Initiative, Robert W. Woodruff Library, Emory University, Atlanta, Ga., www.metascholar.org/highlander. See also Charron, *Freedom's Teacher,* 268–70.

71. Horton to "Fellow Tennesseans," n.d. [1959].

72. Myles Horton to "Dear Friend of Highlander," Nov. 8, 1961, 1, folder 6, box 253, Matthews Papers; Highlander Research and Education Center, "Highlander News," n.p.; Jervis, "Highlander Folk School," 6; Horton, *The Long Haul,* 110, 112; Raines, *My Soul Is Rested,* 399; Reed, *Simple Decency and Common Sense,* 159; Lewis Sinclair [member, board of directors, Highlander Research and Education Center, New Market, Tenn.], letter to the author, May 8, 1998; editorial, *Birmingham (Ala.) Post-Herald,* Oct. 10, 1961.

73. Horton to "Dear Friend of Highlander," Nov. 8, 1961, 1; Bell et al., eds., *We Make the Road by Walking,* xxviii.

74. Myles Horton to "Dear Friend," May 15, 1963, folder: "Circuit Riders," Garman Papers.

75. Raines, *My Soul Is Rested,* 399.

76. Egerton, *Shades of Gray,* 76. See also Campbell, *Providence,* 17.

77. Rabby, *The Pain and the Promise,* 3.

78. Jones and McCarthy, *African Americans in Florida,* 111; Scott Fields, "The Tallahassee Bus Boycott of 1956–58," Teaching American History with a Florida Flavor, Polk County Public

School District, Bartow, Fla., www.polk-fl.net/staff/teachers/tah/documents/floridaflavor/lessons/F-6.pdf.

79. Johns, recorded interview, 7; *St. Petersburg (Fla.) Times,* June 3, 2001; "The Pork Chop Gang," Behind Closed Doors: Dark Legacy of the Johns Committee, ed. Allyson A. Beutke, n.p., www.behindcloseddoorsfilm.com/index2.htm.

80. Bass and DeVries, *The Transformation of Southern Politics,* 108–9; *Pensacola (Fla.) News Journal,* July 1, 1993.

81. Key, *Southern Politics in State and Nation,* 92; Sanders, *Mighty Peculiar Elections,* 78; Klein, "Guarding the Baggage," Ph.D. diss., 19.

82. Johns, recorded interview, 12; *Miami (Fla.) Herald,* June 30, 1993; "Charley Eugene Johns," Florida Governors' Portraits, Division of Historical Resources, Florida Department of State, Tallahassee, http://dhr.dos.state.fl.us/museum/collections/governors/about.cfm?id=39.

83. Karl, *The 57 Club,* 131.

84. McMillen, *The Citizens' Council,* 100.

85. Weitz, "Bourbon, Pork Chops, and Red Peppers," Ph.D. diss., 116–17.

86. FLIC, "Report of the Florida Legislative Investigation Committee to the 1961 Session of the Legislature," n.d., 3, folder 21, box 1, FLIC Records; Steven F. Lawson, "The Florida Legislative Investigation Committee and the Constitutional Readjustment of Race Relations, 1956–1963," in *An Uncertain Tradition,* ed. Hall and Ely, 299.

87. FLIC, "Report of the Florida Legislative Investigation Committee to the 1961 Session of the Legislature," 3; Schnur, "Cold Warriors in the Hot Sunshine," 9; Graves, *And They Were Wonderful Teachers,* 1–2.

88. FLIC, "Report of the Florida Legislative Investigation Committee to the 1961 Session of the Legislature," 3; Stark, "McCarthyism in Florida," master's thesis, 31, 89; *Miami Herald,* June 30, 1993.

89. FLIC, "Rules and Regulations," n.d. [1956], n.p., folder 23, box 1, FLIC Records.

90. Schnur, "Cold Warriors in the Hot Sunshine"; FLIC, "Report of the Florida Legislative Investigation Committee to the 1961 Session of the Legislature," 2.

91. Weitz, "Bourbon, Pork Chops, and Red Peppers," 120–21.

92. Rabby, *The Pain and the Promise,* 35, 66–67; *Tallahassee (Fla.) Democrat,* May 21, 2006.

93. Rabby, *The Pain and the Promise,* 70.

94. Ibid., 71.

95. Hurst, *It Was Never about a Hot Dog and a Coke!,* 120; Caroline Emmons, "A State Divided: Implementation of the *Brown* Decision in Florida, 1954–1970," in *With All Deliberate Speed,* ed. Daugherity and Bolton, 144–45; "U.S. Supreme Court Clears Father Gibson," 292.

96. Raymond A. Mohl, "'South of the South?': Jews, Blacks, and the Civil Rights Movement in Miami, 1945–1960," in *The Civil Rights Movement,* ed. Davis, 114.

97. Ibid., 112; Bush, "We Must Picture an 'Octopus,'" 48–63; Greenbaum, ed., *Jews of South Florida,* xx.

98. Tscheschlok, "So Goes the Negro," 61.

99. "Father Theodore R. Gibson," 91; "U.S. Supreme Court Clears Father Gibson," 292.

100. Taylor, *Black Religious Intellectuals,* 95.

101. FLIC, "Report of the Florida Legislative Investigation Committee to the 1961 Session of the Legislature," 3.

102. *Miami Herald,* June 30, 1993.

103. *Atlanta Journal-Constitution,* Aug. 3, 1958.

104. M. G. Lowman, "A Privileged Record of Race . . . [illegible] . . . in [the] South," handwritten memo, June 21, 1967, folder: "Georgia Commission on Education," box 95, Lowman Papers.

105. *Florida Times-Union,* Feb. 11, 1958.

106. FLIC, "Transcript of Testimony [of Joseph Brown Matthews]," Feb. 10, 1958, 3, folders 13 and 14, box 4, FLIC Records.

107. Braden, *House Un-American Activities Committee,* 26; Fariello, ed., *Red Scare,* 471; Lawson, "The Florida Legislative Investigation Committee," 303.

108. FLIC, "Transcript of Testimony [of Joseph Brown Matthews]," 37, 47.

109. Ibid., 45; Braden, *House Un-American Activities Committee,* 26.

110. FLIC, "Transcript of Testimony [of Joseph Brown Matthews]," 3.

111. Braukman, *Communists and Perverts under the Palms,* 60; *Miami Herald,* Feb. 28, 1958.

112. *Miami Herald,* Feb. 28, 1958; Dunn, *Black Miami in the Twentieth Century,* 191; Weitz, "Bourbon, Pork Chops, and Red Peppers," 128; Judith Poucher, "One Woman's Courage: Ruth Perry and the Johns Committee," in *Making Waves,* ed. Davis and Frederickson, 240–41; Taylor, *Black Religious Intellectuals,* 110.

113. GCE, *Communism and the NAACP,* 2 vols., in both folder: "Lowman, Myers G., 1958," box 671, Matthews Papers; and folder 12, Welch Papers.

114. GCE, vol. 1 of *Communism and the NAACP,* 40–41.

115. Advertising Committee of the GCE, untitled memo [regarding "50,000 Matthews Florida Report"], n.d. [1958]; Advertising Committee of the GCE, untitled memo [regarding "50,000 Matthews Florida Report—Reprint"], n.d. [1958], both in folder: "Advertising Committee, Roy V. Harris, Chairman, 1957," box 22, GCE Records.

116. Carl McIntire, "J. B. Matthews" [introduction], in Matthews, *Communism in Our Churches,* 3, folder: "Pamphlets," box 5, CR Records.

117. "Father Theodore R. Gibson," 92; Tushnet, *Making Civil Rights Law,* 296–98. See also Lichtman, *The Supreme Court and McCarthy-Era Repression,* 161–62.

118. Schnur, "Cold Warriors in the Hot Sunshine," 10.

119. R. J. Strickland to J. B. Matthews, Oct. 6, 1958, folder: "Florida Legislative Investigation Committee, 1958–1962 and n.d.," box 660, Matthews Papers.

120. R. J. Strickland to M. G. Lowman, Apr. 4, 1958, folder: "Florida Legislative Investigating [*sic*] Committee"; Strickland to Lowman, May 12, 1958, folder: "Florida Legislative Investigating [*sic*] Committee"; Charley E. Johns to Lowman, June 10, 1958, folder: "Florida," all in box 38, Lowman Papers.

121. R. J. Strickland, "Report of Organizations, Publications and Findings Pertaining to Communists and Racial Agitation in the State of Florida," n.d. [1961], record nos. 13-0-3-4-1-1-1 to 5-1-1, pp. 3-1-1 to 4-1-1, MSSC Records. Part of the Circuit Riders' literature collected and studied by the Florida committee is located in folder 17, box 17, FLIC Records.

122. FLIC, "Report of the Florida Legislative Investigation Committee to the 1961 Session of the Legislature," 1.

123. Schnur, "Cold Warriors in the Hot Sunshine," 10; Weitz, "Bourbon, Pork Chops, and Red Peppers," 6. On the Johns Committee's investigation of the University of South Florida, see Bertwell, "A Veritable Refuge for Practicing Homosexuals," 410–31; Graves, "Confronting a 'Climate of Raucous and Carnival Invasion,'" 154–76; and Weitz, "Campus of Evil," 35–54.

124. Johns, recorded interview, 8. See also Daniel, *Lost Revolutions,* 156; *Miami Herald,* June 30, 1993; and *Pensacola News Journal,* July 1, 1993.

125. Florida Bureau of Archives and Records Management, *The Black Experience*, 45; FLIC, "Interim Report," Mar. 1964, 1, folder 7, box 145, Matthews Papers.

126. FLIC, "Report of the Florida Legislative Investigation Committee to the 1961 Session of the Legislature," 3; Bartley, *The New South*, 153, 221; Weitz, "Bourbon, Pork Chops, and Red Peppers." See also Florida Special Assistant Attorney General [Ellis S. Rubin], *Report on Investigation of Subversive Activities in Florida*, 7, folder: "Pamphlets," box 5, CR Records.

127. Schnur, "Cold Warriors in the Hot Sunshine," 13.

128. Tomberlin, "Florida and the School Desegregation Issue," 466; *Jackson County Floridan*, June 24, 2009.

129. *Gibson v. Florida Legislative Investigation Committee*, 372 U.S. 539 (1963).

130. "U.S. Supreme Court Clears Father Gibson," 292.

131. Egerton, *Speak Now against the Day*, 553–72.

CHAPTER SIX

1. Key, *Southern Politics in State and Nation*, 229.

2. Ibid.; Cash, *The Mind of the South*, xlviii . See also Watts, *One Homogeneous People*, xxix.

3. Bolton, *The Hardest Deal of All*, xix; Marshall, *Student Activism and Civil Rights in Mississippi*, 2.

4. Key, *Southern Politics in State and Nation*, 230.

5. Smith, *Congressman from Mississippi*, 276–77; Morris, *My Mississippi*, xi.

6. *Laws of the State of Mississippi*, 1956, regular sess., 715, 717, 752–53; "Legislative Acts: Mississippi," frame no. D3 200, roll no. 3, May 1954–June 1958, *FF;* "Editor Calls for 'Positive Thinking' in Mississippi Crisis," 3.

7. *Laws of the State of Mississippi*, 1956, regular sess., 741–44.

8. Ibid., 520–24, 744.

9. MSSC, "State Sovereignty Commission," typescript, n.d. [1959], record nos. 7–0–1–56–1–1–1 to 12–1–1, pp. 1–1–1 to 2–1–1, MSSC Records; Yasuhiro Katagiri, "Invoking State Sovereignty to Resist Federal Civil Rights Laws," in *States' Rights*, ed. Boduch, 103.

10. MSSC, "Report to the Mississippi State Legislature on Activities of the State Sovereignty Commission," n.d. [1959], record nos. 7–3–0–5–1–1–1 to 13–1–1, p. 8–1–1, MSSC Records; Katagiri, *The Mississippi State Sovereignty Commission*, 36–63.

11. *Journal of the Senate of the State of Mississippi*, 1958, regular sess., 174.

12. Ibid., 309.

13. MGLIC, *A Report by the General Legislative Investigating Committee to the Mississippi State Legislature*, 1, folder 4, box 3, Barrett Collection; Williams, "An Oral History with Mr. Kenneth O. Williams," 9–11; *Jackson (Miss.) State Times*, Nov. 22, 1959. The transcript of the author's oral history interview with Williams can be consulted online at Civil Rights in Mississippi Digital Archive, McCain Library, http://digilib.usm.edu/cdm/compoundobject/collection/coh/id/7857.

14. *Laws of the State of Mississippi*, 1958, regular sess., 1170; "Legislative Acts: Mississippi," frame no. D3 220, roll no. 3, May 1954–June 1958, *FF;* Crespino, *In Search of Another Country*, 55.

15. *Journal of the Senate of the State of Mississippi*, 1958, regular sess., 451, 707, 1188; *Laws of the State of Mississippi*, 1958, regular sess., 780; *Journal of the House of Representatives of the State of Mississippi*, 1958, regular sess., 1272–73.

16. *Jackson (Miss.) Daily News,* Mar. 8, 1958.

17. MSSC, "State Sovereignty Commission," p. 11–1–1.

18. MGLIC, *A Report to the 1962 Regular Session of the Mississippi State Legislature,* 4, box 72, Rainach Papers; MGLIC to the governor of the state of Mississippi and the members of the Mississippi legislature, untitled report, n.d. [1960], record nos. 6–7–0–85–1–1–1 to 3–1–1, p. 1–1–1, MSSC Records.

19. Carl McIntire, "J. B. Matthews" [introduction], in Matthews, *Communism in Our Churches,* 3, folder: "Pamphlets," box 5, CR Records.

20. Stanton A. Hall to W. M. Rainach, Mar. 1, 1957, folder 68, box 7; Rainach to Hall, Nov. 2, 1957, folder 68, box 7; Rainach to Joe T. Patterson [Mississippi attorney general], Nov. 2, 1957, folder 97, box 10, all in Rainach Papers; *Baton Rouge (La.) Morning Advocate,* Mar. 11, 1957; *Jackson State Times,* Nov. 20, 1959.

21. Stowe, "Willie Rainach and the Defense of Segregation in Louisiana," Ph.D. diss., 162.

22. J. B. Matthews to Russell L. Fox, Sept. 18, 1957, folder: "Circuit Riders, Inc.—Correspondence," box 14, Lowman Papers.

23. MSSC, "Report to the Mississippi State Legislature on Activities of the State Sovereignty Commission," p. 8–1–1; Cook, *The Ugly Truth about the NAACP,* 1, in both folder: "Association of Citizens' Councils: Folder 1," box 26, Cox Papers; and folder 24, box 2, McCain Collection.

24. Alabama Association of Methodist Ministers and Laymen, "The Birmingham Meeting," bulletin, n.d., 4, box 89, Lowman Papers; William H. Willimon, "A Very Brief History of Segregation in the Methodist Church in Birmingham," Apr. 4, 2005, Weekly Messages from Bishop Will Willimon, North Alabama Conference of the United Methodist Church, Birmingham, www.northalabamaumc.org/Willimon/willimon050404.html; Bartley, *The Rise of Massive Resistance,* 300. On the formation of the Association of Methodist Ministers and Laymen, see also Eskew, *But for Birmingham,* 109; Collins, *When the Church Bell Rang Racist,* 19–20; Harvey, *Freedom's Coming,* 237; and Andrew M. Manis, "'City Mothers': Dorothy Tilly, Georgia Methodist Women, and Black Civil Rights," in *Politics and Religion in White South,* ed. Feldman, 133–34.

25. Alabama Association of Methodist Ministers and Laymen, "The Birmingham Meeting," 2.

26. Crespino, *In Search of Another Country,* 60; Winter, "Division and Reunion in the Presbyterian Church, U.S."

27. Reiff, "Conflicting Convictions in White Mississippi Methodism," 165; Mississippi Association of Methodist Ministers and Laymen, *Information Bulletin,* Jan. 1959, record nos. 10–0–2–17–1–1–1 to 4–1–1, p. 4–1–1, MSSC Records.

28. Sparks, *Religion in Mississippi,* 234; Crespino, *In Search of Another Country,* 60; Charles Remsberg, "Behind the Cotton Curtain," Mississippi Freedom School Curriculum, ed. Kathy Emery, Education and Democracy, n.p., www.educationanddemocracy.org/FSCfiles/C_CC7g_BehindCottonCurtain.htm.

29. Crespino, *In Search of Another Country,* 60; McMillen, *The Citizens' Council,* 29; Ellis W. Wright, "Notice of Special Meeting," open letter to the Jackson Citizens' Council members, n.d. [Feb. 1959], record no. 9–11–1–7–1–1–1, MSSC Records. Though Sparks has maintained in his *Religion in Mississippi* that the Mississippi Association of Methodist Ministers and Laymen was initiated "through the sponsorship of the Circuit Riders, Inc.," it cannot be determined with precision, as far as the Myers G. Lowman Papers and the Circuit Riders, Inc., Records attest, if the Lowman-led Methodist group indeed financially helped the segregationist group when it was organized (see Sparks, *Religion in Mississippi,* 234).

30. Mississippi Association of Methodist Ministers and Laymen, *Information Bulletin,* p. 4-1-1.

31. Ross R. Barnett, "Address by Governor Ross R. Barnett to Statewide Citizens' Council Banquet, Columbia, South Carolina, January 29, 1960," 7, folder 38, box 2, McIlhenny Papers.

32. MGLIC, *A Report to the 1962 Regular Session of the Mississippi State Legislature,* 5; Stowe, "Willie Rainach and the Defense of Segregation in Louisiana," 162–63; Dugas Shands to GCE, Oct. 17, 1957, 1, folder: "Mississippi, Miscellaneous Correspondence," box 26, GCE Records.

33. MGLIC, *A Report to the 1962 Regular Session of the Mississippi State Legislature,* 5.

34. Zack J. Van Landingham [MSSC investigator] to MSSC director, "General Legislative Committee," memo, Sept. 18, 1959, record no. 6-7-0-1-1-1-1, MSSC Records; *Jackson State Times,* Nov. 18, 1959; *Memphis Commercial Appeal,* Nov. 19, 1959.

35. "Excerpts from the Deposition of James Meredith, June 8, 1961," Integrating Ole Miss: A Civil Rights Milestone, John F. Kennedy Presidential Library, Boston, www.jfklibrary.org/meredith/chron_miss_05.html.

36. *New Orleans Times-Picayune,* Nov. 19, 1959.

37. Ruth I. Matthews to W. J. Simmons, Oct. 21, 1959, folder: "Simmons, W. J., 1954–1963 and n.d.," box 680, Matthews Papers.

38. MSSC, "Classification—Cases," typescript, n.d., record no. 7-0-1-1-1-1-1; Zack J. Van Landingham to MSSC director, "Filing System," memo, n.d. [June 1959], record nos. 7-0-1-2-1-1-1 to 2-1-1, p. 2-1-1, both in MSSC Records.

39. MSSC, "State Sovereignty Commission," p. 12-1-1.

40. Van Landingham to MSSC director, "General Legislative Committee," memo, Sept. 18, 1959.

41. Zack J. Van Landingham to MSSC director, "General Legislative Investigating Committee," memo, Nov. 16, 1959, record no. 6-7-0-3-1-1-1, MSSC Records.

42. MGLIC to the governor of the state of Mississippi and the members of the Mississippi legislature, untitled report, n.d. [1960], p. 1-1-1; Katagiri, *The Mississippi State Sovereignty Commission,* 149.

43. MGLIC, *A Report to the 1962 Regular Session of the Mississippi State Legislature,* 5.

44. Ibid.; *Jackson (Miss.) Clarion-Ledger,* Nov. 19, 1959.

45. *Jackson Daily News,* Nov. 19, 1959; Nelson and Roberts, *The Censors and the Schools,* 90; *Jackson State Times,* Nov. 3, 1959.

46. Nelson and Roberts, *The Censors and the Schools,* 90; Edna Whitfield Alexander (Mrs. Harry A. Alexander) to "Dear Chapter Regent and National Defense Chairman," Apr. 22, 1961, record no. 2-41-0-40-2-1-1, MSSC Records.

47. *Jackson Daily News,* Nov. 19, 1959.

48. W. J. Simmons to Lee R. Pennington, Aug. 26, 1955; Pennington to J. B. Matthews, Sept. 1, 1955; Matthews to Simmons, Sept. 3, 1955, all in folder: "Simmons, W. J., 1954–1963 and n.d.," box 680, Matthews Papers.

49. W. J. Simmons to J. B. Matthews, Sept. 6, 1955, 1, folder: "Simmons, W. J., 1954–1963 and n.d.," box 680, Matthews Papers.

50. J. B. Matthews to W. J. Simmons, Sept. 12, 1955, folder: "Simmons, W. J., 1954–1963 and n.d.," box 680, Matthews Papers.

51. W. J. Simmons to Dr. and Mrs. J. B. Matthews, Mar. 18, 1957, folder: "Simmons, W. J., 1954–1963 and n.d.," box 680, Matthews Papers.

52. Ibid.

53. J. B. Matthews to W. J. Simmons, Mar. 24, 1957, folder: "Simmons, W. J., 1954–1963 and n.d.," box 680, Matthews Papers.

54. W. J. Simmons to J. B. Matthews, Sept. 13, 1957; Matthews to Simmons, Sept. 18, 1957, both in folder: "Simmons, W. J., 1954–1963 and n.d.," box 680, Matthews Papers.

55. W. J. Simmons to J. B. Matthews, Jan. 24, 1958; Matthews to Simmons, Feb. 6, 1958; Simmons to Matthews, Feb. 24, 1958, all in folder: "Simmons, W. J., 1954–1963 and n.d.," box 680, Matthews Papers.

56. W. J. Simmons to J. B. Matthews, Apr. 7, 1958, folder: "Simmons, W. J., 1954–1963 and n.d.," box 680, Matthews Papers.

57. *Jackson State Times,* Nov. 18, 1959.

58. MGLIC, *A Report to the 1962 Regular Session of the Mississippi State Legislature,* 14.

59. Ibid., 154; SECALC, untitled transcript of J. B. Matthews's testimony, n.d. [Dec. 17, 1958], 19, folder: "Matthews, John [*sic,* Joseph] B.," box 3, CR Records.

60. MGLIC, *A Report to the 1962 Regular Session of the Mississippi State Legislature,* 14, 17, 20.

61. *New Orleans Times-Picayune,* Nov. 19, 1959.

62. MGLIC, *A Report to the 1962 Regular Session of the Mississippi State Legislature,* 18, 143–44. On Mississippi segregationists' persecution of Beittel, see Katagiri, *The Mississippi State Sovereignty Commission,* 152–57.

63. *Jackson State Times,* Nov. 19, 1959; Waldron, *Hodding Carter,* 282.

64. *Jackson State Times,* Nov. 19, 1959.

65. MGLIC, *A Report to the 1962 Regular Session of the Mississippi State Legislature,* 12, 153; Bartley, *The Rise of Massive Resistance,* 188.

66. MGLIC, *A Report to the 1962 Regular Session of the Mississippi State Legislature,* 19.

67. *Jackson State Times,* Nov. 18, 1959.

68. MGLIC, *A Report to the 1962 Regular Session of the Mississippi State Legislature,* 185–92, 206–7, 237–38.

69. *Jackson Daily News,* Nov. 19, 1959.

70. Ibid.; *Jackson State Times,* Nov. 19, 1959; GCE, *Communism and the NAACP,* 2 vols., in both folder: "Lowman, Myers G., 1958," box 671, Matthews Papers; and folder 12, Welch Papers.

71. *Jackson State Times,* Nov. 19, 1959; GCE, *Highlander Folk School,* folder: "Churches, 1958," box 28, GCE Records. See also Alston and Dickerson, *Devil's Sanctuary,* 237.

72. Aaron E. Henry, "Statement Approved by Board of Directors as the Official Answer of the NAACP to Charges Filed by the Legislative Investigating Committee," Nov. 25, 1959, record nos. 6–7–0–48–1–1–1 to 2–1–1, p. 2–1–1, MSSC Records.

73. Henry and Curry, *Aaron Henry,* 77.

74. Egerton, "Delta Democrat," 23; Benjamin O. Sperry, "Walter Sillers and His Fifty Years inside Mississippi Politics," *Mississippi History Now,* Mississippi Historical Society, Jackson, http://mshistory.k12.ms.us/articles/356/walter-sillers-and-his-fifty-years-inside-mississippi-politics; *Jackson State Times,* Nov. 19, 1959; *Jackson Daily News,* Nov. 20, 1959; Waldron, *Hodding Carter,* 282; Crespino, *In Search of Another Country,* 56.

75. *Jackson Clarion-Ledger,* Nov. 24, 1959; Waldron, *Hodding Carter,* 282–83; Wroten, "An Oral History with Mr. Joseph E. Wroten," 12–14; MSSC, "State Sovereignty Commission Meeting, November 20, 1958," memo, record no. 7–0–1–23–1–1–1, MSSC Records; C. C. Smith, letter to the editor, *Jackson State Times,* Nov. 24, 1959.

76. MGLIC to the governor of the state of Mississippi and the members of the Mississippi legislature, untitled report, n.d. [1960], pp. 1–1–1 to 2–1–1.

77. M. G. Lowman to J. B. Matthews, Aug. 5, 1960, folder: "Lowman, Myers G., 1960," box 671, Matthews Papers.

78. MGLIC, *A Report to the 1962 Regular Session of the Mississippi State Legislature,* i–ii.

79. *Jackson Clarion-Ledger,* Nov. 24, 1959.

80. *Jackson State Times,* Nov. 3, 1959.

81. National Defense Committee of the National Society of the Daughters of the American Revolution, "Textbook Study, 1958–1959," typescript, n.d., folder: "Miscellaneous Leaflets," box 88, Lowman Papers.

82. Nelson and Roberts, *The Censors and the Schools,* 90, 96.

83. Lorayne W. Westbrook to Albert Jones, June 22, 1960, record no. 13–0–1–56–1–1–1, MSSC Records.

84. Lorayne W. Westbrook to Albert Jones, Mar. 14, 1961, record no. 7–0–3–123–1–1–1, MSSC Records.

85. Durr, "The Emancipation of Pure, White, Southern Womanhood"; Durr, *Outside the Magic Circle,* 45; Gillespie, *A Christian View on Segregation,* 3, folder 22, box 1, CC Collection (UM). On Gillespie, see Chappell, *A Stone of Hope,* 110–13; and McAtee, *Transformed,* 19.

86. *Chicago Defender,* Dec. 26, 1959.

87. Sansing, *The University of Mississippi,* 278. On Hooker, see Katagiri, *The Mississippi State Sovereignty Commission,* 67.

88. *Chicago Defender,* Dec. 26, 1959; *Jackson Clarion-Ledger,* Sept. 1, 1959.

89. Silver, *Running Scared,* 67.

90. University of Mississippi, "Reply to Allegations Concerning Certain Members of the Faculty and Staff of the University of Mississippi," typescript, n.d. [1959], record nos. 3–9–1–8–1–1–1 to 58–1–1, pp. 24–1–1 to 25–1–1, 36–1–1; Silver, *Running Scared,* 67; Sansing, *The University of Mississippi,* 278. See also Fox, "Cracking the Closed Society," master's thesis, 141.

91. Silver, *Mississippi;* Barrett, *Integration at Ole Miss.*

92. University of Mississippi, "Reply to Allegations Concerning Certain Members of the Faculty and Staff of the University of Mississippi," p. 38–1–1.

93. Sansing, *The University of Mississippi,* 279; *Jackson Daily News,* Aug. 27, 1959.

94. University of Mississippi, "Reply to Allegations Concerning Certain Members of the Faculty and Staff of the University of Mississippi," pp. 2–1–1, 5–1–1.

95. *Memphis Commercial Appeal,* July 25, 1959.

96. *Jackson Clarion-Ledger,* Aug. 28, 1959.

97. Ibid., Sept. 1, 1959.

98. Ibid.

99. *Jackson Daily News,* Oct. 27, 1959.

100. Ibid.; *New Orleans Times-Picayune,* Nov. 19, 1959.

101. Nelson and Roberts, *The Censors and the Schools,* 91; *New Orleans Times-Picayune,* Jan. 6, 1960.

102. Smith, *Congressman from Mississippi,* 269; MGLIC to the governor of the state of Mississippi and the members of the Mississippi legislature, untitled report, n.d. [1959], record nos. 6–7–0–66–1–1–1 to 48–1–1, p. 1–1–1, MSSC Records.

103. MGLIC to the governor of the state of Mississippi and the members of the Mississippi legislature, untitled report, n.d. [1959], pp. 1–1–1 to 2–1–1.

104. E. Merrill Root to J. B. Matthews, Dec. 14, 1952, folder 7, box 485, Matthews Papers; Root, *Collectivism on the Campus.*

105. E. Merrill Root to J. B. Matthews, May 24, 1953; Root to Matthews, Nov. 23, 1953, both in folder 7, box 485, Matthews Papers.

106. E. Merrill Root to J. B. Matthews, July 13, 1953, folder: "Clergy Incident, July 1953," box 696, Matthews Papers.

107. Root to Matthews, Nov. 23, 1953; J. B. Matthews to E. Merrill Root, Dec. 3, 1953, folder 7, box 485, Matthews Papers.

108. E. Merrill Root to J. B. Matthews, Nov. 15, 1958, 2, folder 7, box 485, Matthews Papers.

109. Ohio Coalition of Patriotic Societies, "Speakers Budget, Canton Seminar, 3–4 October 1953," n.d., folder: "Circuit Riders, Inc.—Correspondence," box 14, Lowman Papers.

110. Ohio Coalition of Patriotic Societies, "Seminar on Socialism and Communism," program, n.d. [Oct. 1953], box 87, Lowman Papers.

111. John Minott, "E. Merrill Root Papers: Biography," typescript, Dec. 1982, 2, folder: "Inventory," box 1, Root Papers; Thorton, "The Legacy of E. Merrill Root"; Nelson and Roberts, *The Censors and the Schools,* 59; Root, "The Murder of Scholarship," 136; "Books Worth Reading."

112. Root, *Brainwashing in the High Schools.*

113. Edna Whitfield Alexander (Mrs. Harry A. Alexander) to Albert Jones, Aug. 17, 1960, record nos. 97–99–2–292–2–1–1 to 3–1–1, p. 2–1–1; Jones to Vincent T. Purser [Citizens' Council member, Gulfport, Miss.], Nov. 2, 1960, record no. 9–11–1–56–1–1–1, both in MSSC Records.

114. Nelson and Roberts, *The Censors and the Schools,* 91.

115. MGLIC to the governor of the state of Mississippi and the members of the Mississippi legislature, untitled report, n.d. [1959], pp. 9–1–1, 13–1–1, 18–1–1, 25–1–1.

116. Ibid., pp. 48–1–1; *Memphis Commercial Appeal,* Jan. 6, 1960.

117. Nelson and Roberts, *The Censors and the Schools,* 77; Thorton, "The Legacy of E. Merrill Root"; Brenner, "Shouting at the Rain," Ph.D. diss., 195.

118. Nelson and Roberts, *The Censors and the Schools,* 93–95.

119. Ibid., 95; Lord, *The Past That Would Not Die,* 77–78; Huey, *Rebel with a Cause,* 151; Minor, *Eyes on Mississippi,* 8–9.

120. Katagiri, *The Mississippi State Sovereignty Commission,* 7–8. See also Bolton, "William F. Winter and the Politics of Racial Moderation in Mississippi," 335–82.

121. William F. Winter, "A Time for Thinking," speech before the Phi Delta Kappa Education Fraternity, Jackson, Miss., Mar. 19, 1964, in *The Measure of Our Days,* ed. Mullins, 141–43.

122. *Jackson State Times,* Nov. 19, 1959; Waldron, *Hodding Carter,* 282.

123. Ruth and J. B. Matthews to Becky and Bill Simmons, draft of Christmas greetings, Dec. 22, 1949 [*sic,* 1959], folder: "Simmons, W. J., 1959–1963 and n.d.," box 680, Matthews Papers.

124. *New York Herald Tribune,* Apr. 12, 1959; *New York Journal-American,* Apr. 12, 1959; *Washington Post,* Apr. 12, 1959; *Washington Daily News,* Apr. 13, 1959; Zack J. Van Landingham to "File," "Dr. J. B. Matthews," memo, Dec. 29, 1959, record no. 6–7–0–59–1–1–1, MSSC Records.

125. J. B. Matthews to George S. Benson, May 18, 1959, folder: "Harding College: National Education Program, 1951–1963," box 663, Matthews Papers.

126. *Washington Evening Star,* Apr. 14, 1959.

127. Matthews to Benson, May 18, 1959.

128. J. B. Matthews to Ruth E. Shallcross and Martin S. Matthews, May 26, 1960, folder: "Matthews, Martin: Correspondence to, 1950–1962," box 698, Matthews Papers.

129. "Myers G. Lowman," typed curriculum vitae prepared by Lowman, n.d. [1959], folder: "Lowman, Myers G., 1959," box 671, Matthews Papers.

130. M. G. Lowman to "Dear Mr. Congressman," Jan. 14, 1959, folder: "Lowman, Myers G., 1959," box 671, Matthews Papers.

131. Lesher, *George Wallace*, 97; Celler, *You Never Leave Brooklyn*, 172–73, 193.

132. "Emanuel Celler," typed tabulation, n.d., folder: "Lowman, Myers G., 1959," box 671, Matthews Papers.

133. Lowman to "Dear Mr. Congressman," Jan. 14, 1959.

134. Goodman, *The Committee*, 427.

135. Jim Wright to M. G. Lowman, Jan. 19, 1959, folder: "Lowman, Myers G., 1959," box 671, Matthews Papers.

136. Hugh F. Miller to Circuit Riders, May 21, 1959, folder: "Lowman, Myers G., 1959," box 671, Matthews Papers.

137. M. G. Lowman to J. B. Matthews, handwritten memo, May 25, 1959; Ruth Matthews to Lowman, June 15, 1959, both in folder: "Lowman, Myers G., 1959," box 671, Matthews Papers.

138. W. Walter Johnson to M. G. Lowman, June 18, 1959; Lowman to Johnson, n.d. [1959], both in folder: "Lowman, Myers G., 1959," box 671, Matthews Papers.

139. Religious Freedom Committee, "Is There a 'Black-List' of Protestant Ministers?: Read This!," flier, n.d. [1960], folder: "Lowman, Myers G., 1960," box 671, Matthews Papers.

140. Westwood Methodist Church, *Westwood Chimes* [church newsletter], May 24, 1960, n.p. [pp. 1–2], in the author's possession by courtesy of Stephen L. Bennett, senior pastor, Westwood United Methodist Church, Cincinnati, Ohio; Department of Christian Social Relations of the National Council of the Protestant Episcopal Church, "Sowing Dissension in the Churches: A Report on Some of the Individuals and Groups Engaged in Attacks on the Leadership of the Churches," typed report, n.d. [Mar. 1962], 16, folder 7, box 83, Matthews Papers.

141. M. G. Lowman, "Throwing Stones at the Person Who Sounds the Fire Alarm," typescript, Jan. 1961, 1, folder: "Circuit Riders," Garman Papers; Department of Christian Social Relations of the National Council of the Protestant Episcopal Church, "Sowing Dissension in the Churches," 17.

142. *Cincinnati Post and Times-Star,* May 7, 1960.

143. Lowman, "Throwing Stones at the Person Who Sounds the Fire Alarm," 1; Department of Christian Social Relations of the National Council of the Protestant Episcopal Church, "Sowing Dissension in the Churches," 17.

144. Department of Christian Social Relations of the National Council of the Protestant Episcopal Church, "Sowing Dissension in the Churches," 16.

145. Ross R. Barnett, "Inaugural Address of Governor Ross R. Barnett," *Journal of the House of Representatives of the State of Mississippi,* 1960, regular sess., 51.

146. James P. Coleman, "Inaugural Address of Governor James P. Coleman," *Journal of the House of Representatives of the State of Mississippi,* 1956, regular sess., 65. Coleman, as the governor in 1956, also said that "those who propose to mix the races in our public schools" might as well try to dry the Atlantic "with a teaspoon" (see "The Judiciary: Mississippi's Best").

147. Polk, *Outside the Southern Myth,* 98.

148. *Laws of the State of Mississippi,* 1960, regular sess., 76; Katagiri, *The Mississippi State Sovereignty Commission,* 65.

149. MSSC, meeting minutes, May 19, 1960, folder 2, box 135, Johnson Papers; untitled minutes [generated by the subsequently named Independent Women's Organization], May 28, 1960, record nos. 7–0–3–4–1–1–1 to 3–1–1, p. 1–1–1, MSSC Records.

150. Robert B. Patterson [secretary, Association of Citizens' Councils of Mississippi] to "All Officers and Members," "Women's Activities," memo, Dec. 30, 1957, folder: "Mississippi, Miscellaneous Correspondence," box 26, GCE Records.

151. McMillen, *The Citizens' Council,* 241.

152. Association of Citizens' Councils of Mississippi, *Statewide Cash Awards,* folder: "Association of Citizens' Councils: Folder 1," box 26, Cox Papers; LJLC, *Subversion in Racial Unrest,* 2 vols.; Cook, *The Ugly Truth about the NAACP;* Brady, *Black Monday.* See also Steve Estes, "A Question of Honor: Masculinity and Massive Resistance to Integration," in *White Masculinity in the Recent South,* ed. Watts, 109.

153. Untitled minutes [generated by the subsequently named Independent Women's Organization], May 28, 1960, p. 1–1–1; Black, *Southern Governors and Civil Rights,* 34; Johnston, *Politics,* 104–5, 121; Johnston, *Mississippi's Defiant Years,* 28; Bartley and Graham, comps., *Southern Elections,* 142; Katagiri, *The Mississippi State Sovereignty Commission,* 69.

154. Minute Women of the U.S.A., "The Minute Women of the United States of America, Inc.," prospectus, n.d., n.p. [pp. 1, 4], folder 2, box 752, reel no. 690, *NR* Records; Carleton, *Red Scare!,* 116.

155. Untitled minutes [generated by the subsequently named Independent Women's Organization], May 28, 1960, pp. 2–1–1 to 3–1–1; untitled organizational chart [generated by the subsequently named Independent Women's Organization], n.d., record no. 7–0–3–1–2–1–1; Independent Women's Organization, minutes, Dec. 8, 1960, record no. 7–0–3–2–1–1–1, both in MSSC Records.

156. Independent Women's Organization, minutes, Dec. 8, 1960.

157. Walter Sillers to Hugh V. Wall [attorney, Brookhaven, Miss.], Oct. 10, 1955, folder 2A, box 11, Sillers Papers; Independent Women's Organization/Paul Revere Ladies, minutes, Dec. 14, 1960, record nos. 7–0–3–2–2–1–1 to 3–1–1, MSSC Records.

158. Independent Women's Organization/Paul Revere Ladies, minutes, Dec. 14, 1960, p. 2–1–1.

159. Ibid.

160. Elizabeth Gillespie McRae, "White Womanhood, White Supremacy, and the Rise of Massive Resistance," in *Massive Resistance,* ed. Webb, 188.

161. Independent Women's Organization/Paul Revere Ladies, minutes, Dec. 14, 1960, p. 2–1–1.

162. Independent Women's Organization/Paul Revere Ladies, minutes, Dec. 15, 1960, record no. 7–0–3–2–3–1–1, MSSC Records.

163. Independent Women's Organization/Paul Revere Ladies, minutes, Dec. 14, 1960, p. 2–1–1.

164. Independent Women's Organization/Paul Revere Ladies, minutes, Dec. 15, 1960; *DeSoto (Miss.) Times-Tribune,* May 11, 2011.

165. Paul Revere Ladies, minutes, Jan. 4, 1961, record no. 7–0–3–1–1–1–1, MSSC Records.

166. *Jackson State Times,* n.d. [1961], record no. 7–0–3–87–1–1–1, MSSC Records.

167. Paul Revere Ladies, minutes, Jan. 4, 1961; MSSC, untitled press release, Jan. 8, 1961 [the first press release of the day], record no. 7–0–2–68–1–1–1, MSSC Records; *Jackson State Times,* Nov. 3, 1959.

168. Mrs. Harry Scrivner [Naomi Scrivner], "Report to Sovereignty Commission," typescript, Jan. 17, 1961, record nos. 7–0–2–82–1–1–1 to 2–1–1, p. 1–1–1, MSSC Records.

169. *Jackson State Times,* Jan. 16, 1961; *Jackson Daily News,* Jan. 16, 1961.

170. MSSC, untitled press release, Jan. 8, 1961 [the second press release of the day], record nos. 7-0-2-69-1-1-1 to 2-1-1, p. 1-1-1; MSSC, untitled press release, Jan. 11, 1961, record no. 7-0-2-70-1-1-1, both in MSSC Records; *Jackson Daily News,* Jan. 13, 1961.

171. MSSC, untitled press release, Jan. 8, 1961 [the second press release of the day], pp. 1-1-1 to 2-1-1; Scrivner, "Report to Sovereignty Commission," pp. 1-1-1 to 2-1-1.

172. Scrivner, "Report to Sovereignty Commission," p. 2-1-1.

173. Ibid.

174. Albert Jones to "File," "Myers G. Lowman's Speaking Engagements," memo, Feb. 19, 1961, record no. 7-0-3-78-1-1-1; MSSC, untitled press release, Feb. 19, 1961, record nos. 7-0-3-78-2-1-1 to 3-1-1, p. 3-1-1; Virgil Downing, "M. G. Lowman Speaking Engagements," report, Mar. 14, 1961, record nos. 7-0-3-79-1-1-1 to 2-1-1, all in MSSC Records.

175. Walter Sillers to Albert Jones, Jan. 9, 1961, record no. 7-0-2-39-1-1-1, MSSC Records; MSSC, untitled press release, Feb. 19, 1961, pp. 2-1-1 to 3-1-1.

176. MSSC, "State Sovereignty Commission," typescript, n.d., record nos. 7-0-1-56-1-1-1 to 12-1-1, p. 11-1-1, MSSC Records; Katagiri, *The Mississippi State Sovereignty Commission,* 38; Williamson, *Radicalizing the Ebony Tower,* 118. See also Walter Sillers to Hal DeCell [MSSC public relations director], Sept. 28, 1956, folder 4, box 5, Sillers Papers.

177. Zack J. Van Landingham to MSSC director, "Possible Negro Informants," memo, Aug. 28, 1959, record no. 9-0-0-45-1-1-1, MSSC Records; Katagiri, *The Mississippi State Sovereignty Commission,* 38–39; Williamson, *Radicalizing the Ebony Tower,* 117–18.

178. Virgil Downing, "Reverend Uriah J. Fields' Proposed Speaking Engagements at State Controlled Colored Colleges in Mississippi," investigative report, Sept. 27, 1963, record nos. 2-109-0-42-1-1-1 to 2-1-1, p. 2-1-1, MSSC Records.

179. Mrs. Harry Scrivner, untitled report, n.d., record nos. 7-0-3-80-1-1-1 to 5-1-1, p. 2-1-1, MSSC Records; Silver, *Running Scared,* 71; Eagles, *The Price of Defiance,* 172.

180. Scrivner, untitled report, pp. 2-1-1 to 3-1-1.

181. *Jackson State Times,* n.d. [1961], record no. 7-0-4-2-1-1-1, MSSC Records. On another occasion, Silver disgustedly termed Lowman's February 1961 speech at the University of Mississippi "the most anti-intellectual performance of the hundreds I have witnessed in Fulton Chapel since 1936" (see Silver, *Mississippi,* 218; and Crespino, *In Search of Another Country,* 59).

182. Silver, *Running Scared,* 71.

183. Ibid.; *Jackson State Times,* Mar. 4, 1961. See also Eagles, *The Price of Defiance,* 172; Slade, *Open Friendship in a Closed Society,* 32–33; and Winter, "Opening the Closed Society," panel discussion, http://blip.tv/mcast/opening-the-closed-society-5619377, online video.

184. Katagiri, *The Mississippi State Sovereignty Commission,* 128–30.

185. MSSC, untitled press release, Jan. 8, 1961 [the first press release of the day].

186. Harned, "An Oral History with Mr. Horace H. Harned Jr.," 13; Harned, letter to the author, Dec. 30, 1994; Harned to MSSC director, Feb. 28, 1961, record nos. 7-0-3-81-1-1-1 to 2-1-1, MSSC Records. The transcript of the author's oral history with Harned can be read online at Civil Rights in Mississippi Digital Archive, McCain Library, http://digilib.usm.edu/cdm/compoundobject/collection/coh/id/3056.

187. Gordon H. Scherer to Albert Jones, Western Union telegram, Mar. 2, 1961, record nos. 7-0-3-84-1-1-1 to 2-1-1, p. 1-1-1, MSSC Records.

188. Albert Jones to Horace H. Harned Jr., Mar. 3, 1961, 7-0-3-82-1-1-1 to 2-1-1, p. 1-1-1, MSSC Records.

189. MSSC, untitled expenditure list for December 1960, record no. 97–6–0–1–85–1–1; MSSC, untitled expenditure list for January 1961, record no. 97–6–0–1–89–1–1; MSSC, untitled expenditure list for February 1961, record no. 97–6–0–1–95–1–1; MSSC, untitled expenditure list for March 1961, record no. 97–6–0–1–97–1–1; MSSC, requisition, Feb. 28, 1961, record nos. 97–99–1–254–1–1–1, 97–99–1–255–1–1–1; MSSC, requisition, Mar. 6, 1961, record no. 97–99–1–232–1–1–1; "State Paying for Anti-Red Lectures," unidentifiable newspaper, n.d. [1961], record no. 7–0–3–135–2–1–1; Albert Jones to Tom Lee Gibson [Mississippi state representative], Mar. 20, 1961, record no. 7–0–3–136–1–1–1, all in MSSC Records; "Lowman Pay Revealed," unidentifiable newspaper, n.d. [Feb. 1961], folder 200.91, box 20, Satterfield Collection.

190. *New Orleans Times-Picayune,* Mar. 5, 1961.

191. *DeSoto Times-Tribune,* May 11, 2011; Jones to Harned, Mar. 3, 1961, p. 1–1–1.

192. *Jackson State Times,* n.d. [1961], record no. 7–0–3–87–1–1–1, MSSC Records.

193. MSSC, untitled press release, n.d. [Apr. 1961?], record no. 7–0–4–31–1–1–1, MSSC Records.

194. MSSC, untitled expenditure list for April 1961, record no. 97–6–0–1–103–1–1; MSSC, requisition, Apr. 20, 1961, record no. 97–99–1–144–1–1–1, both in MSSC Records.

195. MSSC, untitled press release, n.d. [Apr. 1961?].

196. *Clarksdale (Miss.) Press-Register,* Apr. 21, 1961.

197. *Jackson Clarion-Ledger,* Nov. 24, 1959.

198. Ibid., Mar. 13, 1961; Wroten, "An Oral History with Mr. Joseph E. Wroten," 24. See also *Jackson State Times,* Mar. 4, 1961; and Wroten, "Interview with Joseph E. Wroten," 24.

199. *Jackson Clarion-Ledger,* Mar. 13, 1961.

200. John W. Moore to Tom Lee Gibson, Jan. 9, 1962, record no. 2–30–0–39–1–1–1, MSSC Records.

201. John W. Moore, "Communism in the Methodist Church: An Address Delivered to the Congregation of First Methodist Church, Brookhaven, Mississippi, on Sunday Morning, June 4, 1961," typescript, record nos. 2–30–0–40–1–1–1 to 12–1–1, pp. 1–1–1 to 2–1–1, MSSC Records.

202. Ibid., pp. 1–1–1 to 3–1–1, 5–1–1.

203. Ibid., pp. 6–1–1, 8–1–1 to 9–1–1.

204. Ibid., pp. 7–1–1, 10–1–1.

205. Ibid., p. 10–1–1.

206. Myers G. Lowman, "The Right to Know," open letter, May 4, 1961, record nos. 7–0–4–42–1–1–1 to 3–1–1, p. 2–1–1, MSSC Records.

207. Ross R. Barnett to M. G. Lowman, May 17, 1961, record no. 7–0–4–41–1–1–1, MSSC Records.

208. Barnett, "Address by Governor Ross R. Barnett to Statewide Citizens' Council Banquet," 7.

CHAPTER SEVEN

1. *Jackson (Miss.) Daily News,* Apr. 14, 1964; Dittmer, *Local People,* 87–89.

2. Katagiri, *The Mississippi State Sovereignty Commission,* 153–57; MGLIC, *A Report to the 1962 Regular Session of the Mississippi State Legislature,* 18, 143–44, box 72, Rainach Papers.

3. Salter, *Jackson, Mississippi;* O'Brien, *We Shall Not Be Moved.*

4. Williamson, *The Crucible of Race.*

5. Schlesinger, *Robert Kennedy and His Times,* 299; Reeves, *President Kennedy,* 134; Strober and Strober, *"Let Us Begin Anew,"* 299. See also Dudziak, *Cold War Civil Rights,* 159; Borstelmann, *The Cold War and the Color Line,* 159; and Wofford, *Of Kennedys and Kings,* 125.

6. Schlesinger, *Robert Kennedy and His Times,* 299; Guthman and Shulman, eds., *Robert Kennedy in His Own Words,* 96–97; Marshall, recorded interview, 22.

7. Bernstein, *Promises Kept,* 67.

8. *Boynton v. Virginia,* 364 U.S. 454 (1960).

9. Williams, *Eyes on the Prize,* 159; Minor, "A Poignant Summer Reunion," 57; Peck, "Not So Deep Are the Roots," 330.

10. *Freedom Riders,* DVD; Faulkner, *The Mansion,* 53.

11. *Jackson Daily News,* June 23, 1961.

12. Arsenault, *Freedom Riders,* 348.

13. Naomi Scrivner to Wilburn Hooker [Mississippi state representative and MSSC member], July 22, 1961, 2, folder: "Circuit Riders, Inc.—Correspondence," box 14, Lowman Papers.

14. MSSC, "Freedom Riders through July 6, 1961," typed list, n.d. [1961], record nos. 2–144–0–1–1–1 to 9–1–1, MSSC Records.

15. Mrs. Harry Scrivner [Naomi Scrivner], "Report to Sovereignty Commission," typescript, Jan. 17, 1961, record nos. 7–0–2–82–1–1–1 to 2–1–1, p. 2–1–1, MSSC Records. As the research clerk of the Mississippi State Sovereignty Commission, Scrivner also led the commission's "Education and Information Program"—or what the pro-segregation state agency somewhat affectionately called "Mrs. Scrivner's project." Organizationally put under the supervision of the State Sovereignty Commission's Public Relations Department overseen by Johnston, her project had received a total of some $6,000 during the period between July 1, 1960, and December 31, 1961, under the administration of Governor Barnett for the purposes of gathering various pamphlets, magazines, and other printed material "in the subversive field"—including those put out by Lowman's Circuit Riders—as well as showing the poorly edited 16-mm documentary film, *Operation Abolition,* before a host of "patriotic groups" throughout the state. The forty-minute documentary, which depicted the anti-HUAC demonstrations—"the longtime, classic Communist tactics" according to the committee chair, Representative Francis Walter—aimed at the House committee's May 1960 public hearings in San Francisco, was put together from the committee-subpoenaed newsreels and was sensationally narrated by Fulton Lewis Jr., a right-wing radio and television broadcaster. Through a Washington, D.C.–based film production company, the HUAC sold copies of *Operation Abolition* at a price of $100 per reel. Among some of the other responsibilities given to "Mrs. Scrivner's project," the most frightening undertaking was its quasi-book-burning operation. "Upon request," as one of the agency's internal reports indicated, a number of books—textbooks and novels alike—were "screened" by the State Sovereignty Commission to "ascertain whether or not Communism is really treated in its true form" in those publications. And to each one of those books approved by the state agency, Scrivner attached a small sheet of paper stating: "Clearly defines and points out the evils of Communism" (see MSSC, "Education and Information Program," typed report, Aug. 1960, record nos. 7–3–0–9–1–1–1 to 2–1–1; Albert Jones [MSSC director] to Washington Video Productions, Inc., Mar. 10, 1961, record no. 7–0–3–98–1–1–1; Jones, "To the Members of the State Sovereignty Commission, and to the Senate and House of Representatives of the State of Mississippi," typed report, n.d. [1962], record nos. 7–3–0–12–1–1–1 to 7–1–1, pp. 4–1–1, 6–1–1, all in MSSC Records; MSSC,

untitled expenditure list, n.d., folder 10, box 135, Johnson Papers; *Jackson Daily News*, Mar. 4, 1961; *Jackson Daily News*, May 19, 1961; "The Investigation: Operation Abolition"; and U.S. Congress, House, Committee on Un-American Activities, *The Truth about the Film "Operation Abolition,"* 1–4).

16. *Montgomery (Ala.) Advertiser,* Mar. 26, 1961.

17. *Jackson Daily News,* June 29, 1961; *Jackson (Miss.) Clarion-Ledger,* June 30, 1961.

18. *Jackson Daily News,* July 1, 1961.

19. R. J. Strickland to A. L. Hopkins [MSSC investigator], June 27, 1961, record nos. 2–55–3–30–1–1–1 to 2–1–1, MSSC Records.

20. *Jackson Clarion-Ledger,* June 30, 1961.

21. Walter Sillers [Mississippi House Speaker] to Fred Jones, June 7, 1950, folder 2A, box 13, Sillers Papers; McMillen, *The Citizens' Council,* 21, 209; "Mississippi: The Reformer"; *Jackson Daily News,* July 3, 1961.

22. W. J. Simmons to Mrs. J. B. Matthews, June 21, 1961, folder: "Simmons, W. J., 1954–1963 and n.d.," box 680, Matthews Papers. Simmons's sarcasm was matched by the one expanded by the combative editor of the pro-segregation *Jackson Daily News,* James M. "Jimmy" Ward, who often referred to the Freedom Riders as the "Friction Riders" deployed by CORE—the "Congress of Riot Encouragement." Celebrating the one-month anniversary of the initial arrival of the Freedom Riders at Jackson, Ward ran a "facetious editorial" on June 24, 1961, for "the benefit of potential 'tourist' traffic from the North and East." Boasting that Parchman was an ideal place to "HAVE A 'VACATION' ON A REAL PLANTATION," the editorial, with a dark sense of humor, read in part: "ATTENTION: RESTLESS RACE MIXERS Whose Hobby is Creating Trouble. . . . Buy yourself a Southbound ticket. . . . Check in and sign the guest register at the Jackson City Jail. Pay a nominal fine of $200. Then spend the next 4 months at our 21,000-acre Parchman Plantation. . . . Meals furnished. Enjoy the wonders of chopping cotton, warm sunshine. . . . Sun lotion, bunion plasters, as well as medical service free. Experience the 'abundant' life under total socialism. Parchman prison fully air-cooled by Mother Nature" (see "The Press: Mississippi's Voice"; and editorial, *Jackson Daily News,* June 24, 1961).

23. Ruth I. Matthews to W. J. Simmons, June 26, 1961, folder: "Simmons, W. J., 1954–1963 and n.d.," box 680, Matthews Papers.

24. Citizens' Council Forum, untitled press release, July 12, 1961, record nos. 9–11–1–72– 1–1–1 to 3–1–1, p. 1–1–1, MSSC Records.

25. W. F. Minor, "The Citizens' Councils: An Incredible Decade of Defiance," typescript, n.d., folder: "Citizens' Council," box 2, Minor Papers. See also W. J. Simmons to "Dear Broadcaster," n.d. [1959], folder 6, box 41, subseries A, series I, Vandiver Papers.

26. Citizens' Council Forum, untitled press release, July 12, 1961, pp. 1–1–1 to 3–1–1. On Patterson's conviction that the Freedom Riders were "agitating riders" sponsored by the Soviet Union and trained in Cuba, see Luckett, "Yapping Dogs," Ph.D. diss., 165.

27. *Jackson Daily News,* Aug. 1, 1961.

28. Editorial, *Greenville (Miss.) Delta Democrat-Times,* Nov. 1, 1961.

29. *Vicksburg (Miss.) Sunday Post,* Nov. 12, 1961.

30. Circuit Riders, "The People Have the Right to Know," seminar advertisement, n.d. [Aug. 1963], folder: "Lowman, Myers G., 1963, 1964, and n.d.," box 671, Matthews Papers.

31. Patriotic American Youth, "Facts We Would Like to Have You Know," pamphlet, n.d., record nos. 10–104–0–15–1–1–1 to 3–1–1, p. 2–1–1, MSSC Records.

32. Patriotic American Youth, *PAY DAY,* Nov. 1961, record nos. 10–104–0–1–1–1–1 to 16–1–1, pp. 2–1–1, 8–1–1, MSSC Records.

33. Albert Jones to Ross Barnett, May 4, 1962, record no. 10–104–0–10–1–1–1; Jones to Walter Sillers, May 4, 1962, record no. 10–104–0–13–1–1–1; Jones to Wilburn Hooker, May 4, 1962, record no. 10–104–0–9–1–1–1; Erle Johnston Jr. to "File," "Patriotic American Youth," memo, Nov. 20, 1964, record no. 10–104–0–19–1–1–1, all in MSSC Records.

34. Wroten, "Implications of the Violence at Oxford," 5, record nos. 10–86–0–24–1–1–1 to 3–1–1, p. 3–1–1, MSSC Records; *Memphis Commercial Appeal,* June 19, 1962; *Memphis Commercial Appeal,* July 2, 1962.

35. M. G. Lowman, "For Publication as Letter to the Editor," typescript, June 15, 1962, folder: "Circuit Riders Literature (1958–71)," box 1, CR Records; Crespino, *In Search of Another Country,* 63.

36. O. Gerald Trigg, letter to editor, *Jackson Clarion-Ledger,* June 26, 1962.

37. *Memphis Commercial Appeal,* July 2, 1962.

38. M. G. Lowman, untitled press release, July 2, 1962, folder: "Lowman, Myers G., 1962," box 671, Matthews Papers.

39. *Wilmington (N.C.) News,* July 31, 1962; *Jackson Clarion-Ledger,* July 31, 1962.

40. M. G. Lowman, "Editorial Comment," typescript [appeared in a blank space on a reproduced document entitled "Committee on the Judiciary, United States Senate, Eighty-Third Congress, Second Session, on Subversive Influence in Southern Conference Educational Fund, Inc."], n.d. [1962], folder: "Lowman, Myers G., 1962," box 671, Matthews Papers. See also Cunningham, *Agony at Galloway,* 8.

41. Editorial, *Madison County (Miss.) Herald,* July 19, 1962.

42. Ibid.

43. Meredith, "An Oral History with James Howard Meredith," 14. The original version of the transcript of the author's oral history interview with Meredith (entitled "'For Me and My Kind': An Oral History with Mr. James H. Meredith") can be consulted at MDAH (call no. OS/B/M559me); and Special Collections Department, Mitchell Memorial Library, Mississippi State University, Mississippi State (call no. E185.61.M55 1995). The transcript was later published as Meredith and Katagiri, *"Me and My Kind."*

44. Ross R. Barnett, "A Statewide Address on Television and Radio to the People of Mississippi by Governor Ross R. Barnett, 7:30 P.M., September 13, 1962," in both folder 50, box 2, Toler Papers; and folder "Barnett, Ross—Miscellaneous, 1962–1963," Godwin Collection; Barnett, oral statement reported by Paul Cunningham, www.nbclearn.com/portal/site/learn/finishing-the-dream/1962–1963-standoffs, online video; Ransone, "Political Leadership in the Governor's Office," 214; *Gadsden (Ala.) Times,* Sept. 30, 1962; John F. Kennedy, "Radio and Television Report to the Nation on the Situation at the University of Mississippi," Sept. 30, 1962, in *Public Papers of the Presidents of the United States: John F. Kennedy, 1962,* 727–28.

45. Pauley, *The Modern Presidency and Civil Rights,* 212; Katagiri, "Let the Word Go Forth," 276–77.

46. Sorensen, *Kennedy,* 547.

47. Guthman, *We Band of Brothers,* 181.

48. Transcript of telephone conversation between Attorney General Robert Kennedy and Mississippi Governor Ross Barnett, 12:20 P.M., September 25, 1962, folder 12, box 20, Marshall Papers; Hendrickson, *Sons of Mississippi,* 141; Katagiri, *The Mississippi State Sovereignty Commission,* 114–15. On the Kennard incident at Mississippi Southern College, see "Kennard

Plans to 'Devote Rest of My Life' to Improving Miss.," 20–22; Katagiri, *The Mississippi State Sovereignty Commission,* 55–61, 127–28; Katagiri, "But the People Aren't Going to Know It, Are They?," 84–95; Williams, *Medgar Evers,* 163–69; Minchin and Salmond, "The Saddest Story of the Whole Movement," 191–234; and *Student Printz* [student newspaper, University of Southern Mississippi, Hattiesburg], Apr. 26, 2010.

49. Doar, Katzenbach, and Goldin, "John F. Kennedy and Civil Rights," panel discussion, wws.princeton.edu/webmedia, webcast.

50. Sorensen, *Kennedy,* 552; Bernstein, *Promises Kept,* 96.

51. Frederick, *Stand Up for Alabama,* 16; "Nation: What You Believe In"; George C. Wallace, "The 1963 Inaugural Address of Governor George C. Wallace," Jan. 14, 1963, Alabama Governors: George Corley Wallace, Alabama Department of Archives and History, Montgomery, www.archives.state.al.us/govs_list/inauguralspeech.html; "Episode 4: No Easy Walk (1961–63)," in *Eyes on the Prize* series, videocassette.

52. Clark, *The Schoolhouse Door,* 154.

53. Woods, *Black Struggle, Red Scare,* 170.

54. Carter, *The Politics of Rage,* 124.

55. Greenhaw, *Fighting the Devil in Dixie,* 101.

56. ALCPP, "Biennial Report to the Alabama Legislature," June 1965, 4, folder 1, container SG21073, ALCPP Records.

57. Ibid., 3–4; C. Edwin Strickland [ALCPP staff director] to "Dear Commission Member," Mar. 22, 1971, 1, folder 12, container SG21074, ALCPP Records.

58. ALCPP, "Biennial Report to the Alabama Legislature," n.p. [title page], 4; Carter, *The Politics of Rage,* 125, 230; Woods, *Black Struggle, Red Scare,* 171; Raines, *My Soul Is Rested,* 174; Rogers et al., *Alabama,* 563.

59. ALCPP, "Biennial Report to the Alabama Legislature," n.p. [title page]; "Commending Speaker James S. Clark for His Distinguished Service to the State of Alabama," House Joint Resolution № 2, 1999, regular sess., Alabama Legislature website, Alabama State Legislature, Montgomery, www.legislature.state.al.us/SearchableInstruments/1999os/Resolutions/HJR2 .htm; Permaloff and Grafton, *Political Power in Alabama,* 217.

60. Carter, *The Politics of Rage,* 231–32; ALCPP, "Biennial Report to the Alabama Legislature," 2.

61. ALCPP, "Biennial Report to the Alabama Legislature," 3–5, 22; Strickland to "Dear Commission Member," Mar. 22, 1971, 1; Edwin Strickland to Harold Martin [publisher, *Montgomery (Ala.) Advertiser-Journal*], Jan. 5, 1973, 1, folder 13, container SG21074, ALCPP Records.

62. Edwin Strickland to Robert Kennedy, Oct. 10, 1962, folder 1, container SG21074, ALCPP Records.

63. Ed Strickland to George C. Wallace, Mar. 8, 1965, 2, ADAH Digital Archives, Alabama Department of Archives and History, Montgomery, http://216.226.178.196/cdm4/item_viewer. php?CISOROOT=/voices&CISOPTR=2892&CISOBOX=1&REC=11.

64. Applebome, *Dixie Rising,* 99; George C. Wallace, "Statement and Proclamation of Governor George C. Wallace, University of Alabama," June 11, 1963, Governor George C. Wallace's School House Door Speech, Alabama Department of Archives and History, www .archives.state.al.us/govs_list/schooldoor.html.

65. *Kennedy vs. Wallace,* videocassette; Hood, Katzenbach , Sorensen, and Crossley, "The Civil Rights Movement and Integrating the University of Alabama," www.c-span.org/Events/ The-Civil-Rights-Movement-Integrating-the-University-of-Alabama/10737422142-1, online

video; Kuettner, *March to a Promised Land,* 54. To be sure, seven years earlier in February 1956, Autherine J. Lucy had become the first black student to be enrolled at the University of Alabama, taking the courageous first steps toward desegregating the all-white institution. However, due to significant unrest on campus, Lucy's hard-earned enrollment lasted only three days (see "South Worries over Miss Lucy," 28–32).

66. Schlesinger, *Robert Kennedy and His Times,* 325.

67. John F. Kennedy, "Radio and Television Report to the American People on Civil Rights," June 11, 1963, in *Public Papers of the Presidents of the United States: John F. Kennedy, 1963,* 469.

68. John F. Kennedy, "Special Message to the Congress on Civil Rights and Job Opportunities," June 19, 1963, in *Public Papers of the Presidents of the United States: John F. Kennedy, 1963,* 494.

69. "Civil Rights: Timeline, 1963," CongressLink, Dirksen Congressional Center, Pekin, Ill., www.congresslink.org/civilrights/1963.htm.

70. Graham, *Civil Rights and the Presidency,* 61; Lesher, *George Wallace,* 242; Carter, *The Politics of Rage,* 160.

71. "Civil Rights: Timeline, 1963"; Graham, *Civil Rights and the Presidency,* 61.

72. John F. Kennedy, "The President's News Conference of July 17, 1963," in *Public Papers of the Presidents of the United States: John F. Kennedy, 1963,* 574; Bartley, *The Rise of Massive Resistance,* 213, 221; Jacoway, *Turn Away Thy Son,* 279.

73. *Boston Globe,* July 13, 1963; Graham, *Civil Rights and the Presidency,* 61; "The Press: Petulant Plea"; Kilpatrick, *The Sovereign States;* Kilpatrick, *The Southern Case for School Segregation;* Hustwit, "From Caste to Color Blindness," 650–55. See also Roberts and Klibanoff, *The Race Beat,* 119; and King and Kilpatrick, debate moderated by John K. M. McCaffery, www.nbclearn.com/portal/site/learn/finishing-the-dream/1960–1962-freedom-fighters, online video.

74. *Meriden-Wallingford (Conn.) Morning Record,* Aug. 1, 1963; Graham, *Civil Rights and the Presidency,* 61.

75. Barnett, *Ross R. Barnett, Governor of State of Mississippi, before the Commerce Committee of the United States Senate,* record nos. 99–69–0–12–1–1–1 to 9–1–1, pp. 2–1–1 to 3–1–1, 9–1–1, MSSC Records; King, recorded interview. On Barnett's inflammatory testimony, see also "1963 Year in Review—Part 1: March on Washington," UPI Radio: Year in Review, UPI, Washington, D.C., www.upi.com/Audio/Year_in_Review/Events-of-1963/March-on-Washington/12295509434394–5.

76. *New York Times,* July 13, 1963. See also Barnett, "Oral History Interview with Ross R. Barnett," 3; and *Jackson Clarion-Ledger,* July 13, 1963.

77. Raines, *My Soul Is Rested,* 395.

78. Alert Americans Association [La.], "Martin Luther King at Communist Training School" [reprint of *Augusta (Ga.) Courier,* July 8, 1963], record no. 3–85–0–2–1–1–1, MSSC Records.

79. Raines, *My Soul Is Rested,* 395; Barnett, "Oral History Interview with Ross R. Barnett," 3; *Albert Lea (Minn.) Sunday Tribune,* July 14, 1963.

80. U.S. Congress, Senate, Select Committee to Study Governmental Operations with Respect to Intelligence Activities, *Supplementary Detailed Staff Reports on Intelligence Activities and the Rights of Americans,* COINTELPRO, ed. Paul Wolf, n.p., www.icdc.com/~paulwolf/cointelpro/churchfinalreportIIIb.htm; *New York Times,* July 13, 1963. In his rare oral history interview conducted in the late 1960s, Barnett talked about his appearance before the Senate

Commerce Committee in a disgruntled manner, mentioning that "the selfish and greedy liberal politicians" in Congress "tried to please the minority groups" by selling out the white South's "heritage and . . . traditions" (see Barnett, "Oral History Interview with Ross R. Barnett," 7).

81. *Washington Post,* Sept. 14, 1998; *New York Times,* July 16, 1963; "Civil Rights: With George and Sam on Capitol Hill"; Lesher, *George Wallace,* 243; Carter, *The Politics of Rage,* 157–58.

82. *New York Times,* July 16, 1963.

83. Ibid.; Carter, *The Politics of Rage,* 158.

84. *New York Times,* July 16, 1963.

85. Ibid.; Reed, *Faubus,* 102–7, 115–16.

86. *New York Times,* July 16, 1963; *Lodi (Calif.) News-Sentinel,* July 17, 1963.

87. *Lodi News-Sentinel,* July 17, 1963; "History of Arkansas' Attorney General," About the Office, Arkansas Attorney General's Office, Little Rock, www.ag.state.ar.us/about_office_history. html; SECALC, "Hearing before the Special Education Committee of the Arkansas Legislative Council," summary, Dec. 16–18, 1958, 1, folder 46, box 5, ACHR Records.

88. Carter, *The Politics of Rage,* 160.

89. Kennedy, "The President's News Conference of July 17, 1963," 574.

90. *New York Times,* July 26, 1963; "RFK Says Mixers Not Communists," *Jackson Clarion-Ledger* [?], July 26, 1963 [?], folder: "Circuit Riders Literature (1958–71)," box 1, CR Records; O'Rcilly, *"Racial Matters,"* 151.

91. Katagiri, *The Mississippi State Sovereignty Commission,* 67, 109–10.

92. Luckett, "Yapping Dogs," Ph.D. diss., 235–57; John C. McLaurin, "Testimony of Senator John C. McLaurin of Mississippi before the Senate Commerce Committee, Wednesday, July 31, 1963," typescript, record nos. 99–94–0–1–1–1 to 16–1–1, p. 2–1–1, MSSC Records; *Boston Globe,* Aug. 1, 1963; *Meriden-Wallingford Morning Record,* Aug. 1, 1963.

93. GCE, *Communism and the NAACP,* 2 vols., in both folder: "Lowman, Myers G., 1958," box 671, Matthews Papers; and folder 12, Welch Papers; McLaurin, "Testimony of Senator John C. McLaurin," pp. 4–1–1 to 6–1–1, 13–1–1. In sharp contrast to Barnett, Wallace, and McLaurin, Atlanta mayor Ivan E. Allen Jr., a former president of the city's chamber of commerce, appeared before the Senate committee as the sole southern official to testify in favor of the civil rights legislation. In confronting Allen with frustration, the committee member Thurmond implied that the progressive-minded Atlanta mayor was a pawn of "a bunch of leftwingers who favor this bill" (see Kruse, *White Flight,* 205–6; and *Atlanta Journal-Consti tution,* Aug. 26, 2006).

94. *New York Times,* July 16, 1963.

95. John C. Satterfield and M. G. Lowman to Harold H. Velde [HUAC chair], Western Union telegram [confirmation copy], Mar. 12, 1953, folder 5, box 83, Matthews Papers; *Houston (Tex.) Post,* Nov. 3, 1953. Elected to the presidency of the influential American Bar Association in August 1961, Satterfield, during the University of Mississippi desegregation crisis, became one of Governor Barnett's legal advisors. And later, when the Mississippi General Legislative Investigating Committee prepared the state's "official" report on the Ole Miss riots, Satterfield served as the pro-segregation committee's counsel (see Katagiri, *The Mississippi State Sovereignty Commission,* 123).

96. Erle Johnston Jr. to Ross Barnett and all members of the Sovereignty Commission, "Conferences in Washington, D.C.," memo, June 27, 1963, 1, folder 3, box 135, Johnson Pa-

pers. See also John C. Satterfield to Palmer Lipscomb [office of U.S. senator James Eastland, Washington, D.C.], June 28, 1963, record nos. 99–51–0–34–1–1–1 to 3–1–1, MSSC Records.

97. Johnston to Barnett and all members of the Sovereignty Commission, "Conferences in Washington, D.C.," 1–3.

98. Coordinating Committee for Fundamental American Freedoms, "An Analysis of 'the Civil Rights Act of 1963,'" n.d. [1963], vertical file: "Sovereignty Commission, Mississippi State," McCain Library.

99. Coordinating Committee for Fundamental American Freedoms, "Collection of Material Concerning Formation and Activities of the Coordinating Committee for Fundamental American Freedoms in Opposition to the Civil Rights Act of 1963," memo, n.d., 1, folder 4, box 135, Johnson Papers. See also Branch, *Pillar of Fire*, 241.

100. William Loeb to J. B. Matthews, Aug. 6, 1954, folder: "Loeb, William, 1954–1958," box 670, Matthews Papers.

101. Coordinating Committee for Fundamental American Freedoms, "Collection of Material Concerning Formation and Activities of the Coordinating Committee for Fundamental American Freedoms," 1.

102. Erle Johnston Jr. to John U. Barr [executive committee chair, Federation for Constitutional Government, New Orleans, La.], May 4, 1964, record nos. 6–70–0–165–1–1–1 to 2–1–1, p. 1–1–1, MSSC Records.

103. "Civil Rights: The Apologist"; Coordinating Committee for Fundamental American Freedoms, "Collection of Material Concerning Formation and Activities of the Coordinating Committee for Fundamental American Freedoms," 1–2; *New York Times*, Nov. 4, 1963. See also Orr-Klopfer, *Where Rebels Roost*, 421–22.

104. MSSC, "Brief Summary of Activities of the Coordinating Committee for Fundamental American Freedoms," n.d. [1964], folder 8, box 135, Johnson Papers; *Jackson Daily News*, Apr. 25, 1964.

105. *Montgomery Advertiser*, Aug. 21, 1963.

106. Woods, *Black Struggle, Red Scare*, 172; Carter, *The Politics of Rage*, 233.

107. *Birmingham (Ala.) News*, Apr. 5, 1964; Clark, *The Schoolhouse Door*, 202; Erle Johnston Jr. to Paul B. Johnson Jr. [Mississippi governor] and all members of the Sovereignty Commission, "Report of Principal Activities and Policies from January 1, 1964, through August 31, 1964," memo, Sept. 1, 1964, 3, folder 4, box 136, Johnson Papers.

108. Lesher, *George Wallace*, 202.

109. *Birmingham News*, Feb. 28, 1964.

110. ASSC, meeting minutes, Jan. 3, 1964, folder 5, container SG13842, ASSC Records.

111. Citizens' Council Forum, "Facts about Citizens' Council Forum," n.d. [1959], n.p. [pp. 1–2], folder 6, box 91, subseries A, series I, Vandiver Papers.

112. Citizens' Council Forum, activity report, n.d. [1965], record nos. 99–30–0–28–1–1–1 to 4–1–1, p. 3–1–1, MSSC Records; Satterfield, *Citizens' Council Forum*, reel no. 35, videocassette; Synon, *Citizens' Council Forum*, reel no. 57, videocassette.

113. Lowman and Williams, *Citizens' Council Forum*, reel no. 37, videocassette. See also Lowman, *Citizens' Council Forum*, reel nos. 27, 33, 56, 96, videocassettes.

114. John Dittmer, "The Politics of the Mississippi Movement, 1954–1964," in *The Civil Rights Movement in America*, ed. Eagles, 73–74.

115. Hogan, *Many Minds, One Heart*, 78; M. G. Lowman to Arthur J. Moore [Methodist bishop, Atlanta, Ga.], May 17, 1957, folder: "Investigation, 1957," box 22, GCE Records.

116. McAdam, *Freedom Summer,* 4.

117. MSSC, "Report on Mississippi State Sovereignty Commission (1964–1967)," typescript, n.d. [Oct. 1967], n.p. [p. 5], folder 1, box 141, Johnson Papers.

118. Editorial, *Jackson Daily News,* Aug. 28, 1963.

119. MSSC, "Report on Mississippi State Sovereignty Commission," n.p. [p. 5].

120. Johnston, "An Oral History with Mr. Erle Johnston," 24; MSSC, meeting minutes, May 19, 1960, 5, folder 2; Tom Scarbrough, "Lafayette County," investigative report, May 5, 1964, 1, folder 9, both in box 135, Johnson Papers. The entire transcript of the author's oral history interview with Johnston can be consulted online at Civil Rights in Mississippi Digital Archive, McCain Library, http://digilib.usm.edu/cdm/compoundobject/collection/coh/id/4035.

121. Scarbrough, "Lafayette County," 2.

122. Editorial, *Meridian (Miss.) Star,* July 12, 1964. See also Tucker, *Mississippi from Within,* 33.

123. Thrasher, "A White Southerner in the Civil Rights Movement," presentation, www.utm.edu/staff/jabel/watkinswebcast.htm, webcast.

124. Weill, *In a Madhouse's Din,* 122; Lowman, untitled press release, July 2, 1962.

125. *Jackson Daily News,* June 13, 1964.

126. Ibid.; Friedland, *Lift Up Your Voice Like a Trumpet,* 81; Heuser, "Stories from Out Past."

127. *Jackson Daily News,* June 13, 1964.

128. *Cincinnati (Ohio) Enquirer,* June 30, 1964.

129. *Meridian Star,* June 19, 1964.

130. *Vicksburg (Miss.) Evening Post,* June 25, 1964.

131. Belfrage, *Freedom Summer,* 105; Mars, *Witness in Philadelphia,* 80.

132. Cagin and Dray, *We Are Not Afraid,* 294.

133. Johnson, conversation with James O. Eastland, http://web2.millercenter.org/lbj/audiovisual/whrecordings/telephone/conversations/1964/lbj_wh6406_14_3836.mp3, online MP3 audio. See also Newton, *The Ku Klux Klan in Mississippi,* 141. Senator Eastland's self-serving "publicity stunt" theory, to be sure, was widely entertained by his constituency as well. For instance, one white woman in Neshoba County, when interviewed by a news reporter about the disappearance of the three civil rights workers, replied: "Well, I believe it's a big publicity hoax." "But if they're dead," she added heartlessly, "I feel like they asked for it" (see *Neshoba,* DVD).

134. U.S. Senate, Senator James O. Eastland of Mississippi speaking on Communist infiltration into the so-called civil rights movement, 88th Cong., 2d sess., *Congressional Record* (July 22, 1964), 16040. See also Weill, "The Press Challenge of Social Responsibility in Times of Political Upheaval," 387.

135. Editorial, *Jackson Clarion-Ledger,* Aug. 3, 1964. See also Tucker, *Mississippi from Within,* 43.

136. A. L. Hopkins, "Investigation of the Finding of the Bodies of Three Civil Rights Workers Who Disappeared from Philadelphia, Mississippi, on June 21, 1964," investigative report, Aug. 6, 1964, folder 2, box 136, Johnson Papers.

137. *National Guardian (N.Y.),* Aug. 1, 1964.

138. *Jackson (Miss.) Clarion-Ledger/Daily News,* July 1, 1984.

139. Lyndon B. Johnson, "Address before a Joint Session of the Congress," Nov. 27, 1963, American Presidency Project, University of California at Santa Barbara, www.presidency.ucsb.edu/ws/index.php?pid=25988.

140. *Jackson Daily News,* July 16, 1964.

141. Silver, *Running Scared,* 71.

142. Dittmer, *Local People,* 142.

143. *New York Times,* Jan. 19, 1964; Doyle, *An American Insurrection,* 315.

144. University of Mississippi, "Reply to Allegations Concerning Certain Members of the Faculty and Staff of the University of Mississippi," typescript, n.d. [1959], record nos. 3–9–1–8–1–1–1 to 58–1–1, p. 5–1–1, MSSC Records; *Jackson Clarion-Ledger,* Sept. 1, 1959; Silver, "Mississippi," 3–34; Clark, "Comments," 854–55; "Mississippi: The Closed Society."

145. *Memphis Press-Scimitar,* Nov. 8, 1963.

146. Erle Johnston Jr. to Tom Tubb, Dec. 2, 1963, record nos. 99–137–0–8–1–1–1 to 2–1–1, MSSC Records; *Pittsburgh (Penn.) Press,* Oct. 1, 1984. See also Katagiri, *The Mississippi State Sovereignty Commission,* 129–30; Bailey, "The Southern Historical Association and the Quest for Racial Justice," 850–51; and Polsgrove, *Divided Mind,* 218–19.

147. James W. Silver to A. Eugene Cox [former director, Providence Cooperative Farm, Miss.], June 14, 1963, folder 4A, box 6, Cox Collection; Silver, "Mississippi Must Choose," 8, 54–55; Gaston, "Speaking for the Negro," 612–13; Silver, *Mississippi,* 30.

148. Jacob Batte, "University to Honor Former Professor for Courageous Actions," Sept. 29, 2011, *DM [Daily Mississippian] Online,* University of Mississippi, University, www.thedmonline.com/article/university-honor-former-professor-courageous-actions; Sansing, *Making Haste Slowly,* 202; Silver, *Running Scared,* 87, 103–4.

149. ALCPP, *The 1964 Civil Rights Bill,* 3–4, folder 3, container SG21073, ALCPP Records.

150. ALCPP, *Communists in Civil Rights,* 2, 5, folder 2, container SG21073, ALCPP Records.

151. Finley, *Delaying the Dream,* 281; Garrow, *Protest at Selma,* 73–77; Carter, *The Politics of Rage,* 249; Johnson, conversation with Earl Buford Ellington [former Tennessee governor], http://web2.millercenter.org/lbj/audiovisual/whrecordings/telephone/conversations/1965/lbj_wh6503_10_7124.mp3, online MP3 audio.

152. U.S. Senate, Senator James O. Eastland of Mississippi, "Communist Invasion of Mississippi under Banner of So-Called 'Civil Rights' Activities," speech, 89th Cong., 1st sess., *Congressional Record* (Mar. 18, 1965), 5284.

153. Frederick, *Stand Up for Alabama,* 119.

154. U.S. House, Representative William L. Dickinson of Alabama, "March on Montgomery: The Untold Story," speech, 89th Cong., 1st sess., *Congressional Record* (Mar. 30, 1965), 6113–14. See also *Toledo (Ohio) Blade,* Mar. 31, 1965; and Stanton, *From Selma to Sorrow,* 144.

155. Conaway, *Judge,* 144; Jeansonne, *Leander Perez,* 243.

156. "The Continuing Confrontation"; Thayer, *The Farther Shores of Politics,* 119; Conaway, *Judge,* 146; *Hopkinsville Kentucky News Era,* Mar. 31, 1965.

157. *Tuscaloosa (Ala.) News,* May 3, 1964; *Toledo Blade,* Mar. 31, 1965; Jeansonne, *Leander Perez,* 243.

158. ALCPP, "Biennial Report to the Alabama Legislature," 9.

159. Ibid.; Eli H. Howell to Richard D. Morphew [producer, *Citizens' Council Forum*], June 29, 1966, folder 48, container SG13842, ASSC Records.

160. Keitz and Herndon, Inc., to ASSC, production estimate, June 24, 1965, folder 48, container SG13842, ASSC Records.

161. Howell to Morphew, June 29, 1966; Eli H. Howell to Leland Childs, Oct. 28, 1965, folder 1, container SG13843, ASSC Records.

162. Carter, *The Politics of Rage,* 260–61.

163. ALCPP, "Selma-Montgomery March," typed list, n.d. [1965], folder 23, container SG21074, ALCPP Records.

164. Rogers et al., *Alabama,* 573; Frederick, *Stand Up for Alabama,* 123. Among those admirers of the segregationist film were the state's conservative women, including Mrs. James M. Sizemore, dean of women at Howard College in Birmingham. Sizemore, who had attended "the premiere showing" of the documentary held in Montgomery, wrote to Governor Wallace in late August 1965, requesting a copy of the film so that her college would be able to "have a showing . . . at a compulsory convocation" on campus. "My opinion is that this film is extremely worthwhile and that it can straighten out lots of people," the elated college educator complimented the governor (see Mrs. James M. Sizemore to George C. Wallace, Aug. 30, 1965, folder 47, container SG13842, ASSC Records).

165. ALCPP, "Biennial Report to the Alabama Legislature," 15.

CONCLUSION

1. Circuit Riders, untitled press release, n.d. [1966], folder: "'Communist Fronts'—News Coverage of M. G. Lowman's Speech at Pascagoula, Mississippi, March 15, 1966," box 21, Lowman Papers; *Greenville (Miss.) Delta Democrat-Times,* Mar. 17, 1966.

2. *Pensacola (Fla.) News Journal,* Apr. 3, 1966.

3. *New York Times,* July 17, 1966; Ruth I. Matthews to "Dear Family," July 20, 1966, 1–2, folder: "Letters from Family, 1966–1967," box 708, Matthews Papers.

4. Matthews, *Odyssey of a Fellow Traveler;* Carl McIntire, "J. B. Matthews" [introduction], in Matthews, *Communism in Our Churches,* 3, folder: "Pamphlets," box 5, CR Records; Dawson, "From Fellow Traveler to Anticommunist," 306. Only a few months after Matthews's death, in the late summer of 1966, Ruth Matthews contemplated writing a sequel to her late husband's *Odyssey of a Fellow Traveler,* planning to make it a "real[-]life chiller-diller" book on the life of J. B. Matthews. However, the publication of the planned eight-chapter biography of Matthews which, at one point, was even tentatively entitled *The Years of Disillusionment,* never materialized (see Mary Kay [Ruth Matthews's personal friend?] to Ruth Matthews, Sept. 7, 1966; and "The Years of Disillusionment," book outline, n.d. [Sept. 7, 1966?], both in folder: "Biographical, 1963–1967," box 696, Matthews Papers).

5. Ruth I. Matthews to Mary Kay, Sept. 11, 1966, folder: "Biographical, 1963–1967," box 696; Matthews, "Burial Service for J. B.," typescript, n.d. [1966], folder: "Grave-Side Service for J. B. Matthews, 1966," box 708, both in Matthews Papers.

6. "Some Zealots Masked in Moderation"; *Los Angeles Times,* Nov. 30, 2004; *Chicago Tribune,* Nov. 30, 2004; Bales, *The Martin Luther King Story,* 199; Bobby Valentine, "Social Concerns in Churches of Christ: Trends since the King Years, 1950–2000," Mar. 15, 2010, Stoned-Campbell Disciple, ed. Bobby Valentine, Tucson, Ariz., http://stoned-campbelldisciple.blogspot.com/2010/03/social-concerns-in-churches-of-christ.html.

7. Lichtman, "J. B. Matthews and the 'Counter-Subversives,'" 32–33.

8. Church League of America, "Biographical Note: J. B. Matthews," typescript, n.d. [1965?], n.p. [p. 1], folder: "Biographical, 1963–1967," box 696, Matthews Papers.

9. Richard M. Nixon to Edgar C. Bundy, Western Union telegram, Sept. 11, 1967, folder 8, box 22, WHS Files; Bundy to John Clements, Western Union telegram, Sept. 8, 1967, 1, folder 4, box 72, Matthews Papers.

10. Turner, *Power on the Right,* 137.

11. Ibid., 137–38; Edgar C. Bundy to Rosemary [*sic,* Rose Mary] Woods [secretary to the Republican presidential nominee Richard M. Nixon], Oct. 3, 1968, folder 8, box 22, WHS Files.

12. Church League of America, *Catalog of Publications and Training Aids of the Church League of America,* 3, record nos. 6–68–1–4–1–1–1 to 20–1–1, p. 2–1–1, MSSC Records. After Matthews's death in July 1966, at least two university archives—the special collections department at the University of Oregon in Eugene and the Archive of Contemporary History at the University of Wyoming in Laramie—took great interests in acquiring and preserving the Matthews files. The University of Oregon's special collections department was particularly enthusiastic, for it had begun to build its Conservative and Libertarian Manuscript Collections since the early 1960s. Acknowledging Matthews's "service as a distinguished conservative writer," the acquisitions librarian at the University of Oregon wrote to Ruth Matthews in September 1966, imploring her to "consider the permanent preservation of the Joseph Brown Matthews collections in our archives." Later, when the Church League of America was dissolved, the Matthews files were returned to Ruth Matthews who, then in turn, deposited the files with Duke University's Special Collections Library in 1983, seventeen years after her husband's passing (see Edward Kemp to "the Estate of Joseph B. Matthews" [Ruth Matthews], Sept. 29, 1966; Gene M. Gressley [director, Archive of Contemporary History, University of Wyoming, Laramie] to Ruth Matthews, June 25, 1968, both in folder: "University of Oregon and University of Wyoming, 1966–1968," box 708, Matthews Papers; and Janie C. Morris [research services librarian, Rare Book, Manuscript, and Special Collections Library, Duke University, Durham, N.C.], conversation with the author, Durham, N.C., Mar. 8, 2007, the author's memo taken during the conversation).

13. M. G. Lowman, open letter to the Circuit Riders' contributors, Jan. 30, 1965, folder 7; Norman A. Sugarman [assistant commissioner, Office of Commissioner of Internal Revenue] to Circuit Riders, Jan. 6, 1953, folder 5, both in box 83, Matthews Papers. See also Andrew, *Power to Destroy,* 34.

14. *Cincinnati (Ohio) Enquirer,* Feb. 2, 1965. See also "U.S. Opens Tax Drive against Right-Wing Groups."

15. Circuit Riders, "Announcement," Aug. 1966, folder: "Circuit Riders," Garman Papers.

16. *Cincinnati Enquirer,* May 20, 1966; *Cincinnati Enquirer,* Mar. 31, 1967.

17. M. G. Lowman to the Commission on Christian Social Concern of the Westwood Methodist Church, "The Ineptness of Rev. Richard Isler['s] and Rev. David Sageser['s] Interferes [*sic*] with the Aspirations of Cincinnati Negro Citizens," memo, Apr. 25, 1966, folder: "Circuit Riders Literature (1958–71)," box 1, CR Records.

18. Roberta Sue Alexander, "A Place of Recourse: The Changing Role of the Federal District Court for the Southern District of Ohio," in vol. 1 of *The History of Ohio Law,* ed. Benedict and Winkler, 306–307.

19. David B. Sageser [Fort Myers, Fla.], "Myers G. Lowman: A Personal Recollection," e-mail to the author, Sept. 19, 2003.

20. Ibid.

21. Robert A. Geier [administrative assistant to U.S. representative James B. Utt from California] to M. G. Lowman, Oct. 31, 1968, folder: "Correspondence: Incoming," box 2, CR Records.

22. Turner, *Power on the Right,* 38, 41, 48.

23. *Los Angeles Times,* May 22, 1988; Geier to Lowman, Oct. 31, 1968.

24. McGirr, *Suburban Warriors*, 7. See also *Emporia (Kans.) Gazette,* Sept. 24, 1966.

25. *Emporia Gazette,* Sept. 24, 1966; *Los Angeles Times,* May 22, 1988; Turner, *Power on the Right,* 41, 46. See also Schoenwald, *A Time for Choosing,* 136.

26. U.S. House, Representative James B. Utt of California, "Communists Promote Mob Violence," extension of remarks, 88th Cong., 2d sess., *Congressional Record* (July 28, 1964), A3943. See also James B. Utt, *Washington Report* [newsletter to constituents], vol. 1, no. 8, n.d. [1964], record nos. 3–30A-1–78–1–1–1 to 2–1–1, p. 1–1–1, MSSC Records; and U.S. Senate, Senator James O. Eastland of Mississippi speaking on Communist infiltration into the so-called civil rights movement, 88th Cong., 2d sess., *Congressional Record* (July 22, 1964), 16040.

27. *Jackson (Miss.) Daily News,* July 29, 1964; *Jackson (Miss.) Clarion-Ledger,* Aug. 6, 1964; Weill, *In a Madhouse's Din,* 111; ALCPP, *Communists in Civil Rights,* 2, 5, folder 2, container SG21073, ALCPP Records.

28. Geier to Lowman, Oct. 31, 1968; Knott, *Will We Keep Our Freedom?,* n.p., folder: "Americanism Educational League," FC Collection.

29. "Mr. Walter Knott: 'An Incomparable American'" [sidebar], in Reagan, *A Time for Choosing,* n.p., folder: "Americanism Educational League," FC Collection; McGirr, *Suburban Warriors,* 102; Turner, *Power on the Right,* 43.

30. Robert F. Williams, "Needed: A National Mettle of Honor," typescript, n.d. [1973], 1, folder: "Americanism Educational League," FC Collection; McGirr, *Suburban Warriors,* 98–99.

31. McGirr, *Suburban Warriors,* 98.

32. Turner, *Power on the Right,* 43.

33. Ibid.; McGirr, *Suburban Warriors,* 99.

34. Turner, *Power on the Right,* 44; Forster and Epstein, *Danger on the Right,* 90–91; Dochuk, *From Bible Belt to Sunbelt,* 215.

35. William E. Fort Jr. [executive director, Americanism Educational League] to Mrs. J. B. Matthews, Aug. 3, 1966, folder: "Letters of Condolence, July 1966," box 708, Matthews Papers; Herbert A. Philbrick [Americanism Educational League] to "Dear Friend," Sept. 20, 1965, folder: "Americanism Educational League," FC Collection; John R. Lechner to "Dear Friend," Jan. 30, 1951; L. Mills Beam [vice chair, advisory board, Americanism Educational League] to Richard M. Nixon, Feb. 18, 1957; Americanism Educational League, "Thirty Years of Patriotic Service," n.d. [1957], all in folder 11, box 53, WHS Files; Leonard, "Is That What We Fought For?," 467. See also Leonard, *The Battle for Los Angeles,* 209, 216; and "It's a Free Country."

36. William E. Saracino [executive director, Americanism Educational League, Monrovia, Calif.], "Meyers [*sic*] G. Lowman," e-mail to the author, June 13, 2006; Fort to Mrs. Matthews, Aug. 3, 1966.

37. "Interview of Ku King Chang, One of the Most Important Taiwan Chinese Anti-Communists, M. G. Lowman's Guest at Independence Hall, Knott[']s Berry Farm," n.d., film reel, box 100, Lowman Papers.

38. *Emporia Gazette,* Sept. 24, 1966; California Death Records, RootsWeb, Provo, Utah, http://vitals.rootsweb.ancestry.com/ca/death/search.cgi.

39. *Georgia's Official Register,* 1959–1960, 86; Editorial, *Macon (Ga.) News,* Oct. 9, 1959; *Augusta (Ga.) Herald,* Oct. 10, 1959; U.S. Commission on Civil Rights, *Education,* book 2 of *1961 United States Commission on Civil Rights Report,* 69; Bartley, *The Rise of Massive Resistance,* 183; Henderson, *Ernest Vandiver,* 96.

40. Untitled draft of the resolution creating a state legislative investigating committee, n.d. [Feb. 1959], n.p. [pp. 1–2], folder 6, box 41, subseries A, series I, Vandiver Papers.

41. Roche, *Restructured Resistance,* 177.

42. Roy V. Harris to W. O. Brooks, Feb. 13, 1959, folder 6, box 41, subseries A, series I, Vandiver Papers.

43. *Acts and Resolutions of the General Assembly of the State of Georgia,* 1959, regular sess., vol. 1, 5–6; *Georgia's Official Register,* 1959–1960, 86. See also Heale, *McCarthy's Americans,* 267.

44. Bartley, *The Rise of Massive Resistance,* 183; GCE, *Highlander Folk School,* folder: "Churches, 1958," box 28, GCE Records; *Georgia Official and Statistical Register,* 1971–72, 381.

45. *Gibson v. Florida Legislative Investigation Committee,* 372 U.S. 539 (1963).

46. FLIC, "Interim Report," Mar. 1964, 1–2, folder 7, box 145, Matthews Papers; *St. Petersburg (Fla.) Evening Independent,* Apr. 19, 1963. See also *Sarasota (Fla.) Herald-Tribune,* Apr. 25, 1963; and Greenberg, *University of South Florida,* 59–61.

47. FLIC, "Budget," typescript, Jan. 1964, 1, folder 7, box 145, Matthews Papers; *St. Petersburg (Fla.) Times,* May 31, 1963; FLIC, "Interim Report," 2.

48. *Daytona Beach (Fla.) Morning Journal,* Dec. 20, 1962.

49. FLIC, "Interim Report," 3.

50. FLIC, *Homosexuality and Citizenship in Florida,* n.p.

51. FLIC, "Interim Report," 3.

52. Weitz, "Bourbon, Pork Chops, and Red Peppers," Ph.D. diss., 237; editorial, *Miami (Fla.) News,* Mar. 19, 1964; Stacy Braukman, "The Johns Committee, Sex, and Civil Rights in Florida, 1963–1965," in *Freedom Rights,* ed. McGuire and Dittmer, 172.

53. *St. Petersburg Times,* Oct. 1, 1964; Bartley, *The New South,* 221; *Pensacola (Fla.) News Journal,* July 2, 1993.

54. *Sarasota Herald-Tribune,* July 1, 2005.

55. Editorial, *Baton Rouge (La.) State-Times,* June 23, 1969; Jeansonne, *Leander Perez,* 235.

56. Hill, *The Deacons for Defense,* 38; Jones, *The Louisiana Journey,* 320.

57. LJLCUA, *Activities of the "Ku Klux Klan" and Certain Other Organizations in Louisiana,* 89, SLL. See also Sherrill, *Gothic Politics in the Deep South,* 215; and Hill, *The Deacons for Defense,* 143.

58. LJLCUA, *Activities of the "Ku Klux Klan" and Certain Other Organizations in Louisiana,* 89.

59. Katagiri, *The Mississippi State Sovereignty Commission,* 217–18.

60. Ibid., 224–26, 229, 240; MSSC, "Statement of Appropriated Funds and Unexpended Balances, May 1956–June 30, 1972," record no. 97–58–0–22–1–1–1; MSSC, "Financial Statement, July 1, 1972, through June 30, 1973," record no. 97–58–0–2–1–1–1, both in MSSC Records.

61. Johnston, "An Oral History with Mr. Erle Johnston," 38.

62. ASSC, meeting minutes, Sept. 19, 1973, 1–2, folder 8, container SG13842, ASSC Records; Alice T. Ulrich [Government Records Division, Alabama Department of Archives and History, Montgomery], e-mail to the author, Nov. 15, 2000.

63. *Montgomery (Ala.) Advertiser-Journal,* Dec. 24, 1972.

64. ALCPP, meeting minutes, Dec. 17, 1969; ALCPP, untitled resolution, Dec. 17, 1969, both in folder 27, container SG21074, ALCPP Records.

65. C. Edwin Strickland, Mavis Hicks, and R. Y. Ball to "Dear Commission Member," Mar. 22, 1971, 1, folder 12, container SG21074, ALCPP Records.

66. *Montgomery Advertiser-Journal,* Dec. 24, 1972.

67. Ibid.; ALCPP, "Biennial Report to the Alabama Legislature," June 1965, 4, folder 1, container SG21073; C. Edwin Strickland to "Dear Commission Member," Mar. 22, 1971, folder 12, container SG21074, both in ALCPP Records.

68. *Montgomery Advertiser-Journal,* Dec. 24, 1972.

69. Ed Strickland to "Dear Legislator," Sept. 30, 1975; ALCPP, untitled report, Sept. 30, 1975, both in folder 13, container SG21074, ALCPP Records.

70. Rainach, "An Interview with William M. Rainach," Aug. 19, 1977, 17–18.

71. *Shreveport (La.) Times,* Jan. 27, 1978; *New York Times,* Jan. 28, 1978.

72. *Shreveport (La.) Journal,* Jan. 27, 1978.

73. W. M. Rainach, untitled speech before the Louisiana Farm Bureau convention, Alexandria, July 20, 1954, 4–5, folder 442, box 38, Rainach Papers.

74. Ward, *Defending White Democracy,* 183.

75. Simmons, "An Oral History with Mr. William J. Simmons," 74.

76. Gordon Lee Baum [chief executive officer, Council of Conservative Citizens, St. Louis, Mo.], letter to the author, July 2, 1990; *Jackson Clarion-Ledger,* Jan. 24, 1994.

77. Sherrill, *Gothic Politics in the Deep South.*

78. Black and Black, *The Rise of Southern Republicans,* 4, 326.

79. Jeremy D. Mayer, "Reagan and Race: Prophet of Color Blindness, Baiter of the Backlash," in Longley et al, *Deconstructing Reagan,* 79; *Neshoba (Miss.) Democrat,* Nov. 15, 2007.

80. George C. Wallace, "Interview with Gov. George C. Wallace," filmed interview by Callie Crossely, Mar. 9, 1986, transcript, Eyes on the Prize Interviews, Washington University Digital Gateway, Washington University, St. Louis, Mo., http://digital.wustl.edu/e/eyes.

81. *Washington Post,* Sept. 14, 1998.

82. *New York Times,* Aug. 31, 2005; *New York Times,* July 5, 2008.

83. *Washington Post,* Oct. 4, 1983; Romero, "A Brief History of Martin Luther King Jr. Day"; David L. Chappell, "Waking from the Dream: The Battle over Martin Luther King's Legacy," paper, 2008 conference of the Historical Society, Baltimore, Md., June 7, 2008, 16, in the author's possession by courtesy of Chappell, University of Oklahoma, Norman; Link, *Righteous Warrior,* 262; *Boston Globe,* July 4, 2008. See also Garrow, *The FBI and Martin Luther King, Jr.*

84. U.S. Senate, Senator Jesse Helms of North Carolina, remarks, 98th Cong., 1st sess., *Congressional Record* (Oct. 3, 1983), reproduced in Council of Conservative Citizens, *The King Holiday and Its Meaning,* 44, in the author's possession by courtesy of the Council of Conservative Citizens, St. Louis, Mo. See also Cohodas, *Strom Thurmond and the Politics of Southern Change,* 483; and Helms, *Here's Where I Stand,* 161–63.

85. Helms, *Here's Where I Stand,* 163; Miller, *Billy Graham and the Rise of the Republican South,* 149; *Chicago Sun-Times,* Aug. 5, 1993.

86. Cobb, *The Most Southern Place on Earth,* 223.

87. "Asked to Leave the County," 1, 4.

88. Lindsey H. Cox [Memphis, Tenn.], letter to the author, June 17, 1993.

89. Bryant, *Poems of William Cullen Bryant,* 171. Duke, as the leader of the National Association for the Advancement of White People (NAAWP), also opposed the proposed federal holiday to celebrate King's birthday, identifying the civil rights icon as a "Communist sympathizer" in 1983 (see Bridges, *The Rise of David Duke,* 92).

90. Carter, *The Politics of Rage,* 260–61.

91. Martin Luther King Jr., "Our God Is Marching On!," in *A Testament of Hope,* ed. Washington, 230.

92. Key, *Southern Politics in State and Nation,* 675.

93. Goldfield, *Black, White, and Southern,* 104–5; Fairclough, *To Redeem the Soul of America,* 138–39.

94. Goldfield, *Still Fighting the Civil War,* 247.

95. Smith, *Killers of the Dream,* 39, 167; Smith, *The Journey,* 34. See also Hobson, *Tell about the South,* 320.

96. Wilma Dykeman and James Stokely, "Our Changing South: A Challenge," in *We Dissent,* ed. Norris, 10.

97. William Faulkner, "American Segregation and the World Crisis," in Faulkner, Mays, and Sims, *The Segregation Decisions,* 12. See also Bailey, "The Southern Historical Association and the Quest for Racial Justice," 851–52.

98. Shogan, *No Sense of Decency,* 226; Fried, ed., *McCarthyism,* 187.

99. Chappell, *A Stone of Hope,* 259.

BIBLIOGRAPHY

ARCHIVES

Alabama Department of Archives and History: Government Records Division, Montgomery.
> Alabama Legislative Commission to Preserve the Peace Records (microfilm).
> Alabama State Sovereignty Commission Records (microfilm).

Birmingham Civil Rights Institute: Archives, Birmingham, Ala.
> Nat Welch Papers.

Bob Jones University: Fundamentalism File Manuscript Collections. J. S. Mack Library, Greenville, S.C.
> W. O. H. Garman Papers.

California State University: Special Collections. University Archives and Special Collections Section. Paulina June and George Pollak Library, Fullerton.
> Freedom Center Collection.

Cincinnati Public Library, Cincinnati, Ohio.
> Circuit Riders, Inc., literature.

Delta State University: Charles W. Capps Jr. Archives and Museum, Cleveland, Miss.
> Walter Sillers Jr. Papers.

Drew University: General Commission on Archives and History of the United Methodist Church. Drew University Methodist Library, Madison, N.J.
> Records of the Methodist Federation for Social Action.

Duke University: Rare Book, Manuscript, and Special Collections Library (presently David M. Rubenstein Rare Book and Manuscript Library), Durham, N.C.
> Earnest S. Cox Papers.
> J. B. Matthews Papers.

Dwight D. Eisenhower Presidential Library, Abilene, Kans.
> James C. Hagerty Papers.
> White House Central Files (Records as President).

Florida State Archives (presently State Archives of Florida), Tallahassee.
  Florida Legislative Investigation Committee Records.
  Florida Photographic Collection.
Georgia Archives, Morrow.
  Records of the Georgia Commission on Education.
John F. Kennedy Presidential Library, Boston, Mass.
  Burke Marshall Personal Papers.
Library of Congress: Prints and Photographs Division, Washington, D.C.
  Harris and Ewing Photographs Collection.
  U.S. News and World Report Magazine Photograph Collection.
Louisiana State Archives, Baton Rouge.
  Louisiana Joint Legislative Committee on Un-American Activities
    Records.
  Louisiana State University: Louisiana and Lower Mississippi Valley
    Collections. Hill Memorial Library, Baton Rouge.
  Charles A. Reynard–Marian Reynard Baun Papers.
  Vertical file (microfilm): "Louisiana—Legislature—Joint Committee
    on Segregation."
  Vertical file (microfilm): "Louisiana State Sovereignty Commission."
Louisiana State University in Shreveport: Archives and Special Collections. Noel
  Memorial Library, Shreveport.
  Henry Langston McEachern Photographic Collection.
  William M. Rainach Papers.
  Ned Touchstone Papers.
Mississippi Department of Archives and History: Archives and Library Division,
  Jackson.
  Records of the Mississippi State Sovereignty Commission.
——: Audio-Visual Section. Image and Sound Division.
  Citizens' Council Forum Film Collection.
Mississippi State University: Manuscripts Division. Special Collections Department.
  Mitchell Memorial Library. Mississippi State.
  A. Eugene Cox Collection.
  Citizens' Council Collection.
  Godwin Advertising Agency Collection.
  George N. McIlhenny Papers.
  Wilson F. "Bill" Minor Papers.
  Kenneth Toler Papers.
Nashville Public Library: Special Collections Division, Nashville, Tenn.
  Nashville Banner Archives.
New Orleans Public Library: Manuscript Collections. Louisiana Division, New
  Orleans, La.
  Leander H. Perez Papers.

Richard M. Nixon Presidential Library: Richard M. Nixon Presidential Returned
Materials Collection, Yorba Linda, Calif.
    White House Special Files.
Ohio Wesleyan University: Archives of Ohio United Methodism. Leon A. Beeghly
Library, Delaware, Ohio.
    The Christian Advocate Collection.
Princeton University: Public Policy Papers. Department of Rare Books and Special
Collections. Seeley G. Mudd Manuscript Library, Princeton, N.J.
    Fund for the Republic Archives.
Stanford University: Hoover Institution Library and Archives, Stanford, Calif.
    Myers G. Lowman Papers.
    The National Republic Records (microfilm).
    George E. Sokolsky Papers.
State Library of Louisiana: Louisiana Collection, Baton Rouge.
    Louisiana Joint Legislative Committee on Un-American Activities literature.
Tennessee State Library and Archives: Archives and Manuscripts Unit, Nashville.
    Records of the 81st Tennessee General Assembly Special Investigating Com-
    mittee.
Texas A&M University: Manuscript Collections. Cushing Memorial Library and
Archives, College Station.
    Charles Levy Civil Rights Collection.
Tougaloo College: Special Collections. L. Zenobia Coleman Library, Tougaloo, Miss.
    Audiovisual material.
Harry S. Truman Presidential Library, Independence, Mo.
    William Hillman Papers.
University of Arkansas: Special Collections. David W. Mullins Library, Fayetteville.
    Arkansas Council on Human Relations Records.
    Virgil T. Blossom Papers.
University of California at Santa Barbara: Department of Special Collections.
Donald C. Davidson Library, Santa Barbara.
    Center for the Study of Democratic Institutions Collection.
University of Georgia: Hargrett Rare Book and Manuscript Library, Athens.
    Broadside Collection.
———: Richard B. Russell Library for Political Research and Studies.
    Ed Friend Visual Materials Collection.
    Roy V. Harris Papers.
    Richard B. Russell Jr. Collection.
    Herman E. Talmadge Collection.
    S. Ernest Vandiver Jr. Papers.
University of Mississippi: Archives and Special Collections. John D. Williams
Library, University.
    Russell H. Barrett Collection.

Citizens' Council Collection.

James Howard Meredith Collection.

John C. Satterfield/American Bar Association Collection.

University of North Carolina: Southern Historical Collection. Louis Round Wilson Special Collections Library, Chapel Hill.

Delta and Providence Cooperative Farms Papers.

University of Notre Dame: Manuscript Collections. University Archives. Theodore M. Hesburgh Library, Notre Dame, Ind.

Social Issues Collection.

University of Oregon: Conservative and Libertarian Manuscript Collections. Special Collections and University Archives. Knight Library, Eugene.

Circuit Riders, Inc., Records.

E. Merrill Root Papers.

University of Southern Mississippi: Archives and Manuscript Department. William D. McCain Library and Archives, Hattiesburg.

Citizens' Council/Civil Rights Collection.

L. E. Faulkner Papers.

Paul B. Johnson Family Papers.

Erle E. Johnston Jr. Papers.

William D. McCain Pamphlet Collection.

Vertical file: "Sovereignty Commission, Mississippi State."

———: Microfilm Section. Joseph A. Cook Memorial Library.

Facts on Film (microfilm).

University of Sussex: Special Collections. University of Sussex Library, Brighton, U.K.

Harvey Matusow Archive.

Washington Memorial Library: Middle Georgia Archives. Macon-Bibb County Public Libraries, Macon, Ga.

Charles J. Bloch Papers.

Wisconsin Historical Society: Library and Archives Division, Madison.

Highlander Research and Education Center Records.

ORAL HISTORIES

(Except where noted, all oral history interviews are from the Mississippi Oral History Program, Center for Oral History and Cultural Heritage, University of Southern Mississippi, Hattiesburg.)

Ashmore, Harry. "Interview with Harry Ashmore." Recorded interview by Roy Reed, June 20, 1992. Transcript. *Arkansas Gazette* Project, David and Barbara Pryor Center for Arkansas Oral and Visual History, Special Collections, University of Arkansas, Fayetteville.

Barnett, Ross R. "Oral History Interview with Ross R. Barnett." Recorded interview by Dennis O'Brien, May 6, 1969. Transcript. Oral History Program, John F. Kennedy Presidential Library, Boston.

Brady, Thomas P. "Interview with the Honorable Thomas P. Brady, Associate Justice, Mississippi Supreme Court." Recorded interview by Orley B. Caudill, Mar. 4, 1972. Vol. 2, pt. 1, transcript.

Foreman, Gene. "Interview with Gene Foreman." Recorded interview by Gerald Jordan, Aug. 4, 2000. Transcript. *Arkansas Gazette* Project, David and Barbara Pryor Center for Arkansas Oral and Visual History, Special Collections, University of Arkansas, Fayetteville.

Harned, Horace H., Jr. "An Oral History with Mr. Horace H. Harned Jr." Recorded interview by Yasuhiro Katagiri, Nov. 3, 1993. Vol. 355, pt. 2, transcript.

Harris, Roy V. "Politics #3 and #4." Recorded reminiscences, n.d. AVA: 86–1: 2, transcript. Roy V. Harris Papers, Richard B. Russell Library for Political Research and Studies, University of Georgia, Athens.

Johns, Charlie [*sic*, Charley]. Recorded interview by Ray Washington, n.d. [1979?]. [Pt. 1], transcript. Samuel Proctor Oral History Program, Department of History, University of Florida, Gainesville.

Johnston, Erle, Jr. "An Oral History with Mr. Erle Johnston." Recorded interview by Yasuhiro Katagiri, Aug. 13, 1993. Vol. 276, pt. 2, transcript.

Kershaw, Jack. Recorded interview by Ben Houston, June 30, 2003. Transcript. Samuel Proctor Oral History Program, Department of History, University of Florida, Gainesville.

Kester, Howard. "Interview with Howard Kester." Recorded interview by Mary Frederickson, Aug. 25, 1974. B-0007–2, transcript. Southern Oral History Program, Southern Historical Collection, Center for the Study of the American South, University of North Carolina at Chapel Hill.

King, Edwin. Recorded interview by Yasuhiro Katagiri, Aug. 17, 1993. Incomplete transcript.

Marshall, Burke. Recorded interview by T. H. Baker, Oct. 28, 1968. AC 74–215, transcript. Oral History Collection, Lyndon B. Johnson Presidential Library, Austin, Tex.

Meredith, James H. "An Oral History with James Howard Meredith." Recorded interview by Yasuhiro Katagiri, Jan. 11, 1994. Transcript. James Howard Meredith Collection, Archives and Special Collections, John D. Williams Library, University of Mississippi, University.

Meredith, James H., and Yasuhiro Katagiri. *"Me and My Kind": An Oral History with James Howard Meredith.* Jackson, Miss.: Meredith Publishing, 1995.

Moseley, Ray. "Interview with Ray Moseley." Recorded interview by Roy Reed, Nov. 4, 2000. Transcript. *Arkansas Gazette* Project, David and Barbara Pryor Center for Arkansas Oral and Visual History, Special Collections, University of Arkansas, Fayetteville.

Rainach, William M. "An Interview with William M. Rainach." Recorded interviews by Hubert Humphreys, June 28, Aug. 19, and Oct. 7, 1977. OH 17, transcript. Oral History Collection, Noel Memorial Library, Louisiana State University in Shreveport.

Simmons, William J. "An Oral History with Mr. William J. Simmons." Recorded interview by Orley B. Caudill, June 26, 1979. Vol. 372, transcript.

Talmadge, Herman E. "Conversations with Senator Herman Talmadge: Interesting Georgians I Have Known." Interview by Mel Steely and Don Wagner, Mar. 14, 1986. Online transcript. Georgia Political Heritage Program, Irvine Sullivan Ingram Library, University of West Georgia, Carrollton.

Watt, Ruth Young. "Ruth Young Watt, Chief Clerk, Permanent Subcommittee on Investigations, 1948–1979." Recorded interview by Donald A. Ritchie, Sept. 21, 1979. Transcript. Oral History Project, U.S. Senate Historical Office, Washington, D.C.

West, Don. "Interview with Don West." Recorded interview by Jacquelyn Hall and Ray Faherty, Jan. 22, 1975. E-0016, transcript. Southern Oral History Program, Southern Historical Collection, Center for the Study of the American South, University of North Carolina at Chapel Hill.

Williams, Kenneth O. "An Oral History with Mr. Kenneth O. Williams." Recorded interview by Yasuhiro Katagiri, Oct. 13, 1993. Vol. 470, transcript.

Wroten, Joseph E. "Interview with Joseph E. Wroten." Recorded interview by Jeff Sainsbury, Mar. 31, 1992. Transcript. John C. Stennis Oral History Project, Department of History, Mississippi State University, Mississippi State.

———. "An Oral History with Mr. Joseph E. Wroten." Recorded interview by Yasuhiro Katagiri, Nov. 4, 1993. Vol. 476, transcript.

AUDIOVISUAL MATERIAL

(All *Citizens' Council Forum* programs listed below were produced by Richard D. Morphew, Citizens' Councils of America, Jackson, Miss., and are from the Citizens' Council Forum Film Collection, Audio-Visual Section, Image and Sound Division, Mississippi Department of Archives and History, Jackson.)

The American South Comes of Age. Produced by Alvin H. Goldstein. South Carolina Educational Television Network and Division of Continuing Education of the University of South Carolina, Columbia, 1985. 14 videocassettes.

Ashmore, Harry. Interview by Mike Wallace. *The Mike Wallace Interview* series. ABC, June 29, 1958. *The Mike Wallace Interview* Collection, Harry Ransom Center, University of Texas, Austin. Online video.

Barnett, Ross R. Oral statement reported by Paul Cunningham. *NBC Nightly News.* NBC, Sept. 26, 1962. *Finishing the Dream: Learning from the Civil Rights Era.* NBC Learn, New York. Online video.

"Communism versus Capitalism." *The War We Are In* series. Produced by National Education Program, Harding College, Searcy, Ark., 1962. *Moving Images.* Internet Archive, San Francisco. Online MPEG movie.

Doar, John M., Nicholas deBelleville Katzenbach, and Harrison Jay Goldin. "John F. Kennedy and Civil Rights: Fifty Years After." Panel discussion. Woodrow Wilson School of Public and International Affairs, Princeton University, Princeton, N.J., Mar. 2, 2011. Webcast.

The Ends of the Earth: Plaquemines Parish, Louisiana. Directed by Louis Alvarez and Andrew Kolker. Center for New American Media, New York, 1982. Videocassette.

Eyes on the Prize: America's Civil Rights Years. Produced by Blackside, Boston. PBS, Alexandria, Va., 1986. 6 videocassettes.

Faubus, Orval E. Interview by Mike Wallace. *The Mike Wallace Interview* series. ABC, Sept. 15, 1957. *The Mike Wallace Interview* Collection, Harry Ransom Center, University of Texas, Austin. Online video.

Freedom Riders. Directed by Stanley Nelson. PBS, Alexandria, Va., 2011. DVD.

Highlander—Segregation. 1957. Series III, Ed Friend Visual Materials Collection, Richard B. Russell Library for Political Research and Studies, University of Georgia, Athens. Videocassette; and Folder 2, box 3, Records of the 81st Tennessee General Assembly Special Investigating Committee, Archives and Manuscripts Unit, Tennessee State Library and Archives, Nashville. 16-mm film.

Hood, James A., Nicholas deBelleville Katzenbach, Theodore C. Sorensen, and Callie Crossley. "The Civil Rights Movement and Integrating the University of Alabama." Panel discussion. John F. Kennedy Presidential Library, Boston, June 11, 2011. *American History TV.* C-SPAN, Washington, D.C. Online video.

JFK. Produced by A. Kitman Ho and Oliver Stone. Directed by Oliver Stone. Warner Bros., Burbank, Calif., 1991. 2 videocassettes.

Johnson, Lyndon B. Conversation with James O. Eastland, June 23, 1964. *Johnson Tapes: Telephone Series.* Presidential Recordings Program, Miller Center of Public Affairs, University of Virginia, Charlottesville. Online MP3 audio.

———. Conversation with Earl Buford Ellington, Mar. 18, 1965. *Johnson Tapes: Telephone Series.* Presidential Recordings Program, Miller Center of Public Affairs, University of Virginia, Charlottesville. Online MP3 audio.

Johnston, Erle, Jr. Interview by Cal Adams. *Eyewitness News 16: Dateline.* WAPT, Jackson, Miss., n.d. Special Collections, L. Zenobia Coleman Library, Tougaloo College, Tougaloo, Miss. Videocassette.

Kennedy vs. Wallace. Produced by Robert Drew. Direct Cinema, Santa Monica, Calif., 1988. Videocassette.

King, Martin Luther, Jr., and James J. Kilpatrick. Debate moderated by John K. M. McCaffery. "Are Sit-In Strikes Justifiable?" *NBC News Special* series. NBC, Nov. 26, 1960. *Finishing the Dream: Learning from the Civil Rights Era.* NBC Learn, New York. Online video.

Lorch, Lee. Telephone interview by Andy Barrie. *Metro Morning*. Jan. 9, 2007. CBC Radio One, Toronto, Ontario. Online Real Player audio.

The Lost Year: The Untold Story of the Year Following the Crisis at Central High School, 1958–1959. Produced by Sandra Hubbard. Morning Star Studio, Little Rock, Ark., 2006. DVD.

Lowman, Myers G. *Citizens' Council Forum*. Reel no. 27. 1963. Videocassette.

———. *Citizens' Council Forum*. Reel no. 33. 1963. Videocassette.

———. *Citizens' Council Forum*. Reel no. 56. 1963. Videocassette.

———. *Citizens' Council Forum*. Reel no. 96. N.d. [1963]. Videocassette.

Lowman, Myers G., and John Bell Williams. *Citizens' Council Forum*. Reel no. 37. 1963. Videocassette.

The Murder of Emmett Till. Directed by Stanley Nelson. PBS, Alexandria, Va., 2003. Videocassette.

Neshoba: The Price of Freedom. Produced and directed by Micki Dickoff and Tony Pagano. Pro Bono Productions and Pagano Productions, New York, 2010. DVD.

"Responsibilities of American Citizenship." *The American Adventure* series. Produced by National Education Program, Harding College, Searcy, Ark., 1955. *Moving Images*. Internet Archive, San Francisco. Online MPEG movie.

Satterfield, John C. *Citizens' Council Forum*. Reel no. 35. 1963. Videocassette.

Segregation and the South. Produced by George M. Martin Jr. Newsfilm Project, Fund for the Republic, Los Angeles, 1957. Center for the Study of Democratic Institutions Collection, Department of Special Collections, Donald C. Davidson Library, University of California at Santa Barbara, Santa Barbara. Videocassette.

Synon, John J. *Citizens' Council Forum*. Reel no. 57. 1963. Videocassette.

Talmadge, Herman E. Interview by Larry Lesueur and Kenneth Crawford. *Longines Chronoscope: A Television Journal of the Important Issues of the Hour* series. CBS, Apr. 14, 1954. *Moving Images*. Internet Archive, San Francisco. Online MPEG movie.

Thrasher, Sue. "A White Southerner in the Civil Rights Movement." Presentation. Annual Civil Rights Conference. University of Tennessee at Martin, Martin, Feb. 24, 2011. Webcast.

Winter, William F. "Opening the Closed Society." Panel discussion. *MCast Video* series. Meek School of Journalism and New Media, University of Mississippi, University, Sept. 30, 2011. Online video.

FEDERAL AND STATE GOVERNMENT PUBLICATIONS

Acts and Joint Resolutions of the General Assembly of the Commonwealth of Virginia.

Acts and Resolutions of the General Assembly of the State of Georgia.

Alabama Legislative Commission to Preserve the Peace. *Communists in Civil Rights*. Montgomery: Alabama Legislative Commission to Preserve the Peace, 1964.

————. *The 1964 Civil Rights Bill: Its Pattern, Its Architects*. Montgomery: Alabama Legislative Commission to Preserve the Peace, 1964.

Congressional Record.

Florida Bureau of Archives and Records Management. *The Black Experience: A Guide to African American Resources in the Florida State Archives*. Rev. ed. Tallahassee: Florida Bureau of Archives and Records Management, 2002.

Florida Legislative Investigation Committee. *Homosexuality and Citizenship in Florida: A Report of the Florida Legislative Investigation Committee*. Tallahassee: Florida Legislative Investigation Committee, 1964.

Florida Special Assistant Attorney General [Ellis S. Rubin]. *Report on Investigation of Subversive Activities in Florida*. Miami: n.p., 1955.

Georgia Commission on Education. *Highlander Folk School: Communist Training School, Monteagle, Tennessee*. Atlanta: Georgia Commission on Education, n.d. [1957].

————. *Ten Directors of the N.A.A.C.P.* Atlanta: Georgia Commission on Education, n.d. [1957].

————. *Communism and the NAACP*. 2 vols. Atlanta: Georgia Commission on Education, n.d. [1958].

Georgia Official and Statistical Register (formerly *Georgia's Official Register*).

Georgia State Law Department, comp. and ed. *Compilation of Georgia Laws and Opinions of the Attorney General Relating to Segregation of the Races*. Atlanta: Georgia State Law Department, 1956.

Georgia's Official Register.

Journal of the House of Representatives of the State of Mississippi.

Journal of the Senate of the State of Mississippi.

Laws of the State of Mississippi.

Louisiana Joint Legislative Committee. *Biennial Report, 1954–1956*. Baton Rouge: Louisiana Joint Legislative Committee, 1956.

————. *Subversion in Racial Unrest: An Outline of a Strategic Weapon to Destroy the Governments of Louisiana and the United States*. 2 vols. Baton Rouge: Louisiana Joint Legislative Committee, n.d. [1957–58].

————. *Segregation Measures Passed by the Regular Session of the Louisiana Legislature, 1958*. Baton Rouge: Louisiana Joint Legislative Committee, 1959.

Louisiana Joint Legislative Committee on Un-American Activities. *The Case of Dr. Waldo F. McNeir*. Baton Rouge: Louisiana Joint Legislative Committee on Un-American Activities, 1961.

————. *Activities of the Southern Conference Educational Fund, Inc., in Louisiana*. 3 vols. Baton Rouge: Louisiana Joint Legislative Committee on Un-American Activities, 1963–65.

————. *Activities of the "Ku Klux Klan" and Certain Other Organizations in Louisiana*. Baton Rouge: Louisiana Joint Legislative Committee on Un-American Activities, 1965.

Louisiana State Advisory Committee to the United States Commission on Civil Rights. *The New Orleans School Crisis: Report of the Louisiana State Advisory Committee to the United States Commission on Civil Rights.* Washington, D.C.: GPO, 1961.

Louisiana State Sovereignty Commission. *Fifty Sovereign States or Fifty Federal Districts?* Baton Rouge: Louisiana State Sovereignty Commission, n.d.

Louisiana State Sovereignty Commission and Louisiana Joint Legislative Committee. *Don't Be Brainwashed!: We Don't Have to Integrate Our Schools!* Baton Rouge: Louisiana State Sovereignty Commission and Louisiana Joint Legislative Committee, n.d.

Mississippi General Legislative Investigating Committee. *A Report by the General Legislative Investigating Committee to the Mississippi State Legislature Concerning the Occupation of the Campus of the University of Mississippi, September 30, 1962, by the Department of Justice of the United States.* Jackson: Mississippi General Legislative Investigating Committee, 1963.

———. *A Report to the 1962 Regular Session of the Mississippi State Legislature on the Investigation of Un-American Activities in the State of Mississippi.* Jackson: Mississippi General Legislative Investigating Committee, n.d.

President's Committee on Civil Rights. *To Secure These Rights: The Report of the President's Committee on Civil Rights.* Washington, D.C.: GPO, 1947.

Public Papers of the Presidents of the United States: John F. Kennedy. Washington, D.C.: GPO, 1962–64.

U.S. Commission on Civil Rights. *1961 United States Commission on Civil Rights Report.* 5 books. Washington, D.C.: GPO, n.d.

U.S. Congress. House. Committee on Un-American Activities. *Southern Conference for Human Welfare.* 80th Cong., 1st sess., June 16, 1947.

———. House. Committee on Un-American Activities. *Hearings Regarding Communist Activities in the Cincinnati, Ohio, Area, July 12–15, August 8, 1950.* 81st Cong., 2d sess., 1950.

———. House. Committee on Un-American Activities. *Guide to Subversive Organizations and Publications (and Appendix).* Rev. ed. 82d Cong., 1st sess., May 14, 1951.

———. House. Committee on Un-American Activities. *Review of the Methodist Federation for Social Action.* 82d Cong., 2d sess., Feb. 17, 1952.

———. House. Committee on Un-American Activities. *Annual Report of the Committee on Un-American Activities for the Year 1953.* 83d Cong., 2d sess., Feb. 6, 1954.

———. House. Committee on Un-American Activities. *The American Negro in the Communist Party.* 83d Cong., 2d sess., Dec. 22, 1954.

———. House. Committee on Un-American Activities. *Investigation of Communist Activities in the Dayton, Ohio, Area, September 13–15, 1954.* 83d Cong., 2d sess., 1954.

———. House. Committee on Un-American Activities. *Investigation of Communist Propaganda in the United States: Part 4 (Foreign Propaganda—Entry and Dissemination in New Orleans, La., Area).* 85th Cong., 1st sess., Feb. 14, 1957.

———. House. Committee on Un-American Activities. *The Truth about the Film "Operation Abolition": Report (Supplemental to House Report № 2228, Eighty-Sixth Congress, Second Session)*. 87th Cong., 1st sess., 1961.

———. Senate. Committee on Governmental Affairs. *Executive Sessions of the Senate Permanent Subcommittee on Investigations of the Committee on Government Operations: Volume 1, Eighty-Third Congress, First Session, 1953*. 107th Cong., 2d sess., Jan. 2003.

———. Senate. Committee on the Judiciary. Subcommittee to Investigate the Administration of the Internal Security Act and Other Internal Security Laws. *Subversive Influence in Southern Conference Educational Fund, Inc., March 18, 19, and 20, 1954*. 83d Cong., 2d sess., 1955.

———. Senate. Committee on the Judiciary. Subcommittee to Investigate the Administration of the Internal Security Act and Other Internal Security Laws. *The Communist Party of the United States of America: What It Is, How It Works—A Handbook for Americans*. 84th Cong., 1st sess., 1955.

———. Senate. Committee on the Judiciary. Subcommittee to Investigate the Administration of the Internal Security Act and Other Internal Security Laws. *Communism in the Mid-South*. 85th Cong., 1st sess., 1957.

———. Senate. Select Committee to Study Governmental Operations with Respect to Intelligence Activities. *Supplementary Detailed Staff Reports on Intelligence Activities and the Rights of Americans*. Book 3 of *Final Report*. 94th Cong., 2d sess., Apr. 23, 1976.

Wehrkamp, Tim, comp. *Reference Information Paper 107: A Finding Aid to National Archives Records Relating to the Cold War*. Online ed.

BOOKS, BOOKLETS, AND BROCHURES

Abernathy, Donzaleigh. *Partners to History: Martin Luther King Jr., Ralph David Abernathy, and the Civil Rights Movement*. New York: Crown, 2003.

Adams, Frank T. *James A. Dombrowski: An American Heretic, 1897–1983*. Knoxville: University of Tennessee Press, 1992.

Adams, Frank, and Myles Horton. *Unearthing Seeds of Fire: The Idea of Highlander*. Winston-Salem, N.C.: John F. Blair, 1975.

Alford, Dale, and L'Moore Alford. *The Case of the Sleeping People*. Little Rock, Ark.: Pioneer, 1959.

Alston, Alex A., Jr., and James L. Dickerson. *Devil's Sanctuary: An Eyewitness History of Mississippi Hate Crimes*. Chicago: Lawrence Hill, 2009.

Alwood, Edward. *Dark Days in the Newsroom: McCarthyism Aimed at the Press*. Philadelphia: Temple University Press, 2007.

American Civil Liberties Union. *"Testing Whether That Nation."* New York: American Civil Liberties Union, n.d. [1961].

American Coalition. *The American Coalition: Why It Was Organized and What It Does*. Washington, D.C.: American Coalition, 1940.

Anderson, Karen. *Little Rock: Race and Resistance at Central High School*. Princeton, N.J.: Princeton University Press, 2009.

Anderson, R. Bentley. *Black, White, and Catholic: New Orleans Interracialism, 1947–1956*. Nashville, Tenn.: Vanderbilt University Press, 2005.

Anderson, William. *The Wild Man from Sugar Creek: The Political Career of Eugene Talmadge*. Baton Rouge: Louisiana State University Press, 1975.

Andrew, John A., III. *Power to Destroy: The Political Uses of the IRS from Kennedy to Nixon*. Chicago: Ivan R. Dee, 2002.

Applebome, Peter. *Dixie Rising: How the South Is Shaping American Values, Politics, and Culture*. New York: Crown, 1996.

Arsenault, Raymond. *Freedom Riders: 1961 and the Struggle for Racial Justice*. New York: Oxford University Press, 2006.

Asch, Chris Myers. *The Senator and the Sharecropper: The Freedom Struggle of James O. Eastland and Fannie Lou Hamer*. New York: New Press, 2008. Reprint, Chapel Hill: University of North Carolina Press, 2011.

Ashmore, Harry S. *Civil Rights and Wrongs: A Memoir of Race and Politics, 1944–1996*. Rev. and expanded ed. Columbia: University of South Carolina Press, 1997.

———. *Hearts and Minds: A Personal Chronicle of Race in America*. Rev. ed. Cabin John, Md.: Seven Locks, 1988.

Association of Citizens' Councils of Louisiana. *The Citizens' Councils: Their Platform*. Homer: Guardian-Journal, n.d.

Association of Citizens' Councils of Mississippi. *Statewide Cash Awards: Essay Contest for Mississippi High School Students, 1960–1961*. Greenwood: Association of Citizens' Councils of Mississippi, n.d. [1960].

Baer, Frances Lisa. *Resistance to Public School Desegregation: Little Rock, Arkansas, and Beyond*. El Paso, Tex.: LFB Scholarly, 2008.

Bailey, D'Army, and Roger Easson. *The Education of a Black Radical: A Southern Civil Rights Activist's Journey, 1959–1964*. Baton Rouge: Louisiana State University Press, 2009.

Bales, James D. *The Martin Luther King Story: A Study in Apostasy, Agitation, and Anarchy*. Tulsa, Okla.: Christian Crusade, 1967.

Barnard, William D. *Dixiecrats and Democrats: Alabama Politics, 1942–1950*. Tuscaloosa: University of Alabama Press, 1974.

Barnett, Ross R. *Ross R. Barnett, Governor of State of Mississippi, before the Commerce Committee of the United States Senate, Washington, D.C., July 12, 1963*. N.p.: n.p., n.d.

Barrett, Russell H. *Integration at Ole Miss*. Chicago: Quadrangle, 1965.

Bartley, Numan V. *The New South, 1945–1980*. Baton Rouge: Louisiana State University Press, 1995.

————. *The Rise of Massive Resistance: Race and Politics in the South during the 1950's.* Baton Rouge: Louisiana State University Press, 1969.

Bartley, Numan V., and Hugh D. Graham, comps. *Southern Elections: County and Precinct Date, 1950–1972.* Baton Rouge: Louisiana State University Press, 1978.

Bass, Jack, and Walter DeVries. *The Transformation of Southern Politics: Social Change and Political Consequence since 1945.* New York: Basic, 1976.

Bates, Daisy. *The Long Shadow of Little Rock: A Memoir.* New York: David McKay, 1962. Reprint, Fayetteville: University of Arkansas Press, 1986.

Beals, Melba Pattillo. *Warriors Don't Cry: A Searing Memoir of the Battle to Integrate Little Rock's Central High.* New York: Washington Square, 1994.

Belfrage, Sally. *Freedom Summer.* New York: Viking, 1965. Reprint, Charlottesville: University Press of Virginia, 1990.

Bell, Brenda, John Gaventa, and John Peters, eds. *We Make the Road by Walking: Conversations on Education and Social Change—Myles Horton and Paulo Freire.* Philadelphia: Temple University Press, 1990.

Bell, Daniel. *Marxian Socialism in the United States.* Ithaca, N.Y.: Cornell University Press, 1996.

Benedict, Michael Les, and John F. Winkler, eds. *The History of Ohio Law.* 2 vols. Athens: Ohio University Press, 2004.

Benson, George S., and Phil Watson. *Missionary Experiences.* Delight, Ark.: Gospel Light, 1987.

Bentley, Eric, ed. *Thirty Years of Treason: Excerpts from Hearings before the House Committee on Un-American Activities, 1938–1968.* New York: Viking, 1971.

Berg, Manfred. *"The Ticket to Freedom": The NAACP and the Struggle for Black Political Integration.* Gainesville: University Press of Florida, 2005.

Bernstein, Irving. *Promises Kept: John F. Kennedy's New Frontier.* New York: Oxford University Press, 1991.

Black, Earl. *Southern Governors and Civil Rights: Racial Segregation as a Campaign Issue in the Second Reconstruction.* Cambridge: Harvard University Press, 1976.

Black, Earl, and Merle Black. *The Rise of Southern Republicans.* Cambridge: Harvard University Press, 2002.

Blake, John. *Children of the Movement.* Chicago: Lawrence Hill, 2004.

Bloch, Charles J. *States' Rights: The Law of the Land.* Atlanta: Harrison, 1958.

————. *We Need Not Integrate to Educate.* Atlanta: States' Rights Council of Georgia, n.d.

Boduch, Jodie Lynn, ed. *States' Rights.* Farmington Hills, Mich.: Greenhaven, 2006.

Boles, John B., ed. *Shapers of Southern History: Autobiographical Reflections.* Athens: University of Georgia Press, 2004.

Bolton, Charles C. *The Hardest Deal of All: The Battle over School Integration in Mississippi, 1870–1980.* Jackson: University Press of Mississippi, 2005.

Borstelmann, Thomas. *The Cold War and the Color Line: American Race Relations in the Global Arena.* Cambridge: Harvard University Press, 2001.

Boyle, Sarah Patton. *The Desegregated Heart: A Virginia's Stand in Time of Transition.* New York: William Morrow, 1962. Reprint, Charlottesville: University Press of Virginia, 2001.

Braden, Anne. *House Un-American Activities Committee: Bulwark of Segregation.* Los Angeles: National Committee to Abolish the House Un-American Activities Committee, n.d. [1964].

Brady, Tom P. *Black Monday.* Brookhaven, Miss.: n.p., 1954.

———. *Black Monday.* Reprint ed. Winona, Miss.: Association of Citizens' Councils, 1955.

———. *The South at Bay.* Brookhaven, Miss.: n.p., 1948.

Branch, Taylor. *Parting the Waters: America in the King Years, 1954–63.* New York: Simon and Schuster, 1988.

———. *Pillar of Fire: America in the King Years, 1963–65.* New York: Simon and Schuster, 1998.

Braukman, Stacy. *Communists and Perverts under the Palms: The Johns Committee in Florida, 1956–1965.* Gainesville: University Press of Florida, 2012.

Brewer, Vivion Lenon. *The Embattled Ladies of Little Rock, 1958–1963: The Struggle to Save Public Education at Central High.* Fort Bragg, Calif.: Lost Coast, 1999.

Bridges, Tyler. *The Rise of David Duke.* Jackson: University Press of Mississippi, 1994.

Brinkley, Douglas. *Rosa Parks: A Life.* New York: Viking, 2000. Reprint, New York: Penguin, 2005.

Brown, Sarah Hart. *Standing against Dragons: Three Southern Lawyers in an Era of Fear.* Baton Rouge: Louisiana State University Press, 1998.

Brown-Nagin, Tomiko. *Courage to Dissent: Atlanta and the Long History of the Civil Rights Movement.* New York: Oxford University Press, 2011.

Bryan, G. McLeod. *These Few Also Paid a Price: Southern Whites Who Fought for Civil Rights.* Macon, Ga.: Mercer University Press, 2001.

Bryant, William Cullen. *Poems of William Cullen Bryant.* New York: Oxford University Press, 1914.

Buchanan, Scott E. *"Some of the People Who Ate My Barbecue Didn't Vote for Me": The Life of Georgia Governor Marvin Griffin.* Nashville, Tenn.: Vanderbilt University Press, 2011.

Buckley, William F., Jr. *The Committee and Its Critics: A Calm Review of the House Committee on Un-American Activities.* New York: G. P. Putnam's Sons, 1962.

Buhle, Mari Jo, Paul Buhle, and Dan Georgakas, eds. *Encyclopedia of the American Left.* 2d ed. New York: Oxford University Press, 1998.

Burk, Robert F. *The Eisenhower Administration and Black Civil Rights.* Knoxville: University of Tennessee Press, 1984.

Cagin, Seth, and Philip Dray. *We Are Not Afraid: The Story of Goodman, Schwerner, and Chaney and the Civil Rights Campaign for Mississippi.* New York: Scribner, 1988. Reprint, New York: Nation Books, 2006.

Cain, Edward. *They'd Rather Be Right: Youth and the Conservative Movement.* New York: Macmillan, 1963.

Campbell, Will D. *Providence*. Atlanta: Longstreet, 1992.

Carleton, Don E. *Red Scare!: Right-Wing Hysteria, Fifties Fanaticism, and Their Legacy in Texas*. Austin: Texas Monthly Press, 1985.

Carson, Clayborne, Susan Carson, Adrienne Clay, Virginia Shradron, and Kieran Taylor, eds. *Symbol of the Movement, January 1957–December 1958*. Vol. 4 of *The Papers of Martin Luther King, Jr*. Berkeley: University of California Press, 2000.

Carson, Clayborne, Tenisha Armstrong, Susan Carson, Adrienne Clay, and Kieran Taylor, eds. *Threshold of a New Decade, January 1959–December 1960*. Vol. 5 of *The Papers of Martin Luther King, Jr*. Berkeley: University of California Press, 2005.

Carter Dan T. *The Politics of Rage: George Wallace, the Origins of the New Conservatism, and the Transformation of American Politics*. New York: Simon and Schuster, 1995. Reprint, Baton Rouge: Louisiana State University Press, 1996.

Carter, Hodding, III. *The South Strikes Back*. Garden City, N.Y.: Doubleday, 1959.

Cash, W. J. *The Mind of the South*. New York: Knopf, 1941. Reprint, New York: Vintage, 1991.

Caute, David. *The Great Fear: The Anti-Communist Purge under Truman and Eisenhower*. New York: Simon and Schuster, 1978.

Celler, Emanuel. *You Never Leave Brooklyn: The Autobiography of Emanuel Celler*. New York: John Day, 1953.

Ceplair, Larry. *Anti-Communism in Twentieth-Century America: A Critical History*. Westport, Conn.: Praeger, 2011.

Chafe, William H., ed. *The Achievement of American Liberalism: The New Deal and Its Legacies*. New York: Columbia University Press, 2003.

Chappell, David L. *Inside Agitators: White Southerners in the Civil Rights Movement*. Baltimore: Johns Hopkins University Press, 1994.

———. *A Stone of Hope: Prophetic Religion and the Death of Jim Crow*. Chapel Hill: University of North Carolina Press, 2004.

Charron, Katherine Mellen. *Freedom's Teacher: The Life of Septima Clark*. Chapel Hill: University of North Carolina Press, 2009.

Cherny, Robert W., William Issel, and Kieran Walsh Taylor, eds. *American Labor and the Cold War: Grassroots Politics and Postwar Political Culture*. New Brunswick, N.J.: Rutgers University Press, 2004.

Church League of America. *Catalog of Publications and Training Aids of the Church League of America*. Wheaton, Ill.: Church League of America, 1967.

Circuit Riders. *Fifty Years of Un-Methodist Propaganda*. Cincinnati, Ohio: Circuit Riders, 1957.

———. *Information Concerning the Methodist Federation for Social Action*. Cincinnati, Ohio: Circuit Riders, 1952.

———. *Principles and Purposes*. Cincinnati, Ohio: Circuit Riders, n.d. [1953].

———. *Recognize Red China?: An Exposé of the National Council of Churches World Order Study Conference, Cleveland, Ohio, November 18–21, 1958*. Cincinnati, Ohio: Circuit Riders, 1959.

Civil Rights Congress. *America's "Thought Police": Record of the Un-American Activities Committee.* New York: Civil Rights Congress, 1947.

Clark, E. Culpepper. *The Schoolhouse Door: Segregation's Last Stand at the University of Alabama.* New York: Oxford University Press, 1995.

Clowse, Barbara Barksdale. *Ralph McGill: A Biography.* Macon, Ga.: Mercer University Press, 1998.

Cobb, James C. *The* Brown *Decision, Jim Crow, and Southern Identity.* Athens: University of Georgia Press, 2005.

———. *The Most Southern Place on Earth: The Mississippi Delta and the Roots of Regional Identity.* New York: Oxford University Press, 1992.

Cobb, James C., and Charles R. Wilson, eds. *Perspectives on the American South: An Annual Review of Society, Politics and Culture.* Vol. 3. New York: Gordon and Breach Science, 1985.

Cobb, William H. *Radical Education in the Rural South: Commonwealth College, 1922–1940.* Detroit: Wayne State University Press, 2000.

Cohodas, Nadine. *Strom Thurmond and the Politics of Southern Change.* New York: Simon and Schuster, 1993.

Collins, Donald E. *When the Church Bell Rang Racist: The Methodist Church and the Civil Rights Movement in Alabama.* Macon, Ga.: Mercer University Press, 1998.

Committee for the Preservation of Methodism. *Is There a Pink Fringe in the Methodist Church?: If So, What Shall We Do about It?* Houston, Tex.: Committee for the Preservation of Methodism, 1951.

Conaway, James. *Judge: The Life and Times of Leander Perez.* New York: Knopf, 1973.

Cook, Eugene. *The Ugly Truth about the NAACP: An Address by Attorney General Eugene Cook of Georgia before the Fifty-Fifth Annual Convention of the Peace Officers['] Association of Georgia Held in Atlanta.* Greenwood: Association of Citizens' Councils of Mississippi, n.d. [1957].

Cook, James Graham. *The Segregationists.* New York: Appleton-Century-Crofts, 1962.

Cook, Robert. *Sweet Land of Liberty?: The African-American Struggle for Civil Rights in the Twentieth Century.* London: Longman, 1998.

Council of Conservative Citizens. *The King Holiday and Its Meaning: Speech by Senator Jesse Helms.* St. Louis, Mo.: Council of Conservative Citizens, 1998.

Cowan, Walter Greaves, and Jack B. McGuire. *Louisiana Governors: Rulers, Rascals, and Reformers.* Jackson: University Press of Mississippi, 2008.

Crespino, Joseph. *In Search of Another Country: Mississippi and the Conservative Counterrevolution.* Princeton, N.J.: Princeton University Press, 2007.

Crosby, Donald F. *God, Church, and Flag: Senator Joseph R. McCarthy and the Catholic Church, 1950–1957.* Chapel Hill: University of North Carolina Press, 2009.

Cunningham, W. J. *Agony at Galloway: One Church's Struggle with Social Change.* Jackson: University Press of Mississippi, 1980.

Daniel, Pete. *Lost Revolutions: The South in the 1950s.* Chapel Hill: University of North Carolina Press, 2000.

Daugherity, Brian J., and Charles C. Bolton, eds. *With All Deliberate Speed: Implementing* Brown v. Board of Education. Fayetteville: University of Arkansas Press, 2008.

Davidson, Chandler. *Race and Class in Texas Politics*. Princeton, N.J.: Princeton University Press, 1990.

Davis, Jack E., ed. *The Civil Rights Movement*. Malden, Mass.: Blackwell, 2001.

Davis, Jack E., and Kari Frederickson, eds. *Making Waves: Female Activists in Twentieth-Century Florida*. Gainesville: University Press of Florida, 2003.

Deckman, Melissa M. *School Board Battles: The Christian Right in Local Politics*. Washington, D.C.: Georgetown University Press, 2004.

Diamond, Sara. *Roads to Dominion: Right-Wing Movements and Political Power in the United States*. New York: Guilford, 1995.

Dickerson, James. *Dixie's Dirty Secret: The True Story of How the Government, the Media, and the Mob Conspired to Combat Integration and the Vietnam Antiwar Movement*. Armonk, N.Y.: M. E. Sharpe, 1998.

Dickson, Keith D. *Sustaining Southern Identity: Douglas Southall Freeman and Memory in the Modern South*. Baton Rouge: Louisiana State University Press, 2011.

Dies, Martin. *The Trojan Horse in America*. New York: Dodd, Mead, 1940.

Dittmer, John. *Local People: The Struggle for Civil Rights in Mississippi*. Urbana: University of Illinois Press, 1994.

Dochuk, Darren. *From Bible Belt to Sunbelt: Plain-Folk Religion, Grassroots Politics, and the Rise of Evangelical Conservatism*. New York: Norton, 2011.

Donner, Frank J. *The Age of Surveillance: The Aims and Methods of America's Political Intelligence System*. New York: Vintage, 1981.

Dorrien, Gary. *The Making of American Liberal Theology: Crisis, Irony, and Postmodernity, 1950–2005*. Louisville, Ky.: Westminster John Knox, 2006.

Doyle, William. *An American Insurrection: The Battle of Oxford, Mississippi, 1962*. New York: Doubleday, 2001.

Du Bois, W. E. B. *The Souls of Black Folk*. Chicago: McClurg, 1903. Reprint, New York: Barnes and Noble, 2003.

Duck, Leigh Anne. *The Nation's Region: Southern Modernism, Segregation, and U.S. Nationalism*. Athens: University of Georgia Press, 2006.

Dudziak, Mary L. *Cold War Civil Rights: Race and the Image of American Democracy*. Princeton, N.J.: Princeton University Press, 2000.

Duke, David Nelson. *In the Trenches with Jesus and Marx: Harry F. Ward and the Struggle for Social Justice*. Tuscaloosa: University of Alabama Press, 2003.

Dunaway, David King. *How Can I Keep from Singing?: The Ballad of Pete Seeger*. New York: Villard, 2008.

Dunbar, Anthony P. *Against the Grain: Southern Radicals and Prophets, 1929–1959*. Charlottesville: University Press of Virginia, 1981.

———, ed. *American Crisis, Southern Solutions: From Where We Stand, Promise and Peril*. Montgomery, Ala.: NewSouth, 2008.

Dunn, Marvin. *Black Miami in the Twentieth Century.* Gainesville: University Press of Florida, 1997.

Durr, Virginia Foster. *Outside the Magic Circle: The Autobiography of Virginia Foster Durr.* Tuscaloosa: University of Alabama Press, 1985.

Eagles, Charles W., ed. *The Civil Rights Movement in America.* Jackson: University Press of Mississippi, 1986.

———. *The Price of Defiance: James Meredith and the Integration of Ole Miss.* Chapel Hill: University of North Carolina Press, 2009.

Egerton, John. *Shades of Gray: Dispatches from the Modern South.* Baton Rouge: Louisiana State University Press, 1991.

———. *Speak Now against the Day: The Generation before the Civil Rights Movement in the South.* New York: Knopf, 1994.

Emanuel, Rachel L., and Alexander P. Tureaud, Jr. *A More Noble Cause: A. P. Tureaud and the Struggle for Civil Rights in Louisiana—A Personal Biography.* Baton Rouge: Louisiana State University Press, 2011.

Escott, Paul D., and David R. Goldfield, eds. *The South for New Southerners.* Chapel Hill: University of North Carolina Press, 1991.

Eskew, Glenn T. *But for Birmingham: The Local and National Movements in the Civil Rights Struggle.* Chapel Hill: University of North Carolina Press, 1997.

Evans, M. Stanton. *Blacklisted by History: The Untold Story of Senator Joe McCarthy and His Fight against America's Enemies.* New York: Crown Forum, 2007.

Fairclough, Adam. *Better Day Coming: Blacks and Equality, 1890–2000.* New York: Penguin, 2001.

———. *Race and Democracy: The Civil Rights Struggle in Louisiana, 1915–1972.* Athens: University of Georgia Press, 1995.

———. *To Redeem the Soul of America: The Southern Christian Leadership Conference and Martin Luther King, Jr.* Athens: University of Georgia Press, 1987.

Fariello, Griffin, ed. *Red Scare: Memories of the American Inquisition—An Oral History.* New York: Norton, 1995.

Faulkner, William. *The Mansion.* New York: Random House, 1959. Reprint, New York: Vintage, 2011.

———. *Requiem for a Nun.* New York: Random House, 1950.

Faulkner, William, Benjamin E. Mays, and Cecil Sims. *The Segregation Decisions: Papers Read at a Session of the Twenty-First Annual Meeting of the Southern Historical Association, Memphis, Tennessee, November 10, 1955.* Atlanta: Southern Regional Council, 1956.

Feldman, Glenn, ed. *Before* Brown: *Civil Rights and White Backlash in the Modern South.* Tuscaloosa: University of Alabama Press, 2004.

———, ed. *Politics and Religion in the White South.* Lexington: University Press of Kentucky, 2005.

Fellowship of Reconciliation. *That Men May Live: Statement of Purpose of the Fellowship of Reconciliation.* Nyack, N.Y.: Fellowship of Reconciliation, n.d.

Findlay, James F., Jr. *Church People in the Struggle: The National Council of Churches and the Black Freedom Movement, 1950–1970.* New York: Oxford University Press, 1993.

Finley, Keith M. *Delaying the Dream: Southern Senators and the Fight against Civil Rights, 1938–1965.* Baton Rouge: Louisiana State University Press, 2008.

Fite, Gilbert C. *Richard B. Russell, Jr., Senator from Georgia.* Chapel Hill: University of North Carolina Press, 1991.

Forster, Arnold, and Benjamin R. Epstein. *Danger on the Right: The Attitudes, Personnel, and Influence of the Radical Right and Extreme Conservatives.* New York: Random House, 1964.

Fosl, Catherine. *Subversive Southerner: Anne Braden and the Struggle for Racial Justice in the Cold War South.* New York: Palgrave, 2002.

Frank, Lisa Tendrich, and Daniel Kilbride, eds. *Southern Character: Essays in Honor of Bertram Wyatt-Brown.* Gainesville: University Press of Florida, 2011.

Franklin, John Hope. *Race and History: Selected Essays, 1938–1988.* Baton Rouge: Louisiana State University Press, 1989.

Frederick, Jeff. *Stand Up for Alabama: Governor George Wallace.* Tuscaloosa: University of Alabama Press, 2007.

Frederickson, Kari. *The Dixiecrat Revolt and the End of the Solid South, 1932–1968.* Chapel Hill: University of North Carolina Press, 2001.

Fried, Albert, ed. *McCarthyism: The Great American Red Scare—A Documentary History.* New York: Oxford University Press, 1997.

Fried, Richard M. *Nightmare in Red: The McCarthy Era in Perspective.* New York: Oxford University Press, 1990.

———. *The Russians Are Coming! The Russians Are Coming!: Pageantry and Patriotism in Cold-War America.* New York: Oxford University Press, 1998.

Friedland, Michael B. *Lift Up Your Voice Like a Trumpet: White Clergy and the Civil Rights and Antiwar Movements, 1954–1973.* Chapel Hill: University of North Carolina Press, 1998.

Gallen, David, ed. *The Quotable Truman.* New York: Carroll and Graf, 1994.

Garrow, David J. *The FBI and Martin Luther King, Jr.: From "Solo" to Memphis.* New York: Norton, 1981.

———, ed. *The Montgomery Bus Boycott and the Women Who Started It: The Memoir of Jo Ann Gibson Robinson.* Knoxville: University of Tennessee Press, 1987.

———. *Protest at Selma: Martin Luther King, Jr., and the Voting Rights Act of 1965.* New Haven: Yale University Press, 1978.

Gasman, Marybeth, and Christopher L. Tudico, eds. *Historically Black Colleges and Universities: Triumphs, Troubles, and Taboos.* New York: Palgrave, 2008.

Gillespie, G. T. *A Christian View on Segregation: Reprint of an Address by Rev. G. T. Gillespie, D.D., President Emeritus of Belhaven College, Jackson, Mississippi, Made before the Synod of Mississippi of the Presbyterian Church in the U.S.,*

November 4, 1954. Greenwood: Educational Fund of the Citizens' Councils of Mississippi, n.d.

Gilmore, Glenda Elizabeth. *Defying Dixie: The Radical Roots of Civil Rights, 1919–1950*. New York: Norton, 2008.

Glen, John M. *Highlander: No Ordinary School*. 2d ed. Knoxville: University of Tennessee Press, 1996.

Glisson, Susan M., ed. *The Human Tradition in the Civil Rights Movement*. Lanham, Md.: Rowman and Littlefield, 2006.

Goldfield, David R. *Black, White, and Southern: Race Relations and Southern Culture, 1940 to the Present*. Baton Rouge: Louisiana State University Press, 1990.

———. *Still Fighting the Civil War: The American South and Southern History*. Baton Rouge: Louisiana State University Press, 2002.

Goldinger, Carolyn, ed. *Presidential Elections since 1789*. 5th ed. Washington, D.C.: Congressional Quarterly, 1991.

Goodman, Walter. *The Committee: The Extraordinary Career of the House Committee on Un-American Activities*. Special ed. London: Book-of-the-Month Club, 1969.

Graham, Hugh Davis. *Civil Rights and the Presidency: Race and Gender in American Politics, 1960–1972*. New York: Oxford University Press, 1992.

Grantham, Dewey W. *The Life and Death of the Solid South: A Political History*. Lexington: University Press of Kentucky, 1988.

———. *The South in Modern America: A Region at Odds*. New York: HarperCollins, 1994. Reprint, Fayetteville: University of Arkansas Press, 2001.

Graves, Karen L. *And They Were Wonderful Teachers: Florida's Purge of Gay and Lesbian Teachers*. Urbana: University of Illinois Press, 2009.

Greenbaum, Andrea, ed. *Jews in South Florida*. Waltham, Mass.: Brandeis University Press, 2005.

Greenberg, Mark I. *University of South Florida: The First Fifty Years, 1956–2006*. Tampa: University of South Florida, 2006.

Greenhaw, Wayne. *Fighting the Devil in Dixie: How Civil Rights Activists Took On the Ku Klux Klan in Alabama*. Chicago: Lawrence Hill, 2011.

Grubbs, Donald H. *Cry from the Cotton: The Southern Tenant Farmers' Union and the New Deal*. Chapel Hill: University of North Carolina Press, 1971. Reprint, Fayetteville: University of Arkansas Press, 2000.

Guthman, Edwin O. *We Band of Brothers*. New York: Harper and Row, 1971.

Guthman, Edwin O., and Jeffrey Shulman, eds. *Robert Kennedy in His Own Words: The Unpublished Recollections of the Kennedy Years*. New York: Bantam, 1988.

Hall, Kermit L., and James W. Ely Jr., eds. *An Uncertain Tradition: Constitutionalism and the History of the South*. Athens: University of Georgia Press, 1989.

Hare, A. P., and Herbert H. Blumberg, eds. *Nonviolent Direct Action—American Cases: Social Psychological Analyses*. Washington, D.C.: Corpus, 1968.

Hargrave, W. Lee. *LSU Law: The Louisiana State University Law School from 1906 to 1977*. Baton Rouge: Louisiana State University Press, 2004.

Harmon, David Andrew. *Beneath the Image of the Civil Rights Movement and Race Relations: Atlanta, Georgia, 1946–1981.* New York: Garland, 1996.

Harvey, Paul. *Freedom's Coming: Religious Culture and the Shaping of the South from the Civil War through the Civil Rights Era.* Chapel Hill: University of North Carolina Press, 2005.

———. *Moses, Jesus, and the Trickster in the Evangelical South.* Athens: University of Georgia Press, 2012.

Haynes, John E. *Red Scare or Red Menace?: American Communism and Anticommunism in the Cold War Era.* Chicago: Ivan R. Dee, 1996.

Heale, M. J. *American Anticommunism: Combating the Enemy Within, 1830–1970.* Baltimore: Johns Hopkins University Press, 1990.

———. *McCarthy's Americans: Red Scare Politics in State and Nation, 1935–1965.* Athens: University of Georgia Press, 1998.

Heinemann, Ronald L. *Harry Byrd of Virginia.* Charlottesville: University Press of Virginia, 1996.

Helms, Jesse. *Here's Where I Stand: A Memoir.* New York: Random House, 2005.

Hendershot, Heather. *What's Fair on the Air?: Cold War Right-Wing Broadcasting and the Public Interest.* Chicago: University of Chicago Press, 2011.

Henderson, Harold P. *Ernest Vandiver, Governor of Georgia.* Athens: University of Georgia Press, 2000.

Henderson, Harold P., and Gary L. Roberts, eds. *Georgia Governors in an Age of Change: From Ellis Arnall to George Busbee.* Athens: University of Georgia Press, 1988.

Hendrickson, Paul. *Sons of Mississippi: A Story of Race and Its Legacy.* New York: Knopf, 2003.

Henry, Aaron, and Constance Curry. *Aaron Henry: The Fire Ever Burning.* Jackson: University Press of Mississippi, 2000.

Herman, Arthur. *Joseph McCarthy: Reexamining the Life and Legacy of America's Most Hated Senator.* New York: Free Press, 1999.

Hero, Alfred O., Jr. *The Southerner and World Affairs.* Baton Rouge: Louisiana State University Press, 1965.

Hicks, L. Edward. *"Sometimes in the Wrong, but Never in Doubt": George S. Benson and the Education of the New Religious Right.* Knoxville: University of Tennessee Press, 1995.

High, Stanley. *The Revolt of Youth.* New York: Abingdon, 1923.

Hill, Lance. *The Deacons for Defense: Armed Resistance and the Civil Rights Movement.* Chapel Hill: University of North Carolina Press, 2004.

Hinckle, Warren, and William Turner. *Deadly Secrets: The CIA-Mafia War against Castro and the Assassination of J.F.K.* New York: Thunder's Mouth, 1993.

Hobson, Fred. *Tell about the South: The Southern Rage to Explain.* Baton Rouge: Louisiana State University Press, 1983.

Hofstadter, Richard. *The Paranoid Style in American Politics and Other Essays.* New York: Knopf, 1965.

Hogan, Wesley C. *Many Minds, One Heart: SNCC's Dream for a New America*. Chapel Hill: University of North Carolina Press, 2007.

Hoover, J. Edgar. *Masters of Deceit*. New York: Henry Holt, 1958.

Horton, Myles. *The Long Haul: An Autobiography*. New York: Doubleday, 1990. Reprint, New York: Teachers College Press, 1998.

Huey, Gary. *Rebel with a Cause: P. D. East, Southern Liberalism, and the Civil Rights Movement, 1953–1971*. Wilmington, Del.: Scholarly Resources, 1985.

Hughes, Richard T. *Reviving the Ancient Faith: The Story of Churches of Christ in America*. Abilene, Tex.: Abilene Christian University Press, 2008.

Hughes, Richard T., and R. L. Roberts. *The Churches of Christ*. Westport, Conn.: Greenwood, 2001.

Hurst, Rodney L., Sr. *It Was Never about a Hot Dog and a Coke!: A Personal Account of the 1960 Sit-In Demonstrations in Jacksonville, Florida and Ax Handle Saturday*. Livermore, Calif.: WingSpan, 2008.

Hurt, R. Douglas, ed. *African American Life in the Rural South, 1900–1950*. Columbia: University of Missouri Press, 2003.

Hyde, Samuel C., Jr., ed. *Sunbelt Revolution: The Historical Progression of the Civil Rights Struggle in the Gulf South, 1866–2000*. Gainesville: University Press of Florida, 2003.

Iggers, Wilma, and Georg Iggers. *Two Lives in Uncertain Times: Facing the Challenges of the Twentieth Century as Scholars and Citizens*. New York: Berghahn, 2006.

Irons, Peter. *Jim Crow's Children: The Broken Promise of the Brown Decision*. New York: Viking, 2002.

Jackson Citizens' Council. *The Eight Ifs and Your Answer!* Jackson, Miss.: Jackson Citizens' Council, n.d.

Jacobs, Dale, ed. *The Myles Horton Reader: Education for Social Change*. Knoxville: University of Tennessee Press, 2003.

Jacoway, Elizabeth. *Turn Away Thy Son: Little Rock, the Crisis That Shocked the Nation*. New York: Free Press, 2007.

Jacoway, Elizabeth, and David R. Colburn, eds. *Southern Businessmen and Desegregation*. Baton Rouge: Louisiana State University Press, 1982.

Jacoway, Elizabeth, and C. Fred Williams, eds. *Understanding the Little Rock Crisis: An Exercise in Remembrance and Reconciliation*. Fayetteville: University of Arkansas Press, 1999.

Jeansonne, Glen. *Leander Perez: Boss of the Delta*. 2d ed. Baton Rouge: Louisiana State University Press, 1977. Reprint, Jackson: University Press of Mississippi, 2006.

Jenkins, Ray. *Blind Vengeance: The Roy Moody Mail Bomb Murders*. Athens: University of Georgia Press, 1997.

Johnson, Manning. *Color, Communism and Common Sense*. New York: Alliance, 1958.

Johnston, Erle, Jr. *Mississippi's Defiant Years, 1953–1973: An Interpretive Documentary with Personal Experiences.* Forest, Miss.: Lake Harbor, 1990.

———. *Politics: Mississippi Style.* Forest, Miss.: Lake Harbor, 1993.

Jones, Maxine D., and Kevin M. McCarthy. *African Americans in Florida.* Sarasota, Fla.: Pineapple, 1993.

Jones, Terry L. *The Louisiana Journey.* Layton, Utah: Gibbs Smith, 2007.

Karl, Frederick B. *The 57 Club: My Four Decades in Florida Politics.* Gainesville: University Press of Florida, 2010.

Katagiri, Yasuhiro. *The Mississippi State Sovereignty Commission: Civil Rights and States' Rights.* Jackson: University Press of Mississippi, 2001.

Kaufman, Robert G. *Henry M. Jackson: A Life in Politics.* Seattle: University of Washington Press, 2000.

Kellar, William Henry. *Make Haste Slowly: Moderates, Conservatives, and School Desegregation in Houston.* College Station: Texas A&M University Press, 1999.

Kelly, Alfred H., and Winfred A. Harbison. *The American Constitution: Its Origins and Development.* 5th ed. New York: Norton, 1976.

Kempton, Murray. *Part of Our Time: Some Ruins and Monuments of the Thirties.* New York: Simon and Schuster, 1955. Reprint, New York: New York Review of Books, 2004.

Key, V. O., Jr. *Southern Politics in State and Nation.* New York: Knopf, 1949.

Kilbaner, Irwin. *Conscience of a Troubled South: The Southern Conference Educational Fund, 1946–1966.* Brooklyn, N.Y.: Carlson, 1989.

Killian, Lewis M. *White Southerners.* Rev. ed. Amherst: University of Massachusetts Press, 1985.

Kilpatrick, James J. *The Southern Case for School Segregation.* New York: Crowell-Collier, 1962.

———. *The Sovereign States: Notes of a Citizen of Virginia.* Chicago: Henry Regnery, 1957.

Kirk, John A. *Redefining the Color Line: Black Activism in Little Rock, Arkansas, 1940–1970.* Gainesville: University Press of Florida, 2002.

Klarman, Michael J. *From Jim Crow to Civil Rights: The Supreme Court and the Struggle for Racial Equality.* New York: Oxford University Press, 2004.

Klehr, Harvey. *The Heyday of American Communism: The Depression Decade.* New York: Basic, 1984.

Klehr, Harvey, John Earl Haynes, and Kyrill M. Anderson. *The Soviet World of American Communism.* New Haven: Yale University Press, 1998.

Kluger, Richard. *Simple Justice: The History of Brown v. Board of Education and Black America's Struggle for Equality.* New York: Knopf, 1976.

K'Meyer, Tracy Elaine. *Interracialism and Christian Community in the Postwar South: The Story of Koinonia Farm.* Charlottesville: University Press of Virginia, 1997.

Knott, Walter. *Will We Keep Our Freedom?* Buena Park, Calif. [?]: Americanism Educational League, n.d. [1972].

Kruse, Kevin M. *White Flight: Atlanta and the Making of Modern Conservatism.* Princeton, N.J.: Princeton University Press, 2007.

Kuettner, Al. *March to a Promised Land: The Civil Rights Files of a White Reporter, 1952–1968.* Herndon, Va.: Capital, 2006.

Lassiter, Matthew D., and Andrew B. Lewis, eds. *The Moderates' Dilemma: Massive Resistance to School Desegregation in Virginia.* Charlottesville: University Press of Virginia, 1998.

Lassiter, Matthew D., and Joseph Crespino, eds. *The Myth of Southern Exceptionalism.* New York: Oxford University Press, 2009.

Leonard, Kevin Allen. *The Battle for Los Angeles: Racial Ideology and World War II.* Albuquerque: University of New Mexico Press, 2006.

Lesher, Stephan. *George Wallace: American Populist.* Reading, Mass.: Addison-Wesley, 1994.

Leuchtenburg, William E. *The White House Looks South: Franklin D. Roosevelt, Harry S. Truman, Lyndon B. Johnson.* Baton Rouge: Louisiana State University Press, 2005.

Lewis, George. *The White South and the Red Menace: Segregationists, Anticommunism, and Massive Resistance, 1945–1965.* Gainesville: University Press of Florida, 2004.

Lichtman, Robert M. *The Supreme Court and McCarthy-Era Repression: One Hundred Decisions.* Urbana: University of Illinois Press, 2012.

Lichtman, Robert M., and Ronald D. Cohen. *Deadly Farce: Harvey Matusow and the Informer System in the McCarthy Era.* Urbana: University of Illinois Press, 2004.

Link, William A. *Righteous Warrior: Jesse Helms and the Rise of Modern Conservatism.* New York: St. Martin's, 2008.

Longley, Kyle, Jeremy D. Mayer, Michael Schaller, and John W. Sloan. *Deconstructing Reagan: Conservative Mythology and America's Fortieth President.* Armonk, N.Y.: M. E. Sharpe, 2007.

Lord, Walter. *The Past That Would Not Die.* New York: Harper and Row, 1965.

Lorence, James J. *A Hard Journey: The Life of Don West.* Urbana: University of Illinois Press, 2007.

Lovett, Bobby L. *The Civil Rights Movement in Tennessee: A Narrative History.* Knoxville: University of Tennessee Press, 2005.

Lowndes, Joseph E. *From the New Deal to the New Right: Race and the Southern Origins of Modern Conservatism.* New Haven: Yale University Press, 2008.

Lubin, Alex. *Romance and Rights: The Politics of Interracial Intimacy, 1945–1954.* Jackson: University Press of Mississippi, 2005.

Malvasi, Mark G. *The Unregenerate South: The Agrarian Thought of John Crowe Ransom, Allen Tate, and Donald Davidson.* Baton Rouge: Louisiana State University Press, 1997.

Manis, Andrew M. *Macon Black and White: An Unutterable Separation in the American Century.* Macon, Ga.: Mercer University Press, 2004.

———. *Southern Civil Religions in Conflict: Civil Rights and the Culture Wars*. Macon, Ga.: Mercer University Press, 2002.

Mars, Florence. *Witness in Philadelphia*. Baton Rouge: Louisiana State University Press, 1977.

Marsh, Charles. *God's Long Summer: Stories of Faith and Civil Rights*. Princeton, N.J.: Princeton University Press, 1997.

Marshall, James P. *Student Activism and Civil Rights in Mississippi: Protest Politics and the Struggle for Racial Justice, 1960–1965*. Baton Rouge: Louisiana State University Press, 2013.

Martin, John Bartlow. *The Deep South Says "Never."* New York: Ballantine, 1957.

Marty, Martin E. *Under God, Indivisible, 1941–1960*. Vol. 3 of *Modern American Religion*. Chicago: University of Chicago Press, 1996.

Matthews, J. B. *Communism in Our Churches*. Collingswood, N.J.: Christian Beacon, 1958.

———. *Doctor Matthews' Amazing Statement before the Dies' Committee Investigating Un-American Activities*. New York: American Immigration Conference Board, n.d.

———. *Odyssey of a Fellow Traveler*. New York: Mount Vernon, 1938.

———. *Some Facts about the Communist Apparatus*. Searcy, Ark.: Harding College Press, n.d.

———. *The "United Front" Exposed*. New York: League for Constitutional Government, 1938.

Matthews, J. B., and R. E. Shallcross. *Partners in Plunder: The Cost of Business Dictatorship*. New York: Covici Friede, 1935.

Mays, Benjamin E. *Born to Rebel: An Autobiography*. New York: Charles Scribner's Sons, 1971. Reprint, Athens: University of Georgia Press, 1987.

McAdam, Doug. *Freedom Summer*. New York: Oxford University Press, 1988.

McAtee, William G. *Transformed: A White Mississippi Pastor's Journey into Civil Rights and Beyond*. Jackson: University Press of Mississippi, 2011.

McCarthy, Joe. *McCarthyism: The Fight for America*. New York: Devin-Adair, 1952.

McEllhenney, John G. *Two Hundred Years of United Methodism: An Illustrated History*. Madison, N.J.: Drew University, 1984. Online ed.

McGill, Ralph. *The South and the Southerner*. Boston: Little, Brown, 1963. Reprint, Athens: University of Georgia Press, 1992.

McGirr, Lisa. *Suburban Warriors: The Origins of the New American Right*. Princeton, N.J.: Princeton University Press, 2001.

McGuiness, Colleen, ed. *National Party Conventions, 1831–1988*. Washington, D.C.: Congressional Quarterly, 1991.

McGuire, Danielle L., and John Dittmer, eds. *Freedom Rights: New Perspectives on the Civil Rights Movement*. Lexington: University Press of Kentucky, 2011.

McMillen, Neil R. *The Citizens' Council: Organized Resistance to the Second Reconstruction, 1954–1964*. Urbana: University of Illinois Press, 1971.

Meier, August. *A White Scholar and the Black Community, 1945–1965: Essays and Reflections.* Amherst: University of Massachusetts Press, 1992.

Meyers, Robert, ed. *Voices of Concern: Critical Studies in Church of Christism.* St. Louis, Mo.: Mission Messenger, 1966.

Miller, Laura A. *Fearless: Irene Gaston Samuel and the Life of a Southern Liberal.* Little Rock: Center for Arkansas Studies of the University of Arkansas at Little Rock, 2002.

Miller, Steven P. *Billy Graham and the Rise of the Republican South.* Philadelphia: University of Pennsylvania Press, 2009.

Minor, Bill. *Eyes on Mississippi: A Fifty-Year Chronicle of Change.* Jackson, Miss.: J. Prichard Morris, 2001.

Mooney, Booth. *LBJ: An Irreverent Chronicle.* New York: Crowell, 1976.

Morris, Willie. *My Mississippi.* Jackson: University Press of Mississippi, 2000.

———. *Yazoo: Integration in a Deep-Southern Town.* 2d ed. Fayetteville: University of Arkansas Press, 2012.

Mullins, Andrew P., Jr., ed. *The Measure of Our Days: Writings of William F. Winter.* Jackson: University Press of Mississippi, 2006.

Murphy, Paul V. *The Rebuke of History: The Southern Agrarians and American Conservative Thought.* Chapel Hill: University of North Carolina Press, 2001.

Muse, Benjamin. *Ten Years of Prelude: The Story of Integration since the Supreme Court's 1954 Decision.* New York: Viking, 1964.

Myrdal, Gunnar. *An American Dilemma: The Negro Problem and Modern Democracy.* 2 vols. New York: Harper and Brothers, 1944.

Namorato, Michael V., ed. *Have We Overcome?: Race Relations since Brown, 1954–1979.* Jackson: University Press of Mississippi, 1979.

Nasaw, David. *The Chief: The Life of William Randolph Hearst.* Boston: Houghton Mifflin, 2000.

National Education Program. *The Origin and Purpose of the National Education Program.* Searcy, Ark.: National Education Program, n.d.

Nelson, Jack, and Gene Roberts Jr. *The Censors and the Schools.* Boston: Little, Brown, 1963.

Newton, Michael. *The Ku Klux Klan in Mississippi: A History.* Jefferson, N.C.: McFarland, 2010.

Nickerson, Michelle M. *Mothers of Conservatism: Women and the Postwar Right.* Princeton, N.J.: Princeton University Press, 2012.

Norris, Hoke, ed. *We Dissent.* New York: St. Martin's, 1962.

Norwood, Frederick A. *The Story of American Methodism.* Nashville, Tenn.: Abingdon, 1974.

O'Brien, M. J. *We Shall Not Be Moved: The Jackson Woolworth's Sit-In and the Movement It Inspired.* Jackson: University Press of Mississippi, 2013.

O'Brien, Michael. *The Idea of the American South, 1920–1941.* Baltimore: Johns Hopkins University Press, 1979.

Ogden, August Raymond. *The Dies Committee: A Study of the Special House Committee for the Investigation of Un-American Activities, 1938–1944.* Washington, D.C.: Catholic University of America Press, 1945.

Ogden, Dunbar H. *My Father Said Yes: A White Pastor in Little Rock School Integration.* Nashville, Tenn.: Vanderbilt University Press, 2008.

O'Reilly, Kenneth. *"Racial Matters": The FBI's Secret File on Black America, 1960–1972.* New York: Free Press, 1989.

Orr-Klopfer, M. Susan, Fred Klopfer, and Barry Klopfer. *Where Rebels Roost: Mississippi Civil Rights Revisited.* Raleigh, N.C.: Lulu, 2005.

Oshinsky, David M. *A Conspiracy So Immense: The World of Joe McCarthy.* New York: Free Press, 1983. Reprint, New York: Oxford University Press, 2005.

Ottanelli, Fraser M. *The Communist Party of the United States: From the Depression to World War II.* New Brunswick, N.J.: Rutgers University Press, 1991.

Ownby, Ted, ed. *Manners and Southern History.* Jackson: University Press of Mississippi, 2007.

Parent, Wayne. *Inside the Carnival: Unmasking Louisiana Politics.* Baton Rouge: Louisiana State University Press, 2004.

Parks, Rosa, and Jim Haskins. *Rosa Parks: My Story.* New York: Dial, 1992. Reprint, New York: Puffin, 1999.

Patrick Henry Group. *Is the Supreme Court Pro-Communist?: Here Are the Facts as Disclosed by United States Senator James O. Eastland, Chairman, Senate Judiciary Committee.* Richmond, Va.: Patrick Henry Group, n.d.

Patterson, James T. Brown v. Board of Education: *A Civil Rights Milestone and Its Troubled Legacy.* New York: Oxford University Press, 2001.

Patterson, Robert B. *The Citizens' Council—A History: An Address by Robert B. Patterson, Secretary, the Citizens' Councils of America, [and] Executive Secretary, Association of Citizens' Councils of Mississippi, to the Annual Leadership Conference of the Citizens' Councils of America, Jackson, Mississippi, October 26, 1963.* Greenwood, Miss.: Association of Citizens' Councils [of Mississippi], n.d.

Pauley, Garth E. *The Modern Presidency and Civil Rights: Rhetoric on Race from Roosevelt to Nixon.* College Station: Texas A&M University Press, 2001.

Peltason, J. W. *Fifty-Eight Lonely Men: Southern Federal Judges and School Desegregation.* New York: Harcourt, Brace, and World, 1961. Reprint, Urbana: University of Illinois Press, 1971.

Permaloff, Anne, and Carl Grafton. *Political Power in Alabama: The More Things Change.* Athens: University of Georgia Press, 1995.

Perman, Michael. *Pursuit of Unity: A Political History of the American South.* Chapel Hill: University of North Carolina Press, 2009.

———. *The Southern Political Tradition.* Baton Rouge: Louisiana State University Press, 2012.

Phillips, Michael. *White Metropolis: Race, Ethnicity, and Religion in Dallas, 1841–2001.* Austin: University of Texas Press, 2006.

Pizzitola, Louis. *Hearst over Hollywood: Power, Passion, and Propaganda in the Movies.* New York: Columbia University Press, 2002.

Plummer, Brenda G., ed. *Window on Freedom: Race, Civil Rights, and Foreign Affairs, 1945–1988.* Chapel Hill: University of North Carolina Press, 2003.

Polk, Noel. *Outside the Southern Myth.* Jackson: University Press of Mississippi, 1997.

Polsgrove, Carol. *Divided Mind: Intellectuals and the Civil Rights Movement.* New York: Norton, 2001.

Powers, Richard G. *Not without Honor: The History of American Anticommunism.* New York: Free Press, 1995.

Pratt, Robert A. *We Shall Not Be Moved: The Desegregation of the University of Georgia.* Athens: University of Georgia Press, 2002.

Rabby, Glenda Alice. *The Pain and the Promise: The Struggle for Civil Rights in Tallahassee, Florida.* Athens: University of Georgia Press, 1999.

Raines, Howell. *My Soul Is Rested: Movement Days in the Deep South Remembered.* New York: G. P. Putnam's Sons, 1977.

Reagan, Ronald W. *A Time for Choosing.* Buena Park, Calif. [?]: Americanism Educational League, n.d.

Record, Wilson. *Race and Radicalism: The NAACP and the Communist Party in Conflict.* Ithaca, N.Y.: Cornell University Press, 1964.

Record, Wilson, and Jane C. Record, eds. *Little Rock, U.S.A.: Materials for Analysis.* San Francisco: Chandler, 1960.

Reed, Linda. *Simple Decency and Common Sense: The Southern Conference Movement, 1938–1963.* Bloomington: Indiana University Press, 1991.

Reed, Roy. *Beware of Limbo Dancers: A Correspondent's Adventures with the New York Times.* Fayetteville: University of Arkansas Press, 2012.

———. *Faubus: The Life and Times of an American Prodigal.* Fayetteville: University of Arkansas Press, 1997.

Reeves, Richard. *President Kennedy: Profile of Power.* New York: Simon and Schuster, 1993.

Richey, Russell E., Kenneth E. Rowe, and Jean Miller Schmidt, eds. *Perspectives on American Methodism: Interpretive Essays.* Nashville, Tenn.: Kingswood, 1993.

Roberts, Gene, and Hank Klibanoff. *The Race Beat: The Press, the Civil Rights Struggle, and the Awakening of a Nation.* New York: Knopf, 2006. Reprint, New York: Vintage, 2007.

Robinson, Armstead L., and Patricia Sullivan, eds. *New Directions in Civil Rights Studies.* Charlottesville: University Press of Virginia, 1991.

Roche, Jeff. *Restructured Resistance: The Sibley Commission and the Politics of Desegregation in Georgia.* Athens: University of Georgia Press, 1998.

Rogers, Kim Lacy. *Righteous Lives: Narratives of the New Orleans Civil Rights Movement.* New York: New York University Press, 1993.

Rogers, William W., Robert D. Ward, Leah R. Atkins, and Wayne Flynt. *Alabama: The History of a Deep South State*. Tuscaloosa: University of Alabama Press, 1994.

Root, E. Merrill. *Brainwashing in the High Schools: An Examination of Eleven American History Textbooks*. New York: Devin-Adair, 1958.

———. *Collectivism on the Campus: The Battle for the Mind in American Colleges*. New York: Devin-Adair, 1955.

Rothbard, Murray N. *The Betrayal of the American Right*. Auburn, Ala.: Ludwig von Mises Institute, 2007.

Roy, Ralph Lord. *Apostles of Discord*. Boston: Beacon, 1953.

———. *Communism and the Churches*. New York: Harcourt, Brace, 1960.

Russo, Gus. *Live by the Sword: The Secret War against Castro and the Death of JFK*. Baltimore: Bancroft, 1998.

Salter, John R., Jr. *Jackson, Mississippi: An American Chronicle of Struggle and Schism*. New York: Exposition, 1979.

Sanders, Randy. *Mighty Peculiar Elections: The New South Gubernatorial Campaigns of 1970 and the Changing Politics of Race*. Gainesville: University Press of Florida, 2002. Reprint, Baton Rouge: Louisiana State University Press, 2007.

Sansing, David G. *Making Haste Slowly: The Troubled History of Higher Education in Mississippi*. Jackson: University Press of Mississippi, 1990.

———. *The University of Mississippi: A Sesquicentennial History*. Jackson: University Press of Mississippi, 1999.

Schlesinger, Arthur M., Jr. *Robert Kennedy and His Times*. Boston: Houghton Mifflin, 1978.

Schneider, Gregory L. *The Conservative Century: From Reaction to Revolution*. Lanham, Md.: Rowman and Littlefield, 2009.

Schoenwald, Jonathan M. *A Time for Choosing: The Rise of Modern American Conservatism*. New York: Oxford University Press, 2001.

Schrecker, Ellen. *The Age of McCarthyism: A Brief History with Documents*. 2d ed. Boston: Bedford/St. Martin's, 2001.

———. *Many Are the Crimes: McCarthyism in America*. Boston: Little, Brown, 1998.

Sherrill, Robert. *Gothic Politics in the Deep South: Stars of the New Confederacy*. Rev. ed. New York: Ballantine, 1969.

Shogan, Robert. *No Sense of Decency: The Army-McCarthy Hearings—A Demagogue Falls and Television Takes Charge of American Politics*. Chicago: Ivan R. Dee, 2009.

Silver, James W. *Mississippi: The Closed Society*. New York: Harcourt, Brace, and World, 1964.

———. *Running Scared: Silver in Mississippi*. Jackson: University Press of Mississippi, 1984.

Slade, Peter. *Open Friendship in a Closed Society: Mission Mississippi and a Theology of Friendship*. New York: Oxford University Press, 2009.

Smith, Frank E. *Congressman from Mississippi*. New York: Pantheon, 1964.

Smith, Jean Edward. *Eisenhower: In War and Peace*. New York: Random House, 2012.

Smith, Lillian. *The Journey*. Cleveland, Ohio: World, 1954.

———. *Killers of the Dream*. Rev. and enlarged ed. New York: Norton, 1961.

Smith, Mark M. *How Race Is Made: Slavery, Segregation, and the Senses*. Chapel Hill: University of North Carolina Press, 2006.

Sokol, Jason. *There Goes My Everything: White Southerners in the Age of Civil Rights, 1945–1975*. New York: Knopf, 2006.

Solomon, Mark. *The Cry Was Unity: Communists and African Americans, 1917–36*. Jackson: University Press of Mississippi, 1998.

Sorensen, Theodore C. *Kennedy*. New York: Harper and Row, 1965.

Sparks, Randy J. *Religion in Mississippi*. Jackson: University Press of Mississippi, 2001.

Stanton, Mary. *From Selma to Sorrow: The Life and Death of Viola Liuzzo*. Athens: University of Georgia Press, 1998.

States' Rights Council of Georgia. *The Aims and Purposes of the States' Rights Council of Georgia, Inc.* Atlanta: States' Rights Council of Georgia, n.d.

Stockley, Grif. *Daisy Bates: Civil Rights Crusader from Arkansas*. Jackson: University Press of Mississippi, 2005.

Stokes, Melvyn, ed. *The State of U.S. History*. Oxford, U.K.: Berg, 2002.

Strober, Gerald S., and Deborah H. Strober. *"Let Us Begin Anew": An Oral History of the Kennedy Presidency*. New York: HarperCollins, 1993.

Sullivan, Patricia. *Days of Hope: Race and Democracy in the New Deal Era*. Chapel Hill: University of North Carolina Press, 1996.

———, ed. *Freedom Writer: Virginia Foster Durr, Letters from the Civil Rights Years*. New York: Routledge, 2003.

———. *Lift Every Voice: The NAACP and the Making of the Civil Rights Movement*. New York: New Press, 2009.

Summers, Anthony. *Not in Your Lifetime*. Updated ed. New York: Marlowe, 1998.

Sweeney, James R., ed. *Race, Reason, and Massive Resistance: The Diary of David J. Mays, 1954–1959*. Athens: University of Georgia Press, 2008.

Talmadge, Herman E. *You and Segregation*. Birmingham, Ala.: Vulcan, 1955.

Taylor, Clarence. *Black Religious Intellectuals: The Fight for Equality from Jim Crow to the 21st Century*. New York: Routledge, 2002.

Thayer, George. *The Farther Shores of Politics: The American Political Fringe Today*. New York: Simon and Schuster, 1968.

Tindall, George B. *The Emergence of the New South, 1913–1945*. Baton Rouge: Louisiana State University Press, 1967.

Tucker, Shirley. *Mississippi from Within*. New York: Acro, 1965.

Turner, William W. *Power on the Right*. Berkeley, Calif.: Ramparts, 1971.

Tushnet, Mark V. *Making Civil Rights Law: Thurgood Marshall and the Supreme Court, 1936–1961*. New York: Oxford University Press, 1994.

Twelve Southerners. *I'll Take My Stand: The South and the Agrarian Tradition.* New York: Harper and Brothers, 1930. Reprint, Birmingham, Ala.: Oxmoor House, 1983.

Twentieth Century Reformation Hour. *Who Is Carl McIntire?: A Testimony to Christ and a Witness for Freedom.* Collingswood, N.J.: Christian Beacon, n.d.

Vanderbilt University School of Law, ed. *Race Relations Law Reporter.* Vol. 1. Nashville, Tenn.: Vanderbilt University School of Law, 1956.

Vetter, Cyril E. *Fonville Winans' Louisiana: Politics, People, and Places.* Baton Rouge: Louisiana State University Press, 1995.

Waldron, Ann. *Hodding Carter: The Reconstruction of a Racist.* Chapel Hill, N.C.: Algonquin, 1993.

Walker, Paul Robert. *Remember Little Rock: The Time, the People, the Stories.* Washington, D.C.: National Geographic Society, 2009.

Ward, Harry F. *A Year Book of the Church and Social Service in the United States.* New York: Federal Council of the Churches of Christ in America, 1916.

Ward, Jason Morgan. *Defending White Democracy: The Making of a Segregationist Movement and the Remaking of Racial Politics, 1936–1965.* Chapel Hill: University of North Carolina Press, 2011.

Washington, James M., ed. *A Testament of Hope: The Essential Writings and Speeches of Martin Luther King, Jr.* New York: HarperCollins, 1991.

Washington-Williams, Essie Mae, and William Stadiem. *Dear Senator: A Memoir by the Daughter of Strom Thurmond.* New York: HarperCollins, 2005.

Watts, Trent A. *One Homogeneous People: Narratives of White Southern Identity, 1890–1920.* Knoxville: University of Tennessee Press, 2010.

———, ed. *White Masculinity in the Recent South.* Baton Rouge: Louisiana State University Press, 2008.

Webb, Clive. *Fight against Fear: Southern Jews and Black Civil Rights.* Athens: University of Georgia Press, 2001.

———, ed. *Massive Resistance: Southern Opposition to the Second Reconstruction.* New York: Oxford University Press, 2005.

———. *Rabble Rousers: The American Far Right in the Civil Rights Era.* Athens: University of Georgia Press, 2010.

Weill, Susan. *In a Madhouse's Din: Civil Rights Coverage by Mississippi's Daily Press, 1948–1968.* Westport, Conn.: Praeger, 2002.

White, Walter. *A Man Called White: The Autobiography of Walter White.* New York: Viking, 1948.

Whitfield, Stephen J. *The Culture of the Cold War.* 2d ed. Baltimore: Johns Hopkins University Press, 1996.

———. *A Death in the Delta: The Story of Emmett Till.* New York: Free Press, 1988.

Wilhoit, Francis M. *The Politics of Massive Resistance.* New York: George Braziller, 1973.

Wilkins, Roy, and Tom Matthews. *Standing Fast: The Autobiography of Roy Wilkins.* New York: Viking, 1982.

Williams, David S. *From Mounds to Megachurches: Georgia's Religious Heritage.* Athens: University of Georgia Press, 2008.

Williams, Juan. *Eyes on the Prize: America's Civil Rights Years, 1954–1965.* New York: Penguin, 1987.

Williams, Michael Vinson. *Medgar Evers: Mississippi Martyr.* Fayetteville: University of Arkansas Press, 2011.

Williamson, Joel. *The Crucible of Race: Black-White Relations in the American South since Emancipation.* New York: Oxford University Press, 1984.

———. *William Faulkner and Southern History.* New York: Oxford University Press, 1993.

Williamson, Joy Ann. *Radicalizing the Ebony Tower: Black Colleges and the Black Freedom Struggle in Mississippi.* New York: Teachers College Press, 2008.

Wilson, Robert L. *Biases and Blind Spots: Methodism and Foreign Policy since World War II.* Bedfordshire, U.K.: Good News Books, 1988. Online ed.

Winchell, Mark Royden. *Where No Flag Flies: Donald Davidson and the Southern Resistance.* Columbia: University of Missouri Press, 2000.

Wofford, Harris. *Of Kennedys and Kings: Making Sense of the Sixties.* New York: Farrar, Straus, and Giroux, 1980. Reprint, Pittsburgh, Penn.: University of Pittsburgh Press, 1992.

Woods, Jeff. *Black Struggle, Red Scare: Segregation and Anti-Communism in the South, 1948–1968.* Baton Rouge: Louisiana State University Press, 2004.

Woodward, C. Vann. *The Burden of Southern History.* Rev. ed. Baton Rouge: Louisiana State University Press, 1968.

ARTICLES

"The Administration Won't Sneer 'One-Man Gestapo' as Martin Dies Heads Back to Washington." *Pathfinder,* Aug. 20, 1952, 23.

"Along the N.A.A.C.P. Battlefront: Attorney General Cook." *Crisis,* Dec. 1955, 620–22.

Ashmore, Harry S. "A Southern Challenge and Epitaph for Dixie." *Life,* Nov. 4, 1957, 128–30, 133, 135–36, 141, 143–44, 146, 148.

"Asked to Leave the County." *Presbyterian Outlook,* Oct. 17, 1955, 1, 4.

Bailey, Fred A. "The Southern Historical Association and the Quest for Racial Justice, 1954–1963." *Journal of Southern History* 71 (Nov. 2005): 833–52.

Berg, Manfred. "Black Civil Rights and Liberal Anticommunism: The NAACP in the Early Cold War." *Journal of American History* 94 (June 2007): 75–96.

Bertwell, Dan. "'A Veritable Refuge for Practicing Homosexuals': The Johns Committee and the University of South Florida." *Florida Historical Quarterly* 83 (Spring 2005): 410–31.

Bloch, Charles J. "The School Segregation Cases: A Legal Error That Should Be Corrected." *American Bar Association Journal* 45 (Jan. 1959): 27–30, 97–99.

Bolton, Charles C. "William F. Winter and the Politics of Racial Moderation in Mississippi." *Journal of Mississippi History* 70 (Winter 2008): 335–82.

"Books Worth Reading." *Citizens' Council,* Feb. 1956, 3.

Brazeal, B. R. "Some Problems in the Desegregation of Higher Education in the 'Hard Core' States." *Journal of Negro Education* 27 (Summer 1958): 352–72.

Brown, Dewey. "Powerful Voice against the Reds." *Arkansas Democrat Magazine,* Sept. 18, 1960, 2–3.

Brown, Sarah Hart. "Congressional Anti-Communism and the Segregationist South: From New Orleans to Atlanta, 1954–1958." *Georgia Historical Quarterly* 80 (Winter 1996): 785–816.

———. "Redressing Southern 'Subversion': The Case of Senator Eastland and the Louisiana Lawyer." *Louisiana History* 43 (Summer 2009): 295–314.

———. "The Role of Elite Leadership in the Southern Defense of Segregation, 1954–1964." *Journal of Southern History* 77 (Nov. 2011): 827–64.

Bush, Gregory W. "'We Must Picture an "Octopus"': Anticommunism, Desegregation, and Local News in Miami, 1945–1960." *Tequesta* 65 (2005): 48–63.

Carter, Dan T. "The Rise of Conservatism since World War II." *OAH Magazine of History,* Jan. 2003, 11–16.

Carter, Hodding, Jr. "A Wave of Terror Threatens the South." *Look,* Mar. 22, 1955, 32–36.

Chappell, David L. "Diversity within a Racial Group: White People in Little Rock, 1957–1959." *Arkansas Historical Quarterly* 66 (Summer 2007): 181–93.

———. "The Divided Mind of Southern Segregationists." *Georgia Historical Quarterly* 82 (Spring 1998): 45–72.

———. "Religious Ideas of the Segregationists." *Journal of American Studies* [British Association for American Studies] 32 (Aug. 1998): 237–62.

"Circuit-Riding Methodists." Editorial. *Christian Advocate,* Oct. 18, 1951, 11.

"Civil Rights: The Apologist." *Time,* Oct. 31, 1969. Online ed.

"Civil Rights: With George and Sam on Capitol Hill." *Time,* July 26, 1963. Online ed.

Clark, Thomas D. "Comments." *Journal of Southern History* 71 (Nov. 2005): 853–56.

Cobb, William H., and Donald H. Grubbs. "Arkansas' Commonwealth College and the Southern Tenant Farmers' Union." *Arkansas Historical Quarterly* 25 (Winter 1966): 293–311.

Colburn, David R., and Richard K. Scher. "Aftermath of the *Brown* Decision: The Politics of Interposition in Florida." *Tequesta* 37 (1977): 62–81.

"The Congress: The New Chairman." *Time,* Mar. 12, 1956. Online ed.

"The Continuing Confrontation." *Time,* Apr. 9, 1965. Online ed.

Dawson, Nelson L. "From Fellow Traveler to Anticommunist: The Odyssey of J. B. Matthews." *Register of the Kentucky Historical Society* 84 (Summer 1986): 280–306.

"Deaths: David A. Witts, Eighty-Five, of Dallas, Texas, Died Oct. 25, 2006." *Cattleman,* Jan. 2007. Online ed.

"Dies Committee Investigation." *Safeguards against Subversive Activities* [Chamber of Commerce of the United States, Washington, D.C.], Oct. 1938, 1.

Douglas, Davison M. "The Rhetoric of Moderation: Desegregating the South during the Decade after *Brown.*" *Northwestern University Law Review* 89 (1994): 92–139.

Dudziak, Mary L. "Desegregation as a Cold War Imperative." *Stanford Law Review* 41 (Nov. 1988): 61–120.

Dunbar, Leslie W. "The Changing Mind of the South: The Exposed Nerve." *Journal of Politics* 26 (Feb. 1964): 3–21.

Durr, Virginia Foster. "The Emancipation of Pure, White, Southern Womanhood." *New South* 26 (Winter 1971): 46–54.

Dykeman, Wilma, and James Stokely. "McCarthyism under the Magnolias." *Progressive,* July 1959, 6–10.

Dyson, Lowell K. "The Southern Tenant Farmers['] Union and Depression Politics." *Political Science Quarterly* 88 (June 1973): 230–52.

"Editor Calls for 'Positive Thinking' in Mississippi Crisis." *Southern School News,* Mar. 1956, 3.

"Education: Southern Milestones." *Time,* Sept. 8, 1961. Online ed.

Egerton, John. "Delta Democrat." Review of *Hodding Carter: The Reconstruction of a Racist,* by Ann Waldron. *Southern Changes* 15 (1993): 22–23.

———. "Homegrown Progressives." *Southern Changes* 16 (1994): 1, 4–17.

———. "The Trial of the Highlander Folk School." *Southern Exposure: A Journal of Politics and Culture* 6 (Spring 1978): 82–89.

———. "Walking into History: The Beginning of School Desegregation in Nashville." *Southern Spaces,* May 4, 2009. Online journal.

Ethridge, Tom. "Mississippi Notebook: Moderation Is Futile." *Citizens' Council,* May 1956, 2.

"Father Theodore R. Gibson." *Crisis,* Feb. 1961, 91–92.

"Federation Speaks for Itself." *Christian Advocate,* Nov. 2, 1950, 12, 31.

Flynn, John T. "Communists and the New Deal, Part II." *American Mercury,* n.d. [1953], n.p. Reprint ed.

Franklin, John Hope. "The Great Confrontation: The South and the Problem of Change." *Journal of Southern History* 38 (Feb. 1972): 3–20.

Gaston, Paul M. "Speaking for the Negro." *Virginia Quarterly Review* 41 (Autumn 1965): 612–18.

"Georgia: Wrong Target." *Time,* Aug. 4, 1958. Online ed.

Graves, Karen. "Confronting a 'Climate of Raucous and Carnival Invasion': The AAUW Takes On the Johns Committee." *Florida Historical Quarterly* 85 (Fall 2006): 154–76.

"Group against 'Isms.'" *Christian Advocate,* Oct. 18, 1951, 14.

Halberstam, David. "An Address by David Halberstam at the Dedication of the William F. Winter Archives and History Building, November 7, 2003." *Journal of Mississippi History* 67 (Summer 2005): 159–63.

———. "The White Citizens['] Councils: Respectable Means for Unrespectable Ends." *Commentary*, Oct. 1956. Online ed.

Hall, Jacquelyn Dowd. "The Long Civil Rights Movement and the Political Use of the Past." *Journal of American History* 91 (Mar. 2005): 1233–63.

Havard, William C., and Robert J. Steamer. "Louisiana Secedes: Collapse of a Compromise." *Massachusetts Review* 1 (Fall 1959): 134–46.

Herzog, Brad. "A Life in Sum." *Cornell Alumni Magazine*, July–Aug. 2009. Online ed.

Heuser, Fred. "Stories from Our Past: Presbyterians and the Struggle for Civil Rights." *Perspectives*, Jan. 2007. Online magazine.

High, Stanley. "Methodism's Pink Fringe." *Reader's Digest*, Feb. 1950, 134–38.

Hill, Herbert. "The Communist Party: Enemy of Negro Equality." *Crisis*, June–July 1951, 365–71, 421–24.

Horowitz, David A. "White Southerners' Alienation and Civil Rights: The Response to Corporate Liberalism, 1956–1965." *Journal of Southern History* 54 (May 1988): 173–200.

Hughes, C. Alvin. "A New Agenda for the South: The Role and Influence of the Highlander Folk School, 1953–1961." *Phylon* 46 (3d quarter 1985): 242–50.

Hustwit, William P. "From Caste to Color Blindness: James J. Kilpatrick's Segregationist Semantics." *Journal of Southern History* 77 (Aug. 2011): 639–70.

"I'm Just One of a Couple of Hundred." *Time*, Sept. 30, 1975. Online ed.

"Inquiries: Joe Stubs Toe." *Newsweek*, July 20, 1953, 29–30.

"The Investigation: Operation Abolition." *Time*, Mar. 17, 1961. Online ed.

"Investigations of Highlander." *Firing Line* [National Americanism Commission, American Legion, Indianapolis, Ind.], Sept. 15, 1959, n.p.

"It's a Free Country." *Time*, Jan. 15, 1945. Online ed.

Jeansonne, Glen. "Racism and Longism in Louisiana: The 1959–60 Gubernatorial Elections." *Louisiana History* 11 (Summer 1970): 259–70.

Johnston, Joyce. "Communism vs. Segregation: Evolution of the Committee to Investigate Communist Activities in South Carolina." *Proceedings of the South Carolina Historical Association*, 1993, 19–29.

"The Judiciary: Mississippi's Best." *Time*, July 23, 1965. Online ed.

Katagiri, Yasuhiro. "'But the People Aren't Going to Know It, Are They?': The Clyde Kennard Incident in Mississippi and the Redemption of a Southern University." *Humanities in the South*, no. 89 (2002): 84–95.

———. "'Let the Word Go Forth': John F. Kennedy's Presidential Rhetoric on Civil Rights during the South's Second Reconstruction." *Japanese Journal of American Studies*, no. 17 (2006): 263–87.

"Kennard Plans to 'Devote Rest of My Life' to Improving Miss." *Jet*, Apr. 11, 1963, 20–22.

Key, Barclay. "On the Periphery of the Civil Rights Movement: Race and Religion at Harding College, 1945–1969." *Arkansas Historical Quarterly* 68 (Autumn 2009). Online consultation.

King, William McGuire. "The Emergence of Social Gospel Radicalism: The Methodist Case." *Church History* 50 (Dec. 1981): 436–49.

Klibaner, Irwin. "The Travail of Southern Radicals: The Southern Conference Educational Fund, 1946–1976." *Journal of Southern History* 49 (May 1983): 179–202.

"A Kneeling Racist and an Upright Archbishop." *Life*, Apr. 27, 1962, 44.

Kruse, Kevin M. "The Paradox of Massive Resistance: Political Conformity and Chaos in the Aftermath of *Brown v. Board of Education*." *Saint Louis University Law Journal* 48 (Spring 2004): 1009–35.

Leonard, Kevin Allen. "'Is That What We Fought For?': Japanese Americans and Racism in California, the Impact of World War II." *Western Historical Quarterly* 21 (Nov. 1990): 463–82.

Lewis, George. "Virginia's Northern Strategy: Southern Segregationists and the Route to National Conservatism." *Journal of Southern History* 72 (Feb. 2006): 111–46.

Lichtman, Robert M. "J. B. Matthews and the 'Counter-Subversives': Names as a Political and Financial Resource in the McCarthy Era." *American Communist History* 5 (June 2006): 1–36.

Lichtman, Robert M., and Ronald D. Cohen. "Harvey Matusow, the FBI, and the Justice Department: Becoming a Government Informer-Witness in the McCarthy Era." *American Communist History* 1 (June 2002): 43–68.

Lohman, Clarence. "Socialism and Communism and the Methodist Church." *Christian Advocate*, Nov. 2, 1950, 4.

"Long Reach of the Law." *Time*, Dec. 1, 1958. Online ed.

"Looking and Listening: Red-Tagging." *Crisis*, Dec. 1957, 622.

"Louisiana: Jambalaya." *Time*, Jan. 18, 1960. Online ed.

Loveland, George W. "A Greater Fairness: May Justus as Popular Educator." *Journal of Research in Rural Education* 17 (Fall 2001): 102–11.

"The Man in the Middle." *Time*, May 24, 1954. Online ed.

Matthews, J. B. "Communists and the New Deal, Part III." *American Mercury*, n.d. [1953], n.p. Reprint ed.

———. "Red and Our Churches." *American Mercury*, July 1953, 3–13.

Mayer, Michael. "With Much Deliberation and Some Speed: Eisenhower and the *Brown* Decision." *Journal of Southern History* 52 (Feb. 1986): 43–76.

McMillen, Neil R. "The White Citizens' Council and Resistance to School Desegregation in Arkansas." *Arkansas Historical Quarterly* 66 (Summer 2007): 125–44. Reprint ed.

Minchin, Timothy J., and John A. Salmond. "'The Saddest Story of the Whole Movement': The Clyde Kennard Case and the Search for Racial Reconciliation in Mississippi, 1955–2007." *Journal of Mississippi History* 71 (Fall 2009): 191–234.

Minor, Bill. "A Poignant Summer Reunion." *Reckon* [Center for the Study of Southern Culture, University of Mississippi] 1 (Premiere 1995): 54–57.

"Mississippi: The Closed Society." *Time,* Nov. 15, 1963. Online ed.

"Mississippi: The Reformer." *Time,* May 12, 1961. Online ed.

"Mississippi Group Backs Equalization Building Plans." *Southern School News,* Dec. 1956, 7.

"Mississippi LEAC Presents Six-Point Plan to Retain School Segregation." *Southern School News,* Oct. 1955, 4–5.

"Mississippi's Leaders 'Divided' on Proposal for Nullification." *Southern School News,* Jan. 1956, 6–7.

"Nation: The Senator from South Carolina." *Time,* Feb. 2, 1962. Online ed.

"Nation: What You Believe In." *Time,* June 8, 1962. Online ed.

"National Affairs: Racist Leader." *Time,* Dec. 12, 1960. Online ed.

Newman, Mark. "The Georgia Baptist Convention and Desegregation, 1945–1980." *Georgia Historical Quarterly* 83 (Winter 1999): 685–705.

Nutt, Rick. "For Truth and Liberty: Presbyterians and McCarthyism." *Journal of Presbyterian History* 78 (Spring 2000). Online ed.

Olney, Warren, III. "Comment: A Government Lawyer Looks at Little Rock." *California Law Review* 45 (Oct. 1957): 516–23.

Olsen, Margaret Nunnelley. "Teaching Americanism: Ray K. Daily and the Persistence of Conservatism in Houston School Politics, 1943–1952." *Southwestern Historical Quarterly* 110 (Oct. 2006): 240–69.

Payton, Jacob S. "That Man from Texas." *Christian Advocate,* Mar. 6, 1952, 16.

———. "Federation Review." *Christian Advocate,* Mar. 6, 1952, 16.

Peck, Jim. "Not So Deep Are the Roots: Fourteen Years Later." *Crisis,* June–July 1961, 325–31.

"Political Notes: Prince of the Peckerwoods." *Time,* July 1, 1946. Online ed.

"The Presidency: Little Rock's Finest." *Time,* Aug. 24, 1959. Online ed.

"The Press: Blowup at the Mercury." *Time,* Oct. 3, 1955. Online ed.

"The Press: Mississippi's Voice." *Time,* Dec. 22, 1961. Online ed.

"The Press: Petulant Plea." *Time,* Oct. 26, 1962. Online ed.

Quin, Paul. "The Dominance of the Shadow in Southern Race Relations." *Louisiana History* 36 (Winter 1995): 5–30.

Raimondo, Justin. "John T. Flynn: Exemplar of the Old Right." *Journal of Libertarian Studies* 10 (Fall 1992): 107–24.

Ransone, Coleman B., Jr. "Political Leadership in the Governor's Office." *Journal of Politics* 26 (Feb. 1964): 197–220.

"Recommended Literature Available from the Citizens' Council." *Citizens' Council,* Jan. 1961, 3.

Record, Jane Cassels. "The Red-Tagging of Negro Protest." *American Scholar* 26 (Summer 1957): 325–33.

Reiff, Joseph T. "Conflicting Convictions in White Mississippi Methodism: The 1963 'Born of Conviction' Controversy." *Methodist History* 49 (Apr. 2011): 162–75.

Romero, Frances. "A Brief History of Martin Luther King Jr. Day." *Time,* Jan. 18, 2010. Online ed.

Root, E. Merrill. "The Murder of Scholarship." *Freeman,* Oct. 1954, 136–38.

Rossinow, Doug. "The Radicalization of the Social Gospel: Harry F. Ward and the Search for a New Social Order, 1898–1936." *Religion and American Culture: A Journal of Interpretation* 15 (Winter 2005): 63–106.

Routh, Frederick B., and Paul Anthony. "Southern Resistance Forces." *Phylon Quarterly* 18 (1st quarter 1957): 50–58.

Rushmore, Howard. "'Mr. Anti-Communist.'" *American Mercury,* n.d. [1953], 79–86. Reprint ed.

Salmond, John A. "'The Great Southern Commie Hunt': Aubrey Williams, the Southern Conference Educational Fund, and the Internal Security Subcommittee." *South Atlantic Quarterly* 77 (Autumn 1978): 433–52.

Schnur, James A. "Cold Warriors in the Hot Sunshine: USF and the Johns Committee." *Sunland Tribune: Journal of the Tampa Historical Society* 18 (Nov. 1992): 9–15.

Schrecker, Ellen W. "Archival Sources for the Study of McCarthyism." *Journal of American History* 75 (June 1988): 197–208.

"The Self-Bound Gulliver." *Time,* Sept. 13, 1963. Online ed.

"Shoofly Pye." *Time,* Apr. 17, 1964. Online ed.

Silver, James W. "Mississippi: The Closed Society." *Journal of Southern History* 30 (Feb. 1964): 3–34.

———. "Mississippi Must Choose." *New York Times Magazine,* July 19, 1964, 8, 54–55.

Smith, Carol. "The Dress Rehearsal for McCarthyism." *Academe,* July–Aug. 2011. Online ed.

Smith, Lindsley Armstrong. "The Southern Tradition Baying: Race, Religion, and Rhetorical Redoubts." *American Communication Journal* 10 (Summer 2008). Online journal.

"Some Zealots Masked in Moderation." *Life,* Feb. 7, 1964, 76.

"The South: The Authentic Voice." *Time,* Mar. 26, 1956. Online ed.

"The South: D-Day in New Orleans." *Time,* Nov. 28, 1960. Online ed.

"The South Awakens." Editorial. *Life,* July 11, 1949, 32.

"South Worries over Miss Lucy." *Life,* Feb. 20, 1956, 28–32.

Thorton, James. "The Legacy of E. Merrill Root: Poet, Patriot, Warrior in the Battle for Men's Souls." *New American,* June 13, 1994. Online ed.

Tomberlin, Joseph A. "Florida and the School Desegregation Issue, 1954–1959: A Summary View." *Journal of Negro Education* 43 (Autumn 1974): 457–67.

Tscheschlok, Eric. "'So Goes the Negro': Race and Labor in Miami, 1940–1963." *Florida Historical Quarterly* 76 (Summer 1997): 42–67.

"'Un-American Activities.'" Editorial. *Life,* Mar. 26, 1945, 30.

"Uncheckable Charge." *Time,* July 13, 1953. Online ed.

"U.S. Opens Tax Drive against Right-Wing Groups." *Jet,* Jan. 7, 1965, 9.

"U.S. Supreme Court Clears Father Gibson." *Crisis,* May 1963, 291–92.

Webb, Clive. "Charles Bloch, Jewish White Supremacist." *Georgia Historical Quarterly* 83 (Summer 1999): 267–92.

Weigand, Kate. "The Red Menace, the Feminine Mystique, and the Ohio Un-American Activities Commission: Gender and Anti-Communism in Ohio, 1951–1954." *Journal of Women's History* 3 (Winter 1992): 70–94.

Weill, Susan. "The Press Challenge of Social Responsibility in Times of Political Upheaval: Hodding Carter III and the *Delta Democrat-Times* Respond to Freedom Summer in 1964." *Journal of Mississippi History* 72 (Winter 2010): 367–400.

Weitz, Seth A. "Campus of Evil: The Johns Committee's Investigation on the University of South Florida." *Tampa Bay History* 22 (2008): 35–54.

Wiener, Willard. "J. B. Matthews, Former Pal of Communists." *PM Daily Picture Magazine,* Feb. 19, 1943, 2–3.

Williams, H. Randall. "'Grace and Guts': Virginia Foster Durr, 1903–1999." *Southern Changes* 21 (1999): 35.

Williams, T. Harry. "Huey, Lyndon, and Southern Radicalism." *Journal of American History* 60 (Sept. 1973): 267–93.

Winter, R. Milton. "Division and Reunion in the Presbyterian Church, U.S.: A Mississippi Retrospective." *Journal of Presbyterian History* 78 (Spring 2000). Online ed.

Woods, Jeff. "The Cold War and the Struggle for Civil Rights." *OAH Magazine of History,* Oct. 2010, 13–17.

Wroten, Joseph E. "Implications of the Violence at Oxford." *Concern,* Dec. 15, 1962, 3–5.

"York Professor Honored for Civil Rights Activism." *York University Gazette* [Toronto, Ontario], May 8, 1996. Online ed.

Zellner, Dorothy M. "Red Roadshow: Eastland in New Orleans, 1954." *Louisiana History* 33 (Winter 1992): 31–60.

DISSERTATIONS AND MASTER'S THESES

Brenner, Samuel Lawrence. "Shouting at the Rain: The Voices and Ideas of Right-Wing Anti-Communist Americanists in the Era of Modern American Conservatism, 1950–1974." Ph.D. diss., Brown University, 2009.

Clark, Wayne A. "An Analysis of the Relationship between Anti-Communism and Segregationist Thought in the Deep South, 1948–1964." Ph.D. diss., University of North Carolina, 1976.

Crawford, Theodore W. "From Segregation to Independence: African Americans in Churches of Christ." Ph.D. diss., Vanderbilt University, 2008.

Cunnigen, Donald. "Men and Women of Goodwill: Mississippi's White Liberals." Ph.D. diss., Harvard University, 1988.

Flood, Heather M. "Chaos in Clinton." Master's thesis, East Tennessee State University, 2007.

Fox, Lisa Ann. "Cracking the Closed Society: James W. Silver and the Civil Rights Movement in Mississippi." Master's thesis, University of North Texas, 2010.

Klein, Kevin N. "Guarding the Baggage: Florida's Pork Chop Gang and Its Defense of the Old South." Ph.D. diss., Florida State University, 1995.

Luce, Phillip A. "The Mississippi White Citizens['] Council: 1954–1959." Master's thesis, Ohio State University, 1960.

Luckett, Robert E., Jr. "Yapping Dogs: Joe T. Patterson and the Limits of Massive Resistance." Ph.D. diss., University of Georgia, 2009.

McCarrick, Earlean M. "Louisiana's Official Resistance to Desegregation." Ph.D. diss., Vanderbilt University, 1964.

McKenzie, Kristina D. "The Desegregation of New Orleans Public and Roman Catholic Schools in New Orleans, 1950–1962." Master's thesis, Louisiana State University, 2009.

Patenaude, Marc. "Providing for the Common Defense: Internal Security and the Cold War, 1945–1975." Ph.D. diss., Louisiana State University, 2011.

Prechter, Ryan Buchanan. "'The Highest Type of Disloyalty': The Struggle for Americanism in Louisiana during the Age of Communist Ascendency, 1930s–1960s." Master's thesis, University of New Orleans, 2011.

Raimondi, Steven. "The Clinton 12 Chronicles: Unsung Heroes of the Civil Rights Movement." Master's thesis, Excelsior College, 2010.

Sperry, Benjamin O. "Caught 'Between Our Moral and Material Selves': Mississippi's Elite White 'Moderates' and Their Role in Changing Race Relations, 1945–1956." Ph.D. diss., Case Western Reserve University, 2010.

Stark, Bonnie. "McCarthyism in Florida: Charley Johns and the Florida Legislative Investigation Committee, July 1956 to July 1965." Master's thesis, University of South Florida, 1985.

Stowe, William M., Jr. "Willie Rainach and the Defense of Segregation in Louisiana, 1954–1959." Ph.D. diss., Texas Christian University, 1989.

Weitz, Seth A. "Bourbon, Pork Chops, and Red Peppers: Political Immorality in Florida, 1945–1968." Ph.D. diss., Florida State University, 2007.

INDEX